THE GREAT PERSUADER

BOOKS BY DAVID LAVENDER

Non-Fiction

One Man's West
The Big Divide
Land of Giants
Bent's Fort
The Story of Cyprus Mines Corporation
Westward Vision: The Story of the Oregon Trail
The Fist in the Wilderness: The American Fur Company
Climax at Buena Vista: American Campaigns in Northeastern New Mexico, 1846–47
The American Heritage History of the Great West
The Rockies
California, Land of New Beginnings
David Lavender's Colorado
The Great Persuader: A Biography of Collis P. Huntington
Nothing Seemed Impossible: William Ralston and Early San Francisco
California: A Place, A People, A Dream
Winner Take All: The TransCanada Canoe Trail
The Southwest
River Runners of the Grand Canyon
The Way to the Western Sea
Let Me Be Free

Official Bicentennial Histories

Los Angeles Two Hundred
California: A Bicentennial History

Novels

Andy Claybourne
Red Mountain

Books for the National Park Service

Fort Vancouver
Fort Laramie
The Overland Migrations
De Soto, Coronado, Cabrillo: Explorers of the Northern Mystery
Pipe Spring and the Arizona Strip

THE GREAT PERSUADER

By David Lavender

UNIVERSITY PRESS OF COLORADO

Copyright © 1969, 1970, 1998 by David Lavender
International Standard Book Number 0-87081-476-1

Published by the University Press of Colorado
P.O. Box 849
Niwot, Colorado 80544

The University Press of Colorado is a cooperative publishing enterprise supported, in part, by Adams State College, Colorado State University, Fort Lewis
College, Mesa State College, Metropolitan State College of Denver, University of
Colorado, University of Northern Colorado, University of Southern Colorado,
and Western State College of Colorado.

The paper used in this publication meets the minimum requirements of the
American National Standard for Information Sciences — Permanence of Paper
for Printed Library Materials. ANSI Z39.48-1984

Library of Congress Cataloging-in-Publication Data

Lavender, David Sievert, 1910–
    The great persuader : the biography of Collis P. Huntington /
David Lavender.
        p. cm.
    Originally published: Garden City, N.Y. : Doubleday, 1970.
    Includes bibliographical references and index.
    ISBN 0-87081-476-1 (pbk. : alk. paper)
    1. Huntington, Collis Potter, 1821–1900. I. Title.
HE2754.H8L3   1998
385'.092—dc21
    [B]   98-28484
                                                                CIP

07 06 05 04 03 02 01 00 99 98   10 9 8 7 6 5 4 3 2 1

For Fritzi and David

CONTENTS

THE GREAT PERSUADER

1   The Start

A song did as much as anything else to make the exotic name familiar during that feverish winter of 1848–49. *Oh, California*—the ill-defined region had been a part of the United States for less than a year when President Polk, on December 5, 1848, officially told Congress that extensive gold mines had indeed been discovered there—*that's the land for me! . . . I'm going to Sacramento with my washbowl on my knee!* But first the singers had to scratch together resources enough to make the long leap.

One discussion place among hundreds during the snowy winter—*O Susannah!*—was the general store owned by the burly Huntington brothers, Solon and Collis, in Oneonta, a village in the hill country of central New York, where the Susquehanna River gathers up its headstreams. It was fitting that the pair should provide the room, redolent with dried fruit and kegs of butter and oiled harness hanging from the walls. For although the Huntingtons may not have originated the idea of leaving Oneonta for the new goldfields, they were, by February 1849, the plan's leading local proponents.

Solon, to be sure, did not plan on making the trip himself. He was thirty-six, nine years older than Collis. Besides, someone had to stay behind to keep the store, reputedly the most prosperous in Otsego County. He would be along in spirit, however, for in conjunction with a Dr. Case he had agreed to lend passage money to some of those who were going. Even more vitally, he had agreed to let Collis establish a branch store for the Huntingtons if the situation on the Coast seemed to merit it, and inasmuch as Solon was mortgaging some of his personal property to make the examination possible, he naturally would await word of developments with anxiety.

To the more conservative souls of Oneonta, and Collis' wife Elizabeth was probably among them, this headlong abandonment of established securities for the distant unknown must have seemed like madness. What, exactly, did her husband want?

Not many Oneontans of his age, twenty-seven, could boast of having achieved so much, especially after so grim a start. He had been born on October 22, 1821, the sixth of nine children—Solon was the second—in Harwinton township, Connecticut, a remote backwoods community in the Litchfield Hills, fifteen miles west of Hartford. Their father William, six feet two inches tall, was a powerful, surly, improvident man who wasted no time with his children. The family lived in a crowded one-story house on a slope above a swampy valley called Poverty Hollow. In addition to his grudging thirty-acre farm, William Huntington owned a decrepit fulling mill and a one-man shingle mill powered by a water wheel. Neither mill operated very often, generally for lack of materials, and then the father went about the countryside eking out small change as a tinker, sharpening scissors, soldering pans, mending umbrellas, and the like.

His three sons and six daughters began working around the farm and the mills as soon as they were able, fetching and carrying, sewing, weaving, plowing, hauling stones, chopping wood. Education was spotty. The one-room school in the hollow operated about four months each winter, and Collis Potter Huntington missed as many days out of the truncated sessions as his dour father directed, whenever there was more important work to do.

He was big for his age; one schoolmate recalled that "he looked like a perfect mountain to me." When an exasperated male pedagogue took to striking students on the palm of the hand with a ruler whenever they misspelled a word, Collis and another lad (Collis speaking now, in 1896) "went for that teacher and whipped him." Later another teacher, named Ely, sought to eject him bodily from the room for refusing to tattle on a companion. Collis retorted by ejecting the teacher instead.[1] In spite of these youthful rebellions against authority he insisted in his old age that he was not an unruly student, that he did well in arithmetic, history, and geography, but that grammar and spelling defeated him—as his early letters amply testify.

At home things went from bad to worse. His father, a cantankerous disputant thoroughly versed in both the Scriptures and Voltaire, publicly aired his free-thinking views so stridently that he was read out of the church, suffering in consequence social and economic ostracism. Later on, his neighbors having reported to the selectmen of the township that the Huntington children were poorly clad and hungry, the self-righteous overseers took the boys away from the burdened family and bound them out to local farmers, Solon first and then Collis.

Collis was just short of fourteen. Under terms of his apprenticeship, in which he had no voice, he served farmer Orson Barber a full year for a wage of seven dollars a month and keep, meanwhile absorbing from Mrs. Barber compensatory tales about Ben Franklin, who, through frugality and hard work, had risen from rags to riches. This Barber year marked Huntington's premature transition to manhood. When it was over, the fifteen-year-old youth had no desire to return to his father's roof, to farm, or to drone through another school recitation. Instead, he found employment with a neighbor, Phineas Noble, who kept a little store in the front room of his house at Poverty Hollow.

Almost at once young Huntington bedazzled Noble by memorizing both the wholesale and retail cost of every item in the cluttered stock and then effortlessly calculating, without pen or paper or even moving his lips, the profit that could be expected from each piece, either in cash or in barter. Won by the virtuosity, Noble loaded a wagon with slow-moving items and sent the overgrown boy to peddling them door to door through the adjoining countryside. It may well be that it was on such a trip that Collis first encountered a family named Stoddard, who lived in tiny Cornwall, some fifteen miles northwest of Harwinton. They were relatives in a sense, linked to the Huntington clan through old marriages among distant cousins. There were several daughters in the Stoddard family. One of them, Elizabeth, soon began to look mighty good to the anchorless boy.

The next years are obscure. Half a century later, when Collis Huntington was one of the wealthiest men in the United States, he dictated his rambling reminiscences to the legmen of historian Hubert Howe Bancroft of San Francisco, who then wrote an adulatory biography based on them.[2] In that account, the events of the subject's youth are telescoped and tailored to the Horatio Alger expectations of the time: Be earnest, Be diligent, and Succeed. Without question Collis was diligent, but what really went on inside him as he drifted around the countryside, eating and sleeping however he could, are matters he never publicly mentioned.

At some point or another he reached the hamlet of Woodbury, eighteen or twenty miles south of Harwinton, and there worked a time for a merchant named Daniel Curtiss, a distant cousin of both his and Elizabeth Stoddard's. Having saved $175 and having wheedled one letter of recommendation from Phineas Noble and perhaps another from Curtiss, he traveled to New York City. He was sixteen by now, and evidently looked

3

capable. By means of his letters and a down payment in cash he acquired a stock of clocks, watch parts, silverware, costume jewelry, and other easily transportable items. He obtained a wagon and horse and with them became one of the sharp-dealing, suspiciously regarded, but essential cogs in the rural economy of pre-Civil War America—the far-ranging Yankee peddler. As a side issue he bought at heavy discount notes on which country merchants had defaulted, and undertook to collect these as he zigzagged through the countryside.

He left Connecticut far behind—how far is impossible to determine. Some accounts have him reaching Iowa, though Indiana seems a more likely limit. Winters drove him South. One tale pictures him standing, still in his teens, on a sandy spit near the entrance to the Chesapeake Bay and visualizing a bustling city there, but since he was the man who eventually created on that desert site the great ship-building yards of Newport News, Virginia, this presentation may be mere patness for the sake of historical symmetry. Still another tale says that during his years of foot-loose but not feckless wandering he met and traveled briefly with cracked old John Brown, twenty years his senior, in the days when Brown was an itinerant sheep buyer, and absorbed from him some of that fierce radical's violent antipathy toward slavery.

What is clear, just from the nature of things, is that as a boy he learned enough quickness, shrewdness, and hearty plausibility that he could reach a penny half a grab ahead of whoever was trying to beat him. It is easy to characterize such a sharklike life as mere money-grubbing. It is just as easy to glimpse a husky youth, unhappy at home, the juices stirring in him, wanting more from life than Poverty Hollow could offer and yet not knowing, because of the blinders Poverty Hollow had put on him, how to go about getting it. But go he must, absorbing pennies to be sure, but other things besides. He felt under the slow-turning wheels of his wagon the uncompromising actualities of the land, saw the way the roads wound along the streams and then curved across the upper slopes to find the easiest passes. Passes opening onto—what? There was always that wonder, that zest of expectancy . . . shackled to a plodding wagon. Nodding over the reins, he learned patience in spite of the simmerings inside him. He carried books along; later in life he insisted to interviewers that he had always liked to read and this was perhaps one of the few public autobiographical statements he made that was not designed to fit what his interviewers wanted to hear.

He discovered out of necessity how to be genial with strangers, how to spin a yarn and listen to one, roaring with laughter under the smoky beams of a tavern, and still turn aside proffered drinks without giving offense; he was over forty, by his own report, before he tasted liquor, and then only rarely. What lonesome farm girls may have smiled on him, what town bullies, eying his heavy six-foot frame, may have challenged him are, once again, matters we can only surmise. There must have been some affrays; one Oneonta acquaintance later recalled Collis' "vivid recital of personal scrapes . . . with bumptious persons who had, while he was peddling clocks and Yankee notions in the South, affronted him."[3] And yet, though Huntington knew the ways of gregariousness, he liked, so he said, the solitude of a lonely camp beside some country stream where he wrapped himself in his blankets with only the embers of his fire to set the tone of his flickering thoughts.

Penny by penny he prospered. So, too, did his older brother Solon, who, having married, drifted west from Harwinton to Oneonta, New York. There, in 1841, Solon built a store of quarried stone, three stories high with a full basement.[4] Hearing of this shortly after his twenty-first birthday, Collis traveled to Oneonta on a visit. For the moment he was weary of roaming, and the stability he saw appealed to him. He went to work for Solon. He did well—so well that within less than two years he declined to remain a subordinate any longer. On September 4, 1844, when he was not yet twenty-four, he and his brother signed a partnership agreement that was to last for five years. To launch the new firm of S. & C. P. Huntington, Collis contributed, in cash, $1,318.64, a sizable sum in a country town in those days. Solon matched him with an equivalent amount of merchandise and then rented his stone building to the new firm for $150 a year.[5] These details completed, Collis hurried to Cornwall, Connecticut, impetuously resumed his courtship of Elizabeth Stoddard, and married her on September 18.

Small-town domesticity: the new husband purchased at the corner of Chestnut and Church streets a square little house fronted by a veranda showy with fluted columns of wood. Under the sloping eaves there was, instead of an attic, a sort of malformed second story consisting of four cramped, poorly lit, poorly ventilated chambers opening onto a strange central "observatory."[6] Perhaps the newlyweds reassured themselves about the odd arrangement by saying that children would not mind sleeping up there—but, to their lasting disappointment, children never came.

A profusion of lilac bushes grew in the yard. In back of the kitchen there was ample room for wood haulers to drive in with their broad-wheeled wagons and pile up, each fall, twenty cords or more of wood for fending off the hard winters. For exercise Collis sawed and split a little of this mountain of fuel every day before breakfast. He was a homebody. He liked to spend the evenings beside the fire with Elizabeth, and he seldom loitered in one of the town's saloons or billiard parlors on his way back from work.

But he was also a merchant, ill content after his long roamings to wait for business to come to him. He went out into the country after it, to smaller stores for which S. & C. P. Huntington could act as jobbers and to the larger farmsteads, and because much of the area's trade was conducted by barter, the firm soon found itself with quantities of country produce on hand, especially butter and hops. It fell to Collis to dispose of this in New York City and then, because he was on the scene, to order whatever the store would need during the next few months. Four years of such dealings brought him to the favorable attention of several of the city's more solid mercantile houses.

He was a commanding figure physically, his two hundred pounds hardened by outdoor living. His hands were small for his massive body and his great round head was too big, but the self-assurance with which he carried himself kept most people from noticing the disproportion. His eyes were what new acquaintances recalled, gray and searching on either side of his thin-bridged nose. He wore a thick, cropped black beard and by the time he was twenty-seven the boys in the neighborhood were referring to him as "The Old Man," not out of deference to his age but because that was the title farm lads habitually gave the boss, the one who was in charge of things.[7]

Such living was a far cry from the starkness of Poverty Hollow. And yet, as Elizabeth must have seen with dismay, it was not far enough. Life had become placid.

Quite possibly Collis could not have articulated his amorphous discontent to himself, let alone to Elizabeth, any more than could thousands of other young men dissatisfied with scores of other placid American Oneontas during the middle of the last century. But the longings were there, in uneasy suspension. When rumors of gold swept the land late in '48 they crystalized, and Collis Huntington, because of his obvious ability to take care of himself out on the road, became the leader of five other Oneontans eager to rush West and see the new elephant.

Although many such companies drew up elaborate articles of association, elected officers, and sold stock to finance themselves, the Oneonta group was more informal. Each man produced his own funds as best he could. They traveled together primarily for mutual aid along the way, and if any written document was prepared for governing their procedures, it has not survived.

Only three in the party left much mark in Collis' California correspondence. One was Daniel Hammond, whom Huntington described from

6

the lofty eminence of his own twenty-seven years as "a young man of Stirling Qualites." Another was George Murray, bookkeeper for the firm of S. & C. P. Huntington. Murray financed himself at least in part by borrowing from Solon and Dr. Case. And then there was teen-age Egbert Sabin. Egbert's father, the head clerk in the store, was not going to California himself, but he wanted the boy to have the experience. Egbert was to work out his fare by being Collis' helper, with a view, probably, to eventually attaining an interest in whatever enterprise developed on the Coast. As events turned out, Egbert proved to be anything but sterling.

In their own nervous opinion, the six Oneontans were off to a late start. A horde of fortune seekers was ahead of them. During the single month of January 1849, 8,000 gold seekers aboard ninety ships had cleared Atlantic ports for the Pacific by way of Cape Horn. It might be possible for the Oneontans to reduce their lead, however, by following the shortcut used by mail carriers traveling under government contract to San Francisco and Astoria, Oregon. A man in a hurry caught a steamer to Panama (at that time a province of New Granada, as Colombia was then named), toiled across the forty-seven-mile neck of land by native canoe and mule to Panama City, and there boarded one of the three vessels of the Pacific Mail Steamship Company. These ships were just then coming off the ways and circling the Horn to start their shuttle service between Panama and Oregon. It was too late for the Oneontans to catch the first of the vessels, the *California,* which had left New York on October 6 and was due in Panama City toward the end of January. But with luck they might make connections with the *Oregon,* which had left New York in December, or the *Panama,* which did not leave until February. Furthermore, at some point during the spring the *California* would be churning back south for another load.

The main drawbacks of the shortcut were its expenses and the danger of contracting tropical fever. The Oneontans were well enough heeled, however, that they were able to book steerage passage to the Chagres River on the Atlantic side of the isthmus aboard the sumptuous new paddle-wheel steamer *Crescent City,* which suggests considerable advance planning, since all boats were oversold and tickets were at a premium.

From the outset Collis intended to be a trader, not a miner. As soon as he could locate a likely spot in the goldfields for a store, he would set up a branch of S. & C. P. Huntington. Solon would act as buyer and shipper of such goods as could be exported advantageously from the Oneonta area. There was, for instance, a woolen mill nearby and if Collis did establish a store in California, Solon would immediately send him bundles of woolen socks to sell to the miners. Solon also was connected with a local wagon manufactory, and from its shops he would be able to send his brother scores of wagons and wagon parts (wheel spokes, for example), adapting them to whatever specialized conditions Collis found in the West. It might be possible also to ship out kegs of local butter snugly packed in brine. Finally, Solon would keep in touch with New York jobbers with whom they had already established credit, jobbers who could supply whatever agricultural tools and mining hardware Collis asked for.

All this would have to await establishment of the store, however, and Collis was eager to start his trading before then, as soon as he arrived in the goldfields. What should he take with him to that wilderness which neither brother could visualize? The route they had selected helped them decide. Because of the laborious isthmus passage and uncertainties about the roads to the mines, bulky items would not do. The brothers had to depend on compact, light-weight merchandise.

Later commentators have occasionally referred scornfully to Collis' cargo of whiskey. There may well have been some; it was a legitimate article of trade, easily transported and readily sold. Collis' letters to Solon following his arrival in California do not mention whiskey, however. After an all-inclusive reference to the "things" he had brought along, he goes on to name specifically only three: rifles, woolen socks, and medicine, the last no doubt of the patent variety.[8]

In order to buy the goods and to meet Collis' expenses until he was located, the brothers executed mortgages on their property with a man named Ford. It is not clear whether or not the store building was included, but Collis' Chestnut Street home definitely was, though Elizabeth would continue living there until he either summoned her to California or gave up the adventure as a mistake and returned to Oneonta.

Because the original five-year agreement between the brothers was due to expire on September 4, 1849, well before the issue of the experiment could be determined, they drew up another document, dated March 10, 1849. Again their contributions and returns were to be equal, except that Collis' exertions in California were to be recognized by a salary of fifty dollars a month. If matters went badly there, he could leave after half a year and resume his place in the Oneonta store.[9]

The document executed, he kissed childless Elizabeth good-by—*Oh, Susannah, don't you cry for me!*—and with the other impatient argonauts journeyed down the Susquehanna to Unadilla. From there they struck south by stagecoach to Deposit on the Delaware River.[10] The next morning they caught the train to New York City and picked up their steerage tickets—eighty dollars each—on the *Crescent City,* scheduled to leave for

Chagres on the Atlantic side of Panama at 1 P.M., March 15. They did not have advanced tickets for the Pacific leg of the trip. The reason for this potentially disastrous oversight can only be surmised: either space on the Pacific Mail steamers was sold out or schedules were uncertain and they wanted to be free to catch the first ship that came along.

In his money belt Collis carried what he supposed would be ample funds both for the trip and for settling the Oneonta store's outstanding accounts with wholesalers in the city. But when he checked on his freight at the shipping office he was startled by the rates he would have to pay to cross the isthmus. He had better, he decided, keep a backlog of at least $2,000, especially since he would have to support young Egbert Sabin until they had set up shop somewhere in California. Apologetically he asked the wholesalers to wait a little longer for part of their money. Because the Huntington brothers had a reputation for reliability, the creditors agreed.[11]

After making sure his freight was loaded, he shouldered his way onto the jammed ship. Between three hundred and four hundred argonauts milled about the decks and along the passageways. Only three females were aboard—twenty-four-year-old Jessie Benton Frémont, her six-year-old daughter Elizabeth, whom Jessie called Lily, and a hard-faced maid, hired in New York City at the last minute, who soon would be arrested and locked up in a makeshift cell for rifling her mistress' trunk. Daughter of famed Senator Thomas Hart Benton of Missouri and the most glamorous woman of her era, Jessie was on her way to California, escorted by a young brother-in-law, to meet her explorer husband, John Charles Frémont, at the conclusion of his fourth expedition through the western reaches of the continent, this one in search of a usable railroad route to the Pacific.

The structuring of the romanticists slips here. Though Jessie Frémont was definitely not traveling steerage, some tug of presentiment should have led her to notice Collis Huntington and to exchange at least nods with him. In 1856 her husband would run unsuccessfully as the first Republican candidate for the Presidency of the United States on a platform advocating, among other things, government help for building a railroad to the Coast. Collis Potter Huntington, one of the founders of the Republican party in California, would cast his first vote as a Republican for Frémont. A decade later he would help turn Frémont's promised railroad into actuality. He would always admire the Frémonts and would visit them often. When they were in desperate straits late in their lives, he would respond generously to Jessie's embarrassed appeal for help. But if he and Jessie met aboard the *Crescent City*, as drama suggests that they should have, there is no record of it.[12]

At twenty minutes before two, only forty minutes behind schedule, the great paddle wheels on either side of the ship began to churn. The red-shirted passengers crowded along the rail and the throngs waving from the dock, among them Senator Benton, whooped and yelled and wept. One more collection of molecules in America's greatest at-home adventure, the gold rush to California, was off on its erratic course toward unguessable combinations.

2 Almost the Finish

George Murray, the one-time bookkeeper for S. & C. P. Huntington, was smug about his stomach. When the first rollers shook the *Crescent City,* he wrote blithely in a letter-journal he was keeping for his backers, Dr. Case and Solon Huntington, "The majority of the Passengers on board . . . were taken Sea Sick including all *our boys* except *myself* and Vomited considerable and looked as though they would give boot to be set down again in Old Oneonta." The queasiness continued for several days. A preaching scheduled for the stormy morning of Sunday, March 18, was canceled by the disability of "the two Domini's on board . . . together with a large number of other Passengers among them our boys generally except myself." Finally, though, the sun rose "once more clear" and the Oneontans began to sit straighter. Able to eat again, they found "the miserable food . . . Provided for Steerage Passengers" to be intolerable, and by paying extra were allowed to dine in the saloon. "Now we are all in Good Spirits and enjoying ourselves 'tip top'."[1]

The weather growing milder, some of the steerage passengers left their fetid cabins to sleep on the deck. To pass the time they played whist and spun yarns. Soon big, bantering Collis Huntington was popular enough that he was chosen by the passengers as one of a committee of five to speed the crossing of the isthmus.

A transportation system of sorts—by native boat up the Chagres River to the head of navigation at Gorgona and then by mule to Panama City—had been in existence for three centuries. Soldiers and administrators bound for Spain's distant possessions traveled that way from the Atlantic. Jewels, spices, china and other oriental exotics, and gold and silver bullion from Peru and Ecuador crossed regularly from the Pacific. In spite of the route's longevity, facilities remained haphazard, and in 1849 they were overwhelmed by the influx of frantic gold seekers. If the different companies aboard the *Crescent City* were to rush pell-mell into Chagres and bid against each other for what was available, prices and confusion would skyrocket still higher. Avoiding this turmoil was the assignment of Collis' committee of five.

To keep the nervous passengers from suspecting them of favoring their own companies, the quintet named a new committee of fifteen, drawing its personnel from each of the principal groups on the ship. These fifteen appointed two executive groups of three each, with full powers to make arrangements for such persons aboard as subscribed ten dollars apiece to the treasury—two hundred and sixty of the passengers, as matters developed, or well over half. One of the trios was charged with obtaining boats for ferrying the contributors up the Chagres River. The other trio was to hurry on to Gorgona and rent mules for the remainder of the journey to Panama City on the Pacific coast. Huntington, who clearly had impressed the milling wayfarers, was made chairman of the boat bargainers. George Parbert of Geneva, New York, recently a candidate for Congress, was head of the threesome entrusted with procuring mules.[2]

Toward dusk on Friday, March 23, the *Crescent City* hove to a mile or more off the jungle-green mouth of the Chagres River. The water was too shoal for a closer approach, and the confused lightering of men, baggage, mail, and freight to the shore by means of the diminutive steamer *Orus* would begin in the morning. The two transportation committees went ahead, rowed in a native dugout under the dark walls of ancient Castle San Lorenzo, frowning down from one of the headlands.

Chagres was a miserable place of blue mud, some fifty palm-thatched huts, rubbish, putrefying offal, insects, and indolent brown men and brown women clad alike in a single loose white garment.[3] On the opposite side of the river, on a sandy flat, stood a few raw frame buildings, most of them intended as hotels and restaurants for the gold seekers and not yet finished. Probably the committees headed toward one of these. Word got out that they were the great *patrons* in charge of hiring boats for everyone, and a clamorous crowd assembled. The bargainers waved them away. After a leisurely meal, they hired an interpreter. With an indifferent take-it-or-leave-it air such as had served Huntington well during his days of peddling, they announced that they would spend $2,600 to get 260 people to Panama City. Casualness was not the sort of approach the boatmen were used to. Also, the sum involved for their section of the trip sounded, in the aggregate, tremendous. After frenzied haranguing they capitulated.

12

If Huntington really did devise the plan, as he stated in his reminiscences, he made one slip. He entrusted the entire $2,600 to George Parbert, who was to pay each boatman his share only after he had landed his cluster of passengers at the head of navigation. That done, Parbert's trio was to use the remaining money to make arrangements with the muleteers.

Off Parbert went early the next morning with the first wave of lightly encumbered travelers. Huntington stayed behind for three days, until the last of those for whom he was responsible had found boats and had loaded their baggage. This waiting may not have been entirely altruistic, for Collis and young Egbert Sabin also had to extract S. & C. P. Huntington's freight from among the piles of cargo that had been tumbled on the muddy beach and enter into contracts for moving it. As soon as they were sure that the goods were on the way, they joined the last of the stragglers and pressed upstream between thick walls of luxurious green, brightened here and there by tropical flowers and scolding birds.

Before they reached Gorgona they met angry boatmen returning downstream. The men had expected to be paid in American dollars, which commanded a 37 per cent premium over the unstable pesos of New Granada. Instead, Parbert had paid them in pesos and had gotten away before the workers realized that they had been hoodwinked.

Recognizing Huntington as one of the committee who had hired them, the men came clamoring to him. As he picked up the story piecemeal through almost incoherent interpreting, Collis calculated silently. Parbert's manipulation of the exchange rates had cut costs by $3.70 for each of the 260 subscribing passengers—a total of almost a thousand dollars. No wonder the boatmen were disturbed—and yet there was no restitution Huntington could make there in the middle of the river. He broke away from the gesticulating natives and went on, wondering meantime just where that thousand dollars was.

The trip to Gorgona took three days. Sometimes travelers ate in a native hut beside the stream; sometimes they opened their own stores of food and gulped down their meals without leaving the *bongo*. They dozed for a few hours each night either on a mudbank, or, as was more common, humped uncomfortably in the dugouts. It was a hard river to breast with nothing more than pushing poles, and they had to be on the way at dawn in order to utilize every moment of daylight.

(Thanks to letters of introduction from the U.S. ambassador to New Granada, Jessie Frémont, her brother-in-law, who soon suffered from sunstroke, and six-year-old Lily were met at Chagres by an official of the Pacific Mail Steamship Company, whose steamers shuttled between

Panama City and San Francisco. The company was surveying for a railroad across the isthmus. They had special boats and special crews in the river. Jessie's party, remarking the while on the hardships being endured by the unprepared mass of gold seckers, went up the river in one of the company's craft. At Gorgona they were feted by the *alcalde*, or mayor, who served them broiled ring-tailed monkey for dinner.)

The mules the Oneontans mounted at Gorgona were a change but not much relief. The twenty-mile trail over the low mountains was narrow and rough, full of potholes and fallen trees. Here and there they passed dead animals "in different processes of decomposition," wrote one later traveler, "torn and devoured by vultures." By the end of March the rainy season was beginning and mud was everywhere, relieved only in the worst places by cobblestones dumped in long ago by the Spanish treasure packers.

Only twenty miles—but the trip took two hard, wet days. As they neared Panama City, the jungle opened. In the clearings between the trees and the walled city and on toward the beaches sprawled a wretched collection of bamboo hutches and tents made of canvas, Indian rubber ponchos, even blankets and overcoats stitched together with twine. Moving listlessly among the makeshift shelters were knots of sallow emigrants waiting for the next ship north.

The *Crescent City*'s passengers had hoped to catch the Pacific Mail Company's steamer *Oregon* as it moved north on its maiden voyage up the coast. They missed it. There was no recourse then but to join the other stranded travelers and wait. But wait how? In town? Or in the wretched settlement on the beach?

Jessie Frémont, wracked with fever, was given refuge in the home of a wealthy Panamanian widow. Hundreds of less fortunate wayfarers tramped the streets in search of any kind of rentable room in the ancient city, dominated by its incompleted, vine-festooned cathedral of gray stones. Rickety wooden houses leaned toward each other over the narrow streets. Crudely lettered canvas signs, flapping on the whitewashed buildings around the central plaza, advertised beds, food, gambling. Each was crowded, each was expensive. After a process of decision none of them bothered to record, the Oneontans gathered up their baggage from where the brown mule skinners had dumped it—a sweaty, tumultuous procedure —and pitched their tents outside the walls.[4] The arrangement not only let them save money but also enabled Collis to pile his freight where he could watch it. How long they would have to stay there no one could guess. There were already more people waiting for passage than the next regularly scheduled ship could accommodate, and each day additional dozens were arriving.

Throughout this time of frustration the thought of Parbert's unspent thousand dollars kept nagging at Huntington. The fellow was making no effort to restore the money. Moreover, no one was pressing him. The illiterate, unorganized boatmen, who were the chief sufferers, did not know how to go about demanding an adjustment—if, indeed, legal means for hauling a foreigner to the bar on so ambiguous a charge existed at the time in Panama. As for the passengers, they had received the transportation they had paid for. Though tongues no doubt wagged over the trick, the amount involved in each individual instance—$3.70—was so picayune that no one was inclined to fuss. Except Collis Huntington.

As he told the story forty years later, he located Parbert's lodgings in Panama and threatened the fellow so ominously that Parbert promised restitution—not to the boatmen, a step which might have proved impossible, but to the passengers. The agreement extracted, Huntington ordered handbills printed announcing the availability of the money and posted these throughout the city and in the tent colony. Presumably the peculating Parbert was thereupon beset by a crowd of creditors.

Huntington dictated the raw materials of this curious little tale to the uncritical scribes of Hubert Howe Bancroft in either 1888 or early 1889, at a time when he was a millionaire many times over. When the sketch based on the dictations appeared in 1891 (as Chapter II in Volume V of a sprawling series entitled *Chronicles of the Builders*), Huntington's motives for hounding Parbert were ascribed, as might be expected, to unadulterated high-mindedness: though circumstances prevented Huntington's helping the swindled boatmen, at least Parbert should not be allowed to gain.

Conceivably other elements were involved. Rumors may have been flying around Panama City to the effect that all members of the transportation committee had been involved in this misappropriation of other people's money, and Huntington may have attacked Parbert in order to prove his own innocence.

One small clue to the truth behind the story—and a larger clue, perhaps, to Huntington's nature—may lie in the timing. In 1887, only a year before he recounted the tale with the full knowledge that it would soon be published, he and his surviving associates had been ruthlessly grilled by the United States Pacific Railway Commission concerning their multimillion-dollar profits from the construction of the Central Pacific Railroad. The Parbert story, which was not admissible as evidence to the commission, may nonetheless have been designed as an indirect answer to those who

15

read the government's scathing report: "Were the actions of Collis P. Huntington in Panama those of a dishonest man?"

Obviously such a reply (if Collis intended the story as a reply) was begging the point. By 1888, however, years of congressional investigations had turned Huntington into a master of evasion. Again and again he replied to criticisms about the management of the railroad with truthful descriptions of the enormous physical difficulties which had beset its construction, as though there were a balance sheet of credits and debits for ethics like the ones his bookkeepers used in presenting company finances. Thus with Parbert. Honor was honor; if a man dealt righteously with $3.70, would he not (by implication) deal righteously with $3.7 million, or any other amount?

All contemporary accounts of the beach at Panama agree that it was appalling. Rain poured. Mud, mildew, and fungus oozed over everything. Sanitation in the improvised tent city was inadequate. Unwashed raw fruit caused epidemics of dysentery. Malaria swept through the weakened sufferers. There were outbreaks of cholera, threats of smallpox. Some men tried to cure their ailments by indiscriminately swallowing whatever powders, potions, and pills they could find; Huntington's stock of medicines may well have been part of the supply, at astronomical prices. Other stampeders sought refuge in dissipation; Bayard Taylor, who also crossed the isthmus in 1849, was horrified by the vice, depravity, and selfishness that he encountered on all sides.

The demoralization did not touch brawny Collis Huntington. He quickly saw that everywhere along the beach and inside the crowded town men were hungry and ill clad, yet most were either too listless or too unimaginative to reach for remedies. Not Huntington. On the way along the trail from Gorgona he had seen clearings and ranches where provisions, primitive cloth, rush mats, and the like could be purchased, loaded onto muleback, and brought through the soupy mud to Panama for sale.

Unassisted evidently by his teen-age helper, Egbert Sabin, who was sick at least part of the time, he tramped endlessly back and forth, fetching what was available. Once he varied the routine. Hearing of a decrepit schooner on a nearby river, he and a friend walked thirty-nine miles through tropic heat to see her. She was too small and unseaworthy to be used as an escape from the isthmus, but she could still haul produce. They loaded her with sacks of staples, hired as crew a native or two who knew more of the sea than they did, and edged back along the coast toward Panama City. During the five-day trip the friend died of malaria, but Huntington stayed hale. All told, he increased his cash resources by $3,000 during his miserable six-week stay on the fever-ridden beaches—or so he claimed in his reminiscences, which, to be sure, are nowhere marked by understatement.

During April, while he was busy with his trading, a handful of small sailing vessels hove to in the shallow bay out beside the stone sea wall. Though the Oneontans milled and shouted with hundreds of others in front of the shipping offices facing the town's central plaza, they could not get tickets. They had no better luck in May when a cannon booming from the sea wall at 2 A.M. on a moonlit night announced the arrival of the new steamer *Panama* on its way from New York around the Horn to San Francisco. Within hours a sister ship, the *California*, appeared, after having been delayed in San Francisco by the desertion of its original crew. To those who managed to get accommodations, Jessie Frémont's party among them, the double arrivals were providential. But for more than half the desperate waiters on the beach there was no space.

While the steamers were still loading supplies and passengers far out in the shallow bay, a Dutch bark, the *Alexander von Humboldt,* appeared with a load of coal for the fueling station that the Pacific Mail Steamship line was establishing on the nearby island of Taboga. The owners of the bark, men named Leach and Feroud, were aboard, and when they saw the crowds begging for any kind of passage, they decided to rack up several tiers of narrow bunks in the black hold and sell tickets to San Francisco—$175 steerage and $300 for the few first-class cabins.

They announced publicly that they had room for four hundred passengers. Though the figure was more than the bark could safely carry, the ease of the harvest led the owners to keep on selling even after they had reached the promised cut-off point. As the purchasers, including the Oneontans, began crowding aboard, it became evident that the vessel was being dangerously overtaxed. The irate ticket buyers thereupon imprisoned the owners in their own cabin and forbade them to set sail until the excess had been cleared away by lot. They vowed to scuttle the ship if the demand was not met. It was an empty threat. The stampeders were not likely to destroy their best hope of quick departure from the grim beaches. The owners accordingly breathed back defiance and the impasse might have dragged on for days had not an English brig appeared. Eighty-four of the *Humboldt*'s disgruntled ticket holders thereupon gladly transferred to the new ship.

With fatal slowness for some—would-be passengers were dying of fever every day, Collis wrote Solon—Feroud and Leach finished equipping and provisioning the bark. On May 18 the steamer *Panama* sailed with 371 passengers. Two days later the much smaller, far less comfortable

Humboldt beat out of the harbor with 365 fares, plus crew, and bore southwest, searching for the trade winds that would swing her north again.

Before she found them she was becalmed. Day after day the sails hung limply from the three masts. The bored passengers yawned at the magnificent sunsets and listened again and again to the full repertoire of the flute and violin players among them. Slowly their supply of beans, weevilly biscuits, duff, "mahogany beef," as one passenger later described it, and vile-tasting water dwindled. Monotony gave way to apprehension. Committees were appointed to supervise rationing. Huntington seems not to have been included this time. In the few surviving reminiscences left by others, he is mentioned only once. Down in the coal-blackened steerage, where the Oneontans were traveling, he had a fight, cause unstated, with a man named A. D. Starr. Whether it was a physical battle or a mere vocal row is not specified.

On June 26, five weeks out of Panama (the steamers were already in San Francisco), wind finally stirred the sails. Two days later rain fell. Pushing north under full sail, the gaunt mariners reached Acapulco, Mexico, on July 6 and put in to reprovision. When owners Leach and Feroud again proved niggardly about what they ordered, the boisterous passengers took matters into their own hands. After securing the compliance of the officers and crew, they set the owners ashore, ordered and paid for what they wanted, posted notice of a lien on the vessel in hope of eventually recovering their money, and sailed to San Francisco, leaving Feroud and Leach behind.

Shortly before arrival in San Francisco, while the *Humboldt* was groping toward the Golden Gate through a dense fog, those who had financed the food buying began to fear that a lien posted in Acapulco might not be sufficient to secure their money in California. How could they protect themselves? Did they dare seize the vessel, sell it in San Francisco, and reimburse themselves out of the funds thus acquired?

Hoping to justify such an action, the creditors drew up a resolution stating the circumstances and asked the passengers to approve the appropriation of the ship on the grounds of need. To many, the proposal seemed illegal and they opposed it vehemently. In spite of the objections and during a scene of intense excitement, an affirmative vote carried. Shortly thereafter, on August 30, after 102 miserable days at sea, the *Humboldt* entered San Francisco Bay.

Uncertain of his own position in the affair, the captain of the bark (who privately favored the seizure) anchored under the eighteen guns of the war sloop *Warren* and said he would stay there until someone in authority pronounced a verdict. Though California by then belonged to

18

the United States, Congress, torn by dissensions over slavery, had not yet established any form of government for the area. The settlers had established a provisional government of sorts, but its vague jurisdiction certainly did not extend to the high seas. This left the collector of the port the only responsible officer available.

He was in a quandary. At first he refused to let the passengers disembark their baggage, but when the *Humboldt*'s agents in chaotic San Francisco showed no inclination to fight the seizure (in what court, with what funds?) he lifted his ban. Early on the morning of September 1, the passengers collected their belongings, hired water taxis, and were put ashore at the corner of Montgomery and Washington streets. Later the *Humboldt* was sold for $12,000, about one-fifth her worth (scores of deserted ships lacking return cargoes and crews rocked uselessly at anchor in the harbor), and eventually those who had advanced money in Acapulco were repaid.

In talking about the trip to Bancroft's men in 1888, Huntington said blandly that nothing of note occurred during the journey. This is so extraordinary an understatement that one cannot help feeling he was being careful about what he recalled for publication. Was he one of those who, having helped finance the provisioning, advocated seizure? Certainly he had been carrying more money on him than most of the argonauts—the remnants of the $2,000 he had brought from Oneonta, plus $3,000 or more earned in Panama. If his desperate need to reach California had led him to advance some of this sum in Acapulco, he naturally wanted to guarantee its reimbursement in the face of highly uncertain conditions. Yet the steps he and the others took (if he was involved) were not the sort that would further the image of bluff righteousness that he was trying to create in the years following the Pacific Railway investigations. Caution would have been particularly advisable if he gained more from the sale of the ship than he had put into its provisioning.

Whatever the extent of his involvement in the appropriation of the *Humboldt*, the memory of the dreadful hundred days aboard it occupied a special place in his regard. About 1858, those of the passengers who remained in California began to hold irregular reunions. On August 30, 1878, the twenty-ninth anniversary of their dropping anchor at San Francisco, Collis Huntington proposed to the group that they formalize their friendships with an annual anniversary banquet of duff and beans. "That our memories may be kept fresh and green," he wrote in a resolution he submitted to that year's gathering, "we mutually promise to set apart a chair and plate, at each such occasion, for every member subscribing hereto, as well after death as during their lifetime, so long as any of the subscribers hereto are alive."[5]

And so it was done each August 30 for many years, gay reunions amidst an annually increasing number of empty chairs. Frosty Collis Huntington, it would seem, did show occasional touches of sentiment in private, no matter what face he prepared for the public.

3   The Nightmare Cities

Whether Huntington went ashore on August 31, while his baggage was immobilized aboard the *Humboldt,* or whether he spent the enforced delay leaning over the railing as he sized up the astounding town in front of him is uncertain. In any event, he soon estimated what he was up against.

He was in the middle of one of the world's loveliest harbors. The narrows of Golden Gate had widened rapidly into a tranquil, hill-girt bay nearly fifty miles long from north to south. Ships seeking San Francisco worked southward past rocky islets to a sparkling roadstead between the sandy shore and mile-long Yerba Buena, later called Goat Island. At the water's edge, just beyond the forest of bare-masted, abandoned ships, the loveliness ended. Sprawled across the beach and up the sandy slopes behind it was a wild mélange of shelters. The only solid-looking ones were a few Spanish-style adobes built by the original settlers and an occasional large oblong structure, either a hotel or a gambling house or a combination of them, that had been hastily thrown together with lumber costing an astronomical $300 to $400 per thousand feet. Everything else was as flimsy as the shelters at Panama: wooden shanties lined with muslin or paper to keep out the perpetually blowing dust, and a maze of tents that reached up the slopes into the chaparral, where wild flowers bloomed and hungry argonauts could still shoot rabbits for their suppers.

It was a nightmare city. On August 21, only ten days before Huntington looked out at the reckless growth, another merchant, Daniel Wadsworth Coit, had written apprehensively home to his wife, "The town is but one great tinder box. . . . The material is all of combustibles, very dry pine, with a large proportion of canvas roofs; no engines, I mean fire engines; no hooks or ladders; and in fact no water (except in very deep wells) available where it might be most required. Most people have their all at stake under these circumstances. Is it not enough to make a prudent man tremble?"[1]

Surging back and forth along the churned streets was an imprudent tide of young, insecure, womenless men. Most had landed recently after wretched sea voyages; others had just returned from the mountains loaded with gold dust gleaned by backbreaking labor. Both groups were taut with long-pent energy, yet there was nothing familiar, nothing certain on which to expend it. Feeling adrift, they milled back and forth, seeking the assurance of companionship, of bright light in the darkness. The result was a moral chaos that has been endlessly described. "Gambling," wrote lawyer John N. Stone, whose ship had come to anchor on August 28, two days ahead of the *Humboldt,* "is really the business that engrosses the time and attention of the great mass of people. It is open, public, notorious. It monopolizes the best business space and localities . . . while legitimate business occupations are carried on in tents, cloth houses, miserable shanties, and even in the open air, by the wayside and along the beach."[2]

Yet in the midst of the confusion, legitimate business did flourish. By September 1849 there were twenty thousand or so people in San Francisco. All needed food, clothing, shelter. Shovelers were leveling sites for buildings; carters were hauling the sand to the beach and filling in the soft bottoms between stranded hulks that were being used for storage; carpenters were hammering and sawing. Draymen rattled about with groceries. Piers were thrusting out into the shallow water to speed the handling of cargoes. Largest of the docks was the Long Wharf, being promoted, as Huntington may well have learned that day, by Sam Brannan, an apostate Mormon whom Collis would learn to know all too well during subsequent years. Of far greater concern to him right then, however, were the auctioneers who filled the town's plaza, Portsmouth Square, with ceaseless shouts as they sold off, at staggering losses, heaps of ill-chosen merchandise that had been brought from the East in greater quantities than could be absorbed.

One obstacle to normal business was the difficulty of locating equipment and dependable workers. Huntington recognized the problem at once— and the personal threat it offered him. The delay in Panama and the long crawl up the Pacific Coast aboard the *Humboldt* had put the Oneontans in California at least three months behind their anticipated schedule. Winter would soon close the mines. Unless they escaped in short order from the frantic city, their expectations for the year might be lost.

His companions refused to be as concerned about the situation as he

22

was. They had just survived a grueling 102-day voyage, and when they were at last allowed ashore with their baggage, the majority of them hurried toward the Parker House, the most imposing building on Portsmouth Square. There they paid exorbitantly for breakfasts which, under the circumstances, may well have seemed worth every penny. Afterwards some of them sampled the delights of the faro and monte tables and perhaps even went upstairs to rooms which Huntington described years later as "used for the purposes of pleasure."[3]

Not Collis. He found a humbler establishment near the beach at a place called The Point. There on the sand dunes was a tent suburb inhabited largely by Chileans and other Latin Americans. Six weeks earlier Little Chile on The Point had been the scene of brutal violence. Riffraff composed of immigrants from Australia's penal colonies and of soldiers discharged in California at the end of the Mexican War had fallen on the settlement, beating, robbing, raping. Outraged citizens led by Sam Brannan among others had formed a body of special constables, had arrested the leaders of the delinquents, and had run them out of town. For a little while after that San Francisco was relatively law-abiding.

It was still peaceful when Huntington, with teen-age Egbert Sabin in tow, found a restaurant that sold good breakfasts for fifty cents. As they ate, the two wayfarers may have listened to tales of the recent outrages, but as soon as they were finished Huntington led the way back along the cluttered beach. Before long he saw what he was searching for, a lone man struggling to load a pile of boxes and barrels into a schooner beside one of the unfinished piers.

Where was the ship bound? Sacramento? Ah! That was the jumping-off point for the mines, wasn't it? Then perhaps they could do business.

He offered his and Egbert's services in loading the schooner at a dollar an hour each, a modest wage for San Francisco, though it would have been excessive in Oneonta. In return he asked only that the captain find room on the ship to take his goods up the river at the standard rate for the haul.[4]

The ship loaded, he rounded up the other Oneontans and several dozen of the *Humboldt*'s former passengers. On the third or fourth of September they started north, gulls screaming and wheeling above the ship's wake.

As the low brown hills closed around the northern end of the bay, the schooner bent eastward toward the delta of the Sacramento River, a maze of channels between marshy islands and low points, on which grew occasional clumps of trees. There was considerable chop where the thrust of the stream met the tide. As the ship pushed deeper between the reed-grown banks, mosquitoes rose to plague them, and the intense

23

September heat of inland California closed like a fist. They passed little settlements at the foot of rolling swales golden with ripe wild oats. They glanced incuriously at the broad mouth of the San Joaquin, which drained the southern part of the vast interior valley, and, leaving it behind, tacked north up the deep, gentle Sacramento.

The town of Sacramento was located on a wedge of land between the Sacramento and American rivers, on the south side of the latter, just below its junction with the main stream. At first glance the place looked less shocking than San Francisco, an illusion created in part by the tall sycamore and cottonwood trees that shaded and muted its bustle. Actually it was just as raw and even newer than the city by the bay.

Almost surely Huntington picked up the skeleton of its story within hours. After all, that was why he was there: to learn without delay as much as he could about the area and its trading possibilities.

Originally Sacramento had been nothing more than the *embarcadero,* the landing place, for traffic bound to and from Sutter's Fort. An oblong post surrounded by adobe walls eighteen feet high, Sutter's famous trading post stood on a slight rise of ground about two miles back from the main river. Collis must have eyed it appreciatively, for it was the creation of another imaginative trader, a Swiss adventurer, who had arrived in Monterey only a decade earlier with little more to his credit than a fancy military uniform and a glib tongue. After winning a huge land grant from the Mexican Government, Sutter had tamed the local Indians and, utilizing their labor, had carved a primitive commercial and agricultural empire out of the wilderness.

When the first American settlers began trickling into central California during the mid-1840s, the fort acted as a natural magnet. Among the newcomers was Sam Brannan, the wharf builder whose name Huntington may already have heard in San Francisco. Brannan had been an active Mormon and an energetic printer in New York City during the critical years when the church leaders in Nauvoo, Illinois, Mormonism's main establishment, were deciding to flee from their persecutors to refuge in the West—to an isolated land where the faithful could gather and be free. Though only twenty-six years old at the time (1845), Sam had been entrusted with bringing a shipload of the eastern Mormons around Cape Horn. He confidently expected that the midwestern Mormons, who were starting overland at the same time, would end up in California. He was dumfounded when messengers arrived stating that Brigham Young had stopped at Great Salt Lake and that the California contingent was to join them there. Brannan refused. He had smelled opportunity on the Coast, and as he set out in pursuit of it, became all but ubiquitous.

24

From San Francisco, where he was publishing the city's first newspaper, Brannan went to Sutter's Fort to evaluate the field there. By then enough Americans had moved into the area that he and a partner, Charles Smith, decided to start a store for them. Amiable John Sutter granted them a concession and rented them a building inside the walls of the fort. Needing a storage place for the goods they were bringing up from San Francisco, the partners next built a warehouse down at the tree-shaded river landing.

By that time (late 1847) other Mormons than Brannan's group had reached the vicinity. Most of the newcomers had been members of the famed Mormon Battalion that had marched through the southwestern deserts to Los Angeles during the war with Mexico. When peace came and they were discharged, several drifted up to Sutter's in search of work, so that they could join their families beside the Great Salt Lake with cash in their pockets. Sutter hired some of them to go up the South Fork of the American River and help build two mills. One, a flour mill, was located at the edge of the foothills. The other, a sawmill being erected by carpenter James Marshall, lay farther back in the mountains, among thick stands of pine trees suitable for lumber.

The Mormons working at the lumber mill saw the grains of gold that Marshall picked out of the tailrace sometime between January 19 and 24, 1848.[5] Curious but not particularly frenzied as yet, some of them dug experimentally through the gravel near the tailrace until they reached bedrock. Clearing out a space on the surface of the stone, they probed into its tiny crevices with their knife blades. More gold gleamed on the steel points.

Sutter tried to keep the discoveries secret, hoping to gain control of the land, which lay outside his grant, before a rush started. But of course the word leaked. Among the first to hear it were the Mormons working farther downstream at the gristmill. On one of their days off they walked up the river to see what was afoot. They watched their fellows dig and from them learned where gold was likely to occur. The mineral, they were told, apparently washed downstream mixed with masses of gravel during spring floods. The mass settled wherever the current slackened—for example, on the flats between the S-shaped bends of the river, where it bounced off one wall of a canyon toward the other. Because the gold was heavier than the gravel, it settled first and was covered by thick layers of overburden. A quicker way of separating it than probing with knife blades was to use a pan or a rocker, devices recently shown them by whiskery old Isaac Humphrey, a wanderer who had learned mining years before in the goldfields of Georgia.

Their minds full of such talk, the gristmill workers started downstream to their jobs. Along the way they noticed on the south side of the swinging river a flat—soon such places would be called bars—like the one at Coloma, the name of the widening in the valley where the sawmill was located. A secondary channel holding overflow water from the main stream ran along the back of the bar. The result was a sort of island. The gristmill workers named the place Mormon Island, and as soon as they could get another day off from their jobs they returned. They found nuggets there too, some especially fine ones in the riverbed, which they exposed by enlarging the overflow channel and turning the stream through it.

Meantime other Mormons—and other gentiles too—were spreading out to other bars, proving beyond doubt that the gold was not confined to isolated pockets, as had been the case with discoveries made a few years earlier in southern California. Because those first finds had turned out to be fiascos, men in Monterey and in little San Francisco (population 812 in March 1848) had been slow to accept the tales of new discoveries being made farther north. Sam Brannan soon changed that, however. He collected a vial full of nuggets from Mormons who came into his and Charley Smith's store to trade, and in May he took the collection to San Francisco. Waving it overhead, he strode through the streets shouting, "Gold! Gold! Gold from the American River!" After that the rush was on, from the bay area first, then Mexico, the Hawaiian Islands, Oregon, and finally the entire world.

Cynics said that Brannan started the excitement to benefit his store at Sutter's Fort, past which the stampeders must stream on their way to the American River. If so, he succeeded. Business was so good that he soon bought Charley Smith's half interest in the place for $50,000. He moved the stock to a large canvas-covered building near his warehouse at the embarcadero. He next enlarged the warehouse and added branch stores at Coloma and Mormon Island. Before a year had passed he had purchased three sailing ships and was dickering for a steamboat so that he could keep merchandise flowing to him from San Francisco. It was enough, all right, to make a trader used to the slower ways of Oneonta shiver with envy.

Sacramento mushroomed hectically around him. On paper its plan looked orderly. The streets ran at rigid right angles to each other and showed no ingenuity in naming. Front Street, then First, Second, Third, and so on lay parallel to the embarcadero. Streets perpendicular to these were lettered. By the time Huntington and the Oneontans landed, J was the principal thoroughfare. Frame oblongs, shanties, and tents straggled along it for nearly a mile. Neither sidewalks nor paving graced any of the ways, and the gullies that meandered across them here and there were bridged only occasionally by foot planks. No one ever paused to pick up rubbish.

Titles were as chaotic as the streets. Sutter claimed the land by virtue of his grant from the Mexican Government, but he was so easy a mark for fast talkers and so often muddled by drink that his affairs had slipped into a dreadful state. Hoping to circumvent bankruptcy, he had deeded most of his property, including the townsite of Sacramento, to his son, recently arrived from Switzerland. Because this had been a mere gesture, the old man still felt he owned the land and in expansive moments appointed different agents to sell lots. On occasion he even gave away chunks of the city. The son meantime had also appointed agents, with the result that several people were often engaged in selling different buyers the same pieces of property.

Inevitably Sam Brannan got into the act. He threatened to move his store and warehouse to a rival townsite and persuade other merchants to follow—unless the Sutters gave him, free of charge, two hundred lots worth several hundred dollars each. Fearful that he might be able to choke the growth of Sacramento, the Sutters meekly complied.

Having thus rooted himself in the town, Brannan decided to boom it by building the flossiest hotel in California outside of the Parker House in San Francisco. He inveigled Sutter into selling him the half-completed gristmill at the edge of the foothills, tore it down, and hauled the boards to Sacramento. On Front Street between I and J he erected a three-story inn thirty-three feet wide by fifty-five deep, its façade graced with the only wrought-iron grillwork in northern California.

Some of the money that he needed for this and his other enterprises he raised by virtue of his position as an elder of the Mormon Church—at least he said he was still an elder. He collected tithings from church members at Mormon Island—one tenth of all the gold they dug—but there is no record that he ever sent an ounce of it back to Brigham Young in Salt Lake City, where it was desperately needed. A man of infinite contrivances, Sam Brannan was. Not even California has ever seen another promoter quite like him.[6]

When the Oneontans stepped onto the embarcadero, the grand opening of Brannan's City Hotel was only days away. Dodgers advertising band music, free drinks, and fireworks were plastered about the town, but Huntington did not let these prospects tempt him. Seeking information, he and his friends turned down Front Street to the nearest express and livery office. The heat was suffocating. There had been no rain for nearly half a year; the reddish dust in the street, shoe-top deep and as fine as powder, puffed up under the least touch and then settled back in gritty layers on skin and clothing, even on a man's teeth.

At least competition was driving down prices. Having decided that Mormon Island was the closest center of extensive mining, the Oneontans found a drayman who would carry their baggage for a mere $4.30 per man.[7] His freight Huntington left behind until he could determine where to locate his new store.

The men walked, an exhausting, thirsty journey across sunbaked plains. Slowly the foothills took shape through the haze of the valley. Cottonwoods and alders lined the South Fork of the American River; live oaks laid patches of dusky green on the high brown slopes, fragrant with the smell of sunburned grass. After a two-day trudge, they reached Mormon Island, a town as shapeless as if it had been jettisoned from a balloon to splatter against the slope of the valley.

Every cubic foot of the neighboring bottomlands had been shoveled up and washed in simple pans and rockers. Because those primitive processes had not removed the finer bits of gold dust, the area was now being reshoveled into more sophisticated sluices and long toms. Other men, having learned that a few ancient bends of the river had survived erosion higher up the hillsides, were energetically moving the mineral-bearing earth to water level by hauling it in carts or sliding it down long chutes. The stream, shrunken by the annual summer drought, was used and reused until it emerged below the town as liquid mud.

A newcomer had difficulty establishing himself among the intent, grimy mass of men who were so industriously tearing up the valley. A would-be miner either had to buy a claim from someone already there or else wander around the edges of the camp in search of an opening that earlier prospectors had overlooked. Although a laborer could choose among a score of menial jobs offering high pay, he soon discovered that living costs were equally inflated; besides, no one had come to California merely to work for day wages. Merchants also found profits elusive. The best a man could do was build a bough-sheltered booth or a dark little log cabin, display the untested wares he had brought with him, and learn by experience which articles moved and which did not. As one disgruntled inhabitant of Mormon Island put matters in a letter to his family in Iowa, "Say to all my friends: stay home. Tell my enemies to come."[8]

Soon convinced that Mormon Island did not offer the financial heaven they had crossed Panama to find, the Oneontans decided to climb to the Dry Diggings, off beyond the ridges to the southeast. These placer mines, located among pine trees in high little mountain valleys, were called dry because not enough water flowed through the creeks during summer to support extensive washing operations. Activity should pick up, however, at the beginning of the rainy season.

To the trader the scattered Dry Diggings offered another advantage. Most of the camps were located on or near the Carson Route, southernmost of the three main overland emigrant trails into California. It was a new route, winding up the Carson River from present-day Nevada and skirting the southern reaches of Lake Tahoe. It had been opened just the year before by members of the Mormon Battalion who were hunting an easier way to Utah than the familiar central trail, the Truckee Route north of Tahoe, where the cannibalistic Donner tragedy had occurred during the winter of 1846–47. Finally, it was considerably shorter than the Lassen Trail that entered the Sacramento Valley far to the north. Thus, though the Carson Route was new, it was populous. Of the estimated 21,000 people who reached California overland during the late summer and early fall of 1849, approximately 8,000 came by the Lassen Trail, 7,000 by the Truckee, 6,000 by the Carson.[9]

By mid-September, the influx of immigrants was nearing a peak—gaunt, ragged, hard-used men, many afflicted with scurvy, all of them in need of supplies for mining or just for staying alive.

Like many another gold-rush peddler, Huntington decided to buy the most likely items he could find in Sacramento, haul them to the mountains, and catch the ill-supplied newcomers as they were fanning out to the mines. After he had skimmed that cream, he could settle down in the Dry Diggings to batten on the winter activities.

At that point, on September 14, just when he needed complete flexibility, Egbert Sabin was attacked by severe cramps and, as Huntington wrote it, "diareah." Though miserable, he was in no danger. If he co-operated, the others could press on with their work . . . if.

Huntington was dubious. By then he was well acquainted with this lad, in whom he had already invested hundreds of dollars. Egbert was a compulsive glutton. With forebodings, Huntington put him to bed in the Oneontans' community tent at Mormon Island and told him that during the next few days while the hale members of the group were exploring the Dry Diggings, Egbert was to eat nothing but beef, boiled rice, tea, and toast. He placed a supply of the provisions beside the stove and with Dan Hammond climbed off across the ridge to the Dry Diggings. There he picked the camp of Weaverville as the best spot in which to launch his trade. But he would have to hurry to catch any of that year's emigrants.

Back to the tent at Mormon Island he went, hopes high. There he found Egbert sicker than ever. He thundered questions at the pasty-faced boy and received only evasions in reply. Later, Egbert confessed to Dan Hammond that on the evening of the second day of his illness he had crawled feebly out of bed and had "bakeed a cake and eaten the Same Shortned with lard and sweetened with molasses, witch caused his Relaps."[10]

They dragged him up the hill to Weaverville, but he was never much help around the makeshift store. Each time he regained enough strength to move around, he went on another eating spree and collapsed again. Then, in October, the rains began. Completely disgusted, yet fearful that the lad could not survive the winter unattended in their canvas shelter, Collis took him to Sacramento and put him to board at the Pomona House, a passable hostelry run by a man named Philander Hunt.

Egbert recovered and in November went back to Weaverville, where Dan Hammond and Leroy Chamberlin, another Oneontan, could keep an eye on him between shifts with their sluice boxes. Huntington did not go with him, for by then he too was ill, downed by a combination of causes.

He was exhausted. In addition to his wayside trading post at Weaverville, he had set up another at Mud Springs and a third at Marthelness Creek, now unidentifiable. He had been jumping without pause from one place to another, then rushing down to Sacramento for odds and ends that someone asked for. During the mellow days of Indian summer the trips had been pleasant. "I would take my blanket," he recalled years later, when nostalgia was softening the hardships, "and lay down and picket my horse. I used to enjoy it very much. There was a kind of vastness about it. . . . I could see how the Indians liked that kind of life."[11] Soon, however, the onslaught of damp weather, increasing nervousness, and a spartan diet as unbalanced in its way as Egbert's, left him susceptible to viruses. It may have been typhus, which swept Sacramento shortly after the advent of the 1849 rainy season. Or it may have been an awakening of a latent amoebic dysentery that he had picked up in Panama. Whatever it was, it felled him.

Years later he remarked laconically that it was not good to be confined to bed in a tent—a wet tent, moreover, stuffed with goods awaiting disposition. His weight dropped from 200 to 125 pounds. Although his friend from the *Humboldt,* Dr. John F. Morse, and another medical man, Dr. James Stillman, had built a rough plank hospital fifty feet long and forty wide in Sacramento, it was always overcrowded. Huntington stayed away and nursed himself.

On January 9, 1850, while he was still shaky on his feet, a fresh deluge dropped onto the rain-soaked soil and triggered one of the most notorious of Sacramento's long series of floods. By midnight, wrote one

30

recent arrival, "the water was from 4 to 7 feet deep in the houses, destroying everything perishable in the shape of goods. . . . Everything that water would spoil was lost." Another stunned resident wrote, ". . . the whole country as far as the eye can reach is under water, nothing but a wild sea all around." Though lifeboats from the dozens of steamers and sailing vessels tied to the embarcadero were used for rescue work, many drowned. Invalids as sick as Collis had recently been were found floating about on their sodden mattresses. Hundreds sought refuge in the anchored ships or crowded into the top floors of the two-story houses.

The muddy water stayed high for more than a week, but the surge only increased the nightmarish frenzy of the place. People conducted business on their housetops; lots completely under water kept on changing hands at unheard-of prices. Men in rowboats descended on knolls where Sutter's cattle had taken refuge, killed and butchered the animals and hawked the dripping meat through the stricken town without the least intention of ever accounting to the owner. Everywhere there were wild drinking bouts, as if in defiance of this wet end to high expectations.[12]

By unrecorded means Huntington found shelter for part of his merchandise and hired George Murray, who had been driven by high water down from Mormon Island, to dispose of as much of it as he could. Then, long before Murray thought that travel was safe, Huntington started by rowboat across the flooded plains to see what was happening to his stores in the mountains.[13]

It was discouraging. The rains, far more excessive than usual, had hindered mining instead of helping it. The diggings were nearly deserted, prices had plummeted. Of the goods he had brought all the way from New York, only the woolen socks and the patent medicines had paid the cost of their freight; a batch of rifles, from which he had hoped a great deal, were still on his hands, worth less than two dollars each. Even the items he had purchased in Sacramento after learning more about the local needs had failed to withstand the exorbitant transportation costs and the unanticipated drop in demand.[14]

And then there was Egbert. The lad had fallen so ill after his return to Weaverville that Dan Hammond had summoned a Dr. Smith, who prescribed the most expensive drugs in town and, like everyone else, cautioned the patient about his diet—to no avail. "While hardly able to walk," Collis sputtered by letter to Solon, the boy had repeatedly sought out an unco-operative "dealor in provisions" named Sheldon Fogus and had bought from him, charging the bills to Huntington, "Pickeled Onions Pies made of Dried apples, dried Peaches Cold Boiled Beans Salt

Cod fish Salt mackerel molasses Cakes &c," in consequence of which "he experienced Sevrel relapses."[15]

Matters were so bad that Huntington hired a covered wagon drawn by oxen, made a bed in its bottom, and sent Egbert back to Philander Hunt at the Pomona House. Hunt in his turn summoned Dr. Morse, and those bills, too, went to Collis Huntington, at gold-rush rates. Before he was through with his apprentice, who returned next to nothing in the way of help, Huntington had expended on boat tickets, board, lodging, allowances, drugs, and doctors upwards of $2,700.[16]

Egbert stowed out of the way in Sacramento, Collis surveyed the sodden Dry Diggings and asked himself what next. Give up? His Yankee jaw set hard behind his wiry black whiskers. No. There was money to be made in California, but only if one planned. In his anxiety to make a fast killing he had spread himself thin in unstable camps where a heavy rain or even the rumor of a strike on the other side of the hill was enough to wash customers out of reach in a twinkling. Would it not be wiser to concentrate his efforts in a distributing center like Sacramento, frenzied though that town was, and act as a jobber?

To do this he would have to find additional help and financing. In his dogged, persuasive way, he soon located both. Young Dan Hammond, who had experienced no better luck at mining than Collis had at trading, agreed to work a year without pay in return for a third interest in the enterprise. Another third went to Edward Schultz, recently arrived from Pensacola, Florida, in return for $5,000. Collis' contribution consisted of such stock as he had on hand and the remnants of the cash that he had brought from Oneonta and had earned in Panama. Inasmuch as Solon shared fifty-fifty in whatever profits Collis earned in California, he was also, in effect, a sleeping partner in the new firm of Huntington, Hammond & Schultz.

The agreement formalized on paper, the new partners rented a lot on K Street for $1,800 a year. On it they erected a building which, though starkly simple and roofed at first with canvas only, cost $1,000.[17] By March 1850, while the streets were still swampy and the miners were still killing time in such favored gaming places as Jim Lee's notorious "Stinking Tent," they were ready to face another year.

4 The Education of a Gold-rush Merchant

Even granting the many justifications for failure, it was hard to explain to Solon why a year's effort had produced no income for S. & C. P. Huntington. The elder brother needed money badly—George Murray could not repay any of his loan, either—and the strain of putting him off is evident in the letters Collis sent him on March 25, 1850, and again on June 17.

It had been a difficult year, Solon: sickness, floods, high freight charges to the mines, goods unsuited to the market. And Egbert. One can't help a flood. But Egbert! By early March, Dr. Morse had revived the boy enough so that he could come to the new store to live with the proprietors and, presumably, help a little. Then, on the second day, "he commensed vomiting and had a very severe Pain in his Bowels and soon began to Purge." The same old story: "molasses cake, Som Dryed aple Pie . . . an orange and . . . Some nettle Greens." Enough was enough. When Egbert could walk again, Huntington took him to San Francisco, put him on a ship, and sent him home. Nearly three thousand dollars wasted, Solon.

Uncharacteristic self-pity touched him:

I should hav bin to home long eare this if I had com alone and on my own act [account] for I hav Suffered mutch in this Country, mutch in Sickness and mutch in helth and how could it be otherwise how can one leave for som of the best yeares of his life his nearest and deares frends and a quiate Home and loving Wife Without looking back With bitter Regret.

To that he added stoutly, with more than a touch of a martyr's relish, "I shall Stay untill I have Sattisfied my Self and all others conserned

33

that I hav don the best I Could under the Sircumstanses. . . . God Speed the time of my return."

The letters that he must have been writing at this same time to Elizabeth have not survived and so we cannot know how he accounted to her.

In spite of such complaints, it is impossible to read the more typical of his hastily penned letters and believe that he really wanted God to speed him back to quiate Oneonta. Conservative though he became in his later years, as a twenty-eight-year-old he responded with an adventurer's zest to the strangeness and the uncertainties surrounding him. He assured Solon that he meant to do a safe business—"I Shal not cast all on one throw and become Rich or poore on the issue"—but in California in the early 1850s it simply was not possible to conduct safe businesses.

Prices fluctuated violently. The sudden opening of a new mining district might create insatiable demands. Shortages led speculators to rush orders across Panama to New York, and then, just as imbalances were swinging to adjustment, more shiploads would arrive than could be absorbed. Or else none would come. Vessels plowing the 17,000-mile route around Cape Horn occasionally sank or were delayed for repairs. Although the isthmus offered a tempting shortcut, transshipping charges were expensive, and awkward cargoes had a way of lying forgotten on the docks at Chagres for months on end. Collis was so concerned about one rush order for Ames shovels that he urged Solon to accompany the goods to Panama in person, to make sure there were no delays.[1] For good cause Californians were among the most vociferous supporters of increasingly frequent proposals that the government help finance a railway across the continent.

Problems with freight continued after the merchandise had reached the Coast. Each transfer point was a potential bottleneck. Helter-skelter heaps of goods piled high whenever trade routes to the interior were blocked by floods or droughts, by shortages of shallow-draft river boats, or by the failure of mule trains to appear on schedule. Adequate storage space for these delayed shipments did not exist, and weather damage threatened. Moreover, speculative goods were generally bought with borrowed money. Because available capital was limited, interest rates at times reached a staggering 10 per cent a month and seldom dropped below 3 per cent a month—at least 36 per cent a year on ordinary transactions. (No wonder Collis had preferred giving Schultz a third interest in the store rather than borrowing what he needed.)

34

Faced with long delays, desperate entrepreneurs often avoided spoilage losses or excessive interest charges by auctioning off their immobilized material for whatever it would bring. Whether or not the buyers obtained a bargain depended on their ability to break the jam and start traffic flowing again. Hence Sam Brannan's eagerness to own his own boats in spite of the enormous investment involved.

Collis, who acted as principal buyer for Huntington, Hammond & Schultz, overcame some of the trade's disadvantages by learning to gauge demands based on seasonal rhythms and, especially, on the needs of each new wave of immigration. (Mail traveling by way of the isthmus brought information about the size of the annual overland influx long before the travelers themselves had crossed the Continental Divide.) His letters to Solon were sprinkled with instructions about hurrying: "Send the Grind Stones & fixtures as soon as bosible on a Clipper ship so that they will be here in the Spring by the time pepol begin to move." When Solon failed him he railed angrily: "When I order goods I do it on what I think the market will be Six months after I do so and I hav Rarely mised in my judgment."[2]

Another way to overcome price fluctuations was to wander among the wholesale houses of San Francisco, ears alert to trade gossip. He insinuated himself easily. He was big and bluff and hearty. As a sort of character tag he wore an enormous straw hat that he had picked up in Panama, a shapeless thing whose wide brim flopped down to his shoulders. Before he was thirty he was known throughout the mercantile colonies of both San Francisco and Sacramento as Old Huntington, an adjectival form of respect that still persists in such expressions as "you old so-and-so," and "Here comes good old Joe," remarks that have nothing to do with age.

During his wandering and yarning he gathered up clues about price trends. Meanwhile he watched the black arms of the signal tower on Telegraph Hill. When they flipped up to tell the city that a ship was approaching, he excused himself from the others and hurried to Clark Point, the north end of the cove that still embraced most of San Francisco. He kept a dory at the point. Raising the sail, he slanted across the sparkling water, risky enough in a high wind, and intercepted the approaching vessel. If a shouted conversation revealed that it carried available goods of the sort he wanted, he asked for a ladder. After securing the dory, he scrambled aboard to make a bargain that sometimes enabled him to ship salable items to Sacramento at rates his competitors could not match.[3]

Even after a man had purchased merchandise, it still was not safe.

35

Huntington was in San Francisco on the morning of July 14, 1850, when the third of the city's long series of major fires broke out in a bakery at the rear of the Merchants' Hotel. Before noon, four blocks in the heart of the city, from Kearny Street to the water's edge, had been gutted—a five-million-dollar loss, Collis wrote Solon. "One man that I was acquanted had just built a store at an expense of forty Thousand Dollars and had filed it with goods. . . . So he told me at night and the next day at noon he Sed that all the Property he had in the World was the close that he had on, and his Coat was all most burnt of[f] at that."[4]

Although Sacramento was as inflammable as its sister city, the first threats to property there came not from fire but from belligerent squatters. On paper all titles within the town limits (and far beyond) derived from a land grant which the Mexican Government had awarded to John Sutter. Sutter in turn had passed on big chunks of the townsite to speculators intent on running up prices. To many of the incoming Americans this was anathema. They had grown up on a frontier whose philosophy held that every man had the right to forge ahead of settlement and pre-empt whatever piece of real estate he wanted—but no more than he could manage himself. In their eyes, victory in war had washed out foreign claims to the area and the land was open to settlement in time-honored American ways. They built houses on whatever unoccupied lots they desired and then defied either Sutter or those who had bought from Sutter to evict them.

During '49, Sam Brannan and other landlords occasionally retorted by demolishing offending cabins. Later, in early 1850, they acted more legally, obtaining writs of eviction from the courts and handing these to the sheriff for execution. Convinced that the municipal government was subservient to the moneyed classes, the squatters retorted by holding mass meetings to raise funds for hiring lawyers and for conducting election campaigns in support of friendly candidates.

One of the leaders of the squatter movement was James McClatchy, an elderly radical who had once worked for Horace Greeley on the New York *Tribune*. In Sacramento McClatchy continued as Greeley's local correspondent, and also acquired a small paper of his own. During the course of setting his editorial policies, he crystallized his economic philosophies into a coherent enough system that a few years later he would attract as a disciple a young reformer named Henry George, future author of *Progress and Poverty* and promulgator of the idea of concentrating all taxes—the "Single Tax"—on real estate. Before very long Collis Huntington, too, would enter into a political alliance with James

McClatchey. Nothing under the sun, it would seem, is wholly impossible.

On August 13, 1850, McClatchy and one Michael Moran came to the aid of a squatter whom the Sacramento sheriff was trying to turn out of doors. Arrested, they were lodged in the city's only jail, a rat-infested ship moored to the embarcadero.

The next morning a mob gathered to free them. Mayor Bigelow summoned a posse of citizens to defend the jail. The upshot was a battle that raged up and down Sacramento's main street. During it four men were killed and several wounded, among them the mayor, one of whose arms later had to be amputated. The next day the sheriff was slain in another riot. Thereafter the Law-and-Order Party, as its members called themselves, gained control and restored order.[5]

Though Collis Huntington may have been chasing ships in San Francisco Bay at the time—no surviving letter of his mentions the riots—nevertheless, as the proprietor of valuable merchandise housed within a stone's throw of the fighting, he must have faced some of the principles involved. In a clash between fundamental concepts of property tenure, did theory or the power to occupy constitute right? How significant was it that the victorious landlords of Sacramento were able to rely on political as well as economic backing? Was Sam Brannan's or James McClatchy's brand of Americanism the proper one? Or was it wiser to take a midway stance and weave through the turmoil according to the expediencies of the moment?

The antics of the federal government throughout this period added to the demoralization. Although three years had passed since the conquest of California, Congressmen engrossed in wrangling over slavery had not yet provided for a territorial government. Wearied of waiting, the people had elected delegates to meet in Monterey in September 1849 and skip the territorial stage of government by drawing up a state constitution. The voters overwhelmingly ratified the anti-slavery document that resulted and sent it to Washington for consideration. Still nothing happened. For another year Californians managed themselves as best they could under an unofficial government. Not until October 18, 1850, when the Pacific Mail steamer *Oregon* entered San Francisco Bay with flags flying and cannons booming, did they know that their state had at last been admitted to the Union.

Spontaneous celebrations filled the streets. In the midst of the rejoicing, the steamer *Sagamore,* destined for Sacramento, blew up beside one of the docks with an appalling roar, killing thirty or more people. Many of the injured were carried to the city hospital, which stood adjacent to a famous whorehouse. They were scarcely bedded down when a fire broke out in the bordello. The flames consumed both it and the hospital. The maimed and scalded victims of the steamboat explosion were picked up again and carried outside, to lie unsheltered on improvised cots in the October cold while the fire roared on through the poorer sections of the city.[6]

Other disasters coincided with the news of statehood. Cholera, a periodic scourge in the East and Midwest, reached California by ship during the fall of 1850. Sacramento's first case was a man who dropped writhing on the new levee on October 20. Soon sixty cases were cropping up each day. In a single week 188 of the victims died. By November 9 the toll was said to have reached 600, including seventeen doctors—an estimate, since no one was keeping accurate records. In any event, it was bad enough that four fifths of the city's terrified populace fled from the town.[7]

Collis Huntington joined some 250 other passengers in sailing aboard the small steamer *Antelope* for Panama. Was fright making him forsake his partners in the Sacramento store? Or had he arranged this trip to visit Elizabeth, and also his wholesalers in New York City, long before the outbreak? There is no evidence, except for the indirect observation that concern over physical safety seems not to have controlled his actions during other emergencies.

He found only a few changes in Oneonta. A fourth child, Henry Edwards Huntington, had been born to Solon on February 27, 1850, and Uncle Collis probably swung the baby in his big arms with no premonition that Henry would one day be his heir apparent. About this time, too, Solon's and Collis' mother left her dour, contentious husband in Harwinton and came to Oneonta with fifteen-year-old Ellen to live with Solon's family. From that point on Collis' letters contain frequent, affectionate references to her. By contrast, he never mentioned his father, who did not die until 1861.

Oneonta's soft domesticity soon palled. In March Collis told Elizabeth it was time to pack up. Sacramento!—a name almost as forbidding to her ears as Samarkand might have been. Only a year earlier (on March 25, 1850) Collis had written Solon that Sacramento supported forty gambling houses but few churches. Of its ten thousand inhabitants, only six hundred, he said, were females "and Som foure fiths of those are Harlots." More recently, the place had been torn by street fighting and swept by disease. Although the impatient husband almost surely played down such details, Elizabeth may well have blanched at the prospect. In any event, he finally agreed to take her younger sister Hannah along for

38

company, no small consideration since fares for the long journey came close to $500 each.

Just before they left, the shade of bilious Egbert Sabin rose again. On learning that Dan Hammond had not only taken his place as Collis' helper but had been given a third interest in the firm, the young man decided that he had been mistreated and instituted a suit for damages against S. & C. P. Huntington. To Collis the action was a monumental affront. For more than a year, until Solon settled matters out of court, it goaded him to passionate screeds in his letters about the many witnesses he could round up to testify concerning Egbert's egregious eating habits and about Collis' expensive patience in dealing with them. At the moment, however, there was nothing to do but gather his women together and go on with his schedule.

They treated themselves to a three-day stopover in Havana and then caught the mail ship *Falcon* to Chagres. They crossed the isthmus as Collis had done, by native boat and muleback—"a fine trip," Elizabeth wrote home in some surprise. "The scenery is delightful, so different from any that I have ever seen before, and any quantity of beautiful flowers. . . ."[8] Instead of enduring a six-week halt in Panama, like the one Collis had experienced two years before, they were delayed only two days. Collis, moreover, was an agreeable traveler, so much so that during their pause in Acapulco the ship's captain invited the threesome to join him and his wife in a call on the local governor. For Elizabeth, used to the humdrum ways of Oneonta, it was an exciting insight into what California had done for her burly, one-time peddler husband.

They passed through the Golden Gate on May 5, 1851. If their vessel docked, as most ocean ships did, at the Long Wharf that Sam Brannan and his associates had built, the sight must have seemed to Elizabeth and Hannah as foreign as Panama City. The sea end of the mile-long dock, booby-trapped for its entire distance with large holes in the abused planking, was lined with squat paddle-wheel steamers and graceful clippers discharging cargo, and with river sloops loading for Sacramento and Stockton. Farther in, the wharf was lined with gambling shanties and cramped saloons and with a wilderness of "cheap-John" traders bawling out offerings of everything from secondhand clothing and hardware to fish and poultry. Another visitor that same May described the thoroughfare between the crazily tilted shops as "narrow and crowded and full of loaded drays, drunken sailors, empty packing-cases, run-away horses, rotten cabbages, excited steam-boat runners, stinking fish, Chinese porters, gaping strangers. . . ."[9]

On the day the Huntingtons landed, the confusion was worse than usual.

Twenty-four hours before, San Francisco had been blackened and staggered by her fifth major fire, this one more devastating than its predecessors. Fifteen hundred buildings, including the entire business district, had been consumed. "There were," Elizabeth wrote home, "several gentlemen who came on board to meet their wives and families which said that every dollar they was worth had gone with the flames." Underneath those tales of personal disaster ran disquieting rumors of arsonists setting the blaze so that they could loot the town. Others thought the conflagration was the criminals' way of retorting to growing agitation for a vigilante committee to supplement the weak police force.[10] Surprisingly, however, no one was discouraged. Before some of the ashes had cooled off enough to be carted away, San Francisco began to rebuild.

As soon as the Huntingtons and Hannah Stoddard had reached Sacramento, Collis went looking for a home. He found what he wanted on Second Street near the river, far enough from Sacramento's tinder-dry heart to be safe from a San Francisco-style conflagration—"a cottage built Gothic style with two Piazzas with folding doors opening upon them, the first floor consists of a Parlor, hall, Dining room, & kitchen, with two large Chambers, & a good well close by the kitchen."[11] Nearby he bought, as an investment, a similar cottage that he could rent out. He closed the deals promptly; within three days the family had moved into the Gothic cottage and had started housekeeping.

All was not a second honeymoon, however. When he went over the accounts in the store, he discovered that business had fallen off badly. The frenzied days of the stampede, when men had been willing to pay fantastic prices for whatever they needed, were over. Although mining projects requiring heavy capitalization were underway in the mountains —the damming of rivers to bare their gold-flecked channels, hydraulic sluicing with giant hoses, the deep-tunnel mining of quartz lodes—their harvest would not come for some time. Agriculture was attracting attention, too, but those returns also lay in the future. Meanwhile the market sagged under a glut of goods brought in by belated speculators who had not foreseen the end of the placer rush. Canned clams for which Collis had paid six dollars in New York dropped to $2.75. Whiskey skidded from $2.50 a gallon to twenty-five cents.[12]

Since the closest kind of dealing would be necessary for Huntington, Hammond & Schultz to show a profit, the partners agreed that Collis should spend the summer months in San Francisco, selling the firm's surpluses, trading slow items for faster-moving ones, and clinching whatever bargains appeared. He comforted Elizabeth by promising that he would come home each weekend, which at least was oftener than he had been able to see her when a continent had lain between them.[13] To allay her nervousness—incendiary plots were feared in Sacramento, and a citizens' watch patrolled the streets every night—he prevailed on Dan Hammond to sleep at the cottage during his absences.[14] To Dan it was a pleasant prospect. He already had an eye on Hannah; before the year was out, they were married.

In San Francisco, Huntington found new tensions building. On June 10, the vigilante committee proposed earlier came into formal existence, led by Sam Brannan, the idol of the crowds, and by William Tell Coleman, a prominent wholesale grocer whom Collis almost surely knew. During the summer there were four public hangings, one in June, one in July, and two on the afternoon of Sunday, August 24, 1851.

The excitement spread swiftly to Sacramento, where a committee modeled after that of San Francisco was formed June 25. By coincidence, the activities of the Sacramento group also came to a climax on Sunday afternoon, August 24. Some days earlier, the local courts had sentenced to death three men convicted of an outrageous robbery. The governor, however, pardoned one of the trio. Dissenting from that judgment, the vigilantes seized the fellow and to the rhythm of muffled drumbeats marched him behind the sheriff's posse to a gallows standing in a grove of trees near Collis' home. After the two men in the sheriff's custody had been executed, the vigilantes hanged their prey to the same beam—"just back of my house," Collis wrote Solon, "in plain sight." He approved: "Property is quite safe hear to what it wos before thay wos strung up."[15] There is no way to determine the extent of his actual involvement (he would join another vigilante group a few years later), nor Elizabeth's thoughts as she perhaps watched through her curtained windows a scene far different from anything Oneonta had prepared her for.

Between alarms Huntington was traveling back and forth between the two cities, bargaining industriously and now and then dashing off in his dory to meet incoming ships. A wry irony may have attended one sailing. Quite possibly he watched the ship Tagus, bearing goods for Huntington, Hammond & Schultz, go aground at North Beach, two miles from the wharves, and begin to break up. Whether he saw the misadventure or only heard of it, he had to arrange for salvage operations. Only about a third of his firm's goods were retrieved undamaged, but insurance held actual monetary loss to about $700. The figure of course did not take into account lost time and trade, but inasmuch as prices were still depressed, Huntington, Hammond & Schultz were not as dismayed by the accident as they might have been during more prosperous times.[16]

41

Fall intensified the economic slump. The annual influx of overland immigrants, normally a stimulus to trade, dropped off disastrously—from 45,000 in 1850 to scarcely a thousand in 1851.[17] Though many discouraged storekeepers in San Francisco and Sacramento began giving up at that point, Huntington saw hope in the situation. His reasoning was based on the enormous number of wagons, costing several hundred dollars apiece, which were used throughout California. A principal source was the vehicles brought across the continent each year by the immigrants. Light travel in 1851 meant a shortage of wagons in 1852.

To Solon, who owned part of a wagon manufactory, he rushed off orders for thousands of wheel spokes, fellies, axle trees, chains, wagon boxes, and twenty large lumber wagons. Not junk; the days when buyers would take practically any kind of merchandise were past. The wagons, he emphatically told his brother, must be of "the *best* quality . . . Ironed in the best manner. . . . Be very particular about the timber and hav it thuraly Seasoned for if it is not after making a Sea voyge it will scrink so as to make a Waggon allmost worthless."[18]

He did not believe, moreover, that California had lost its charm for settlers. On November 10, 1851, he wrote Solon, without explaining his reasoning, "I think next year thare will be a vary large emagration to this Country and . . . most kinds of goods will be high." On that assumption he ordered extravagantly: butter in five-thousand-pound lots, comparable amounts of dried codfish and haddock, ten thousand pounds of ham, dozens of pints of peppermint essence and bitters "in hansom Bottles," "as many good Woollin Socks as you can by," a hundred grindstones, shovels, axes, harness, plows, blasting powder.[19]

Most of these orders were for his own account. Early in 1852 Huntington, Hammond & Schultz dissolved. The two-year venture, launched with an investment of $5,000 each in 1850, returned the partners $18,000 each in goods and cash.[20] Presumably this figure also included the proceeds from the sale of the rough plank store building that Collis had erected on a rented lot.

On his own at last, Huntington purchased the lot he once had leased. There, at 54 K Street, he erected at a cost of $12,000—perhaps ten times that much in today's terms—what he and Elizabeth considered to be one of the handsomest brick edifices in Sacramento. "We Shall not hav enny more Rent to pay," he wrote Solon, "and Shall not be in as mutch danger of Burning up as we wos in the old Store." To top off his well-being he also scratched together another thousand dollars and with it built a house that he rented for $150 a month.[21]

His estimate of the future proved sound. Mining and agriculture picked up. In the fall, 52,000 people, the largest immigration to that point, poured into California. Feeling prosperous at last in spite of the notes he had signed for building materials and merchandise, Huntington made arrangements to leave for New York on December 1. He wanted to talk in person to his principal suppliers, Israel Minor & Company and Van Antwerp & Massol. He was also worried about Solon. His brother, who was strapped, wanted to end their awkward arrangement whereby Collis still held a half interest in the Oneonta store and Solon a half in the California venture, which, after years of disaster, the younger brother now seemed intent on mortgaging to the ears.

Collis, too, was willing to end their arrangement. His permanent return to Oneonta, which he once had wished God to speed, was beginning to look more and more remote, and under the circumstances the maintenance of a refuge in the East no longer seemed so prudent as it had in 1849. The segregation of their accounts would be complex, however, and he wanted to discuss it in person.

November 2, 1852, election day in Sacramento, brought a violent interruption to the proposed trip. As ballots were being counted while a high north wind howled through the streets, arsonists, so it was believed, set the city afire.

Alarm bells brought merchants, clerks, volunteer firemen, and spectators running to the heart of the business district. Spears of flame arched from roof to dry roof of the buildings that stood shoulder to shoulder along J and K streets. Wind-spun embers started fresh blazes in the piles of merchandise that storekeepers dragged from doomed structures into the plank-paved thoroughfares, which also began to smoke. Avaricious draymen whipped their frightened teams through the crowds, asking and receiving fifty dollars and up for hauling a single wagonload of movable property to the safety of the levee, where the more timid of the populace were congregating.

Huntington tried to save his stock of goods, five thousand dollars' worth of which had just arrived the day before, by defending the "fireproof" building which housed the material. Flailing wildly with wet blankets and sacks, he, Elizabeth, some of their clerks, and even the servant girl who worked for Elizabeth plunged into the inferno. When the servant girl's sunbonnet took fire on her head, Collis ordered the women into the street. Elizabeth was so exhausted that she fell and had to be carried to safety. Collis kept trying, "untill," he wrote Solon, "the Back Counter wos all on fire and I saw that no effort of mine could Save it and then I wraped a wet Blanket around me and . . . left the Store through a Sheet of flames and Saw the earnings of years consumed eaven to the last dollar." For days afterwards his seared eyes pained him. His loss, a local newspaper estimated, was $50,000.

Others suffered as sorely. Next door to him, a store belonging to Mark Hopkins and E. H. Miller, Jr., two of whose clerks were severely injured, was destroyed at a loss of $55,000. "A Mr. Brigam," Elizabeth wrote to Collis' sister, "who was a very smart young man was burned to death on the same Block." Over on J Street, a dry goods and clothing store belonging to Charles Crocker and his brother—Charles was absent on a trip East—was obliterated. By contrast, the white brick warehouse and store of Stanford & Brothers, located on the other side of the Huntington lot from the Hopkins-Miller establishment, was spared.[22]

With fortitude comparable to that shown by San Franciscans after their disasters, the people of Sacramento began to rebuild. Merchants who had saved some of their stock or who, like Huntington, were able to obtain more on credit in San Francisco, moved the material into temporary shelters roofed with canvas and started selling again, mostly on trust since the majority of their customers had also been burned out.

Raising funds for a new building was more difficult. Although skimping hurt Collis' pride, he did not dare try to duplicate the building he had lost. In its place he settled on a plain, narrow cube twenty feet wide, a hundred feet deep, and two stories high, with open ground to the side onto which he could expand when conditions warranted it. Though he had learned that brick walls, of themselves, did not make a building fireproof, they were safer than lumber, and so he laid out money for them, too. By cutting every corner and doing much of the work himself, he was able to hold costs to about $2,000.[23]

About the middle of December, just as the season's first hard rains were beginning to fall, he moved such goods as he possessed from his tents into the new building. As had happened in 1850, the deluge did not abate. By Christmas Day the upper part of the levee, built as a protection after the earlier inundation, had crumbled and the outskirts of the city were flooded. Throughout the first part of January, 1853, the overflow kept spreading, a vast stagnant pond covering every street, for now the intact sections of the broken levee were acting as a dam, holding water inside the city instead of out. The council ordered the obstacle cut. Slowly the water drained away and commerce began to move again, dragged about through the ashes and mud on flat-bottomed stone boats, since wagons could not yet negotiate the muck. Elizabeth, who had been helping more than her strength warranted, took a violent ague and had to go to bed.[24]

And yet she was able to write home, underscoring occasional words with determined strokes of her pen, "While we have our Health and credit left us we will stay and try to get up again. . . . You know that Collis is not the one to be very easily discouraged. . . . This is no place to get disheartened in. Say to Mother that she must not worry about us for we have a great deal of courage yet and there is not a person in California that has more true friends than Collis has."[25]

Friends in California did not solve Huntington's problems in New York. As soon as one of his principal suppliers, Israel Minor & Company, heard of his troubles, they not only declined to advance him more credit but began pressing him for what he already owed.[26] Toward the beginning of March, after Elizabeth's health had improved enough for him to leave her, Collis decided that he would have to reschedule his interrupted trip East and work out new arrangements.

He was a good salesman. He called first on another of his suppliers, Van Antwerp & Massol. By the time he was through talking, Florian Massol had agreed to go West with him as a partner, putting up whatever funds were necessary to launch the new firm of Huntington, Massol & Company in Sacramento. In return, the Californians agreed to do all their buying through Van Antwerp & Massol, except for certain items —wagons and woolen socks among them—that Collis had always bought through Solon. The contract, which was executed on May 1, 1853, was to run for two years.[27] As soon as it was signed, Huntington called on Israel Minor & Company and informed them with some vindictiveness that although they would be paid eventually, meanwhile receiving full interest, they were at the bottom of his list of creditors and would receive no more of his business.

In Oneonta he gave Solon a note for $3,300 to balance off the values of their half interests in each other's concerns. By then he was heavily encumbered, but Solon seemed even more impoverished and Collis tried to lighten the load by offering to take the older brother's nine-year-old son Howard to California and raise him. The parents demurred, probably with some horror: Sacramento for a nine-year-old! But though frustrated there, Collis was able to expend some of his family affection on his youngest sister, Ellen. She was seventeen then, the only bookish member of the large family, and had exhausted the possibilities of the local schools. Collis, uneducated himself, vowed to send her through college, no matter how much he deprived himself and Elizabeth in order to do it.[28]

On returning to Sacramento, he found that trade remained dull in the still wounded city. To conserve cash, he moved out of the Gothic cottage, which he rented, and set up housekeeping with Elizabeth on the cramped second floor of the cubical store building, behind whose counters she almost surely lent a hand after her own work was done. Stumbling across a bargain in lumber, he borrowed enough money to put up four cheap shacks on lots he owned. Though he soon had close to six hundred dollars a month in rents coming in, expenses and interest charges remained high. But at least he was staying ahead of the wolf. To Solon, fretting about the $3,300 note, he promised grimly, "I hav had all that I could do to get along but"—the pen stroked vigorously—"if I liv I Shall win Sure."[29]

These are the years that led Huntington to recount in his old age the sort of tales that are so often exhibited as examples of the essential barrenness of self-made millionaires. "Young man," he reputedly snapped at a hotel clerk who overcharged him twenty-five cents on a bill running into hundreds of dollars, "you can't follow me through life by the quarters I have dropped." And then there was the employee who did not stoop to retrieve a four-penny nail. Huntington reprimanded him fiercely, not because of the value of the nail but because a worker who let himself be careless about small matters would also prove careless about large ones— if ever the errant employee chanced to reach that stage.[30]

And indeed during those niggardly years Collis did grow hard and cold and calculating, cheery on the surface because his dealings demanded that, Old Huntington still, a local character in his floppy Panama hat, but underneath, suspicious and alert. Yet in some ways he remained remarkably unsullied. He lived in what one writer described as a city notorious for having on every principal corner "a gilded palace of infamy," but there is no indication that Collis Huntington ever worked off his energies or soothed his frustrations behind their inviting doors, even during his long separations from Elizabeth. On every corner, too, the shadiest schemes were concocted, from open thievery to smiling frauds. During the 1850s Huntington was never involved. Every debt he incurred was paid in full, without his turning to various possible devices for shaving corners and cutting interest. Very seldom did he ask for an extension in time. Among wholesalers and bankers in San Francisco, New York City and, to an extent, Boston, his reputation remained impeccable.[31]

Less could be said of his new partners. Taking advantage of their exclusive contract and of Florian Massol's presence in California, the New York house of Van Antwerp & Massol juggled their methods in such a way as to charge the Sacramentans, so Collis wrote his brother on October 15, 1854, "from 10 to 100 per cent more for goods than outher houses." Outraged, he asked Solon to establish contacts with new suppliers, not including Irsrael Minor & Company.

46

He also set about finding a new Sacramento partner for replacing Florian Massol. It was an easy search this time and led not across the continent, as in the case of Massol, but next door, to Mark Hopkins, a man eight years and seven weeks older than Huntington, but destined, despite the difference in their ages, to be the firmest friend Collis would ever have.

The union with Hopkins marked a final retreat from his earlier yearning to return to Oneonta. California was home now, and the shift in attitudes would involve him in local affairs to an extent he had no way of foreseeing at the time.

Comparable adjustments were occurring throughout the state. The frenzied adventurers of the boom days, who had been too busy trying to fill their pockets to pay attention to civic matters, had either left the region or had settled down on farms and in steady jobs. The result was a new set of values stubbornly opposed to the criminal carelessness of the stampedes.

The most immediate of the problems faced by the slowly emerging leaders of the new order was the clearing away of corruptions that during the years of indifference had permeated all levels of politics. Another painful readjustment would be the shrinking of overexpanded credit brought about by the earlier speculative booms. And always there was the desperate struggle to end the economic and psychological ills created by distance—distance from families, friends, and business associates in the East, at a time when it took a letter from home a full month to cross the Isthmus of Panama and heavy freight three months or more to circle Cape Horn.

Leadership in the struggle fell largely to the state's lawyers, who were trained in politics, and to the merchants, who by the nature of things desired stability.[82] Inevitably Huntington and Hopkins became, through the compatibilities of their natures—compatibilities Collis had not found in prior associates—partners in politics as well as in storekeeping. Politics, and not shared business interests, next aligned them with other merchants seeking comparable goals.[83] The import of those bonds was far greater than is generally realized. Although it is superficially true that four men called merchants on the census rolls—Huntington, Hopkins, Leland Stanford, and Charles Crocker—banded together to build the Central Pacific Railroad, it was not their common commercial experiences but, as we shall see, their shared political efforts that enabled them first to sense and then to seize the construction opportunities that suddenly appeared in front of them.

5 California Ferment

Like Huntington, Mark Hopkins had a mercantile background. When he was twelve or so his father had moved with his wife and eight children from the eastern shore of Lake Ontario to St. Clair, Michigan, and there had opened a store. After the elder Hopkins' death in 1828, Mark, aged fifteen, had left school to help two of his older brothers run the establishment. On coming of age, he tried storekeeping on his own in Lockport, New York, east of Niagara Falls. That venture palling, he studied law with another brother but did not take to it and eventually landed in New York City as a bookkeeper. Later in life he would look like the miser he was reputed to be, frail and stooped, his sharp face adorned by a stringy beard. During his New York days, however, he weighed a sturdy 160 pounds and stood five feet ten and a half inches tall. He had a straight nose, a direct glance; his dark hair and beard were neatly cropped. Women probably would have called him handsome.[1]

He was prosperous enough by then and old enough—thirty-five in late 1848—to have been settled in his ways. But there was a streak of restlessness in him. He had never married, and when word of the California gold discoveries reached the East Coast he had no hesitation about breaking old ties. With twenty-five friends he formed a mining company. Each put $500 into the venture. With this they bought supplies and mining equipment that none of them knew how to use. In January 1849 they set sail around Cape Horn, the beginning of a miserable 196-day trip plagued by storms, bad food, limited water, and a tyrannical captain.

They docked at San Francisco in August. Like many another company, Hopkins' group could not agree on its next step. After fruitless quarrels, they separated. Mark, a Dr. James Stillman, and three others purchased a longboat, into which they loaded their share of the community supplies.

In suffocating heat they rowed up the Sacramento River past Sacramento City, on and on until they had reached Peter Lassen's ranch—farther, they said later, than a comparable boat had ever ascended before.

The river growing too shoal for further navigation, they traded the longboat for two wagons and several worn work oxen. Slowly they started toward the mountains. The did not go far. The long ocean voyage followed by the ordeal on the river had drained their strength. Hearing adverse reports of what lay ahead, they gave up the adventure and returned to Sacramento City, arriving in November, at the beginning of the rainy season.

Stillman joined Dr. John F. Morse, who had been on the *Humboldt* with Huntington, in building the city's first hospital. Hopkins invested the last of his funds in merchandise and hauled it through stormy weather to the Dry Diggings. He had as little luck trading there as Huntington was having at the same time in the same vicinity. Whether or not they met at the Diggings is uncertain.

In February 1850, as Hopkins was returning to Sacramento, wondering what to do next, he encountered beside the road E. H. Miller, Jr., with whom he had struck up a friendship during the trip around Cape Horn. After an enthusiastic reunion, the pair agreed that as soon as they could wind up their other affairs they would open a store together in Sacramento.[2]

After a short stay on J Street, they moved to 52 K, next door to Huntington. Their new building, like Huntington's, was destroyed by the fire of 1852, but they, too, immediately rebuilt. Out of shared interests and troubles, Old Huntington and Uncle Mark, as the clerks called Hopkins, developed an abiding affection for each other. Thus when Huntington grew dissatisfied with Massol, he turned first to Hopkins, who agreed to a new partnership.[3] The shift brought no rupture with E. H. Miller, Jr. He formed a new association with other merchants, meanwhile retaining the friendship of both Hopkins and Huntington; later, during their railroad careers, Miller would be one of their most dependable subordinates.

The new partnership could not take effect until the expiration of Huntington's contract with Massol. Hopkins, meantime, had another project in mind, one he had been contemplating since a buying trip to New York City in 1851. In the summer of 1854 he went East again by way of Panama and resumed wooing his cousin, Mary Frances Sherwood, aged thirty-six, with whom he had probably been corresponding throughout the years. On September 20 they were married. Mark had just turned forty-one.[4]

The newlyweds arrived in Sacramento in November, nearly half a year ahead of the time when Mark and Collis Huntington would launch their enterprise. The interim gave Hopkins ample leisure to buy and furnish a house (no second-story living for him and his wife), settle accounts with Miller, discuss the future with Collis (they had decided to switch from general merchandising to heavy hardware for farms, foundries, and mines), walk around town to absorb what was going on, talk politics, and, that subject palling, to discuss the coming railroad.

The transportation project had been devised two years earlier, in 1852, by Colonel C. L. Wilson as a means of bringing freight to certain Sacramento River steamboats which he owned. His plan was to thrust tracks twenty-two and a half miles northeast along the American River to a place called Negro Bar. Once a placer camp, Negro Bar had become a distribution center. Roads for stagecoaches and freight wagons fingered out from there to all the mining towns adjacent to the various forks of the American River. At Negro Bar, Wilson would cross the river and push his rails northward along the base of the foothills, intersecting additional supply roads en route, until he reached California's third-largest city, Marysville, a major distribution point located at the junction of the Feather and Yuba rivers, some forty miles from Negro Bar. When completed, his sixty-mile line—he called it the Sacramento Valley Railroad—would dominate the supply lanes to eight counties, whose 239,000 people imported 162,700 tons of freight a year.[5]

It was a dazzling scheme, but unproved—no one had yet dared try to build a railroad in California, thousands of watery miles from the source of supplies on the Atlantic Coast. For more than a year Wilson could not get the project off the drawing board. Then finally, in October 1853, a drastic reorganization put a few thousand dollars in his pocket. Off he went to New York. His first goal was the hiring of an engineer to make feasibility studies. If these turned out to be as optimistic as he was sure they would, he could then present the figures to construction firms that might be prevailed on to build the road partly for the sake of the speculative profits it offered.

The engineer he approached was one whom Huntington and Hopkins would soon know very well—Theodore Dehone Judah, just turned twenty-eight when Wilson sounded him out in March 1854. A graduate of Rensselaer Polytechnic Institute of Troy, New York, Judah had already begun to win approval from his associates for his work on suspension bridges and difficult railroad grades near Niagara Falls. He was wiry, nervous, incurably sanguine. He was also ambitious. According to his wife Anna, he was even then dreaming of becoming involved in building a railroad to the Pacific Coast. That chimera and the fact that he had a brother living in San Francisco induced him to accept Wilson's offer. He and Anna arrived in Sacramento in May 1854.[6]

The thought of immediately building all the way to Marysville—sixty miles at one swoop—was a little more than Wilson's courage could face. Forty miles to the supply roads serving the Auburn area would do for a starter. So Judah surveyed only the first twenty-two and a half miles to Negro Bar and eighteen more due north to a road junction that eventually would become the town of Lincoln. This almost level stretch, he estimated, could be graded and equipped with both track and rolling stock at an average cost of $43,500 per mile. After making a rough count of the wagons traveling the same forty miles, he concluded that the road's gross revenue would come to $2,063,000 per annum and that annual profits would amount to $1,300,000, or more than 70 per cent per year of the total cost! Persons used to the slow-moving East would, he admitted, view such figures "with astonishment." But such was California—and such was Theodore Judah, perennial optimist.

On the strength of his estimates, the Sacramento Valley Railroad entered into a $1.8 million construction contract with Robinson, Seymour and Company of New York. The agreement contained certain interesting provisions that Huntington and Hopkins almost surely noticed at once. Only $300,000 in cash were committed at the outset by the railroad company. Two hundred thousand more dollars would come from promissory notes issued by the company and payable on the completion of specified amounts of track. Another $700,000 was to be paid to the construction firm in the form of 10 per cent, twenty-year bonds; the builders would sell these at a discount in order to raise additional working funds. The remaining $800,000 were to be paid for by capital shares of railroad stock, issued at par.

This stock provision, common among canal and railroad builders in the East, was potentially mischievous, for it brought to the contractors a sizable block of votes in the management of the company for which they were working. As stockholders they could make sure that they obtained favorable terms as builders. And finally, if the finished railroad succeeded as well as Judah predicted, the stock would soar in value and the already well-rewarded builders could sell out at a thumping profit.

Work began swiftly. The men in charge of construction, brothers John P. and Lester L. Robinson, arrived in Sacramento early in 1855. A hundred workers were hired; scores of picks and shovels were purchased, some conceivably from Huntington & Massol. On February 12, graders moved down R Street along Judah's line of yellow stakes and began shoveling dirt.

Sacramento was enthralled. To an extent difficult to realize today, railroads had captured the popular imagination as beacons of progress, as guarantors of prosperity. And yet, oddly, few people envisioned the new steam marvels as offering anything more than regional magic. There was no concept of broad networks under a single management. Builders simply thrust toward a logical goal without reference to other projects. Even gauges—the width between rails—varied erratically from line to line. The main thing, in the eyes of the boosters, was to get rid of muddy wagon roads and speed the flow of golden commerce between related towns.

Although Huntington and Hopkins may not have attended the ceremonies that launched the grading, they almost surely discussed the impact that the Sacramento Valley Railroad might have in their partnership, due to take effect within six weeks. But one can't talk about shoveling forever, and meantime the perennial subject of California's ferocious politics was competing as usual with all other topics for the city's attention.

As was true elsewhere in the nation, the state's dominant Democratic party was rent by feuds between northern and southern sympathizers. In California, the leader of the northern wing was a former stone mason and fireman from New York, David C. Broderick, who had learned the tactics of brass knuckle politics in Tammany Hall. Leader of the proslavery southern element, the Chivalry Wing, called "Chivs," was the incumbent United States Senator, Dr. William M. Gwin, a handsome six-foot physician and lawyer from Tennessee.

In January 1854 Broderick had begun a campaign to have the legislature unseat Gwin, although the Senator's term did not expire until March, 1856.* As part of his maneuvering for votes, Broderick had Sacramento named state capital, the legislature's first permanent home after seven moves in six years. The triumph drew forth a parade of welcome from local citizens, caused a burst of building, and attracted a large following of both hangers-on and cultural elite to Sacramento. But it did not bring victory to Broderick, for Gwin's friends in the legislature held his seat for him.

Broderick continued the battle during the Democratic state convention, which assembled during the summer in Sacramento's First Baptist Church. The struggle, which was marked by fistfights, brandished pistols, and jostlings that caused several hundred dollars' worth of damage to the church building was again inconclusive.

* In those days U. S. Senators were elected not by direct popular vote, but by the state legislators.

52

In January 1855, the regularly scheduled date for the senatorial election, Gwin offered himself to the legislature as a candidate to be his own successor. Broderick easily blocked him. Gwin then blocked Broderick's candidacy. Neither man would accept a compromise candidate. Fifty ballots failed to break the deadlock, and on February 16, 1855, four days after grading had begun on the Sacramento Valley Railroad, the legislature adjourned, having made no provision to fill Gwin's seat at the expiration of his term. As matters developed, the impasse would continue for two years, to the disgust of the electorate. Throughout this turbulent period California's single Senator in Washington was another Democrat, John B. Weller.[7]

There were other dissatisfactions. Persistent rumors told sordid tales of mismanagement in the state prison, corruption in construction contracts, purchased votes, and, on the local level, brazen laxness among self-servers holding office as a reward for party obedience. These soft spots, together with suicidal intra-party feud, should have made the Democrats vulnerable. But the strength had gone out of the challengers, the Whigs, whose supporters had melted away in California, as they had throughout the nation, after the party's compromse on the Fugitive Slave Law and General Winfield Scott's defeat in his 1852 bid for the presidency.

Into this vacuum came the new American party, imported from the East, nurtured in a score of secret meeting halls scattered through the mining communities, and spread from there to the cities. The group advocated the exclusion of Orientals, a lively issue in California, a check on the immigration of other foreigners, and the rejection at the polls of all but native-born Protestants. Party members, who recognized each other by secret signs and handshakes, were called Know-Nothings, for whenever they were grilled about the group they always disclaimed knowledge of it.

The party appealed to Mark Hopkins, mostly because he had no place else to turn. Like Huntington, he was a Whig. Both were deeply opposed to slavery. Huntington's antipathy had sprung from what he had seen during his peddling days in the South and from what he had heard from John Brown, if he actually did travel for a time with Brown, as legend attests. Hopkins' indignation had been sparked more recently by the so-called Andy case.

Andy was a Negro whose master had brought him from Mississippi to the goldfields to help dig. On returning home in 1852, the owner had freed Andy, giving him a signed paper testifying to the manumission. His own man at last, the black had stayed in the mountains until he had gleaned a few hundred dollars' worth of gold dust. With the earnings he purchased a wagon and a team of mules, intending to become a drayman.

53

At that point a man named Skags overpowered him, destroyed the paper of manumission, and said that he intended, as a representative of Andy's owner, to return him as a fugitive slave to Mississippi. The presumption was that Skags had invented the whole story as a means of obtaining a slave for himself.

Apprized of the situation by a Negro worker seeking help for Andy, Hopkins sought out a Whig lawyer named Cornelius Cole, an intense, tight-lipped former New Yorker of about thirty-five, his wedge-shaped chin decorated with luxuriant whiskers. Assisted by another anti-slavery lawyer named Edwin Bryant Crocker, Cole carried the case to the state supreme court—without avail. California's strong southern element had pushed through the legislature an even more stringent fugitive slave law than the nation's, and the justices, finding no firm evidence of manumission, upheld the law (which Cole had hoped to prove unconstitutional) and remanded Andy to Skags. Off he went with the unhappy Negro, never to be seen again.[8]

Outraged by the decision, Hopkins was ripe for any sort of effective political tie that would let him express himself. He joined the Know-Nothings. Though the Know-Nothings were as divided over slavery as were the other major parties, they at least offered an alternative to the squabbling Democrats, neither branch of which Hopkins could stomach.

Another merchant who joined the Know-Nothings that year was lawyer Edwin B. Crocker's younger brother, fat Charles Crocker, who ran a dry goods store over on J Street. Early in 1855, about the time that the strife-torn Democratic legislature adjourned without having been able to agree on a United States Senator, the two men, Hopkins and Crocker, announced themselves as candidates on the Know-Nothing ticket for seats on the Sacramento city council. Municipal elections were scheduled for April 2.

Charles Crocker had been born in Troy, New York, on September 14, 1822, and thus was eleven months younger than Huntington, nine years younger than Uncle Mark Hopkins. There were six children in the Crocker family, five boys and a girl. Edwin was the eldest and by far the most intellectual. Because the father's business, liquor wholesaling, was relatively prosperous, Ed was able to go through Rensselaer Institute, the same engineering college that Theodore Judah attended a few years later. Then, in 1836, hard times fell, and the father went bankrupt. Following the example of many another debtor, he took his family West to Indiana. There, helped by his younger children he broke out a farm on a quarter section of land adjoining the Potawatomi Indian reservation.

A small coincidence is involved in the proximity. A few years after the Crockers arrived, the Potawatomis sold their holdings to the government and moved to a new reservation near the similarly relocated Delawares and Wyandots in northeastern Kansas. Charles Crocker, still in his teens, signed on with the local militia that escorted the dispossessed Potawatomis partway toward Kansas. Years later, in 1861, appropriation of part of the Potawatomi lands in Kansas would be a crucial element in helping involve Charles Crocker, albeit indirectly, in railroad building. But more of that later.

Not long after the Potawatomi episode in Indiana, Charles quarreled with his father and left home. During the next ten years he did menial labor on nearby farms, rafted logs, and worked in a sawmill, where he fell in love with the boss's daughter, Mary Deming. He could not marry, however. For one thing, he was helping his brother Edwin, who had not taken to engineering as a profession and wanted to switch to law. Charles helped finance the transition out of his meager wages.

As soon as Ed was established as E. B. Crocker, barrister, he repaid the loan by helping his younger brother and a friend build a forge for making bar iron from ore in a mine on which they held a lease. Profits were niggardly. Meanwhile, Ed, a radical abolitionist, was threatened with arrest (so legend says) for helping runaway slaves. He fled town a step ahead of the sheriff and, having heard just then of the California gold discoveries, journeyed to Sacramento, where he hung up his shingle.

Charles decided to follow. He sold his forge, formed a small company of adventurers that included his brothers Henry and Clark—"I was a natural leader in everything," he boasted to Bancroft many years later —and in March 1850 started overland.

The trip was comparable to that endured by thousands of other emigrants that same summer. When human obstacles appeared, Charles blustered them aside. He had grown into a 240-pound mountain of a man, five feet eleven inches tall, bull-voiced and given to explosions of energy followed by periods of extreme lassitude.

He mined with modest success during the winter of 1850–51, then switched to retailing boots, shoes, and mining supplies in small stores in two different camps. Very soon he sold these at a profit and with George Backus as a partner built a larger store in Sacramento, dealing in dry goods, carpets, clothing, boots, and shoes. As soon as the place was running smoothly, he returned to Indiana and on November 25, 1852, wed his sweetheart, Mary Deming. Although he did not know it at the time, his new store in Sacramento had already been destroyed by the blaze that had swept the city earlier in the month.

After a miserable trip West by way of Panama—Mary was seasick the entire distance—the honeymooners reached the muddy devastation of Sacramento. Partner Backus had had enough, but with a courage as stubborn as Huntington's, Charles took in his brother Clark as a new partner, borrowed what money he could, and rebuilt. During the construction of the new store, an edifice twenty-five feet wide by sixty-three feet deep, Charles and Mary lived in a shed they erected against one of the outside walls of brother Ed's small, undamaged house. As soon as the store was finished, the Crockers, like the Huntingtons, saved rent money by moving into an apartment on the second floor. As a sign of increasing civic prominence, Charles succumbed to the fad for beards and grew a set of chin whiskers that hung from his heavy jowls like an oriole's nest.[9]

Just what led him into politics remains unknown, but in any event he joined the Know-Nothings and agreed to run with Mark Hopkins for a seat on the Sacramento city council.

Economic discontent aided their campaigns. An abnormally dry winter shrank the state's streams and threw thousands of placer miners out of work. Simultaneously, the last of the juice evaporated from the erratic up-and-down speculative frenzies that had marked the opening days of the stampede. As was happening throughout the nation, credit tightened. On February 18, two days after the adjournment of the legislature, the steamer *Oregon* reached San Francisco with word that the great banking firm of Page, Bacon & Company in St. Louis had failed. A run on the San Francisco branch of the company closed its doors. The panic spread. On Black Friday, February 23, 1855, every insurance company in the city and every bank but one suspended business.

In time many reopened, but what had been considered the giant, Adams & Company, never did. All told, some three hundred businesses failed in San Francisco, and a comparable number in Sacramento. On April 2, the shaken voters of the capital city turned the Democrats out of office and elected to their council the full slate of Know-Nothing candidates.[10] The exultant winners then began laying plans to capture the entire state in elections scheduled for November.

Victory at the polls did not help storekeeping. Huntington and Hopkins must have weighed and reweighed their plans to link and enlarge their adjoining store buildings as soon as their partnership took effect on May 1. Was it not wisdom to mark time? Yet they had already placed extensive orders for plows, wheelbarrows, fence wire, sheet iron, gas pipe, belting, rope, pitch tar, blasting powder, wagon axles, picks, kegs of nails, even coal. Orders could not be canceled; the material was already on its way by ship from the East, and they would need space for storage.

56

Besides, it was not the nature of either man to hold back, once committed. They decided to press ahead.

(The Sacramento Valley Railroad was in a comparable position. Work had started and the company felt obliged to press on. The barriers were formidable. As was customary at the time, investors had been allowed to purchase stock in the railroad for a down payment of only 10 per cent of par. When management sought to raise funds by assessments and by calling for additional payments, scores of stockholders defaulted. As the treasury neared depletion, founder Wilson was ejected and a new board of directors was installed. C. K. Garrison, who had twice been mayor of San Francisco and was connected with the Vanderbilts, became president. Vice-president was a one-time army officer who would return to the ranks in another war—William Tecumseh Sherman. In 1855, Sherman was an official of the only bank in San Francisco that had not shut its doors. Even this array of talent could not restore confidence, however. In October the Robinson brothers attached the company's tracks and equipment as security for their construction contract. A trustee, J. Mora Moss, assumed charge for the stockholders. Track laying was ordered stopped at Folsom, the new name of Negro Bar. The halt left engineer Judah without a job. No matter. He immediately found another whose main requirement was optimism, a quality he possessed in abundance. But this is getting ahead of the story.)

The decision to remodel the Huntington-Hopkins store buildings turned Collis and Elizabeth out of their second-story apartment, and gave her an opportunity to spend the spring and summer visiting her family in Connecticut. She proved a persuasive booster for California. When she returned in mid-September 1855, her brother William Stoddard and his wife were with her.[11]

The trip home was a terrifying experience. Prone to seasickness, Elizabeth chose to travel the shorter Nicaragua route, even though a railroad had recently been completed across the Isthmus of Panama. Two days after her overcrowded steamer started north along the Pacific Coast—there were 650 passengers and crewmen aboard—cholera began to rage. One shaken traveler told Collis, probably with exaggeration, that he counted eighty-nine bodies thrown overboard in three days and that a total of between 250 and 260 of those aboard the ship perished.[12]

Elizabeth's journey underlined the dread with which most Californians regarded their isolation from home. If one went by sea, the threat of fire and shipwreck was ever present; during the early years of the 1850s several steamers had run aground and had broken up, and in 1853 the *Independence* had burned off Baja California with a loss of 125 of the

300 persons aboard. Physically, the overland journey was an even greater ordeal. One had to use his own equipment, spend three to five months on the trail, and run the risk of Indian attack. In 1855, uprisings on the plains, the nationwide depression, and the free soil-slavery turmoils in Kansas held the number of overland emigrants, which once had reached as high as 50,000 a year, to a few hundred. The state's overriding need, Senator Weller cried to Congress, "is an increase of population." And that would come only with better transportation.[13]

By the middle of the 1850s the majority of the American people favored a transcontinental railroad—in the abstract. Dissension arose when rivals discussed means of expediting it. What route should the line follow? Who should build it? How should it be financed?

Southerners hoped that a line through the southwestern territories would divert California trade to them and open new states that would help them regain their ebbing political power. Northerners, equally eager for Californian and even Asiatic commerce and fearful of a further spread of slavery, demanded a central or northern route. Within these regional disputes swirled local animosities between cities eager to anchor the road to themselves: Chicago, St. Louis, Memphis, Vicksburg, New Orleans.

Economic discussions filled pages of the *Congressional Globe*. Once the route was determined, should the government build the railroad through the undeveloped deserts and mountains, or should the nation aid private companies in doing the work—companies which afterwards would own the road and retain its profits? What form should the aid, if any, take—loans or subsidies of land and cash? Was it constitutional for the government to spend money on internal improvements within a state, or would government participation in the job, if any, be limited to the territories through which the road passed?*

On March 2, 1853, Congress authorized the War Department to conduct "surveys" of the principal cross-country routes under discussion—except for the main emigrant trail up the Platte Valley and through Nevada, a neglect excused on the grounds that the central way was already well known. Private pressure groups added examiners of their own: Iowa promoters sent young Grenville Dodge through Nebraska;

* Governor Clinton DeWitt was hooted down for suggesting in 1817 that the federal government aid New York State in building the Erie Canal. When the government later began offering public domain land to midwestern canal and railroad builders (the idea was that the canal or railroad involved would increase the value of all nearby lands and that the builders were entitled to a part of the increment), the grants were first made to the states, who doled them out to the corporations. States' rights, in short, were so touchy an issue that many people did not even want federal handouts.

Missourians led by Senator Benton dispatched Frémont on another trip through the Colorado Rockies.

The exploratory trips added immeasurably to the nation's knowledge of western geology, topography, paleontology, ethnology, and whatnot. Each group reported that a railroad given adequate funds could be built along the route it had explored. Their estimates of cost were vague guesses, however. As Theodore Judah and many other practical engineers scornfully pointed out, the explorers had conducted fleeting reconnaissances only; they had not made the kind of detailed studies a construction firm would need, and none of the antagonists was likely to be convinced by the data they presented.

Anticipating inconclusiveness even before the reports were published, a group of San Franciscans ran advertisements in the city's newspapers announcing that on December 14, 1854, there would be a mass meeting to discuss what might be done to speed the advent of an Atlantic-Pacific railroad. The conclave's decision was startling. Because of the North-South feud, particularly as it was boiling up in Kansas (the area favored by most San Franciscans as the starting point for the road), nothing could be accomplished for the time being. That cold reality faced, the gathering then roared through a resolution advocating, as a stopgap, a federally built, army-protected wagon road over which emigrant wagons could travel in safety and along which passenger stages and mail coaches could speed, bringing letters oftener than once every two weeks, as was the schedule by steamship.

A committee of twenty-five, John D. Frémont and William T. Sherman among its members, was appointed to attack the problem. Their first step was to put pressure on Congress. Prodded by the committee, the California legislature passed resolutions urging federal wagon roads. The committeemen also supported a mammoth petition calling on Congress for the same action. During the summer of 1855, seventy-five thousand Californians affixed their signatures. (Wagon roads, declaimed the Sacramento *Union* on June 15, 1855, in support of all this activity, were "harbingers of the . . . great and magnificent scheme, a railroad to the Pacific.") The finished document was bound in two leather volumes, stamped with gold leaf, and entrusted to Senator Weller for transmittal to Washington—by far the largest petition submitted to Congress in well over a century. There were private efforts as well. William T. Sherman, committeeman and new vice-president of the Sacramento Valley Railroad, wrote his brother John, a Congressman of Ohio, urging John's support of the wagon road bill, reflecting the while that if the highway materialized in the proper place, his little railroad up to Folsom would profit as a feeder for transcontinental stagecoaches. In fact, some day it might even follow the wagon road over the Sierra Nevada toward the East—a heady prospect for a bankrupt rail company!

The notion of a transcontinental wagon road over the mountains raised familiar doubts about the constitutionality of federal work within state borders. The committee therefore decided that Californians should build that section of the road themselves—if the legislature would vote the necessary funds. This the lawmakers obligingly did on April 28, 1855.

Local jealousies immediately paralyzed action. Three different regions vociferously presented themselves as the logical starting points for the trans-Sierra road. Their only accomplishment was to block passage of a bill which would have appropriated money for the necessary surveys.

Careful surveys, it should be pointed out, really were necessary in spite of the fact that tens of thousands of emigrants had brought wagons over the mountains during the preceding decade. The emigrants, however, had made the journey late in the summer, after snow had disappeared, when they could avoid the deep canyons and rough lateral ravines by clinging to the high ridges between the rivers, where they did not need a graded highway. An all-winter road would have to compromise, angling across side hills to stay out of the canyons and venturing above the snow line for no greater distance than was absolutely necessary. Though everyone familiar with the mountains recognized the problem, none of the competing regions was willing to let state money be spent examining a rival section. The rival's way just might be preferable!

Citizens of El Dorado County, which stretched from Folsom on past Placerville, were particularly annoyed by the stalemate. In their minds the Sacramento Valley Railroad as a feeder for the wagon way made their section the logical choice. Digging into their own pockets, they raised money enough to send Sherman Day, a hale, fifty-year-old state senator from Sacramento, and engineer George Goddard, also of Sacramento, into the mountains late in the summer of 1855. After tramping through the high country in the vicinity of the old Carson emigrant route south of Lake Tahoe, the pair emerged declaring that they had found at Johnson Pass the best crossing anywhere in the range.

Although the surveyor-general of California, who had also spent time in the mountains that summer, disagreed with them, Day's voice was influential. The legislature called for bids on a road over Johnson Pass to the Carson Valley in what is now Nevada but was then part of Utah Territory.

A curious and prophetic episode followed. Submitter of the low bid was a certain L. B. Leach of Stockton. The legislature accepted his proposal and then, after a fruitless search, discovered that no such person existed. He had been invented as a delaying device either by steamship lines fearful of losing their government mail contracts or by jealous towns opposed to the Folsom-Placerville-Johnson Pass route. No one bothered to investigate, for the delay had served its purpose. During the pause lawyers of the Pacific Mail Steamship Company had been attacking the whole wagon road bill on technical grounds, and in 1856 the state supreme court declared the act void.[14] Discouraged Californians reflected that if neither the state nor the federal government could smooth away the rough spots impeding legislation, easy transportation to the East might be a long time coming.

None of the jealousies and self-defeating legislative maneuvers, none of the stopgaps and counterproposals was lost on engineer Theodore Judah, who once had supposed, in his innocence, that the main problem facing the construction of a Pacific railroad would be physical difficulties. Nor, it might be added, were the lessons wasted on Charles Crocker, Mark Hopkins, Collis Huntington, or a new next-door neighbor of the latter two, hulking Leland Stanford.

6   Upstairs at 54 K

Remodeling a store, Collis wrote Solon, was slower than erecting a new building and almost as expensive. Not until mid-November 1855, two months after Elizabeth had returned from her eastern visit, were they able to give up boarding with some of Elizabeth's relatives in Sacramento and move, thankfully, into a new apartment on the second floor.[1]

The flat did not occupy the whole of the space. In what remained and in a shed out back, the proprietors fitted up a dormitory for their help and for customers down from the hills.

The arrangement was practical rather than magnanimous. In the opinion of Huntington and Mark Hopkins, Sacramento was still wild enough to tempt young men. After a night on the town a clerk was likely to show up for work heavy-eyed, careless, and so destitute, if he had been gambling, that the store's cash box was a temptation. To counter the problem, the hardware company required its help to sign contracts agreeing to stay off the streets from suppertime until after breakfast the next morning. In return the firm provided board for the men (Elizabeth probably did some of the cooking), subscribed to newspapers, and provided a shelf of right-minded classics through which the clerks could browse at the end of their twelve-hour shifts.[2]

Collis' own spare time was increasingly taken up by politics. The Know-Nothing party, which had captured the governorship and the majority of the state legislature during the fall elections, had proved more tolerant toward California's strong pro-slavery element than he liked. Seeking still another alternative, he and a handful of other disgruntled former Whigs took to meeting on the second floor of the hardware store, either in the Huntingtons' living room or, more probably, in an office adjacent to the apartment. Two lawyers soon emerged as spokesmen

62

for the group. One was Charles Crocker's brother, E. B. Crocker. The other was Ed Crocker's crony, Cornelius Cole.

As a student, Cole had read law in Auburn, New York, under the one-time governor of the state, William Henry Seward, who later, as an anti-slavery Whig, had become a United States Senator. When the Whigs' power began to dwindle, Seward switched to the new Republican party in the hope that in 1856 he would be nominated as the first Republican candidate for the presidency of the United States. In connection with his campaign he recemented contacts with his former protégé, Cornelius Cole, and sent Cole batches of his Senate speeches for distribution in California. The center of Cole's activity became the second floor of the Huntington & Hopkins hardware store.[3]

The little group who met there picked March 8, 1856, as the date for launching the Republican party of California. Defiance set the timing. The Democrats were holding their state convention in Sacramento, and on the evening of the eighth an outdoor rally, dominated by Senator Gwin's Chivalry Wing, was scheduled to meet in front of the Orleans Hotel on Second Street, scarcely a block from the hardware store.

Predictably the speakers at the rally abandoned their prepared texts and took to belaboring the nearby "black Republicans" as "unholy and un-Christian demagogues . . . fanatics and madmen, unprincipled knaves banded together to destroy and dissolve the Union."[4] The ranting stirred the listeners to such howls of outrage that the handful of men who slipped into the hardware store for their own meeting may well have felt awed by the emotions their work had released. They may have felt, too, as they listened to the yells outside, that the document presented to them for signing was, under the circumstances, unnecessarily restrained.

Believing that the time has fully come for the organization of a Republican Party in the City of Sacramento and the State of California, we hereby mutually pledge ourselves to each other, and to our Country, to unite in carrying out the great principles of Republicanism; hereby declare that while we have no intention of interfering with Slavery in the present Slave States, yet we are firmly opposed to its further extension, and to the admission of any more Slave States; and will use all our efforts to redeem the Federal Government as well as that of California, from the domination of the Slave Power.

Sacramento   March 8 1856

E. B. Crocker signed first. Alexander Nixon, a doctor, was second; Cornelius Cole, third. C. P. Huntington was thirteenth. All told, twenty-two men—a newspaper reporter, two magazine subscription agents, a policeman, three clerks, an engraver, a carpenter, a plasterer, various merchants—subscribed to the declaration. The name of E. H. Miller, Jr., Mark Hopkins' one-time partner, was there. Hopkins' signature was missing, however, as was Charley Crocker's. As members of the Know-Nothing city council, they probably felt discretion was called for, at least until their terms expired on April 2. Also missing from the roll of organizers, in spite of what his biographers would later state, was Leland Stanford.[5] The lapses were temporary, however. Soon all three—Hopkins, Charles Crocker, and Stanford—would be deeply involved in the group's activities.

The party advertised in the local papers that its first public rally would be held on April 19 at Sacramento's favorite outdoor political rendezvous, on Second Street in front of the Orleans Hotel. The gathering was not a success. Hoodlums overturned the speakers' stand and scattered the listeners. Commenting on the disorder, the Sacramento *Union* of April 21 remarked that while "we deprecate the formation of a Republican party in this state," it was best to let its adherents expose their barrenness by talking. Riots would elicit sympathy. "Let their meetings be broken up a few times as that one was last Saturday night, and we shall not be surprised to hear of Republican organizations all over the state."

In spite of the suggestion, persecution continued enthusiastically. On May 10 ruffians disrupted a second attempt by the Republicans to gather in front of the Orleans Hotel, and on the thirteenth pranksters plastered the city with handbills that could hardly have read like a joke to the nascent party:[6]

TO ARMS

To All True and Patriotic Americans!

Whereas Sundry Persons in this Community have commenced the agitation of subjects which are treasonable, and which have a tendency to excite and disturb good citizens, and destroy the amity which exists among us as brethren, and to weaken our love for the glorious CONSTITUTION and laws of the land; And whereas said agitators are TRAITORS,

Now, therefore, all good Citizens are called on to attend a PUBLIC MASS MEETING, to be held at the Orleans Hotel on Saturday, to devise means to protect the public welfare, by appointing a Committee to HANG ALL THE LEADERS, and as many of the attaches of said TRAITORS as may be deemed necessary to restore the public quiet and put a stop to such treasonable practices.

Before the meeting could be held, a far more serious form of vigilantism seized the attention of the citizens and of Collis Huntington. Late on the afternoon of Wednesday, May 14, a popular San Francisco newspaper editor, James King, who liked to call himself James King of William, was gunned down in a San Francisco street by a corrupt politician named James Casey, in retaliation for King's scathing editorials denouncing him. Immediately after firing the shot, which did not kill King at once, Casey surrendered himself to the police, who, he had reason to believe, would protect him. They took him to the county jail, a formidable brick and stone structure on the side of Telegraph Hill, and when a mob began to gather, a mass of deputy sheriffs lined up in front of the building to defend it.

At this the city's long resentment against corrupt police officers, peculating supervisors, venal judges, and untouched criminals came to a head. The result was a gigantic vigilance group led by veterans of the 1851 organization. The chief once again was William T. Coleman.

Swiftly Coleman organized his flood of volunteers into an army—companies of one hundred men each, ten companies to a regiment. Shaken by the mounting opposition, the police requisitioned some cannon from ships in the harbor and mounted them where they could command the jail. Meanwhile other citizens opposed to vigilante activity formed what they called a Law-and-Order Party and also began to arm.

Newly built telegraph lines flashed word of the threatening clash to other cities throughout the central part of the state. On Thursday, May 15, a feverish mass meeting assembled in front of Sacramento's Orleans Hotel and roared through resolutions calling for the formation of a similar group to clean out their own city and to send armed reinforcements to Coleman in case he needed help. Details of organization were entrusted to an executive committee whose corresponding secretary was Collis P. Huntington.[7]

On May 18, the San Francisco vigilante army marched against the jail in such strength that the authorities abandoned thoughts of resistance and handed over both Casey and a notorious murderer named Cora. While the two men were being tried on May 20, James King of William died. As his enormous funeral procession moved through the streets on the twenty-second, Casey and Cora were hanged in front of the vigilantes' headquarters. On May 24, Huntington wrote to Coleman, asking for guidelines that would help the Sacramento group establish its own procedures.

Tension mounted swiftly. By the end of the month Coleman had about nine thousand men under arms, drilling regularly. Backed by this extraordinary power, the San Francisco committee began holding trials that in time hanged two more men and banished several. It also reorganized the police department and shook up the city government.

After long vacillation, John Neely Johnson, the Know-Nothing governor who had assumed office in January, issued a proclamation denouncing the activity as unlawful and ordering the vigilantes to disband. When they declined, he placed San Francisco under martial law and directed William T. Sherman, banker, railroad official, and commander of the second division of California militia, to restore order.

The task proved hopeless. Militiamen refused to report for duty; the commander of the federal arsenal declined to issue munitions without an express order from the President of the United States. Completely frustrated, Sherman resigned and was replaced by Volney Howard.

Howard stepped into command with reckless boasts about using the Law-and-Order Party to help the militia drive the vigilantes into the bay. Colemen's men dared them to try. Fearful of outright civil war, twenty-five Sacramentans led by John B. Harmon called on both Johnson and Coleman, urging moderation. Presumably Harmon's delegation also waited on the Sacramento vigilantes.

What effect the peacemakers actually had is impossible to determine. In any event, the Sacramento vigilantes seem not to have hanged anyone, so far as records go, though they undoubtedly frightened into hiding many citizens who in their minds were undesirable. Though Johnson declined to revoke his declaration of martial law for San Francisco, he did little to enforce it. Coleman's housecleaners, conducting themselves with remarkable dignity, wound up their work and disbanded in mid-August, leaving generations of historians to debate the morality of their actions within the context of American traditions about fair and open trials.

Huntington's own opinions have not survived. As a vigilante he presumably approved this rough insistence on goals, not means, as the ultimate consideration. Seen against that background his statement, made years later to Hubert H. Bancroft's scribes, to the effect that the bribery of Congressmen was justifiable if it persuaded them to do "right"—such thinking then emerges with a blunt and consistent logic.[8]

In Philadelphia, meanwhile, the convening Republicans had bid for midwestern and far western support by introducing into their platform a plank that ignored the debate about the constitutionality of federal aid within state boundaries and called for unqualified government support in the building of a railroad all the way to the western ocean. As their choice of a President the Republicans then by-passed William Seward and nominated an explorer closely identified with California, John C. Frémont.

The group at 54 K Street, Seward men all, swallowed their disappointment and prepared to support Frémont. One move was to install a printing press in the loft next to the Huntingtons' apartment and start issuing a morning paper, the *California Daily Times*. The nominal editor was Cornelius Cole. The working editor was James McClatchy, one of the leaders of the squatter riots of 1851. The sound of the clanking must have mingled oddly in Elizabeth's ears with the gentler clatter of her dishwashing.

As was true of most political newspapers of the era, the columns of the *Times* were not marked by restraint. "We have all the gamblers and prostitutes in the state against us," cried one editorial, "and also the whole herd of office seekers, who have long fattened at the public crib. Then again we have all the 'Chivalry' opposed to us. That delectable crowd of brandy-drinking, pistol-shooting, swearing, swaggering gentry, who turn up their noses at all honest labor." As for the Know-Nothings, from whose ranks Hopkins and Charley Crocker had just defected, they were "the sea-serpent party . . . eely and oily . . . destitute of backbone."[9]

Name-calling was to amuse and attract readers. Votes would have to come from a more positive program. In California, slavery did not seem to be the key, even though slavery had been the only point mentioned by the founding fathers in their declaration of March 8. Instead, the strategists at 54 K Street decided to concentrate on the railroad. "We are in favor," declared the *Times* of August 28, 1856, "of Frémont and the Pacific Railroad; we have nothing to do with abolition—nothing to do with slavery; we are willing to have it stay where it is." The railroad issue, by contrast, seemed so persuasive that one early Republican wrote a friend that he really believed it alone would spell victory: "The people of this State have dwelt upon the subject . . . until it has become a kind of mania with them."[10]

The opposition, declining to be sidetracked by the mildness about slavery, continued to deride the Republicans as "nigger worshippers." Hoodlums again and again broke up Republican rallies. There was not much fighting back, except on one occasion at Folsom, when Collis Huntington rallied a force that drove the hecklers from the field and, as Bancroft later put matters, "Vindicated the right of free speech."[11]

In general, however, Collis stayed behind the scenes, leaving public appearances to his associates—the Crocker brothers, Mark Hopkins, E. H. Miller, Jr., and, as the campaign quickened, Leland Stanford.

Like Hopkins, Crocker, and, in a sense, Huntington, Stanford was a New Yorker, having been born near Albany on March 9, 1824. His father, who sired seven other children, kept an inn on the post road to Schenectady, cut firewood for the Albany market, and on occasion farmed. Although Leland soon learned to swing an ax, his childhood was less laborious than that of the other merchants with whom he became associated. He was well educated. When he decided at the age of seventeen to prepare for the law his family sent him first to Clinton Liberal Institute near Utica and later to Cazenovia Seminary, a coeducational Methodist academy just outside of Syracuse.

Interested always in politics, Stanford joined academic debating societies, took part in schoolboy anti-slavery demonstrations, and listened avidly to whatever famous orators appeared in the neighborhood. He preened himself on being a hand with the girls. One Cazenovia coed with a "lovely face and splendidly developed bosom" would, he boasted to one of his brothers, "run away with me to the other end of the world I believe if I would only let her."[12]

In 1845, aged twenty-one, he began reading as an apprentice in an Albany law firm. After being admitted to the bar in 1848, he proposed to Jane Lathrop, a mild little girl with protuberant eyes. She accepted, but her possessive family did not want her to leave home quite yet, and so Leland traveled alone to Port Washington, Wisconsin, north of Milwaukee, and there hung out his shingle. To advertise himself, he ran for district attorney as a Whig in a heavily Democratic county. Trounced, he kept plugging away. After two years he was well enough established that he was able to batter down parental opposition, marry Jane, and take her to Port Washington to live.

He did not really like the law. When a fire destroyed his office and law library on March 16, 1852, he was too indifferent to begin again, as Crocker, Hopkins, and Huntington would do when wiped out by fires in Sacramento that same year. Instead, Stanford decided to follow his older brothers to the goldfields.

The decision caused consternation in his wife's family. California! And her father ill! Did she want to be the death of him? Jane yielded to their clamor and told her husband that he would have to make the trip alone.

After visiting his brothers briefly—they had gone into the mercantile business at 56 K Street, next door to Huntington—Stanford moved into the mountains to open a one-room branch store for the firm at Cold Springs, halfway between Coloma and Placerville. When that camp lost population to newer rushes, he shifted to Michigan Bluff, high above the canyon of the Middle Fork of the American River.

People liked him. He was a burly, solid six-footer with a swarthy complexion, coarse features, and dark hair. He spoke with slow deliberation. A cropped beard increased his appearance of ponderous dignity. There was nothing pretentious about him, however. For two and a half years he personally swept out his store each morning. At night he made his bed on one of the counters and slept there alone. Impressed by these things and by his legal training, the residents of Michigan Bluff elected him their justice of the peace.

Learning in May 1855 that his father-in-law had died, he went to Albany for Jane. During his absence his brothers decided to embark on a new enterprise in San Francisco. To free their hands, they made Leland manager of their Sacramento store. He ran the venture from 56 K Street for less than a year and then shifted his trade—groceries, liquor, grain, and miners' supplies—to an imposing new $14,000 edifice on Front Street, where he could be nearer to both the river wharves and the tracks of the Sacramento Valley Railroad.

To digress briefly: the railroad, which had opened for business early in February 1856 (two trains twice a day between Sacramento and Folsom, passenger fare $2.00, freight $3.00 a ton), was in perilous shape. Construction costs, estimated by engineer Theodore Judah at $43,500 a mile, had averaged $60,000, though how much of the discrepancy was due to Judah's optimism and how much to the favorable contracts that Lester L. and John P. Robinson, as heavy stockholders in the road, saw to it that they received as builders is impossible to say. Still, California's first railway *was* operating, and to signalize the event the directors decided to hold a grand excursion on Washington's birthday. For ten dollars an excursionist received a ticket good for the round-trip ride between Sacramento and Folsom, all he could eat at a giant outdoor barbecue in the latter town, and entrance to an all-night dance in Folsom's new Meredith Hotel.

Response was sensational. More than a thousand merrymakers, many of whom had never before ridden a train, came from as far away as San Francisco to crowd aboard all the rolling stock the Sacramento Valley Railroad could muster. There were two trains. One consisted of the line's six passenger vehicles, each forty feet long. The other, made up of open flatcars hastily equipped with benches, was rendered unpleasant, according to a finicky reporter from San Francisco, by the rushing wind and the great number of tobacco chewers aboard. But the speeches at the

69

Folsom barbecue were stirring and the band lively; when the trains started home at 5 A.M., everyone agreed that it had been a momentous occasion.[13]

It did not, however, help very much toward reducing the railroad's staggering debt.

As election time drew near in the fall, the Republicans at 54 K Street dug deeper into their pockets and added an evening weekly to the daily morning paper being printed beside Collis' apartment. About the same time, they secured the services of a famous orator, Colonel E. D. Baker, and with him as their drawing card staged a climactic rally in San Francisco's Forrest Theater—a glittering occasion in which Stanford, Hopkins, Charles Crocker, and E. H. Miller, Jr., but not Collis Huntington, played leading roles.

It was wasted effort. Buchanan polled 52,000 votes from California's Democrats; Fillmore, 35,000 from the Know-Nothings; Frémont, 20,000 from the Republicans. Mournfully the *Times* wrote, just before expiring, "The chief reason for regret . . . is the effect on the railroad question." And to show where his affections still lay, Cornelius Cole named the son that was born to him on December 31, 1856, William Henry Seward Cole.[14] So much for Frémont's efforts.

Not everything was lost, however. Congress, controlled now by Democrats, was at last showing signs that it would help finance a cross-country wagon road within the territories. The states concerned would then be responsible for building connecting links to the federal highway.

Where would the government road end? In California, the question was complicated by the difficulty of crossing the Sierra Nevada mountains. The state's northern communities, hoping to turn traffic their way, plumped for one of several passes north of Lake Tahoe. This meant, in turn, a terminus for the federal road somewhere along the northern part of California's eastern border. Lobbyist in Congress for this view was Dr. O. M. Wozencraft of San Francisco. Wozencraft not only hoped that a road in the north would further interests he held in that area, but he also yearned to be appointed engineer in charge of building the western sector of the federal highway through the territories.

Opposed to the northerners were California's central counties. They favored a federal road down the Humboldt River of Nevada to Carson Valley, the traditional emigrant trail. The connecting state road would then run from Sacramento through Placerville and over Johnson Pass, south of Lake Tahoe—the route that Sherman Day and George Goddard had surveyed late in the summer of 1855. Lobbyist for this proposal was

John Kirk of Placerville, who also hoped, as a reward for success, to be named engineer in charge of the western end of the federal highway.[15] Sacramento residents in general favored Kirk as against Wozencraft.

Floating about on the periphery of the struggle and eager to turn whatever developed to his own advantage was Theodore Dehone Judah. As noted earlier, the decision of the Sacramento Valley Railroad to halt at Folsom had left Judah without a job. He had soon found another, surveying a line for the paper San Francisco & Sacramento Railway, designed to run from the west bank of the Sacramento River, opposite Sacramento City, southward to the moribund town of Benicia on the north shore of San Francisco Bay. From Benicia water transport would carry passengers and freight on to San Francisco.

In a report of his activities, issued on February 7, 1856, as a lure for prospective stockholders, Judah presented Californians with a brand-new idea.[16] In spite of Democratic arguments about unconstitutionality, the federal government should lend its aid to the building of feeder railroads within the state of California, for the advent of a rail network west of the Sierra, he argued, would assure the completion of a transcontinental railway, since the feeders would guarantee its nourishment. In Judah's mind the step was certain to come very soon, and he so stated in his report. There was precedent for government intervention. Congress had already given millions of acres of fertile land to the states of Missouri and Iowa. They in turn had passed it on as a form of aid to railroads building within their borders. Could not California claim the same consideration? And would not the San Francisco and Sacramento Railway be certain to share in the largesse?

Until capital appeared for building this hopeful feeder, Judah was again out of work. To fill his time, he and Anna went East, arriving in Washington in April 1856. He listened with boredom to the debates over the wagon road bills, applauded when Congressman James Denver of California introduced still another transcontinental railroad measure in the House, and with varying degrees of optimism mailed long comments about the activities back to the Sacramento *Union,* whose editor, a close personal friend named Lauren Upson, saw to it that they were printed.[17] Although Collis Huntington was engrossed by many other things that summer, it is inconceivable that he did not notice the outpourings, though how impressed he may have been is another matter.

Exasperated by the endless talk in Congress and hoping also to attract attention to himself, Judah wrote and had printed late that year (where the money came from during his periods of unemployment is a mystery) a pamphlet entitled "A Practical Plan for Building the Pacific Railroad."

There were two main obstacles in its way, he said: lack of the sort of precise information a capitalist would need before investing his money, and, second, the impossibility of obtaining this information so long as the different sections of the country refused to settle on a common route. The way to obviate the problem, he continued, was to conduct a true *railroad* survey of the central route through the West—not a useless zoological reconnaissance like the so-called railroad surveys of 1853— and then test the feasibility of the chosen path by building a preliminary wagon road along it. If facts and not sectional emotionalism showed the route's practicability—Judah was sure the facts would—then private capital would take over the project and complete it without the need of additional help from the government other than grants of land.[18] Or so he reasoned, neatly bundling into a single package his obsession for the railroad and Congress' current enthusiasm for wagon ways.

In January 1857 he mailed copies of his pamphlet to every member of Congress and to the heads of whatever administrative departments might be concerned. The effect was nil. Railroad legislation foundered as usual, but interest in wagon roads remained high. In February the lawmakers, tiptoeing gingerly through the sectional briar patches Judah wanted to avoid, authorized the spending of $250,000 on two projects in the Southwest and $300,000 to start work on a wagon road along the central route. The latter highway was to begin quite constitutionally in Nebraska Territory and run through South Pass to a western terminus at, surprisingly enough, isolated Honey Lake. Since Honey Lake lay near the eastern border of northern California, the designation was a victory for Wozencraft's northern faction.

President Pierce, who signed the bill on February 17, 1857, left the problem of staffing the job to his successor, James Buchanan. Two days after the new President's inauguration, Judah wrote him a typically airy letter recommending Theodore Judah as engineer for the western sector of the road.[19] California's lone Senator, Democrat John B. Weller, plumped for Wozencraft. Gwin's Chivalry Wing of the still torn Democratic party backed Kirk.

Buchanan, friendly toward Gwin, tapped Kirk for the assignment that Wozencraft felt should have come to him.

The unexpected selection of the Placerville resident led proponents of the Johnson Pass route—Collis Huntington was active among them— to start devising some means of canceling out Honey Lake's designation as the terminus of the federal road. The plan they concocted went like this. Voters in Sacramento and El Dorado counties would be prevailed on to pass a special bond issue financing the construction of a first-class

72

wagon road across the mountains at Johnson Pass. Kirk could then sing the road's praises, pointing out meanwhile that it was far better than any crossing in the vicinity of Honey Lake. Thus bemused, Congress would shift the terminus to Carson Valley.

Caught completely by surprise, Wozencraft's Honey Lake faction could think of no better riposte than to try to defeat the bond issue. On May 29, 1857, a handful of them managed to drive a stagecoach from Oroville to Honey Lake, the first such vehicle ever to cross the Sierra Nevada. Obviously they must have followed a usable road. In view of that did the voters of Sacramento and El Dorado counties suppose that Congress would listen to Kirk? Did the taxpayers in the central counties want to raise their annual bills for thirty years by passing a needless bond issue?

The road boomers of Sacramento and Placerville, the latter the seat of El Dorado County, retorted by calling mass meetings in each town. At these gatherings the voters authorized a board of distinguished citizens, their names carefully selected in advance, to travel the proposed route from Placerville to Johnson Pass—by stagecoach in order to match the Oroville demonstration—and afterwards report their findings. Collis P. Huntington was among the inspectors chosen at Sacramento.

The examiners assembled in Placerville, where several hundred excited residents gathered to watch their meticulously staged departure. Leland Stanford made a speech; a guard of militiamen fired a parting salute. The august board then climbed into a coach driven by no less a personage than Jared B. Crandall himself, president of the Pioneer Stage Lines, the most powerful of California's far-flung transportation companies.

The ride proved rough. According to a reporter who went along, the passengers frequently had their skulls cracked against the roof. On steep pitches they had to dismount and walk. Occasionally they had to push, an effort at which brawny Collis excelled. Some of the drops that they skirted above the canyon of the South Fork of the American River made them catch their breath. In due time, however, they reached the top of Johnson Pass. There they held a merry picnic and came back with glowing words of approval.[20]

The bond issue passed easily and Sacramento celebrated—prematurely, it developed. Although Kirk did what he could to follow through, Congress declined to budge and the federal road eventually (1860) ended at Honey Lake.[21] Private efforts by mail contractors to draw attention to the local road that was scratched across Johnson Pass with the bond money were no more successful. Postmaster General Aaron Brown, a Tennessean, saw to it that the lion's share of the mail subsidies went to John Butterfield, traveling a long southern route through Texas and Arizona.

To Collis Huntington all this was an illuminating introduction to the devious art of manipulating political agencies. He had helped win the bond issue but had lost the main campaign. In national matters local triumphs were seldom decisive. Although later rivals of his in California would sometimes forget that apparently obvious fact, Huntington never again did.

It is not likely that he supposed, during the latter part of the 1850s, that he would one day be in a position to exert pressure on a national level. After the wagon road episode, his life became so uneventful that in only a few instances did his name appear in the Sacramento newspapers. In the fall of 1857, for instance, he was one of eighteen men— Leland Stanford, Mark Hopkins, Charles Crocker, and E. H. Miller, Jr., were among the others—who donated $100 each to found what became the Sacramento Public Library. Shortly thereafter he and Eizabeth traveled to New York to consult with suppliers and visit their families. After their return Huntington became associated with the State Agricultural Society, whose main function was to promote an annual fair in the capital city.[22] It is a sketchy outline, yet from it a few generalities may be hypothecated. By small-town standards Huntington was relatively prosperous. He was interested in improving his community and was respected by his fellow townsmen. Like most of them he had survived disaster and turmoil, and as he approached his thirty-eighth birthday on October 22, 1859, the habit of contentment may have become so ingrained in him that he seldom paused any more to think that it was not for this sort of placidity that he had left Oneonta ten years before.

What finally broke him loose, indirectly to be sure, was his political involvement, and even there the beginnings hardly seemed auspicious. Defeat followed defeat. In September 1857 Stanford ran a poor third as the Republican candidate for state treasurer. In spite of that he agreed to be a candidate for governor in the state elections of 1859.*

It was a year of wild bitterness. In 1857 the leaders of the feuding Democratic factions, David Broderick and William Gwin, had made a secret, scandalous deal whereby each had been elected to the United States Senate. There they began fighting again, Broderick supporting among other things the admission of Kansas to the Union under an anti-

---

* In those days Californians elected a governor every two years. Timing was such that a fourth-year campaign never coincided with the national elections but always preceded it by a year—a fact of some importance to Huntington's and Stanford's careers, as will be developed.

slavery constitution while Gwin followed a pro-slavery line. The clash swirled back to California, grew fouled with personal recriminations, and tore the state Democratic party asunder once again. The issue became completely irreconcilable when Broderick and Gwin each backed different Democrats for the governorship.

The vicious campaign that followed seemed to leave the balance of power in Republican hands. Again and again anti-slavery men urged Stanford and his backers to withdraw from the race and throw their support behind Broderick's candidate, John Currey. Even Horace Greeley, powerful editor of the New York *Tribune,* who had crossed the continent by stagecoach during the summer of 1859—the trip over Johnson Pass with driver Hank Monk frightened him almost out of his wits—urged the course on Stanford by means of a public letter printed in the San Francisco newspapers.

There were anxious consultations in the unofficial party headquarters upstairs at 54 K Street, for it was obvious that voters were going to line up on one side of the fight or the other, and the Republicans, working by themselves, had no chance whatsoever of winning a single major office. A Currey victory achieved by their help would bring them immediate rewards. On the other hand, if they supported Currey and he lost, their party would be wrecked, yet they wanted to hold it together for the sake of William Seward's second attempt at the presidency during the national elections of 1860. Deciding finally to reject Broderick's overtures, Stanford and his fellow candidates, including Charles Crocker, who was running for a seat in the legislature, kept stumping the central counties in a forlorn cause.

They were right in shying away from Currey. At the elections on September 7, 1859, Gwin's candidate, Milton Latham, swept into the governorship with 62,255 votes. Broderick's man, Currey, trailed badly with 32,298. Stanford picked up 10,110.[23] Crocker did no better in his race.

The decision to stick it out left the little coterie in Sacramento— Stanford, Cole, the Crocker brothers, Mark Hopkins, Dr. Alexander Nixon, and Collis Huntington—with an unshakable grip on the Republican party machine. But of what value, they must have wondered privately, was a machine that had attracted barely one tenth of the total vote?

Almost at once two seemingly unrelated events, occurring within a week of each other, forecast the answer.

Shortly after the election, Broderick entered into a violent quarrel with an ardent supporter of Gwin's, David S. Terry of the state supreme court. Choosing an isolated farm on the peninsula south of San Francisco as a field of honor, they dueled with pistols at 5:30 A.M., Tuesday, September 13. Broderick fell mortally wounded.*

Intense excitement swept the state, followed by a revulsion toward the sort of politics that led to such naked furies.[24] The Republicans could hardly fail to gain from the reaction. A strengthening of the Republican position would, in turn, almost surely focus fresh attention on the problem of transcontinental railroads.

That matter, too, was engrossing the state. On September 20, one week after the Broderick-Terry duel, a convention of delegates from the entire Pacific Coast met in San Francisco to discuss what could be done, in the words of their own steering committee, about "the refusal of Congress to take efficient measures for the construction of a Railroad from the Atlantic States to the Pacific."

In hindsight the relationship between the forces is clear, but it is not likely that the little group of men who habitually met at 54 K Street to gossip and plan really grasped the possibilities at the time—not, indeed, until they were brought face to face with them by that fabricator of giant dreams he was never able to implement, Theodore Judah.

* One of Broderick's seconds during the affray was David D. Colton, a name that eventually would become the core of the most disastrous scandal ever to involve Collis Huntington. But once again this is getting ahead of the story.

7 The Catalyst

After his failure to land an engineering job with the transcontinental wagon road, Judah returned to California and a series of unsatisfying local surveys. The first was for the California Central, a line designed to finish what the Sacramento Valley Railroad had left undone—run north from Folsom to Marysville.[1] Having finished that forty-mile survey, Judah in 1858 ran another that was only nineteen miles long. This one also began at Folsom, then wriggled northeast through the foothills to the mining camp of Auburn, seat of Placer County. Who employed him on the Auburn survey is uncertain. It does not really matter, because the cost estimates he submitted were so high that the promoters backed off.

The collapse dismayed the residents of Auburn and of Nevada City, thirty-two miles farther north.* They had been talking railroad since 1852 and were determined to have a line in spite of Judah's chilling figures. Taking a deep breath, a group of them incorporated what they called the Sacramento, Placer & Nevada Railroad, and hired Sherman Day, locator of the wagon road across Johnson Pass, to find a more feasible route to Auburn than Judah's.

Day succeeded. Thus heartened, the incorporators of the Sacramento, Placer & Nevada set about raising enough local money to start the

* To clear up problems of nomenclature: the town of Placerville is the seat of El Dorado County, southernmost of three elongated counties that sprawl from the Sacramento Valley across the crest of the Sierra Nevada Mountains to California's eastern boundary. Placer County is just north of El Dorado; its seat, as stated above, is Auburn. Nevada County, whose seat is Nevada City, is just north of Placer; it had nothing to do with the territory of Nevada, which was carved out of the western part of Utah in 1861. Endlessly duplicated names (Springfield for example) are one of the unimaginative characteristics of the settlement of North America.

project rolling. Under California law it was a cumbersome procedure. First the state legislature had to pass a special act authorizing the county supervisors to prepare a bond issue; the supervisors in their turn scheduled a special election, at which the question was submitted to the taxpayers.

During 1859 both Auburn town and Placer County hewed through the legal thickets and scheduled the necessary elections for June 4, 1860. If the measure passed, then Auburn and Placer County would deliver $150,000 worth of bonds to the Sacramento, Placer & Nevada—but only after thirteen miles of track had been laid from Folsom toward Auburn.[2] Hopefully, the prospect of receiving the bonds would give stability to the company and hence would lure in enough private capital to start the railroad.

The device worked, attracting the attention of those busy contracting brothers, John P. and Lester L. Robinson, builders of the Sacramento Valley Railroad, and of the faintly mysterious San Francisco banking firm of Pioche, Bayerque & Company. It also prepared the way for enmities that would pursue Collis Huntington until he died, even to providing a name for Frank Norris' bitterly anti-capitalistic railroad novel, *The Octopus*. But this is getting far ahead of the story.

F. L. A. Pioche of Pioche, Bayerque & Co. was a Frenchman out of Chile. After scouting California during the gold rush, he had gone to Paris, where he had persuaded several financiers to form a pool of capital into which he could dip whenever he encountered likely investment opportunities in western mines, real estate, and related enterprises. He wove complex webs. The briefly rich silver-mining town of Pioche, Nevada, would be named for him. During the early 1860s, when Napoleon was endeavoring to establish a French empire in Mexico under Maximilian, Pioche and his San Francisco partner, J. B. Bayerque, would be suspected of conspiring, under cover of the Civil War, to detach California from the Union and join it to French Mexico. So many intricate manipulations gave F. L. A. Pioche headaches—literally. In 1872 he shot himself, reputedly because of their excruciating pain.

By 1858 Pioche, Bayerque, and Lester L. Robinson had gained control of the Sacramento Valley Railroad. (J. P. Robinson was the road's superintendent at the then munificent salary of $5,000 a year.) Operations were proving profitable. In 1858 the stubby little twenty-two-mile line cleared ninety thousand dollars, but interest charges on its floating and bonded debts kept the company from paying dividends. Because of those debts, the company did not want to extend the Sacramento

Valley Railroad, and yet they did want the increased profits that would accrue from a longer line. Thus they were interested in the possibility of building, partly with town and county money, the nominally independent Sacramento, Placer & Nevada from their own railhead at Folsom on to Auburn and, eventually, to Nevada City. Not the least of the attractions was the fact that they would be able to use their own rolling stock on the extension and thus materially reduce the cost of getting trains into Auburn. As soon as they were reasonably sure that the bond issue would pass, they began to discuss construction contracts with the officials of the hopeful line. Their intention was to gain control and turn the Sacramento, Placer & Nevada into a debt-free extension of their own debt-ridden Sacramento Valley Railroad.[3]

Judah meanwhile, having failed to get a nineteen-mile line off the drawing board, had turned once more to his obsession, a nineteen-hundred-mile railroad from somewhere in the Mississippi Valley to the Pacific. Early in 1859, he and a close friend, Lauren Upson of the Sacramento *Union,* began writing editorials and making speeches in favor of an official convention of railroad-minded delegates from the entire Pacific area. The California legislature fell in line and on April 5 passed a resolution calling for the state-supported meeting in San Francisco which was mentioned at the end of the preceding chapter.

Response was enthusiastic. On September 20, delegates assembled from nearly every county in California, from the new (February 1859) state of Oregon, and from the territories of Washington and Arizona. But if the geographic spread was notable, concord was not: "The prejudices of localities," reported the Sacramento *Union* on September 24, "have already and strongly broken out, and today there is no harmony of interest."

Judah, the guiding power of the convention, tried to pour oil on the water: "Let us adopt as our motto, 'the Pacific Railroad wherever it can be soonest and best built.'" Soonest and best, he continued, repeating the argument already advanced in his 1857 pamphlet, "A Practical Plan for Building the Pacific Railroad," were points to be determined not by emotion but by careful engineering surveys. Let the federal government spend $250,000 underwriting an examination that would "enable us to speak understandingly of the relative merits, length, and cost of the various routes and upon this information" adopt the proper way.[4] That vexatious question solved, then let the government subsidize the construction of the road by granting land to the builders, guaranteeing 5 per cent interest on twenty-year company bonds, and remitting tariff duties on imports connected with the job.*

In actuality Judah was not as impartial about routes as he pretended. He offered no remonstrance when the convention passed a disruptive resolution favoring a central route up the Platte Valley and through what is now Nevada. This pleased the delegates from Oregon and Washington, who thereupon joined northern California in pushing through another resolution favoring a branch line from Puget Sound to a junction with the main road somewhere in the vicinity of Great Salt Lake.

The delegates from southern California and Arizona objected vehemently. They wanted the main line, and supported their stand against a central route by pointing to the formidable, snow-beset Sierra Nevada mountain range. How was it to be crossed, especially since the obstacle lay almost entirely within the state of California and, according to prevalent constitutional theory, would have to be surmounted without federal aid? In southern California, they argued, the mountains were not so awesome.

An argument began then about passes north and south of Lake Tahoe. Judah quieted it, having learned from the wagon road quarrels of 1857 that the mere mention of routes was enough to create paralyzing local jealousies. Instead, he and his supporters concentrated on methods of providing adequate state aid for whatever route was chosen. Caught up by his glowing predictions of the gains which a transcontinental road would bring to the entire Pacific Coast, regardless of routes, the delegates whooped through resolutions calling for California to donate fifteen million dollars to whatever company breached the Sierra anywhere (which left southern California out), and for Oregon to give five million dollars to the company that attacked the Cascade Range farther north. These resolutions were mere recommendations for legislative action, of course, and not commitments.

After five days of oratory, the convention adjourned with an agreement to reconvene in Sacramento in February 1860, at which time the legislature would be invited to attend the sessions. Meanwhile the group's executive committee was to print and distribute 25,000 pamphlets explaining the convention's activities. The committee also appointed Theodore Judah to be its accredited lobbyist in Congress. He sailed for the East Coast on October 20.

Instead of instructing Congress, he ended up being edified. The country as a whole no longer questioned the desirability of a railroad across the West. The swift growth of the Pacific states had raised the costs of

* The best rails, for example, came from England.

roundabout mail deliveries to San Francisco and Portland by way of Panama or even southern Arizona to exorbitant figures. Indian troubles on the plains and in the Northwest, and the so-called Mormon War that sent columns of troops into Utah during 1857–58 had demonstrated a need for military flexibility. The opening of Japan and new commercial treaties with China had reinvigorated a long-standing American hope that oriental merchandise could be drawn into Pacific ports and thence carried overland to the East. Moreover, as soon as the railroad was built, towns would spring up and land values would increase all along the line.[5]

Even the question of routes was no longer a major issue, except to obstructionists in the South. As the delegates in San Francisco pointed out, of an estimated $960 million invested in American railroads, $818 million lay in the North, and those northern roads would not want a southern outlet to the Coast, especially since the San Francisco Bay area and Oregon were by far the most populous sections of the Pacific littoral. Mormon converts were meanwhile steadily swelling the population of Utah. Kansas had attracted a hundred thousand residents. More tens of thousands were streaming across the central plains toward the new goldfields of Colorado. Guided by those considerations, Samuel R. Curtis of Iowa, chairman of the House Select Committee on the Pacific Railroad introduced into the House of Representatives in April 1860, while Judah listened from the galleries, a bill limiting the transcontinental project to a single road through the central part of the West.

Curtis had been connected with railroad promotion in Iowa since at least 1852. The jealousies there, the schemes for preference, and the mechanics that had been developed for applying pressure to government agencies made comparable antics in California look like the palest sort of naïveté. From Iowa's turbulent activities Curtis had learned that until competing local interests were satisfied, there could be no united front against southern opposition. Nor were the local interests as isolated as they might appear. Powerful railroad systems were beginning to emerge in the East. Behind the Iowa railroads stood financiers from Chicago and New England. They wanted *their* lines to hook onto and benefit from whatever Pacific railroad developed. Behind the local railroads in equally turbulent Missouri stood other financiers from St. Louis, the Ohio Valley, and Pennsylvania. They wanted the weight of preference to swing *their* way. Resolving those rivalries was the aim of Curtis' bill of 1860—a maneuver that opened wide the eyes of the country boys from the Far West.[6]

The great fat shibboleth of the transcontinental line, which was to justify the shorter local roads, was accorded the showier part of the ceremony. First, Curtis provided the Pacific road with a virgin birth. Prominent men selected by Congress from throughout the country were to meet in solemn convocation, determine the amount of capitalization necessary for building and equipping the line, prepare bylaws, elect directors, and issue stock in accordance with regulations laid down by the government. Conception thus accomplished, the incorporating commissioners would step aside and let the new directors assume control, choose their own officers, and get on with the job.

The company would need inducements, of course. One bait was the old lure of land grants. By 1860, however, the nation in general had learned that much western land was of poor quality and that returns from real estate were likely to be too low and too long delayed to attract financiers interested in relatively quick returns from heavy investments. To lighten the burden of waiting until land and operating revenues were achieved, Curtis proposed a generous government loan of sixty million dollars, about one half the estimated cost of the project. The loan was to be in the form of 5 per cent thirty-year bonds which the railroad could sell on the open market in order to raise cash for construction. The government, moreover, would not call on the railroad for the payment of interest until the bonds matured.* Private investors (or so the promoters of the Curtis bill hoped) would also buy enough of the company's own stocks and bonds to provide the other sixty million needed to complete the project.

In apparent accord with prevailing constitutional theory, the railroad to be built with this money was to be confined to the territories. Obviously, then, feeders would have to link the main line to the states— and therein lay the heart of Curtis' maneuvering. He proposed two feeders running westward like the forks of a Y. One was to start at an undesignated spot on the western border of Iowa, the other at an undesignated spot on the western border of Missouri. (Thus Chicago would be happy, St. Louis would be happy, everyone but the deep South would be happy.) The forks were to meet at still another undesignated spot two hundred miles west of the Missouri River, either in the Kaw Valley of Kansas or the Platte Valley of Nebraska. That junction spot would be the actual beginning point of the great Pacific Railroad.

This airy arrangement breathed not a word about surveys to pick routes. The silence was so contrary to Judah's thinking that he may well

* This part of Curtis' proposal differed from Judah's in that it called for a government loan. The Pacific Railroad Convention had asked only that the government guarantee the interest on the company's own bonds.

have asked Curtis to explain it. What innocence! Surveys would come after the Iowa and Missouri companies concerned had decided on the main route. St. Louis promoters, for example, might carry their point for a direct line through Kansas to Denver. (John Evans and other Colorado boosters were already hard at work behind the scenes, advocating just that.) Or Chicago and Des Moines interests might win a direct line farther north along the old emigrant trail through Nebraska to Great Salt Lake. The main point now was to pass a broad general bill and later stitch the details onto it.

Judah, as we shall see, was not convinced. As an engineer, he still believed that a gathering of geographic facts by means of a survey was the way to begin. But politicians, he was learning, did not always work quite so methodically.

Still another point must have raised his eyebrows. Under Curtis' bill, the feeder lines as well as the main road were to receive land and loans directly from the government, even though one of the branches would traverse part of Kansas, which was slated to become a state within a matter of months. And since there must also be a feeder at the west end of the main line, the bill provided for that, too—land grants within the state of California plus a loan of $18,000 per mile for building from navigable water to the base of the Sierra Nevada mountains and $24,000 per mile from the base of the mountains to the summit. This sum would be in addition to whatever aid the California legislature provided—up to $15 million according to the last talk Judah had heard. Such totals were enough, all right, to quicken a man's pulse.

Constitutionality? Ah, well, times change. Samuel Curtis was a Republican. In 1860 the House of Representatives was controlled by Republicans, and they were earnestly advocating the radical theory that when states lacked sufficient resources to complete projects of national importance within their borders, then the federal government should lend its assistance.

Who was to build these government-financed feeders? The bill was vague about that, too, although it had spelled out in detail the methods by which a brand-new, untainted corporation was to be formed for constructing the main line.

It was another revealing silence, as Judah soon realized. The tail was wagging the dog. The most active lobbyists behind the Curtis bill were not interested in the main line (whose feasibility west of Great Salt Lake many of them doubted anyway) but in garnering national funds for building local branches that could batten off local traffic and land grants whether the main line was ever finished to the Pacific or not.

Intricate maneuvers by rival local lines eager for preference were already afoot in both Missouri and Iowa, but it is unlikely that Judah concerned himself with them. His head was too full of whirling thoughts about the California feeder. Who was to build it?[7] The state's pioneer Sacramento Valley Railroad? The still nonexistent Sacramento, Placer & Nevada, which hoped to start work as soon as the scheduled town and county bond issues were passed on June 4, 1860? Or perhaps the San Francisco & San José, a paper line with which Bay area promoters had been struggling on and off since 1852?

Or—and his pulse must have leaped—would it be best to form an entirely new corporation for this express purpose?

Such a happening would bring down on the new firm's head the full venom of the companies already formed. But weren't the bounties rich enough to make the fight worthwhile?

Disappointment awaited the schemers. Southerners tacked onto the main act a provision calling for a route through the Southwest as well as one through the central area. The measure was then sent back to committee for further consideration. Normally this would have meant burial. Curtis' supporters staved off the death, however, by entering on the calendar for the coming session an order that the bill be again presented to the House for debate on December 3, 1860.

Curtis was confident that in December the bill would pass. One sign of shifting sentiment was the passage, in June 1860, of an act granting federal aid to an overland telegraph line. Political trends were even more propitious. The national Democratic party was profoundly split between the Douglas and Breckinridge wings. The Republicans, on the other hand, were united. By the time Judah and his wife left the East for California they had learned the results of the new party's convention held in Chicago in May: Abraham Lincoln for president on a platform that called, among other things, for full government support of the Pacific railway, without quibbles over state or territorial limitations. Moreover, the Republicans were a northern party and would have little patience with southern attacks on a railroad bill advocating a central route—the route Judah had always favored.

He must be ready with a feeder route when the time came. "Oh, how we used to talk it all over and over on the steamer en route to California in July, 1860," Anna wrote years later without really understanding the intricacies that were involved.[8] But she did know that her husband was on fire to get into the mountains and find a usable pass. For he still insisted on the value of surveys.

Would not the California plum go, in all logic, to whatever company could produce profiles and maps proving that it had found a way across the mountains? In addition, would not the maps silence the last geographic objections of those who insisted that only in southern California could the western ranges be crossed?

On arriving in California, he prepared for the convention a laundered report of his activities in Washington and submitted a bill of forty dollars to cover the cost of certain printing he had ordered.[9] He next (so far as the tangled sequence of his activities can be unraveled) paid a call on bankers Pioche and Bayerque and their shadow, promoter Lester L. Robinson.

He may have gone in answer to a summons. They were following with keen interest new developments in the Washoe district of what would soon be set aside as Nevada Territory. During the latter part of the previous summer, as Judah already knew, word had begun trickling back to California about the discovery of a gigantic deposit of gold and silver ore high on the barren sides of Mt. Davidson. Winter had slowed the initial stampede, but not high-blown rumors of continuing rich strikes. The Comstock Lode, as the deposit was called, was clearly destined to be one of the great mining bonanzas of the world. As soon as snow was gone from the High Sierra in the spring of 1860, the rush redoubled.

Most of the fortune hunters followed the thoroughfare that Collis Huntington had helped promote in 1857, a steep narrow road winding from Placerville over Johnson Pass to Carson Valley. By 1860 it was in wretched shape. It had not achieved its purpose, and the discouraged supervisors of El Dorado County had thereupon declined to vote adequate funds for its maintenance. Private companies holding toll franchises to other sections of the highway had naturally followed suit. As a result the unrepaired road was totally inadequate for the stampede to Washoe. When the grades disintegrated still more under the continuing jam of grinding wheels, sulphurous demands for better transportation began to arise.

So choice an opportunity was not lost on the voters of Auburn town and Placer County. On June 4, 1860, they not only authorized $150,000 worth of bonds for luring the Sacramento, Placer & Nevada Railroad as far as Auburn, but also added another $25,000 to help build a pair of trans-Sierra wagon roads. One was to climb toward the summit of the mountains between the Middle and North forks of the American River. The other was to begin at the mining town of Dutch Flat north of the North Fork and cross wherever it could.

Although the proposed wagon route between the Middle and North forks of the river was out of reach of the Sacramento, Placer & Nevada

Railroad, the Robinson brothers and their bankers were very interested in the highway out of Dutch Flat. If the road was built, its principal feeder from the west would be the Sacramento, Placer & Nevada.

The Sacramento, Placer & Nevada was no longer a mere paper concern. On the strength of the successful town and county bond elections, its officers were already soliciting stock subscriptions in Sacramento and San Francisco and hoped to start grading from Folsom toward Auburn in 1861. Meanwhile, the Sacramento Valley Railroad already fed the Johnson Pass road along the South Fork. Thus, if the Robinsons and Pioche, Bayerque & Co. also achieved control of the new wagon road out of Dutch Flat, they could practically monopolize freight haulage to and from Washoe, a volume already running into thousands of tons per year.

The promoters put Judah back on the payroll of the Sacramento Valley Railroad as an engineer, and told him to go into the mountains and hunt out a route for the wagon road from Dutch Flat. They may have suggested the old emigrant highway over Truckee Pass and down past Donner Lake. It had been popular once, but the mountains were rugged there, especially in winter. It might be better, therefore, to strike north from Dutch Flat, hook onto a rough road that already led from Marysville eastward over Henness Pass, and repair that route.* Anyway, they wanted Judah to look over the ground as quickly as might be and hurry back with some sound engineering estimates.[10]

Judah's response is an exasperating mystery. Did he stay silent about the prospects of a federally built railroad in the hope that *he* could control whatever developed, and did he accept the survey job from the promoters as a way of getting into the mountains and making his maps at someone else's expense? Or did he blurt out everything he knew in the hope of obtaining the support of these influential San Franciscans?

The latter conjecture seems, as a pure guess, to be the more likely. But if Judah did talk, his arguments failed to impress his listeners. The California promoters probably knew of the Curtis bill's return to committee, an action redolent of fatality. Why should they chase the chimera of federal aid that might never materialize? Besides, a mere $28,000 per mile would not cover one third of the cost of the heaviest construction in the mountains. Nor was state aid likely to make up the deficit. At the joint meeting of the legislature and the Pacific Railroad Convention in February, strong taxpayer opposition had developed to the

---

* This Marysville-Henness Pass-Little Truckee River road was used by the California Stage Company lines, chief competitor of the Pioneer line that ran through Placerville.

proposed grant of fifteen million dollars. It was much more realisitic, in the opinions of the Robinson brothers and Pioche, Bayerque & Co. to build their short line Sacramento, Placer & Nevada through easy country with funds already in sight and finish the crossing of the mountains with a cheap wagon road. Judah had better settle for that. And, oh yes, while he was at it, he ought to drop in at express and freight offices in the little towns in the area he examined and suggest that they send their business by way of the Sacramento Valley Railroad's terminus at Folsom. Some of those back country teamsters were still driving their wagons all the way to Sacramento.

Judah was used to having big dreams shrink to small tasks. He accepted the offer (with or without revealing his broader plans) and traveled to Auburn, nestled among hills tawny with sun-smitten grass and dotted by groves of shiny-leafed, evergreen live oaks. Beyond Auburn, the road climbed steeply, seeking the upper levels of the long, high ridge that divided the North Fork of the American from the Bear River to his left. The massive ridgetop was rough, a sequence of broad, high timbered knobs divided from each other by wide gaps, or saddles. To avoid climbing over those knobs, the wagon road slanted along their tree-covered sides from one gap to the next. Some of the drops beneath the wagon wheels looked fearful—as much as fifteen hundred feet at a place called Cape Horn, two miles above Illinoistown.* Such sights had made the thought of a rail line preposterous to timid observers. Judah, however, knew well enough that grading above a fifteen-hundred-foot drop was not a great deal harder, relatively speaking, than above fifteen feet. What interested him were those widely spaced saddles in the ridgetop. By weaving in and out of them, *his* railway—he was already coupling the possessive to the noun—could ascend toward the ultimate crest of the mountain on an even grade not in excess of the capabilities of the locomotives of his time. Without that long ridge the climb might have been impossible.[11]

Existing stage roads ended at Dutch Flat. Judah evidently rented horses and with a helper or two prowled the high country, looking not just for wagon roads but for railway grades as well. He apparently returned to Sacramento on schedule with information for his employers about a wagon road to the Henness Pass highway but with little concrete data that would further his ambitions for a railway. Into his discouragement came a letter from a Dutch Flat druggist, Daniel W. Strong, called Doctor by his customers because of his virtuosity with prescriptions.

* Illinoistown would shortly be renamed Colfax after the vice-president of the United States.

Some weeks earlier, on June 26, so Strong wrote, forty-seven civic-minded residents of the Dutch Flat area had contributed from one to fifteen dollars each (only nine of the contributions amounted to ten dollars or more) for locating a good wagon road over Donner Summit.[12] What motivated the contributors is not clear. Perhaps they feared that using county money to build a mere connection with the Henness Pass route would leave them isolated on a branch highway, and they wanted to find a way that would place their town firmly on the main route. On returning from this survey, Strong had learned through livery stable gossip that Judah had also been searching among the timbered crags, asking more questions about possible railroad grades than about wagon ways. If that was true, then Strong could point out exactly where such a route could best be located.[13]

The day after the letter arrived, Judah was on his way back to Dutch Flat, apparently without saying a word of what he was after to the Robinsons or to Pioche and Bayerque. Strong led him up the vast ridge that divides the North Fork from the Bear and, farther on, from the looping headwaters of the South Yuba. Thanks to key saddles like Emigrant Gap several miles on beyond Dutch Flat, a railroad could maintain the same even grade that Judah had noted farther down the slope—and it may be that a knowledge of these gaps, which Judah had lacked time to ferret out, was Strong's contribution to the reconnaissance. Neither of them ever said exactly what geographic keys they uncovered on the ride.

Gaps were only part of the story. This vital east-west ridge reached the summit of the main north-south Sierra chain on what amounted to a plateau. Southward, the Sierra crested twice—parallel ridges with a deep valley between them, so that a railroad in that vicinity would have to drop down and then climb again, obviously a heavy expense. Here, however, there was only one summit, thanks to the forces of erosion. A little south of the explorers Lake Tahoe lay cupped between the two summit ridges. Tahoe's drainage, the Truckee River, flowed north a short distance and then, bending northeast toward Nevada, carved a deep natural gateway through the eastern ridge. Thus a railroad climbing up from Dutch Flat would have to surmount only the western summit, and its chief engineering problem would lie in finding a way down a thousand-foot rocky wall past lovely Donner Lake and along Donner Creek to the canyon gateway formed by the Truckee.

Though the route was feasible it was not necessarily better than other ways farther north. Judah made quick reconnaissances of Henness Pass at the head of the Yuba and of the Johnson Pass country south of Lake

Tahoe, in El Dorado County. According to Anna Judah, Strong went with him on both those long rides. Charles Marsh, a prosperous merchant, mine owner, and ditch operator of Nevada City, joined them on the Henness exploration.[14] So far as Nevada City was concerned, Henness was a preferable location, but after looking over both crossings Marsh agreed that Donner Summit (or Truckee Pass, the names being synonymous) was a better way and offered to persuade his neighbors of the truth.

By that time October was half gone and Judah wanted to bring a company into existence before Congress began its debates on the Curtis bill in December. This involved considerable doing, for California statute was strict on the subject of railroad corporations. The company had to be capitalized for enough money to build the proposed line, a cost Judah placed at $8.5 million—or 85,000 hundred-dollar shares. In addition, no company could be incorporated until there was actual cash in the treasury; a minimum of ten subscribers had to pledge themselves to buy at least $1,000 worth of stock for each mile of the contemplated road. Since Judah estimated the distance from navigable water at Sacramento to the state line to be 115 miles, he was faced with rounding up promises for $115,000, a formidable sum since many people did not think the railroad was physically possible.

Fortunately, only 10 per cent of the $115,000 had to be paid down in cash at the time a subscriber made his pledge. Balancing this leniency, however, was a grim declaration about stockholder responsibility: under California law stockholders in a corporation were "individually and personally liable" for the debts of the corporation in proportion to the amount of stock they owned—a deterrent well calculated to dampen high-flying speculation.

Not many unsophisticated investors knew of this liability law, and, for the sophisticated, there were loopholes. Ignoring the potential penalties, Strong, Marsh, and Judah made a rough map of the proposed railway, which they named the Central Pacific, and then rode from camp to camp— Dutch Flat, Illinoistown, Grass Valley, Nevada City—begging for enough stock subscription at one hundred dollars per share (ten dollars down) to launch the company. Eventually they gleaned pledges totaling $46,500, leaving a little less than $70,000 still to go.[15]

All of this is passing strange. Naïve though Judah often appeared to be, he could hardly have expected to raise enough money in the remote towns of the Sierra foothills to launch a company. Nor could he have supposed that Congress would consider his hasty horseback reconnaissances—the very sort of examination he had once derided—as *surveys* in proof of the road's practicability. But they were a lever. The list of subscribers and the rough profiles he had drawn of the Donner Pass ridge would give him something to point to while he talked to San Franciscans capable of giving him the kind of backing he needed. Or so he hoped, blinded meanwhile by his own soaring enthusiasm.

He prepared his pitch with care. In an eighteen-page pamphlet dated November 1, 1860, he described the route he had found after months of exploration. He outlined the bounties he expected from Congress and tossed off bright figures about potential revenues from operations. He waved his mountain subscriptions like a hawker of patent medicines displaying testimonials: See what has already been done! With disarming candor he admitted why he was in a hurry: "It is important that this organization be effected before the sitting of the next Congress, that they may deal with a company already in existence." He tried to forestall any possible resentment on the part of Pioche, Bayerque & Co. by saying that he was willing for his new line to "connect with the Sacramento Valley Road at Folsom, or the California Central Road at Lincoln." And then he finished blandly, "It is not considered necessary to make an urgent appeal for subscriptions, but simply to present a plain statement of the facts to a few persons of responsibility and influence. . . . To this end your cooperation is respectfully solicited."[16]

Hopefully he sent the flyer to a selected list and followed it with personal calls. According to his wife's recollections he very quickly arranged for a meeting with key men in the office of a prominent San Francisco attorney. Such contacts were far more in accord with the way significant amounts of money were raised than were street-corner solicitations in small villages. In high excitement he wrote Strong on November 14, 1860, "I drop a hasty line to say that I have struck a lucky streak, and shall fill up the list without further trouble. I have got one of the richest concerns in California into it. . . ."[17]

Instead, he met a violent rebuff. First, the Robinsons fired him from his job as engineer for the Sacramento Valley Railroad. The ostensible reason was that he had published without permission survey information that he had gathered while on their payroll. A deeper reason was that in spite of being an employee of the Sacramento Valley road, he was promoting a company whose success, however unlikely, would end not only the Sacramento Valley's subsidiary, the Sacramento, Placer & Nevada, but the proposed wagon road by way of Henness Pass as well.

As a result he arrived at his meeting with his prospective backers in bad odor with Pioche, Bayerque & Co., one of San Francisco's major banking houses. Conceivably this lent a hostile tone to remarks fired at

90

him about his optimism concerning congressional action of the once delayed Curtis bill, the inadequate nature of his reconnaissances across the mountains (he said he could build the line for $70,000 a mile, but how did he really know?), and a complete lack of data about the fearsome difficulties of keeping the Sierra road free of snow, if ever it was built.

Other, deeper forces were again at work under the objections. Most San Francisco capitalists were already involved in enterprises that would be hurt by a transcontinental railroad—steamship lines, wagon, stage, and express companies. Besides, there were quicker ways to make money out of Nevada than building a railroad. Stocks in the new Comstock mines were soaring, and interest rates were back up to 2 and 2.5 per cent per month. Why sink money in a railroad that would not begin to pay for years, if ever?

Judah left the meeting stunned and angry. He'd show them, he told Anna. They'd be sorry. "I shall never talk nor labor any more with them."[18] It was like a small boy's petulance, and in many ways—both in his enthusiasms and his tempers—Theodore Judah forever remained almost childish.

The only recourse left was for him to forget big money and seek out, in the time that remained to him, enough small subscribers to round out the subscriptions he needed. The place to do it was not San Francisco, looking complacently toward its established sea lanes, but Sacramento, facing inland toward the mountains. He prevailed on Lauren Upson of the *Union* to publish a notice of a meeting at the St. Charles Hotel on J Street, and with his resilient optimism surging again he gathered together his charts and maps for still another effort.

Surely someone would be there who would listen to him.

8 The Incredible Leap

When Judah arrived in Sacramento, the habitués of the upstairs rendez-vous at 54 K Street were in an expansive mood. Their insistence on keep-ing the Republican party intact during the disastrous campaign of 1859 had paid off spectacularly. Though their favorite, William Seward, had lost the nomination, Republicanism in general had triumphed. Charles Crocker had won a seat in the legislature—he weighed 250 pounds by then, yet had conducted a lively campaign at country dances—and in the California presidential contest Lincoln had squeaked past Douglas and Breckinridge by narrow margins. In the eyes of some observers, the Pacific railroad and not slavery had been the key factor leading to success.[1]

Stanford, the titular head of the party, was now able to speak out on a national level. The men at 54 K Street meant for him to do so. Because of California's off-beat election schedule, there would be no vote for United States Senator until 1863, no vote for representatives until 1861. Thus every member of the California delegation in Washington was a Democrat. In order to make sure that Republican wishes about patronage were heard, it was decided that Stanford should leave for the East in January, to consult with the President-elect.[2]

Against this pleasing background Collis Huntington opened his copy of the *Union* one day late in November 1860, and read Judah's call for a railroad meeting in the St. Charles Hotel. He had probably met the en-gineer before: they lived in the same town, and Hopkins and he sold the kind of equipment Judah used. Furthermore, Daniel Strong of Dutch Flat had already tried to sell Huntington and Hopkins shares in the new rail-road, but they had turned him aside with remarks that they were still try-ing to recover from the disastrous fire of 1852.[3] These talks with Strong, however, had come before the Pony Express' arrival with the word of

Lincoln's election, and perhaps the situation had changed. Together with the newly elected Republican assemblyman, Charles Crocker, Huntington wandered over to the hotel to hear what Judah had to say.

Underneath the speech ran a note of desperation. Judah had to form a company almost overnight, conduct a survey, and find money enough to build several dozen miles of railroad, for the federal loan would not be forthcoming until the company had proved its responsibility by completing a specified amount of work.

When foot-draggers pointed out the last fact, Judah replied querulously that he had already answered the question in his circular of November 1. State and county aid would surely be forthcoming at once. He would start with that. In costly areas he would compromise, laying temporary track on grades as steep as 250 feet per mile.* Then as fast as "appropriations [can] be procured from the Government, the work for [permanent] grading can be carried on, and . . . the track moved over on to it." It was a slippery expedient, and he doubted that it would prove necessary. The company's franchise alone would attract capital, he said. Eastern financiers would require only evidence enough to show that the Westerners could really breast the mountains. As a trained engineer, he knew the Donner route would work. Nonetheless he had to produce exact figures. He proposed to use the down payments made for stock subscriptions to finance the survey. A mere ten dollars per share, gentlemen . . .

A grocer or farmer in the audience asked whether produce usable by the surveyors—grain for horses, potatoes and flour for the men—would be acceptable as down payments.⁴ Judah winced and said yes. A few men shuffled up to the desk and wrote down their names. Others watched Huntington, a leading merchant of known sagacity, to see what he would do.

He sat motionless. To anyone who knew the ways of finance—and he and Hopkins by this time were each year handling heavy equipment worth tens of thousands of dollars—Judah's presentation must have sounded like a child's playhouse fantasy. Still, underneath the impractical approach there was a sounder basis than mere zeal. Judah knew railroading; he had watched Congress in action and could call many members by name; he had found a route that probably was workable. It was a rare mixture, worthy of further exploration. As soon as the gathering had dispersed, Huntington stepped over to the discouraged

* This was more than twice the maximum allowed in the bill that finally passed Congress.

man and arranged for a meeting, either upstairs at 54 K or at the home of Collis' brother-in-law E. D. Prentice—accounts vary.

Either at that gathering or at a subsequent one, Judah played his ace. The survey he wanted his listeners to finance would be useful, he said, not only for the railroad but for a preliminary wagon way from Dutch Flat across the Sierra to Virginia City on the Comstock Lode. Such a wagon way would produce revenue from toll charges while the railroad was being built, and would be useful for bringing supplies to workers engaged on the larger project. Thus their investment would be protected, for if anything happened to the railroad, they would still have the wagon way. Competition was no worry. Because of the single summit at Donner Pass, their route would be more popular with teamsters than the existing highway over Johnson Pass or the longer road over Henness Pass that the Robinson brothers were talking about. A perfect deal. They couldn't lose![5]

Not that he supposed the railroad would fail to materialize. No! And back he circled to his conviction that Curtis' bill, or a variation of it, would soon pass Congress, if not during the current lame-duck session, then surely during the first regular session to meet after Lincoln's inauguration.

Surely?

Yes. Judah leaned forward to explain and for the first time, probably, Huntington and his associates became aware of the intense manipulations with which local lines in the Midwest were fostering a transcontinental railroad as a means of furthering their regional ambitions.

Huntington grew thoughtful. Here, patently, was an opportunity for horse trading. If the bosses of the Republican party of California—most of them sitting right there at 54 K Street—put their weight behind the Midwesterners, would not the Midwesterners return the favor by encouraging the government to name the Central Pacific as the official feeder line in the West?

Again and again, long after Judah had gathered up his portfolios and had gone home, Collis and Mark Hopkins wore the small hours away, talking, talking. Another $7,500 would put the Central Pacific over the top, guaranteeing funds enough to cover both the survey and the necessary lobbying in Congress. Only $7,500—750 shares of $100 stock, 10 per cent down, pledged by three men in addition to themselves, or 150 shares each.

Judah? Ah, yes. They would have to take him in as an equal, of course, paying him for his preliminary work and for his surveying with a bookkeeping entry of another hundred and fifty shares. If the engineer needed money

94

to live on meanwhile, they could afford to give him a salary of $100 a month.[6] So argued Collis Huntington, the born plunger, excitement racing in his veins. Think of it! A transcontinental railroad in their grasp for only fifteen hundred dollars!

Hopkins was more cautious. Fifteen hundred dollars did not sound like much. On the other hand, they were hardly wealthy. Sacramento tax rolls show that Huntington's real estate and personal property together were assessed in 1861 at $8,680. Though the hardware store did a good business, most of it was on credit. Its assessed valuation for 1861 was $21,405.[7] And the survey was just the opening of what might prove a bottomless sink. That was a mighty big mountain they were talking about.

But think of the opportunity! Judah was in their hands now. He might slip loose if they kept him dangling too long. Their prospects for a favorable hearing in both the national capitol and at the statehouse in Sacramento were as bright as anyone's in California. By controlling the survey and afterwards the board of directors, a tight little group of them could move a long way toward controlling the entire company. Ah, Mark! If ever they were going to amount to more than country hardware dealers, this was the time.

Hopkins finally agreed. Jauntily Collis set out to find three more men willing to risk $1,500. More colossal self-confidence can scarcely be imagined. Huntington was depending utterly on congressional favor, yet had only secondhand information about how Congress worked. Neither he nor Hopkins had had the least contact with railroad construction or operation, and Judah's experience was limited to engineering details.

Yet he dared offer an empire for $1,500 down.

A gold brick? Men like Darius O. Mills, Sacramento's leading banker and a good friend of Collis', thought so and refused to participate. In the end Huntington had to settle for small-town entrepreneurs like himself: James Peel, an engineer about whom little is known, and James Bailey, a prosperous Sacramento importer of watches, clocks, and jewelry. After hesitating for several days, Stanford finally succumbed. When he did, the list was complete—and then Peel backed out. Doggedly Huntington searched again and this time made contact with Charles Crocker.[8]

Smaller investors added their bit, among them, Cornelius Cole, who subscribed for ten shares—$100 down. A more valuable contribution was Cole's friendship for William Seward, who appeared destined for a place in Lincoln's cabinet. On December 1, 1860, Cole sent Seward via Pony Express a long letter offering a few words of advice about patronage and a great deal about the need for a Pacific railroad.[9]

The letter must have reached the New York Senator about the time the Curtis bill passed the House, December 18—two days before South Carolina seceded. How much effect the missive had is problematical. In any event, on January 5, 1861, after Gwin of California had offered a comparable railroad bill to the Senate, Seward supported it with a ringing speech. Gwin, of course, was a southern sympathizer and his railroad proposal became a sort of bedraggled olive branch held out by northern senators in hope of quieting secessionist talk. Everything the South wanted concerning railroads was put into amendments and shoveled into the proposed measure. This enabled the Far North to demand and win matching concessions: a government-supported railroad from Puget Sound to Lake Superior and land grants for a Pacific Coast line from Sacramento to Portland and Puget Sound.

This Santa Claus bagful of promises, enough to founder the treasury of even a nation at peace with itself, passed the Senate thirty-seven to fourteen and was sent to conference so that discrepancies with the House bill could be smoothed away. The House Republicans proved less conciliatory than the senators and measure died.[10]

News of the collapse came as a rude shock to 54 K Street. Until then events had been sailing along according to expectations. Stanford had left on January 21 to confer with Lincoln. Unquestionably he had been briefed about people he should see concerning the Central Pacific's aspirations to be named in the act as the official railroad of the Far West. The winter being unusually dry, Judah had then hurried ahead with his survey, running it during March from Folsom northeast toward Dutch Flat. Thus the company would be ready for whatever Congress did. But Congress, hamstrung once again by southern complications, had done nothing.

While the associates were absorbing this, word arrived by way of Pony Express and the western end of the Overland Telegraph that the attack on Fort Sumter had made civil war inevitable. What did this portend? Might not the next Congress be too absorbed by emergency measures to heed still another railroad bill? Should they not suspend operations and conserve their funds until they saw what was likely to happen?

Judah at least and perhaps Huntington argued vehemently against such timorousness. With southern obstructionism ended, a railroad bill was virtually guaranteed. Besides, the potential competitors they had feared all along were beginning to stir. Assured of county support and backed by Pioche, Bayerque & Co., the Robinson brothers were preparing to grade the line of the Sacramento, Placer & Nevada as far as Auburn. From Auburn they sent surveyors into the mountains to re-examine the route from Dutch Flat through Henness Pass. Was a local rail and wagon way their only goal?

Nearer the coast, the promoters of the San Francisco & San José had begun grading south. They made no secret whatsoever of their expectations that *their* line would become the western end of the great Pacific railroad, if and when the national system was built. If Congress proved friendly, would they be content to stop at San Jose and wait for the main line to come to them?

Meanwhile the businessmen of El Dorado County, hoping to keep Nevada traffic flowing through their district, had run a survey for what they called the Sacramento & Placerville from Folsom to Placerville. Pioche, Bayerque & Co. probably had a finger in that, too, and in plans to improve the wagon road over Johnson Pass. Suppose *they* attracted congressional attention?

Faced with such threats, the Central Pacific dared not hesitate before shoring up its own resources. The state capital looked like the place to begin. Polls by the Republican managers at 54 K Street indicated that Stanford might well be nominated for governor and win the election this year, if he consented to run. Off went urgent letters, advising him to hurry back from the East in time for the state convention, to be held in Sacramento on June 18.[11] Judah meantime was told to press ahead with his Donner Pass survey as fast as the retreating snow allowed.

The next step was to turn the informal Central Pacific Railroad into a legally recognized corporation. This entailed finding new subscribers to replace those in the mountains who had lost their nerve during the winter and had dropped out.[12] Someone, Huntington probably, undertook to call on his Sacramento neighbors, chat with them about the grand survey underway in the mountains, drop a few prominent names— Stanford for one—and then give his listeners an opportunity to get in on "bedrock," as California idiom put it. The approach worked. Dr. John F. Morse, who had sailed from Panama to San Francisco on the brig *Humboldt* with Huntington in 1849, took five shares. The mercantile houses of Lord, Holbrook & Co. and Millikin Brothers each took ten. So it went until 1,250 shares were accounted for—well above the 1,150 legal minumum. Of those 1,250 shares, the original contributors to the survey—Judah, Hopkins, Stanford, Crocker, Bailey, and Huntington—held 900.

A meeting to elect a board of directors was then called for April 30—at 54 K Street inevitably. To no one's surprise each of the original contributors was given a place. All were Sacramentans. To keep the mountain counties through which the road passed from feeling voiceless, Huntington added to the board the names of Charles Marsh of Nevada City and Daniel Strong of Dutch Flat.[13] Both had helped Judah during his preliminary reconnaissance. Moreover, a firm friendship had developed between Judah and Strong, and perhaps Huntington hoped that the addition of the pharmacist would keep the touchy little engineer from complaining that he was being smothered by the Sacramento political clique. And finally, for reasons not now recoverable, there was Lucius A. Booth, a wholesale grocer who seems to have sat in on most of the company's early discussions, even though he held only ten shares of stock.

Before the company's articles of incorporation could be filed with the secretary of state, this new board had to elect a slate of officers. They delayed several weeks, awaiting Stanford's return from the East. After he was back and had been duly named on June 19 as the Republican candidate for governor, the nine directors met at 54 K Street. Stanford, appointed temporary chairman, named Judah and Strong as a nominating committee. The two brought in a slate that designated Judah as chief engineer, James Bailey as secretary, Mark Hopkins as treasurer, Collis P. Huntington as vice-president, Leland Stanford as president.

Huntington was displeased. He wanted the presidency for himself and with a thrust of his cold gray-blue eyes let Strong know as much. The druggist and Judah stood their ground. Shrugging, Huntington chose not to make an issue of the point and the slate was declared elected.[14] There would be no open breach between the two top men until their climactic sundering in 1890. Long before then, however, Collis Huntington's private letters to Hopkins would show clearly that he never considered Leland Stanford an adequate man for the job given him that day.

On June 27, Secretary Bailey filed articles of incorporation with the state, and the Central Pacific was a true company at last. With one fair summer day following another in the mountains, Judah stepped up the pace of his survey. Stanford, accompanied nearly everywhere he went by Cornelius Cole, concentrated on his gubernatorial campaign. Huntington and Booth turned to patriotic affairs.

Secessionist sentiment was strong in California. As a retort, northern sympathizers formed energetic Union clubs, modeled after Eastern prototypes, and used them as cohesive units around which to build pro-war demonstrations. The Union Club of Sacramento spent $2,500 on a tumultuous Fourth of July celebration. Huntington and Booth were both members of the three-man finance committee responsible for the emotional and highly successful show.[15]

Not all was well with the railroad. Because of lack of funds, Judah did not continue the survey deep into Nevada, as he had originally proposed, but halted as soon as he was sure he could spiral tracks from Donner Summit down Donner Creek into the canyon of the Truckee River. By early August he was back in Sacramento boasting of his accomplishments to the editor of the *Union,* who on August 7 reported to the town with due awe, "When the Pacific RR next comes up in Congress, Californians will be able to say to members, We are now prepared to lay before you a perfectly reliable report of a complete survey over the mountain, by a competent engineer. The problem as to crossing the Sierra Nevada has been solved!"

Unmentioned in this rosy report were certain chilling truths about cost. Among other things, Judah had discovered that to hold to his average grade of 105 feet per mile he would have to bore eighteen tunnels totaling 17,410 feet in length; the longest would be 1,370 feet. His original guess at mileage—115—had risen under actual measurement to 140. His estimate for the cost of building to the border jumped from $8.5 million to almost $13 million, or approximately $88,000 a mile. So stark a total made the loan of $28,000 a mile offered by the Curtis bill look considerably less alluring than it had when Judah had been talking in terms of an average outlay of $70,000 a mile. He must have squirmed uncomfortably while presenting the figures, and in self-defense he finally persuaded Crocker, Huntington, and Stanford to ride with him over the proposed route and see for themselves why the estimates had risen so.

They skirted the beetling cliffs of Cape Horn high above the North Fork—a route across those precipices had been one of the hardest of all to plot, Judah said—and on among the evergreens and pinnacles to the summit, 7,000 feet above sea level. Years later Stanford told members of Congress' Pacific Railway Commission that the view from Donner Pass down 1,200 feet to deep blue Donner Lake and then 2,000 feet up to the wind-swept, snow-streaked peaks on either hand was "very formidable." Yet the three merchants, who knew nothing of construction, decided to push ahead.

Wouldn't it have been safer just to write off their $1,500 as a bad investment?

No, Stanford said. They still had faith in county, state, and federal aid. Moreover, continuing mineral strikes made Nevada's future seem as ripe as California's had in 1850. If the legal freight rate of fifteen cents a ton per mile remained in effect, "we could afford to build the road with the prospect of the further developments of Nevada." In short, the Californians, like the promoters in the Midwest, were attaching their hopes like a tail to the kite of a government-sponsored transcontinental line. If it materialized . . . no, they weren't willing to quit yet.[16]

Judah was in a fever to leave immediately for Washington and start working with his Midwestern friends on a new measure to replace the Curtis bill.* The other directors restrained him. "Election and politics so monopolize everything here now," he wrote Strong on September 2, "that our people have very little time to talk railroad matters." Still, he recognized the necessity. "A good deal depends on the election of Stanford," he added to Strong, "for the prestige of electing a Republican ticket will go a good ways toward getting us what we want."[17]

On September 4, Stanford swept into office with an ease that surprised even Republicans. With him he carried three Republican Congressmen, Frederick Low, Timothy G. Phelps, and Aaron Augustus Sargent, the latter a thirty-four-year-old newspaper editor from Nevada City, seat of one of the counties that would immediately benefit from the building of the Central Pacific.

The election over, Judah put the finishing touches on his maps, made notes for an elaborate report that he would have printed and distributed in Washington, and arranged for a salary increase to $150 a month. He drew $1,500 toward expenses and filled a portfolio with company stock valued, on the face of the certificates, at a hundred thousand dollars. This he could distribute as need warranted.[18] In October he sailed. With him were James Bailey, secretary of the Central Pacific Railroad, and (not by coincidence, probably) Aaron Augustus Sargent. For the rest of his life, Sargent's fortunes would be intimately linked with those of the Central Pacific Railroad.

An oblique remark made by Charles Crocker and quoted in the Sacramento *Union* of September 26, 1861, suggests that Huntington rather than Bailey had been delegated to travel to Washington with Judah and Sargent. If so, plans changed abruptly. The reason apparently was the discovery that Judge Timothy Dame, Peter Donahue, Alexander Houston, and other incorporators of the San Francisco & San José Railroad, and contractor Charles McLaughlin, who was grading the line to San Jose, were also journeying to Washington.

Almost surely the San Franciscans meant to offer themselves to Congress as builders of the western end of the great Pacific railroad. If they were chosen, they would no doubt come to some understanding about rights-of-way with the other San Francisco-dominated railways already at work in the foothills, either the Sacramento, Placer & Nevada, which was grading from Folsom toward Auburn on the north side of

* Curtis had resigned his seat to join the Union Army.

the American River system, or the Sacramento & Placerville, which had run a survey as far as Placerville on the south side.

The prospect caused consternation at 54 K Street. The men from the Bay City were not without political resources of their own. Most of San Francisco's great businesses (and that included Donahue's Union Iron Works) had been founded during the days when Democrats had controlled California politics. They still retained their Democratic orientation.[19] Only a few months earlier, on April 2, 1861, Bay City commercial interests had helped see to it that the California state legislature elected a Democrat, James McDougall, to the United States Senate to succeed William Gwin.* The other senator was Democrat Milton S. Latham, who had been elected to fill the vacancy created by Broderick's death. Against those two men the Central Pacific's Republicanism would not count heavily, should a Democratic rival appear on the scene.

It so chanced that at this very time the first territorial legislature of Nevada, predominantly Republican in cast, was gathering in Carson City, across the Sierra. Among the legislators' duties would be the granting of charters to private companies interested in providing public services.

Someone at 54 K Street, Huntington perhaps, suggested that a Nevada railroad franchise in the hands of the Central Pacific or of a CP subsidiary—in effect a seal of approval from the Nevada legislature—would not only discourage rivals but would also help convince Congress that the Central Pacific, on its toes and ready to go, was the logical recipient of federal aid. Moreover, the Nevada franchise could be used as a trump in bargaining with the Dame-Donahue-McLaughlin syndicate. If the San Franciscans would not interfere, through Senators Latham McDougall, with the naming of the Central Pacific in the railroad bill, then the CP would assign to the San Francisco & San José or a subsidiary whatever land and bond bounties were granted the CP between Sacramento and the Bay City—a move that would let the San Franciscans control the approaches to their town, a generous plum surely. If, on the other hand, the San Franciscans declined to be allies, then the Central Pacific, armed with its Nevada franchise, would put pressure on the Republican Congressmen and the Republican legislature in Sacramento to block any further expansion by the San Francisco & San José.

But first there had to be a Nevada franchise.

* Like the Broderick-Gwin struggle, the election was bitterly contested and resulted in another fatal political duel, this one fought with rifles at forty yards.

101

The normal way of reaching Carson City was to travel by a Pioneer line stagecoach from Folsom through Placerville and over Johnson Pass. Potential rivals—the Robinson brothers of the Sacramento & Placerville—were at work there, however, and the directors assigned to visit the Nevada legislature—Strong, Crocker, and Governor-elect Stanford went with Huntington—may have feared that the sight of them crowding into a public conveyance would alert the opposition. Besides, they wanted to visit Dutch Flat and solicit stock for their proposed Dutch Flat and Donner Lake Wagon Road.* Accordingly they made arrangements by telegraph for a wagon to drive up a rough lumber road that wound through Truckee Canyon from Nevada, and meet them at Donner Lake, the road's end. They then took a Sacramento Valley Railroad train to the Dutch Flat stagecoach terminus at Folsom.

At Folsom they almost surely paused to contemplate a new locomotive steaming northward along the tracks of the California Central, which recently, on October 13, had opened for business as far as Lincoln, a dozen miles away. This short line, in which Sam Brannan, founder of Sacramento City, was heavily interested, was aiming toward Marysville. From Marysville it might veer up the Yuba River to Yuba Pass. Or, having reached Marysville, it could join forces with the new California Northern, organized in January 1861 to build north to Oroville and at that point turn along the Feather River toward Beckwourth Pass south of Honey Lake.

Either alternative opened the way to possible competition—and a possible alliance with the San Francisco & San José against the CP . . . unless the California Central and the California Northern could somehow be bought off. Could they, for example, be prevailed on to consider themselves as segments of the transcontinental's branch line to Portland and Seattle? After all, why run the Northwest's feeder line through nonproductive deserts to Salt Lake City? Why not push it due north through the fertile Sacramento and Willamette valleys, where there would be lucrative traffic? In other words, make allies of the two short lines by promising Brannan and the other directors that if they went north instead of east, Aaron Sargent would name them as recipients of federal largess in the bill he planned to introduce into the House of Representatives. Well, it was something to consider.[20] But first there was the matter of Nevada.

* In spite of the name Donner Lake, the road builders intended, if circumstances seemed propitious, to push the wagon way on as far as Virginia City. Hence it was necessary for them to sign up enough stock subscribers to meet the incorporation requirements of both California and Nevada.

On the ponderous quartet went—Huntington, Stanford, and Crocker each weighed more than two hundred pounds and Strong, not much less. After completing their errands in Dutch Flat, they mounted reluctant horses provided by the druggist and in biting October winds rode over the "very formidable" pass to icy Donner Lake on the other side.[21] The wagon that was to have met them had been delayed. They camped out twenty-four hours waiting for it, the first time, probably, that they had slept on the ground for years.

When the belated vehicle appeared, its driver was entrusted with taking the saddle horses back to Dutch Flat. With Strong acting as teamster, the others rattled down the lumber road beside the river to Truckee Meadows, about where Reno now stands. Trying to make up for lost time, they pressed on until long after dark, bedding down finally in a haystack. The next day, as they were pushing south across a sagebrush desert, one of the overloaded axles cracked. Out of deference either to Stanford's dignity or groans of misery, the other three let him gingerly drive the crippled wagon while they dismounted and hiked to a wayside tavern known as Honey Lake Smith's. There they procured a new vehicle for the rest of the journey.

The next day, October 25, the Carson City correspondent of the Sacramento *Union* duly noted that C. P. Huntington, Governor-elect Stanford, and "jolly Charley Crocker" of the California legislature had "arrived in town late last night and today have been hob-nobbing around with our Governor, and seeing the lions pretty largely."

"Our Governor" was handsome, portly James Nye, an ex-police commissioner of New York City who had labored well for Lincoln and had been rewarded with this Nevada appointment. Most impressive of Nye's lions was a long-bearded, thirty-four-year-old giant named William Morris Stewart, a brand-new Republican married somewhat uneasily to the daughter of a former senator from Mississippi. Before joining the rush to Washoe, Stewart had been a colleague of Aaron Sargent's in Nevada City. As in the case of Sargent, his fortunes too would soon be inextricably linked with those of the Central Pacific Railroad.

Smaller lions included Orion Clemens, secretary of Nevada Territory, and Orion's younger brother, Sam Clemens, who a little later would begin writing for the Virginia City *Territorial Enterprise* under the pseudonym Mark Twain.

Years afterward, in *Roughing It*, Twain left an account of that first legislature and its meeting place, a large stone building provided rent-free just outside the city limits by old Abe Curry. Curry also "furnished pine benches and chairs for the legislature, and covered the floors with clean saw-dust by way of carpet and spitoon combined. . . . A canvas partition to separate the Senate from the House of Representatives was put up by the Secretary at a cost of three dollars and forty cents."

Among the legislators meeting in Curry's hall was a man named Hannah, once of Sacramento. As a favor to old acquaintances, Hannah agreed to introduce into the legislature a bill granting to the "Nevada Central Railroad" a franchise that included a two-hundred-foot right-of-way down Truckee Canyon and on across Nevada toward Utah. An interesting clause in the right-of-way provision prohibited any other railroad from building within two hundred feet of the grant's outer edges, an innocent-sounding detail which effectively excluded would-be rivals from the natural gateway provided by the Truckee Canyon.

Hannah's proposed franchise was instantly attacked by certain legislators who were presumed to be under the thumb of San Francisco businessmen. The Sacramento *Union*'s correspondent was outraged. "Shortsighted and narrow arguments were urged against the bill," he fumed on October 28; ". . . the language of boys rather than that of grown men."

If San Francisco interests were in fact responsible for the opposition, they made a serious mistake. They stayed at home. The visitors had invaded the battlefield in person. Thus they were able to contact an influential Nevadan, J. H. Todman, who wanted to build a short-line railroad from Virginia City to the California border and there connect with whatever system breached the Sierra. Huntington and company convinced Todman—no doubt he was duly impressed at being approached by the governor-elect of California—that the Central Pacific, whose representative was already bound for Washington, was the only company in existence capable of doing the job. No doubt they played up the wagon road, too. It would be a feeder for him well before the railway could cross the summit. Completely bemused, Todman undertook to concentrate his resources on the legislative committees concerned.[22]

The Californians next turned their attention to a franchise for the Dutch Flat and Donner Lake wagon highway. This proved easier. Everyone was winning toll road franchises. "The ends of them," Twain wrote later, "were hanging over the boundary line everywhere like a fringe."

Assured that the railroad franchise would pass, the directors of the Central Pacific returned home without waiting for the formality of Governor Nye's signature. (He affixed it to the charter on November 25, 1861.) In Sacramento, the group capitalized the Dutch Flat and Donner Lake Wagon Road Company for $100,000 and on November 27, 1861, filed articles of incorporation with the California secretary of state, little realizing the troubles which this simple and, in their minds, eminently logical move was going to precipitate on their heads.[23]

In a hurry still, Collis then boarded a river steamer with Elizabeth and went to San Francisco. There, presumably, he called on Sam Brannan and persuaded the apostate Mormon that the Nevada franchise gave the Central Pacific first call on Congress's attention and that the California Central's future lay north toward Oregon rather than east in competition with the CP. This step achieved, the Huntingtons next caught ship for Panama and the East.

They reached New York City on December 24, spent Christmas Day in the drab Merchant's Hotel in the commercial district, and then separated.[24] Elizabeth went to Connecticut to visit relatives. Collis boarded a train for war-beset Washington.

He found Judah discouraged. The engineer said that although his survey maps and Anna's Sierra paintings, both on display once more in an unused room in the Capitol building, had attracted many visitors, nothing concrete had happened. So far, the House's Select Committee on the Pacific Railroad, the only group that could report a bill to the representatives, had not even met. Congress was spending all its time listening to "everlasting buncombe . . . on the eternal colored man" and had no interest in railroad matters.[25]

In spite of the indifference, Aaron Sargent prepared a long speech rehashing the same arguments that had been used over and over in favor of the railroad: the government would save upwards of seven million dollars a year in transporting troops, munitions, and mail; the western Indians would be quelled; emigration to the Coast would be speeded; the intervening territories would be developed; trade with the Orient would jump; California's loyalty to the Union would be assured; foreign aggressors would be confounded; the nation's prestige would soar. In mid-January 1862, he managed to secure the floor during a dull debate on an unrelated subject and with grim perseverance delivered his oration to, so Judah later reported to the *Union,* "a beggarly account of empty boxes."

The effort had its effect. The House added Sargent's name to the select committee. A week later the group held its first meeting of the session and after fierce intramural disputes appointed a three-man subcommittee to draft a new Pacific railroad bill for submission to the House. Aaron A. Sargent was appointed chairman of the subcommittee. Its other two members were James A. Campbell of Pennsylvania and Richard Franchot of New York.

An extraordinary piece of Huntington luck was at work there. Richard

Franchot, a native of Otsego County, New York, had been a close friend of Solon's and Collis' during Collis' storekeeping days in Oneonta. Later Franchot had moved to Schenectady and had become president of the little Albany and Susquehanna Railroad Company. A Republican, he was elected to Congress in 1861. Rather than run again in 1863, he joined the Union Army. He was destined to remain familiar with Congress, however, for until his death in 1875 he would move in and out of the legislative halls as chief lobbyist of the Central Pacific Railroad.

Judah was named clerk of Sargent's subcommittee. A bit later he was named secretary of the Senate's Committee on Pacific Railroads, of which Senator McDougall of California was chairman. (More Huntington luck: a distant relative, coarse old Ben Wade of Ohio was also a member of the Senate committee.) Undoubtedly Theodore Judah knew as much about the problems facing a transcontinental railway as anyone in the land. Undoubtedly the members of the depleted Congress, the southerners having departed, were overworked and needed help in meeting the extra burdens imposed on them by the war. Undoubtedly Judah was industrious and dependable. Still, he did bring to his new jobs a certain amount of what today would be classed as "conflict of interests."

Lobbyists of many midwestern lines buzzed around the committeemen, hoping to have their roads named in either the House or Senate bills as the official feeders for the eastern end of the transcontinental railway. Most active of these contenders was the incredible Leavenworth, Pawnee & Western.

This paper railroad had been created in 1855 to run from Leavenworth on the northeastern boundary of Kansas westward a hundred miles to the vicinity of Fort Riley and from there to, vaguely, the summit of the Rockies. Save for a perfunctory survey to Fort Riley, it had done no work. Then in 1860 it had been captured by four Kansas promoters: Thomas Ewing, Jr., the mastermind of the group, A. J. Isaacs, James C. Stone, and James H. McDowell. They needed a railroad in order to implement a dazzling scheme.

Home seekers pouring into eastern Kansas were annoyed at finding some of the area's best lands in the hands of the Delaware and Potawatomi Indians—the same Potawatomis that Charles Crocker as a teenager had helped herd out of Indiana to new homes in the West. The tribes were destined one way or another to lose some of those holdings. The contribution of Ewing and his cohorts was a brand-new method of euchring them. The Kansas promoters pushed through the Senate of the United States bills allowing them to buy several hundred thousand acres from the two tribes at a ridiculously low price. Their pious plan (and it was spelled out explicitly in the bills) was to sell the lands that they thus acquired to American homemakers at a high figure and use the profits for building a railroad, the Leavenworth, Pawnee & Western, that would benefit all the white settlers of the region.

John Palmer Usher, a lawyer hired by the Indians, denounced the deal as a "gross, heartless fraud," but the Senate let it stand. Usher thereupon transferred his allegiance to the successful promoters. Shortly afterwards he was named Lincoln's assistant secretary of the Interior.

The bill did contain one joker. Before the promoters could obtain full title to the lands involved they had to build a specified amount of railroad as an evidence of good faith. They had no funds for doing this, but that was no worry. They could get money from the federal government by having the Leavenworth, Pawnee & Western named in the Pacific railroad bill as a feeder for the transcontinental line. With this end in view, Ewing and company on January 6, 1862, appointed Henry Bennett to represent them in Washington. By no sheer coincidence Bennett was an intimate friend of John Palmer Usher, assistant secretary of the Interior. The new lobbyist reached Washington shortly after Huntington did.

To lend persuasiveness to his arguments, Bennett carried with him sheaves of LP&W stock certificates, not entirely valueless since the stock could be converted into Kansas Indian land if the deals went through. At least four United States senators and four United States congressmen received gifts of this stock. Among the latter was seventy-year-old Thaddeus Stevens, one of the founders of the Republican party of Pennsylvania.[26] Lame, harsh, sarcastic, and a brilliant parliamentarian, Stevens had used his position as chairman of the House Ways and Means Committee to make himself the most powerful single individual in Congress. He was also a partner in a lucrative Pennsylvania iron works that manufactured, among other things, railroad rails.[27]

Another recipient of the stock Bennett scattered around was the clerk of the Pacific railway committees, Theodore Dehone Judah. He received 1,200 shares, worth, at face value, $60,000—but considerably less on the market.[28] The reason is obvious. The LP&W wanted the good will of the California delegation in Congress. Conversely, the Central Pacific hoped that the Kansas and Missouri delegations, over which Ewing's group exerted considerable influence, would look kindly on them when the name of the Central Pacific bobbed up in the railroad bill.

During those hectic weeks Judah disbursed Central Pacific stock with a nominal, but not actual, value of $66,000.[29] In this case the names of the recipients are not known. No evidence survives to indicate that either Collis Huntington or Thomas Ewing, Jr., ever personally touched a single share of the migrating certificates. Both of them were in Washington at the time, however, and it is a little difficult to believe that they were unaware of what Judah and Bennett were doing.[30]

When the House and Senate committees reported bills to their different bodies, the names of the Leavenworth, Pawnee & Western and the Central Pacific appeared in clear black type as recipients of the lion's share of federal favor. Inevitably there were going to be objections from other lines. In an effort, evidently, to soften these plaints, the bill also threw out sops in the form of land grants to (so far as western railroads were concerned) the California Central, the California Northern, the Nevada Central—and also to Dame's and Donahue's San Francisco & San José.

"Instead of conciliating the friends of different local interests," Judah wrote back to the Sacramento *Union,* the bill's shotgun generosity "set them all quarreling." The main resentment in the East centered on the fact that the bill would let the LP&W build through the heart of Kansas to a point of its own choosing on the 102d meridian (the border between Kansas and Colorado). In effect this all but allowed the LP&W to designate the starting point for the transcontinental Union Pacific, a patriotic name already selected for the company which was to build from the 102d meridian westward through the territories to a junction with the Nevada Central—i.e., with the Central Pacific. All of this suited St. Louis and Denver, but not New England and Chicago. Those interests, unappeased by the little branches allowed them, wanted a starting point farther north and nearer the Iowa roads they controlled.

The fierce attacks and counterattacks that swirled around this first version of the bill led Justin Morrill of Vermont to comment sourly that capital was not interested in building the Union Pacific through uninhabited territories, but only in grabbing off the subsidies at either end. Anyway, he added, the nation could hardly afford both guns and railroads. Why not wait until after the war?[31]

Recognizing that the bitter feuds created by the bill's excessive generosity were likely to kill the measure, its proponents began trimming the package—or, as Judah put it in his report to the Sacramento *Union:* ". . . some changes of detail were made, some sharp points rounded out." Among the potential recipients of aid that were eliminated in the West were the California Central and the California Northern. They were told that they would be considered in later bills, as indeed was done; even so, the removal may well have looked to Brannan like a double cross after the promises Huntington had made in California. Out went, in addition, the San Francisco & San José. To calm Dame, Donahue, Houston, and McLaughlin, Huntington offered them the bargain he had already determined on before leaving California: if they would accept the elimination without stirring up the opposition of California's Democratic senators, the Central Pacific would unobtrusively assign to them the right to build the 175-mile stretch from Sacramento south around the Bay to San Francisco, along with whatever land grants and bond bounties went with that right.[82] Realizing that they were in no position to fight back, the San Franciscans agreed.

To help keep things looking clean, out went the Nevada Central as a designated road. In fact, by the time all the sharp corners in the West had been rounded off, the only railroad remaining in the revised bill was the Central Pacific.

The LP&W, which had suffered the most acidulous attacks in Congress, allowed the starting point of the Union Pacific to be pulled northeast from the Colorado-Kansas border to a point on the 100th meridian in the Platte Valley of Nebraska, near today's Cozad—a major concession that Judah is said to have engineered.[83] Other adjustments not relevant to Huntington's story followed. Where compromise could not be produced, the issue was sidestepped—anything to get the bill through. When, for example, the Missouri and Iowa contenders could not agree on the company that should build the central feeder branch or on the point at which it should start, the legislators handed the disputed line over to the supposedly impartial (and still unformed) Union Pacific, and charged the President of the United States with the ticklish duty of selecting the starting spot.

As soon as the new bill had been hammered into shape, Huntington grew restless. A keen reader of men, he was confident that this leaner second version would pass and he preferrred not to listen to the tedious debates that would precede success. Judah and Bailey were capable of handling interim emergencies. Besides, time was wasting. He had let Hopkins assume the full burden of the hardware store long enough. He wanted to get on with the essential wagon road the moment he heard that the railroad bill had passed. Most of all, he missed Elizabeth and his home.

As a member of California's State Board of Agriculture he accepted from the Patent Office quantities of new-type seeds, including tobacco seed, to be tested in California's warm central valleys.[84] He paid a visit to Oneonta, settled some hardware company business in New York, and in mid-March 1862 set sail with Elizabeth for Sacramento.

It had been a remarkable trip. During every waking hour of it he had followed with utter absorption the arts of political and financial manipulation as practiced by the experts who swarmed around him and Judah. In the sometimes subtle, sometimes brass-knuckled school of Washington's wartime politics, among promoters and developers drawn from every section of the nation, he had learned where his own particular genius lay—a flowering that could never have occurred within the confines of his hardware store. From relative obscurity, he, and his associates with him, had leaped into potential prominence, for $1,500 down.

The next step would be to learn whether they were capable of handling this vast project which their boldness, persistence, energy, and adroitness was on the point of delivering to them.[35]

9 Preparations

The Huntingtons reached San Francisco aboard the steamer *St. Louis* on April 7, 1862, and repaired immediately to Sacramento. They were worried. By occasional dispatches over the newly completed Overland Telegraph and by letters traveling through Panama, they knew that the town had recently been devastated by the worst of the area's many floods.

On January 9, after a month of rain, the levees had begun to break. An old ship hulk, still used as the city jail, sank so rapidly that there had scarcely been time to remove the prisoners. The river steamer *Gem* floated off into an orchard. The next day, January 10, Leland Stanford and his wife traveled to his inaugural ceremonies in a rowboat. On returning, the celebrants entered the square, pretentious, iron-fenced governor's residence through a second-story window.

Because most kitchens were inundated, cooking was impossible. Tired of crackers and cold cheese, the legislators shifted operations to San Francisco. Eventually they returned, but scores of disgusted citizens did not. Among them was Cornelius Cole. At the beginning of the flood, he, his wife, and their four children had desperately piled carpets and overstuffed furniture onto tables, had moved upstairs for three weeks of cheerless living, and then had abandoned Sacramento for a new home in Santa Cruz.

Ed Prentice, owner of the Plaza Grocery and husband of Elizabeth's sister Clarissa, was not so lucky. He sustained severe injuries while trying to move some barrels of foodstuffs out of reach of the flood waters, and on March 21, about the time the Huntingtons sailed from New York, he died.[1]

California had not dealt kindly with Clarissa Prentice. Of six children

111

born over a period of nine years, two boys had died in Sacramento in their infancy. Now she and her four remaining children were left without support. The eldest of the little ones was ten; the baby, Clara, had just turned one.

Elizabeth Huntington, almost forty and without children of her own, was captivated by the child. Couldn't she and Collis take Clara to the upstairs apartment at 54 K?

Collis, as sorrowful as Elizabeth over their childlessness, agreed. Gradually the temporary arrangement became permanent. Clarissa Prentice stayed a semi-invalid, and the Huntingtons in effect became Clara's parents. Until she was well into her teens—and this may say something of the Huntingtons' yearnings—the child remained unaware that they were not her real father and mother.

While Elizabeth went through the upheaval of adjusting to a baby, Collis turned his energies to helping Mark Hopkins ready the flood-ravaged store for the normal spring upturn in business. Favorable reports kept arriving meanwhile from Judah and Bailey in Washington. The House would probably pass the railroad bill in spite of Justin Morrill of Vermont, who regularly complained that here was a work involving scores of millions of dollars "and yet amendments are offered and voted in, according to the will of the gentlemen having charge of the measure, without the slightest apparent interest or attention upon the part of the majority of the House." The country as a whole favored the measure, however, and with that support behind them, Congressmen from California, Kansas, Iowa, and Pennsylvania (an iron-making state) on May 7 won the House's approval of the bill.[2] As soon as the Senate concurred, work on the grandest construction project yet undertaken within the United States could begin—in the midst of a ferocious war.

The first step for the Central Pacific would be, as we have seen, the building of the Dutch Flat toll road, both for the sake of its revenues and, eventually, for speeding materials to workers in the mountains. Throughout the spring the partners worked hard at raising the necessary cash. As soon as snow had melted from the pine-clad slopes, Huntington picked up a new engineer, Samuel S. Montague, and with him hurried into the moist foothills. There, without fanfare, they set into motion the precursor of the Pacific railroad. By June 4 Collis was back in Sacramento.[3]

Slowly the news they needed drifted in. The Senate passed an amended version of the House's railroad bill. The House accepted the Senate's changes, and at 9:30 P.M. on July 3, a climactic telegram arrived from

112

A. A. Sargent. "The President has signed the Railroad Bill. Let California rejoice."[4]

Torchlight parades snaked through the streets of both San Francisco and Sacramento. But what the specifics of the bill were no one knew until a copy arrived by mail from Sargent early in August.[5]

The men at 54 K Street read it avidly. The first part was largely irrelevant to them: detailed instructions concerning the appointment of 163 incorporating commissioners responsible for electing officers and selling enough stock, par value $1,000 a share, for launching the Union Pacific Railroad Company on its way from the 100th meridian in the Platte Valley of Nebraska west toward California.[6] This same Union Pacific Company was also charged with building two branches from the Missouri River to the 100th meridian, a northern one from Sioux City, Iowa, and a central one from somewhere near Council Bluffs, the exact site to be determined by President Lincoln. The southern branch was to be built by the Leavenworth, Pawnee & Western in conjunction with various Kansas and Missouri lines.

In the West the only designated feeder was the Central Pacific. The Central Pacific, the Union Pacific, and the branch lines were given identical bounties. These rights included rights-of-way, permission to use stone and timber on the public domain free of charge, and, for each mile of track built, 6,400 acres of government land in alternate square-mile sections checkerboarded throughout ten-mile strips on either side of the railroad. This land grant did not seem as exciting then as it does now. Much of the dry western soil was unfit for cultivation unless irrigated, and even the best of it could not be sold until settlers had begun moving West in numbers.

More to the point were the government loans. For each mile of track completed across the flat lands of Kansas and Nebraska, and around San Francisco Bay to the base of the Sierra Nevada mountains, the government would advance to the railroads concerned $16,000 in thirty-year, 6 per cent bonds. For 150 miles west of the east base of the Rockies and 150 east of the west base of the Sierra—"said [bases] to be fixed by the president of the United States"—the loan would leap to $48,000 per mile. In the arid country between the two mountain ranges, the loan was to be $32,000 a mile.

Provisions for repayment were haphazard. As soon as the railroads were completed (a term left undefined) they were to start setting aside 5 per cent of their annual net earnings (another undefined designation) as a sinking fund for meeting interest charges and retiring the bonds as they matured. Meeting interest when? Semiannually as the coupons were

113

clipped? Or after the railroads had started earning money? Or could all interest payments be deferred until the bonds fell due and then be paid off in one lump sum?

The act breathed not a word about these points. Whether the silence was inadvertent or resulted from behind-the-scenes manipulation by the promoters cannot be said. In any event, Congress shirked its responsibilities, the builders took advantage of the lapse, and the way was prepared for a titanic battle which would help blacken the closing years of Collis Huntington's life. In 1862, however, he was concerned not with the vague future but with more immediate threats inherent in the ill-drawn bill.

There were several. For instance, the government bonds issued for track building were to constitute a first mortgage on the entire property of the railroads receiving the aid. As Huntington at once realized, this provision automatically reduced the company's own bonds to the status of second mortgages and would make the securities difficult to sell—and yet they had to be sold since the government loan would not by itself cover the cost of construction. Furthermore, forty miles of track had to be completed before any U.S. bonds could be claimed. Even then the builders could not ask for the full sum. Twenty-five per cent of the money due for finishing the easy portion of the project—from the Missouri River to the 100th meridian and from the western terminus to the base of the Sierra—and fifteen per cent of the sum due for the remainder of the line would be retained by the government until the entire transcontinental was in running order. Congress's intent was, of course, to keep the companies at work by dangling carrots in front of their noses. In the builders' view, however, the withholding provisions meant added difficulties in raising funds when money for construction was most needed. No slack at all was allowed. Fifty miles of the track had to be completed within two years of the company's agreeing to the terms of the act.

There were other jokers in the bill. During the debates preceding its passage, opponents had accused the branch lines of using the Pacific railroad as a blind for building local empires with national money. None of the roads, the doubters charged, cared a hoot about the long, unprofitable stretch between the mountains. Let the still unformed Union Pacific worry about those lean miles. But suppose private investors refused to support the UP, in spite of its government bounties. What then?

Congress had aimed a double-barreled shotgun at the possibility. Section 10 of the act stated that if the Leavenworth, Pawnee & Western reached the junction point at the 100th meridian ahead of the Union Pacific, it could, either alone or in conjunction with the other eastern branches, push on to California. Similarly, if the Central Pacific reached Nevada before the other roads appeared from the East, it could keep on building until it met them.

Not only could, but *should*. Section 17 decreed that if either the Union Pacific *or* the other companies failed to build a continuous line between the Missouri and Sacramento rivers by July 1, 1876, then "the whole of said railroads . . . their furniture, fixtures, rolling stock, machine shops, lands, tenements . . . shall be forfeited to and taken possession of by the United States." In other words, if the eastern railroads failed, the Central Pacific could be forced, under pain of forfeiture, to build the entire transcontinental by itself.

From one standpoint the prospect was breathless, and Judah, the dreamer, had been enthralled by it during the drawing up of the bill. But to Huntington, the hardheaded realist, the risk of being held responsible for other people's failures was appalling. He could not believe that the promoters he had met in the East had really wanted the forefeiture provision, and perhaps, if all of them worked together, they could effect amendments to the bill during forthcoming sessions of Congress. Certainly it was a matter to be considered.

And finally there were the local venoms distilled by the act's implicit acceptance of Judah's route over Donner Summit. Residents of El Dorado County, fearful of losing the thirteen million dollars' worth of Nevada traffic that passed through their area each year, were being particularly vociferous. Donner Pass, they proclaimed loudly through their newspapers and to their state legislators, was too rugged for a railroad. Had not wagon trains abandoned the Donner Trail years before in favor of the easier Johnson Pass-Placerville route south of Lake Tahoe?

Residents of the Marysville-Oroville area, which would benefit directly from the railroad only if it crossed the Sierra far north of Donner, were raising a similar shout. Look at the heavy snowfall that blanketed Donner Summit each year. Trains could not operate under such conditions. By contrast, the passes farther north were lower and hence less subject to winter blockade.

After his ineffective efforts a few years earlier to change Congress' mind about the Honey Lake terminus of the national wagon road, Huntington doubted that these local clamors would sway Congress. But they might create trouble at home by upsetting the California legislature when it began considering state aid of the railroad. The attacks might also create hesitation among prospective purchasers of stock. And so the directors of the Central Pacific decided to quiet the opposition by re-examining, or at least pretending to re-examine, every crossing of the Sierra. Intermittently between August 22 and October 1 they ran a series of advertisements in the Sacramento *Union* stating that they would consider every mountain pass called to their attention by competent surveyors. In the meantime they sent forth into the mountains several groups of their own.

Huntington took an active part in this campaign of pacification. Theodore and Anna Judah and Aaron Sargent returned to Sacramento from Washington on August 17.[7] A few weeks later the engineer, the Congressman, Collis Huntington, and Charles Marsh set forth in buggies to examine some of the crossings of the range north of Donner. First they traveled from Downieville up the rough road over Yuba Pass. This route they rejected at once. Reaching the long ridges leading to the gap would necessitate high, expensive trestles over several deep gorges, and the pass itself was not appreciably lower than Donner. As a substitute, it had no advantages.

Yuba thus eliminated, the travelers reined their teams north to the Middle Fork of the Feather River. They struck the stream where it coiled gently through lovely mountain meadows. To their right, up easy grades, was Beckwourth Pass, 1,800 feet lower than Donner. That much difference in altitude could reduce not only the snow problems but also the cost of hauling trains uphill—unless there were complicating factors.

Complications, one surmises, were exactly what the "surveyors" planned to discover. They did not want to move their line as far north as Beckwourth because the shift would preclude their seizing the mine traffic of Virginia City. Yet they dared not say this publicly lest they provide ammunition for those who charged that they were interested solely in local revenues. Thus their answer was to find something wrong with the approaches to the pass.

There were two ways of climbing toward Beckwourth from Oroville in the Sacramento Valley. One, perfectly feasible from a construction standpoint, was to go up the North Fork of the Feather River and then loop back to the Middle Fork. This, however, would add at least sixty-five miles to a road striking for the north edge of Great Salt Lake—and even more miles to one driving toward the lake's south shore, a possibility under discussion at the time. Thus, ostensibly on the grounds of distance, the North Fork was ruled out.*

That decision reached, only the Middle Fork of the Feather remained

* A few years later a rival railroad that was not concerned with Virginia City traffic seriously considered the North Fork route but, as the text will show, was unable to start construction. In the early 1900s the modern Western Pacific did build across Beckwourth Pass and down the North Fork. So distance alone (distance that would have increased congressional loans) was not the obstacle that the Central Pacific pretended in 1862 when defending the Donner route into Nevada—a route that would command Comstock mine traffic.

116

to be disposed of. Down the stream the surveyors went. At Nelson Point the mountains closed around them. No one, they were informed by local residents, had ever penetrated the notorious gorge into which the river plunged below the point.

In view of the California placer miners' indefatigable persistence in following streams wherever they flowed, these local assurances could hardly have seemed convincing. They were enough for Sargent and Marsh, however; those two contented themselves with driving the buggies to Oroville along the Quincy-La Porte wagon road used by the miners of the area. But Judah, whose long search for a railway route surely had made him familiar with the chasm's reputation, and Huntington, who probably knew of it at least by hearsay, decided to make a good story for the newspapers by looking at the canyon in person.

Hiring a Chinaman to help carry their food and blankets, they struck out afoot on the rough journey. Later they described the abyss to a reporter from the Sacramento *Union* as "one of the most fearful man ever looked upon . . . walls rising from two to three thousand feet. . . . The canons [sic] of the forks of the American and Yuba Rivers, if dropped into the chasm, would be almost lost to sight." Often the explorers had to climb high up the cliff faces to circumvent rapids too tumultuous for wading. It took them seven days to travel what they estimated to be seventy miles. For a middle-aged man habituated to town living it was a muscle-stiffening experience, but Huntington, over six feet tall and still as strong as a bull, conceivably ended up enjoying the outing, though he did not bother saying so to inquiring reporters. What Judah and he did declare for public consumption was that no railroad would ever be built through that gorge.[8] None ever was.

The other reconnoitering parties also reported that every route save Donner was impractical for a railroad.[9] The Central Pacific would therefore follow its original plan of building northeast through Newcastle, Auburn, Dutch Flat, and Donner Summit.

Public announcement of the decision brought the associates at 54 K Street an immediate visit from John P. Robinson of the Sacramento Valley Railroad and its extension toward Auburn, the Sacramento, Placer & Nevada. The Central Pacific, the visitor said, would be paralleling the SVRR as far as Auburn, an obvious handicap to both roads. An equitable solution woud be for the CP to buy the Sacramento Valley holdings and use a line already built as the starting link of the transcontinental system.

The men at 54 K declined. Later Judah published a long list of reasons why.[10] The Sacramento Valley Railroad and its extension were heavily overcapitalized and, because of the January floods, badly in need of repairs. The lines were built of English rail, whereas the Act of 1862 specified that the transcontinental must run on American iron. The SVRR line to Auburn was eight miles longer than the route projected by the Central Pacific. And so on. But the main reason was the illogical fact that the CP could draw federal aid for building a new road but not for taking over an existing one. Thus the government itself had made a wasteful duplication of facilities inevitable.

Robinson answered the refusal with threats. Unless the Central Pacific played ball, he and his backers, Pioche & Bayerque would attack the company both in San Francisco and Washington, no idle braggadocio since John and Lester Robinson were closely linked with a construction firm headed by a brother of Governor Horatio Seymour of New York. Furthermore, the route over Donner Summit was not as superior as the CP's surveys pretended to show. A workable railroad grade had already been staked out on the south side of the American River from Folsom through Latrobe and Shingle Springs to Placerville. By pushing that line, the Sacramento & Placerville, on over Johnson Pass to Virginia City, the Robinsons could cut deeply into the Nevada revenues anticipated by the Sacramentans. How much was getting rid of that opposition worth?[11]

Nothing, Huntington and his associates snapped back. So long as the Central Pacific held the trump card of congressional favor, investors would not risk sinking money in still another line over the Sierra.

Turning their backs on Robinson, they plunged again into their complicated schedules. Charles Crocker, new president of the Dutch Flat and Donner Lake Wagon Road Company, advertised in the Sacramento *Union* for bids on additional work on the highway. The old building that the Stanford grocery had once occupied next to 54 K was remodeled as an office for the Central Pacific. Judah and his brother Charles led field parties into the valley to begin engineering studies for every culvert and curve.

The results of the field work were, naturally enough, the consuming interest of the neophyte railroad builders. Until forty miles of track were built and federal funds became available, they had to find financing somewhere else. Exactly what would these obligations amount to?

For the sake of the figuring, Judah broke the line across the state into three fifty-mile sections, and then began calculating eastward from the levee at the foot of I Street. The answers he reached were frightening.

Although the city of Sacramento would donate to the company enough swampy land along the American River for essential buildings and would grant the CP permission to use the levee as a right-of-way out of town,

118

the railway would still have to fill the low acres and riprap the embankments with granite hauled in from the foothills. Three and a half miles east of the town they would have to erect long trestles across ground inundated by each of the American's recurrent floods, and then leap the stream itself with a bridge nearly four hundred feet long.

For the next twenty miles the grading would be light, but as soon as the road penetrated the foothills, deep cuts and heavy fills would alternate with dismaying frequency. Because usable timber in the High Sierra would still be out of reach, redwood for trestles and for the 2,500 ties that supported each mile of track would have to be shipped in on river boat from the coastal mountains. They would need locomotives and flatcars for hauling materials—and also freight, baggage, and passenger cars, for the company planned to put regular trains into operation as soon as the railroad reached the first settlements outside of Sacramento. All this material—thousands of tons of rails and spikes, bulky engines, and at least the wheels and axles for cars (some of the woodwork could be done in Sacramento)—would have to be purchased in the East, where costs were jumping fast under wartime demands, and shipped past Confederate raiders seventeen thousand miles around Cape Horn.

Judah drew a deep breath. The first fifty-mile section would be the cheapest, he said, and yet because of the heavy work at its mountainous end—well, $3,221,496 was as close as he dared pare it. Moreover, those fifty miles had to be completed within two years. This meant that material would have to start flowing without delay. That, in turn, necessitated an immediate source of money.

State and county help would not be available soon enough. The legislature, which had adjourned before the passage of the federal act, would not reconvene until January 5, 1863. Although Governor Stanford would push aid bills as diligently as the proprieties allowed, routines were slow and months might pass before decisions resulted.

There was only one possible way to rush the financing: to issue stock, whose market by the nature of things would be limited primarily to central California, and to sell first-mortgage bonds to financiers in the East. Unfortunately, as Huntington pointed out, the bonds would be backed with nothing more tangible than the company's franchise and undoubtedly would sell far below par.

Judah took exception. Surely the road's expectations were worth something. He'd had men out counting wagon traffic again, and he estimated that the Central Pacific could promise investors a net income of $736,490 a year as soon as the tracks touched the mountains. Once the line had reached Virginia City, Nevada, the annual net would soar, according to his figures, to $3,654,240.

And then his obsession broke in again. Nevada? A trickle. Exuberantly he declared that the congressional act authorizing the road "virtually conceded to your company the right to construct at least half of the Pacific Railroad without absolutely compelling them to do so. It becomes important, therefore, that a Railroad survey be made from the eastern boundary of the state eastwardly to, say, Salt Lake. . . ."[12]

Huntington glowered. To him the threat of forfeiture in Section 17 of the act looked very much like compulsion if the other roads failed, and Judah's characteristic lightness in skimming over the point annoyed him. Asking for the whole West before they were even sure of being able to fund a bridge across the American River! Let's work within the range of our immediate possibilities, he told the others, and not spread ourselves so thin that we lose control of what we build. There'd be time later to talk of Salt Lake.[13]

That cramping decision reached (as Judah regarded it), the directors began wrestling with the unfamiliar problem of issuing $1.5 million of 7 per cent twenty-year first-mortgage bonds. How could the flossy looking paper be rendered attractive in the skeptical East?

One method was to permit conversion of the bonds into government securities of the same denomination as soon as the federal bonds were available.[14] Another step, they decided, would be the launching of an intensive stock-selling drive in Sacramento and San Francisco. Success would not only bring funds to the company, even at the customary small down payment of 10 per cent at the time of subscription, but would also create an atmosphere of confidence.

Into these labors there came, by coincidence, an appeal for contributions to the United States Sanitary Commission, the Civil War equivalent, roughly, of the American Red Cross. Among the committee of thirteen appointed to conduct the drive in Sacramento were Huntington, Stanford, Charles Crocker, and E. B. Crocker. Their campaign ran from September 24 to November 21. It netted $17,000, one of the most successful fund projects, from a per capita standpoint, conducted by the Sanitary Commission during the war[15]—but meager enough compared to what the company hoped to do for itself.

Their goal was the immediate subscription by the public to three million dollars of Central Pacific stock, par value $100 a share. The campaign began with an announcement in the *Union* of October 16, 1862, that the company would open its books for subscriptions in Sacramento on October 22 and in San Francisco on October 28.

For publicity the company relied on an enthusiastic editorial in the *Union* and on a special report, issued by Judah in October, and filled with his usual glowing predictions. Results were exhilarating. On the first day of the drive, so reported the *Union,* eager investors pledged themselves to take 3,642 shares. On the twenty-fourth the directors actually walked the streets in person, knocking on the doors of prosperous citizens. By the twenty-ninth the *Union* was predicting "that at least a million of stock will be taken in Sacramento." And so far no reports had come in from San Francisco!

Under the act of 1862 the companies named as recipients of federal largesse had to accept in writing, within six months of the act's passage, the terms laid down by Congress, including time requirements, forfeiture, and all the rest. By the end of October only four months had gone by. And yet the associates were so encouraged by the start of the stock subscription drive and were so eager to start material moving from the East that they decided to wait no longer. On November 1 they dispatched their letter of acceptance. They were committed now—so totally committed, Huntington would remark a few weeks later to Oliver Ames of Boston, that if failure occurred anywhere along the line, no one would bother even to stoop over and pick up the pieces.[16]

And then the bad news began to drift in. No one in the Bay area was buying Central Pacific stock.

The company's agent there was Marcus D. Boruck, editor of a weekly newspaper, *Spirit of the Times.* Boruck wrote fervid stories in support of the grand project. On November 7 the Sacramento *Union* tried to support him with a long, pained editorial about the short-sightedness of the neighboring community. A correspondent signing himself "Railroader" (probably Judah) wrote an exhortatory letter to the San Francisco *Bulletin.* None of it availed. In twenty-two days Boruck sold a total of fourteen shares of stock, 10 per cent down, to three different customers— $140 income.[17] This was not going to look good to financiers in the East, where San Francisco was deemed to be the only city of consequence on the Pacific Coast.

The reason for the failure seemed clear. On the face of things, San Franciscans were being asked to support a railroad that would end at Sacramento and—hideous to contemplate—might even make Sacramento a greater city than theirs. These fears were intensified by whispers spread by the powerful San Francisco steamship, express, stagecoach, telegraph, and river-boat interests that wanted no competition from a trans-Sierra railroad—and by the owners of the Sacramento Valley Railroad, who had reasons of their own for helping the Central Pacific to fail.

A wry irony lay behind the swift spread of these objections. During the maneuvers in Congress prior to the passage of the act of 1862, Huntington and Judah had sought to secure the co-operation of Donahue, Dame, McLaughlin, and Houston, the San Franciscans who were building a railroad south to San Jose, by assigning to them, as individuals, whatever rights the Central Pacific won between Sacramento and San Francisco. Thus San Francisco really was the terminus of the Pacific Railroad. The associates had not quite dared say so as yet, however. The assignment would not be binding until confirmed by Congress in the form of an amendment to the act of 1862. Fearful that public talk of the transfer in advance of confirmation might strike Congress as presumptuous, the men concerned had stayed silent.

Now, however, it seemed necessary to speak out. After anxious discussions, the Central Pacific's directors openly announced on December 4, 1862, that they were turning over their land grant and bond rights between Sacramento and San Francisco to the men who were building the San Francisco & San José. On December 13, the assignees incorporated the Western Pacific Railroad for building a connecting link from San Jose around the south side of the Bay to Stockton and thence to Sacramento.*

Lauren Upson of the *Union* tried to be exuberant about the development. "It is to be hoped," he editorialized on December 22, "that the capitalists, property owners, and business men of that city will now subscribe liberally for the stock of the CPRR of California." But the capitalists and businessmen still had their own axes to grind. New whispers began to the effect that the Central Pacific would probably not be able to complete its ill-chosen route over Donner Summit or keep the tracks clear of snow if by chance it succeeded. The Western Pacific was a sham; its route was so roundabout that it would never be able to compete with water transport, and Sacramento would still be the terminus of the Pacific road—if the road materialized. Why take such chances with stock in so shady a firm? Far better investments were available in the Comstock mines of Nevada and in loaning out money at the standard rate of 2 per cent a month.

The directors of the Central Pacific could not wait to see the results of these conflicting tugs. Someone had to go East, sell bonds as well as he could, buy materials, find ships, and start the equipment moving. Because Huntington had had some experience in purchasing hardware for his and Hopkins' store and in floating loans to pay for it, he was

* This Western Pacific of the 1860s had no connection whatsoever with the modern railroad of the same name.

122

chosen to make the trip. He was also to visit Washington and, with Sargent's help, press for recognition of the assignment to Dame and the others. Too, he might contact officials of the eastern branches of the transcontinental, all of whom were having trouble getting started, and talk over other possible amendments to the act—a relaxing of time requirements, a striking out of the forfeiture clause, and an elimination of the provision withholding some of the bonds until the entire road was in running order. But the main problem was equipment. To pay for it he was entrusted with fifteen hundred crinkly new $1,000 company bonds. How much they were actually worth would depend on how good a salesman he proved to be. Still, it was something just to hold that green sheaf in his hands and think back to the days, ten years before, when all he'd had in the world were the ashes of his little general store.

Talk of buying rails raised the question of building the roadbed. Should the railroad do its own work or turn the job over to a contracting company?

The prevailing method throughout the United States was to contract the work to an outside firm willing to accept part of its pay in the form of company securities. The Robinson brothers had followed this method in building the Sacramento Valley Railroad, and by holding onto the stock they received, they had obtained a commanding influence in its management. That, too, was standard practice.

Cash being short in the tills of the Central Pacific, the associates were willing to listen when Charles Crocker offered to resign as a director of the CP and form a comparable construction firm, to be known as Charles Crocker & Company, for building the line. Years later he testified that there was no "& Company." Because of the antipathy toward the Central Pacific in San Francisco and the consequent difficulty in selling securities, no one would take the risk of joining him if part of the pay was to be in railroad stock and bonds.

Experience? Crocker had employed a handful of laborers during his iron-mining days in Indiana: "I knew how to manage men; I had worked them in ore-beds, in the coalpits, and . . . had worked myself along with them."[18]

In spite of this confident statement he began cautiously. Either he did not want to wade out too far all at once, or his friends were not yet convinced that his recent years in a dry goods store had qualified him for the undertaking. Although Huntington was delegated to buy enough equipment for fifty miles of track, Crocker's first contract was for only eighteen "units," a unit being approximately one mile.

123

Unit costs varied widely. Thus $100,000 were allotted to the four-hundred-foot bridge over the American River, together with approach trestles totaling another 5,000 feet. The average cost, however, including the bridge, was only $22,222 a mile, or $400,000 altogether. Crocker was to receive $250,000 of this sum in cash. For the balance he accepted $100,000 in company bonds and $50,000 in stock.

Some contractors furnished the iron and work trains along with grading, bridge building, and track laying. In Crocker's case the railroad provided all materials save lumber. Even so, his price does not seem exceptional.* Nevertheless a hue and cry immediately arose that the other directors of the Central Pacific were secret partners in Charles Crocker & Company in order that they might help bleed the railroad by awarding themselves exorbitant construction contracts. Early in 1863, after Huntington had gone East, a committee of fourteen Central Pacific stockholders investigated the charges of interlocking directorates and reported them baseless.[19] Crocker and his associates, in short, unlike the Robinsons, had not yet grasped the possibilities inherent in awarding themselves lush construction contracts through dummy corporations, and were doing their honest best to pare costs. They were pared so close, indeed, that if the securities Crocker received sank much below par he was likely to lose everything he had.

Eighteen units were set as the extent of Crocker's contract because this distance would bring the Central Pacific into contact with the California Central, one of the lines which Huntington and Judah had tried, without success, to include in the act of '62 as a recipient of federal bounty. The junction point was Grider's Ranch, later Roseville, about halfway between the hamlets of Lincoln and Folsom. At the latter point the California Central made connections with the CP's most determined enemy, the Robinson brothers' Sacramento Valley Railroad.

Like the Central Pacific, the California Central was in the throes of raising money. The floods of January 1862 had battered it close to bankruptcy and in desperation the original officers had appealed to Sam Brannan, a principal stockholder, to bail them out. Brannan, the founder of Sacramento, was still making money hand over fist in his bank, mercantile houses, vineyards, and in a new distillery in the lovely Napa Valley north of San Francisco Bay. Though he was sinking a large

---

* A decade earlier, Judah had estimated that grading *and* equipping the Sacramento Valley Railroad through comparable ground would average out at $43,500 a mile. The Robinson brothers actually spent close to $60,000 a mile on the work. Another comparison: the railroad from Boston, Mass., to Albany, N.Y., cost from $43,000 to $56,000 a mile.

124

part of these profits into the construction of a flamboyant resort hotel at Calistoga Hot Springs, he agreed to take on the railroad as well. The California Central's chief handicap was undernourishment. Its founder, C. L. Wilson, had intended to push it from Folsom north to Marysville, where it would connect with the California Northern. He had been able to reach only as far as Lincoln, however, a mere eighteen miles from Folsom, and those eighteen miles did not produce enough revenue to keep the short line afloat.

Brannan decided that salvation lay in finishing the track as far as Marysville. In order to have a debt-free road to begin with, he formed a new company, the Yuba Railroad. He named himself president of the Yuba and James P. Flint as vice-president.[20] By no coincidence, Flint was connected with the Boston brokerage firm of Flint, Peabody & Company, noted for its success in marketing railroad securities. Brannan's hope was that Flint, Peabody & Company would sell enough Yuba Railroad securities to finance extending the California Central's tracks on to Marysville. Large amounts of traffic would then flow over the united lines and, presto, all problems would be solved.

Huntington decided to call on Brannan and Flint. He did not particularly relish Brannan. The one-time Mormon swaggered offensively, drank heavily, and carried on extramarital high jinks that were a scandal even in San Francisco's demimonde. He was aggressive and shrewd, however, and if the Yuba Railroad did reach Marysville, he would be in a fair way to control the traffic of most of Northern California. He still lacked an outlet to Sacramento City and navigable waters, however, and so would have to use the tracks of either the new Central Pacific or of the Sacramento Valley Railroad. Naturally Huntington hoped to convince Brannan that the Central Pacific would soon offer the better way. Furthermore, Collis hoped that he might find, through James P. Flint, a marketing outlet for his own fifteen hundred $1,000 bonds.

Although Huntington had failed to produce the land grant that he had promised the California Central earlier in the year, Brannan and Flint received him graciously. He still might help them. After all, Stanford was governor of California, and the Republican party controlled the state's three congressional seats. Sargent, Huntington's good friend, was chairman of the House of Representatives' Select Committee on Railroads and as such might exert considerable influence in determining the matter of the transcontinental's gauge, or width between rails. The matter was of considerable economic importance to Brannan.

No standard gauge existed in the United States at the time. California law specified five feet. Some midwestern roads were as wide as six, while many of those in New York and around Chicago were four feet, eight and one half inches between rails. President Lincoln had been assigned the responsibility of selecting the gauge for the transcontinental, and the California Central naturally hoped he would pick the California standard, so that when the transcontinental was built, they could move their cars onto it without awkward transfers. Huntington said that the still unbuilt Central Pacific did not really care which gauge was used (state law would have to yield to federal in case of discrepancy), but as a favor to good neighbors he and Sargent would be glad to plump for five feet. That way the California Central would be spared the extra expense of having to rip up and realign its rails.

Talks between the companies evidently were amiable, for Flint and Huntington agreed to travel East together aboard the same Panama-bound ship, the *Golden Age,* departing on December 10, 1862.[21] Unwilling to risk little Clara to the rigors of the crossing, Elizabeth stayed at home, contenting herself with the thought that her husband would be back for the next annual meeting of the CP board of directors, scheduled for July 4, 1863. As matters developed, her decision was probably wise.

There were 550 passengers and $1,575,599 in gold and silver bullion aboard the *Golden Age.* As the steamer passed through the harbor mouth onto the open sea, a winter storm lashed out of the north. One of the two propeller shafts broke. As the ship heaved almost out of control in the gray tempest, the terrified passengers could hardly have helped remembering that a sister steamer, the *Golden Gate,* had sunk five months before with a loss of 233 lives and $1,400,000 in treasure.[22] Huntington probably recalled, too, the dreadful bark *Humboldt,* which had first brought him to California, and Elizabeth's encounter a few years later with the cholera death-ship from Nicaragua.

This time the travelers were luckier. The storm abated and the *Golden Age* limped back to San Francisco for repairs. That was the end of the excitement on that trip. Still, it was small wonder that the people of the Coast yearned for a railroad.

10   The Quagmire

When Huntington reached Washington, he discovered with some uneasiness that the eastern branches of the transcontinental had not made the least move toward building. Thomas Ewing, Jr. and the promoters of the Leavenworth, Pawnee & Western were busily trying to sell their franchise to a syndicate headed by John C. Frémont and a boisterous young freebooter named Samuel Hallett. As for the Union Pacific, only half of the incorporating commissioners had appeared in Chicago on September 2, 1862. There they had capitalized the company for $100 million and had offered stock to the public at $1,000 a share. During the four months that followed, agents of the company sold thirty-one shares. The act of 1862 specified that two thousand shares must be subscribed before the railroad could become a legal corporation.

The backers of both the LP&W and the UP felt they would have a better chance of achieving their aims if Congress were to liberalize the act of 1862 by relaxing time requirements, eliminating the clause concerning forfeiture and the one requiring that a portion of the government bonds be withheld until the entire road was built, and by inserting a new provision allowing the companies' own bonds to be offered as first mortgages on the road—in effect reducing the government securities to second mortgages. Thomas C. Durant, the vice-president and chief lobbyist of the Union Pacific, believed, moreover, that the sale of UP stock would quicken if its statutory price were reduced to $100 per share.

Huntington and one of the directors of the new Western Pacific, Charles McLaughlin, who was also in Washington, said that they would ask the California delegation in Congress to support the price reduction if Durant would urge his congressional friends to approve the CP's assignment of its Sacramento-San Francisco franchise to the incorporators of Western Pacific.

At first all seemed promising. The amendments were clustered into a bundle, introduced to the Senate by James McDougall of California, and accepted on February 25, 1863. In the House, however, a companion bill was lost during the rush to adjourn and there the matter died.[1]

Almost on the same day Huntington received another rebuff over the question of gauges. On January 20, shortly after reaching Washington, he, Senator McDougall, and Representative Timothy G. Phelps of California had accompanied several other railroad men and legislators to a meeting of the Cabinet. There the one-time peddler of Yankee notions had met the President of the United States—an exciting moment, surely—and had helped push the case for a five-foot span between rails with enough eloquence that Lincoln had approved it.[2]

Lincoln's word, it turned out, was not final. Representative Erastus Corning of New York, who was also president of the New York Central Railroad, counterattacked vigorously in favor of a gauge of four feet, eight and one half inches. On March 3, 1863, as the clocks in the House ticked toward adjournment and the bill allowing amendments to the act of 1862 lay unattended, Corning's colleagues responded to his pleas with a special act that overruled Lincoln's decision and made the New York Central's gauge the standard for the transcontinental. Huntington's record as a lobbyist so far stood at exactly zero.

He was in a glum frame of mind when he journeyed to Boston, where he had been earlier with Flint, making arrangements for marketing $1.5 million in Central Pacific bonds. Another shock awaited him in the brokers' office. The war and a treasury law making paper money legal tender had brought chaos to the country's financial establishment. During the conflict a paper dollar would at times sag as low, in terms of gold, as thirty-five cents, depending on the misfortunes of the Union Army. Bonds of all kinds reflected the depreciation and often could be sold only at staggering discounts, especially in the case of unbuilt railroads.

On top of this, Flint, Peabody & Company had been turned sour by the failures in Washington. Indeed, the whole transcontinental system appeared to be in jeopardy. Under the circumstances, the brokers said smoothly, they had decided to let the CP offering rest—it was worth practically nothing anyway—while they pushed California Central and Yuba Railroad bonds instead.

Huntington, who on the face of things was in no position to fight back, reacted explosively. "There was always," an acquaintance said many years later, "something tigerish and irrational in his ravenous pursuit. He was always on the scent, incapable of fatigue, delighting in his strength and the use of it, and full of the love of combat. . . . If the Great Wall of China were put in his path, he would attack it with his nails."[3]

Furiously he demanded the return of the bonds.[4] With them he stalked to the office of Oliver Ames, whose company manufactured more shovels than any other firm in the United States, no small item in an era when earth was moved not by machines but by human muscle. Huntington had never before met Oliver or his brother Oakes Ames, a member of Congress from Massachusetts, but he and Hopkins had handled thousands upon thousands of Ames shovels for California prospectors, and would be in a position to handle thousands more if construction work on the Central Pacific ever hit full stride.

Having learned from Flint, Peabody & Company how heavily his bonds would be discounted on the market, he did not try to sell any to Ames. Instead, he offered a fistful of them as security for a loan of between $100,000 and $200,000—whatever Ames would agree to. This loan, Huntington hoped, would enable him to establish credit and make down payments on equipment to be sent West. Later, after the California legislature had authorized state and county aid, as he expected it would, the bonds should rise in value and be marketable for cash he could use in completing his payments for material.

It was a shaky bridge to depend on, for the only real strength supporting it was his past business dealings in Sacramento and two letters of recommendation, one from D. O. Mills, a leading California banker, the other from Orville Lambard, partner in Sacramento's largest foundry and a brother of Charles A. Lambard, well-known Boston capitalist.

Ames, fourteen years older than Huntington and big-framed and rugged still, told his visitor to return the next day. During the interval he checked on Huntington & Hopkins' record. He found not a single instance of an overdue bill, not even during the lean years of 1855–56, when nearly every other California firm that handled Ames shovels had either delayed payment or had defaulted entirely. The next morning he agreed to make the loan, but exacted from Collis a promise that Huntington would personally guarantee the interest payments on the bonds if the Central Pacific at any time failed to meet those semiannual obligations. Of equal importance, he gave Huntington letters of introduction to leading manufacturers of locomotives and rails.[5]

Prices were shocking. The act of 1862 specified that the Pacific Railroad had to run on American rails. Under impact of the war, quotations on rails had soared from fifty-five dollars a ton to $115 and would soon go higher. The cost of spikes, switches, wheels, couplings, and locomotives had risen in proportion. Every item then had to be sent around Cape Horn at wartime freight rates; Huntington, for instance, paid out $2,282 just to ship the Central Pacific's first light-weight engine to Sacramento. Whenever Confederate sea riders were active, insurance climbed sevenfold.

To the men blandly listing these figures, Collis P. Huntington was a rough frontiersman from beyond the farthest mountains. But his store had always paid its bills and his letters of introduction were as good as if he had sauntered down off Beacon Hill. The manufacturers hemmed and hawed and then sold him five thousand tons of rail and the spikes, chairs, frogs, switches, and other hardware to go with it; six locomotives, six passenger cars, two baggage cars, fifteen boxcars, and twenty-five flatcars. In payment—the bill came to $721,000—they accepted, at unrecorded discounts, the company's bonds, once again requiring, as Ames had, that Huntington and his associates personally meet the interest payments as they fell due, in case the Central Pacific proved unable to do so.[6]

This first mingling of personal and company obligations obviously was risky, but Huntington felt he had no choice. During the repeated financial crises of ensuing years, he and his associates would march farther and farther down the same muddy path. Soon the Central Pacific's affairs would be inseparable from even their own household accounts. Partly for that reason the Big Four, who personally bet everything they had on the road, came to regard it as personal property, while the government, which had lent its assistance (and then abrogated its responsibilities as custodian), continued to insist that the line was a public trust. The fierce dichotomy that resulted would not be resolved during Collis Huntington's lifetime. But once again that is getting far ahead of the story.

During April, while Huntington was still negotiating with manufacturers and shippers, he received via telegraph the welcome news that California's Republican legislature, prodded by Governor Stanford, was acting as generously as desired. In accord with statutory requirements, the lawmakers authorized Sacramento and Placer counties to vote on the issuing of bonds that could be used for purchasing capital stock in the Central Pacific. San Jose and San Joaquin counties would vote on bonds benefiting the Western Pacific. San Francisco's election dealt with both railroads.[7]

As a climax to these gestures the legislature on April 25 agreed to donate to the Central Pacific the full fifteen million dollars in state bonds originally recommended by the Pacific Railroad Convention of 1859. The bonds were to be issued at the rate of ten thousand dollars per mile after the completion of specified amounts of track. In return the railroad agreed to transport, without charge, convicts bound for prison, display products intended for the annual state agricultural fair, and militia in times of war or insurrection. The company also promised to deed to California a granite quarry which occupied a piece of railroad land. All this was cleverly put in the form of a contract in the hope of evading the California requirement that a public vote be held on measures committing the state to projects costing more than $300,000.

Opposition flared. Some rose from local jealousies—El Dorado County did not wish to lose its Nevada traffic—and some from normal taxpayer dislike of using public money for promoting private enterprise. The great majority of the state's people wanted a transcontinental railroad, however, and the obstructionism probably would have been smothered without trouble if at that critical juncture the Robinson brothers, their bankers Pioche, Bayerque & Co., and various anti-railroad businessmen in San Francisco had not united to kill off the Central Pacific by depriving it of the local sustenance it needed for building its first forty miles of track. If the Central Pacific died, then hopefully the Dutch Flat and Donner Lake Wagon Road would also, and the commerce to Nevada would then continue to flow without ripples along established channels.

In the Robinsons' grand strategy not just the Central Pacific but even the city of Sacramento was slated for extinction. Their Sacramento Valley Railroad had been at loggerheads with the city council for years. High taxes were a principal bone of contention. The company claimed that the council was deliberately harassing it in order to hold the votes of the swarms of local draymen who transferred freight and passengers from the river docks to the railroad's depots. The city retorted that the railroad in its arrogance refused to heed orders that it repair street crossings and alter its embankments so as to reduce the danger of floods.

Early in 1863, rioters yelling execrations at the railroad ripped up a stretch of tracks within the city limits. Charging that the council had inspired the disorders, the company resolved to leave the city, whose affections were clearly oriented toward the Central Pacific anyway. On the pretense that the Sacramento River landing was filling with silt, the directors of the SVRR began building new landing facilities four miles downstream. They also laid out a new town in conjunction with the docks. This town they named Freeport, a direct allusion to Sacramento's high levee taxes.

From Freeport they pushed rails around Sacramento to a junction

131

with their old line to Folsom. Their intent was clear—to intercept both river steamers and the Western Pacific, if ever that railroad was built. Freeport would then become the great river port of central California. Folsom in its turn would become the hub of the mountain railroads, for while the Freeport line was building, the directors also kept slowly pushing their extension on the north side of the American River up the hills toward Auburn. Simultaneously they set to work grading a difficult corkscrew line, the Sacramento & Placerville, up the steep pitches south of Folsom.

Success would open various options to the new system. The Robinsons could try to capture the north side traffic to Nevada by thrusting a wagon road from Auburn through Dutch Flat to Henness Pass. On the south, meanwhile, it could use its Sacramento & Placerville line as a feeder for the Pioneer Company stages and for Wells Fargo, both growing fat on Virginia City freight, and thus retain the support of those powerful corporations.

That was the conservative possibility. More dazzling prospects lurked in the background. Should the SVRR succeed and the Central Pacific collapse, the former might inherit Congress' bounties and become the western end of the transcontinental. If Pioche, Bayerque & Co. allowed. . . . But that, rumor whispered, would never happen. According to scare talk emanating from no one knew where, Pioche and Bayerque were secret emissaries of Napoleon III and wanted no transcontinental crossing, even by their own railroad. They would let its south-side extension reach Placerville for the sake of the Nevada traffic, but there they would stop it. For if the Pacific Coast states had no firm link with the rest of the U.S., the Far West would be ripe for swallowing by the new French-Mexican empire under Maximilian.[8]

Whatever the truth, none of these schemes would succeed unless the Central Pacific failed. Immediately after the legislature had acted, therefore, the opponents of the state bond issue devised a test case so that its constitutionality could be tried before the supreme court of California. At the same time energetic campaigns were mounted to defeat the county bond elections at the polls.

In Placer County, whose voters had recently approved bonds in favor of the Robinsons' Sacramento, Placer & Nevada extension toward Auburn, the opposition came within a hair of triumphing. In Sacramento, the Central Pacific won more handily. The culminating contest was San Francisco, where the largest amount of money was involved—$600,000 in bonds for the purchase of Central Pacific stock, $400,000 for the Western Pacific.

132

Three main arguments were used against the proposal. First, under California law, stockholders in a bankrupt company were liable for its debts in proportion to the amount of their holdings. Since the Central Pacific could not possibly cross the mountains, the nay-sayers argued, San Francisco might find herself subject to staggering obligations. Second, the railroad probably did not intend to cross the Sierra anyway, but was building the railroad with public money as a feeder for its Dutch Flat and Donner Lake Wagon Road. And finally, Sacramento, not San Francisco, would be the true beneficiary of the Bay City's generosity.

These arguments, obviously, were not bound together by logical consistency. It was enough to get voters to believe any one or another of them.

On May 15, three days before the election, Stanford tried to quiet the last objection by writing a long letter to the most antagonistic of the San Francisco newspapers, the *Alta California,* knowing that because of his position as governor the editor would not dare omit it. In his missive the president of the railroad declared, with perhaps more condescension than he intended, that although Congress had named the Central Pacific as sole recipient of federal aid, ". . . the Company, in a 'friendly spirit, made San Francisco the terminus of the road by assignment. . . . For my own part, I am free to say I have never doubted what would be your answer when called upon for county aid."

The flaw in Stanford's argument was Congress' failure to confirm the assignment. Meantime the other objections were being advanced with such energy—"the lowest tactics of the political adventurer" were used, the *Union* clucked[9]—that friends of the company began to fear they needed more persuasive ways of gaining favor than letters in the *Alta California.* Nine purported eyewitnesses later swore affidavits to the effect that on election morning, Asa Philip Stanford, one of the governor's older brothers, traveled from polling place to polling place in a buggy, handing out gold pieces to voters who promised to support the bonds.[10]

The election carried by a margin of almost two to one. Triumphantly the railroad declared that obviously it had not needed to buy votes.[11] The reply of course begs the issue. Phil Stanford, whom Huntington later characterized as a "damn fool,"[12] could hardly have predicted so easy a victory and in his nervousness may have decided to make sure—if, indeed, the alleged passing of the gold really did take place.

The triple victory at the polls resulted in no immediate flow of cash. In each instance the Robinsons or one of their associates went to the courts. There they declared that their rights as taxpayers were being violated, and they asked that injunctions be issued restraining the county

133

supervisors from delivering the bonds until the legality of the issues could be determined. The injunctions were granted.[13] County aid was thus blocked along with state aid, and the company could only look wistfully toward what might have been $16,150,000 in bonds—enough, even at discount rates, to give solid support to their own first-mortgage bonds and carry them on over the mountains to the lucrative traffic of the Comstock Lode.

On May 21, while the injunctions were falling thick and fast, Stanford hurt the railroad's case still more by naming E. B. Crocker, brother of Charles and a stockholder in the Central Pacific, as chief justice of the California Supreme Court, to fill the unexpired term of Stephen J. Field, who on Stanford's recommendation had recently been elevated to the bench of the Supreme Court of the United States.[14] Crocker's appointment would run only until the end of the year. Probably it was a political payoff, not an effort to help the railroad, for he would step down before any of the railroad cases reached the court. Even so, the timing of the move was ill calculated to lend luster to the image of either the railroad or the Republican party.

The Robinsons were succeeding, for confidence in the Central Pacific began to melt away under the heated attacks. Stock could not be sold either in San Francisco or across the mountains in Virginia City, where the company's brokers reported that three months of effort resulted in the sale of exactly one share. In need of funds to meet his payrolls, Charles Crocker himself crossed the Sierra and called on potential investors, but failed miserably.[15]

To raise cash for current bills the company began levying assessments on the early purchasers of stock. At the time of subscribing, the buyers had paid only 10 per cent down and were legally bound to liquidate the balance in additional 10 per cent installments at the call of the company. Dozens defaulted, however, rather than sink more money into what now looked like a hopeless venture. By mid-July 1863, eight months after the *Union* had declared that a million in stock would be sold in Sacramento alone, President Stanford admitted to the annual meeting of stockholders that only a little more than $600,000 still stood on the books.[16]

It did Huntington's peace of mind no good to learn, during this period of economic shrinkage, that because of Stanford's bumbling the founders of California's Republican party were being pried out of their once heady positions of power.

Engineer of the defeat was John Conness, a Democrat from unfriendly El Dorado County, whom Stanford had trounced for the governorship in 1861. Several months after that election Conness had proposed to Stanford that they form a new, patriotic, unbeatable organization formed by a fusion of Republicans and Democrats loyal to Lincoln's war aims. Its name, the Union Party, was a gauge of its rationale.

After some weeks of hesitation, Stanford agreed, confident of his ability to keep the reins of the expanded group in his own hands. After all, hadn't he drubbed Conness in '61?

There was no true cohesion within the new organization. In January 1863, three of its incompatible bedfellows offered themselves to the legislature as candidates to replace Democrat James McDougall in the United States Senate. Two of the hopefuls were Republican Congressmen and good friends of the Central Pacific Railroad, Aaron A. Sargent and Timothy G. Phelps. The third was John Conness.

Phelp's friends, acting perhaps without either his or Stanford's knowledge, were detected in so noisome a bribery scandal that the whole Republican organization suffered and Conness was easily elected. His next step was to eliminate the three old-line Republicans in the House of Representatives. The taint of bribery made Phelps easy to dispose of. A second Congressman, Frederick Low, was wooed away from Stanford by Conness' promise to make Low the next governor of California. As nominees for replacing Low and Phelps in Congress, Conness offered the names of two Union Democrats. His only concession to the Republicans was a reluctant agreement to let Cornelius Cole be nominated as a Congressman in place of Aaron Sargent.[17]

The elections that year were particularly important because of a new constitutional amendment extending the governor's term in office and that of the members of the upper chamber of the state legislature from two years to four. Stanford should have been on his toes. According to the Sacramento *Union* of June 4, however, he and his followers went to the Sacramento County nominating caucus "so confident in their strength that . . . they seemed to be in the convention without having any fixed line of policy mapped out." The governor was dumped in favor of Low by his own home county and thereupon withdrew from the race, a disaster that occurred at about the time Huntington was embarking for home by way of Panama.

He reached Sacramento late in June. It was good to see Elizabeth again, to pick up little Clara and exclaim over how the child had grown. It was good to saddle a horse, ride out and view the spidery bridge leaping the American River, then cross on the ferry, inspect the grading and imagine the raw scar after the rails were down and the first engine he had bought, the *Governor Stanford,* was steaming along them toward the mountains.

135

But it was not good to come face to face with the antagonistic factions into which the board of directors had split during the strain of the past months.

Judah led one group. Behind him stood Daniel Strong of Dutch Flat, who had helped locate the route over Donner Summit; James Bailey, who had gone to Washington with the engineer to help lobby for the act of 1862; and grocer Lucius Booth. Opposing this quartet were Mark Hopkins and Charles Marsh, openly backed by Charles Crocker, although Crocker was no longer a member of the board. Stanford, engrossed with his political problems, wavered between the two camps.

Today it is not possible to unravel all the strands of the quarrel. The Dutch Flat and Donner Lake Wagon Road, on which two hundred men were working that summer, was involved. Judah, who had recommended the project originally, owned no stock in it and perhaps was piqued at being left out. Certainly he resented the fact that some of the money raised for the Central Pacific was being diverted to the wagon road on the ground that the highway would eventually assist the railroad with toll revenues and access to the right-of-way. When government money became involved, however, Congress might not agree with that reasoning; and as the rift in Sacramento deepened, Judah grew increasingly high-minded about staying within the bounds of the law.[18]

He developed other scruples. At the western base of the Sierra Nevada Mountains the government loan to the Central Pacific would jump from $16,000 a mile to $48,000. Determining exactly where this financially critical point lay was the responsibility of the President of the United States. In reaching his decision Lincoln obviously would have to depend on scientists familiar with the California scene.

One generally accepted point was an outcropping of a Sierra-type granite located twenty-two miles from Sacramento. It occurred to someone —Stanford perhaps—that if the granite was a legitimate marker, then why not a fan of reddish earth that ran from the foothills as far out onto the valley floor as Arcade Creek, only seven miles from Sacramento?

As governor of the state, he asked California's official geologist, Josiah D. Whitney, to look into the matter. Charles Crocker, equipped with maps prepared by the railroad, served as Whitney's guide during a buggy trip to the creek in question. After glancing around at what appeared to be dead-level ground, the geologist remarked that of course the Sacramento River was the ultimate base of the region's tilt, and added that under the circumstances Arcade Creek seemed to him as fair a place as any to begin. On June 29, about the time that Huntington reached

Sacramento, the state surveyor-general, J. F. Houghton, following a somewhat different line of reasoning, reached the same conclusion.[19]

Assuming, for the sake of argument, that the granite outcrop twenty-two miles from Sacramento was a more realistic base, the Whitney-Houghton opinion brought the railroad a gain of fifteen miles, or $240,000 in government bonds, which in the market would net considerably less than that.* Since Judah had estimated that some of the construction in the Sierra could cost more than $100,000 a mile, against which only $48,000 per mile in subsidies were available, a compensating gain in the flatlands seemed fair to men whose hope of state and county aid had been chilled by the Robinsons' injunctions. Yet Judah, the company's engineer, refused to endorse the findings of the chief geologist and surveyor-general of the state.[20]

Further and fiercer dissension rose out of Judah's objections to Crocker's construction contracts. Why he opposed them is uncertain. Though an investigating committee had cleared the CP directors of a charge that they were sharing in the contracts, Judah may still have believed that Huntington, Hopkins, and Stanford were secretly involved—while he wasn't. Or, and this seems more likely, his standards as a professional engineer may have been offended by the quality of Crocker's work.

There were frequent explosions. On May 13, Judah wrote Strong, "I had a blowout about two weeks ago . . . called things by their right names and invited war; but counsel of peace prevailed and my head is still on. . . ." After Huntington's return there was another "big row" but "I carried my point and prevented a certain gentleman from becoming a further contractor on the Central Pacific at present."[21] As a result of this victory the next thirteen units to Newcastle were awarded to six different contractors at a total cost for grading, masonry, ties, and track laying of $505,685.[22] Crocker was not entirely eliminated. He received the two last—and hardest—units.

As Huntington toured the line in temperatures that soared each day to more than a hundred degrees in the shade and as he listened to the sweaty bickering as each faction tried to sell its story to him, he found Judah's professed high-mindedness harder and harder to swallow. Because the engineer had laid out a line beside a slough where new embankments would have to be erected, Crocker's subcontractor for the section was dutifully importing, over the Sacramento Valley Railroad,

* One hundred and fifty miles east of the west base of the mountains, the government loan dropped to $32,000 a mile, and not back to the $16,000 that prevailed west of the base. Thus the shift benefited the Central Pacific $16,000 a mile, not $32,000 as is sometimes said.

endless tons of granite for filling the bog. In Huntington's opinion work like that was best postponed until the money pinch was relieved. Meantime, let the tracks go up I Street in spite of possible quarrels with the city over crossing repairs. And then there was the depot. Judah had drawn plans for an elaborate structure, but that, too, could wait until they knew where the money was coming from.

Money—there was the crux. How were they to keep operating until the state and county bonds were released? Judah and Strong, whose resources were meager, wanted to raise funds by mortgaging, at rates of up to 2 per cent a month, the equipment Huntington had purchased in the East. Though better heeled, Bailey and Booth wanted to keep their jewelry and grocery businesses separate from the railroad and hence supported the first two.

Huntington disagreed. He had paid for the equipment with first-mortgage bonds, some of them so heavily discounted that the interest on them would, in effect, run to 1 per cent or more a month. Judah's proposal, added to those obligations, would not only create a crushing interest load but would also impair the credit standing Huntington had so laboriously created in the East. It was better, he felt, to assess the stockholders more rapidly than originally intended and then dig into their own pockets until they could sight relief somewhere ahead.[23] Since none of them were wealthy men, this obviously was going to be a strain on all their businesses.

Attempts at discussion resulted only in heightened anger. Their very personalities prevented compromise. Judah, thin and short, seemed compelled to assert himself truculently in the company of opponents who, save for lean, tall Mark Hopkins, were bluff, overfed, overriding six-footers.

One mode of perhaps unconscious defiance was his habit of referring to the Central Pacific as "my" road. He had worked at the dream for a decade. He had found the route and had borne the brunt of the tedious details involved in lobbying the bill through Congress. Yet the merchants with whom he was forced to deal wanted, as he saw things, to take his creation from him and relegate him to a back seat as a hired hand.

Huntington had no patience with this attitude of Judah's. He felt that he and his associates had been more than fair. They had picked up the engineer after everyone else had brushed him aside. His salary had risen steadily from an initial $100 a month to $5,000 a year. He had a stock-option plan for purchasing five hundred shares of $100 stock at half price.[24] Yet he remained dissatisfied. He had a hunger for deference that struck Huntington as "cheap dignity" and methods of dealing that in Collis' opinion were little better than "low cunning."[25]

Almost inevitably the conflicts about policy precipitated a battle to control the board of directors. Huntington easily pulled Stanford to his side and then the issue was joined, four against four—Huntington, Hopkins, Stanford, and Charles Marsh against Judah, Strong, Bailey, and Booth.* To break the impasse each side struggled to round up enough proxies so that it could elect additional supporters of its policies to the board. Knowing that the Huntington faction was firmly entrenched in Sacramento, Judah urged Strong to be diligent in the mountain counties.[26] The effort was unavailing. When the annual meeting ended late on July 14, the board's two new members were Asa Philip Stanford and the builder of Sacramento's first hospital, Dr. John Morse, who had come to California aboard the *Humboldt* and had been Collis Huntington's close friend ever since.

Control thus assured, Huntington struck hard. He tore up Judah's plans for a depot and decreed that a shed which could also serve as a storage place for tools would do until further notice. He ordered the grading shifted from the embankment to I Street. He demanded that the entire board put up its share of the money needed to keep the work going. When Bailey, the most affluent of the opposition, refused, Huntington swung astride a horse, rode out to the different construction camps, and halted the work. It was dark before he returned to Sacramento; a full moon was shining and he was humming to himself.

The next day, as he recalled events years afterwards, there was "a good deal of hubbub."[27] Although the Huntington faction could have had its way simply by outvoting the others, he decided instead to get rid of them completely. If the objectors did not like the way things were going, he said bluntly, why did they not buy out the majority? He for one was willing to sell. His allies nodded. So were they, provided that Judah could produce enough to compensate them for the cash, time, and energy they had expended so far.

It hardly seemed likely that Judah could. The outlook was too gloomy. So far not a rail had reached Sacramento, and yet the act of 1862 specified that by November 1864—only sixteen months away—the Central Pacific must have fifty miles of track in running order. How could the company possibly succeed? It was already so short of money that it

---

* The original board had consisted of nine men, but Charles Crocker had resigned on taking over the construction contracts. He was always privy to the board's discussions, however.

had awarded grading contracts for only thirty-one miles. Yet it must build forty miles in order to collect its first federal bonds.

Judah, overly optimistic as always, did his best nevertheless. Assuming that the Western Pacific would jump at a chance to gain control of the Central Pacific rather than remain its stub end, he and Bailey called on Charles McLaughlin. McLaughlin, who had been in Washington with Huntington and who understood the situation thoroughly, shook his head. If Old Huntington wanted out, he, McLaughlin, certainly did not want in.[28] No better luck awaited the pair elsewhere in San Francisco, and by the end of the summer they were back in Sacramento empty-handed.

The rest is fuzzy. Apparently Huntington insisted that inasmuch as the dissenters had failed to buy, now they must sell—and evidently not for cash, either. For his five hundred shares of stock in the still unbuilt road, Judah received $100,000 in Central Pacific bonds. What Bailey, Booth, and Strong received for their interests is unrecorded. It is known that Bailey sold his share of the franchise of the Nevada Central Railroad to Phil Stanford for $10,000 cash; Judah disposed of his interest in the same franchise to Charles Crocker for the same sum. Then, in September 1863, Bailey was replaced on the board of the Central Pacific and as secretary of the company by E. H. Miller, Jr., who had kept store with Mark Hopkins before the latter had joined up with Huntington.[29]

All this seems final. And yet Stanford repeatedly stated that Judah remained as chief engineer of the company until his death. Evidently, too, Judah's option to buy remained open, if he could raise enough money in the East. To that end, he and Anna sailed early in October, an ill-fated voyage.[30] In Panama he contracted tropical fever. On November 2, 1863, two days after reaching New York, the catalyst of the Pacific railroad was dead. If any settlement remained to be effected with his widow, it was quickly done—she was ever afterwards bitter toward the associates—and the Big Four, as they soon became known, were then firmly in control, to save the Central Pacific as best they could.

Even before Judah's departure from Sacramento, a few deceptive signs of hope had started fluttering. In September the courts directed the supervisors of Sacramento and Placer counties to exchange $550,000 in bonds for 5,500 shares of CP stock, as authorized by the voters concerned. (The $600,000 worth of San Francisco bonds remained blocked by litigation, however.) Also in September the bridge over the American River and the grading as far as the junction with the California Central at Roseville-to-be was pronounced ready for rails. Shortly thereafter ships carrying iron in hundred-ton lots began docking at the levee.

On October 5 the first locomotive, the wood-burning *Governor Stanford* arrived dismantled aboard the schooner *Artful Dodger*. The special low-slung track-laying cars that Huntington had ordered were delayed, however, and so the Goss and Lambard foundry of Sacramento was ordered to improvise substitutes. Thus the first rails of the transcontinental, eight rods of them that first day, were not spiked into place until October 26.

Imported machinists finished assembling the first locomotive, gay with brass and red and gold paint, on November 9. Stanford, armed with baskets of champagne, invited the bigwigs of the city to meet near the toolshed on I Street for a ride in the tender out to tracks' end at Twenty-first Street. Huntington was not on hand to help play host. Years later he explained his absence by saying that he had no desire to "jubilate . . . Those mountains over there look too ugly." So they did. But he had also been summoned for jury duty, and according to the *Union* of November 10, he was cooped up in the courthouse listening to a case.

He did not miss much. Excited boys and loiterers along the right-of-way could not resist the temptation to leap aboard the slowly moving locomotive, and by the time it had reached the shed there was no room aboard for the invited guests. It was no loss. The engine's steam valves were not functioning properly, and so the first run anywhere on America's first transcontinental line was postponed a day. The second attempt went more smoothly—still no Huntington, however—and at the end of the tracks toasts were drunk to everyone involved in the feat, including a solemn salute to the memory of Theodore Dehone Judah.[31]

Save for its publicity value, Huntington saw scant reason for spending money on champagne. True, the company safe now held $550,000 in county bonds, but they could be sold in the East only at heavy discounts. Furthermore, the company would have to accept greenbacks in pay. California, however, had declined to abide by the paper-money law. Work done on the Coast had to be paid for in gold. Early in November 1863, one paper dollar was worth only seventy-five cents in gold and so there went another 25 per cent discount off the face value of the bonds. Nor was that all. Workers were streaming off the job toward new silver strikes near Reese River in central Nevada, and it looked as if both the railroad and wagon road would have to raise wages to hold their laborers. In short, the bonds and the eighth 10 per cent assessment on outstanding stock, announced in the *Union* of November 13 as falling due the next month, would hardly be enough, even added together, to complete the thirteen new units of grading between Roseville and Newcastle.

On top of that, the company, which had $7,000 in its treasury, owed Crocker $48,000. The only way to pay him was in stock and bonds—and the stock was all but unsalable. Crocker said that in the future he would accept additional certificates as worth only fifty cents on the dollar. Unless the request was granted, the track laying to Roseville could not be finished. And so of course it was granted.[32]

The only possible way out was to join the eastern branches on the transcontinental in pressing for increased government aid. As Huntington knew from dispatches in the *Union*—and probably from private letters as well—Thomas C. Durant had finally succeeded in selling subscriptions to enough stock in the Union Pacific to justify incorporating that company. Concurrently, John C. Frémont and Samuel Hallett had bought control of the Leavenworth, Pawnee & Western. Renaming their acquisition the Union Pacific Railway, Eastern Division, in order to capture reflected sheen from the publicity attending the true UP, they were in quest of a loan of five million dollars for launching construction.

Both companies were eager to pass the liberalizing amendments to the act of 1862 that had died in the House of Representatives the previous March. By joining forces with them in Washington, Huntington might bring additional benefits to the Central Pacific as well.

How long the work might take Collis did not know. But he did know that he'd had enough of living alone in hotels for months on end as he drove himself relentlessly back and forth. This time he wanted Elizabeth and Clara with him.

The jury duty finished, they began to pack. On November 21 they bade farewell to their friends—and to Clara's mother, too, presumably—and shut the door of the upstairs flat at 54 K Street behind them. When they would open it again, if ever, they had no way of telling.

11 Anticlimax

The Huntingtons, three-year-old Clara in tow, reached the East in mid-December and quite probably spent Christmas in Oneonta with Solon's family. They were eager to show themselves off as foster parents, and Solon was just as proud of his eldest son, Henry Edwards Huntington, then a lad of thirteen.* In addition, the visit provided Collis with an opportunity to sit down for an earnest talk with a long-time Otsego County friend of his and Solon's, Congressman John B. Steele.

Another extraordinary coincidence had occurred. During Collis' first appearance in Washington, Judah and he had been helped by the presence, on the House of Representatives' Select Committee on the Pacific Railroad, of Richard Franchot, a one-time Oneontan who had moved to Schenectady and there had been elected to Congress. Shortly after the passage of the railroad bill of 1862 Franchot had resigned to join the Union Army. By amazing chance, his place on the select committee had been filled by another Huntington friend, John B. Steele, elected in the fall of 1862.

Nor was Steele the end of it. When freshman Congressman Cornelius Cole had reached Washington in the fall of 1863—on odd year because of California's offbeat election schedules—he, too, had been named to the select committee as the sole surviving Republican from the Golden State. Cole did not like Huntington particularly, but he would be helpful nonetheless. Most of his constituents wanted a transcontinental railroad. Furthermore, Collis was sure that the new Congressman would remain loyal to the leaders of the sadly battered California Republican party—to Stanford, the railroad's president, and to E. B. Crocker, who, now that

* An elder brother, Howard, had died April 10, 1860, aged sixteen.

his brief term as chief justice had ended, was about to become the Central Pacific's attorney in battling the San Francisco injunction suits. And still that wasn't all. Another member of the House Select Committee on the Pacific Railroads was Oakes Ames. Oakes's brother Oliver, it will be recalled, had recently loaned Collis nearly $200,000. For that reason and for the impact it would have on the sale of shovels, Oliver and Oakes were both interested in seeing the Central Pacific succeed. And, finally, the chairman of the committee remained Thaddeus Stevens, whom Huntington had grown to know and admire during his first experience at lobbying in 1862.

The opportunity for a little missionary work in Oneonta before Congress reconvened must have been overwhelming. Look at it this way, Steele. The entrepreneurs who had agreed to risk building the transcontinental were not going to receive what the government had promised. For example: the Central Pacific was by now working well within the foothills and hence was entitled to a $48,000 loan, in bonds, for each mile of track laid, as soon as forty miles had been finished and approved.*

Sounded like a grand sum, didn't it? Actually, it was an illusion. The Central Pacific would have to sell those 6 per cent government bonds in the East; no one would buy them in California, where money was scarce and brought 2 per cent a month. Moreover, on sales in the East the railroad would have to accept payment in greenbacks, according to the law. California had rejected that ruling, however. Work done on the Coast had to be paid for in gold. Yet at that very minute a paper dollar in New York would bring only sixty-five cents in gold coin. So what was a thousand-dollar bond really worth?

There was another penalty, Steele. Under the act of 1862 the government would not pay out the full amount of the bonds as they fell due but would retain 15 per cent until the entire system was completed. Thus at the time cash was most needed for difficult work in the mountains the company would receive not $48,000 per mile, but only $40,800 in bonds. In coin this would amount to $26,500—if the bonds were sold at face value in greenbacks, which probably would not be the case.[1]

So drastic a shrinkage was almost entirely due to the government's own fiscal policies. Did not simple fairness demand an adjustment?

* On January 12, 1864, some two weeks after the presumed conversation, Lincoln accepted the recommendation of California's state geologist and surveyor-general and named Arcade Creek seven miles from Sacramento as the base of Sierra Nevada. By that time the Central Pacific graders had already passed the granite outcroppings which conservative observers considered a more appropriate point.

As Steele no doubt knew, a large segment of the country looked on the transcontinental as an urgent national necessity and therefore shared Huntington's view. According to testimony offered later on behalf of Oakes Ames, Lincoln himself felt that the act of 1862 should be altered in order to bring it more nearly in line with the intentions of Congress at the time of its passage.[2] In view of these strong forces behind him, Huntington perhaps should have left well enough alone. It was not his way to trust to chance, however. Congress contained a dismayingly large proportion of inept, vacillating, unpredictable men.[3] It was well, therefore, to be on hand when the amendments to the first act were prepared by the committees; when they were presented to Congress; and especially when they were discussed.

Because of the war, the job might drag out for several months. Even so, Collis decided against renting a house until the family could return to Sacramento. Instead, he established residence in New York City's Metropolitan Hotel.[4] Elizabeth, gentle and unprotesting and accustomed to a yardless flat above a hardware store, accepted the arrangement without ado. After all, a small hotel suite in the heart of a noisy city was no more cramped a place in which to bring up a healthy child than an apartment above a hardware store.

As an office Collis rented a single room within walking distance of the hotel. It was located in an obsolescent building at—surely he recalled the numbering of the Sacramento hardware store when he signed the lease—54 William Street. A little distance away on the same street was a very different office, luxuriantly carpeted and paneled, where the vice-president of the Union Pacific, Thomas C. Durant, was also preparing to approach Congress.

Tall, lean, dark, and hawk-eyed, Durant was given to flamboyant clothes and outbursts of nervous volubility. He was not quite two years older than Huntington. Educated as a doctor, he had taught a short time at Albany Medical College and then had drifted into an uncle's grain exporting firm, where he had first felt the lure of stock speculation. During the 1850s he had plunged into promoting railways across Iowa. His initial interest in the Union Pacific had arisen from a hope that a connection with a transcontinental might revive his somnolent Iowa interests.

When it looked as if the necessary number of stock subscribers would never rally around the railroad, he saved it by personally financing most of the down payments required by law. In addition he used personal funds to finance engineer Peter Dey on a reconnaissance of the Platte Valley as far as the Rockies so that he could have tangible figures to present his stockholders at their first meeting on October 29, 1863. On December 2 he staged elaborate groundbreaking ceremonies at Omaha.* Now his pockets were empty and would stay that way unless Congress extended additional aid.

On the surface, then, Durant's situation looked much like Huntington's— a desperate need to escape from liabilities incurred under the act of 1862. What Huntington did not know when he first went to Durant's office to discuss railroad legislation was that the vice-president of the Union Pacific had no interest in acquiring and managing a railroad, but only in milking it during the process of construction.

As we have seen, the theory behind such operations was simple. The contractors who built the road accepted their pay in cash, bonds, and stock. They bid high enough that the cash and bonds alone would cover costs and allow a reasonable profit. The railroad stock, generally taken in at a fraction of its par value, was the speculative reward for their risks. Either it could be held until the contractor acquired enough to control the road, or it could be sold on the market for immediate dividends. The major flaw in the scheme, from the standpoint of railroad service, was the tendency of the contractors to boost profits by doing cheap work; and inasmuch as the contractors were also officials of the railroad, who was to bring them to heel?

Congress had sought to preclude this sort of operation by ruling that stock in the Union Pacific had to be sold at par for cash. The act added, moreover, that if the road failed, the holders of stock would be personally liable for the company's debts in proportion to the amount of their holdings—a provision intended to keep shareholders intent on the health of the railroad rather than on that of the construction company.

Durant planned to sidestep the ruling about individual liability by finding a company whose charter let it deal in stocks and bonds without being held responsible for the failure of the firms whose securities it handled. Thus there would be no individuals to attack in case of trouble. This handy agency would also act as a construction company. Its bills for work could, under the law, be considered as the equivalent of cash and thus exchangeable for stock at par—at least on the company's books. Actually, these bills could be manipulated so as to make the stock cost the promoters as little as they chose. Having collected the stock through

---

* By now, it was recognized that the Union Pacific would build the "branch" from Omaha to the 100th meridian as well as the main line from the meridian on west.

Durant, incidentally, was endeavoring, during this time, to copper his bets by insinuating himself into the management of the Union Pacific, Eastern Division. In the end the effort proved unsuccessful.

bookkeeping transactions, the construction company could then dispose of it at whatever price the market would bring and declare dividends for its own stockholders out of the profits realized.

Early in 1864, at about the time Huntington was beginning his own quest for funds, the schemers found the very firm they wanted, a dormant investment company called the Pennsylvania Fiscal Agency. On March 2, 1864—and Huntington knew none of this at the time—Durant's associate, Cornelius S. Bushnell, purchased the agency for the sake of its very liberal charter. George Francis Train, another associate, whose tastes were even more flamboyant than Durant's, dreamed up what he considered an impressive title for the acquisition—Crédit Mobilier. The speculators were now ready—providing Congress relaxed its purse strings—to start their milking.

Except for the supposed safeguards built into the Union Pacific's charter, Durant and company probably would have been as blatant with their operations as was the Union Pacific, Eastern Division, nee Leavenworth, Pawnee & Western. The rambunctious reagent of that company, which held its charter from the Kansas legislature and not from Congress, was young Samuel Hallett. After Frémont and he had acquired control of the line, Hallett set up his own construction company without bothering about disguises. Blandly he then awarded himself a contract for forty miles of grading and track laying.

It so happened that Thomas Ewing, Jr., and the other promoters of the original LP&W had already granted contracts covering much of the same ground to the Montreal firm of Ross & Steele. When the Canadians declined to leave, Hallett through devious channels of influence obtained troops from nearby Ft. Leavenworth. These he used to drive his opponents from the field. The construction which his company then began to push to completion was so shoddy that Hallett's own chief engineer, O. A. Talcott, wrote President Lincoln stating that no government bonds should be awarded for the work.[5]

All this was too much for Frémont, who precipitated a stockholder fight that led to conflicting boards of directors, one headed by Frémont and the other by John D. Perry, of whom we will hear again. Standing behind Perry and Hallett were certain Philadelphia and St. Louis capitalists who hoped to amend the act of 1862 in such wise that the Eastern Division could relegate the UP to the status of a branch line and have the Eastern Division become the main stem of the transcontinental. To the schemers the quality of Hallett's construction work did not matter greatly. Their chief consideration was to get a jump on the still stationary Union Pacific.

147

In view of all this conniving in the East, it is interesting to note what was going on at the same time in the Far West. Like the Eastern Division, the Central Pacific held its charter from a state legislature and hence was not subject to the congressional hedges surrounding the UP. Because of Judah's intransigence, however, not one construction company but six were working on the thirteen-mile stretch between Roseville and Newcastle. They were taking 17.5 per cent of their pay in stock and were very unhappy about it.[6]

Because of the new silver strikes at Reese River in central Nevada, labor was hard to hold. The contractors bid against each other for men and for such adjuncts as teams and hay. Supply deliveries to the many small units were chaotic; expenses soared. One of the contractors went broke and Charles Crocker had to assume his obligations. By the time Crocker had finished that section and his own two units of work, he was so near bankruptcy, he said later, that he would gladly have settled the account for one clean shirt and absolution of his debts.[7]

Ironically, the company would have liked to have pushed on beyond Newcastle, no matter how sour the contractors felt. Nine more miles would make the Central Pacific eligible for government loans, and never again would winter weather be so propitious. One mild, dry day succeeded another without interruption. Workers on the Dutch Flat and Donner Lake Wagon Road, several Chinese among them, crossed the summit of the Sierra with only occasional layoffs because of snow. The Robinson brothers kept 150 men pushing the grades of the rival Sacramento & Placerville steadily up the slopes beyond Folsom toward Latrobe: by summer they would have more track laid than the Central Pacific— thirty-eight miles as compared to thirty-one.

Only nine miles! The Central Pacific scratched out a dab of preliminary grading beyond Newcastle and then quit for lack of funds. True, Huntington had taken half a million dollars in Sacramento and Placer county bonds East with him, but the greenback discount squeeze was so severe that he was doling out only as many of the securities as he had to in order to ship necessary equipment to the West Coast. The rest of the bonds he was holding in hope of a rise in prices.

All this while nearly sixteen million in bonds approved by the state legislature and by the voters of San Francisco County lay just out of reach. Would the company lawyers break through the legal thickets surrounding the issues? E. B. Crocker feared not. Fresh from his vantage point as chief justice, he warned Stanford that the supreme court of California probably would not uphold the constitutionality of the state-aid bill. The railroad had better compromise the matter.

148

The fate of the San Francisco bond issue was equally uncertain. Though the voters had approved it, local officials were making a great to-do in the courts over the liability that the city and county would assume if they became the owners of Central Pacific and Western Pacific stock. Once again, in Ed Crocker's opinion, compromise was called for—and this compromise, too, would have to be approved by the legislature, since the legislature had outlined the terms of the original bond proposal.

Reluctantly the directors prepared to have their representatives introduce the necessary bills. They knew by then that Judah's original estimate of $8.5 million for surmounting the Sierra was far short of the mark. In order to raise the additional amounts necessary, they would have to obtain legislative permission to increase their capitalization to twenty million dollars. There was where the compromise came in. If the legislature would pay, as a donation, 7 per cent interest on $1.5 million of those bonds—$105,000 a year for twenty years, a total of $2.1 million—the company would drop its insistence that the state fulfill the original contract.

The compromise proposed in connection with San Francisco was not quite so drastic. As originally approved by the voters, the county supervisors would issue $600,000 in bonds in exchange for 6,000 shares of Central Pacific stock, $400,000 for 4,000 shares of Western Pacific stock. The officials, however, were balking at the liability provisions. Very well then. If the city and county would donate outright $400,000 in bonds to the Central Pacific and $250,000 to the Western Pacific, the railroads would drop their demand that the stock sale be consummated.

All this was cold comfort to Huntington, waiting in the East for Congress to reconvene after the Christmas holidays. He could not be sure that Stanford still retained enough influence to push the compromise measures through the legislature, or that the enemies of the road would withdraw their injunctions even if the bills passed. Furthermore, $2.5 million in Far West bonds, all of them subject to heavy discount in the East, would scarcely chip what lay ahead in the Sierra. No, Huntington's reliance had to be on Congress—not for the sake of devious construction firms, as in the case of Durant and Hallett, but for simple survival.

About the time he reached Washington, an event occurred that caused him some uneasiness. James McDougall, the California senator with whom he had worked effectively in 1862, had turned into such a notorious and ineffective rumpot that his colleagues decided to maneuver him out of his committee positions. As his replacement on the Senate's

Committee on Pacific Railroads they picked another Californian, John Conness, resident of El Dorado County, a region bitterly hostile toward the Central Pacific. Conness, it will be remembered, was the man who had engineered the defeats of both Leland Stanford and of Aaron Sargent, Judah's stalwart supporter during the lobbying for the act of 1862.

Huntington did what he could to cultivate the new senator, a delicate bit of balancing since he had to keep from offending Cole and the other outraged Republicans back in California.[8] Among other gestures he gave the name *Conness* to a new locomotive that he had ordered from the Mason Works in Taunton, Massachusetts, the largest locomotive yet sent to the West.[9] To counterbalance this sycophancy, he named another locomotive for Sargent.

Washington was a dismal city that winter. Frequent rains turned the crowded streets into quagmires. Passengers were assisted from mired hansom cabs by Negroes who shuffled back and forth through the misty winds carrying long planks. The moral climate was just as drizzly. Although Gettysburg had been fought and won, few observers yet appreciated the battle's significance and it seemed as though the war had sagged into a hopeless stalemate, insatiably draining blood and treasure from both combatants.

Corruption oozed everywhere. One notorious example was Secretary of the Treasury Salmon P. Chase. At the very time that he was trying to win the Republican nomination by crying out in horror at Lincoln's "shoddy contractors and swarms of official leeches," Chase was also selling illegal trade permits to his friends and indulging in shady maneuvers over government bond issues with financier Jay Cooke. Lending luster to this dubious milieu was Chase's beautiful, statuesque daughter, Kate Chase Sprague, recent bride, for the sake of his money and political power, of the all-but-treasonable senator from Rhode Island, William Sprague.[10]

Anyone who had spent the decade of the 1850s in Sacramento was no stranger to political malfeasance. Even so, Washington shook Collis Huntington. To help him learn his way around, he hired two of Durant's henchmen, James Stewart and Alexander Henry, paying them eleven thousand dollars for their services. It was the poorest bargain, he testified later, that he ever made.[11]

The normal routine for lobbyists was to confer with interested senators and representatives concerning the preparation of bills desired by the firms they represented. This was legitimate so long as no untoward means were used to win the friendship of the lawmakers. As soon as a preliminary draft of a bill had been prepared, it was read to the appropriate chamber of Congress. If it struck the listeners as meriting consideration, it went back to committees for further study, was revised in the light of additional evidence, and again brought onto the floor for final debate.

The interests behind the Pacific railroad helped draft two different bills. The proposals were so very discrepant, indeed, that one is led to the conclusion that the Senate version represented the least the railroads would settle for, and the House presentation, the most they hoped to get. The intent, evidently, was a compromise somewhere between the two. As will become apparent, Huntington naturally gravitated toward the more familiar House committee and, in spite of his wooing of Conness, remained unaware of the inner discussions in the Senate group.

The Senate bill was reported out of committee first, in mid-April. Collis hurried to Washington for the debates. This time he took Elizabeth with him, for Cornelius Cole's wife, Olive, had promised to introduce her to Lincoln at the next presidential reception.

"I was proud to present Mrs. Huntington," Olive Cole wrote later, "for she was beautiful and tall, with a sweet womanly face, and on that day wore a superb black gown with diamond earrings and brooch." The fete disappointed Elizabeth, however. A jostling crowd surrounded the President. He looked haggard. One of his new white gloves was ripped at the thumb from shaking so many hands. She had time to exchange only a word with him before the ill-mannered crowd thrust her aside.[12]

A rush of war measures sidetracked discussion of the railroad bill. Uneasy about Clara, Elizabeth returned to New York City, leaving Collis to pass the time as best he could at the city's center of intrigue, the Willard Hotel. It was not, in 1864, a pleasant spot. Offensive odors filled the noisy corridors. "The carpet [of my room]," Cornelius Cole wrote Olive in December, "has been brussels some day, but the brussels are now worn off and it has every appearance of being a coarse canvas carpet. . . . Everything is dirty except the old tattered diaper which covers the bureau." But the bar and dining room hummed. Politicians, lobbyists, everyone in search of a favor, anyone with a rumor to leak, all gathered—"a maelstrom of political bargaining and sale, a place where the noisy, cumbersome machine of politics was oiled and greased."[13]

Collis was a homebody by preference. But the mining camps, the waterfront at San Francisco, and the launching of the Republican party of California had taught him to be at ease amidst gossiping, scheming, wait-for-the-breaks men. He was big and bluff and hearty. Although he seldom drank more than an occasional glass of wine, a sybaritic pleasure he had only recently begun to allow himself, he did not look down his nose at those who did. He was a marvelous yarn spinner, mining-camp style;

the subject matter of his tales, one acquaintance recalled, was apt to be "outré in mixed society and the humor runs toward the forbidden."[14]

For a month he dawdled around Washington, visiting the Capitol nearly every day, until finally, on May 18, the Senate took up its version of the railroad bill. Its main feature proposed abandonment of the government loans entirely in favor of letting the companies concerned issue their own first-mortgage bonds at the following rates: $24,000 a mile on the flat terrain west of the Sierra and east of the Rockies, $96,000 a mile within the mountains themselves, and $48,000 in the desert country between the ranges. To make these bonds readily salable, the government would pay the first year's interest on each issue, 6 per cent, and guarantee the rest. The land grant remained at 6,400 acres per mile.

Under these terms the objectionable withholding feature connected with government bonds automatically vanished. Time limits for completing the work were extended, and the forfeiture clause was eliminated. So far, so good. And then suddenly Huntington sat bolt upright in the gallery chair where he was listening. Tucked in among the other provisions was a clause that said the Central Pacific was to halt as soon as it reached California's eastern boundary.[15]

Furiously he sought out Durant. Was the Union Pacific trying to hog the continent?

Durant had just that in mind—for Crédit Mobilier, however, rather than for the railroad. He knew as well as Huntington did that the relatively easy desert stretches between the Rockies and the Sierra offered the fattest opportunities for construction profits—assuming that Congress passed a generous enough bill. In order to seize as much of that desert land as possible, he had smuggled past Senator Conness the directive halting the Central Pacific at the California border. Huntington had waked up in time, however, and through his connections with the House select committee was still able to cause trouble. Durant, who was not yet ready to risk a fight that would expose the Crédit Mobilier scheme, decided to placate him.

How much did Collis want?

Huntington's position was weaker than Durant realized. The Union Pacific is said to have spent $435,000 easing the legislation it wanted through Congress.[16] Comparable charges concerning the act of 1864 were never leveled at the Central Pacific. For one thing, the company had no such sums available.

As Collis well knew, money raising in California was going badly, in spite of a propitious start. On March 19 Stanford and Crocker had hooked up a gaily furbished train and had taken two thirds of the state's lawmakers and their families on a grand excursion to tracks' end a little beyond Roseville.[17] In April the legislature passed both compromise bills the railroad wanted: the state-aid measure paying the interest on $1.5 million of company bonds and a companion act allowing San Francisco to donate $400,000 in bonds to the CP rather than spend $600,000 buying stock.

Very promising—but just as Crocker was writing exultantly to Cole, *"We have got it,"* the road's enemies challenged both measures. A test suit carried the state-aid bill to the supreme court for a determination of its constitutionality. The belligerent officials of San Francisco defied the legislature and refused to deliver the bonds to the railroads (the Western Pacific had also been included in the compromise) and that issue, too, had to await settlement at law.

With that knowledge in the back of his mind, Huntington was uncertain how far he dared push Durant. He finally determined on the new mines at Reese River as a goal, for by the nature of things Nevada traffic was oriented toward California and it was logical to demand at least that much. He got out his maps, measured the air-line distance from the state border to the infant town of Austin, and told Durant, "One hundred and fifty miles."

Durant yielded and on May 23, as the record of debates in the *Congressional Globe* clearly shows, both of California's senators, McDougall and Conness, arose in support of an amendment to the Senate bill that would allow the Central Pacific to push 150 miles into Nevada. Assured by McDougall that "the representatives of the Union Pacific as well as of the Central Pacific concur," the senators accepted the change and a few hours later passed the act by a vote of twenty-three to five.

Though Huntington had saved the Nevada mining traffic, he was not pleased. The Comstock mines appeared to be on the point of running out of ore. Their stocks had broken sharply. On April 1, for example, shares in the Gould & Curry, one of Virginia City's largest, had been selling readily at $4,550. Immediately thereafter, prices began a disastrous nose dive; by the end of July, the stock had shrunk to $900. The Bank of California, whose branch in Virginia City was the mainstay of the Comstock, was tottering. As for Reese River, there was no real way of telling yet what the district might turn into.

Meanwhile, under the Senate's bill, the Union Pacific was assured of fifteen hundred miles of track. The Central Pacific was allowed only three hundred miles, nearly half of it across one of the most formidable mountain ranges in America. Yet Durant had been reluctant to give up even that much. Why? Huntington, who still knew nothing definite about

153

Crédit Mobilier or the vast construction racket Durant wanted to stitch to it, was not sure. But obviously Durant was ravenous. It behooved Collis to mend his fences and use the House bill for protecting even those niggardly miles of Nevada sagebrush that he had managed to hang onto.

As usual, horse trading was necessary. The vigorous young states of Minnesota and Oregon, supported by strong interests in New England, were demanding, as they did each time a transcontinental bill appeared, that they, too, be connected by rail. Since Representative John McBride of Oregon was a member of the thirteen-man House committee, their voices could not be ignored. Procedures for incorporating the Northern Pacific accordingly were whipped together (Sam Brannan was named as one of the incorporating commissioners from California) and the new company was promised the largest land grant in American history— 12,800 acres for each mile of track laid in the states through which it passed and 25,600 acres per mile in the territories.

This grand gesture assured the UP and CP of the co-operation of the northerners. Durant, Huntington, and their associates, however, had no interest in seeing a competitor spring alive in the north. They'd rather run their own branch lines up into those areas. Quietly, therefore, they forgot their own differences long enough to help economy-minded Congressmen render the apparent generosity ineffective. The Northern Pacific was granted neither loans nor bonding privileges based on mileage— just land. Since the huge acreage would remain virtually worthless for years after it was earned, the Northern Pacific would have to raise money for construction through the sale of stock. From their own experiences, Huntington and Durant knew how difficult that would be.

The northerners taken care of, the promoters of the central route set about improving their own bonding situation. The House bill introduced to Congress on June 16 relegated the government securities authorized by the act of 1862 to the status of second mortgages and allowed the railroads to issue their own first-mortgage bonds in amounts equal to the government bonds. This in effect allowed the roads to realize a total of $32,000 in the flatlands, $64,000 in the country between the mountains, and $96,000 in the major ranges—as compared to the sums of $24,000, $48,000, and $96,000 authorized by the Senate. There was to be no retention of any of the bonds against the completion of the entire system. And the land grant was doubled, to 12,800 acres per mile checkerboarded on strips extending twenty miles to either side of the tracks.

The old requirement that 10 per cent of net operating profits and all moneys received from the government for transporting mail, troops, and supplies be placed in a sinking fund for debt retirement was cut in half. Again nothing specific was said about interest payments; by that time it was generally assumed that the accrued amount would not be paid until after thirty years, when the principal also fell due. Like the Senate, the House eliminated the clauses calling for forfeiture of every one of the railroads if a continuous line from the Missouri to the Sacramento had not been completed by 1876.

Since Thomas Durant had been openly suggesting most of these amendments for some months past, it is questionable whether Huntington's influence that June was as persuasive as he liked to remember.[18] There were a few clauses, however, that showed his hand. The distance the Central Pacific's track layers had to cover each year was halved. Moreover the CP could collect bonds as soon as twenty miles of track were in working order. Since the railroad's iron was then on the point of entering Newcastle, nearly thirty-one miles from Sacramento, this meant that the moment the act was approved and signed, Huntington could ask the government for $1,258,000 in bonds, par value.*

Still another clause said that if Hallett's and Perry's Eastern Division reached the 100th meridian ahead of the Union Pacific, it could, under certain conditions, forge on west until it met the Central Pacific. The ostensible purpose behind this provision was to keep the eastern roads hard at work. The ultimate result, however, might well be an extravagant race between the UP and the Eastern Division that would lead conservative investors to eye both companies with suspicion.

Tucked in among the welter of amendments was a curious provision designed by Durant to speed construction—and the collection of bonds. The number of men who could be kept gainfully at work along any railhead was necessarily limited by sheer crowding. To loosen things up, the new act would allow construction crews to leapfrog ahead and grade disconnected segments of twenty miles each. As soon as one of these blocks of grading was finished, but before the track was laid, the company concerned could collect two thirds of the bonds due for the work, even though the railhead itself was far to the rear.

This same clause let Huntington salvage a little of his pride by putting a limit on Durant. The UP's construction workers, the act said, could skip westward no more than three hundred miles from Salt Lake City. It so happened that three hundred miles was the distance from Salt Lake to the Reese River silver mines clustering around the new town of Austin.

* Some red tape would be involved before he could collect. The work would first have to be approved by government inspectors, none of whom had yet been appointed.

If the Central Pacific must stop in central Nevada, then the Union Pacific must halt there, too, and not use the twenty-mile grading privilege to skip on to the California border. Huntington, in short, had learned that the only way to get along with Durant was to watch him. It was a lesson he remembered in his dealings with every other railroad entrepreneur he encountered during the rest of his life.

For five hot, soggy days, the House acrimoniously debated the bill. Elihu Washburne of Illinois and William Holman of Indiana attacked it as a treasury raid of "sublime audacity . . . the greatest legislative crime in history."[19] Rumor swept through the city that ruthless power was promoting the bill. When the final vote was called on the night of June 21, the House seethed with more excitement than one would expect from a piece of technical railroad legislation. According to Washburne's recollections, the galleries were packed with lobbyists, male and, so he specified, female as well. Some of the visitors even defied the guards and pushed onto the floor of the chamber itself. Voting was conducted in a "tempest of wildest disorder."[20]

The bill carried and a conference committee, which included both Senator Conness and Representative Cole, was named to adjust differences between the measures. The outcome was a total victory for the House version with its generous bonding and land privileges. Only two clauses were carried over from the Senate version. One was the amendment restraining the Central Pacific from building more than 150 miles into Nevada. In conjunction with the House's restraints on the Union Pacific, this in effect set the middle of Nevada as a meeting place for the roads, yet avoided naming a specific junction point—a desirable vagueness then since the routes across the territory had not been determined. In time, however, vagueness about a meeting place would become a costly plague.

On July 2, 1864, Lincoln signed the act into law.

Years later, Huntington insisted that from the beginning he never intended to abide by the Nevada limitations.[21] In view of his circumstances at the time, however, one wonders. He did not even know yet that the Central Pacific could cross the mountains, let alone penetrate Nevada—many people were sure it couldn't—and he may well have consoled himself, and his associates, that he had made the best he could out of a bad bargain. The decision to fight back probably grew slowly, as luck began to mend. Concerning this, however, no sound evidence survives and the point remains conjectural.

In still other ways the bill must have seemed anticlimactic to Huntington. True, time and repayment requirements had been relaxed. The

156

threat of forfeiture was removed. Land and bonding opportunities appeared, on the face of things, to be doubled. Actually, however, events had made the new monetary provisions as illusory as the old.

Just before the passage of the railroad bill, Grant's drive toward Richmond had been checked with disastrous casualties. On July 11, 1864, shortly after its passage, the guns of Jubal Early's counterattacking Confederates were clearly audible in Washington. Along with several other valiant Congressmen, Cole volunteered to take a musket, join a citizens' army, and help man the barricades.

The impromptu militia never marched. Early withdrew and the capital rejoiced. Government funding, however, had been shaken disastrously. Although Huntington might have raised cash by hypothecating the bonds now due him from the government under the terms of the new act, the move would have been folly. He would have had to accept greenbacks, and on July 11, when Early's guns were audible at the Treasury building, a paper dollar was worth only thirty-three cents in gold coin. In California, where only gold was acceptable, the Central Pacific's $1.25 million in federal bonds would purchase only $400,000 in work and horse feed. The company's handsome new first-mortgage bonds would fare no better. Under the circumstances, and except in cases where eastern manufacturers were willing to deal in greenbacks, he had no choice but to wait for values to rise.[22]

In view of what was happening on the Coast, where for seventeen straight days there was not a single dollar in the Central Pacific's coffers, the experience promised to be an uncomfortable one.

12   Breakthrough

More ironies were at work in California. On June 6, 1864, Central Pacific freight and passenger trains began operating on regular schedules between Sacramento and Newcastle. A week or so later the Dutch Flat wagon road was completed to Virginia City.[1] Attracted in part by the novelty, long lines of wagons began creaking along the new route.

The builders might well have expected congratulations. Instead, San Franciscans who were opposed to the railroad used the opening of the highway as an excuse for rushing to press a thick pamphlet entitled "THE GREAT DUTCH FLAT SWINDLE!! *The City of San Francisco Demands Justice!!*" Pages were filled with long descriptions of Phil Stanford's alleged bribery of voters at the bond election of May 1863. The railroad, the pamphlet went on, was a sham anyway. It could not possibly be built across Donner Summit. Talk of its becoming part of the grand Pacific railroad was a pretext for raiding the taxpayers of enough money to build only as far as Dutch Flat. The intent was, quite baldly, to lure freight for the wagon road and so pour tolls into the pockets of Huntington, Hopkins, and the brothers Stanford and Crocker. Surely, the argument concluded, the judges who were reviewing the bond issues would never be hoodwinked into supporting such a fraud.

The attack was not limited to words. Aided by El Dorado County and Placerville city bonds and backed by the McLanes of Wells Fargo and by Pioche, Bayerque & Co., the Robinson brothers had pushed their Sacramento & Placerville extension to Latrobe, seven miles farther from navigable water than the Central Pacific had yet reached. Soon (by mid-August) their trains would be operating out of Freeport, the new town they had built below Sacramento—all this to the anguish of the capital city, which saw itself in deep distress if the CP failed to meet the challenge.[2]

During this same period an engineer named F. A. Bishop, an associate of the Robinsons but ostensibly working for a yet unincorporated entity to be called the San Francisco & Washoe Railroad, was trumpeting that he had surveys to prove the feasibility of linking Freeport to Carson Valley by way of Johnson Pass at a cost of only $8.7 million. By contrast, Leland Stanford himself had confessed that it would cost the Central Pacific thirteen million dollars just to reach the state line—if ever it managed to cross Donner at all, which possibility Bishop vehemently doubted.[3]

Target of Bishop's remarks were delegates to Nevada's constitutional convention, then meeting in Carson City to prepare a set of laws under which the territory could be admitted to the Union as a state. Supporters of the Johnson Pass route had inserted into the proposed constitution a paragraph authorizing a donation of three million dollars in Nevada bonds to the first railway that connected the new state with the navigable waters of either the Missouri or Sacramento rivers. The Robinsons hoped, through Bishop, to pass the provision and, with this three-million-dollar prize dangling in front of them, make money raising easier for their own railroad.

Fearing any gesture that might bring encouragement to the enemy, Leland Stanford hurried to Carson City. There he went to work on portly Governor James Nye and on long-bearded William M. Stewart, the leading Republicans at the convention. Through them he, a Californian, won permission to address the delegates on July 13 and instruct them as to what Nevada wanted in its own constitution.

It was an adroit presentation. Never once did Stanford evince the least alarm over the possibility that the Robinsons might cross Johnson Pass. Instead, he concentrated on the fact that the Central Pacific alone had been designated by both the Congress of the United States and the legislature of California as the western end of the transcontinental. For Nevadans to suggest in their state constitution that another road was worming, however feebly, into the picture would merely confuse investors and retard the sale of Central Pacific securities. Thus, instead of speeding a railroad, the proposed bonus might actually delay it.[4]

Disconcerted by the argument, the Nevadans eliminated the provision —but immediately thereafter also rejected Stanford's follow-up plea that the new state join California and the federal government in offering aid to the Central Pacific alone.

In spite of the Nevada setback, the Robinsons kept pushing their

159

road toward Placerville. Needing rails, they started to rip up their own Sacramento, Placer & Nevada extension from Folsom to Auburn, which the Central Pacific's shorter, better line to Newcastle (within five miles of Auburn) had rendered obsolete. Scenting opportunity for obstructionism on their own part, the directors of the CP helped a quarry owner named Griffith obtain an injunction halting the removal on the grounds that the value of his property was being destroyed. Deputy sheriffs were posted beside the tracks to see that no more iron was removed.

John Robinson thereupon found a justice of the peace who obligingly issued warrants for the arrest of the deputies on the charge that they were carrying concealed weapons and disturbing the peace. Out went a posse. The deputies called on the county militia for reinforcements. In the scuffle one man was shot in the ear, another was pricked by a bayonet. Then into the fray marched Sheriff McClatchy of Sacramento County, who once had printed the state's first Republican newspaper in the loft at 54 K Street. On orders of the state supreme court, McClatchy jailed Robinson and seventy others for defying a legal injunction, a sweep that considerably overstrained local accommodations. In the end Robinson had the restraining order set aside and got the rails, but not before his embarrassments had provided Sacramentans with several loud guffaws.[5]

A bit later the Robinsons suffered a more serious humiliation. A race, with San Francisco newspapers serving as the baton, was arranged between the rival railroad and stagecoach lines that linked the Sacramento River to Virginia City. The Central Pacific and special relays of the California Stage Company coaches won handily over the Robinsons' road and the Pioneer Stage Lines—twenty-one hours to almost thirty-five. Grumbles that the winners had hired freight wagons to block strategic points of the Placerville road were quieted when regularly scheduled trips over the Donner route continued to maintain a marked superiority.[6]

The achievement turned increasing amounts of traffic to the victors, so that between July and December the Central Pacific netted $47,265.37 above operational costs (but without provisions yet for debt retirement). Although toll returns from the Dutch Flat wagon road are not recoverable, they must have been commensurate.

Among other observers impressed by these victories was Sam Brannan. He had recently pushed his extension of the California Central, the Yuba Railroad, to within seven miles of the California Northern at Marysville. A closing of the gap would result in a seventy-mile run northward to Oroville, the longest operating system in the state.

Brannan could have supported either the Central Pacific, whose tracks he crossed at Roseville, or the Sacramento Valley Railroad, whose tracks he joined at Folsom. He chose the Central Pacific—Huntington, it will be remembered, had been cultivating him for years. Henceforth, all northern California traffic would go into Sacramento over the Central Pacific. On November 10, 1864, he also sold to the CP certain surplus equipment created by his road's apparently imminent consolidation with the California Northern—four locomotives, twenty-three flatcars, four passenger coaches, three boxcars, and one baggage car. In exchange he received two hundred shares of Central Pacific stock and promises of sixty $1,000 San Francisco bonds and twenty-five $1,000 company bonds on which the state would pay the interest.[7]

Sam Brannan, in short, was confident that the courts would soon order those disputed bonds released.

He was right. On January 3, 1865, the supreme court upheld the constitutionality of the state-aid bill. It was no panacea, however. The $1.5 million in company bonds on which the state was to pay 7 per cent interest eventually brought the Central Pacific only $980,000 in gold.[8] It was enough, however, to start work rolling again. On January 7, the company advertised for five thousand laborers.

One jam-up after another, both in the East and in the West, accompanied this sudden resumption of work. According to rumor, the busy opponents of the Central Pacific spread scare tales and even money to such good effect that fewer than two thousand men answered this appeal for workers. Winter weather, too, chilled recruiting. Others signed on merely to earn enough to cross over the hill to the Nevada mines. Those who did stay, principally turbulent Irishmen, felt that they could have things their own way and grew high-handed.

Remembering the meek Chinese he had employed on the wagon road, Crocker persuaded his tall, fierce-visaged superintendent of construction, J. H. Strobridge, to try fifty of the Orientals. Before long thousands were at work—to the temporary embarrassment of Leland Stanford who, as governor, had railed against the competition of these "dregs of Asia" with honest white workingmen. He recovered, though, when he saw how well the Chinese performed and how tractable the Irish turned as soon as their jobs were threatened.[9]

Along with workers, Crocker needed black powder for blasting. Off went an urgent telegram for Huntington to ship five thousand kegs. To speed procurement along, Collis called on the Secretary of War to ask for permits. Stanton proved unco-operative. "He looked up like a hog, as he was"—hog was Huntington's favorite epithet for opponents; his later correspondence is sprinkled with the term—and refused. Well, there was one more avenue. Huntington used it with no least hint of the diffidence he had felt during his early days in Washington. Off he marched to President Lincoln, and soon shiploads of the necessary powder were on their way West.[10]

Financing was far more complex. Costs of construction were skyrocketing. Just beyond Newcastle lay Bloomer Cut, a trench eight hundred feet long and sixty-five feet deep that would have to be gouged out of hard, cemented gravel by pickax and black powder. And Bloomer Cut was a mere foretaste. In order to maintain grade, Crocker's timbermen, using at first pine imported from the Northwest, would have to erect an almost endless sequence of trestles, one as long as 878 feet; others were seventy feet high. The antlike Chinese, filling tiny two-wheeled carts by hand, would have to heap up one massive fill after another. At Cape Horn men would have to be lowered in baskets to chip out the roadbed. Higher, there would be fifteen tunnels, culminating in a summit bore 1,659 feet long, pushed ahead with hand drills and black powder at a rate of from eight to twelve inches a day.*

In the most difficult places, costs would rise to $150,000 a mile. Many stretches would devour $100,000. The maximum revenue allowable was $48,000 a mile in federal bonds, matched by an equal number of the company's own first-mortgage bonds. These face-value figures stayed illusory, however. Although Grant was grinding away again toward Richmond and greenbacks were rising in value, $96,000 in bonds per mile would still yield only $72,000 in gold.

In addition to this sum, the company could draw on $950,000 in county bonds, for at long last, in April 1865, the supreme court ordered San Francisco to add its $400,000 worth of compromise bonds to those already delivered by Sacramento and Placer counties. This $950,000 worth of bonds yielded $650,000 in gold, or another $5,420 a mile for the remaining distance across the mountains.[11] Interest of $105,000 a year from the state would bring the total to roughly $80,000 a mile in gold. It was not enough. The farther the company built into those rugged mountains, the farther behind it would fall financially.[12]

On top of this there was the problem of the competing line in California—the combined Freeport, Sacramento Valley, and Sacramento & Placerville system, which by then had pushed on as far as Shingle Springs, within eight miles of Placerville. Although the Robinsons remained as grim as ever, some of their associates were wearying of the fight. One of them, George Bragg, approached Huntington with an offer

---

* Continued meticulous surveys shortened Judah's original route by five thousand feet and eliminated three tunnels. This is no reflection on Judah's engineering. Constant revisions are a part of every rail and highway project.

to act as agent in persuading Lester Robinson, F. L. A. Pioche and J. B. Bayerque to sell their controlling stock interests. It would cost, Bragg estimated, $800,000, part of which could be paid in the form of Central Pacific bonds.

In order to get rid of the enemy's continual harassment, Huntington agreed, athough this meant adding appreciably to his already staggering commitments.*

Where was so much money coming from?

The sale of capital stock was no answer. The Dutch Flat swindle pamphlet, opposition newspapers like the San Francisco *Alta California,* and engineers like F. A. Bishop, to say nothing of the Robinsons, had succeeded in convincing cautious investors that the Central Pacific would never cross Donner Summit. Only Sacramentans stayed loyal—of the road's 297 shareholders, 230 lived in the capital city[13]—and Sacramento's capacity was limited. After producing something less than a million dollars, stock sales, despite hard pushing, had come to a dead halt.[14]

If only it were possible to borrow money in advance on the unbuilt line! This, however, would require special legislation. Under the acts of 1862 and 1864, payments to the railroads were yoked hard and fast to the progress they made. Twenty miles of road had to be approved by government inspectors before a single government bond could be issued as a loan on work already completed. And until government securities had been authorized, the companies concerned could not issue their own first-mortgage bonds in equivalent amounts.

Twenty Sierra miles! The county securities the Central Pacific held in its till and those due it from the government for the thirty-one miles already completed were not enough to do the job. And beyond that first twenty miles lay nearly a hundred more to the state line and the flatter lands of Nevada. Somehow Congress had to be persuaded to liberalize its terms once again.

Huntington carried the argument to Cornelius Cole. Linking progress and payment in the Sierra, he said, was manifestly unfair. Consider those fifteen tunnels. Each one would be a bottleneck. The only way to speed progress would be to work at both ends simultaneously. Mean-

---

* The sale, consummated in August 1865, did not include the San Francisco & Washoe. In 1866 that company obtained the assistance of a federal land grant, but the Robinsons fell into a quarrel with the McLanes of Wells Fargo and the road never managed to push from Placerville on across Johnson Pass. Eventually the government took back the land for non-compliance, and in the 1870s the company quietly expired.

while other crews could be scattered out in between, building trestles, digging cuts, heaping up fills—preparing the roadbed, in short, so that the rails could be laid without wasted time as soon as each tunnel was holed through and work trains could come up from below with the iron. Surely Congress could appreciate the months, even years of time that this method of attack would save.

Cole admitted the force of the argument but pointed out the criticism to which Congress would be subject if it were to advance large sums, without check, in advance of actual work. The lawmakers might compromise, however. They might permit the railroads, the Union Pacific and Eastern Division as well as the Central Pacific, to issue their own company bonds for, say, a hundred miles in advance of a continuous line of track.

A hundred miles—that would make $4.8 million in greenbacks immediately available. Another $4.8 million would come from the government in five installments as each twenty-mile segment of track was completed. Considering the excessive wartime costs of material and of freight around South America, and the payroll demands of the ten thousand laborers they would need in the mountains, the figure did not seem any too generous. But at least it would give them a fighting chance. After sounding out Durant, who of course was agreeable to any kind of money-raising amendment, Huntington asked Conness and Cole to begin the necessary committee work.[15]

The bill passed and was signed into law by Lincoln on March 3, 1865. The next day, March 4, Huntington and Charles McLaughlin, who was also in Washington (and who the previous October had finally won congressional approval of the Central Pacific's assignment of its Sacramento–San Francisco rights to the Western Pacific), celebrated by attending the President's second inaugural. Records do not indicate whether Elizabeth was with them or back in the Metropolitan Hotel with Clara.

The passage of the amendment helped bring Durant's carefully nurtured Crédit Mobilier scheme into view. Until then he had worked deviously. First, the Union Pacific had awarded, at his behest, a hundred-mile construction contract to Herbert M. Hoxie, an Iowa political pal of Durant's. The terms of the agreement were so flagrant that the UP's own chief engineer, Peter Dey, resigned in disgust. Later, Hoxie's contract was extended, under the same liberal terms, to the 100th meridian, the beginning point of the original Union Pacific. Immediately thereafter Hoxie assigned this new 247-mile contract to Durant, Cornelius S. Bushnell, and three other associates, who guaranteed enough money to launch

164

construction. For the sake of appearances, however, the contract still remained in Hoxie's name.

No building followed. There were disagreements over the route the railroad should follow out of Omaha. More pertinent, the Union Pacific had supply problems of its own—not so formidable as the Central Pacific's, but dismaying nevertheless. No railroads had yet crossed Iowa. Material purchased at inflationary prices had to be hauled several hundred miles by wagon or brought up the undependable Missouri aboard fleets of shallow-draft steamboats. Because no trees other than scattered, soft cottonwoods grew on the plains, timber for ties and trestles had to be imported from Wisconsin and Minnesota, or else cottonwood had to be "hardened" with injections of zinc chloride. Firewood for locomotive fuel had to be floated hundreds of miles down the Missouri. Like Huntington, Durant did not know where to find money enough for all this.

A partial solution came with the March amendment, which let the Union Pacific issue $1.6 million in company bonds against an unbuilt hundred-mile stretch of track up the flat valley of the Platte. Promptly the Durant-Hoxie construction contract was transferred to Crédit Mobilier. Lavishly, Crédit Mobilier then began buying locomotives, cars, rails, and lumber, contracted for their delivery, and hired hundreds of graders. The government directors assigned to keep an eye on progress clucked disapprovingly over Crédit Mobilier's terms with the UP, but finally let the arrangement go through. On July 10, 1865, the Union Pacific laid its first rails. By that time the reinvigorated Central Pacific had reached Clipper Gap, forty-three miles northeast of Sacramento and 1,751 feet above sea level.

These early exertions broke Crédit Mobilier. A drive for more stock subscriptions to the Union Pacific failed as miserably as the CP drives in California. To obtain more money, Durant, after long negotiations, enlisted the support of Oliver Ames, the shovel manufacturer who not long since had loaned Huntington money, and of his brother, Congressman Oakes Ames. Like Cole, Oakes Ames was a member of the House's Select Committee on Pacific Railroads and had helped Cole implement the March amendment.

With them the Ames brothers brought into Crédit Mobilier a handful of other capitalists, including Charles A. Lambard. Charles's brother, Orville Lambard, lived in Sacramento and was part owner of a foundry that did a great deal of iron fabricating for the Central Pacific. Together the Lambards owned 320 shares of Central Pacific stock—the largest block held by any private investor outside of Charles Crocker & Company.

165

Furthermore, by meeting all their assessments, the Lambards had paid par for the shares—$32,000.[16]

Conceivably these many interlockings could have produced a certain friendliness between the Union Pacific and the Central Pacific, if the aggressive vice-presidents of the two roads had been so disposed. Neither was.

Whether or not an awareness of Crédit Mobilier led Huntington and his associates to try to emulate its quick-goal profits through Charles Crocker & Company is impossible to determine. The idea may have occurred to them earlier. From the beginning, Crocker and the smaller contractors who had worked on the road between Sacramento and Newcastle had taken part of their pay in the form of Central Pacific stock. Though the situation of the minor contractors is not clear, Crocker after September 1863 had accepted his shares as worth only fifty cents on the dollar. In spite of this deflation, the stock appears to have been, during those first transactions, an honest part of the remuneration and not frosting on a cake already amply paid for with cash and railroad bonds.

Eventually, though, the associates must have begun to wonder. Stock manipulation by firms engaged in canal and railroad construction was one of the oldest money-making dodges in the United States. It was by this means that the Robinsons and their bankers had gained control of their Sacramento system, and had paid themselves fancy profits, to boot.[17] An even more notorious example had been provided by Sam Hallett of the Eastern Division. In the spring of 1864, Hallett had fired his engineer, Orlando A. Talcott, for writing President Lincoln about the wretched work that Hallett's construction firm was doing in Kansas for Hallett's and Frémont's railroad. One thing had led to another until, in October, Talcott slipped up behind Hallett in an alleyway in Wyandotte, Kansas, killed him with a shot in the back, and escaped. The resultant scandal led Frémont finally to wash his hands of the mess and sell out to John D. Perry's rival faction. To those connected with railroad building the uproar also revealed illuminating details about the profits Hallett had been planning to garner through Eastern Division capital stock absorbed by his contracting firm.

There were other urgings toward imitation. California law forbade a railroad issuing more bonds than capital stock. Thus, when Congress allowed the companies concerned in the transcontinental to issue bonds for a hundred miles in advance of their railheads, the Central Pacific was all but obliged to release, on the dot, $4.8 million in stock, plus another

166

$48,000 worth for each mile the track advanced, plus still more for secondary bond issues.

All that paper required by law—and all of it quite unsalable, as matters stood!

Since it could not be sold, why not use it as frosting in return for the gigantic risk that they were undertaking—and, as the associates frequently pointed out during subsequent investigations—in partial recompense for the benefits which their success would confer upon the entire Pacific Coast?

Thus motivated, the directors of the Central Pacific allotted, without competitive bidding, every foot of the construction from Newcastle eastward to the state line to Charles Crocker & Company. As it had been doing since September 1863, Crocker & Company accepted three eighths of its pay in Central Pacific stock valued at fifty cents on the dollar. In April 1866 the stock was further devalued to thirty cents. This of course sugared the frosting still more, though none of it would become available until the railroad succeeded and values began to rise.

Just how rich the frosting really was depends, of course, on what the true costs of construction amounted to and the extent to which these expenses were met by cash and bonds. The more stock that was paid out in excess of actual costs, the higher the future profits would be. Concerning these things there are no records, nor were numerous congressional investigating committees ever able to turn up any.

In 1887 Charles Crocker testified that he had sought for partners to join him in the work but no one had dared take the risk; therefore, there had been no "& Company." In a technical sense this was true. No written agreement named any associates or apportioned any of the company's profits and liabilities. Nonetheless Crocker quite patently had reached some sort of agreement with his brother Ed, with Huntington, Hopkins, and Phil and Leland Stanford—but not, evidently, with the other directors of the Central Pacific: Charles Marsh, E. H. Miller, Jr., and John Morse. They were left out of the understanding. Soon, indeed, Marsh and Morse were eased out of the company entirely.

A remarkable amity acted in place of legal phraseology for holding the surviving sextet together. Each assumed, on the basis of his knowledge of the others' past dealings, that his five partners would keep promises pledged by only a nod of the head. Each was confident that if one of them died or became incapacitated, the others would close ranks without a ripple, protecting his heirs the while. Only in the case of Phil Stanford did any reason develop for altering the arrangement.[18]

It had to be that way. For when the rails finally reached the state line in 1867, Crocker held in unspoken trust for the five associates remaining after Phil Stanford's removal, Central Pacific stock worth, at face value, fourteen million dollars, all of it collected through his construction contracts. If there had not been some sort of understanding he would soon have controlled the railroad.[19]

Stimulated by the release of the state-aid and county bonds, by the borrow-in-advance legislation, and, probably, by their belated realization of the profit possibilities inherent in the construction contracts, the track builders leaped ahead. Thanks to a mild spring, Charles Crocker faced little physical trouble in dotting the foothills with construction camps peopled largely by Chinese. On April 12, 1865, his brother Ed wrote Cole that they had two thousand men and three hundred wagons at work. "I tell you, Cole, we are in dead earnest about this R. R., and you take 6 or 8 men in real earnest, and if they have any brains and industry, they will accomplish it rapidly."[20]

The force kept growing. As it did, Crocker pushed his camps deeper into the mountains. Now the Dutch Flat road proved its usefulness in speeding ingress to the right-of-way. Late in the summer he set up a camp at the site of the summit tunnel and ordered his patient coolies to start chipping away at nearly a third of a mile of solid granite. By the end of the year, seven thousand Orientals, 2,500 Irish, and more than a thousand teams were strung up and down the long slopes.

Trains were running as well. Gross revenues rose from $11,040 for January to $65,925 for October. After making provisions for interest payments and debt retirement, the books still showed an operating net for the year of $27,233.44.

The fevered activity enthralled a potent group of traveling reporters—Samuel Bowles, publisher of the Springfield, Massachusetts, *Republican,* Albert Richardson, special correspondent of Horace Greeley's widely read New York *Tribune,* and, as a sort of freeloader on the trip, Schuyler Colfax, speaker of the House of Representatives. During their leisurely ride across the continent, the journalists and their entourage had been very scornful of the Union Pacific's lack of progress. After visiting the Central Pacific's railhead aboard a special train provided by Leland Stanford, they were agog and told their readers so in a series of highly flattering stories.

Far more to the point was a report from George M. Gray, a highly respected engineer whom the company had hired to study the railroad's chances of crossing the mountains along the route surveyed. After walking and riding across the entire line, Gray wrote, "I feel confident that your railroad can be constructed over the Sierra Nevada within two years from next Spring . . . at a cost which will favorably compare with other important railroads, long in successful operation."[21]

The stories by the journalists and the optimism of engineer Gray helped Collis persuade the vigorous young New York City bond house of Fisk and Hatch (no relationship to the notorious Jim Fisk) to assist him in marketing his badly depreciated Central Pacific securities. Almost surely, too, Gray's confidence turned Huntington's restless mind back toward those flat desert miles through Nevada and western Utah. Only two years to reach them, Gray had said!

Would the Union Pacific be able to cross the Rockies during the same two years? It seemed unlikely. Although Durant's surveyors were working in the vicinity of Salt Lake City and his graders were pushing well into Nebraska, the track layers were far behind. By the end of 1865 they had succeeded in placing only forty miles of rail on land almost as smooth as a tabletop. And out on the plains, the Sioux and Cheyenne Indians were up in arms. Under the circumstances the Central Pacific could almost surely reach central Nevada well ahead of the Union Pacific. Should it then sit still and wait for the other road?

To Collis the answer was clear. No matter how costs were padded in the Sierra, government limitations on the number of bonds that could be issued, coupled to the greenback squeeze, precluded any great amount of profit. Moreover, by issuing bonds for a hundred miles in advance of their railhead, the associates were automatically knocking some of the props out from under the funding program that would be necessary for building the last hundred miles. They needed room, down on the Nevada flats, where loan privileges ran up to $64,000 a mile ($32,000 from the government plus a matching $32,000 in company bonds) to catch up with themselves. To achieve this Collis must once again go to Congress, this time in request of an amendment striking out the 150-mile limitation Durant had forced on him in 1864.

He no longer doubted his ability to manage Congress. His swiftly matured confidence shows clearly, if indirectly, in a letter that he wrote to his brother Solon on December 8, 1865.

A few months earlier, Solon had bought several shares of Central Pacific stock, and now he was nervous about them. Just what, he asked Collis by letter, were the prospects?

Hang on, Collis replied. Little stock would reach the market because state, county, and federal aid, plus company bonds and operating revenues would be ample to finance the road. (Thus, clearly, the engrossing of Central Pacific stock through Charles Crocker & Company was by December 8 an established policy.) Within twenty-four months, he went on, the road would have reached the Nevada mines, at which point operating profits ought to be 24 per cent on the investment. And that was just a beginning. Very soon thereafter the railroad would also be trafficking with the Mormons of Utah and the new gold mines of Idaho. So he said, although as yet not a word had been breathed to Congress about breaking the 150-mile limit.[22] Obviously he expected no trouble when the matter arose.

He had scarcely laid down his pen from writing Solon when he learned that the congressional hopper for 1866 was going to be filled with railroad-aid bills. Still sanguine about transcontinental prospects despite his experience with the Union Pacific, Eastern Division, John C. Frémont had become president of a firm called the Atlantic & Pacific. This road proposed to build from Springfield in the southwestern corner of Missouri off through Indian Territory (today's Oklahoma) to the neighborhood of the thirty-fifth parallel, which it would follow through Albuquerque to the California border in the vicinity of present-day Needles. From Van Buren, Arkansas, a branch would run west to meet the main stem in Indian Territory. Companies unaided by federal grants would link these starting points, Springfield and Van Buren, to St. Louis and Memphis.

In California a firm called the Southern Pacific Railroad Company was incorporated to build from San Francisco south through the coastal counties to San Diego and then east to the California border and a meeting with the Atlantic & Pacific. Both of these roads wanted federal assistance. Their supporters used several of the arguments that had been trotted out in support of the Union Pacific–Central Pacific system. The new roads would save the cost of their building by providing quicker transportation of troops and mails, they would develop the Southwest, and so on. Two new arguments accompanied the old ones. The southern transcontinental would help reconstruct the war-prostrated South. And because the route was largely free of snow, it would be a much more efficient system than the central line—an argument which, as later events showed, really worried Huntington.

Another group of Californians, led by a slippery surveyor and promoter named Simon G. Elliott, had simultaneously formed an organization called the California & Oregon, designed to strike north through the Sacramento and Willamette valleys to a connection with the Northern Pacific at Portland. Thus the CP's northern, as well as its southern, flank was threatened.

There were other dangers. A third California group, heir of the old San Francisco & Sacramento, had just announced its intentions to build

170

a direct line from Vallejo on the north shore of San Francisco Bay to Sacramento and thence to Marysville. Either this road (eventually it would be known as the California Pacific) or the California & Oregon or even the older locals, the California Central, the Yuba, and the California Northern, could, as Huntington had learned from his surveys in the Feather River country, veer off through Oroville over low, easy Beckwourth Pass and meet the Union Pacific somewhere along the Humboldt River in north-central Nevada. Such a junction, if the UP fostered it, would leave the Central Pacific isolated.

One way to obviate the Beckwourth Pass threat was for the CP to drive east and halt the UP far enough from California that the potential rivals would lose interest in trying to pursue. This, too, involved breaking the 150-mile limit. Expansion would also help answer the threats of the northern and southern transcontinentals. Entrench the Central Pacific solidly by refusing to let it become a mere appendage of the UP and then, that strength achieved, swing around to confront the newcomers. This, of course, was always Huntington's way: seize and then protect.

Because Oakes Ames of Crédit Mobilier was also a member of the House of Representative's Select Committee on the Pacific Railroad, Huntington decided to steer clear of that group, even though it meant offending Cole. Instead, he took his problem to Senator Conness, whom Cole detested, and dumped the problem of drawing up the necessary amendment into Conness' lap.[23] That done, he went back to his endless chores, both for the railroad and for the hardware store.

The store was flourishing. Huntington purchased goods with greenbacks in the East; Hopkins sold for gold in the West, taking advantage of the exchange premiums. Nor was that all. When bargains appeared, Huntington snapped them up with Central Pacific money. All of it was repaid.[24] Still, the state of California and the city and county of San Francisco might well have looked askance at this use of the bonds which they had donated, after so much controversy, for railroad purposes alone.

Although Huntington later told Congress that the hardware store made no profits by dealing with the railroad, the statements will hardly bear scrutiny. For instance, there was the matter of many thousands of shovels. Originally he had bought them from the Ames Shovel Company, labeling them Charles Crocker & Co. both for safekeeping and for satisfying Crocker's vanity. Later he located a cheaper brand, the Colony, that seemed as good. He began substituting, selling Colonies to the railroad through the store, "so we could make some money on them," he wrote Hopkins, meantime drawing a sour satisfaction from doing an indirect injury to Ames, who "was being mean in Congress."

As for Crocker, if he objected to the sideline profiteering, let him. "It would be well," Collis wrote Mark, "to have Crocker understand that we you & I have something to say as to what should be used. if it had not bin for you & I my opinion is that the Central Pacific would hav gone to *Devil* before this."[25]

At times the hurly-burly of commerce palled and he grew homesick. "I would much like to go to California," he told Mark, and even wondered briefly about the possibility of their changing places for a year. Such moods were rare, however. When Mrs. Hopkins told Collis, during a visit to her old home in New York, that Stanford was boasting that the railroad's eastern business had reached such a volume that he, Stanford, would soon have to take personal charge of it, Huntington let out a snort of disgust. "I don't think thar will be much of a shower."[26] He could handle Congress and the financiers without that sort of help, thank you.

At one time or another all the Stanfords managed to annoy him. Charles, an older brother who had been in California but then had returned to New York, deprecated the Central Pacific to Richard Franchot, who was helping market the railroad's securities in the Schenectady area— and then, in April 1866, after the construction drive over Donner Summit was going full steam, had nerve enough to want to buy a piece of Charles Crocker & Company. "He is a *Bilk*," Collis railed to Hopkins, and the associates turned down the request.*

In California, meanwhile, Phil Stanford was agitating for a distribution of the securities that Charles Crocker & Company had already amassed. Hopkins and Huntington opposed the move. For one thing, the securities, if kept together, could be a tremendous backlog in the race that was shaping up with the Union Pacific. For another, Huntington did not trust Phil Stanford's judgment. If Phil got hold of so many securities at once, there was no telling what he might do: "build a wind mill of jigantic proportions . . ." Huntington sniffed to Hopkins, "or some other foolish thing that would not only put the securities out of the companies reach but very likely bring the company into bad odor before the public." There was, needless to say, no distribution. When Phil proved obstreperous, the others bought him out in an unrecorded transaction.[27]

A far graver worry was the shifting pace of the construction race. After two abnormally dry winters, torrential rains drenched the Sierra. Roads

---

* They also rejected Delos Emmons, who had married one of Elizabeth's sisters. Collis, ever addicted to nepotism, recommended that Emmons be allowed to buy into the construction company. The others refused.

became impassable to all except floundering strings of pack mules. A landslide wiped out a long section of grading; forward progress all but ceased.

The Union Pacific at this same time was picking up speed. Demobilization at the end of the war let the company flesh out its construction crews from top to bottom. Thousands of Irishmen picked up shovels and sledge hammers. General Grenville Dodge became chief engineer. Another general, John Casement, and his brother Dan took over the track laying. Though few people in the Midwest believed that the railroad would succeed in completing its first hundred miles of track within the time specified by Congress, these men met the requirements and then raced on west without pause, to cut off the Eastern Division before it could gain the 100th meridian, and, on the basis of that triumph, press on to an eventual junction with the Central Pacific.[28]

The Eastern Division, thoroughly reorganized by John Perry after Hallett's murder, proved a welcome ally to Huntington. It, too, wanted to amend the acts of 1862 and 1864 in such wise that it could push on to Denver before swinging north to join the main line of the Union Pacific in what is now southern Wyoming. So much track—more than six hundred miles—would make it a parallel line to the UP rather than a branch. This independence, together with the prospect of seizing the mining traffic of Colorado, would, Perry hoped, improve the sale of his securities to such an extent that he could outrace the UP, meet Huntington's road somewhere beyond the Rockies, and so become part of the main transcontinental system.

Provisions facilitating these plans were incorporated into the bill Senator Conness was helping prepare for the benefit of the Central Pacific. Unexpected benefits to Huntington arose from this amalgamation. For when debates were held on the various amendments on June 18 and 19, 1866, the senators, like many a reader since then, became confused trying to distinguish between the Union Pacific *branch* line from Omaha to the 100th meridian, the Union Pacific *main* line from the 100th meridian on west, and the Union Pacific, Eastern Division, which had no corporate connection whatsoever with the other two. Eventually the Senate let the Eastern Division go to Denver and gave it generous land grants along the way, but refused—probably through the machinations of the Union Pacific—to extend it bond loans in addition to those already authorized from Kansas City westward to the 100th meridian.

These points absorbed so much time and confusion that no one noticed when Conness stood up at his desk and told a flat and flagrant lie. The 150-mile limit on the Central Pacific, he said, had not appeared

173

in the original version of the act of 1864. "It was stolen in through the corruption of some parties [he probably meant Durant, as most of the senators realized] and the clerk who eventually made the report. . . . What I say cannot be contradicted." Actually, the statement could easily have been contradicted by anyone who bothered to turn back the pages of the *Congressional Globe*. None did. The discussion slid away into more wrangling about the various Union Pacifics, and Conness was not challenged.

The Union Pacific did object to the relaxation of the 150-mile limit, but ineptly, through a letter written by John Adams Dix, the road's respected figurehead president, to a friendly senator. The Union Pacific, Dix said, hoped to obtain financing in Europe by mortgaging its entire line as far as the meeting place in central Nevada. Any shift of that junction point would jeopardize the negotiations. On hearing this statement read aloud, Huntington's good friend, Santa Claus-bearded William Morris Stewart of Nevada reared up and roared out that the UP had no right to issue bonds for more than a hundred miles in advance of its railhead. This was not exactly what Dix had been talking about, but no one seemed to notice that point, either. The senators were still trying to sort out the various Union Pacifics.[29]

The amendment to end the 150-mile limit passed, along with those favoring the Eastern Division. Utterly outraged, Senator John B. Alley of Massachusetts, a boon companion of the Ames brothers and a holder of Crédit Mobilier stock, accused Huntington of using bribery to win the victory. Pinning him with those chill gray-blue eyes, Collis retorted that he had taken money along to use if necessary, but after sitting in the gallery and studying every face in the Senate with a spyglass, he had decided that there was only one man there corrupt enough to sell his vote—"and you know devilish well I didn't try it on *you!*"[30]

The House concurred in the bill and on July 3 President Johnson signed it. On July 27 he signed other bills bestowing generous land grants (but no bond loans) on the Atlantic & Pacific, the Southern Pacific, and the California & Oregon.* The central route was now wide open to competition. At the moment, however, Huntington's concern was dead ahead, with Durant.

---

* One of the chief supporters of these roads, all of them potentially hostile to the Central Pacific, was Congressman Cornelius Cole, a purported friend of Stanford and his associates. The reason is not hard to find. Cole was a sub rosa stockholder in the California & Oregon.[31] Presumably he received the stock in exchange for his help in the House of Representatives. Presumably, too, Huntington was unaware of this conflict of interest. At least none of his letters mentions it.

He signaled his intentions by adroitly buying, under Durant's very nose, at bargain prices, several thousand tons of rail. Next, in a single wily maneuver, he rounded up twenty-three ships for transporting the iron around the Horn.[32] He could hardly have been clearer if he had sent Durant a telegram: *Look out! Here we come!*

The crowing continued in the West. On July 4, one day after President Johnson signed the amendment, Crocker's tracklayers reached Dutch Flat. Shortly thereafter his drillers holed through the first and lowest tunnel. As a triumphant retort to all San Franciscans who had accused the railroad of being the great Dutch Flat swindle, Stanford staged a mammoth excursion and picnic at a point two miles beyond Dutch Flat. Only the guests relaxed, however. The Chinese kept chipping at the granite roadbed; sawmills whined over pungent-smelling ties. Foot by foot Crocker's teamsters dragged a huge hoisting engine up the Dutch Flat wagon road to the site of the summit tunnel and began sinking a shaft so that drillers could attack the bore not only from both ends but from the middle as well.

Durant retorted to Stanford's excursion with a spectacle of his own. Contrary to all expectations, his tracklayers had reached the 100th meridian, 247 miles west of Omaha, in October, well ahead of the Eastern Division. To signalize the event he gathered together two hundred guests—Congressmen, generals, editors, financiers, and their ladies—loaded them into nine cars, and chuffed them up the Platte Valley to tracks' end. Bands played, Pawnee Indians danced, buffalo steaks sizzled. For added excitement the entrepreneurs even staged a raging prairie fire.

Let Huntington—and the country—take note: 247 miles in 182 working days. The Central Pacific had spent four years reaching Cisco, ninety-two miles from Sacramento. They were, to be sure, remarkable miles; Cisco stood in shaggy mountains nearly six thousand feet above sea level. But the hardest part, and the longest tunnels, still lay ahead, in the final thousand-foot, granitic climb to the divide. And exceptionally heavy snows were already beginning to sift down through the evergreens with dismaying frequency.

As awareness of these facts spread, it began to look to people who knew railroading as though Huntington, the plunger, had gained no real advantage from challenging the UP's 150-mile limit. Congress might break legal barriers for him. But there was nothing that Congress or any other human agency could do to hold back the dread winters of the High Sierra.

13   The Tentacles Begin to Grow

On February 14, 1867, Andrew Johnson's new (September 1866) Secretary of the Interior, Orville Hickman Browning, made a singularly naïve remark. Why not, he suggested, let the Union Pacific and Central Pacific railroads meet at a point precisely 78.295 miles east of Salt Lake City?[1] This would allow each company to draw equal sums in government bonds.

Browning could hardly have taken himself seriously. Before his appointment to the Cabinet he had been a Republican senator from Illinois and after that a lobbyist in partnership with Thomas Ewing, Jr., Judah's friend and one of the original promoters of the old Leavenworth, Pawnee & Western Railroad. As lobbyists, he and Ewing had made a nice living by trading "on their influence with the leaders of the Republican party in securing special favors for contractors."[2] After such a background, Browning must have been aware that the builders of the transcontinental were not interested in sharing profits but in dominating them.

Miles alone meant rich returns from construction contracts. For Thomas Durant, who had once tried to stop the Central Pacific at the California border, that was reason enough for absorbing more ground than his rivals. It was not enough for Huntington, however. He was intrigued by the contingent benefits that would flow from a meeting well to the east of Salt Lake City—as far east, if possible, as Green River in present-day Wyoming.

For one thing, there was coal. So far as Huntington knew, no coal existed in California. What was used on the Coast came by ship around Cape Horn, a dreadful expense for a railroad. Yet the alternative—using the wood of the Sierra Nevada mountains for hauling trains across the deserts of Nevada and Utah—might prove even more costly. Meanwhile, in the Wasatch Mountains east of Salt Lake City, there was an area denoted on the maps of the time as "The Great Coal Basin." There the Central Pacific could not only fuel its locomotives, but could also mine more trainloads for sale in California.

This was only a beginning. In December 1866, the government-subsidized San Francisco, China, and Japan Mail Steamship Line inaugurated service across the Pacific. In San Francisco, Leland Stanford was called on to signalize the event with one of his sonorous after-dinner speeches. The Golden Gate, he declared to his audience on December 31, could now gather unto itself "the commerce of a people more numerous than the people of all Europe and America. . . . As an auxiliary to that end, the Pacific Railroad will . . . perform the chief part." Whereupon he forgot the steamship line and launched into a eulogy of the railroad. "The financial problem has been solved. . . . The physical one is in a fair way for solution." And he added with a blythe confidence that would soon return to haunt him, "The provision made to encounter snow is amply sufficient." Ah, the glory of it: "Mr. Chairman, behold the result! . . . California will then commence a career of prosperity hitherto unexampled; and here on the Bay of San Francisco will be . . . one of the great cities of the world."[3]

The speech was not candid. The ex-governor's euphoric listeners, somnolently digesting their banquet, supposed that he was talking about San Francisco, and he knew that they so supposed. Actually, the board of the Central Pacific had no such thing in mind. What's more, Stanford seems to have been vindictive about the matter.[4] Throughout the Central Pacific's career, the leading citizens of San Francisco had been unfriendly toward the Sacramento-based railroad. Very well. They'd learn, to their own deep pain, that it was not in the geographic logic of things for their smug city to be the entrepôt for oriental goods bound eastward.

Until then, San Francisco had been lucky. Ever since the beginning of the gold rush, various promoters had sought to establish ports on the northeastern or eastern shores of the great bay, nearer to the interior. For one reason or another all had failed. As a result, San Francisco, logical or not, had maintained her dominance.

Within a decade the pattern had become so frozen in Bay area thinking that the Pacific Railroad Convention of 1859 had automatically assumed that the transcontinental would of course come to the city's doors on tracks laid around the southern tip of the elongated bay. The federal enabling act of 1862 had assumed the same route. But when subsidized steamships at last started plying the Pacific, the directors of the CP began

177

to stir. Why send east-bound Asiatic goods clear around the Bay by rail when the very ships that brought them from the Orient could go straight across the inland sea in a fraction of the time?

Out came the maps. Two possibilities presented themselves. The Central Pacific could bridge the Sacramento River opposite the city of Sacramento and then drive southwestward to Carquinez Strait, the narrow mouth through which the Sacramento River flows into the northern part of the Bay. There, either at moribund Benicia or Vallejo, the associates could build a deep-water port for receiving ocean traffic.

Another possibility was for the railroad to push due south from Sacramento to the San Joaquin River in the vicinity of Antioch. After bridging the river there, it could veer off through Walnut Creek to the then-drab, marsh-bordered shantytown of Oakland. Out in the narrow waist of the Bay, halfway between Oakland and San Francisco was a three-hundred-acre island that now serves as a pier of the Bay Bridge. The first Spanish-speaking inhabitants of the region had named the spot Yerba Buena. The less melodious Americans called it Goat Island. Its western site bordered water deep enough so that ocean-going ships could berth there. On the Oakland side, by contrast, the water was shoal. After examining the bottom and finding it solid, engineers of the Central Pacific reported that a causeway capable of carrying loaded trains was economically and financially feasible. Why not make Goat Island the port?

Both routes presented drawbacks. The California Pacific, last of several railroads to try to build from the northern shore of Carquinez Strait to Sacramento, held a franchise through the area west of the Sacramento River. Incorporated in 1865, it had finally raised money enough to start grading out of Vallejo in December 1866. Conceivably it would sell its franchise, but the price might be high. Not all of the coincidences in Collis Huntington's life were fortunate. One of the early directors of the California Pacific was A. D. Starr, with whom Huntington had had a rousing fight in the mephitic hold of the *Humboldt* during the brig's tedious journey from Panama to San Francisco in '49. Starr might be glad to fight again if he thought he saw a way to put a painful hammer lock on the vaulting ambitions of the Central Pacific.

The hurdle in the way of the other route was the United States Government. It held Goat Island as a military reserve. Several squatters, some of whom asserted rights stemming from the days of Mexican sovereignty, also claimed ownership to parts of the island. So far, the government had made no move either to build installations of its own or to dispossess the squatters.

In view of the neglect, Huntington, who had proved his adroitness at prying what he wanted out of Congress, felt he could win a grant to the island without undue trouble. This would be far cheaper than buying the California Pacific, but would take time. The necessary bills would have to be prepared, steered through the appropriate committees, and presented to both houses of Congress at the proper time. Still, the prize ought to be safely in the bag by the end of the year. The east-bound traffic of the Orient could then be steered to the Central Pacific's docking facilities on Goat Island without touching San Francisco. West-bound traffic would feed from the island into San Francisco over the Central Pacific's own ferry system. Adjacent Oakland would become the great city Stanford had forecast to the banqueters. As a corollary, arrogant San Francisco would dwindle, as Stanford foresaw matters, to a docile appendage.

As a first step in the program, the Central Pacific on March 21, 1867, filed with California's secretary of state the plat of a route running from Sacramento through Antioch to Goat Island. The directors then held their breaths, waiting for protests. There were none. Surprised and relieved, E. B. Crocker wrote to Hopkins from San Francisco on March 29 and again on April 1, that "our Goat Island movement seems to please the people generally."[5] The powers of self-deception, it would seem, are almost limitless. But more of that later on.

Building a port on Goat Island would be costly. To justify the expense, the Central Pacific would want a lion's share of the freight rates charged for forwarding the traffic that landed there. This involved controlling as much trackage as the Union Pacific did. From that consideration rose still another motive for reaching Green River ahead of the westward pushing Union Pacific.

And, finally, there had to be some way of blocking an end run by the UP. That railroad might slant off along the old Oregon Trail to Portland and then try to lure oriental commerce in through the mouth of the Columbia River. From Portland, the UP could forward eastern freight to San Francisco either by coastal steamer or by a rail line thrusting south through the Willamette and Sacramento valleys.

By reaching Green River ahead of the Union Pacific, the CP could close the Oregon Trail and then claim for itself the right to build to Portland by whatever route . . . if any . . . seemed most expedient.

Those were the prizes. And yet in February 1867, right while the strategy was taking shape, Orville Browning had supposed—or had pretended to suppose—that nothing more was involved than equal loans of government bonds.[6]

Early in the spring, the Central Pacific ordered its surveyors to push eastward across Utah, searching both north and south of Great Salt Lake for the best route. It was an exercise in supreme optimism. Back in the Sierra, snow was piling to unprecedented depths.

Wisdom dictated that work be suspended. But storms were roaring across the plains, too, and the Union Pacific was not quitting. The associates drove ahead, even though their engineers warned that costs would leap at least 50 per cent. They underestimated. The worst of those winter miles drained $245,600 each from the company's treasury.[7]

For a while Charlie Crocker's straw bosses attacked each new fall of snow with hordes of Chinese shovelers, trying to clear a way so that graders could keep on leveling the roadbeds and building up the retaining walls. It was no use. There were forty-four storms that winter, and several nights when the thermometer dropped to twenty below zero. Finally the only place where men could work was inside the tunnels, chipping away at granite so hard that it bent the steel of their drills. In order to haul away the debris left by each blast, the ever-patient Chinese had to dig out rabbit warrens of passageways underneath the drifts. Amazingly they stayed at it even after a series of avalanches had flattened some of their camps. Twenty died in a single snowslide. Small wonder that Huntington declared after the winter was over that "it would be all the better for us and the State if there should be a half a million [Chinese] come over in 1868"[8]—a sentiment to which few other Californians of the time would have subscribed.

Bringing up supplies was an ordeal. Stanford, who on December 31 had declared that snow was no problem, watched five locomotives linked in tandem struggle in vain to push a plow through the blockading drifts. Thereupon he called a strategy huddle with Charles Crocker and Arthur Brown, the engineer in charge of the railroad's timber work.[9] The entire mountain crossing, they decided, would have to be covered. Pilot sheds of heavy timber built at the worst places—a total of five miles of them—were scheduled for the ensuing summer of 1867. As soon as the best design for withstanding the shock of avalanches was determined, the rest of the line across the divide—thirty-seven twisting miles—would be roofed. That, too, would be costly.

The thousands of graders left idle by snow were moved down the Truckee River toward Nevada. (All told, 13,500 laborers were kept at work that winter; the payroll averaged about $450,000 a month.) There, in lighter drifts, they went to work again. Iron for forty miles of track was sledded to them across the summit. Three locomotives and forty cars were taken apart, loaded first on sleds and then on mud wagons, moved twenty-eight miles, and reassembled into work trains. Gaunt teams of mules and oxen, hauling food for the men and hay for themselves, floundered along behind.

It was a prodigious effort—and it did not produce the kind of progress that yielded very many government bonds. During 1867 the Central Pacific completed a meager twenty-one miles of track. (Green River, here we come!) Those twenty-one miles entitled the company to a million dollars, face value, in government bonds and the right to issue another million of their own first-mortgage bonds—enough, altogether, to build about nine high-Sierra miles.

It was Huntington's job to make up the difference. He still had a satchelful of the company bonds that the law of 1864 let him draw in advance of construction. They had little appeal, however, among banks and investment houses, for they represented unlaid track out in Nevada, and the fierce winter had reconvinced many people that the road would never reach that far. Even the house of Fisk and Hatch, which had agreed to market the company paper issued on rail lying within California, declined to handle that outside the state.[10]

Collis took to knocking on doors himself. As an ally he recruited his old Otsego County friend, Richard Franchot, one-time president of a railroad between Albany and Schenectady and later a Congressman. Franchot helped teach Huntington what Jay Cooke had learned while marketing government securities during the Civil War: not all the money was in the banks. Ordinary people could be persuaded to put their savings to work in investments that seemed sound. Franchot began contacting prospects in upper New York State, where he was well known; Huntington followed suit in New York City and Boston. Sometimes they offered Central Pacific stock as a bonus to tempt purchasers. The move was ill judged, as a later chapter will indicate. But for the time being it helped, and they were able to dispose of two or three bonds here, four or five there.[11]

Hoping to broaden the market, the company turned simultaneously toward Western Europe. Now that the American Civil War had ended, foreign capital was again looking for profit possibilities in frontier mines, irrigation projects, and railroads. Stanford was useful here. In order to obtain recommendations that would lend a convincing sheen to CP offerings, he worked diligently among California's leading financiers—D. O. Mills, W. C. Ralston, T. Parrott, and, in particular, ex-Senator Milton Latham, manager of the London and San Francisco Bank. In

181

April he took Latham and a party of eight "ladies and gentlemen" to tracks' end at Cisco and then on a sleigh ride over the summit to Donner Lake. They were delighted. "Have a bully letter from Latham," Stanford reported triumphantly.[12]

Letters were not enough, however. Satisfactory outlets in Europe were not established until Huntington completed arrangements, through Fisk and Hatch, with Philip Speyer & Company, American representative of L. Speyer-Ellisen & Co. of Frankfurt, Germany. Meanwhile the money demands of the Sierra push were too voracious to be fed by small-lot bond sales, even fortified by the road's earnings. (The CP's local trains netted $663,000 in 1866 and a thumping $1,140,000 in 1867.) Stanford, whose gold mine on Shutter Creek had developed into a better-than-average producer, was able to raise, on the security of the mine, hundreds of thousands of dollars in California. Huntington borrowed millions in the East.[13] When he could, he used the county securities he still held in the company till as collateral. When government bonds were selling slowly, he borrowed on them. When he had to, he pledged his own and his associates' personal credit, and that of the Huntington & Hopkins hardware store. He had an instinct for bargains in money. Whenever he sensed that interest rates were about to rise (they were much more volatile in those days than now), he borrowed heavily at the lower rates and loaned out the money himself until the railroad's creditor's began dunning him.[14] It was a dazzling performance—but risky. As Stanford recalled the situation years later, "We passed the mountains in pretty nearly crippled condition."[15]

Green River indeed!

Finding money was only part of the pressure. Shiploads of supplies had to be kept moving around Cape Horn to both the railroad and the expanding hardware store. Political trips to Washington were frequent. For weeks at a stretch, Elizabeth scarcely saw her husband.

Hopkins, whose duty it was to inventory the railroad materials as they arrived, forward them to Crocker, keep the involved accounts, and on the side run the hardware company, had suggested as early as 1866 that they find relief by selling the store to their clerks. Huntington hesitated for more than a year. Finally, on March 29, 1867, after reaching Green River had become an obsession, he consented. He could not bring himself to face the actual details of cutting loose, however. In his all but indecipherable handwriting—Collis once drawled that he prided himself on being able to write a letter in half the time the recipient could read it—he dumped the arrangements into Hopkins' lap.

"I do not think I could sell all my interests their and walk out of the old store without droping a tear on the threshold for the old place is some how dear to me with all my losses their by fire and flood." By the end of November details were complete. The two founders each retained a tenth interest in the firm. The new company, which battened on increasing amounts of railroad business, kept the original name and became Huntington, Hopkins & Company.[16]

Until the spring of 1867 Huntington, unaided, had conducted millions of dollars' worth of railroad and hardware business out of a single small room at 54 William Street. The arrangement was exasperating at times. "Their is allmost allways some one in talking to me," he wrote Mark, "and you know how difficult it is for me to write when I am disturbed by persons talking . . ." In May he added another room and a book-keeper. By year's end there was a clerk—but he still scribbled off a large part of his voluminous correspondence with his own hand.[17]

His orientation was entirely in the East now. His mother and sisters, the girls married now, lived in various parts of rural New York, mostly around Oneonta, and in Connecticut, where Elizabeth's relatives also resided. Tiring of the Metropolitan Hotel after nearly four years there, he yielded to Elizabeth and let her start shopping for a home. She looked carefully, not finding what she wanted—a comfortable residence at 65 Park Avenue—until September. What the property cost is uncertain. Huntington paid for it with $50,000 worth (face value) of the Central Pacific stock being held in trust for him by the railroad's construction firm, Charles Crocker & Company.[18] Crocker at that time was accepting the stock as worth only thirty cents on the dollar.

Back in California, Stanford and E. B. Crocker had become enthralled with the idea of buying the Western Pacific, to which the Central Pacific had assigned its Sacramento–San Francisco rights in the vain hope of allaying the hostility of the Bay City's financiers.* It was not an enthusiasm shared by the other associates; they preferred to strengthen themselves in the north. The disputes that resulted led, circuitously enough at times, to a calculated policy of trying to monopolize the railroad traffic not just of California but of the entire Pacific Coast. Since many of the records have been lost, or perhaps destroyed, the

* Actually, as noted earlier, the Western Pacific was projected to run from Sacramento only to San Jose at the southeastern tip of the Bay. The link from San Jose north was the San Francisco & San José Railroad Co. Originally, control of both roads had rested in the same hands and so it has been convenient to speak of them as a single line. That situation ended in 1867, as will become evident.

course of events is not fully clear. One thing is apparent, however. Considerable skulduggery was involved on every side.

Shakiest of the lines in northern California was the all but nonexistent California & Oregon, brainchild (as noted earlier) of surveyor Simon G. Elliott, whose chief resources seem to have been a glib command of railroad lingo, a convincing exterior, and unlimited gall. After mapping out a route to Oregon and forming a company with San Francisco's respected C. Temple Emmet as its figurehead president, Elliott had gone to Washington in quest of aid. There, with the help of Cornelius Cole (in return for which Cole received a sheaf of California & Oregon stock), he had obtained the promise of a land grant from Congress. He would rather have had a loan of government bonds.

Like all congressional land grants, the conveyance of this one was contingent on Elliott's building a specified amount of track within a specified time. At this point the air ran out of the promoter's balloon. Realizing that Elliott could not produce as much as he had promised, Emmet's San Franciscans dumped him. Unabashed, Elliott hustled off to Oregon and tried to revitalize the scheme from that end—but the Oregon adventure is another story.[19]

During Elliott's struggle with Emmet, the California & Oregon somehow incurred obligations to the Central Pacific. As security the Central Pacific took a mortgage on the land grant. The amounts involved probably were modest; the grant was contingent, not actual. But it gave the CP a handhold on the vise, and although Emmet would squirm at times in the future, he never managed to get loose.[20]

According to the road's enabling legislation, the California & Oregon was to begin its construction at an unspecified point on the CP east of Sacramento and run north. Success would make it a rival of the system that Sam Brannan had tried to form out of the California Central-Yuba Railroad, and the California Northern. The California Central and Yuba roads, it will be recalled, ran from Roseville to within seven miles of Marysville. The California Northern ran from Marysville up the Feather River to Oroville. In spite of the short gap between the roads they had worked in harmony and had looked forward to an eventual junction. It did not happen, however. Brannan's amorous, alcoholic, and speculative excesses finally caught up with him. His California-wide empire began crumbling. His creditors closed in.

Scenting opportunity, Colonel C. L. Wilson, founder of the California Central in 1853, discoverer of Theodore Judah, and (until the Robinson brothers ousted him) the railroad's first president, endeavored to regain control. In the process he became involved in an injudicious legal battle with the Central Pacific. The CP won a stiff monetary judgment against him, and Wilson began thrashing wildly for an escape. One spasm led him to the Union Pacific. Would that road finance him and the California Northern in building across Beckwourth Pass to a junction with the UP in north-central Nevada?

Huntington, headed in his own mind for the Green River, was not worried by this outdated attack. "It takes a cool brain," he wrote E. B. Crocker, "and a heap of cash to work up such a programme, and Wilson has neither." Still, the man was an annoyance. He leaked the story of what he was trying to do to Nevada newspapers. Gleefully they broadcast the possibility that the CP might be circumvented by the new system. When the rumors were reprinted in the East, the price of CP bonds shivered and Huntington wrote truculently to Hopkins to "keep them [the Nevada newspapers] in oure interest by giving them a small advertisement. . . . I do not suppose you can keep all the Damned Bohemias quiate but I wish you would come as near it as you can."[21]

Far more worrisome was the possibility that Wilson might somehow pull the California Central, the Yuba, and the California Northern together (the owners of the California Northern were offering it for sale to the highest bidder), and, in conjunction with the California & Oregon, strike for Portland and a junction there with the Union Pacific. Huntington, of course, did not intend to let the UP reach Oregon. But if his drive to Green River failed, command of a Sacramento–Portland road, which would also do considerable local business, might prove to be a valuable second line of defense. During the early months of 1867, accordingly, he kept urging on his associates the wisdom of rounding out their control of the California & Oregon, the California Central, the Yuba, and the California Northern.

Charles Crocker and Hopkins agreed. Ed Crocker and Stanford did not. They wanted to sell their judgment against Wilson and their mortgage on the California & Oregon land grant to whatever "party of the right sort will work in harmony with us," and then concentrate their resources on acquiring the Western Pacific.[22]

The Western Pacific had also fallen victim to inner squabbles. It had laid about twenty miles of track from San Jose north to what was then called Vallejo's Mill and is now the town of Niles. From Niles it had started grading east and northeast toward Stockton. At Stockton it would bridge the San Joaquin River and then head due north again for Sacramento.

Progress had been halted by a falling-out between the two chief officers, Alexander Houston and Charles McLaughlin. Houston won judgment against McLaughlin and withdrew from the company. Having sole command of the road was no gain to the latter, however. Broke, he could not pay his subcontractors and was ready to sell to the first bidder who offered enough to let him escape with a whole skin.

Stanford and E. B. Crocker somehow got the idea that San Francisco interests meant to buy the line, hook it up with the California Northern and Wilson's California Central (in his desperation Wilson was promoting that plan, too), and thus bring the traffic of northern California into San Francisco by going clear around the southern tip of the Bay.

Such a plan ignored the California Pacific, the new road mentioned earlier as building north from Vallejo (the town, not the mill) beside Carquinez Strait. The California Pacific's first goal was the hamlet of Davis. At Davis, the tracks would fork. One branch would go east, bridge the Sacramento River at Sacramento, and, if the builders so desired, continue northeast to meet the California Central at Lincoln. The other fork would thrust from Davis north to Marysville. A trip from either Marysville or Sacramento to San Francisco via this new road (the last twenty-two miles on a ferryboat from Vallejo) would be half as long as one by way of the Western Pacific. Moreover, the California Pacific's route was dead level; the WP's was hilly.

In spite of the California Pacific's marked geographic advantages, Stanford and E. B. Crocker did not think that its officers could raise enough money to finish the construction. Turning their backs on it—foolishly, as events turned out—they concentrated on obtaining the Western Pacific. It was essential to the CP, they said. The WP, along with the San Francisco & San José was, E. B. Crocker wrote, "the butt end of all railroads coming directly into San Francisco." By controlling the butt end they could exact tribute from any line that might try approaching from the south, through either the San Joaquin Valley or the coastal counties.

There was also the matter of Oakland, destined in Stanford's mind to become the great entrepôt of the Pacific Coast as soon as the CP had built its terminal facilities on Goat Island. Ramshackle Oakland was, at that time, the domain of Horace W. Carpentier, notorious land speculator and a leading figure in the development of the state's early telegraph lines. Carpentier held title to all of Oakland's waterfront. He also had an exclusive franchise to construct all warehouses, piers, and docks within the town limits.[23]

The incorporation of the Western Pacific in 1862 had created high excitement in Oakland and in neighboring Alameda to the south. Led by an eloquent, nimble, and contentious San Francisco lawyer, Alfred A. Cohen, promoters financed a ferry pier on Carpentier's Oakland land and started pushing a short-line railroad from the landing eastward through the town, aiming for a junction with the Western Pacific.

South of Oakland, across an unmanageable slough, was the marshy town of Alameda. To keep Alameda from being developed by a rival, Cohen and his cohorts built a ferry landing there, too, and started another railroad toward the Western Pacific. The idea was for the Oakland and Alameda short-lines to meet a few miles out in the country and then continue as a single trunk to a junction with the Western Pacific at Niles.[24] Being a mere defensive screen, the Alameda branch would be little used. Traffic would be manipulated so as to flow from freighters in the Bay through Oakland to the Western Pacific and thence to the Central Pacific at Sacramento, all to the great benefit of Horace W. Carpentier's long stretch of Oakland waterfront real estate.

The dream collapsed. Neither Cohen nor Carpentier could raise enough money to complete either short-line railroad. Work sagged to a halt before they had even achieved a junction. In hope of salvaging his tideland property, Carpentier offered part of it to McLaughlin if the latter would finish the project. McLaughlin, however, lacked funds for buying out Cohen's group. Next, Carpentier turned desperately to Stanford. Would the Central Pacific finish the short lines in exchange for a part of his mud flats?

At that point the associates were still content with Sacramento as a terminus, and Stanford brushed the proposal aside. But then the Goat Island plan took shape. Oakland began to glitter, in Stanford's mind, as the shining city of the West. He decided that perhaps the Central Pacific had better reconsider and build the short lines as a means of laying hold of some of that strategic waterfront real estate. Rather condescendingly he sought out Carpentier—and was amazed to find the Oakland promoter completely indifferent. Carpentier would not even bother to go talk to Cohen about the still incompleted lines.

Stung by the chilly reception, Stanford seems not to have tried to discover the reason for Carpentier's change of attitude. After all, so Stanford thought, the Western Pacific was the key to the situation. As soon as the associates controlled it, they would have a noose around Oakland, and could dictate terms to both Carpentier and the Cohen group. In his mind, this reasoning added still more luster to his proposal that the associates buy the Western Pacific.

Huntington, Hopkins, and Charles Crocker remained unimpressed. They felt that the first order of business was to gain control in the north

187

and then run a line, often discussed, from Sacramento through Antioch to Goat Island. That route offered a much shorter approach to San Francisco Bay, and to San Francisco, too, than did the Western Pacific's roundabout loop through San Jose. The longer line could not compete with them, and so why waste good money buying the franchise and building it, even for the sake of its government bonds? Carpentier would come around, once Goat Island loomed as a threat to his holdings.

For weeks the four associates who were in California argued and argued—and got nowhere. "I would give a good deal if Huntington could only be here for a few days to consult," E. B. Crocker wrote in a quandary to Hopkins on April 6, 1867.[25] Huntington not only wasn't there but, having spoken his mind, declined to reply to the telegrams and letters the others poured out to him.

Made stubborn by his strange silence, Stanford and E. B. Crocker went ahead on their own, drawing up what seemed to them a highly advantageous contract for the purchase of the Western Pacific. Since both of them were lawyers, they did not summon professional assistance. McLaughlin was represented by William B. Carr, later to become, with railroad help, one of the giant land barons of the San Joaquin Valley. Suavely Carr informed the prospective purchasers that the San Francisco & San José line had disassociated itself from the WP and was not part of the bargain. In their eagerness, Stanford and Ed Crocker accepted the omission, even though it meant that they would not then be able to control the butt end of all lines approaching San Francisco.

Their failure to investigate McLaughlin's reasons for withholding the SF&SJ would, in the light of coming events, prove to be as egregious a piece of carelessness as Stanford's failure to inquire into Carpentier's sudden aloofness concerning his Oakland tidelands.

Terms were quickly agreed on. Little cash was involved. The Central Pacific took over the Western Pacific's franchise and with it the right to collect government bonds for the construction—an opportunity, in other words, for further stock engrossment. It also acquired rolling stock and twenty miles of iron, worth an estimated fifty thousand dollars. In return the Central Pacific reassigned to McLaughlin the land grant that went with the franchise. It was of uncertain value. Much of it was in conflict with earlier Mexican grants covering the same area, but if McLaughlin worked fast he might be able to sell off a tidy part of the property before protests began. The purchasers could then fight out the problem of titles with the United States Government, which had presumed to own clear title at the time of making the grant.

Proudly the bargainers showed the papers to Charles Crocker and

Mark Hopkins. Those two refused to approve unless Huntington agreed. Huntington, however, still did not answer the telegrams they sent.[26] Ed Crocker and Stanford all but jigged in an anguish of frustration. Such obstructionism after everything had been prepared, Ed Crocker wailed to Hopkins, "makes the biggest kind of fools of the Gov. & I." Stanford grew so outraged that he finally vowed to carry out the trade on his own.[27]

The threat may be what broke the impasse, for the associates made a careful point of presenting a front of unchipped unity to outside view. In any event, Huntington acquiesced, and on June 8, 1867, the Central Pacific took back the line it had so willingly shed a few years earlier. Ever afterwards the Western Pacific was called "The Governor's Road."[28] One suspects that Huntington, whose opinion of Stanford's acumen had dropped another notch, intoned the phrase derisively. Stanford, though, was always proud of it.

14 Overconfidence

Engrossed in the debate over the Western Pacific, the directors of the Central Pacific let themselves be caught napping. A group of capitalists long hostile to them formed what they called, with joyful mockery, the Terminal Central Pacific Railroad Company.* Its franchise covered a line from Vallejo, where it would connect with the California Pacific, south to Goat Island. In addition to this franchise, the directors of the new line also acquired, by special act of the state legislature, title to 150 acres of submerged land bordering Goat Island—land the Central Pacific must have for reaching its projected new terminal facilities.[1]

So! Now what was the terminal of the great Central Pacific?

The Terminal Central Pacific Railroad was a midget so far as miles went—only thirty-two from Vallejo to Goat Island. Since Vallejo could be turned into a good port, there seemed no reason for extending the new line to Goat Island—unless it was a bald attempt to checkmate the Central Pacific and thus force it to keep its terminus at Sacramento. If the move succeeded, the California Pacific would control a gigantic flow of commerce. It would pick up transcontinental traffic from the Central Pacific with its branch from Davis to Sacramento. Its northern branch from Davis to Marysville would provide an outlet for the California & Oregon—and in so doing would encourage all the northern

---

* Among its board members were E. P. Flint and his father J. P. Flint, for whom Huntington had had no use since his first bond-selling troubles in Boston. The Flints, still bondholders in the California Central, were aiding Wilson in his efforts to break that road free of the CP vise. Another Terminal director was Alpheus Bull of the California & Oregon, who wanted to shake the C&O loose from the same grip. Still another was J. Mora Moss, once heavily interested in the Sacramento Valley Railroad; with the Robinson brothers, Moss had fought the CP for as long as the majority of bondholders allowed and was still bitter about the road's surrender.

190

roads to stay independent of the CP. Then, having absorbed the freight, the California Pacific would carry it to Vallejo. That town, not Goat Island, would become the Bay area's great port and the receiver of traffic from the Orient. The Western Pacific, as a corollary, would be rendered next to useless.

As the shocked directors of the Central Pacific burrowed deeper into the situation, they detected a new spoor. It led eventually to one of the canniest manipulators in San Francisco, Lloyd Tevis. Tevis, a one-time barrister, had made a fortune speculating in mines, real estate, telegraph lines, shipping firms, even ice companies. Now, apparently, he had scented new opportunities. But what, exactly?

So far as the associates could discover, Tevis had no monetary interest in the California Pacific or in Vallejo or in any of the struggling northern roads. Why, then, did his shadow keep appearing behind the new Terminal Central Pacific, whose chief value lay in helping the other lines block the giant Central Pacific? Certainly he was not prompted by altruism. For, as Huntington wrote E. B. Crocker, "Lloyd Tevis was never known to work for anyone but Lloyd Tevis."[2]

In due time a devious ploy emerged. Tevis and certain colleagues in San Francisco had taken over the Southern Pacific Railroad. This unbuilt line had been incorporated in 1865 and had won a land grant from Congress in 1866. The original design of the SP had been to build south through the coastal counties to San Diego and then east to the California border. There it would meet the Atlantic & Pacific, also a recipient of an 1866 congressional land grant, and form with it a new transcontinental.

The founders of the Southern Pacific, who were required to build fifty miles of track within two years or forfeit the grant, proved unable to sell enough bonds to finance the work. They called on Tevis for help. At once he launched a new program.

Senator Conness, who was obligated to Tevis, prepared a bill relaxing time limits for construction. If it emerged from committee and was passed, the SP would be allowed two more years in which to build only thirty miles of track. At about the same time the railroad blandly sent to Secretary of the Interior Browning a map showing a route quite different from the one Congress had authorized in 1866. Under this new plan the Southern Pacific would swing away from the coastal route originally approved, drop inland into the San Joaquin Valley, and then head for the border without coming anywhere near San Diego or Los Angeles. The reason for the shift was plain. Old Spanish and Mexican land grants clouded titles throughout the coastal valleys. The Southern

Pacific, whose only aid was land, wanted to push out where titles were clear.

Speculating about Tevis' motives in all this was a frustrating exercise, for the man always operated obscurely. Still, on the face of things, certain answers seemed to explain his support of the obstreperous little Terminal Central Pacific. He was trying to boom the southern route as the nation's chief transcontinental. One step was to shut the CP out of Goat Island and thus reduce that road's effectiveness as a receiver of oriental traffic. Then, if the Southern Pacific developed a harbor of its own contiguous to San Francisco, it could pick up the commerce of Asia and hurry it eastward to a junction with the Atlantic & Pacific.* Meanwhile the formidable Sierra would serve as a second ally. Passengers and shippers of heavy freight from the East, apprehensive of drifts like the ones currently piling high on Donner Summit, would choose to use the new, snow-free southern tracks. Very conceivably, in short, Tevis might be envisioning the Southern Pacific as the western link of the nation's finest transcontinental.

In hindsight, several straws in the wind became significant. Among the members of the SP's new board of directors was William B. Carr. Carr had "helped" Stanford and E. B. Crocker work out the details of the purchase of the Western Pacific—minus the San Francisco & San José, which the SP would need to control in order to reach San Francisco. Why hadn't the Sacramentans wondered more about the omission? The San Francisco & San José was probably already in Tevis' hands—or soon would be.

Another new director of the Southern Pacific was Horace W. Carpentier, owner of Oakland's waterfront. Of course Carpentier had turned unfriendly. Tevis had made him believe that the Terminal Central Pacific would keep the Sacramentans out of Oakland. Tevis may even have promised that the Southern Pacific would run a branch up the San Joaquin Valley to a terminus on Carpentier's waterfront property. Why back a loser? Carpentier had decided to go onto the board of the Southern Pacific. So far as he was concerned, the CP would not get anywhere near the water.

Well, it was something to know what the opposition consisted of. There was no real community of interest between Tevis and the disgruntled incorporators of the Terminal Central Pacific. The San Francisco speculator was using the CP's enemies for his own ends. He would drop

* The Suez Canal was, at this point, well on the way to completion. Curiously, none of the California railroad builders paused to wonder what effect this might have on the flow of Asia's traffic.

them the minute it seemed useful to do so. And Huntington was without resources of his own, both in and out of Congress and in the state legislature. With sunny self-confidence he set about putting himself into so strong a bargaining position that even Lloyd Tevis would have to listen.

In the process he never forgot his main goal, Green River. The Central Pacific's surveyors were ordered to work on east of Salt Lake City, looking for a line through the Wasatch Mountains. (Like the surveyors scouting for the Union Pacific, they found that the most practical line by far would not touch Salt Lake City at all, but would by-pass it to the north, through Ogden.) Meantime, after nearly two years of effort, drillers finally holed through the summit tunnel in the Sierra Nevada.

The work was by no means done. The bore would not be widened enough for trains until November. And below it, near Donner Lake, yawned a rough seven-mile gap where no iron had yet been laid. In spite of those remaining obstacles, Huntington's spirits leaped. Now to push bond sales! He hired a publicity expert, Richard Colburn, to send glowing stories about the conquering of the mountains to newspapers throughout the nation. He had garish posters plastered to the walls of depots everywhere. As fast as he received E. H. Miller's audits about each month's profits on the operating part of the line, he had them printed in eastern newspapers, paying for the insertions when editors balked.[3]

He acted the part of confidence—gold-headed walking stick, dark cutaway coat, light trousers, his graying beard neatly cropped like General Grant's, his big, Olympian head held high, its growing bald spot covered by a pearl-gray topper, size seven and three quarters. "It is well understood here," he wrote Ed Crocker, "that the directors of the Central Pacific are rich and have put into the road from one-half to one and one-half million dollars each, and have taken most of their pay in stock"[4]—a falsehood that also appeared to explain what was happening to Central Pacific stock, very little of which was appearing on the market. Actually, of course, the stock was pouring into Charles Crocker & Company at the rate of thirty cents on the dollar. Later it would be divided among the five associates, who, except for C. Crocker, were also the directors of the Central Pacific.

Bond sales perked up. Fisk and Hatch agreed to handle the paper issued against the unbuilt line in Nevada. Inquiries began coming in from Europe, particularly Germany. To speed the interest, Huntington had

193

circulars prepared extolling California's wine-making potentials and sent them throughout the grape-growing areas of Germany and France.[5]

Let Tevis ponder all this!

The other directors were equally excited by the breakthrough in the tunnel. Stanford rushed across the mountains to further the development of a town, later named Reno, which the company planned to promote beside the Truckee River. Huntington was annoyed. Why Stanford? he asked Hopkins. "I look on that intrest as one of great magnitude and it seems to me Stanford has not one qualification nesessary to work it up."[6]

Even more engrossing to the California directorate, now that a profitable drive across Nevada at last loomed ahead, was the replacing of Charles Crocker & Company with a new construction firm modeled after Crédit Mobilier. Huntington objected. He liked the easy, informal arrangement that had surmounted the Sierra, but when the others outvoted him, he went along.[7] The result was the Contract & Finance Company. Formally incorporated on October 28, 1867, it was capitalized at five million dollars in hundred-dollar shares. Charles Crocker was elected president. The five associates—Stanford, Hopkins, Huntington, and the Crocker brothers—held ten thousand shares apiece.

Promptly Stanford, Huntington, Hopkins, and E. B. Crocker of the Central Pacific awarded to Charles Crocker, E. B. Crocker, Stanford, Huntington, and Hopkins of the Contract & Finance Company contracts for building eastward into Utah. Remuneration was set at $86,000 per mile, payable half in cash and first-mortgage bonds on the CP, and half in CP stock valued at thirty cents on the dollar.

In awarding themselves this contract, the associates figured that the work would actually cost about $47,000 per mile. The remaining $39,000 in stock would represent clear profit, if and when the stock became marketable. The developing race with Union Pacific kept prices from being normal, however. The cost of the road across Nevada and Utah leaped to slightly more than $64,000 per mile—and $64,000 was the maximum the CP could borrow for that section of track, $32,000 in government bonds and $32,000 in the company's own first-mortgage bonds.

By their figuring, the associates thus lost $17,000 a mile.[8] The only way to recoup was to make sure that when CP stock reached the market, it would sell for more than thirty dollars a share—a value which, in 1867, it did not have. As we shall see, awareness of this need would soon drive Huntington to involved, fierce, and often recklessly dishonest schemes in order to protect the value of the railroad.

All that was in the future, however. At the time of its formation, the Contract & Finance Company, like Charles Crocker & Company, was simply one more variant of a time-tested device for making money by paying yourself more for doing a piece of work than you would pay an outsider. The matter became questionable, of course, when the payments were made with public funds.

Years later, after the Crédit Mobilier scandal had broken and railroad construction firms were in evil repute throughout the land, the surviving associates in the Central Pacific solemnly swore that they had formed the Contract & Finance Company because the Central Pacific was broke. It could not pay its contracting firm. To raise money for the rush across Nevada the associates tried to sell C&F stock to outside capitalists. They named wealthy people whom they had approached to no avail. Some of those people, D. O. Mills and Lloyd Tevis among them, testified that they had indeed considered the stock in both the railroad and the construction company to be poor investments. Therefore, the associates said piously, they had been forced to subscribe to all of the C&F stock themselves. Otherwise the railroad could never have been built.[9]

Possibly the railroad did need money. Both Huntington and Stanford said that by the time the tracks had crossed the Sierra, the CP's floating debt stood in excess of six million dollars. Even if the figure is accurate, however, there is no indication that the associates were having any trouble raising funds during the fall of 1867, when the Contract & Finance Company was organized. Quite the contrary. In letter after letter, Huntington gloated about the new ease with which he was selling bonds. People at last believed the railroad was possible. "If 1868 should be financially like 1867," he wrote Charles Crocker on December 27, "I can supply you with what money you will need to lay 350 miles of road"—a remark that hardly sounds desperate. The Sierra was behind them. Why take in more partners? Or, as he wrote Charlie in another letter, help would have been welcome earlier, but now "if you see your way across the mountains I would not part with the least portion of the control of any of our franchises."[10]

Finally: stock in a firm no one would touch could hardly have been very valuable. Yet a note among Stanford's papers, written in his own hand and dated May 30, 1868, seven months after the birth of the Contract & Finance Company (and two weeks after the birth of his only son), shows that Stanford valued each share of C&F stock at $1,000.[11] (Par was $100 a share.) No, the Contract & Finance Company was not a desperation measure, formed as a last resort. It was a way of tidying up a loose arrangement, Charles Crocker & Company, which might grow sticky in event of accident to one of the participants. But it had to seem desperate later on, to keep the public from gagging over it as they had gagged over Crédit Mobilier's excessive profits at the expense of the government.

There were other reasons for Collis' euphoria that fall. Both the Union Pacific and Crédit Mobilier were wracked by a violent dispute between the Ames brothers and the Durant faction. Both sides sought Huntington's good will. The Ames brothers suggested that the Californians join the Union Pacific in the building of a great central city somewhere in the Weber Valley of Utah, northeast of Salt Lake City, where they proposed that the rails meet. A month later, Oliver Ames offered Huntington a place on the Union Pacific board. Durant's henchman, ex-Congressman John Alley, countered by offering him a piece of Crédit Mobilier. *"No, I thank you!"* Collis said, underscoring the words.[12] Let them squabble. If they broke, then Green River would be a certainty and the Central Pacific would rule the roost.

It was time to start cleaning up the peripheral matters—control of the northern roads, control of Goat Island. The way to get rid of Wilson was to start buying California Central bonds at depreciated prices; then, when the interest payments were not met, the bondholders would demand a foreclosure sale and buy the line themselves. The acquisition flowed with only a single ripple. While Huntington was buying hundred-dollar bonds in New York and Boston at fifty to sixty dollars each, Stanford was paying full price in San Francisco. "I was not particularly well pleased," Huntington wrote. But matters ironed out, and by February 1868 the California Central was in their pockets.[13]

The next step was to obtain mastery of Goat Island. That done, the assets of the hostile Terminal Central Pacific would be limited to a piece of submerged tideland whose only value was its nuisance potential. If necessary, the legislature probably could be persuaded to end even that by using eminent domain to condemn a right-of-way to the island.

Collis bared his knuckles. "Mr. Donnelly, MC, and a first-class man on the Land and Railroad Committee, and a good friend of the Central Pacific Road, was a little short of cash and I loaned him $1000. He says that Flint's Goat Island bill shall sleep in the Land Committee. . . ."[14] "The last time I went to Washington . . . I talked Goat Island with [Senator Nye of Nevada]. He said that we ought to have it and that he would do all in his power to get it for us. I told him that he ought to have an interest in the new city [Reno] that must grow up on the Truckee. . . ."[15]

And then there was Cole, now a senator. He and Collis had grown to detest each other. ("The fact is there is no good feeling in Cole; his heart is cold and his blood is white, and I do not nor *cannot* like him.") But when needs were stark enough, feelings did not count. Cole's brother George killed a man named Hitchcock. Cornelius wanted Huntington to line up a famous trial lawyer named James T. Brady to defend George, fee $5,000. Hmmm, said Collis. It so happened that the "the Co. wanted Goat Island for its Western Depot and . . . if he thought it was right for the Co to have it, and would work to that end, I would make an arrangement with Brady, &c. Cole said that he would."[16]

So it went, pressure here, persuasion there. "I have also talked with Senator Williams [of Oregon] and he is with us. I am well acquainted with Mrs. Williams." . . . Congressman Axtell of Oregon was unfriendly. Banker D. O. Mills had a talk with him. Axtell became friendly. "I have employed him as our attorney (confidentail)," Huntington wrote Crocker. Franchot went to work, too. All told, Collis said, he and Franchot, whom he was paying $25,000 a year in Central Pacific stock, presented their case in person to seventy members of Congress.[17]

Even before the campaign against the Terminal people was fully underway, he had no doubt of its outcome. "I would not," he wrote Hopkins on November 19, "give them ten cents to get out of the way."[18]

And finally, blockades were a strategy the Central Pacific could also employ. San Francisco had grown to the point that no railroad could be allowed to cross the city proper to docks near the Golden Gate. The tracks would have to stop somewhere south of the city. Quietly the associates prepared a bill for introduction into the state legislature during its session early in 1868. Under the terms of this bill the state, which controlled the submerged lands in that part of the Bay, would sell to the Central Pacific and Western Pacific railroads*—at fairly stringent terms; the stakes were high—6,620 acres of tidelands stretching from Mission Bay at the southern edge of San Francisco southward for three and three-quarters miles. This astonishing acquisition, if it became a reality, would effectively keep all railroads but those controlled by the Sacramentans from reaching deep water in the vicinity of San Francisco.[19]

Now what would Tevis do with his Southern Pacific?

A happy fall—until November 20. That day Huntington got his first inkling that the Union Pacific suspected his intentions concerning Green River and was preparing to block him not just short of there, but out of all Utah.[20]

* The Western Pacific still held a congressional franchise which allowed it to build to San Francisco, even though the San Francisco & San José already ran up the peninsula.

15   The Race Heats Up

"I have," Huntington wrote Charlie Crocker, "a way of finding out what is done in the Union Co's office." Later letters were more explicit. "I have sent men that they did not suspect, to inquire." . . . "I called on a lady friend and she told me that C. S. Bushnell (one of the Union men) called on her the evening before and he told her that they had made up their minds to build 400 miles of road that year." In Washington he paid John Boyd, an assistant doorkeeper in the Capitol building, to keep an eye on meetings between Union Pacific officers and Congressmen. Shortly thereafter Boyd saw Thomas Durant, Oakes Ames, and Grenville Dodge go into the room of the Committee of Ways and Means. Boyd followed, in Collis' words, "to put things in order *sorter* and he said . . . they all agreed to push the work without much regard to cost, and he said that Durant remarked that he would be damned if he would not prevent the Central Pacific from coming more than 200 miles east of California."[1]

Was such talk mere gossip? Collis checked with various iron works to learn how much rail the CP was ordering for delivery during the spring of 1868. The figure confirmed the rumors—36,000 tons, or enough to lay more than 350 miles of track.[2]

Such distances were impossible—or so he thought until he investigated further. During the summer, trains had reached Council Bluffs. Only a short ferry trip across the Missouri River now interrupted rail connections between the Union Pacific's contractors and their eastern suppliers. In spite of occasional Indian attacks, material was flowing smoothly across the plains. And out at tracks' end highly organized crews under Jack Casement were setting new records in placing rails. "By all I can learn," Huntington wrote glumly to Charles Crocker on January 13, 1868, "they have a man that can lay more track in a day than any other man in the United States."

He should have learned sooner. In October the Union Pacific had run a special excursion train through Nebraska to advertise its accomplishments. But Huntington had been engrossed in selling bonds, gathering in the railroads of northern California, scheming to get Goat Island, and fretting about Tevis. The significance of the excursion failed to impress him. And now the Union Pacific was ready to start crawling up the slopes of the mountains between Cheyenne and Laramie.

Three hundred and fifty more miles in a single year! Out came his maps. His big fist must have clenched in dismay. Green River was lost.

Worse, Durant was serious about halting the CP out in the profitless sagebrush of Nevada. Huntington's behind-the-doors informants revealed those details, too. The laws of 1864 and 1866 gave both railroads the right to grade three hundred miles in advance of the end of a continuous line of track and collect part of their government bonds on the completion of each twenty-mile segment of grading. During the coming year, the Union Pacific planned to use its 36,000 tons of iron for pushing within a hundred miles or so of Ogden. It would then send laborers ahead a legal three hundred miles and begin grading in the vicinity of Humboldt Wells, Nevada (now just plain Wells).[3] If the Secretary of the Interior decreed that the UP grading was on the legal line of the transcontinental railroad, then the Central Pacific would be forced to meet the UP at Humboldt Wells—or even farther west if Durant could effect more stringent restrictions.

Feverishly Huntington developed his counterattacks. The UP's hardest work lay ahead in the Wasatch Mountains. The rival road would have to build tunnels there; the longest, 772 feet, was well east of Salt Lake, at the head of Echo Canyon near the present Utah-Wyoming border. Drilling the huge bore would slow the westward-pushing road considerably. And that, of course, was the reason that Durant wanted to send graders out as far in advance of tracks' end as the law allowed—to claim ground in Nevada while the tunnel workers were still held up in the Wasatches.

Was there any way in which the Central Pacific could get graders into the Wasatch Mountains before UP workers advanced toward Humboldt Wells? Out came the maps again. The sight was still dismaying. The laws were hinged to *continuous* track. The Central Pacific line, which reached as far as the California-Nevada border, was not continuous. It was broken by that seven-mile gap near Donner Lake. According to the law, Crocker's graders would earn no bonds if they advanced more than three hundred miles beyond that gap, or approximately to the site of present Elko, Nevada.

199

Echo Summit in the Wasatch Mountains was another three hundred miles beyond Elko.

Most of the miles were flat, however. Work could leap ahead as soon as construction trains were able to roll unobstructed down into Nevada. Telegraph wires crackled: *Close that gap.*

Hopkins wrote back that because of the heavy snowfall in the Sierra, Huntington should not count on the junction's being made until August.

Collis went wild. "I would make that connection in April," he railed, "if I was compelled to melt the snow in tin kettles."[4]

Letter after letter flew to Charles Crocker. "Buckle on your armor for the fight, for the ground once lost is lost forever." The chief objection Huntington found with the new agreement between the Central Pacific and the Contract & Finance Company was its failure to require the construction firm to build at least four hundred miles during 1868. "Never before was mortal in so great a need of speed" . . . *"Tell Charlie,"* he wrote both E. B. Crocker and Hopkins, underlining the words, *"to let out a link!"*[5] Never mind how the work was done. "Let the paint and putty men come afterwards." . . . "When a cheap road will pass the commissioners, make it cheap."[6] But do it quietly lest the Union Pacific be alerted.[7]

Charles Crocker responded that if he was sent the money and the iron fast enough, he would, "by the Eternal," lay an average of at least a mile a day throughout '68. "That," Huntington told him exultantly, "has the ring of pure metal. . . . So now prepare to lay what iron you have there and 40,000 tons more this season, as you shall have it if Old Ocean don't get her back up. . . . I expect to ship thirty-seven [locomotives] between this and the first of June, with material for 400 cars. . . . Would it not pay to work two sets of hands in the long summer days, four hours on and four hours off, and so getting sixteen hours of work out of the day?"[8]

Summer was still a long way off. Meanwhile snow was piling as deep as it had the year before. Crocker did not even try to keep the tracks open above Cisco, on the western slope. Material of every sort, including hay at $120 a ton, went across the mountains on sleds and then along the Truckee River in mud wagons. It was slow, laborious, expensive. Even so, Crocker managed to keep 14,500 men at work, most of them Chinese. He pushed his graders from the Truckee River over toward the Humboldt, the key path on the way through northern Nevada. They were in the desert now, and water had to be hauled to some of the construction camps from as far away as forty miles.

Go, go, go! To be sure of having enough money to push the expensive

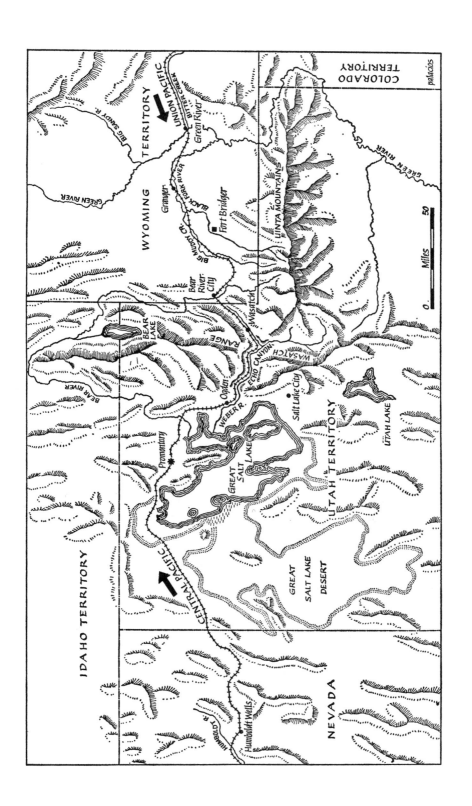

work during the laggard spring, Huntington went out among the financial houses and borrowed from German investors half a million dollars against company bonds that he could issue *when* the gap was closed. He sold, at prices between ninety-eight dollars and par, certificates for almost $1.5 million worth of government bonds.[9] The bonds were due on track already laid in Nevada, but he could not collect them *until* the gap was closed. Obviously, the New York financial establishment trusted him. In turn, he trusted his associates in the West not to slack off in the least.

Even so, the requirements were hopeless. As his frenzy subsided, he realized that there was no legal way by which he could reach the Wasatch Mountains in time to checkmate the Union Pacific.

Could he do it illegally?

He called for more maps—those which Central Pacific surveyors had made the preceding fall. The plats showed two routes. One ran south of the Great Salt Lake, threaded Salt Lake City and bent north to Weber Canyon, where it swung east again. The other ran north of Salt Lake, then dropped south through Ogden to Weber Canyon. This northern route missed Salt Lake City by thirty miles. Brigham Young and the Mormon hierarchy would object strenuously to having their capital by-passed. From an engineering standpoint, however, the northern route was preferable—and would be quicker to build. Huntington determined then and there to defy Young and run the line north of the lake.*

He put a dot of red ink at Humboldt Wells, where the road must finally veer either north or south of the lake. With a pen he drew a red line northeast to Monument Point at the northern extremity of the lake. From Monument Point the line curved across the Promontory Mountains and south around the lake through Brigham City to Ogden. There the lengthening red mark struck the Weber River, whose tumultuous canyons it followed eastward high into the Wasatch Mountains. Presently the stream forked. The red line turned up the northern fork, Echo Creek, toward the summit of the range.

As soon as the map was finished, Huntington sent it, through the helping hand of Thomas Ewing, Jr., to Ewing's former lobbying partner, Secretary of the Interior Orville Browning. With the map went a letter explaining the red line. The line, the letter stated, was based on long and careful engineering studies. (Actually the red line was the result of nothing more than a preliminary reconnaissance.) Without mentioning the seven-mile gap near Donner Lake, Huntington went on to say that CP tracks had reached the Big Bend of the Truckee River. (Actually they would not

---

* Union Pacific surveyors had also recommended a northern route, as Huntington knew through what he called in another context "my usual source."

202

reach that point, present-day Wadsworth, until July 9.) He reported that the distance from the Big Bend of the Truckee to Humboldt Wells was about 240 miles. (It is three hundred miles.) From Humboldt Wells to Echo Summit, he added, was something less than three hundred miles. In other words, as soon as Central Pacific track had reached Wells—and the whole implication of the letter was that track laying was rushing ahead at a record pace—then its graders could advance up the Weber River into Echo Canyon.

The graders, he finished, would of course work only on a legal line. Therefore Huntington asked the Secretary to approve the line as drawn in red on the accompanying map.[10]

His object was clear. As soon as Browning had approved the line, then the Central Pacific could spread workers along the entire reaches of it while Huntington argued—and he knew how to be convincing—that the ground was his. The Union Pacific could come no farther and still be on an approved, legal route.

The entire manipulation was based on bald dishonesty. Huntington could be that way under stress. For example, when cautious bond buyers asked him what the Central Pacific planned to use for fuel in the treeless, coalless deserts of Nevada, he replied suavely (and untruly) that the tracks passed near extensive beds of superior peat and that peat was perfectly satisfactory for firing locomotive boilers. "That seemed to satisfy the parties asking," he wrote Hopkins.[11]

He described the map scheme to his partners with equal candor:

The only way to keep them [the UP] from occupying the ground . . . [is] for us to go and occupy the whole distance into Weber Canon as soon as we get within, say, 400 miles, of course claiming that the distance is inside of 300, and I would suggest that you jointly get a lot of teams and material and send them on to the Upper Humboldt, but before they stop let them reach Weber Canon . . . and I would make up my mind to hold all the line to Weber Canon as arbitrarily as though it was held by the great I am.[12]

Meanwhile it was up to him to procure the necessary materials and ship them West. He placed orders for rails at every rolling mill in America that was not already swamped with demands from other lines in the nation's expanding network. Troubles immediately developed. First ice and then floods halted shipments by canal and river. The Spuyten Duyvil mill in Pennsylvania, which was rolling seventy-five tons a day for him, burned to the ground. He cashed bonds and loaned the mill owners money so that they could rebuild as rapidly as possible. Overstrained machinery in some of the other mills broke down. "It does seem as though the Devil was among our iron," he wrote Crocker. Tentatively he identified the devil. "I sometimes think the Union people have something to do with it, and I have watched but have not yet made any connections."[13]

In the West, Crocker and Stanford accepted his strategy without question. Crocker took a survey trip as far as Humboldt Wells to study the appalling logistics involved in spreading thousands of men across the desert hundreds of miles from any base of supplies. In mid-May he reported that he could do it if iron and other supplies reached him faster than was currently the case. So Stanford wired Huntington to investigate the costs of shipping rail and even locomotives across the Isthmus of Panama.[14] They were appalling—more than $8,000 for a single locomotive and other materials in proportion—but the need for speed was so great that Huntington went ahead with the arrangements.

Nature interposed another delay. Stanford was supposed to hurry straightway to Salt Lake City and make arrangements with Brigham Young for graders to work up Weber Canyon—without admitting to Young as yet that the CP intended to by-pass Salt Lake City. He delayed his start. After eighteen years of childlessness, Jane Stanford was pregnant. The child was due any moment, and the nervous husband kept postponing his departure. On May 14, a frail son, immediately named Leland Stanford, Jr., was born to the pair. Under the circumstances the ecstatic father decided to ignore the pressures awaiting him in Utah.

At that point Secretary Browning created further obstacles. He approved the line that Huntington had suggested only as far as Monument Point at the northern end of Great Salt Lake.* Sorely disappointed, Huntington took the bit in his teeth. He'd go ahead without approval. "With money enough," he wrote Hopkins grimly, "we can get the line located to any point, and so located we would take and hold all that we wanted."

His work reflected his determination. "I am loading iron on ships as fast as possible, working night and day. . . . I think sometimes I have too much to do, but I guess not; men don't wear out." He sent up smoke screens to conceal his purpose from Durant. Once men whom he knew to be agents of the UP tried to worm from him some hint as to the CP's plans

---

* By then the gap near Donner was almost closed and rails had reached almost to Reno, then called Lake's Crossing. Perhaps Browning thought that rails had reached Reno. Even so, Monument Point was still 450 miles away, or 150 miles farther than Browning should have approved. Presumably the excess reflects the deliberately inaccurate figures that Huntington submitted with the map.

for 1868. He grumbled to them that his associates in California were too involved with the Western Pacific (whose tracks the Contract & Finance Company had started laying) to push the main line as hard as he wished. "I think," he wrote Stanford, "I have thrown the Union folks so much off the track that you can get possession of the line to Echo Canyon before they mistrust that you are after it, that is, if you move with despatch."[15]

Unlike Crocker and Stanford, Hopkins objected to the illegalities—on pragmatic, not moral grounds. They were risking millions of dollars, but the premises were shaky. Was it wise?

Huntington waved the caution aside. He meant to take possession at least as far as the Wasatch coal mines "and swear that it is not 300 miles from the end of our line of completed road and then, before anyone can prove to the contrary, push our work so that we would be within the 300 miles. *It is an important matter and we should be bold.*" In no other way, he added in a later letter, could they beat Durant, "a man of wonderful energy, in fact reckless in his energy."[16]

Conceivably Hopkins thought that Huntington, too, was reckless, for on May 29 Collis announced to his associates, "I shall go to Washington tomorrow (Sunday) night and shall get the line located to Weber Canon if it costs $100,000."[17] Meantime the men in the West were to act as if approval had already been won.

Crocker obediently prepared to move three thousand Chinese, their carts, horses, tools, tents, and commissary shacks several hundred sunblistered miles up the Humboldt to occupy upper Nevada—a staggering migration whose true motives and almost incredible implementation have been too little noticed. Stanford was directed to go to Salt Lake City and arrange with Brigham Young for men to grade both ways from Ogden. It had to be done fast, before the UP realized what was afoot.

Thus beset, Stanford finally made arrangements to leave his new son. As a gesture of affection, he gave his wife nine million dollars' worth of Contract & Finance stock, just in case an accident happened to him out in the wilds, and then departed reluctantly by train and stagecoach for Utah.[18]

On reaching Salt Lake City he learned that representatives of the Union Pacific had already contracted through Brigham Young for Mormons to grade from Echo Summit to the mouth of the Weber, and from the latter point another thirty miles north or south, as engineering studies determined.[19] In other words, the Union Pacific also dreaded letting Young know that they, too, had determined to skirt the northern shore of the inland sea.

All this left Stanford in a quandary. Did he dare hire men to go into Weber Canyon alongside UP graders and start work on a line not yet approved for the Central Pacific? Besides, would a single Mormon anywhere listen to him when Young learned, as he soon must, that the Central Pacific meant to go north? Had this trip across the desert been anything more than a fool's errand? While he puzzled, he did nothing.

Huntington's first reaction to the UP's contract with Young was to grow even more reckless. Health may have had something to do with his feverishness. He was tense and nervous and awoke most mornings with a splitting headache.[20] He kept flailing around, nevertheless, and expected others to keep moving also. Stanford's delay in reaching Salt Lake City exasperated him, and in no surviving letter does he so much as mention Leland, Jr. As for Young's contract with the Union Pacific, it was up to Stanford to bribe him to break it: "I would make Young *see it is for his interest* to work with and for us, and although it ought to have been done long ago, I think there is an even chance that it can still be done, if the effort . . . be made."[21] Nor did he just scold. He called on Browning and told him that the Union Pacific was building substandard track in Wyoming, which indeed it was.[22] The road should not be accepted by the government's examining commissioners. That is to say, the UP did not have a continuous line, merely a pretense of one, and should not be allowed to send graders across the Wasatches until the line in Wyoming was brought up to standard.

What calmed him down is hard to say. Perhaps it was Hopkins. Or it may have been Thomas Ewing, Jr., with whom Huntington was still working. In any event he was made to face certain stark facts. Congressman Oakes Ames and other UP representatives in Washington had at last learned of the map to Echo Summit and were protesting vigorously. Badgered by them, Browning growled to both sides that he would of course stick to the law and would not approve either group's line for more than three hundred miles in advance of its railhead.[23]

Abruptly Huntington did an about-face and decided, in his own words, "to play virtuous." Telegrams flashed along the wires for Crocker's three thousand Chinese to advance no farther than the law allowed. To Hopkins, Collis added with glum cynicism that for the time being, "we had better take the *high ground* and confine ourselves to the law until we see where we can make more to break it than to keep it."[24] But even though the Salt Lake venture had proved abortive, he did not forgive the slothfulness of Leland Stanford, who had already gone scooting home without Huntington's knowledge. "We want," he sneered to Crocker, "a first-class man at Salt Lake. One that is up in the morning and that does not knock off until after noon—a man that can handle Mormons."[25]

Crocker settled his migrating Chinese down in the Palisade Canyon stretch of the Humboldt and let them tackle a particularly difficult seventeen-mile reach of grading. Supplying them that far in advance of work trains (more than two hundred miles at the beginning) was fantastically expensive, but there wasn't much use marching them all the way back again. Besides, Huntington was working on another scheme and might want to start leapfrogging again at almost any moment.

The new plan was based on an extraordinary sophistry. Somehow or other Collis had got the notion that the Union Pacific meant to descend the Wasatch Mountains to the vicinity of Ogden by following the south side of the streams that flow down Echo and Weber canyons. Perhaps Central Pacific surveyors had reported seeing Union Pacific stakes there; or perhaps his "usual source" in the UP office (a person never identified) showed him maps to that effect. In any event, he decided that the Central Pacific line should go up the north side of both Weber Canyon and its tributary Echo Canyon, to the summit. There the line would butt up against the site of the western portal of the Union Pacific's yet-to-be-drilled summit tunnel.

His reasoning went as follows. As soon as the Central Pacific was within three hundred miles of the summit, Huntington would present Secretary of the Interior Browning with a new map of the Central Pacific's surveyed line up the *north* bank of the canyons. He would prevail on Browning to approve this line. It would then be the legal, unalterable route of the transcontinental. On breaking out of its tunnel, the Union Pacific would find itself without authorized ground to build on.

No doubt Union Pacific graders would be working in Weber and Echo canyons long before Central Pacific laborers arrived—Samuel Reed of the Union Pacific had just signed contracts with Brigham Young for the grading—but no matter. The enemy would be on the *south* side of the creek. Their work would not count. The UP would be left dangling at the end of nowhere.

One glaring oversight marred what seems today an almost childish artifice. Echo and Weber canyons are narrow and tortuous. Anyone familiar with the gorges would wonder about a railroad's keeping steadily to just one bank of the small streams. Would not the tracks cross from side to side? Whenever the UP grade crossed to the north, would it not be on the legal line? Whenever the rugged terrain forced CP graders to the south bank, would they not be off Browning's approved line?

207

Was it, indeed, possible to decree "legal" lines from rough survey maps for such a canyon?

The questions seem not to have occurred to Huntington. He was overworked and ill. His doctor told him that his heart was enlarged and that he must ease off and spend more time out of doors.[26] He refused. He was obsessed.

A telegram from engineer S. S. Montague stoked his fever still higher: "Recent surveys show a decided improvement in line from north end of Salt Lake to Echo Summit. We are making location as rapidly as possible. Maps and profiles are now being made."[27]

"Just what I want!" Huntington exulted to Crocker, convinced by the telegram that he could keep the legal line well to the side of whatever grade the UP worked. The next question was to learn whether Browning would be a party to the plot. Off Collis went to Washington to learn. He worked through Ewing. Money almost certainly passed. Huntington had been prepared to spend $100,000 on winning approval for the first map; presumably he considered the new plan worth a comparable sum. In any event he wrote to Charles Crocker that Ewing "talked with the Secretary . . . and had no doubt but that the whole thing could be carried out as per my programme, and I am satisfied it will be if no one finds out so as to outbid me."[28] What the amount of his bid was he never indicated.

Ewing did suggest one restraint. The map should be presented to Browning in October. By then Congress would have adjourned for fence mending prior to the national elections of November. Fewer people, including Congressmen beholden to the UP, would be around Washington to ask embarrassing questions.[29]

This meant that by October the Central Pacific track should have reached within three hundred miles of Echo Summit. Could it be done? Again Collis made himself believe what he wanted. After all, there were hopeful signs. On June 16, Ed Crocker had wired triumphantly, "The track is connected across the mountains!" Supplies were flowing directly to the tracklayers without the necessity of an awkward transfer to wagons at the gap near Donner Lake. To be sure, tracks' end was, as July opened, six hundred miles from Echo Summit. Could Crocker build nearly three hundred miles of track in a little more than a hundred days—or, if not that, at least enough so that Huntington could claim three hundred miles to Browning? Of course he could. He must—it was that simple. Collis thundered behests at him: *Work on as though Heaven was before you and Hell was behind you!*[30]

He was a stubborn, fierce, ruthless driver. He meant, even at the ruin of his health, to win this war, and he intended for everyone associated with him to fight with the same wild zeal. It was the only way to forestall ruin. Stock prices would not hold up in the future if the Union Pacific dominated the western end of the transcontinental. They would not hold up if competitors could find easier, less snowy routes either to the north or south. That was another part of the battle: protecting his flanks while he fought Durant in Utah. And in that war, too, his ingenuity and energies were taxed to the utmost.

16   Guarding the Flanks

In the West, the year 1868 opened to the rumbles of political trouble for the railroad. Some of this unfavorable reaction was the result of Collis' own exuberant activities in the East.

It will be recalled that when the summit tunnel in the Sierra Nevada had finally been holed through, the investment firm of Fisk and Hatch had at last agreed to market Central Pacific bonds secured by a mortgage on the yet-to-be-built track in Nevada. In support of this sales drive the brokers had issued glowing prospectuses about the railroad's earning potential. Huntington had backed up the activity by hiring a publicity expert and broadcasting to newspapers everywhere stories about CP's earnings. Readers throughout the land could have learned, had they wished, that in 1866 the line had netted $663,000. In 1867 the figure soared to $1.1 million.[1]

To investors this looked lovely. To county taxpapers in California who had voted bonds for buying stock in the railroad—and who were receiving no dividends on that stock—the figures seemed less lustrous. If the CP really was prospering, should they not receive part of the melon in the form of lower passenger fares and lower freight rates? Yet the Central Pacific insisted on maintaining the maximum fares set by the state years before in an effort to encourage construction—ten cents a mile for passengers and fifteen cents a ton-mile for freight.

Placer County had still another grievance. When the railroad had asked the voters for help in 1863, it had proclaimed that taxes on CP tracks, depots, and other facilities would be more than enough to meet the 8 per cent interest on a bond issue of $250,000. Then, having buttoned the bonds safely in their pockets, the directors stubbornly resisted every effort to raise the assessed valuation on the railroad's

210

property above a meager six thousand dollars.[2] Nor was that all. Opponents of the railroad charged that the directors had not cashed the bonds as expected, but were still holding some of them, even though the work was then being done far out in Nevada.[3] Suspicions leaped. Why hadn't the bonds been used for railroad work in the counties that issued them? Were the taxpayers simply feathering the nests of the railroad builders?

The railroad of course denied that its operating profits were as real as they appeared. Everything was being poured back into the vast work still ahead. Until the work was done, the company could not survive either higher taxes or lower rates. As for the county bonds, Huntington had been able to raise more money in the East by using them as collateral for loans than by selling them at the stringent discounts that prevailed. Thus they were filling their functions, whether cashed immediately or not.

To the taxpayers such explanations seemed abstruse and hollow. The railroad had surmounted its chief hurdle, the Sierra Nevada. There was no sound reason for a householder in the mountain town of, say, Colfax to continue paying high taxes and high freight bills for the sake of a transcontinental whose traffic would speed past his home without doing him the least good.

Here, obviously, were explosive issues. Local politicians quickly took advantage of them. On January 4, 1868, a bill that would have almost halved rates was introduced into the state legislature.* A resolution in the state senate asked for an investigation of the Central Pacific in order to determine whether proper use was being made of the interest money donated by California's taxpayers.

The press took up the clamor. Hostility from the *Alta California* and other newspapers in San Francisco was predictable, but the sudden about-face of the railroad's oldest friend, the Sacramento *Union,* dumfounded the associates. The attacks began on February 7, 1868, at the close of an editorial advocating reduced rates. The words stung. The directorate of the Central Pacific, the writer charged, "has not been remarkable for meekness of spirit. . . . If they are allowed to take the

---

* In December 1867, the Congress of the United States also received a bill designed to reduce rates on the Pacific railroads. To defeat the legislation, Representative Oakes Ames "sold" Crédit Mobilier stock at par to certain willing Congressmen. The stock was worth more than par and the Congressmen were allowed to pay for it out of future dividends to be declared by Crédit Mobilier. Later, Ames's activities ballooned into one of the most odorous scandals in American political history. There is no evidence that Huntington was associated with Ames in attacking that particular bill.

reins in their own hands now in the infancy of their power, what may not be apprehended from them when all their machinery is rounded out and completed?"

Back in New York Huntington growled in exasperation. "I wish," he wrote Crocker, "we could come nearer controlling that paper than we do."[4]

An attempt at control evidently was made. At least the *Union* declared righteously on December 9, 1869:

> About two years ago Governor Stanford, in behalf of the Railroad Company made an infamous proposition to the proprietors of the Union to advocate or withhold opposition to a scheme to be presented to the Legislature for the benefit of the company. . . . We rejected the offer and opposed the project when it was brought before the Legislature. From that time to this the influence of the company has been used to annoy us and injure us in every possible way. They have descended to means utterly contemptible. . . .

The associates countered the charge with various explanations. Charles Crocker said that the proprietors of the *Union* had turned hostile because one of them was ejected from a Central Pacific passenger coach while trying to board it, contrary to regulations, with a hunting dog and gun. Huntington suggested that his partners foolishly took the railroad's printing away from the *Union*'s job presses and awarded it to a firm headed by H. S. Crocker, a brother of Charles and Ed. Hopkins saw more sinister motives. He was convinced that emissaries of the Union Pacific not only paid the editors of the Sacramento *Union* for the attacks but were also behind the unfriendly resolutions in the legislature.[5] The reader may take his choice.

The hostile bills were safely tabled—methods unknown—but the railroad nevertheless found the limelight embarrassing. For it had bills of its own pending in the legislature. The principal one concerned the company's request, mentioned in a previous chapter, that it be permitted to purchase 6,620 acres of waterfront and tidelands south of San Francisco.

To everyone's surprise, the original bill, when introduced to the legislature on March 5, 1868, had been radically modified. It now included among the grantees both the Southern Pacific and the San Francisco & San José. Yet Tevis of the Southern Pacific was supposedly battling the associates!

Enemies of the railroad jumped to the conclusion that the Central Pacific had bought control of the SP and SF&SJ. Cries of monopoly arose. On March 6, 1868, Stanford issued a statement vigorously denying

212

the accusations. Neither the Western Pacific nor the Central Pacific nor any of the men connected with those roads was associated—he said—with either the Southern Pacific or the San Francisco & San José.[6]

Technically Stanford was telling the truth, but only because negotiations had not yet crystallized. And that raises the question of Lloyd Tevis. What had swung him away from the Terminal Central Pacific into the embrace of the associates?

Details of the wooing have not survived. It would appear, however, that the master bluffer of San Francisco had been up to his old tricks. It may be that he had never intended to build the Southern Pacific, but had used it only as a lure to bring the directors of the Central Pacific running to him with offers. If so, he succeeded.

He had not invested as much money in the Southern Pacific as Stanford & Company had assumed.[7] Probably he had been afraid to. His position was vulnerable. The greatest weakness was the land grant, the Southern Pacific's only source of aid. The original incorporators of the road had, it will be remembered, shifted the line from the coastal counties eastward into the San Joaquin Valley. They wanted the land grant shifted to accord with the line, and the government at first appeared amenable. Residents of the coastal counties were objecting, however. They hoped that if the Southern Pacific's new officers could not prevail on Congress to change the grant's location, the line would return to them.

Tevis had little strength in Congress. Senator Conness was obligated to him—but Conness was also a friend of Huntington's. Furthermore, both Conness and Conness' candidate for the governorship of California, George C. Gorham (who owned stock in the Southern Pacific), had recently been defeated. A waning political star would be no great help in Washington, especially if Collis Huntington chose to oppose the shift of the land grant. Nor could Tevis count on any aid of consequence from the eastern end of the transcontinental, the Atlantic & Pacific. So far the Atlantic & Pacific had not been able to raise enough money to spike down a foot of rail.

The SP's own financial position was further weakened by the threat of competition in the San Joaquin Valley. Stanford had recently incorporated the San Joaquin Railroad Company, designed to run from Stockton, where it connected with the Western Pacific, south to the vicinity of present-day Bakersfield. The San Joaquin planned to ask Congress for a land grant of its own.[8] If it won the aid and began to build, it would be in a position to cut across the line of the Southern Pacific and perhaps force the Atlantic & Pacific to join with it rather than with Tevis' road.

Tevis' only counter had been the little Terminal Central Pacific and its right-of-way north to Carquinez Strait, blocking the approaches to Goat Island. He made the most of the obstruction. As soon as Stanford and E. B. Crocker realized that he was aiding the enemy, apparently for the sake of securing oriental trade to the Southern Pacific, they scurried to him with proposals. How much did he want for the Southern Pacific? How much for the San Francisco & San José, which they had only recently let slip through their fingers?

When Huntington learned of the precipitate discussions on the West Coast, he was displeased. For one thing, it was clear by then that Tevis did not control the two railroads. Several men were involved, and Collis was averse to any situation in which many voices were entitled to speak out. For another, he did not believe that the Atlantic & Pacific and hence the Southern Pacific were, as yet, a serious threat. Land grants were a poor lever for raising sizable sums of money. "At this time," he wrote Hopkins, "it seems to me we do not want [the Southern Pacific]." To Crocker he added, "As for our buying the San José Railroad . . . I would not do it."[9]

Cutting into the discussions and changing his mind abruptly came a totally unexpected element, the Union Pacific, Eastern Division. That line, intended originally as a branch of the main Union Pacific, was laying track from Kansas City toward Denver. By law it was supposed to join the UP near Cheyenne and thus remain subordinate to the northern road. But as the so-called Eastern Division progressed from one wild Kansas cattle town to another, the line's president, John D. Perry, who had wrested control from Frémont in 1863, began developing oceanic ambitions of his own. Why couldn't the Kansas line avoid the UP and become a full-blown transcontinental?

Fueling Perry's ambitions was Thomas A. Scott, vice-president of the Pennsylvania Railroad. Since the close of the war, Scott had been wondering how best to link the eastern and western coasts with a continuous line under one company's control. His plan shaped up like this: to thrust the Pennsy from Philadelphia to St. Louis and then acquire a line across Missouri to Kansas City. At Kansas City the eastern giant would hook up with the Union Pacific, Eastern Division. Instead of swinging north to Cheyenne, the UPED would veer off through southern Colorado, New Mexico, and Arizona into southern California. From there it would move on to San Francisco as best it could. This did not involve kowtowing to local interests. Neither Perry nor Tom Scott had the least intention of letting some unbuilt paper road, either the Southern Pacific or the San Joaquin Railroad, stand in the way of their monumental concept.

Scott's field general was William Jackson Palmer. Palmer had begun his business career as private secretary to J. Edgar Thompson, president of the Pennsylvania Railroad. A dour young Scot of his own age, Andrew Carnegie, was functioning at the same time as the private secretary of Thomas A. Scott, the Pennsy's vice-president. The Civil War interrupted the parallelism. Though born a Quaker, Palmer drummed up a regiment of Union cavalrymen and galloped off to the front as their general. When the war was over, the Union Pacific, Eastern Division, acting on Thompson's recommendation, hired Palmer as chief engineer on the theory that he could fight the embattled Cheyenne Indians of Kansas with one hand and lay track with the other. He succeeded very well.

When Perry of the UPED and Scott of the Pennsy began talking of the Pacific Ocean, Palmer was the man they selected, in June 1867, to survey the proposed line. It was a strenuous trip—Indian ambushes, lost trails, stolen livestock, near starvation, fierce weather.[10] Early in '68 Palmer was in San Francisco, talking noncommittally to Tevis of the Southern Pacific and Stanford of the San Joaquin Railroad about the western end of the proposed southern route. Having filled them with wild surmises, the easterner boarded a Central Pacific train for Cisco, transferred to a sleigh for surmounting such snowdrifts as his proposed line would never have to battle, and went to Philadelphia to report.

Having learned these things, Huntington changed his mind and agreed that the associates had better snap up the Southern Pacific in a hurry ahead of whatever the UPED had in mind. But he still would not enter into a fifty-fifty arrangement with the Southern Pacific's current owners. Hopkins, Stanford, the two Crockers, and he should each own a one eighth interest, enough to give them control. No more than three other men, each owning another eighth, should be included. That was still more voices than he liked, but under the circumstances it was the best he could do.

Tevis undertook to ease the minority stockholders out of the Southern Pacific and consolidate ownership in the hands of the eight men whom Huntington named. Curiously, Tevis was not one of them. In addition to the five associates, the new owners were to include three of the SP's original incorporators—William B. Carr, George C. Gorham, and a man named Grantley.[11] Tevis' motives in this strange venture are obscure. One guess is this: in return for his co-operation, he was promised a share in the 6,620 waterfront acres that the Central Pacific, Western Pacific, Southern Pacific, and San Francisco & San José roads hoped to obtain south of San Francisco.

Even four railroads would not need that much land—ten square miles—for depots, docks, and marshalling yards. The excess, ememies guessed, was to be used for speculative purposes. (They were probably right. On January 27, 1868, Huntington had written Hopkins, "The water front for three of four miles above [Mission Bay] will in time be very valuable. . . . Strike for a large slice.") Lloyd Tevis, who had founded his fortune on real estate speculation, may well have been tempted by the hope of a piece of that lush acreage.

If so, he was disappointed. As noted earlier, the appearance of the bill authorizing the purchase raised a storm of opposition. In vain Stanford denied that the Central Pacific owned either the Southern Pacific or the San Francisco & San José. Enemies continued to scoff; the press remained vociferous. Cried the San Francisco *Bulletin,* "The scheme is an outrageous one. . . . This immense property will be worth eventually as much as the Pacific Railroad itself." The *Alta* declared that if the railroads had asked for the whole state of California, the effrontery could hardly have been greater.[12]

Thus beset, the legislators scrambled for cover and on March 30 ended up donating, not selling, to the Western Pacific and to the Southern Pacific thirty acres each of Mission Bay property.* In return the grantees were to spend $100,000 each reclaiming the land. And once that had been done, they were to keep their tracks three hundred feet away from the water's edge—a curious restriction that was evidently designed to let San Francisco's draymen collect fat fees for transferring freight from ships to railroad cars. The two roads accepted the grant, but its niggardliness made Goat Island look better than ever to Collis Huntington as a receiving point for oriental traffic.

The reduction of acreage from 6,620 to sixty dampened whatever speculative plans Lloyd Tevis may have had in the area. In Oakland his luck was better. There Horace Carpentier's holdings were consolidated into the Oakland Water Front Company. This company conveyed part of its land to the city of Oakland, to quiet that municipality's objections to being shut away from its own waterfront. Another five hundred acres, including half a mile of waterfront for docks, went to the Western Pacific. In return, the Western Pacific promised to build a connecting line from Niles to Oakland and to spend $500,000 developing the five hundred acres.

The rest of the area remained in the hands of the Oakland Water

---

* Only two grants were made because by then it was generally known that the SP controlled the San Francisco & San José, and that the WP was controlled by the Central Pacific. Also, suspicions were rife about additional interlockings. Making grants to all four roads would have seemed like indefensible duplication.

Front Company. Its chief officers and principal stockholders were Carpentier, Stanford, who was fronting for the Central Pacific, and Lloyd Tevis.[13] Thus at least half of Tevis' bluff with the obstreperous little Terminal Central Pacific had worked. Though he had missed out south of San Francisco, he had acquired within the city limits of Oakland, and at very little expenditure of cash, a sizable share in a valuable piece of industrial real estate.

Nor was that all. With Charles Crocker he obtained control of the moribund Pacific Express Company. The Central Pacific granted to that company exclusive rights for carrying express on its trains. Using this contract as a bludgeon, Tevis forced down the stock of mighty Wells, Fargo & Co and bought control. As president of the newly acquired company, he increased its capitalization from ten million dollars to fifteen. He gave $1.5 million of this watered Wells Fargo stock to Stanford, Huntington, Hopkins, and the Crocker brothers for the express monopoly once enjoyed by the Pacific Express Company. Later, by similar means, Wells Fargo obtained comparable contracts with the Southern Pacific. The stockholders all received fat dividends each year. Everyone was content. A very nimble operator was Mr. Lloyd Tevis. But this is getting us far ahead of Huntington's sudden concern with the UPED.

In mid-March, after negotiations for the purchase of the Southern Pacific had been launched, but well before they were completed, Huntington received a summons from Perry of the Union Pacific, Eastern Division, and from Thomas A. Scott of the Pennsylvania Railroad to meet them in Washington. Collis was not used to orders of that nature, but this time he heeded.

It was his first confrontation with Tom Scott, the man who later would become his most formidable—and respected—opponent. Three years younger than Huntington, Scott had hewn out a comparable rags-to-power career. His father, a destitute tavern keeper, had died when the lad was ten. Tom left school, clerked in a store, then became helper to a station agent of the Pennsylvania Railroad. He rose fast. At the age of thirty-seven he was made first vice-president of the line. Smooth-shaven in a wilderness of beards, handsome and debonair, he had, like Huntington, an infinite capacity for work. Many nights he never went to bed, but catnapped upright in a chair between appointments with a stream of underlings ordered to come to him with their reports at unearthly hours.

Grandly Perry and Scott informed Collis that they were going to build a southern transcontinental to San Francisco. First, they would ask Congress for permission to cut the UPED away from the Union Pacific. That achieved, they would build through Kansas to Denver and from Denver southward to the thirty-fifth parallel in New Mexico. They would then continue west along routes currently assigned to the moribund Atlantic & Pacific and to the Southern Pacific.

And if those railroads objected? Huntington asked.

They couldn't, the others said. The A&P had not built a foot of track since its incorporation. The SP was in scarcely better shape: its land grant was in jeopardy because of its shift in routes. If all the facts were pointed out to Congress with proper care, the lawmakers would revoke the grants to A&P and the SP, and would reaward them to the new transcontinental. After all, the UPED and the Pennsy were both roads of proven ability.

To do the work, Perry, Scott, and their friends planned to set up a single construction company. Just one. There would be no dividing of profits and responsibilities and no costly races, as in the case of the Central Pacific and the Union Pacific. Because Huntington and his California associates were good railroad men and owned the franchise for an unbuilt road through the San Joaquin Valley, they would be allowed to buy stock in the new construction company and thus share in the profits.

To Huntington the purpose of the meeting was now obvious. Perry and Scott hoped to silence in advance any objections he might be tempted to raise in Congress. They were offering to buy him off without giving him or his associates any real voice in the affairs of the southern line. The schemers thought that he would be humble because they were sure that the Central Pacific could not possibly reach Salt Lake City ahead of the Union Pacific. The CP would then be an inconsiderable stub end of the UP, wagging forlornly out in the desert. The associates, in the minds of the easterners, ought to jump at a chance to get away from the wreckage and make a little money by accepting a small part in the southern construction company. Take it now or lose the chance, they said in effect. Obviously they did not yet know that the Central Pacific was negotiating for control of the Southern Pacific, and Huntington saw no present need for enlightening them.

Collis could match a grandiose approach any day. Blandly he said that the Scott-Perry idea sounded fine—with alterations. He and his associates, backed by some of the richest men in California (whom he did not name), would build the San Joaquin Railroad to the south-eastern border of California. They would retain full control of that line. And *then* they would take a share of the construction company that built the UPED from Denver to the California border. As for the legislation that the UPED hoped to get from Congress, Huntington's western senators could block it at will. What's more, the easterners knew it. It was time they realized, too, that he meant to beat the UP to Salt Lake City. In short, they had better reconsider their offer.

This was not the answer that Perry had had in mind. The meeting broke up. Then, almost immediately, Scott, "who," Huntington wrote Ed Crocker, "is very sharp," returned and let it be known that he wanted this southern transcontinental badly enough to bargain. They spent the next several weeks talking about it.[14]

At first Huntington seems to have been bluffing when he talked about building part of a second cross-country road when he was not sure he could finish the first. Why should he risk defying men of such stature? There were several possible reasons. Perhaps he was instinctively trying to protect the Central Pacific by blocking all other railroads from entering California. Possibly he was hoping to get hold of a bigger share of the southern construction company than the easterners appeared willing to grant. Or he may just have been a born gambler, feeling out the opposition before he decided how to bet his own cards.

In any event, the talks with Scott forced him to face issues that until then had only nagged at the edges of his attention. Sooner or later other transcontinentals were going to be reaching for San Francisco. Furthermore, the past two fierce winters had convinced him that no other railroad, even in the north, was likely to encounter snow problems more formidable than those that plagued the CP's crossing of the Sierra Nevada. The Central Pacific, in short, could not expect to dominate cross-country traffic. That being so, investors were not likely to scramble for its stock when finally the enormous blocks being accumulated in the Contract & Finance Company were put on the market. And if the stock did not sell well, then the dreams of Midas-like wealth in return for all the risks and labor went glimmering.

If other railroads could not be kept out of California, then the obvious answer was to control all those that entered. But though the concept was simple, implementing it would not be. All along the way he would be beset by giant financial combinations intent on breaking his control and by politicians fearful of the strangling powers of monopoly.

As he was thinking on these matters, he received a gloomy letter from Hopkins, describing the vituperative attacks made on the company during its abortive attempt to win the 6,620 acres south of San Francisco.

219

Everyone, Hopkins said, was in favor of a railroad until it was built. Then they started attacking it for trying to maintain itself.

True enough, Huntington replied. And since they were going to have to fight anyhow, why not do battle with the public on every railroad in the state, "as it is not much more fight and there is more pay." Whereupon he outlined his plans for controlling not only the southern approaches but also the northern ones through the California & Oregon. In addition, the Central Pacific should thrust branches from northern Nevada into both Oregon and Montana. Meanwhile they must acquire Goat Island. Above all, they must reach the Wasatch Mountains ahead of the Union Pacific.[15]

The whole West is ours! The fierceness of the drive alarmed Charles Crocker, who wailed to him by mail, "Do you ever stop to think where you are leading us?"

"I do not expect to lead you at all," Huntington replied softly. *But . . . :* "[I] think that there will be three overland roads and that they will all center at San Francisco, and I am disposed to think that for overland traffic the Salt Lake route will be the least valuable of the three and that we can control the west ends of them all just as well as not do it, and if it can be done I am in favor of doing it."[16]

And so the talks with Perry, Scott, and Thompson, the president of the Pennsy, went on and on, often past midnight, in various hotels. At first Huntington considered using the Southern Pacific, when it was acquired, as the western end of the new route, hoping in this way to have the shift in the grant legalized as part of the legislation authorizing the new transcontinental. Then he changed his mind. The SP wasn't theirs yet. Also, he may have feared that hanky-panky about the controversial grant would reduce the chances of passing the new transcontinental bill; strong opposition was already building in the country against further congressional handouts to the railroads.[17] In any event, on April 18 or 19 he traveled to Washington and there, with the help of Senators Stewart and Conness, drew up a bill for aiding the UPED with land grants as far as the Colorado River and the San Joaquin Railroad from that same stream northward through the Central Valley to Stockton. Thus both the Southern Pacific and the San Joaquin might be able to absorb generous chunks of the public domain.*

The bill, as finally drawn, was presented to Congress on June 6, 1868. It was immediately and viciously attacked by senators and representatives who, Huntington knew, were under the influence of the Union Pacific.

* The San Joaquin Railroad would run down the east side of the broad San Joaquin Valley, and the Southern Pacific down the west side.

The reason was obvious. The UP wanted no competition from a southern line. Huntington's joining the enemy in furthering such a route did nothing to endear him to the Ames brothers, Dodge, Durant, and the rest. According to the charter which the San Joaquin Railroad held from the state, its tracks were to begin at or near Stockton. This in turn suggested a terminus on the eastern side of San Francisco Bay, at either Oakland or Goat Island. The strategic value of both spots thus doubled; one or the other of them (or both functioning as a unit) might end up being the grand entrepôt not only for the Central Pacific but for the new southern transcontinental as well.

The associates, the Oakland waterfront safely in their hands, had already started talks with grandiloquent A. A. Cohen (we will hear of him later) about purchasing two ferry slips on the east side of the Bay. One slip was in Oakland, the other in Alameda to the south. As stated earlier, an abbreviated railroad led from each slip a few miles toward the interior. The associates purchased those little railroads, too. The next step would be to push the diminutive lines on to the southeast and connect with the Western Pacific at Niles.

Through those roads and through the Southern Pacific, when it was acquired, they had three sides of the Bay tightly blockaded. The only gap lay in the north. In this gap were the still anaemic California Pacific, limping north from Vallejo, and that unbuilt exasperation, the Terminal Central Pacific, with its legislative grant to 150 acres of submerged land north of Goat Island and its franchise to build from Oakland north to Carquinez Strait.

In spite of the acquisition of the Oakland property, Huntington's determination to have Goat Island remained as strong as ever. Better docks could be built on its west side than at Oakland's shallow waterfront. At Goat Island, the railroads would be free from vexatious municipal regulations. But mostly he did not want any other rail line to have it.

The leaders of the Terminal Central Pacific, whose Washington representative was a shrewd horse trader named William B. Hyde, were resourceful. Many eastern Congressmen were objecting to a grant of the island to any railroad on the grounds that it should remain a United States military reserve. Hyde decided therefore not to ask for the island, but merely for permission to quarry stone there. The Terminal Central Pacific would then use this stone for constructing a small island atop their submerged 150 acres.*

* The plan was perfectly sound from an engineering standpoint. During the 1930s, Treasure Island, home of San Francisco's World Fair, was built approximately on the site of the Terminal Pacific's original grant.

Huntington immediately entrained for Washington and there prevailed on friendly Congressmen to kill Hyde's bill in committee. Then he had Senator Nye of Nevada introduce to the Senate a bill granting all of Goat Island to the Central Pacific.

During the same period he was conferring with Ewing about obtaining Browning's approval of the new CP line from Monument Point to Echo Summit. He was buttonholing legislators concerning aid to the UPED and the San Joaquin Railroad. He sought to quiet objections to changing the location of the Southern Pacific's land grant. Each errand concerned a major decision by the government; each one would have absorbed the full energy of a less durable man. Huntington, outwardly calm, strode from room to room, hall to hall. Then back to New York he rushed, to order material, catch up on his endless correspondence, untangle shipping snarls, borrow hundreds of thousands of dollars, sell millions in bonds. One letter to Hopkins, written June 6, is typical of many: "It will take hard work and as much as $200,000 in cash to get a bill [aiding the new southern transcontinental] through, but you understand all this, and I hope, see it clearer than I do today, for I went to Washington Wednesday night, rode all night in the cars, was at work in Washington until three o'cock in the morning Thursday and returned Friday (last) night, and am about as near used up today as I ever was in my life."[18]

It was during this hectic period that Tevis finally completed the purchase of the Southern Pacific. Huntington learned of the acquisition just after he had returned to Washington to confer again with Ewing about the best way to handle Secretary of the Interior Browning. While hanging around the anterooms, he learned that Browning had decided to cancel the land grant to the Southern Pacific because of its shift in routes. Ten minutes after he picked up that disturbing news, along came a telegram from Stanford stating that the associates at last owned the SP. But now there was no land to go with it.

Again Huntington had to tamper with the Secretary's judgment. He proved equal to the occasion—and so did the malleable Mr. Browning. As we know, the Secretary told Ewing that the bizarre location scheme for Weber Canyon seemed feasible. In addition, Browning on that same day rescinded his order revoking the Southern Pacific grant and restored the full amount of land—not on the original route as specified by Congress but just where Huntington wanted it, along the proposed new line through the San Joaquin Valley. No surviving letters indicate what considerations led to the Secretary's sudden and remarkable change of mind.

222

Although Tevis' holdings in the Southern Pacific were negligible, he was named as president of the new corporation. Fire alarms of monopoly were resounding on all sides and the purchasers wished to conceal the truth about the SP's ownership lest they be embarrassed during future negotiations with state and national officials. In the East, Huntington blandly spread the word that he was simply a financial and purchasing agent for the reorganized railroad.*

Still other triumphs seemed to be shaping up. In spite of undercover opposition by Cole, the Goat Island bill passed the Senate twenty-eight to eight. Now for the House!

Huntington's insistence on the island left him exposed. Congressmen Donnelly of Minnesota, a member of the House's railroad and land committees, had already hit Collis for a thousand dollars. Now he asked for ten. "I finally gave him $5,000. . . ." Huntington wrote E. B. Crocker. "He has been very true to us but I did not like the way he called for it. . . . I have had such a headache the last two or three days that I can hardly think, much less write."

In his eagerness he even asked Representative Oakes Ames to support the Goat Island bill. Ames agreed—but when the roll was called in the House he voted with the opposition.

The bill failed. Huntington confronted Ames in the Willard Hotel in a storm of passion:

> I told him he was a treacherous old cuss and that I would follow him as long as I lived. . . . I got him mad, as I wanted to, thinking if I did I would get some truth out of him; and he went on and said that he did not work for me; that he thought the Union Company would want a part of that island. . . . I really unearthed the old skunk.

The next day a friendly Congressman showed Collis a map drawn by William Hyde of the Terminal Central Pacific. It showed a rail line running from Goat Island to Vallejo and thence up the Sacramento Valley. From the valley's upper end it veered off through southern Idaho into Wyoming, to meet the Union Pacific. "That," Collis growled to Stanford, "was why Ames wanted a part of Goat Island."[19]

The bill that would have aided the southern transcontinental also failed, and the UPED—it soon changed its name to Kansas Pacific—was forced to remain subordinate to the UP. Unless the Atlantic & Pacific was

---

* By this time the Southern Pacific needed financing and equipment. In conjunction with a vague entity known as the Santa Clara and Pajaro Valley Railroad, it was grading slowly toward Gilroy, a farming hamlet thirty miles south of San Jose.

somehow revived, neither the San Joaquin nor the Southern Pacific had much of any place left to go.

To Huntington, hammered by headaches and sick with dizzy spells, that defeat, too, was largely attributable to the Union Pacific crowd.

Well, he'd humble them yet, somewhere out in the rugged canyons of eastern Utah.

17 Scheming for Victory

Charles Crocker and his swarming thousands of Chinese were not able to meet the demands for speed that Huntington placed on them during the summer and fall of 1868. Bottlenecks in the supply routes were the chief reason. Huntington at one point during the summer had thirty ships on the ocean loaded with locomotives, cars, rails, spikes, fishplates, and whatnot. At San Francisco all that material had to be transferred to river boats for the trip to Sacramento.* Arrived there, it then had to be shifted again, this time to freight trains.

Jams developed. Why can't you get the iron to Sacramento? Collis snarled in one letter to Crocker. "You knew what was coming, and I had supposed that Mr. Stanford had not much else to do but to attend to the reshipment of material and draw checks on me."[1]

The single line over Donner Summit, relieved by only occasional sidings, was a dispatcher's nightmare. Construction trains hauling imported material as well as ties and stone from the mountains vied for clearance with regularly scheduled freight and passenger trains bound for the Nevada mines. Arthur Brown's timbermen, who that summer kept twenty-five sawmills busy while building eighteen miles of snowshed over the line, snarled matters still more with their clutter.

Greenhorns ran too many of those crowding trains. California, railroadless until recently, had no backlog of experienced engineers, conductors, and brakemen. Wrecks were frequent. They, too, clogged the single line that each week extended farther from its base of supplies. Precious hours were often wasted out in the heat and the alkali dust be-

---

* During this period work was also being pushed on the Western Pacific, from Sacramento toward San Jose. Huntington was that road's purchasing, financial, and shipping agent, too.

cause a trainload of rails arrived long before the necessary ties appeared or because carloads of fishplates were rushed through while the rails were still stalled back in the hills.

To top off the troubles came new silver strikes in Nevada's remote sagebrush hills. Hundreds of workers vanished from Crocker's construction camps. Replacements got a free ride as far as tracks' end and then disappeared in their turn.

To relieve the jam Stanford in early August traveled again to Salt Lake City. Working through Brigham Young, he made a contract with the firm of Benson, Farr & West (in which Young held an unpublicized interest) to grade west from Monument Point into Nevada. The agreement broke the letter of federal law, for on August 22, when the Mormons began moving toward their new job, tracks' end was still 375 miles short of Monument Point. But it was advancing steadily, and, as Stanford realized, no one was likely to note the premature work in time to complain.

The Mormons took their own tents, teams, scrapers, and wagons with them. Hay, food, and other supplies would be sent to them from the farms around Ogden and Brigham City. Supplying them that way, from the east, relieved pressure on the line from California. Moreover, the stable Mormons were not likely to skip away to the mines. The prospects were so pleasing that Stanford tried to prevail on Benson, Farr & West to grade two hundred miles west of Monument. They declined. One hundred miles was as far as they would commit themselves in those grim deserts.

The negotiations completed, Stanford hurried home. Huntington was furious. He had wanted the president of the company to stay in Salt Lake City, ready to counter any move that the Union Pacific might make.

Mounting tensions were creating a dangerous change in Huntington's plan for the location line that he hoped Secretary Browning would approve. Time was one problem. Collis had not anticipated the Union Pacific's swift advance across Wyoming. By fall, UP tunnel workers were chipping away at the 772-foot bore at the head of Echo Canyon. Mormon graders hired through Brigham Young were strung along both Echo and Weber canyons. Before the year was out, iron would reach the summit tunnel, and then the UP would be entitled to send graders three hundred miles ahead, far out into Nevada. Survey parties were already working out a route for them around Great Salt Lake toward the west. If that line was legally occupied by the enemy, the Central would be reduced to insignificance, and the men who had backed it with so much exertion during the past five years would be irretrievably ruined.

At first, as we have seen, Huntington had hoped that his legal-line scheme would nullify any such disastrous advance by the enemy. Let the UP graders work on west. If they did not stick to the approved route, their roadbed would not be accepted. But when warming himself with that thought, he had been counting on Crocker's coolies reaching within three hundred miles of Echo Summit by mid-October, the target date for Browning's pronouncement. Then, at the moment the line was officially approved, Central Pacific graders would occupy all three hundred miles, up to the western portal of the summit tunnel. By the end of August, however, it was evident that in October Crocker would still be at least five hundred miles short of the mountains.

How could that two-hundred-mile gap across northern Utah be filled? In his quest for a solution Huntington turned to the Pacific Railroad Act and its amendments. Were there any weaknesses in the law?

He studied the documents carefully. He decided finally, and with some reason, that the act merely forbade the companies from drawing bonds from the government if they worked beyond the three-hundred-mile limit.* If they did not ask for bonds, why could they not work wherever they wished?

Durant brought the problem to a head. The moment the vice-president of the Union Pacific learned of Stanford's contract with the Mormons for grading a hundred miles west of Monument Point, he rushed to Utah, declaring, so Huntington wrote Mark Hopkins on September 14, that "he will grade alongside us" north of the lake. The thought was chilling. Would not a grade *alongside* the CP's work be so close to the proposed legal line that it, too, would be acceptable? "I have telegraphed for Stanford to go there. . . . Some one of *us* [not engineers like Montague or construction foremen like Strobridge] must be there soon after the 1st of October to take possession of the line . . . up to the west end of the tunnel."[2]

Huntington meant absolute, literal possession. Gone was the plan of simply letting the Union Pacific grade the wrong line. Stanford was to prepare hundreds of men and teams for immediate action. The instant Browning approved the CP route, Stanford was to string that army along more than five hundred miles of desert and mountains from north-central Nevada to the tunnel in Wasatch Mountains.

Get possession!—those were the nine points of law that Collis Huntington understood best. And then stand firm, buttressed by lawyers and friendly Congressmen, while the opposition stormed.

* In this connection it is well to remember that only a few months earlier Huntington had assumed that the law was definite and that in order to send graders out more than three hundred miles from the railhead he would have to lie about distances. (See pages 208–12.)

He was that kind of fighter, a slugger lacking in what might be called peripheral moral vision. He saw only what was necessary for success. He did not see qualifying ifs, ands, or buts. In his mind the location-line scheme had ceased being a sophistry and was now a clear and justifiable defense of property rights. Central Pacific men had found and surveyed the route. Browning had agreed to stamp his seal of approval on it. The moment that happened, no rails could be legitimately laid anywhere else. The only road that could possibly show a superior right, Collis argued, would be a road that came from the East with a *continuous* line of track. The Echo tunnel, however, would block the UP's track for months to come. If, during those months, Stanford's army of occupation asked for no bonds they would be within their rights, as Huntington defined the rights. His problem would be to raise money enough to do the job without government aid.

As he sat looking at the maps and figures spread out on his desk, the strategy was perfectly clear to him. He supposed that it would be perfectly clear to Stanford also. And so he never really explained the changed concept to his associates. For one thing, he was not adroit with written explanations. When matters grew involved, so did his prose.[3] He simply told Stanford to make preparations and then wait for a telegram which would read: "Go and see him!" This would mean that Browning had formally approved the line. Immediately on receipt of the signal Stanford was to launch work at key spots along the five-hundred-mile line.

The company president ignored the instructions. He did not even answer Huntington's letters.[4] In the absence of evidence we can only speculate why. Scruples about the law? Possibly, though such hesitations were not characteristic of Stanford. More probably he simply wondered why Old Huntington was working himself into such a lather. The UP's grading would not count, would it, so long as it was not done on the approved line? Furthermore, Stanford may well have resented the peremptoriness of Huntington's orders. After all, who was president of the company? Finally, he did not like Salt Lake City. He preferred the warmth of his extensive circle of sycophants in Sacramento and San Francisco, and he was still enthralled by the joys of belated fatherhood. In view of all that, why rush things beyond the letter of the law? For Huntington nowhere explained to him the new construction he had recently read into the Pacific Railroad acts. As a result, Stanford indulged both his dislike of Huntington and his penchant for doing as little hard work as possible, and stayed home.

As noted earlier, Collis' new strategy called for a considerable expenditure of money without any prospect of a quick return in government bonds issued for completed work. At first, the contingency did not worry him. Finances were in good shape. Although Crocker was not laying track nearly as fast as Huntington wished, he was living up to his promise to put down a mile of iron a day during 1868. Each of those miles brought with it $32,000 in government securities. During the year Collis visited the Treasury Department fourteen times to pick up a total of nearly ten million dollars in bonds, as contrasted with three deliveries in 1867 for a total of $2.1 million. With the securities went the right to issue an equivalent amount of the company's own first-mortgage bonds.

Fistfuls of crinkly green paper for the first time since work had started —and suddenly the price fell! Throughout the United States, the glow was beginning to fade from the industrial boom that had followed the war. As investors grew cautious, they began to take a second look at the extravagant race of the transcontinental railroad builders. Like Tom Scott and John D. Perry, many of them believed that the Central Pacific was losing and would end up stranded in the Nevada deserts. Fresh spates of an old rumor appeared: as soon as the Union Pacific had swept around the north shore of Great Salt Lake, it would ignore the Central Pacific entirely, drive into northern California, and, through an understanding with the California Pacific, achieve its own terminus on San Francisco Bay—possibly even on Goat Island. The Central Pacific was doomed.

Investors who had readily bought CP bonds early in the year began dumping them onto the market. The price sagged. To boost it back and thus restore confidence, Huntington ordered Fisk and Hatch to buy up, a par, every bond that was offered.[5] It was a dangerous expedient. Soon the railroad's unsecured debt with the brokerage house was running upwards of a million dollars. But there was no turning back now.

On October 13, he went nervously to Washington, assuming meanwhile that Stanford was waiting with his army of occupation in Utah. He delivered his portfolio of maps to Browning and added to them a long letter. The tracks of the Central Pacific, he wrote, had reached Reese River in Nevada and were advancing at a rate of three miles a day.* Progress would quicken still more as soon as the rails reached the grading which Mormon contractors were working on west of Monument Point. "I think it quite safe to say that the CP will be in

* The facts: when he wrote the letter, the railroad was still approximately seventy-five miles short of Reese River. Between October 6 and October 18, inclusive, the railhead advanced twenty-four miles, or an average of slightly less than two miles a day. Huntington knew this at the time of writing from telegrams regularly sent him about progress—telegrams still preserved in the Central Pacific telegram book in the Stanford University Manuscripts, Stanford Library.

operation to Salt Lake [i.e., Monument Point on the north shore of the lake] within 80 days from this date"—or shortly after the first of the year. Blandly he assumed, or pretended to, that of course the Central could grade as far as it liked if it drew no bonds beyond three hundred miles. But he wanted to be sure that his men worked where they were supposed to and nowhere else—on a line authorized by the government. "If the Honorable Secretary will approve the location as per the maps here presented, so that the company can get men and materials on the heavy work before winter sets in, the road will be completed to Echo Summit by the 1st of June."[6]

By statute the Secretary of the Interior was empowered to establish the legal line of the Pacific Railroad without consulting anyone else. At the last minute, however, he decided to cover himself by presenting Huntington's proposal to the full Cabinet. He suggested, moreover, that before the meeting took place Huntington should "see" Postmaster General Alexander Randall and Secretary of the Treasury Hugh McCulloch. In addition, Browning's former partner, lobbyist Tom Ewing, undertook to call on the President of the United States, Andrew Johnson. What form their arguments took is anyone's guess.[7]

Fearful that emissaries of the Union Pacific might suspect that something was afoot, Collis tried to pretend that he never left New York. He darted down to Washington on six successive days, made his calls late in the afternoon, then returned by night train to New York, where he made sure that he was seen in the office the next morning. Then back to Washington he went just long enough for another call.

The Cabinet discussed his presentation for the first time on Friday, October 17. McCulloch and Browning both "pitched into" it, to use Collis' words, and after a heated argument, decision was postponed until the following Monday, October 20. Gloomily Huntington returned to New York. "I think the chances are against us," he wrote his associates.

On Sunday, October 19, Stanford finally gathered himself together and left Sacramento for Utah.[8]

That same night Huntington again boarded one of the bone-jarring sleeping cars of the time and went to Washington, to await the results of the Cabinet meeting held Monday morning. After it was over, Browning wrote in his diary, ". . . the unanimous opinion was that the location should be accepted so that work might progress this winter."

Had a representative of the Union Pacific been present, he might well have suggested that the Central was not the only railroad capable of working during the winter. Mormon graders under contract to the Union

Pacific had for some time been blasting out tunnels and excavating grades in Echo and Weber canyons and would continue to do so without pause. Durant had fulfilled his threat about grading alongside the CP and had sent workers as far west as Humboldt Wells, Nevada. Why hadn't the Cabinet considered those matters when voting to speed up the work by heeding the Central's request?

Huntington had no intention of letting the Union Pacific raise those disturbing points any sooner than necessary. He wrung from Browning a promise that the Secretary would withhold word of the decision from the Union Pacific as long as possible![9] Triumphantly he then wired Stanford: *Go and see him!* To make sure that there was no slip, he sent a duplicate of the message to George Gray, the Central Pacific's consulting engineer, who was also presumed to be in Salt Lake City.

Back in New York, he rushed off an exultant letter to Charles Crocker.

I did it. The line from Humboldt Wells to Echo Summit is approved and is the legal line for the road to be built on and a road built outside of it will get no Government bonds. I telegraphed to Stanford . . . and I hope before this reaches you that you will have men on the whole line between the end of the completed line and the tunnel, as you knew about what time it would be approved and no doubt have matters so fixed that it will not take long to get men onto the line.[10]

He was aware, of course, of the plan's grave weakness. In spite of the Cabinet, the courts might decide, on appeal from the Union Pacific, that graders could not work more than three hundred miles in advance of tracks' end. Therefore Crocker must get that close to the tunnel before the Union Pacific discovered what was afoot.

By God, Charley, you must work as man has never worked before. Our salvation is in you. Let out another link. Yes, a couple, and let her run. Don't mind Durant's blowing; *say nothing, lay the iron on the approved line.*[11]

It was a colossal bluff, for surely Durant would react as soon as Stanford moved graders east of Ogden into the canyons. And what he did would surely be more than mere blowing. But never mind that now. Huntington was the tormented fighter still, trying to break back into the middle of the ring. That achieved, he would wonder about the rest of the

231

attack. "Milk for babes," he growled in another letter to Crocker, "but strong food for men."

His optimism increased when he learned that the Union Pacific was all but bankrupt, and trying to raise money by offering certificates to government bonds not yet due for completed construction work. On October 27 he wrote Hopkins with fierce joy, "As soon as you get the line covered . . . telegraph me and I will knock the certificates so they cannot use them." The whole West would be theirs yet!

Throughout this time Stanford was traveling slowly eastward, first by train to the railhead and then, for more than a week, in a buggy driven by one of his men. Along the way he stopped frequently to calculate what forces would be necessary to do the grading within the normal three-hundred-mile limit. Why hurry? He was still following Huntington's original concept of letting the Union Pacific go ahead with its work while the CP quietly confined itself to the legal line.[12]

It took him twelve days to reach Salt Lake City. In reporting on his trip to Hopkins, he said not a word about any telegram from Huntington, although the message "Go and see him" had been sent ten days before his arrival in the Mormon capital. At his leisure he visited Echo and Weber canyons. There he received a considerable shock. In traversing the narrowest parts of the gorges, the UP graders were blasting out the new roadbed first on one side of the stream and then on the other. This meant that for at least part of the way, *they* were on the legal line.

There was, Stanford told himself, nothing he could do about it. The canyons were beyond the Central's current three-hundred-mile restriction, and his job for the present (as he understood things) was simply to arrange for such grading as could be done without straining the law too far—say, in view of Crocker's recent progress, to the mouth of Weber Canyon, a few miles east of Ogden.*

He visited Brigham Young and soon had the necessary contracts arranged.[13] At some point during this period, George Gray told him about the telegram that he had received: "Go and see him."[14] It did not upset Stanford. Hadn't he already done all that he was supposed to do?

Learning in New York of the misadventures, Huntington exploded. Why on earth had the company president been dawdling so when he knew that Browning's decision had been due at any moment? Furthermore, what did Stanford mean by saying that there was room in the

---

* On November 1, 1868, the Central Pacific railhead was at Winnemucca, Nevada, roughly 385 miles from Ogden. Stanford was willing to fudge that much since it would take the new graders time to assemble equipment and move out to the job. During that time the railhead would of course be advancing.

canyons for only a single line? Such a statement did not accord with information sent Collis by Montague's surveyors earlier in the year—or at least it did not accord with Huntington's interpretation of the information.[15] Something was wrong—and at the moment Huntington chose to blame Stanford. Things *had* to be the way Collis wanted them.

It was not too late yet, he wrote. Browning would not publicize the legal-line decision until the middle of December. That gave the associates another month in which to bring things to a head. Possession! As soon as that was solidly accomplished, there would be no way for the Union Pacific to break their hold.

Furiously he wrote to Stanford, "If it is in the power of *God,* man or the devil to get our rail laid to within three hundred miles of Echo by, say, the tenth of December . . . then I would take possession of the line [now]. . . . As soon as you get at work [as far as] the tunnel let me know and I will have it in all the papers here. I think if I could tell it today, I could break the Union Pacific."[16]

Stanford refused. "How can we justify ourselves and what good can come to us in going 60 miles beyond the Pt. the Act of Congress permits?" Besides, as he had pointed out over and over, the UP workers in Weber Canyon were grading "for the most of the way as near to our line . . . as we could build ourselves."

Forget the canyons, he told his vice-president. The most they could count on covering was the section that he had already contracted to be graded—from the mouth of the Weber gorge on around the lake to Monument Point. To protect that section still more, he had hired a Mormon bishop, Chauncey West, to buy up certain key rights-of-way from farmers on both sides of Ogden. For the rest, the associates would have to pray for deep snow in the mountains to delay the enemy, for already the UP was building an eight-mile shoofly track around the unfinished Echo tunnel. As soon as that was finished and two other shooflies were constructed around short tunnels in the gorges themselves, Jack Casement's tracklayers would swarm down the canyons to the flats near the lake. Then, unless nature had blocked them high in the mountains, they would be in a position to roll along the grades Durant was stretching westward.[17]

Prayer! "It is a fearful position to be in," Huntington rumbled, "when one has to trust vital, material things to Providence only."[18] He preferred his own methods. Once again he ordered Stanford into the canyons and once again Stanford refused. Finally, in December, the argument reached such an impasse that Huntington agreed to meet his associate in the West and settle the control of policy on the battleground itself.

18   By the Skin of Their Teeth

Before leaving for the West, Huntington did what he could to bolster his strength in Congress. He loaned five thousand dollars to Cole, although he detested California's senior senator as much as ever, and he hired flamboyant, red-bearded, athletic Roscoe Conkling of New York, the "pouter pigeon of the Senate" (Carl Schurz's term), as the Central Pacific's legal counsel in the East.[1]

He also picked up one tidbit of good news. Several weeks earlier, Browning had dispatched two groups of special investigators to look into continuing newspaper charges about substandard construction work all along the Pacific railroad. The men who investigated the Union Pacific returned a highly critical report, saying that an expenditure of $6.4 million would be necessary to put the road into acceptable shape.[2]

The trio who examined the Central Pacific were more lenient. They were Lt. Col. R. S. Williamson, a United States Army engineer who had been making railroad and topographical surveys in California for the government since 1853; Sherman Day, a one-time California State engineer whom Collis had known since the days of the wagon road surveys in 1857—and Lloyd Tevis! The three men estimated that $310,000 would put the Central Pacific in tiptop shape. "The road," they stated to Browning, "is being constructed in good faith, in a substantial manner, without stint of labor or equipment, and is worthy of its characteristic as a great national work."[3]

Even Huntington was surprised at the praise. He told Crocker, who had shepherded the trio during their examination, "I think you must have slept with them. There is nothing like sleeping with men, or women either for that matter."[4]

At the last minute Elizabeth decided to go West with him. She

234

naturally wanted to look at the work that was making her husband's name familiar throughout the nation. More than that, she wanted to share what little of the great adventure she could. Collis had grown almost like a stranger of late. He was frequently away from home; when she did see him, he was often aloof and irritable. But during this transcontinental dash, uncomfortable though it would surely be, she and Collis might be close together again, as they had been during the harsh, happy days in early Sacramento.

They left New York by train on December 17. Stanford came as far east as Omaha to meet them. Together the trio swayed and rattled in a special Union Pacific car across Nebraska and through the high, chill deserts of Wyoming. At Green River they disembarked. Trains ran seventy miles farther, if one counted the dangerous eight-mile shoofly recently built around the unfinished tunnel at Echo Summit so that supplies could reach the tracklayers in the head of Echo Canyon. The condition of those seventy miles was so wretched, however, that Durant did not want the travelers to see them. He said, very apologetically, that passenger coaches were not running beyond Green River. The travelers accordingly changed to a stagecoach that Stanford had waiting and dashed behind relays of special horses into Salt Lake City.

They spent two or three days, Christmas included, in unfamiliar surroundings. Then, while Stanford stayed in Utah to push the work, the Huntingtons boarded another special coach. Again relays of special horses were waiting every few miles. Off they rocked, traveling night and day, not along the railroad route, but over the regular stagecoach road through central Nevada to Reno.

The trip was a shock to Huntington. Maps and schemes in a room in the Willard Hotel in Washington were one thing. The winter realities of the West were something else. Grudgingly Huntington admitted to his associates that Stanford had been at least partly right: an attempt to gain possession of his so-called legal line in canyons already filled with Union Pacific workers would have done more harm than good.

As for the raw, parallel grades that were running side by side from the mouth of Weber Canyon off around the north shore of the lake, some new stratagem was necessary. The railheads of the two competitors had by then reached almost within three hundred miles of each other, the CP at Elko, Nevada, and the UP, thanks to the shoofly around the Echo Summit tunnel, well down Echo Canyon. Thus each road was entitled to send graders almost to the other's railhead—and each was doing so. The desert was spotted with truculent crews working diligently in opposite directions. The Central Pacific could claim Browning's approval for its route. But the UP could counter that it was acting under a higher law, the Pacific Railroad acts, as passed by Congress.

The Union Pacific, however, was gasping for finances. The emergency was so acute that Huntington feared that the overstrained company might of its own accord offer a compromise—a junction halfway between the railheads as they existed at a prescribed date. Ames, Durant & Company had one powerful argument on their side. They had built twice as much track as the Central. As soon as they reached halfway down Weber Canyon they would be a thousand miles from Omaha. At Elko, the Central Pacific was a paltry 468 miles—rough miles, to be sure—from Sacramento. To yield half of the remaining distance to the shorter line might appear in Washington like commendable generosity, and pressure would be put on the CP to accept.

Actually, such a division would strand the Californians out in the salt flats near the Utah-Nevada border. The UP would garner the traffic of Salt Lake Valley; it would dominate transcontinental policies and freight rates; it would be in a position, if finances revived, to strike off through northern Nevada and northern California to its own terminus on the Pacific Ocean.

For a year Huntington had been fighting to avoid just that, and the prospect of being forced into so disastrous a "compromise" put him into a fresh passion. He railed at his partners, especially Charles Crocker, for their delinquencies.[5] Back in October, as they well knew, he had assured Browning that by the first of the year the Central's tracks would have reached Monument Point on the north side of Salt Lake. If the promise had been kept, Ogden would be only eighty miles away and he could point out to Browning the fairness of letting the Central Pacific build on into the fertile valleys east of the lake. Instead, the track was almost two hundred miles from Monument Point—280 miles from Ogden. How could he explain that to the Secretary, especially now that the UP was all but knocking at Ogden's door?

Well, there was no choice but to keep trying. Could Crocker reach Monument Point in another forty-five days?[6]

Charlie spread a big, pudgy hand. It was winter now. In spite of the new snowsheds, supply trains might slow up. The frozen ground was hard to work and the grading went slowly. There was one positive factor, however. A hundred miles west of Monument Point they would pick up a good roadbed already prepared by the Mormons. Without the need of supplying graders, on whose heels they were practically walking now, progress should quicken. Certainly he and Strobridge would do their best.

236

The best had better be good enough, Huntington growled, or they would all be in the poorhouse.

For his part, he would hold the Union Pacific at bay in the Wasatch canyons. He would attack the shoofly around the tunnel as unacceptable by the government within the meaning of continuous track and thus he would prevent the delivery of bonds to them. He would insist further that whatever work the UP had done off the approved line was equally unacceptable. And because the enemy, by sheer chance, had graded on parts of the authorized route in the canyons—a route first surveyed by the CP—he would sue them for trespass. It would be expensive. But taken together the devices would freeze the UP's funds. Unless he was badly mistaken, the scare would bring Old Ames around in a hurry to talk of a better compromise than a splitting of distances. But the plan would not work unless the track reached Monument Point by the end of February.

At least they understood each other now. With that small satisfaction to cheer his return journey, Huntington left Sacramento on January 7 and by train and stage raced East, arriving in New York at 5 A.M., January 19.[7]

A new shock awaited him there. At about the time that he had left New York, the Ames brothers and Grenville Dodge had learned of Browning's approval of the Central's route as the only legal line. Promptly they had stormed into Washington with evidence purporting to show that the CP "line" was a fraud, based on a mere reconnaissance and not on the sound engineering studies that an acceptable line demanded. Badgered thus, the Secretary retreated and said that he had approved a general route only and not one specific line. Then, having been burned once, he declined to approve the maps the UP men thrust at him. Instead, he appointed a special four-man commission to meet in Salt Lake City, study both roads and their grades, decide which was preferable, and make recommendations about a satisfactory meeting point.[8]

On learning of these developments, Collis rushed to Washington in his turn. Browning met him frostily. "If their road is as good as yours and if they get to Ogden before you get to Monument Point, they ought to have the road."

"The Union Pacific," Collis decided in his chagrin, "has outbid me."[9] But he would not—could not—quit. He wrote letters to the President of the United States. He urged his partners to greater effort. "For God's sake, push the work on. . . . If I was there I would not take off my clothes or change my shirt until the rails were laid to Ogden City." He prepared the trespass action against the Union Pacific. "I think by commencing this

237

suit we can cripple them. . . . I have felt for the last 100 days as though I would like a hell of a fight with someone." He told Hopkins to stall the new commissioners Browning had appointed. "Keep back the report as long as you can"—at least until he had lifted the CP into the saddle again.[10]

The relentless assault worked. Twice Oakes Ames and other Union Pacific officials came to his hotel room in Washington to discuss a meeting place. As Collis had anticipated, Ames's first offer was to split the remaining distance between railheads. "I'll see you damned first," Collis told him bluntly.[11] As a counteroffer, he named the mouth of Weber Canyon, east of Ogden. Ames replied with equal incivility. In subsequent interviews Collis backed up to Ogden itself. Beyond that, he growled at his visitors, he would never budge.

Actually, he was not as confident as he sounded. The UP by then (mid-February) had pushed its rails almost through Weber Canyon, and Ogden was only a few miles away. Central Pacific bonds were not selling, because of a general expectation of a Union Pacific victory. If he thought Ames would consent, Collis confided to Crocker, he was ready to give the enemy a million dollars in exchange for the right to enter Ogden.[12]

And then, suddenly, he had a brand-new inspiration about how to make the Central Pacific line the legal route as far as Ogden. Telegrams flew again. Had the Mormon graders hired by Stanford completed the roadbed between Monument Point and Ogden? Practically, the answer came back. Ah! Then he would ask, as he was entitled to, for two thirds of the bonds due on the eighty miles between Monument Point and Ogden. If they were granted to him—and not to the UP for the grading it had done beyond Ogden—then he was in the clear, for obviously the government would not pay duplicate subsidies.

He sent in the request through normal channels, to make it look all the more legitimate. Browning turned it down. Collis stormed into his office. After long conversations, Browning agreed to present the question to the Cabinet. This he did on February 26. The members attending, all of whom were going to be unemployed after Grant's approaching inauguration, agreed in principle to advancing the bonds Huntington wanted. To protect themselves, however, they asked the Attorney General for a ruling. They met again on Monday, March 1, to hear his decision and cast their votes. Afterwards Browning wrote in his diary, "It was unanimously decided that the company was entitled to them under the law and Secy [of the Treasury] McCulloch was directed to issue the bonds."

Collis picked up the securities the day before the inauguration, on

March 3—$1,333,000 worth. Five hundred thousand of this sum he had to leave at the Treasury as security for the satisfactory completion of the road to Ogden. He surrendered them happily. *Ogden!* Let the Union Pacific try to dislodge him now![13]

He stayed around for the inauguration, then went back to New York. To Hopkins he boasted by mail, "This was the biggest fight I ever had in Washington, and it cost a considerable sum, but I thought it of so much importance that I should have put it through at a much higher price if it had been necessary."[14]

The Union Pacific directors would protest, of course, but he thought he had a way to placate them. It was a familiar obsession and one that Ames himself had suggested earlier—a new city. Let the two roads meet a few miles outside of Ogden and at the point of junction create the great metropolis of the West. The various directors would own the choicest lots and would make fortunes from real estate speculation.[15]

He was too canny a fighter to drop his guard at the first gleam of victory. He kept exhorting Crocker to push on at top speed—the pace was creeping up toward five miles a day, now that the tracklayers had reached the Mormon grade—and he warned Stanford against letting the UP lay iron on even a foot of roadbed prepared for the Central: "It would be well to have a few good rifles. . . ."[16] The last fear was unfounded. Neither line attempted to jump the other's grade. But the workers did torment each other with occasional barrages of stones. Now and then, also, an explosion just chanced to go off when the enemy was close by. Actually, if these clashes were as serious as later accounts have sometimes suggested, they left curiously little record in the surviving letters of the CP's directorate.

The climactic warfare took place in the East. The Union Pacific rejected Huntington's attempts at placation through a jointly owned city. They prevailed on Congressman John Bingham of Ohio to introduce into the House of Representatives a resolution charging that the Central's grading between Monument Point and Ogden was completely substandard and that the bonds issued to Huntington had been "hastily, wrongfully, and illegally approved by the late Secretary of the Interior." Why had Browning been so liberal? To find the answer, Bingham demanded a full-scale investigation by Congress.[17]

Huntington immediately wired Stanford to forward engineering evidence that the grading was sound. He urged friendly senators to block any bill that the House might pass as a result of the resolution. This, he warned his associates, was going to be "a sharp, bitter fight."[18]

To their great good luck the battle never came to a head. The Union Pacific was mired in serious financial and legal troubles. Young Jim Fisk, partner of Daniel Drew in a notorious stock raid on the Erie Railroad, had decided to gain control of the Union Pacific. He bought a few shares of stock and then opened suit, declaring that the railroad was bankrupt and demanding the appointment of a receiver. All was done as he wished. A complaisant friend of Fisk's, William Marcy Tweed, Jr., was named by a complaisant judge as receiver on the plaintiff's behalf. At this, certain disgruntled holders of Crédit Mobilier stock, who felt that the interlocked Union Pacific-Crédit Mobilier directorate had shortchanged them during the distribution of dividends, leaped into the fray.[19]

The sound of the uproar carried quickly to Congress. On hearing it, the Central Pacific's task force went swiftly to work. Senator William Stewart of Nevada, six feet four, adorned with a grizzled beard that covered half his chest, led the assault. Stewart, Mark Twain remarked (Twain once served for a few weeks as the senator's secretary), had more brass in his constitution than the Colossus of Rhodes. While Oakes Ames listened stolidly, he began dropping hints about the shortcomings of the Union Pacific in general and the Crédit Mobilier in particular. Other recriminations flew back and forth, and it began to look as though the Union Pacific as well as the Central Pacific would be included in a sweeping congressional investigation.

Neither side wanted that. Ames and Huntington decided to compromise after all. They met at the home of Representative Samuel Hooper of Massachusetts, holder of considerable Union Pacific and Crédit Mobilier stock. Hooper, part owner also of an iron mill, had bought fifty shares of Central Pacific stock during Huntington's first crucial foray into New England in search of finances. Hooper, in short, was not exactly disinterested, but at least he represented all three parties immediately concerned in the troubles—the government and both railroads.

The talks began in the evening on April 8, lasted until 4 A.M., adjourned for a few hours, and were finally concluded late at night on April 9.[20] During them Huntington and Richard Franchot stood off practically the entire Union Pacific directorate. The Ames brothers yielded first. Durant, outvoted, stamped away swearing that he would not abide by the agreement the others patched together. Later, when lawyers for the contestants tried to smooth off the rough edges of the memoranda that had been drawn up at the talks, more sparks flew. A new impasse developed and final peace was not achieved until November, when the impatient government at last intervened to bring about accord.

Victory, if any, was Huntington's. He gained the right for the Central Pacific to continue around the lake as far as his proposed new city. The metropolis, which the Union Pacific agreed to help promote, was to be located five miles north of Ogden. The two groups of course did not want word of the yet unborn city to leak out, lest the Mormons of Ogden object and speculators come swarming in too soon. Hence it was unmentioned in the account of the compromise sent to Congress on April 10; the junction point, the message said somewhat vaguely, would be "at or near Ogden."

By the time of the agreement the UP had already laid iron well beyond Ogden. Partly out of resentment over the way Huntington had collected bonds for the grading on that stretch, the Union refused to halt. After acrimonious debate Huntington agreed that the rival road could continue to lay iron as far as Promontory, Utah. The Central Pacific would then purchase the road between Promontory and the site of the proposed metropolis. For this 47.5-mile stretch of track, the CP paid $2,840,000. Part of the sum was made up of the government bonds that Huntington had drawn from McCulloch on March 3.[21]

Until the metropolis was built, the Central wanted the right to enter Ogden. Therefore it leased the five miles of Union Pacific track lying between the site of the unborn town and the city of Ogden. The peculiar arrangement—a purchase of 47.5 miles of track and a 999-year lease of five more miles—has long baffled commentators. The cause was Huntington's stubborn dream of new cities, but since this particular town never materialized (the reasons will be noted later), neither he nor the other would-be participants felt like discussing the matter in public, and so they let the motives behind the seemingly strange lease-sale remain obscure.

Congress formally approved the compromise, and with that as justification, called off its own threatened investigation. The long, extravagant battle was over.

The Central had escaped from the desert by the skin of its teeth. Stewart's pyrotechnics in the Senate had been the immediate cause of the favorable outcome, and Huntington was always scrupulous about paying for services rendered. On May 17 he wrote E. B. Crocker:

Stewart . . . has always stood by us. He is peculiar, but thoroughly honest and will bear no dictation, but I know he must live, and we must fix it so that he can make one or two hundred thousand dollars. It is to our interest and I think his right.

The result of the suggestion was a gift to Stewart of fifty thousand acres of "average value" land in the San Joaquin Valley, located near the new right-of-way of the Southern Pacific. Title of course was conveyed through a dummy trustee.[22]

During the furor in Congress, the four commissioners whom Browning had appointed to investigate the entire Pacific railroad returned to Washington. They submitted conflicting reports. Blickensderfer, a Union Pacific engineer, and Gen. Gouverneur Warren were highly critical of the work done by both roads. It would cost, they said, $4.5 million to put the CP in decent shape, $6.8 million to bring the UP up to acceptable standards. Lt. Col. R. S. Williamson and Lewis Clement, a Central Pacific engineer, were more kindly. They felt both roads were adequate as they stood and could be improved gradually as increasing amounts of traffic dictated.

No one heeded the remarks. At Congress's request, President Grant had appointed a board of "Five Eminent Citizens" (Congress' term) to make still another examination of the oft investigated transcontinental. Thus the Williamson-Clement report was wholly redundant. Still, Huntington appreciated its kindly remarks. While Williamson and Clement lingered in the East after turning in their reports (both were Californians), Collis paid their expenses. The tab came to seven hundred dollars—fair enough for an obsolete paper.[23]

Meanwhile the rails were hurrying closer and closer to their physical wedding at Promontory. Thanks to the snowsheds in the Sierra, the mountain crossing stayed open most of the winter. Delivery procedures had finally been hammered into shape. Grades were ready and waiting. Perhaps because he was still smarting under Huntington's continued criticism of his slowness, Crocker decided to show once and for all how much track he could lay in a single day—an astounding ten miles, laid on April 28 after everything had been prepared in advance.

On May 10, following awkward delays caused by rainy weather and strikes by unpaid Union Pacific workers, officials from both railroads gathered at Promontory to tap the famous golden spike into place. The first blows were designed to trip a telegraphic signal, but the hammer swingers missed and the operator had to simulate the dramatic moment with his key. From coast to coast cannons boomed, celebrants paraded, fireworks reddened the sky.

Huntington, sitting as usual in his New York office, ignored them all. He may have been thinking of the days when Green River had been his goal and of the enormous shrinkage that had occurred since then. If only

242

it could have been! Reaching for a pen, he scrawled off, on May 10, right while the ceremonies were underway, a letter to Charles Crocker:

> I notice by the papers that there was ten miles of track laid in one day on the Central Pacific, which was really a great feat, the more particularly when we consider that it was done after the necessity for its being done had passed.[24]

As Leland Stanford would learn in his turn, Collis Huntington was not of a disposition either to forgive or to forget.

19 New Vistas in Virginia

Shortly after the linking of the rails at Promontory, Huntington received, in his cramped office at 54 William Street, a call from Harvey Fisk and Alfrederick Hatch. He greeted them warmly. During the past few years the brokerage firm of Fisk and Hatch had helped him dispose of some fifty million dollars' worth of Central Pacific and U. S. Government bonds. In addition, the two men had supported the price of the company bonds by buying them up in the open market whenever quotations began to sag. For these latter transactions the Central Pacific owed Fisk and Hatch about a million dollars, a debt recorded only by notations scrawled on small slips of blue paper.[1] Under the circumstances, Huntington was disposed to listen whenever the two men chose to make a recommendation.

They were, in effect, making one now, for they brought with them and personally introduced to Huntington an ebullient young promoter named H. Chester Parsons.

In 1869, Parsons was twenty-eight years old, nineteen years younger than Collis Huntington. The discrepancy in ages bothered the young man not at all. He was used to charging where others went gingerly.

A native of Vermont, he had served with distinction as a cavalry officer during the war. He was wounded three times, officially cited for gallantry in action, and mustered out as a colonel. During one of his cavalry sweeps through Fairfax County, Virginia, southeast of Washington, D.C., he had met a southern belle named Nellie Loomis. A storybook romance sparked. After the war he returned to Virginia and married Nellie. Scenting financial as well as romantic interests in the rebuilding South, he decided to stay below the Mason-Dixon line. Soon he was deeply involved in promoting railroad lines and coal and iron mines in both Virginia and West Virginia.

244

His visit to Huntington was on behalf of the hard-luck Chesapeake and Ohio Railroad Company. The line's ancestor, financed largely by state and county money, had started creeping northwest from Richmond in 1836. Known eventually as the Virginia Central, it had reached the mountains near Covington (Virginia, not Kentucky) when the War between the States broke out. During the conflict its tracks were repeatedly torn up, its buildings and rolling stock burned. Even so, it had tried to rouse again as soon as the conflict was over. The principal figure in this stubborn renascence was Williams C. Wickham. Wickham was something of an anomaly in Virginia, being both a Confederate brigadier general and a Republican.

Wickham managed to stitch together, on paper, three small systems. One was the old Virginia Central. The other was the state-controlled Blue Ridge Railroad. The third, which consisted only of a charter from the state of West Virginia, was the Covington and Ohio. To this combination Wickham gave the descriptive name, Chesapeake and Ohio. His intent was to tap the Ohio River in the western part of West Virginia. There the C&O would pick up commerce from the entire Ohio Valley and carry the freight through Richmond to a port, unlocated as yet, near the mouth of the Chesapeake Bay. Since the port would be ice-free and since the railroad's grades through the mountains would be easier than those faced by the trans-Allegheny lines in Pennsylvania, the C&O was destined, in Wickham's mind, to become the dominant railroad of the East.[2]

On October 1, 1868, the directors of the C&O issued ten million dollars' worth of thirty-year 7 per cent bonds. Simultaneously they set workers to scratching out twenty-two miles of track from Covington through rough mountain country to White Sulphur Springs, West Virginia. The idea behind the construction was to prove their vigor and thus stimulate the sale of bonds.

They misjudged. Competition for capital was fierce, both in the United States and in Europe. Railroads were being promoted everywhere. New industries throughout the East were offering stocks and bonds at alluring figures. Growing cities were bidding for money in order to create municipal improvements. Hordes of bonanza wheat farmers at the edge of the plains were mortgaging their holdings at rates of 15 to 18 per cent a year. In so rapacious a money market, one more issue of railroad bonds could not hope to attract attention unless surrounded by some special aura. The Chesapeake and Ohio, floundering through deep Jerry's Run near the West Virginia border, did not have the necessary radiance. In the spring of 1869 its directors found themselves with a treasury full of unsold bonds and a million-dollar debt on their abortive stretch of new track.

At this point H. Chester Parsons, twenty-eight years old, offered to produce a savior. By unrecorded stages he reached Harvey Fisk and Alfrederick Hatch. They thought well enough of what he told them that they agreed to introduce him to Collis Huntington.

In the office at 54 William Street Parsons spread out his maps and charts and graphs. One exhibit was probably an endorsement which Robert E. Lee had given to the company on September 21, 1868: inasmuch as the Chesapeake and Ohio would furnish the best route from the Mississippi Valley to the Atlantic, it "may therefore become one of the most prominent of the eastern branches of the Pacific Railroad." Surely that prediction would interest Huntington. But if it did, he gave no sign. All through the interview he sat silent, shaggy and massive, staring at Parsons out of those unreadable gray-blue eyes. The brash young man left the office considerably deflated, convinced that he had failed.[3]

Fisk and Hatch reassured him. It was a matter of timing, they said. Let the notion simmer for a while.

Financially, Huntington was in no position to undertake another major construction job. Except for the bonds being withheld by the government pending formal acceptance of the Pacific railroad, the Central Pacific had used up all its resources. In addition to a million dollars due Fisk and Hatch, the CP owed Philip Speyer & Company (American Branch of a potent Frankfurt, Germany, brokerage firm) another $1.25 million. Other notes were scattered here and there, especially in a Newark savings bank. Semiannual interest payments on upwards of twenty million dollars in company bonds would soon be due. Against these sums stood an operating net for 1869 that Hopkins forecast at about $1.5 million—hardly enough to help.

Far more serious were the obligations of the Contract & Finance Company. Its floating debt stood somewhere in the neighborhood of $3.5 million. Securing those obligations were personal notes signed by the five associates, notes that bore from 12 to 15 per cent interest a year.[4]

Heavy drains on the Contract & Finance Company were bound to continue. The Western Pacific had to be finished between Sacramento and San Jose. Branch lines recently purchased in Oakland and Alameda had to be hooked up to the Western Pacific at Niles. Money was needed to construct terminal facilities at Oakland and, if Congress proved amenable, at Goat Island. More funds had to be found to improve the submerged sixty acres of land recently donated by the state at Mission Bay south of San Francisco; to make the first payment on the option to purchase the San Francisco & San José Railroad; and to buy hundreds of thousands of dollars' worth of rolling stock for the new transcontinental trains.

And that was just a beginning. As soon as the Western Pacific and its branches were completed, the Contract & Finance Company would have to begin work on three more roads. To meet charter requirements it would have to push ahead with the Southern Pacific. It would have to start the San Joaquin Valley road south through the valley for which it was named, and the California & Oregon north from Marysville. Meanwhile, the special commission of Five Eminent Citizens appointed by President Grant was about to leave on an inspection trip to determine how much work both the Union Pacific and the Central Pacific would have to do to bring their tracks up to acceptable standards. Conceivably the amount could run into several million dollars. Huntington was so nervous about the matter that he called on one of the commissioners, Gen. Hiram Walbridge. Afterwards, in what seems a blatant hint that Stanford tamper with the general's judgment, he wrote the CP president that Walbridge was "a good fellow and I think he will look out for our interest if it is for his interest to do so."[5]

From a financial standpoint, in short, young Parsons had picked a poor time for calling on Huntington. Brokers Fisk and Hatch surely realized this. Psychologically, however, the situation was very different, and they probably realized that, too.

For one thing, Huntington was suffering a natural letdown. His great project was finished. He had saved the Central Pacific by the narrowest of margins, but instead of being able to relax for a moment in contemplation of what he had achieved, he was being harassed by pettiness.

Much of the trouble stemmed from the brothers Lambard, Charles of Boston and Orville of Sacramento. After acquiring a few shares of Central Pacific stock during its early years, both men had become involved in railroads inimical to the Central Pacific's progress.

The western brother, Orville Lambard, had joined Col. C. L. Wilson and Sam Brannan in trying to push the California Central and its extension, the Yuba Railroad, north to Marysville. As noted earlier, they had fallen seven miles short of their goal. Afterwards, floods had damaged the short section of the Yuba that did exist to such an extent that it became all but inoperative. Meanwhile, the Central Pacific had acquired the California & Oregon, holder of a valuable land grant from Congress. The associates wanted to pick up the California Central and the next-to-worthless Yuba, make them the first leg of the California & Oregon, and then start pushing northward. In spite of Wilson's resistance, Huntington had soon absorbed the California Central. The Yuba proved thornier, however, because of the intransigence of Orville Lambard, who owned $250,000 worth of badly depreciated Yuba bonds.

Orville intended to make Huntington pay through the nose for those bonds. He had a powerful weapon. His brother, Charles Lambard, was a heavy stockholder in both the Union Pacific and in Crédit Mobilier. While Charles nodded agreement in the background, Orville proclaimed throughout New York's financial district that he was going to use the Yuba as a link in a new trans-Sierra system that would give the Union Pacific an independent entry to the Coast. It was a worn threat by that time. The muscle behind it amounted to little more than rusty rails and the Yuba's franchise. Even so, Lambard was able to hurt the price of Central Pacific securities. Collis struggled with him for months, trying to get his bonds at a reasonable price.[6] He was still struggling, and sick of the wrangle, when Parsons called.

Charles Lambard was an even greater nuisance. From the beginning he had opposed the settlement which had saved the Central Pacific's corporate life—the agreement whereby the Union Pacific was to sell the Central enough track so that the CP could reach the fertile valleys of northern Utah. He found fault with all the terms, refused to accept the price the Ames brothers had established, and persistently interfered in all related matters. After Huntington had won a concession from Oakes and Oliver Ames that the two railroads would share equally in revenues arising from cross-country traffic, Lambard upset the arrangement. The UP's tracks were longer, he argued (ignoring Collis' retort that the CP's grades were far more rigorous), and rates should reflect that fact. The upshot was an increased share in each ticket for the Union Pacific and, in consequence, higher rates for both passengers and freight than Huntington thought were justifiable.[7]

The long, scratchy arguments that accompanied these disputes corroded even Huntington's monumental patience and left him ready to listen to any new proposal that would challenge his imagination rather than his temper. Of this, too, Fisk and Hatch were aware.

He had been working on such a project all spring, but in late May it was on the point of collapse. Apparently on his own initiative, he had devised a plan for New York City's first subway.* He would excavate

---

* A standard California denigration of the associates still says that they had shopkeepers' minds, that they dealt with railroad matters as they had once dealt across their counters with dried fruit, hair ribbons, and monkey wrenches. Actually, Huntington's achievements in New York in financing the western half of the nation's single greatest construction project to that time, had released in him a creative imagination of singular daring. He visualized enormous projects not for their own sake so much as for the challenge (and profit) involved in putting together the capital necessary to finance them. This, after all, was the lush era of the nation's headlong plunge into industrial capitalism, and a new kind of entrepreneur was called for. Collis Huntington rode in the van and relished every bruising minute of it.

Broadway from the Battery to Ninth Avenue and then follow Ninth Avenue to 150th Street. At Union Square a branch line would strike up Fourth Avenue to Harlem.

The plan called for four railroad tracks along the Broadway section, express trains inside and locals outside. Promenades and basement stores would line the underground tracks. Because electric locomotives had not yet been invented, motive power would have to be provided by steam engines. Ventilation would be furnished by parallel iron grills five feet wide between surface sidewalks and the street. Entrance to the subway would be by two flights of stairs in each block.[8]

In March 1869 bills granting the necessary franchises were introduced into the assembly at Albany. The New York *Times* was agog. "The scheme," the paper editorialized on April 3, "is enormous in its proportions. Nothing at all comparable with it has been done or attempted in any large city in the world. But . . ." And then the objections began.

The idea was half a century premature. Alarmists wondered what would happen to traffic flow along the streets concerned while work was underway. What about the disruption to sewer mains, gas and water pipes? Where would the excavated earth be disposed of? Costs would be exorbitant.

Perhaps those questions could have been answered. But Boss Tweed was something else. Proponents of surface streetcar lines and of elevated railroads (the first "El," powered by steam locomotives, was built the following year) enlisted his support. Huntington's bills jammed up in legislative committees, and he was just coming to a full realization of the odds against him when Parsons arrived. It is even conceivable that Fisk and Hatch hurried the young promoter to Huntington in order to give their chief client a new and attainable target for his sometimes frightening energies.

Finally, there was a certain balm of recognition in Parsons' approach. By his own choice, Huntington had been largely ignored during the celebrations that marked the completion of the Pacific railroad. He had not seen fit to go to Promontory, where he would have had to stand in the background while President Stanford clumsily swung a sledge hammer at the golden spike. Now Charles Crocker was reaping headlines in his turn by taking his family with him in a private car back over the route he had covered in 1850 in a covered wagon—a four-day journey compared to one of more than a hundred days only twenty years before. Inasmuch as the other associates had arrived by sea, Crocker was the only one who could really play up the contrast, and he was making the most of it. Arrived in New York, he passed out to the crowd of journalists who met his special train "blooming flowers . . . strawberries, oranges, and luscious cherries from California brought upon Alaska ice."

It made good copy. But when the Virginians wanted a railroad, they did not turn to Crocker or Stanford or any of the Union Pacific-Crédit Mobilier group. They came to Huntington—came when he needed a boost.

In view of later developments, it would be interesting to know exactly what Huntington envisioned for the future on the day that he first looked at Parsons' maps. The system the drawings showed was, on the face of things, relatively modest: two-hundred-odd miles of track restored to good running order between Richmond and Covington, twenty-two miles of shoddy construction between Covington and White Sulphur Springs, and another two hundred miles of surveyed right-of-way from White Sulphur Springs to a still undetermined point in Cabell County, West Virginia, beside the Ohio River. Pure hope as yet was a southeastern extension from Richmond down the peninsula to some undesignated spot near Hampton Roads at the mouth of the Chesapeake Bay.

This was the period of Huntington's life when he was fascinated by the speculative opportunities inherent in railroad-created towns. The proposed Chesapeake and Ohio offered two tantalizing sites. One was a river port on the Ohio. From it West Virginia coal and lumber could be dispatched to all parts of the Ohio and central Mississippi valleys. To it the same regions could send produce of all kinds for shipment to the Atlantic seaboard. The second site was a complement of the first—an ocean port which, having captured the export-import traffic of the Midwest, might rival the great harbors farther north.

Did he glimpse anything more? He may have. During this period, he and Elizabeth were occasional visitors at Pocaho, the Hudson River estate of Gen. John Charles Frémont and his glamorous Jessie, with the latter of whom Collis almost surely exchanged reminiscences about their simultaneous crossing of the dreadful Isthmus of Panama in 1849.[9] With Jessie's husband, Huntington undoubtedly shared railroad talk.

Frémont, it will be recalled, had been involved first in the Kansas Pacific and later in the Atlantic & Pacific. He had lost heavily in both ventures, but, always sanguine—and always injudicious—he was trying again. In 1869 he was the president of the Memphis, El Paso and Pacific, which held valuable land-grant rights (eighteen million acres) in Texas. Shortly before Parsons called on Huntington, the Memphis, El Paso and Pacific had also acquired for $600,000 in stock the grandiloquently named San Diego and Gila, Pacific and Atlantic Railroad, which had surveyed a roadbed east from San Diego Bay to Yuma, Arizona, where the Gila River debouches into the Colorado. The Memphis, El Paso intended, in other words, to build to the West Coast along the thirty-second parallel, the route Jefferson Davis had recommended in 1853. Any such road obviously became a potential competitor of the Central Pacific and thus bore watching.

In addition, Frémont was dickering for the control of a series of roads that ran from Memphis east to Norfolk, Virginia, on the Chesapeake Bay. Those disjointed roads were not in his clutches, but his high-pressure bond salesmen were telling investors in France that they were. The salesmen were also proclaiming that here at last was the making of a true transcontinental spanning the entire American continent from Norfolk to San Diego.

It is scarcely credible that Huntington, who possessed an almost uncanny cunning for discovering the secrets of his rivals, did not learn of this sweeping plan. If he did, he saw at once that the extension of the Chesapeake and Ohio to, say, the Mississippi, would reduce the effectiveness of the eastern end of Frémont's proposed transcontinental. The vision, like Frémont's, may have extended even farther. After he had checkmated Frémont, why could not he, Collis Huntington, link the Chesapeake & Ohio and the California systems and so become the builder of the first transcontinental?

In time, he would fight to achieve just that, the world's most gigantic railroad system. The seeds of it were implicit in Frémont's plans—and also in the maps that Parsons showed him that June of 1869. If the actual scheme flowered in Huntington's mind that early, however, there is no record. He was, above all, a realist. Financing two hundred miles of railroad through West Virginia was all that he could swing right then. The rest would have to wait.

He told Parsons that he would consider the proposal. Parsons, as we have already noted, equated the words with a polite brush-off. Fisk and Hatch, who knew Huntington well, were more hopeful.

The brokers were right. Huntington needed the challenge of a new project. And at that particular time in his career it was a staggering challenge. He controlled little liquid capital himself. He would have to obtain the backing of richer men than he, yet men who would be willing to let him take charge of affairs. To do this he would have to extract from the Virginians an enormous price for his help—so enormous that potential supporters would have to take notice.

He submitted his proposal to Parsons on June 9, 1869. The Chesapeake & Ohio was to recall the ten million dollars' worth of 7 per cent bonds that it had recently issued and substitute fifteen million dollars of 6 per cent bonds. Huntington, or his agents, Fisk and Hatch, were to have the marketing of the bonds at a price to be determined. A syndicate that Huntington would form would buy the first million of the offering. This would restore the road's faltering credit and establish confidence in the rest of the issue. The syndicate was also to receive a controlling interest in the road's common stock, eight million dollars' worth (face value), payable in four equal installments during the building of the road across West Virginia. The financiers were also to receive another two million dollars in the stock of the subsidiary Blue Ridge Railroad.[10]

Obviously the stock (and the prospective river and sea ports, which Huntington did not mention) would be the reward of the risk. In return Huntington offered intangibles backed by the reputation he had acquired during the past half dozen years: his syndicate, having taken control of the Chesapeake & Ohio from its former board, would "devote whatever skill, experience, and influence we possess to secure the early completion of the road, the extension of its business connections, and the establishment of its finances on a satisfactory basis."

Even granting the C&O's perilous condition, the terms were harsh. Furthermore, no syndicate as yet existed. Huntington wanted a solid, attractive proposal in hand before he approached anyone. Parsons of course did not know that. He assumed Huntington himself could furnish whatever resources were necessary, and he saw no other hope for the C&O. Nervously he skimmed back and forth between New York and Richmond, arguing vehemently. At last he prevailed on President Williams Wickham and the other reluctant directors of the C&O to invite Huntington to White Sulphur Springs for further conferences.

The meetings were held during the first two weeks of July 1869. Bitter terms? True. But Huntington refused to compromise. Desperate, the Virginians capitulated. As soon as they saw the color of the syndicate's money, they said in effect, they would relinquish control of the company.

With that promise reduced to writing and folded inside his coat pocket, Huntington returned to New York. Not another sound came from him for four suspenseful months.

The financial market was soft that summer, and Huntington had trouble finding men to join him in the venture. Strangely, he did not breathe a word of the plan to his California associates, not even to Charles Crocker, who was in New York at the time. The reason for the aloofness in the case of Stanford and E. B. Crocker seems clear: Huntington disliked Stanford acutely, and Ed Crocker had just suffered a paralytic stroke that had all but incapacitated him. As for Hopkins and Charles Crocker—well, Collis could hardly pick and choose among his associates, and besides, he probably was anxious to stretch his wings this time entirely on his own. The Californians could join him, on his own terms, once the C&O began reaching westward.

Counting himself, he finally persuaded six men to contribute $100,000 each toward the syndicate. Brokers Fisk and Hatch and an attorney named Joseph R. Anderson were three of them. Another was William Aspinwall, who had founded the Pacific Mail Steamship Company shortly before the gold rush and then had built an immensely profitable railroad across the Isthmus of Panama. The sixth member was A. A. Low, designer and builder of fabulous clipper ships.

Five more men agreed to put up $50,000 each. Among them was Jonas Clarke, a returned forty-niner and New York real estate speculator whom Huntington had known in California as a fellow vigilante during the wild days of 1856. Another was David O. Stewart, a New York merchant with whom Huntington had dealt during Collis' storekeeping days.[11] Fatefully enough, as matters developed, both David Stewart and William Aspinwall had purchased a few shares of Central Pacific stock during the formative period of the railroad, when Huntington had been struggling to raise money by every means possible.

This eleven-man syndicate was $150,000 short of the one million that Huntington had tentatively promised to the Virginians. Before he was able to round out the sum, he had to go to California to attend a critical meeting of the Central Pacific's board of directors. He said nothing about the trip to the impatient Virginians, and as the stock market shivered into fall they began to despair. As we shall see, his silence proved to be a shrewd bit of maneuvering—assuming, of course, that it was deliberate and not just a reluctance to admit inadequacy. But first, California.

20 Consolidation In California

The trip West was something of a royal progression. Elizabeth and Clara, then nine years old, traveled in one private car with Collis. Charles and Mary Crocker and some of their children were in another. Scattered among them were various guests: General Franchot, the Central Pacific's chief lobbyist in Washington, Congressman John Farnsworth of Illinois, and other dignitaries. Squads of lesser flunkies—cooks, porters, butlers, maids, and governesses—attended them all.

Somewhat ill at ease in the gathering were Mr. and Mrs. Alban N. Towne and their seven-year-old daughter Evelyn.[1] Towne, the self-educated son of a Massachusetts millwright, had just turned forty. Until a few days before he had been general superintendent of the Chicago, Burlington & Quincy. By offering him the then munificent salary of $13,000 a year, Huntington had lured him away from the Burlington to take full charge of operating both the Central Pacific and the Western Pacific. The liberality shocked Crocker and Stanford, but Towne turned out to be one of the best investments the associates ever made.

Also west-bound in a private car attached to a different train was Oliver Ames, president of the Union Pacific. Ames and his staff were scheduled to meet with the directors of the Central Pacific, settle the matter of turning over the track between Promontory and Ogden, and pick the official junction point of the two railroads. The junction selected, the directors of the two companies would then quietly buy up, on their own account, the surrounding land and launch the city that in Huntington's mind would become the great metropolis of the West.

He was counting on giant transportation interchanges to foster the new town. First, the CP and UP would lure the Utah Central, then under construction in the south, into the new community. Branch lines would be thrust north into Idaho and Montana. The Union Pacific and the Central Pacific would jointly build a major road into the Northwest, to head off Jay Cooke's Northern Pacific. All this, of course, would destroy nearby Ogden, population 1,400. But never mind—the Mormons weren't deserving of a grand interstate transportation metropolis anyway.[2]

Stanford, coming from the West, met the party at Promontory. The private cars were shunted onto a desolate siding. While the women endured a cindery boredom, the men rode a slow work train back toward Ogden, inspecting the roadbed. Crocker proved obstreperous. He was suspicious of the rival company, which had tried to block the Central Pacific in the desert, and as a result he did not like their roadbed, either. He found many points that, in his estimation, the UP would have to improve before the CP would accept the tracks. Stanford agreed. In fact, the two men told Ames that the Central Pacific would be better off if it built its own road into Ogden and let the UP do whatever it pleased with its substandard grade.[3]

A few miles outside of Ogden the train halted so that the unfriendly group could tramp through the sagebrush, purple mountains to one side, distant gleams from the salt sea to the other, and select a townsite. They achieved no real agreement on that point, either.[4] Crocker, for one, stubbornly opposed the building of either a community city or a community line into the Northwest with the Union Pacific. If such things were to be, let the Central Pacific control them. He simply did not believe that shared work would end the feud. Instead, their quarrels would, in his opinion, be intensified.

Ames went sulkily East. The Californians continued on to Sacramento and a series of directors' meetings wherein, hopefully, they would discover means of staving off ruin.

Except for the generous salaries that the directors had paid themselves, seven years of labor had brought them none of the profits they had anticipated. For a while they had hoped that the relative cheapness of building across Nevada would compensate them for the flood of dollars they had poured out in surmounting the Sierra. The gain had not come. To meet the exorbitant cost of the race to Promontory, Huntington had been forced to sell every available company and government bond as fast as he could lay hands on it. Even this had not been enough.[5] The swollen floating debts referred to in the last chapter still hung over both the Central Pacific and the Contract & Finance Company—debts whose exact amount cannot be reconstructed because of the deliberate destruction of records some years later.

Only a few flimsy shields existed to blunt the sharp edges of those obligations. One was the Central Pacific's land grant. Land sales, however, were certain to move slowly. Not an acre could be marketed legally until after the government had surveyed each square-mile section in the grant and had issued titles, called patents. The surveying was moving at a snail's pace. Besides, much of the acreage was so arid that prospective purchasers were not likely even to look at it. Thus the only way to realize a quick return from the land was to use it as security for an issue of land-grant bonds that could be sold on the open market.

Although the Union Pacific was resorting to the expedient, Huntington was reluctant to follow suit. Land-grant bonds had very little allure. In order to attract buyers, the paper would have to bear high interest— 10 per cent or so—and be sold at a discount. Eventually, too, the bonds would have to be either redeemed at full price or refunded. Relief from present pains, in Collis' opinion, should not have to cost that much in future prospects.

Another expedient was income bonds issued against anticipated earnings. The Union Pacific was trying that, too, but again Huntington was reluctant, and for the same reasons. As for trying to borrow against the road's physical plant—track, buildings, rolling stock, and so on—the prospects were hopeless. Those resources were completely blanketed by the Central Pacific's own first-mortgage bonds and by the government's loan of second-mortgage bonds.

Most of all, Collis wished to protect the value of the road's capital stock against the harmful effects of excessive bonding. This stock, which had been paid over to the Contract & Finance Company in partial recompense for the building of the road, was the associates' best hope of recovery.

Some 385,000 shares of $100 par value were involved. The figures reflected two increases in capitalization that had been authorized as the demands of construction grew increasingly insistent. The first expansion, completed on October 8, 1864, had lifted the ceiling from the $8.5 million originally recommended by Judah to twenty million. On July 23, 1868, the figure had leaped again, from twenty million to $100 million, with a corresponding right to issue one million shares of $100 par value stock. The figure was excessive, for there were contractual limits on the amount of stock the Contract & Finance Company could accept; as already indicated, the maximum came to roughly 385,000 shares by the time the job was done.

This was a tantalizing amount of crinkly new paper. Charles Crocker would gladly have laid hands on his portion at any momer brother Ed had just been incapacitated by a stroke, and Jolly (feared a similar fate for himself—he said—unless he relaxed. mind the associates ought to use income bonds, land-grant bonds, or anything else they could dream up to reduce the floating debt and then sell the stock for whatever it would bring. After all, it had cost them next to nothing, since company and government bonds together had paid the major part of construction expenses, except, of course, for the floating debts.

The others declined. Since the stock had never been listed on any exchange, there was no way to know what it might bring when offered in large blocks. Years later, in 1896, Huntington told congressional investigators that at the completion of the road, its $100 par value stock could not have been sold at five dollars a share.[6] He was making a point and therefore the figure may have been an exaggeration; at its lowest ebb, Union Pacific stock never dropped below nine dollars. But even if the entire block of Central Pacific stock could have been sold at ten dollars, with no need to devote part of the proceeds to clearing up old obligations (a highly unlikely situation)—even then each of the five associates would have made only about $780,000 for seven years' work. They had glimpsed much more than that during the high moments of their drive toward Green River, and three of them at least—Hopkins, Huntington, and Stanford—intended to keep on fighting to reach those alluring vistas.

The question was how best to do it. The search for an answer led them into a close review not just of the Central Pacific but also of the several properties that they had been acquiring piecemeal through the past several years.

From the outset they had sought to maintain the value of the Central Pacific, and hence of its stock, by eliminating possible competitors. In order to get rid of the Robinson brothers, they had purchased the Sacramento Valley line, which ran from Sacramento through Folsom to Shingle Springs near Placerville. Next, Stanford and Ed Crocker had overridden Huntington's opposition in order to obtain the Western Pacific, thinking that this would block out any southern transcontinental searching for an inlet to San Francisco. But they had let the San Francisco & San José slip through their fingers; to remedy that, the associates had secured control of the Southern Pacific. This in turn brought them an option to purchase the SF&SJ and also a franchise that would let them build to the Colorado River, there to check the Atlantic & Pacific. As a final bulwark in the south they had incorporated the San Joaquin Railroad. It was a paper entity still, but possessed a franchise that permitted it to reach southward toward Bakersfield and freeze approaching competitors out of that area.

In the north they had absorbed the California Central and the Yuba, and had acquired the franchise of the California & Oregon. These three acquisitions they planned to amalgamate into a unit that could block either an end run through northern California by the Union Pacific or a California thrust by the Northern Pacific, currently being revived under Jay Cooke's supposedly magic touch.

To gain an outlet to San Francisco Bay the associates had obtained five hundred acres of choice waterfront real estate in Oakland, on which they had agreed to spend $500,000 in making improvements. They had then sought to connect the Western Pacific to Oakland by purchasing for $814,936, two dinky short lines and their ferry slips. One short line ran southeast from Oakland and the other, southeast from Alameda, a hamlet separated from Oakland by a bothersome tidal estuary.[7]

Besides being expensive in themselves, the acquisitions had entailed a certain amount of construction. The biggest job was the completion of the Western Pacific, which on September 6, 1869, shortly before the directors gathered for their meeting, was formally opened between Sacramento and San Jose. At the same time work was pushed on the Oakland and Alameda short lines. The two branches met like arms of a Y at a place called Melrose and then continued as a single trunk to join the Western Pacific at Niles. The Alameda part of the Y was finished, as was the Western Pacific, on September 6. On that day a bunting-bedecked Central Pacific train chugged up to the Bay bringing eleven transcontinental passengers from the East, the first to touch Pacific waters by rail. They were greeted with flags, flowers, cannon shots, and cheers, but, so far as Alameda was concerned, the excitement was short-lived. The Oakland arm was scheduled for completion in November, and because of the property the associates held there, that branch became the CP's main outlet to the Bay.[8] The Alameda extension was just a way to keep competitors from sneaking close to navigable water from the southeast.

Smaller bits of construction involved the California Central and Yuba. Their tracks, which formed a continuous line north from Roseville, were repaired and, during the early summer of 1869, extended seven miles farther north to Marysville. The two small roads were then incorporated into the California & Oregon, which, so far, had built nothing. Southward, meantime, the Southern Pacific had crept out of San Jose through twenty-five miles of fertile farmland to Gilroy. At Gilroy the work was halted by a dilemma which, as we shall see, was going to give the associates endless trouble.

The purchases and projects outlined above had been a severe drain on the associates' resources, and more work still had to be done in order to meet various franchise, land-grant, and contract requirements. The California & Oregon had to start pushing north; the San Joaquin had to move south. The promised $500,000 in improvements at Oakland had to be at least inaugurated. The Oakland requirements, the associates decided, could best be met by building a two-mile-long railroad pier reaching into navigable water near Goat Island. Until Goat Island was acquired from Congress (Huntington still meant to battle for that), the pier would serve as the terminus of the transcontinental. Later Goat Island would become the region's great entrepôt, and then the pier could be turned into a causeway leading to it.

After outlining the bleak facts, Huntington laid out a program. First, Stanford was to provide statistics on population, climate, agricultural possibilities, and so on for publicity purposes. Using the figures to support his sales talks, Collis would raise funds for construction by bonding both the California & Oregon and the San Joaquin roads. Lest his partners expect too much, he warned that bonds on incomplete roads were hard to sell. He would need time to persuade brokers, particularly in Germany, a favorite source of capital, that his offerings were sound. Meanwhile the associates had to prepare to meet upwards of $600,000 interest on the Central Pacific's first-mortgage bonds, due in January, to say nothing of other payments due on the floating debts of both the CP and the Contract & Finance Company. The Californians must realize, in short, that for a while they would have to move very slowly with the different projects.

Just how much could they spend? they asked him.

He named what seemed a trivial figure, $380,000.

They protested. They could not build even the Oakland pier with that.

They could start, Huntington retorted, doing just enough to maintain appearances. Speed could pick up as soon as he was able to start money flowing again.

He must have awed them with his vehemence. They agreed. Evidently they did it merely to keep him quiet, for, as we shall see, he was hardly out of sight when they began spending money almost as recklessly as they had during the race to Promontory.[9]

So many different projects, each working away at its own program, raised questions of organization. Would it not be better to consolidate all of the roads, except the Southern Pacific, under a single management?*

Efficiency was only one of the lures tempting the associates to consolidation. A stronger appeal was the possibility of stock manipulation. By considering the different lines as extensions of the Central Pacific, CP stock could be issued against them, too, and added to the 385,000 shares already held in Contract & Finance Company pool. (As matters worked out, the total eventually jumped from 385,000 shares to 542,000 shares.)[10] Moreover, each share of the augmented pool would be worth more than each original share, because the Central Pacific with feeder lines would look more attractive than the Central Pacific without any.

A dewier bit of stock watering can hardly be conceived. It was dangerous, however, for it involved the equities of the Central Pacific's minority stockholders.

During the formative years of the company, it will be recalled, the associates had tried assiduously to raise funds by selling shares in the enterprise. Sacramento and Placer counties had traded $550,000 worth of county bonds for 5,500 shares of stock. San Joaquin and Santa Clara counties had also exchanged bonds for Western Pacific stock.

Many individuals were concerned. Sam Brannan had accepted two hundred shares of Central Pacific stock as part payment for rolling stock. During a door-to-door canvas for funds, more than two hundred residents of Sacramento had subscribed for shares. Huntington and Franchot had sold some in New York, Boston, and Albany. On occasion, Huntington had used small stock bonuses as a sweetener when urging manufacturers to accept his depreciated bonds in payment for material. He had used $50,000 worth (par, not actual, value) of his own shares in order to purchase and furnish his home at 65 Park Avenue, New York. Stanford's brothers, Philip and Charles were shareholders. An indeterminate amount of stock had gone to Congressmen as an expression of gratitude for their votes.

Thus at the time the associates had realized that they could build the

---

* Grantley, George Gorham, and William Carr still held a three eighths interest in the Southern Pacific. Taking them into the expanded Central Pacific would create difficulties, and as yet the associates were not in a position to buy them out. Another obstacle to the SP's formal consolidation with the CP was the related San Francisco & San José, which the associates did not yet control but on which they held, through the Southern Pacific, an option to buy. Most important, the Southern Pacific might some day make connections with another transcontinental at the Colorado River. If that occurred, the SP would be part of a competing system and hence might prove an awkward bedfellow if included in the same organization as the Central Pacific. For all those reasons the SP was omitted from the consolidation.

road with bonds alone and had decided to issue no more stock to out-siders, there were perhaps ten thousand shares of CP stock floating around loose. These shares were based, moreover, on the company's original capitalization of $8.5 million. Since then, authorized capital had been increased twice—to twenty million and then to $100 million—but there is no evidence that the minority stockholders had been offered any adjustment.

That was not the worst of it. The directors of the Central Pacific had awarded themselves, as directors of the Contract & Finance Company, very lush contracts for building the road. And then they had wasted the money in a mad race with the Union Pacific. Either matter might justify a demand that the Central Pacific and Contract & Finance Company open their books to inspection. Since considerable sums of government money—county, state, and federal—were involved, this might prove embarrassing.

Finally, there was the manner in which the many short-line acquisitions had been obtained. Most had been purchased by the Contract & Finance Company, using Central Pacific bonds paid to it for building the CP. Just where had so many bonds, supposedly devoted to construction alone, come from?

As indicated earlier, the demands of the race to Promontory had absorbed more bonds than the associates had anticipated. Therefore, in order to purchase the short lines in California, the Contract & Finance Company had borrowed heavily from the Central Pacific. One wonders (in the absence of records) whether the C&F perhaps borrowed even more bonds from the Central Pacific than the railroad was entitled to issue under the terms of the congressional acts of 1862 and 1864.[11]

All of these things had a direct bearing on the value of the stock that had been sold during the days when the total capitalization of the railroad had been a modest $8.5 million. The matter was, however, as amorphous as fog. No one had any sound idea what a share of the old stock was worth, or what a share of the new stock based on the proposed amalgamations would be worth at the time of issue. Presumably there would be an increase in value. Therefore it was just possible that some shareholder might ask the courts to allow him to examine the books so that he could discover what had been going on and what his rights were.

There had been warnings of this. Legislators had already risen in the California assembly to inquire about the source of the money being used to acquire so many California short lines. Were state or county funds, granted for the construction of the main line only, being used for these unauthorized purposes? Were the diversions of money, if any, causes for criminal action against the associates?

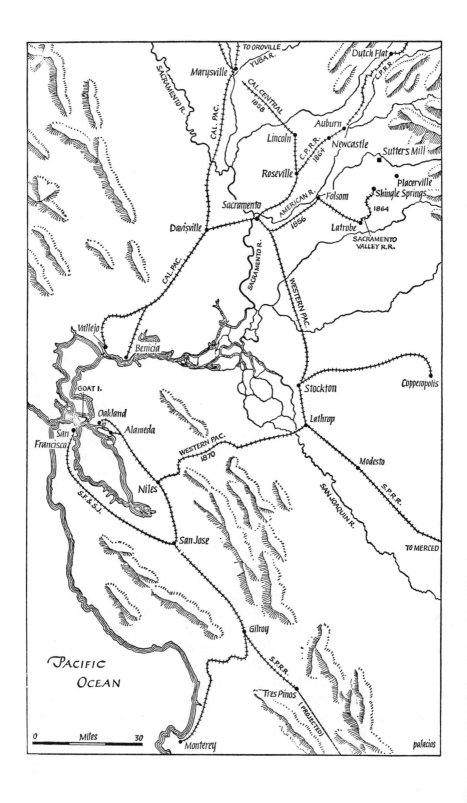

TO OROVILLE
YUBA R.
Dutch Flat
C.P.R.R.
SACRAMENTO R.
Marysville
CAL. PAC.
CAL. CENTRAL 1858
Auburn
Lincoln
C.P.R.R. 1864
Newcastle
Sutters Mill
Roseville
Placerville
Shingle Springs
Folsom
1864
AMERICAN R.
1856
Sacramento
Latrobe
Davisville
SACRAMENTO VALLEY R.R.
CAL. PAC.
SACRAMENTO R.
WESTERN PAC.
Vallejo
Benicia
Stockton
Copperopolis
GOAT I.
Lathrop
Oakland
Alameda
San Francisco
Niles
WESTERN PAC. 1870
Modesto
S.P.R.R.
SAN JOAQUIN R.
S.F. & S.J.
San Jose
TO MERCED
PACIFIC OCEAN
Gilroy
S.P.R.R.
Tres Pinos
(PROJECTED)
0   Miles   30
Monterey
palacios

Some lawmakers had introduced bills demanding a formal investigation. Stanford's cohorts had promptly buried them in committee. The ease with which it was done and the inchoate nature of the stock with which they were dealing perhaps made the associates overconfident. In any event, they voted to go ahead with the consolidation.

The intricate details were to be worked out in the West. Then, as soon as the new issue was ready, Huntington would undertake to have it listed on the New York exchange. The listing would immediately open several options to the associates. They could use the stock as collateral for working loans, a privilege not accorded unlisted stock. A value per share would be established. They could then sell enough to pay off their debts, divide the rest, and do with it as they chose. Or, if they liked, they could keep it in a pool and be content with whatever dividends they voted themselves. They would be doing this, moreover, with 542,000 shares and not with the original 385,000 shares collected from the Central Pacific, a potential difference of many millions of dollars.

Need and greed appear to have blinded most of the five men.

Only Huntington seems to have worried about possible stockholders' suits. As a way of forestalling them, he suggested that each minority shareholder be given a 10 per cent stock bonus at the time the new issue was floated. This might keep the recipients quiet until the stock was listed and regular cash dividends began, at which time, if dividends were high enough, the shareholders would probably subside for good. But, he said, the bonus should not apply to the Contract & Finance Company. The contemplated reorganization would add, by itself, a sufficiency to the firm's holdings; additional watering would reduce the effectiveness of the scheme.

Stanford objected to the restraint. They, too, should have a bonus, he argued hungrily, but the others voted him down and followed Huntington.[12]

Insofar as the plan for consolidation did not face the problem of the minority stockholders, it was untidy, to say nothing of its ethics. If anything went wrong, solutions would have to come through improvisation, the hallmark of speculative promotion. Leap today; worry tomorrow—without that cheerful recklessness, there probably would not have been a California gold rush of such proportions, and certainly the advent of the Pacific railroad would have been long delayed. But a dependence on extemporizing can breed trouble. As will become evident, the residue of the associates' carelessness about their minority stockholders still interferes with objective estimates of their work.

Two other shaggy situations were left uncombed during the September-October meetings. One was the rival California Pacific Railroad; the other was the associates' own Southern Pacific.

The first, the California Pacific, had recently built from Vallejo on the north side of Carquinez Strait northeast to Davisville, now Davis. There the tracks forked. One branch ran east to Sacramento and was opened in time to blunt the celebrations that heralded the Central Pacific's belated touching of salt water at Oakland. For one thing, the California Pacific had the better route. It was flatter than the Central's hilly path via Stockton and Niles, was nearly fifty miles shorter, and nearly two hours quicker. Predictably, most local traffic traveled over the California Pacific. Some transcontinental passengers even disembarked from the Central at Sacramento and finished the run on the rival line.

The California Pacific's branch to Marysville, finished a short time later, promised to be equally vexatious. It offered marked savings in both time and distance over the associates' new California Central-Yuba-California & Oregon link-up and hence would handle increasing amounts of wheat shipments from the Sacramento Valley. What freight it did not seize by rail, it would take by boat, for its owners had just bought the California Steam Navigation Company and thus controlled most of the shipping on the Bay and on the navigable waters of the Sacramento and San Joaquin rivers. There was talk, too, that the California Pacific planned to fulfill the long-standing threat of building through northern California and southern Idaho to a junction with the Union Pacific.

In brief, the rival road opened a wide gate in the associates' would-be wall around the Bay. Hence it was a marked threat to the stock values that they hoped to create through the consolidation of their lines.

It would seem that merger terms could have been worked out if the contending parties had wished. There is no indication that they did. For one thing, the associates knew that the California Pacific was heavily in debt and had been forced to cut sharp corners during the construction of its lines. They did not want to assume those burdens through a merger. Moreover, if they waited, they might be able to pluck up the rival company on their own terms. On the other hand, if the California Pacific showed signs of unexpected resiliency—well, they would improvise to meet that, too. And thus, by postponing a decision that needed making, they created another source of trouble for themselves.

Finally, there was the dilemma that faced the Southern Pacific. Since this quandary would lead in time to the most infamous event in the history of California railroading, the so-called massacre at Mussel Slough and its literary sequel, Frank Norris' fiercely critical novel, *The Octopus,* it will be useful to review here the situation that confronted Huntington and his partners in the fall of 1869.

As first chartered in 1866, the Southern Pacific was to run south through the coastal counties to Los Angeles and on to San Diego. From San Diego it was to swing northeast and meet the Atlantic & Pacific at the Colorado River in the vicinity of present-day Needles. The Southern Pacific's aid from Congress (like the Atlantic & Pacific's) was limited to land grants.

Because old Mexican land grants covered much of the area to be served by the SP, relatively little land turned out to be available. In 1867, therefore, the company changed routes. As mapped, its new line would head southeast from Gilroy through the hamlet of Tres Pinos, would cross a low range of mountains near the head of San Benito Creek, and then would drop through Priest Valley to the vicinity of present-day Coalinga. There it would bend almost due east through good sheep and wheat-raising country—Mussel Slough and Hanford—to Visalia. From Visalia it would dip south to Bakersfield before veering off through the Mojave to the Colorado River and its junction with the Atlantic & Pacific.

This proposed route, which missed Los Angeles and San Diego entirely, was shorter and less mountainous than the original line. It also passed through long stretches of the San Joaquin Valley, where superior land was available.

The Department of the Interior accepted the change. As noted some chapters back, residents of the coastal counties thereupon raised so strenuous a protest that Secretary of the Interior Orville Browning backed down and decreed that the grant to the Southern Pacific would not be allowed unless the road was built along its original line. This pronouncement came almost on the very day in 1868 that the associates acquired control of the SP. Huntington promptly strode into the Secretary's office and protested in his turn. He had winning ways with Browning, as witness the "legal-line" maneuvers during the race with the Union Pacific. After a short hesitation for the sake of appearances, Browning restored the grant to the railroad.

Shortly thereafter a new administration had been elected. Fresh protests by the coastal counties were pressed on Grant's new Secretary of the Interior, Jacob Cox. Huntington, who had sensitive antennae for unwelcome trends, anticipated an unfavorable ruling. He was right. In November, shortly after the conclusion of the directors' meeting, Cox announced that the grant along the revised line had again been revoked.

All this while, when no one could possibly know whether hundreds of square-mile sections of the southern part of the San Joaquin Valley would belong to the railroad or would remain in the public domain, wheat farmers and livestock raisers were moving into the Mussel Slough region and taking up homesteads. A clash would be inevitable if ever the railroad recovered the grant once again and tried to claim the homesteads. But this is getting ahead of the story.

In 1869, Huntington was not sure that he wanted to resist Cox. The situation had suddenly been altered by the grandiose plans of John C. Frémont's Memphis, El Paso and Pacific, mentioned in the last chapter, and by that line's western extension from Yuma, the San Diego and Gila. San Diegans were ecstatic and boasting that as soon as the new railroad was completed through the snowless country of the south, their fine harbor would snatch control of Asian traffic away from San Francisco Bay.

San Francisco, however, still dominated the California commercial scene. Any cross-country railroad would want to reach the city. And a friend of Frémont's, Gen. William S. Rosecrans, goat of the Union Army's defeat at Chickamauga, was eager to provide Frémont with the means.

Rosecrans had picked up for a song considerable real estate south of Los Angeles and near San Diego. He had then moved to California in 1867 with thoughts of running for governor, but had changed his mind on being appointed ambassador to Mexico. Diplomacy did not interfere with his promotional proclivities. As soon as he was convinced that Frémont really intended to build to San Diego, he incorporated what he called the California Southern. It was designed to run north from San Diego to San Francisco, and, eventually, become part of Frémont's system.

With this paper club Rosecrans created massive uncertainties among the associates, for he announced publicly that if the Southern Pacific did not build through the coastal counties to San Diego, he would. On the other hand, if the Southern Pacific did build near the coast, Rosecrans would swing into the San Joaquin Valley. There he would be in a position to thrust east to a meeting with the Atlantic & Pacific (if that road ever got stirring) and, simultaneously, north to San Francisco.

Huntington had heard many people talk about more railroad than they were able to build. Rosecrans worried him, however. Residents of the coastal counties, thoroughly alienated by the Southern Pacific's cavalier dismissal of their hopes, were solidly behind the general. Frémont listened to him because Rosecrans promised an inlet into San Francisco. And finally, the general-ambassador had influence both in Congress and with President Grant.[13]

The associates did not know how to respond. Should they go down the coast, where at least some of their original land grant would be available? Or should they cling to the new route, build a branch to Yuma in hope of blocking Frémont there, and in the meantime do what they could to void Cox's anticipated revocation of their valley grant? Or should they attempt the almost hopeless task of raising enough money to construct both routes?

Gilroy, where the SP's tracks ended, was the fork in the road. They could build no farther until they had decided, yet they were too bedeviled to make up their minds. In the end they stalled. It saved money, of which they had very little right then. Later, they would improvise in the light of what the enemy did; after all, Frémont might have troubles of his own.

Meantime, quite unknown to the associates, one more farmer here and another there were taking up homesteads around Mussel Slough, on land that the Southern Pacific might or might not own. Naturally, in the event of conflict, the homesteaders would insist that the land was rightfully a part of the public domain. Just as naturally, the railroad would insist that it had been theirs ever since the date of the grant's first award in 1867. If, in 1869, the associates had not temporized, some of the misunderstandings might have been cleared up before violence erupted—a gratuitous speculation, to be sure, since it is based on privileges of hindsight not available to the associates.

Their meetings in Sacramento lasted for a month.[14] The decisions—and lack of decisions—which emerged would help alter the destinies of an entire state. For men who less than a decade before had been obscure merchants, it was a startling spin of Fortune's wheel, and one wonders how they viewed themselves in their new position as minor demigods. How, for that matter, did their contemporaries see them?

Already opinions concerning the associates were completely polarized and would stay that way throughout the rest of their lives. Reactions to a banquet that was held during this period will epitomize the clash in attitudes.

Shortly after the associates had assembled in Sacramento, they received from 155 of the town's leading citizens an invitation to attend an all-male testimonial dinner at the Golden Eagle Hotel on September 28. The purpose of the ceremony was "to express to you in person our high esteem and the appreciation of the people of this city for the great enterprise which you inaugurated and carried through to triumphant conclusion."

At the banquet the honored guests were extolled to the skies. It was the outstanding social event of the season, and yet the Sacramento *Union,* the town's leading newspaper (and one of the most influential in the state) took no notice of it—until October 1. On that day the *Union* reprinted, with approval, an editorial from the *Inland Empire* of tiny Baker City, Oregon, whose citizens blamed the Central Pacific for not letting the UP build a branch line through their town to Portland:

> The owners and directors of the road are simply cold-hearted, selfish, sordid men. . . . There is not but one in ten today but that despises [them] . . . If wealth accumulated in utter selfishness . . . is entitled to glorification then this public dinner is appropriate and in good taste; but beyond this the Directors of the Central Pacific are entitled to no praise.

Publicly expressed sentiments as contradictory as those must have stirred tensions of identity within the associates and, even more painfully, within their families. What were they, public benefactors or public monsters?

No one faces himself for long as a monster. On being goaded sufficiently, both Huntington and Stanford declared time and again to probing reporters that they had done more to further the development of California than had any other group of men in the state's history. Support for the view was clearly visible in the number of farms, factories, and cities that sprouted beside their rail lines. Fortified by those statistics, the associates were inclined to dismiss contrary estimates as the product of either envy or political expediency. Whipping the railroads was, after all, one of the favorite vote-gathering ploys of the Granger era.

The charge that they had built the roads not for the good of the state but to grub up money for themselves was particularly infuriating. True, the associates stood to make millions, eventually, from a relatively paltry initial investment of a few thousand dollars, but to assume that such gains were wrong was to concede that at some point or another a ceiling appeared above which profits were no longer "fair."[15] Predictably, the associates rejected the philosophy. If they were willing to run risks, they were entitled, in their minds, to the full enjoyment of whatever gains the risks produced.[16] Risks, furthermore, were not to be measured by quantity alone. As long as the partners were putting everything they possessed into this adventure, what difference did the size of the investment make? Was Napoleon's collapse any more desolating than a storekeeper's? Under those circumstances, should not success, if it came, be equally unrestrained?[17]

But, critics retorted, no success whatsoever would have been possible

268

if the public had not granted them loans, cash, and land. As a consequence were they not obligated to look upon their enterprise as a public trust, subject to public regulation?

This argument, too, the associates rejected. They had made a contract with the government to build a railroad. They had completed the job according to specifications. In their estimation the road was now private property, as sacrosanct under the American system of individual liberty as was any other private property.

Detractors fumed at the stance and argued again and again in newspaper editorials and legislative speeches that if property rights were to become as vested as the railroad tycoons pretended, the public would have no recourse when those rights were ballooned into intolerable monopoly. No state could allow such a thing to happen to its transportation systems.

To this the associates retorted with a point painfully learned during their race with the Union Pacific. Competition was warfare and chaos. No one won. Even the public lost, because the price cutting and the manipulations for advantage subordinated orderly growth, economical work, and long-range planning to the expediencies of the moment.

Self-defense and the survival of the fittest, their attitudes proclaimed, were the first law of economics as well as of nature.[18] In fulfillment of that law they would do, with no sense of wrong, whatever was necessary to protect their great achievement against erosion by politicians ("demagogues" was Huntington's favorite term), competitors, or raiding speculators, just as they would have protected their homes against robbers or wild animals. If this involved breaking unjust laws (and the associates would define injustice to suit themselves), then they would do it.[19]

In 1870 there was nothing exceptional about such a philosophy. Most leaders of America's burgeoning post-Civil War industrial establishment shared it to varying degrees. In California the trait was even more marked than in the East. The dominant group of the state's economy was a hardy, aggressive band of adventurers who had rushed West to exploit the goldfields. When those had proved less enduring than anticipated, they had turned with equal feverishness and equal combativeness toward such other resources—land, irrigating water, and transportation of all kinds—as best lent themselves to quick engrossment. Monopoly achieved, the next logical step was to protect it against the complaints of those who had been elbowed aside—the envious, the weak, the malicious, the incompetent, as they considered those whom they had outdistanced.

In the fall of 1869, at the directors' meetings in Sacramento, Collis Huntington committed himself fully to monopoly and all that it entailed.

Given his nature, the context of the times, and the precarious situation of the railroad, it is inconceivable that he would have chosen otherwise, even though the decision was certain to bring him a lifetime of verbal abuse. Well, abuse, too, was part of the price. There would be occasions, though, when he and those around him would find the cost a hard one to have to keep on paying.

21   Blackmail and Other Ailments

The Huntingtons left Sacramento on October 22, 1869. In New York Collis found a financial establishment still staggered by Jay Gould's assault on the gold market a month before. In Richmond, Gen. Williams C. Wickham and the other promoters of the Chesapeake & Ohio were desperate. They were sure that because of the collapse of the stock market Huntington would not be able to put together the syndicate he had promised.

The assumption was another stroke of Huntington luck. He was unscathed personally, for he seldom speculated in stocks. On the other hand, he had not been able to raise the full million dollars that he had led Wickham to expect. Subscriptions to the syndicate still stood at $850,000. That was where the luck came in. Against the background of Wickham's gloomy expectations, $850,000 shone like a rainbow. On November 25, the Virginians accepted it in full payment of Collis' promises. Shortly thereafter the Chesapeake & Ohio was completely reorganized with Collis Huntington as president and Gen. Williams C. Wickham as vice-president and general superintendent. Huntington nominees held seven places on the eleven-man board of directors. Not until then did Collis inform his California partners of his new venture. It would not, he assured them, detract in any way from his work for the Central Pacific.

The first contracts to build in West Virginia were let in March 1870. Work began in May. Huntington, held down by politics in Washington and a spate of threatened lawsuits in New York, did not manage to inspect the line until summer. He then rode over most of it on horseback, looking colossal on a long-legged mount big enough to support his bulk. Where the mountain canyons were too rough for trails, he ran the rivers with his engineers in a plunging bateau. Though he was forty-nine

271

by then and completely adjusted to city living, he seemed as vigorous as during his years in the goldfields.

He could not have been reassured by all that he saw. Fifteen tunnels were projected, aggregating 23,649 feet in length. An enormous fill would have to be heaped up in Jerry's Run. There were long stretches beside West Virginia's roily rivers where lifting the roadbed above flood level would involve cutting high shelves out of loose, exfoliating sandstone slabs.[1] It would be a tough, expensive job, and he must have wondered whether fifteen million dollars in discounted bonds would be enough.

Other prospects were more pleasing. With Delos W. Emmons, who had married one of Elizabeth's sisters, he scoured the edges of the Ohio River, looking for cheap land and favorable docking facilities where the western terminus of the new road could be located. They found what they wanted west of the mouth of Guyandot Creek. Through agents Huntington quietly purchased some five thousand acres, formed the Central Land Company, put Emmons in charge, and on February 27, 1871, incorporated the town of Huntington, West Virginia. To insure instant population, he and Emmons placed the C&O's shops inside the city limits and built two rows of houses to rent to employees.[2]

Nepotism did not end there. During his inspection of the line, Huntington had noticed a struggling sawmill just outside St. Albans, some thirty-five miles east of Huntington townsite. Fine stands of pine grew nearby and if the sawmill were enlarged, it could supply ties and bridge timbers to the Chesapeake & Ohio. Afterwards it could start marketing lumber throughout the region served by the tracks. He bought the property, laid out plans for expansion, and summoned his favorite nephew, Solon's eldest son, Henry Edwards Huntington, to take charge. At that time Ed Huntington, as Collis generally referred to him, was twenty years old and bored with his job in a New York City hardware firm.[3]

At the eastern end of the Chesapeake & Ohio, plans were underway for driving a tunnel underneath Richmond in order to reach docks beside the James River. (The city was helping with a bond issue of $300,000.) That was as far as finances would reach. For the time being, Collis' plan of extending the tracks to another potential townsite at the mouth of the Chesapeake Bay would have to be postponed. Even so, Virginians were agog at what was being done. In February 1871, the Richmond *Dispatch* declared, "If enterprise, the masterly control of means and force, and a wonderful rapidity of railroad construction entitle a man to the crown of railroad king, that crown belongs . . . to a man remarkable alike for his reticence and modesty . . . Mr. Huntington."[4]

In Oneonta, where Huntington frequently went to visit his family and to look at bits of real estate that he owned there, the *Herald* was even more excited. After predicting that Collis' next project would be the uniting of his lines into a true transcontinental, the editor cried, "We therefore nominate him for president in 1876, as all his roads will unquestionably be completed by that time, and C.P. will have nothing to do."[5] Neither C.P., who was devoid of Stanford's interest in politics, nor anyone else took the boomlet seriously. Still, in view of the constant run of difficulties that had plagued him since his return from California, the eulogies must have made pleasant reading.

He had not expected so overwhelming an onslaught of troubles. At the directors' meetings in Sacramento, his partners had agreed to economy. In addition, operations seemed promising; during its first full month of business the Western Pacific had netted $93,700, while at the same time the Central Pacific had cleared $579,642.[6] More balm had come from the report of the Five Eminent Citizens whom President Grant had dispatched to inspect the road prior to its acceptance by the government. After the trip the group had said that although the Union Pacific must spend $1.58 million bringing its track and equipment to passable standards, the Central Pacific need spend only $576,650. On the strength of the committee's praise Huntington was able to collect the remaining government bonds that the Secretary of the Treasury had been withholding as a guarantee of the road's satisfactory completion.

There had been exasperations, to be sure, most of them caused by what was, in Huntington's mind, Stanford's genius for folly. The first clash arose over the Utah townsite. On November 19, 1869, Collis, Oliver Ames, and Cornelius Bushnell had finally signed a compromise agreement concerning the CP's taking possession of the tracks that the UP had built from Ogden to Promontory. They had also agreed on the junction point of their rails. All that remained was to gain control of the land where the new metropolis of the West was to be built. Exultantly Collis ordered Stanford to hurry to Utah and buy "8 sections [5280 acres] of land for the town before it is known that our point of meeting is not Ogden."

Stanford, supported by Charles Crocker, chose instead to present the problem to Brigham Young. Young urged Ogden as the junction point, and Stanford bought 150 acres there. "I would rather have nothing," Huntington snapped at his colleague, and added petulantly, "It does seem as though the fates are against our making any money out of town sites."[7] They were indeed. Stanford having failed, emissaries of the Union Pacific undertook to acquire the desired land. That done, Congress was prevailed on to designate the undeveloped site as the official junction point of the rails. The Mormons promptly objected. Their intense opposition and a belated realization that ample water for the new city would be hard to find killed the scheme. In 1875, Huntington finally surrendered and let the Central Pacific begin building permanent yards, shops, and depots in Ogden on the land that Stanford had originally purchased.[8]

Still other grudges against Stanford built up in Huntington's unforgiving mind. He was slow about sending the statistics Huntington needed in connection with marketing the bonds of the California & Oregon Railroad. His carelessness, in Huntington's opinion, had let profits on the Sacramento Valley branch line between Folsom and Shingle Springs dwindle toward the vanishing point.[9]

In December the accumulation of grievances exploded in a letter to Hopkins.[10] California's one-time governor, Huntington railed, was a millstone around the company's neck—lazy, pompous, vain, and foolish. "I think we are all to blame for allowing him drift with our interests. . . . We let him go on and fool away millions of dollars for us." Unless Hopkins would take the responsibility for shaping Stanford up, Huntington would walk out of the firm.

No follow-up to the correspondence has survived. Either Hopkins was an efficient peacemaker, or Huntington was distracted by a gathering of far more ominous problems than those that Stanford represented.

The first blows were delivered by Collis' own associates. Impelled by considerations that cannot now be recovered, they decided to ignore the promises of economy they had made in October. Instead, they pressed ahead full speed with the construction of the California & Oregon and with the Oakland Long Wharf. There were floods of other bills, notably for the last eighteen miles of snowshed built to shelter the CP tracks in the High Sierra. By December the associates had called on Huntington not for the $380,000 that they had agreed to, but for $950,000.

The operating revenues which Collis had been holding against January interest payments were diverted to these unexpected needs and he had to borrow once again. If the drain kept up, he warned, "we shall all go to the Devil." There was no abatement. By March 1870 he had sent to California $1.68 million in gold and $317,281 in currency, and had paid out, for rolling stock, repairs to the hastily built line in Nevada and Utah, and materials ordered from eastern supply houses another $946,229. Tighten up, he ordered his associates furiously, and at last, toward summer, they did.[11]

Normally he would have been able to raise some of the funds he needed by selling bonds on the new San Joaquin road and on the

274

California & Oregon. But the money market was constricting. Meanwhile scores of unbuilt railroads were offering paper at high discounts, and investors were wary. To top the difficulties, along came Ben Holladay, the one-time stagecoach king who had sold out to Wells Fargo and then had started gathering in shipping and railroad lines in the Northwest. Among his acquisitions was the Oregon Central, which held a land grant from Congress and a franchise to meet the California & Oregon somewhere near the boundary between the two states.

Holladay gave the Oregon Central a new name, the Oregon & California and flooded the German market, which Collis was trying to open, with cut-rate offerings—sixty-five dollars for a $100 Oregon & California bond. "Fraud!" Huntington growled. He was sure that the man was using the similarity in names in order to cash in on the reputation of the California & Oregon, which was known to have a solid link-up with the only Pacific railroad in the United States.[12] If that really was Holladay's intent, he failed. He merely confused investors. As a result, the bonds of both companies moved very slowly, until the outbreak of the Franco-Prussian War in July 1870. After that they did not sell at all.

Simultaneously, the owners of the San Francisco & San José grew restive. Did, or did not, the Southern Pacific intend to take up the option on their line?

Of course the Southern Pacific intended to. The company did not dare let that vital link become available to someone else—to General Rosecrans, for instance. Pressed for action, Huntington offered the impatient railroaders one million dollars down and $100,000 a month until the purchase price of $3.25 million was met. Stanford overrode him. For unknown reasons he raised the down payment to $1.5 and then let Huntington worry about finding the money.

Collis could not do it. He was overloaded with obligations, and the most he could raise for this particular purchase was $500,000. A major crisis threatened until Lloyd Tevis, nominal president of the Southern Pacific and part owner of the San Francisco & San José, persuaded his partners to be less adamant. Late in the summer of 1870 they accepted Collis' proffered $500,000 and the Southern Pacific took possession of the SF&SJ. For his services Tevis demanded and received, over Collis' objections, an undivided one twentieth interest in whatever land grants the Southern Pacific became entitled to.[13] In time his take amounted to some 320,000 acres. Part of the acres were irreclaimable desert sand. But a goodly share lay in the fertile southern end of the San Joaquin

Valley and helped make Lloyd Tevis, together with his partner James Ben Ali Haggin, one of the great landholders of California.

Congress heaped up more problems. Budget watchers began to ask why the Union Pacific and the Central Pacific were not paying interest on the 6 per cent bonds that the government had loaned them. By the end of 1870, the Union Pacific was $2.5 million in arrears; the Central Pacific and the Western Pacific together, almost $3.5 million.

The railroads answered that Congress, when authorizing the loans in 1862 and 1864, had not intended that the interest be paid until the bonds matured. (The language of the bills was ambiguous on the point.) Repayment of principal and interest combined, the company officials went on, was to be met through a sinking fund. The fund was to be fed by the government's placing into it each year half of the compensation due the railroads for hauling troops, mail, and other government supplies. In addition, the companies were supposed to place into the fund 5 per cent of the net proceeds achieved after the completion of the roads.

What, the questioners asked, was the state of the funds?

They were anaemic. The companies blamed the government. The United States, they said, was sending a disproportionate amount of material over the Panama route. Moreover, the need to place 5 per cent of their net proceeds in the sinking fund had not risen and would not until the railroads were completed—that is, until the repairs recommended by the Five Eminent Citizens had been finished and accepted by the government.* Nor was that all. The government was withholding, for the sinking fund, 50 per cent of all payments due the roads for transportation services, yet was ignoring that subtraction when figuring the companies' receipts. A true net should show the deductions. For those various reasons, the Union Pacific and the Central Pacific were not yet prepared to put any such sums into the sinking funds as arbitrary bureaucrats said that they should.[14]

The truth of the matter was that both roads were in a trap. To keep up the price of their bonds, they had to broadcast favorable statistics about earnings and prospects. These reports provided critics with free ammunition. And yet, though earnings seemed high, both roads were actually mired in debt. To survive they had to fight off every drain, even as little a one as 5 per cent of their apparent income.

Stockholders as well as Congressmen were turned curious by the

---

* It should be noted that when Huntington asked the Treasury, in November 1869, for the last bonds due the Central Pacific, he argued that the road was, in effect, completed. His tune changed completely when the sinking fund came under discussion.

glowing sales propaganda that Huntington broadcast in his eagerness to sell bonds. On December 16, 1869, a Mr. Pruyn of Albany, holder of 250 shares of Central Pacific stock, appeared in Huntington's office at 54 William Street. He was followed the next day by a Mr. Winston of Boston. Both referred to figures they had been hearing and asked why they were receiving neither dividends nor annual reports. Collis tried to placate them with a promise of a 10 per cent stock bonus that would come to them when the consolidations in California were completed. The bonus, he added, would be accompanied with a full financial statement. In some agitation he then wrote Stanford to hurry the consolidation along. There should also be, he said, a report that would "clarify things." The failure of the associates in California to be more businesslike—his pen drew harsh lines beneath the words—"*is hurting us very much.*"[15]

Pruyn and Winston were mere rumbles. The thunderclap came a few weeks later. Sam Brannan, who owned two hundred shares of Central Pacific stock, called on Stanford, quoted what he had heard about earnings, and tried to sell Stanford his stock for something like par. Brushed off, he prepared to strike back. Learning how the Contract & Finance Company had operated, he called exultantly on a lawyer named Moses G. Cobb and set about drawing up a suit whose ostensible purpose was to force the associates to render a full accounting.

While Cobb was at work, he received a visit from two other attorneys, John B. Felton and William H. Patterson. They introduced themselves as representing a group of ten stockholders, mostly residents of New England. Leading spirits of the group were Charles A. Lambard, director of both the Union Pacific and Crédit Mobilier, and his brother, Orville D. Lambard of Sacramento. Another of the group was Anna Judah, Theodore Judah's widow, holder of twenty-five shares. Anna had been rendered so bitter by the associates' misappropriation of her husband's dream, as she saw it, that on the day Stanford drove the golden spike at Promontory she had shut herself into her home and had refused all visitors.

Like Brannan, the Lambard brothers had decided to sue for an accounting. For the sake of added strength before the court, they had obtained the support of eight other stockholders. Now their attorneys proposed to Cobb that they all join forces.

Together the lawyers concocted an extraordinary document. By adding up the face value of the county, state, and federal donations and loans that the associates had received; by grossly overestimating the amount of land covered by the Central Pacific's grant (10,041,600 acres as against the 6,890,404 which the railroad actually obtained) and valuing each acre at five dollars (the government valued it at $2.50); by at-

277

taching astronomical values to the CP's acquisitions; by tossing in the old Donner Pass wagon road and the Wells Fargo stock that the associates had received in exchange for an exclusive express contract—by reaching for everything remotely connected with the road, the complainants reached a grand total of $225,855,618.17 as the value of the assets which the associates had garnered unto themselves through the Contract & Finance Company. The suit averred further, with equal disregard of obvious facts, that the building of the road to Promontory had cost a mere $19,222,956.66⅔. Profits thus amounted to exactly $206,632,661.50⅓. Moreover, so the plaintiffs charged, only 7,345 shares of Central Pacific stock had ever been legally issued. Thus Brannan, as owner of two hundred shares, was entitled to 200/7345ths of the total, or $5,688,888.89 plus 272,213 acres of land. The cut of the others would of course be proportionate to their holdings.[16]

It so happened that Brannan's attorney, Moses Cobb, also acted on occasion as attorney for Lloyd Tevis. By no mere chance, probably, word reached Tevis of what was afoot. Instantly he communicated with the associates.* They panicked.

The fear did not arise because of the absurd figures. Even the antagonistic Sacramento *Union* gagged a little and remarked that the charges seemed "exaggerated." Somewhat naïvely the reporter took motives at face value and added, "The purpose of the plaintiff appears to be to compel the Directors to show their books in Court."

Huntington was more cynical. At least part of the motive behind the suit, he thought, was the ill will that Charles Lambard bore him because of the difficulties that Collis had caused the Union Pacific. "Blackmail!" he termed the action on several occasions, with no apparent awareness of the self-accusation implicit in the statement—namely, that he and his fellows had put themselves into a position where they could be blackmailed.[17]

Their most pressing anxiety concerned Sacramento and Placer counties, holders of 3,000 and 2,500 shares of Central Pacific stock, all of it paid for with county bonds. How had those bonds been used? It could be an awkward question and might even lead to criminal charges of the misappropriation of funds. Therefore it must be silenced.

* Conceivably Tevis took the step as a way of reinforcing his request that his services in acquiring the San Francisco & San José be recognized by a one twentieth interest in the Southern Pacific land grant. (The matter of the down payment for the SF&SJ was then under discussion.) Huntington had been opposing the exorbitant commission that Tevis wanted, but of a sudden no more objections were heard. The coincidence in timing is suggestive, but unsupported by surviving records.

Immediately on receipt of Tevis' warning and before the plaintiffs were aware that there had been a leak, Hopkins called on the supervisors of Sacramento County. Banker D. O. Mills of San Francisco, acting at Stanford's behest (and rewarded, it was charged later, with $50,000 in Central Pacific first-mortgage bonds) called on the supervisors of Placer County. Both sets of officials sold the stock back to the railroad for a total of about half a million dollars. In view of their impoverished treasuries, they probably preened themselves—until the truth emerged. Then it was too late.[18]

In the East, Huntington called on Charles Lambard, who said blandly that he wanted a thousand dollars a share for his two hundred shares. Collis growled back, so he wrote Hopkins on April 9, 1870, a dramatic refusal: "Let the fight go on and damn the man who first cries 'Enough!' . . . I was rather eloquent, for I felt hurt, as I knew we had done nothing but what was right and honorable."* The Glidden brothers and John M. S. Williams, Boston shipbuilders, jarred him back into gold-camp speech. They wanted $1,500 for each of their jointly held 125 shares. He said he'd see them in hell first.[19]

In the West, Stanford opened negotiations with Brannan and Orville Lambard. This kept the enemy from filing the suit and gave the associates time to scurry around, buying up the stock of minority shareholders before they should learn of the action and be tempted to join the hue and cry.

Some of Collis' encounters were embarrassing. Among the shareholders whom he approached were William Aspinwall and David Stewart, members of the syndicate that had taken over the Chesapeake & Ohio with him. Pretending sheepishness, he told them that in selling them the Central Pacific stock years before, he had been too sanguine. It was not a good investment. Besides, there had been an overissue. The CP was calling in the excess, and as a favor to them—he did not want to be guilty of injuring old friends—he'd buy their stock back for what they had paid (par), plus interest on their money. Skeptical, they asked what he was offering other holders for their stock. He replied that if *he* paid anyone more than he was offering them, he would make up the difference. The "he" is underscored because the point became expensive later on.

He followed the gambit with every other stockholder of record in the East—par plus interest, so that in most cases he was actually only

* An aside: at about this time occasional literary allusions begin to crop up in Huntington's letters. Somehow he had been inspired, at almost fifty years of age, to polish a few of the deficiencies left by his incompleted schooling.

279

paying back what the company had received in days of even greater need. It took endless time. He combed directories, chased heirs, hunted up ex-Congressmen, and then visited most of them in person, for he was reluctant to send an agent on errands of such delicacy.

He had certain bargaining advantages. Charles Lambard and most of his fellow plaintiffs also held Union Pacific stock, which was worth no more than ten to fifteen dollars a share at the time. They could well believe that the Central Pacific stock would command little more on the market. Thus par plus interest was, at the time, a real bargain. Moreover, Lambard's position in Crédit Mobilier was not beyond reproach, and Collis quite possibly threatened a counter-exposure if the plaintiffs' action against the associates ever reached public view. In any event, he talked Lambard down from an initial demand of a thousand dollars a share to $125—a total of $25,000, and even that hurt, he wrote Stanford on June 30, 1870. Although records are incomplete, the others seem also to have lowered their sights considerably.[20]

Stanford was less successful. His settlement with Orville Lambard is unrecorded, but Huntington wrote angrily that it was too high. Orville having succeeded, a few others did also.[21] Brannan, however, over-reached. Offered $750 a share, he demanded a thousand. (Contrast this with his suit's request for nearly six million dollars, or $30,000 a share.) Refused, he vindictively filed his suit in the San Francisco district court. It did him scant good. His personal affairs had grown hopelessly tangled. His wife won a divorce and in the settlement was awarded her former husband's rights in the suit. One story has it that James Ben Ali Haggin, Tevis' partner, then called on her and persuaded her to drop the action in exchange for $85,000—$425 a share. By that time the scramble for stock had cost the associates well over a million dollars.

Learning of the high settlements on the Coast, Aspinwall, Stewart, and a few others sued some years later on Collis' promise to pay them as much as he gave anyone else. *He* hadn't paid those high sums, he quibbled, and hired his good friend, ex-Senator Roscoe Conkling of New York, to defend him. The plaintiffs, represented in one of their suits by a rising young attorney named Joseph H. Choate, won a settlement of $400 a share—with interest, $515 a share.[22]

Money was the least of the damage, however. Copies of Brannan's complaint reached all corners of the world. Its figures hurt bond sales in Germany, were trumpeted by the press during the Crédit Mobilier scandal, and furnished ammunition not just to Aspinwall and his fellows but to additional suits by the associates' ancient enemy, John P. Robinson, and by San Joaquin County (the latter two of whom did not collect). The worn figures were used as testimony before half a dozen congressional committees. They helped convince many Californians that the railroad was indeed the *bête noire* of their state. And although the associates did their best to rebut the "evidence," they did not dare show the truth as it stood in their books, and so never really convinced very many people that their hands were clean.

22   The Desperate Years

The paper work connected with the consolidation of the lines around the Bay was finally completed in the summer of 1870.[1] Immediately thereafter the associates were faced with hurrying through a comparable consolidation in the south, where a new threat had arisen.

Early in 1870, Frémont's grandiose Memphis, El Paso and Pacific collapsed, partly because of the fraudulent activities of its bond salesmen in Europe. The vacuum was not allowed to remain unfilled, however. A bill was introduced into Congress that would let a new corporation, the Texas & Pacific, follow the thirty-second parallel route originally assigned to Frémont's road.* The same bill proposed to give the new road generous land grants in Louisiana, New Mexico, Arizona, and in California, where the San Diego & Gila was clinging desperately to the T&P's coattails. The act, if passed, would also allow the Texas & Pacific to buy any railroads it encountered along the way. This provision was designed to let the new road lay hands on grants that the state of Texas had once offered to Frémont's Memphis, El Paso and Pacific, grants since forfeited. (As a once independent nation, Texas controlled the public lands within her borders and Congress had no authority over them.)

Behind the Texas & Pacific loomed the formidable figure of Thomas A. Scott, vice-president of the Pennsylvania Railroad. Scott had had transcontinental ambitions since before 1867. That year, it will be recalled, he had sought to use the Kansas Pacific as an outlet to the Coast and had frightened the associates into acquiring the Southern Pacific as a means of holding him at bay. The government's refusal to amend the KP's charter had ended the immediate threat but not Scott's limitless

---

* The original name was Texas Pacific, but in 1872 it became the Texas & Pacific. For the sake of consistency, this account uses the latter designation throughout.

282

ambition. When his Washington lobby revealed its sponsorship of the Texas & Pacific bill, Huntington was instantly alerted. Once again the associates must man their bulwarks in the south.

The first step was to settle the matter of the Southern Pacific's route and land grant. Hoping to nullify the revocation order that Secretary of the Interior Cox had issued late in 1869, Huntington turned his persuasive powers on friendly senators and congressmen. Would they introduce into their chambers a joint resolution stating that "the Southern Pacific Railroad of California may construct its road and telegraph line as near as may be on the route indicated by the map filed [in 1867]"— the route that slanted away from the coastal counties into the San Joaquin Valley. Congress complied on June 28, 1870. The legislature in Sacramento soon followed suit. After five years of uncertainty both the route and the land grant were at last buttoned up.

"The map filed" led to a meeting place at the Colorado River near present-day Needles with the thirty-fifth parallel route, the still semi-moribund Atlantic & Pacific. Scott's much more dangerous Texas & Pacific, however, was aiming along the thirty-second parallel toward a vital crossing of the Colorado River at Yuma. Accordingly, Huntington had an amendment tacked onto the Texas & Pacific bill which would allow the Southern Pacific to build a branch line by way of Los Angeles to that same spot. This "branch" was to receive as much public land per mile in California as was granted in the same state to either the Texas & Pacific or its satellites. Congress then settled down to almost a full year of debate about the bill.

For an undisclosed sum and a promise to build (at some conveniently unspecified time) a coast line to San Diego, Huntington next purchased the franchise of General Rosecrans' California Southern.[2] Somehow or other he also got rid of Messrs. Grantley, Gorham, and Carr, each of whom had, until then, been holding a one eighth interest in the Southern Pacific. The associates now had firm control of everything in southern California except the San Diego & Gila, which was in the hands of Tom Scott.

Those acquisitions completed, Huntington journeyed to California in the fall of 1870. There, on October 12, the Southern Pacific, the San Francisco & San José, the Santa Clara & Pajaro, and the California Southern were consolidated into what eventually became one of the giant corporations of the United States, the Southern Pacific Railroad Company. Huntington was elected president; initial capitalization was set at fifty million dollars.

In spite of that good round sum, the directors had other commitments to meet and could authorize only token scratches of work to be done for the Southern Pacific during 1871. One was a twenty-mile thrust that followed the mapped line from Gilroy southeast toward Hollister and the hamlet of Tres Pinos. The other covered a somewhat shorter distance from Gilroy along the promised coast route toward Pajaro.

At the same meeting the directors also decided to push the California & Oregon as far north, in 1871, as Red Bluff, California, and the San Joaquin as far south as Merced, in order to capture the huge wheat harvests that were beginning to pour out of California's fertile Central Valley. Fortunately, the earnings of the Central Pacific were holding up. Otherwise the associates would hardly have dared risk even that much construction—a total of about 120 miles of relatively easy work.

All of this was a matter of great indifference to Jolly Charley Crocker. He and his invalid brother Ed had had enough. They wanted out. If their partners would not buy their holdings, then they would offer the securities somewhere else. The threat left the remaining three associates with little choice. But they did not have to like it.

Haggling lasted from October 1870 through May 1871, in Sacramento and in New York. At its end Huntington, Hopkins, and Stanford agreed to give each Crocker $900,000 for his one-fifth interest in the group's undivided assets—the Contract & Finance Company, the unsold bonds of the California & Oregon, San Joaquin, and other short lines, the charters, franchises, and the Central Pacific land-grant bonds which, over Huntington's opposition, were soon to be issued to relieve immediate debt pressures. The sum was to be paid in three years in installments of $300,000 to each brother, a total of $1.8 million.

The sale did not cover the Crockers' portion of the Central Pacific stock held in the Contract & Finance Company's enlarged pool. The brothers kept that for a nest egg. Hopkins was bitter. The two men had forsaken the company at a difficult time, taking with them an immediate "fortune of a vast sum, and a reasonable expectation from C. P. stock of many million more, so yoked with our interest in like property that we must realize to them their expectations, or do worse for ourselves."[3]

While the haggling with the Crockers was going on, Scott's lobbyists in Washington grew impatient over the delay with the Texas & Pacific bill. Move along, boys!—and, so charged the New York *Sun* years later, "the air of Congress was thick with its bonds, falling like snowflakes."[4] In March 1871, the bill passed. What Huntington's role was, if any, remains unknown, though he was one of the beneficiaries. The same bill that allowed the Texas & Pacific to build from Marshall, Texas, through Fort Worth and El Paso to San Diego also allowed the Southern

Pacific to build to Yuma, and promised it twenty sections of land (12,800 acres) per mile for each mile of track constructed.

Tom Scott and his coterie next arranged for the state of Texas to reinstate its generous land grants to the remnants of the old Memphis, El Paso and Pacific and, also, to another defunct road. By questionable dealings with the receiver who was handling the affairs of the Memphis road (a receiver whose appointment had been engineered by the Scott lobby) the promoters then arranged to buy both roads for a few hundred thousand dollars. With them they gained a right to millions of Texas acres, title to be transferred as construction proceeded.

The building was to be performed by a Crédit Mobilier-Contract & Finance Company-type construction firm. The money paid by the railroad for the construction was to be raised by floating an enormous issue of bonds secured by Texas and United States public land. Engineer in charge of the building was Gen. Grenville M. Dodge, erstwhile chief engineer of the Union Pacific and one of the Central Pacific's chief antagonists during the race toward Promontory.*

Here then was a challenge comparable to the one that Collis had risen to during the yeasty days of building the Central. But this time his interest flagged. Building the Central Pacific had brought troubles and enmity. Where was the end? He could not glimpse it, and in his discouragement suggested to his partners that they find relief from their burdens by selling one of the systems, either the Central Pacific or the Southern Pacific. They agreed, Stanford with considerable reluctance.

It was not to be a cheap sale, however, and in order to maintain the value of what they were offering they found themselves forced to meet a series of onslaughts from all sides. There is some significance in the way they reacted to the attacks. Mere promoters, having decided to sell, probably would have cut corners. The three partners, by contrast, pushed doggedly ahead on the presumption that if they were not offered what the properties were worth, they would keep them. Hence they wanted the value of the roads to remain intact in every way—or even to increase. There was to be no marking of time while sales were promoted.

The first serious attack came from the California Pacific. In May 1871 that company found enough English capital to form the subsidiary California Pacific Eastern Extension. It then announced its intention to

---

* Tom Scott, curiously enough, became president of the faltering Union Pacific at about the same time that the Texas & Pacific bill passed. The next year, realizing that he could not conveniently mastermind two inherently hostile systems, he resigned from the Union Pacific and was openly elected president of the Texas & Pacific, whose destinies had already been secretly in his hands.

parallel the California & Oregon as far as Redding, California, before swinging east to a junction with the Union Pacific. Through a short line out of Stockton, the Stockton and Copperopolis, the California Pacific also threatened the associates' San Joaquin road. Tom Scott may not have had a finger in any of this, but he certainly watched it with amusement and pleasure.

Another man who was pleased was the associates' old enemy, James W. Simonton of Western Union and the Associated Press. Joyfully he telegraphed every shred of unfavorable news to financial papers throughout the world, and felt the headiness of power when the price of Central Pacific and California & Oregon bonds began to tremble.[5]

The threat had to be stopped, yet Huntington, Stanford, and Hopkins lacked money enough for an honestly competitive countermove. Instead, they called on their ingenuity. They announced that the Central Pacific would build a first-class, highly modern line from Sacramento to Vallejo directly beside the California Pacific's extravagantly built, poorly maintained tracks.

This was a marvelous bluff. The Central Pacific was heavily involved with the Western Pacific and its Oakland properties. A line to Vallejo would, in effect, be self-competition. The California Pacific had not anticipated anything so reckless, and immediately its president, Milton Latham, hurried around to see Huntington in New York. Collis easily convinced his visitor that the Central Pacific was in earnest. Well, then, Latham asked, could not an understanding be reached?

Indeed it could be—a most involved and illegal one. Latham's acquiescence was purchased, several lawsuits charged later, with a bribe of $250,000. Be that as it may, Latham in July 1871 signed an agreement whereby the Contract & Finance was to rebuild the California Pacific's substandard lines under terms which the contracting road could not meet. The work was paid for with a new issue of California Pacific bonds. Through foreclosures and then sleight-of-hand stock manipulations, the Central Pacific obtained control of its rival under an ostensible leasing agreement. The whole business completely ignored the rights of investors holding California Pacific securities, many of whom lived in Europe. Outraged, they sued and sued, but never managed to upset the complex agreements.

The attacks were worrisome, nonetheless, for, to borrow Huntington's own mixed but surprisingly candid metaphors, he disliked "so much dirty linen on the outer wall, as we have glass in our windows, and all railroads are built on curves, and I have no doubt [the] complaint will go to the Railroad Committee of the House of Representatives to show . . . how much crime can be committed by railroad rings under cover of contracting companies."[6]

With the California Pacific removed, the obstreperous little Terminal Central Pacific found itself with no potential outside connections that it could use for threatening the transcontinental. Even so, it managed to exact a good price, $250,000, before it left the battlefield, transferring to the Central Pacific its sole assets—150 acres of submerged tidelands near Goat Island and a franchise to build from Oakland north along the Bay shore (a line which the Central Pacific did build some years later). Huntington, who knew a good obstructionist when he saw one, put the deceased line's chief lobbyist, William B. Hyde, on the Central Pacific payroll.

The way should have been open then for the acquisition of Goat Island, a piece of real estate which Huntington believed would add millions of dollars to the value of the Central Pacific.* But when Huntington had a bill introduced into the House looking toward that end, he stirred a great clamor in San Francisco. Protests poured in on Congress.

Start a counter-campaign, Huntington urged Hopkins. Prepare messages and petitions for important men to sign—but don't use Western Union. Simonton would see to it that the telegrams never reached their destination. (Telegraph companies in those days were quite capable of that sort of thing.) Huntington himself spent hours trying to win the support of Horace Greeley of the New York *Tribune*. In a sense he hurt himself with his own intensity. The battle caught the attention of the nation, and Goat Island began to seem like a pearl of inestimable price. If the Central Pacific failed to win it after so much glaring publicity, security prices would be injured, or, as Huntington put the matter to Hopkins on March 27, 1872, "It would hurt us three times the value of the Island to get beat at this time."[7]

On April 24, the House passed the bill by a vote of 101 to 86. In

---

* A bill granting the island to the railroad had been defeated in 1870 largely by the efforts of Senator Cornelius Cole of California. Huntington had thereupon given five thousand dollars to Representative A. A. Sargent to distribute as campaign funds among California legislators running for office in the election of September 1871. The idea was that, if elected, they would send Sargent to the Senate in Cole's place in March 1873. Since Stanford, who retained some influence in Republican circles, disliked Sargent, Huntington warned Hopkins to say nothing of the donation. —March 7, 1871, *Collected Letters*, Vol. II. Sargent won Cole's seat, but only in the face of what he considered Stanford's opposition, and an enmity was fanned alive that twenty years later would have violent repercussions.

287

San Francisco, a disputatious Committee of One Hundred, formed a short time earlier to consider the city's railroad situation, wrung its hands in despair. If the Senate followed suit, the principal shipping interests of the Bay might move to the island and to nearby Oakland—which, of course, was what Huntington hoped.

In a letter partly churlish and partly imploring, the Committee of One Hundred tried to buy off the railroad. If San Francisco's voters were to approve a three-million-dollar bond issue at the election in November, would the railroad use the money to build a bridge across the southern part of the Bay (about where the San Mateo automobile bridge now runs) and develop as its terminus the sixty acres of Mission Bay property, so far unused, which had been donated to the Western Pacific and the Southern Pacific some years earlier? Stanford replied with an adroit letter that did not really commit the railroad to anything. The bond issue was nevertheless placed on the ballot—and was defeated.[8]

California's two senators, Cole and Eugene Casserly, were cleverer than the committee. Calling on President Grant, they told him that the Goat Island question was hurting the Republican party in California and furnishing ammunition to Grangers everywhere—an undesirable development during a presidential election year. Grant thereupon sent out word that he did not want the Goat Island bill presented to the Senate until after the elections.

Huntington was furious. He and Casserly engaged in a shouting, well-watched altercation in the Marble Room of the Willard Hotel. Defiantly he sent Senators Conkling and Wheeler and Congressman Sargent to Grant with rebuttals. The President declined to budge, and the bill was dropped. Though Huntington tried to revive it in March 1873, when Sargent was at last sitting in Cole's Senate seat, the Crédit Mobilier scandal had broken by then and no politician, however venal, would touch so controversial a railroad measure. It died in committee and was never revived again.*

Farther south, progress was more satisfactory, thanks partly to one of Stanford's few bursts of creativity. In the summer of 1870, it will

* As a substitute for the island, the railroad developed extensive wheat-shipping facilities at Port Costa beside Carquinez Strait. It replaced the Oakland Long Wharf with the famed Oakland Mole, wide enough to hold eleven rows of tracks. And it transferred its main business offices to a ponderous granite building at Fourth and Townsend streets, San Francisco, near its trans-Bay ferry slips and the Southern Pacific depot.

be recalled, both Congress and the California legislature had confirmed the Southern Pacific's route from Gilroy southeast through Hollister and Tres Pinos into the San Joaquin Valley. Meanwhile, the San Joaquin Railroad, by then a subsidiary of the Central Pacific, was building straight south through the valley itself. As surveyed, the tracks would intersect somewhere near the small town of Visalia.

From Visalia both lines could, so far as their charters were concerned, continue south side by side to Bakersfield. Obviously, however, one road would be enough. Moreover, the Southern Pacific was the logical choice to do the building inasmuch as it was entitled to 12,800 acres for each mile constructed, whereas the San Joaquin road would receive no land whatsoever.

As Stanford studied his maps, he had an inspiration. There was little chance that the Southern Pacific could develop much traffic beyond Tres Pinos. Why not forget that barren stretch, skip a hundred miles on to Visalia, and build south from there? The linked SP and CP (through its subsidiary, the San Joaquin) would then control the growing wheat traffic of the entire valley. Moreover, the Southern Pacific would be within striking distance of Los Angeles. If the directors threatened to skirt that community on the way to the Colorado River, the desperate citizens would probably respond with an offer of some of the ready cash that the railroad so badly needed.

At their meeting in the fall of 1871, the directors approved the plan, along with a pious resolution to fill the gap from Tres Pinos to Visalia at some later date.[9] (Actually, the gap was never closed.) As a practice maneuver, emissaries of the railroad then traveled to Visalia and asked its citizens how much land and how many bonds they would donate if the company made their town the junction point of the Central Pacific and Southern Pacific railroads.

Until and unless the Tres Pinos gap was filled, the junction would be a mere corporate designation invisible to the naked eye. Unimpressed, the local farmers declined to offer anything. Disgruntled, the railroad then withdrew seven miles and created its own town of Goshen. At that point the Central Pacific ended and the Southern Pacific began, a matter of indifference to shippers and travelers but of considerable, as we shall see, importance to Huntington's later financial and political problems.

Los Angeles proved more amenable. Word was leaked to the leading merchants of that dusty hamlet (population 6,000) that the difficulties of breaching the mountains north of San Fernando might tempt the railroad to by-pass them on its way to Yuma. The distraught Angelenos reacted as expected. In the summer of 1872 representatives hurried

289

north to confer with the directors, who were then meeting in Sacramento. Under what terms would the Southern Pacific bring its line through their city?

The answer was foreordained. State law allowed cities and counties to support railroads with bond issues amounting to no more than 5 per cent of the city's or county's assessed valuation. In the case of Los Angeles County, the maximum came to $610,000, and that was what the Southern Pacific demanded. Since a tunnel under the mountains north of San Fernando would cost more than that by itself, the request was perhaps not unreasonable. But then the directors added that they would want, in part payment of the sum, the $250,000 worth of bonds which Los Angeles owned in a twenty-two-mile rail line, the Los Angeles and San Pedro, that connected the village with the seacoast at Wilmington, near San Pedro.

Letting a San Francisco-oriented railroad control rail access to the town's ocean shipping was obviously putting Los Angeles into a transportation trap. Many merchants were so eager for a railroad, however— a yearning that afflicted most towns without one—that their representatives agreed to place the measure on the November ballot.

Huntington told his new man, William Hyde, to take charge of instructing the voters. Hyde soon found that he had his hands full. Dapper Tom Scott, a spellbinder par excellence, had gone to San Diego that summer to wring more concessions from the town for the Texas & Pacific. Hearing of the Southern Pacific's maneuvers in Los Angeles, he visited the hamlet in person and said that he would extend his line north from San Diego if the citizens of Los Angeles subsidized him not to the full extent of the law but by a mere $377,000. That measure, too, went onto the ballot. Meanwhile back-country farmers grumbled that they were not going to vote extra taxes for the benefit of any railroad; after all, locomotives consumed neither hay nor barley, as freight horses did.

Hyde, working with a heavy hand, alienated many people and spent more money than Huntington thought he should.[10] But he had one compelling argument, which he persuaded a respected judge and real estate promoter to present for him. Would the people of Los Angeles rather be an important stop on a transcontinental line to San Francisco, with connections to the state capital at Sacramento, or be the tag end of a branch from San Diego, whose merchants had already shown a jealous desire to retard Los Angeles' growth?

In comparison to the subsidy battle, the Grant-Greeley presidential campaign paled to insignificance in Los Angeles. Torchlight parades, fireworks, band music, and frenzied oratory boomed first one side and then the other. On election day the county farmers rejected both subsidy proposals, but Los Angeles carried the day for the Southern Pacific, 1,896 votes to 650 for Scott.[11] It looked like a handsome plum—but it could not be plucked unless the company built fifty miles of track at a time when Huntington could not see where the next dollar was coming from.

Of far greater concern to Huntington than the San Francisco and Los Angeles elections were the scandals connected with Crédit Mobilier. The unsavory tale had been brought into the open by a stockholder's suit not unlike those that the associates had recently sidestepped. Inconveniently for the Republicans, Grant's presidential campaign was then under way—and the suit was full of Republican names. Campaign oratory and literature immediately began to resound with the names of politicians accused of accepting Crédit Mobilier stock under suspicious circumstances. Vice-president Schuyler Colfax was besmirched, as were two future presidents, James Garfield and Rutherford B. Hayes, Speaker of the House James G. Blaine, Senator Patterson of New Hampshire, and various lesser fry.

The shock was not enough to topple Grant's Republicans. Still, a face-saving gesture was needed. Means apparently were at hand. A committee headed by Congressman J. W. Wilson of Indiana was already investigating the uses that the railroads had made of government money and could easily have extended the scope of its inquiries. But this wasn't enough for the embarrassed House of Representatives. It appointed a fresh group of sleuths under Congressman Luke Pollard of Vermont and directed it to concentrate on Crédit Mobilier.

As has happened with other self-righteous gestures by Congress, the investigations turned into something of a witch hunt. Competition added to the zest; Wilson was eager to outshine his Johnny-come-lately rival, Luke Pollard. Early in 1873 he put Huntington on the stand for a rigorous grilling. California's two senators, lame-duck Cole, smarting from his defeat by Sargent, and Casserly, who felt ill treated in connection with Southern Pacific matters, came joyfully to Wilson's aid. "These hell hounds," Huntington characterized them to Hopkins. He was angered, too, by the unfavorable publicity that the investigations triggered in California. "Why is it that we have so many enemies out there?" he demanded of Hopkins. "Do we do all that we can to quiet them? I think not," and he went on to suggest ways of reaching certain editors.[12]

Although his letters reveal the extent of his distress, he proved imperturbable on the witness stand. Unable to pry exact figures about the costs and profits connected with the Pacific railroads from him (or from anyone else), Wilson produced a report filled with critical rumblings but devoid of accusations specific enough to sustain legal action.

Pollard's somewhat more dignified hearings had meantime unearthed enough evidence of irregularities inside Congress that a scapegoat was necessary. Because Representative Oakes Ames had sold Crédit Mobilier stock at advantageous prices to his colleagues, he was chosen for the sacrifice, along with a henchman, Congressman James Brooks of New York. Both, said the Pollard report, should be expelled from the House. Congress, ever prone to sympathy for its erring members, softened this to a resolution of censure. A few weeks later, and probably not entirely by coincidence, Oakes Ames died of a heart attack.

The turmoil reawoke the associates' fear of a public display of the Contract & Finance Company books. For one thing, the timing was inconvenient. In desperate need of money, Huntington was hoping to have the watered stock of the consolidated Central Pacific system listed on the New York Exchange so that he could use it as collateral for loans.

Listing requirements demanded a statement of the cost of the road, its bonded and floating debts, the amount of stock issued, and the number of shareholders. By adroit juggling of accounts, Huntington had come up with a cost figure for all construction to that time of $144,778,986—something more than Brannan's $19 million or the Wilson Committee's estimate of $35 million. He had sworn further that although twenty-seven people owned most of the stock, a great deal more was scattered about in small lots, mostly in California. And so on.[13]

Obviously an opening of the books would lead the exchange, as well as the government, to ask embarrassing questions. Yet that, oddly, was not what frightened the associates most. A revelation that the great bulk of the stock was clustered in five hands would invite additional stockholder suits of the Brannan kind—suits that might tear control of the road away from the builders. Or, as Huntington put it anxiously to Hopkins, they were "much more likely to be struck by black-mailers . . . than we would be if the stock was scattered amongst a large number of holders."[14]

The ultimate decision was to finish working up a set of figures for the exchange and then to burn the fifteen volumes of Contract & Finance Company books in the basement of the railroad office. They did it just in time. During the summer of 1873, the New York *Sun* picked up a copy of the Brannan complaint and on July 19 used its figures, somewhat altered, as the basis of a front-page story under the headline "THE ACME OF FRAUD . . . $211,299,328.17—GOBBLED!" Nine days later the Wilson Committee once again put Huntington on the stand, and this time demanded to see the Contract & Finance Company books. There were none, Collis replied sorrowfully. The company was being dissolved and Hopkins, admittedly a peculiar man, had incinerated the records as wastepaper no longer worth saving.

As matters developed, Central Pacific stock was not listed on the exchange that disastrous year. The reason was not Huntington's figures but the California law concerning the liability of stockholders for their proportionate share of their company's entire debt—and a loud fuss was being raised just then concerning the huge amounts that both the Union and Central Pacific lines owed the government. Brokers were wary. They were in no mood to underwrite the stock at even twenty-five cents a barrel, Huntington reported disconsolately.[15] Even after the associates had declared a 3 per cent dividend in the hope of making the shares attractive, there seemed no possibility of placing them on the market at a value anywhere near what Huntington needed, whether as collateral or as a talking point in his efforts to sell either the Central Pacific or the Southern Pacific or both. Accordingly he postponed plans for offering the stock.

The decision led him to intensify his efforts to dispose of one or the other of the railroads.[16] Without stock to use as collateral, a sale seemed the best path toward salvation. Each week the situation was growing more critical. By the fall of 1873, the railroads' floating debts stood at about five million dollars, all of it bearing high rates of interest. Bond coupons fell remorselessly due twice a year. Construction bills on both the San Joaquin and Southern Pacific roads remained largely unpaid. Such securities as he had to offer, chiefly San Joaquin, California & Oregon, and Southern Pacific bonds, did not move, nor could he use them as collateral to borrow what he needed at reasonable rates of interest.

There had to be a sale—but gradually Collis faced up to the fact that there was not going to be one. The money market was as tight for prospective purchasers as it was for him. Potential customers (including Tom Scott, who wanted the Southern Pacific so that his Texas & Pacific would have a clear run into San Francisco) found that they could not raise the sums that Huntington insisted on as a minimum.

That situation acknowledged, he concentrated with almost frantic desperation on day-to-day expedients that might avoid the receiverships threatening each of his lines.[17] He did not succeed with the Chesapeake & Ohio. Construction costs in West Virginia had soared beyond estimates and, because of the nationwide depression, traffic in coal and lumber did not meet expectations. Moreover, the road had, at Huntington's behest, mired itself still deeper in debt in order to buy franchises and bits of track in Kentucky, hoping to extend its line from Huntington, West Virginia, on through Lexington to Louisville. When the crash came, the unfinished piers of a bridge in the Big Sandy River on the Kentucky border were mute testimony of what had happened to that dream.

He failed also to succor Fisk and Hatch. He was deeply obligated to them. Throughout his meteoric rise toward fortune, the brokers had supported him almost without question. In 1873, the Central Pacific owed them $1.7 million; the Chesapeake & Ohio, more than two million dollars. After Jay Cooke's shattering collapse in September, while wild panic was shaking financial New York, they begged Huntington for a settlement that would save them. Though he appealed to every source he knew, he could not raise the necessary amounts, and Fisk and Hatch became one more of the nation's long list of insolvent brokerage houses.

But—and one suspects that in those days of stark choice this was where his heart really lay—he did save the Central Pacific and Southern Pacific. None of their paper went to protest, though there were times when he produced the necessary funds only minutes ahead of the deadline. He succeeded because the depression had not yet paralyzed California. The Central Pacific was having its best year to date. Mining had revived in Nevada; the wheat harvest was enormous. The railroad netted that year more than five million dollars. By ignoring necessary repairs and by letting small contractors wait for their pay, Hopkins kept a flow of gold and currency moving steadily eastward.

Each of the associates added his own personal resources to the funds on which Huntington could call. Each of them borrowed heavily on personal securities in order to raise still more money for emergency demands. When Crocker came into Huntington's office and demanded the second payment due on his note, he was told that there was no money. He thereupon returned the $300,000 that had been given him as his first payment in 1871 and rejoined the firm as its second vice-president, simultaneously turning over to Huntington all the personal assets that he could command.[18] He was eager to go to work, too, but Huntington did not know quite what to do with Jolly Charley. Accordingly he dispatched Crocker and Maj. R. P. Hammond, figurehead president of the California Pacific, on a round-the-world selling trip.[19] In Asia they were to persuade shippers that a combination Pacific steamer-railroad run to the East Coast offered more advantages than did the new Suez Canal, which most oriental exporters were using. In Western Europe, the emissaries were to line up agents who would promote immigration to California and, hopefully, sell farms out of the still fallow land grants owned by the California & Oregon, the Central Pacific, and Southern Pacific. The pair were also instructed to placate, if possible, the holders of California Pacific bonds. On none of these errands did they prove particularly successful.

Meantime Huntington was working his way out of the thickets. At year's end, when he was able to gather in nearly a million dollars for meeting bond coupons due in January 1874, he knew that the worst was over. He prepared again to put Central Pacific stock on the market, this time not just as a device for raising loans but as a means by which the partners could at last realize a full measure of profit from their long struggle.

Full profits, in turn, pointed straight toward a showdown with Tom Scott. In spite of heavy losses of his own, the Pennsylvania Napoleon had managed to save the Texas & Pacific and its construction company. Now he was determined to enlist the support of the United States Government, which owed the prostrate South some help with internal improvements. With that backing he would then build to the Coast, there to break the Big Four's monopoly and seize as much cross-country traffic as he could for the Texas & Pacific. It promised to be as titanic a battle as the one that the associates had waged only a few years before with the Union Pacific.

23 New Battlefields

In 1874 the associates were not well braced for a sustained battle with so resourceful an antagonist as Tom Scott. Although the Central Pacific's immediate financial crisis had been weathered, the funding of additional construction would be difficult, perhaps impossible. Meanwhile, as seemed chronic, other troubles were heaping up. Unexpected competition threatened to absorb the oriental trade that Crocker was traveling around the world to revive. Congress continued to resound with demands that the Union Pacific and Central Pacific be forced to begin payments on their debt to the government. In California, where Republican Newton Booth, an anti-railroad governor, occupied the state capitol, legislators vied with each other in introducing bills designed to curb the yet unbridled railroad. All these matters had to be attended to before Scott could be challenged.

The first of the new crises was the revolt of the Pacific Mail Steamship Company. The line, its Atlantic and Pacific segments linked by an independent railway across Panama, had been turned into a giant by California's gold rush. During the 1860s it showed its muscle by winning from Congress a mail subsidy that enabled it to extend its service westward to the Orient and eastward to England. Yet, though its ships plied half the world, the key link in the system remained the stubbornly independent Panama Railroad.

At first it seemed that the completion of the Pacific railroad might shatter the company's prosperity. Slowly, however, shippers learned that heavy freight moved less speedily over the railroad than anticipated, particularly in winter. By cutting rates, the Pacific Mail Steamship Company found that it could compete by way of Panama. Once again oriental traffic in tea, rice, silk, and sugar began moving across the isthmus—except for what went through the Suez Canal.

296

This pained the associates. From the beginning one of their sustaining motives had been a vision of trainloads of Asiatic commerce moving through their own tightly controlled port on Goat Island. They could not get the island. They did not want to lose the commerce, too. In conjunction with the Union Pacific, they worked out, at considerable cash cost to themselves, traffic-sharing agreements with the Pacific Mail Steamship Company. This brought part of the oriental traffic back to their Oakland wharves. Crocker had then been sent abroad to drum up more trade.

The arrangement with the Pacific Mail Company held until the fall of 1873. At that point the ocean firm rejected an extension of its contract with the railroads and announced that henceforth all its traffic to and from the Orient would travel by way of Panama. One of the prods behind the revolt was the Panama Railroad. Far more galvanic, however, was the enigmatic figure of Jay Gould. He had recently acquired enough stock in the Pacific Mail Steamship Company that in 1873 he was able to squeeze some of his associates, including Trenor W. Park, onto its board of directors.* At the same time Gould gained control of the badly managed, heavily encumbered Union Pacific.[1]

Essentially the Pacific Mail and the Union Pacific were competitors. In the routines of the day, Gould's control of both companies would have been a way of achieving rate monopolies. That was not what happened, however. Instead, Gould declared war on himself, using his steamship line to undercut his railroad. In the process he of course undercut the Central Pacific as well.

Huntington understood the ploy at once. Gould was a manipulator who cared little for a property as such. He would play his two new companies off against each other in order to affect the prices of their stock as suited his purposes at the moment. What harm this wrought to the Central Pacific was of no concern to him.

Grimly Huntington prepared to strike back. Crocker, who had reached London on his round-the-world jaunt in behalf of the railroad, was summoned to New York in July 1874.[2] Stanford met the other two associates there. (Hopkins, too ill to travel, stayed home.[3]) After a series of agitated conferences, the trio decided to form a rival ocean line. At first they called it the Overland, Pacific, and China Steamship Company. Recruiting the services of Captain George Bradbury, who had served for a few months as president of the Pacific Mail Steamship Company before being dumped by Gould, they sent him to England to

* Park was a gold-rusher and early-day (1856) California Republican. In 1872 he bought Stanford's profitable gold mine in Amador County for $400,000.

297

charter vessels. Stanford and Crocker thought they would need at least seven ships. Huntington shook his head. Times were hard. In his opinion three would be enough to put a crimp in Gould's stockjobbing, as Collis called it.[4]

A steamship line that fed Asiatic traffic to the Central Pacific would inevitably feed the Union Pacific also. It became necessary, therefore, to consult with Gould, however reluctantly, about rates and schedules for the new company.

As soon as the great manipulator learned what was afoot, he demanded a share in the firm for the Union Pacific, intending to use it, too, in his juggling of stock prices. Night after night he came to Collis' house at 65 Park Avenue, to cajole and threaten in his barely audible, insistent voice. He was fifteen years younger than Huntington, a bald, bearded, secretive gnome who looked startlingly like one of Snow White's dwarfs. His ways were subterranean, too, and with them he would repeatedly shake New York's financial structures. But he did not shake Collis Huntington.

Huntington's victory was not complete, to be sure. He had to scrap the Overland, Pacific, and China line and form instead the Occidental and Oriental Steamship Company, of which the Union Pacific owned 50 per cent. The Occidental and Oriental company was to be based in San Francisco, however, and its board was dominated by men of Huntington's choosing—not including himself. He did not want, he wrote, any responsibilities toward the steamship company that might warp "my judgment [so that] I cannot do what seems best for the C. P."[5] One cannot imagine Jay Gould ever voicing such a sentiment about the UP.

Though not a member of the O&O board, Collis clearly had a great deal to say about its management. When it began service in 1875 it used three ships, not seven. As Huntington had foreseen, three were enough to bring Gould into line. He consented, in return for his share in the O&O company, to let the Pacific Mail resume traffic-sharing agreements with the railroads. That done, the two ocean lines fell into each other's arms. They established non-competitive sailing schedules, used the same agents, loaded and unloaded at the same docks. Despite those interlockings, however, no one ever forgot that the basic intent behind the O&O was to keep Jay Gould co-operative so far as the Central Pacific was concerned—a minor nineteenth-century marvel, for it was the first time that the country's most notorious speculator had been leashed for very long.[6] And even then he needed continual watching.

Huntington was not quite sure that the rapport with Gould would last. Accordingly he made a few probing gestures toward gaining control of the Union Pacific in the hope that he could eliminate the man entirely.[7] Word of the gestures leaked out. At the same time, it became known that he was looking for some way of extending the Chesapeake & Ohio to St. Louis. His gropings coincided with Wall Street talk that Tom Scott, recently elected to the presidency of the Pennsylvania Railroad, intended to hook that property to the Texas & Pacific and form a nationwide system. Huntington's gestures sent rumors sweeping through the Street that the Big Four planned to checkmate the Pennsylvania Napoleon by welding the Central Pacific, Union Pacific, and Chesapeake & Ohio into a comparable giant.[8]

Huntington repeatedly denied any such intent. It must have hurt him to do so, for surely the concept had crossed his mind. It was out of reach, however. He and his associates simply could not command enough money. Fortunately, from their viewpoint, neither could Tom Scott during those hard depression years. The showdown fight, when it came, would be on the somewhat smaller battlefield of the American Southwest.

Throughout the jockeying with Gould, Huntington was doing all he could, with scant success, to improve the Central Pacific's shaky credit structure. His first move was to complete, early in 1874, the delayed listing of the Central Pacific's stock on the New York Exchange. That done, he rigged a few bids so as to command a respectable public quotation on a few shares. They brought from 68 to 68.5—at a time when Union Pacific stock was bringing less than thirty. Encouraged by the success, he persuaded Speyer & Company to take a thirty-day option on two million dollars' worth at sixty-one, provided that the brokers place the stock on the Amsterdam Bourse. Once again, however, California laws imposing personal liability on shareholders frightened European investors away and Speyer dropped the option.[9] Obviously some radical move would have to be made if he hoped to sell enough stock in the near future to reduce the Central Pacific's onerous floating debt.

Because of his anxiety, he walked into a trap in his own front yard. In 1873, it will be recalled, the CP directorate had sought to draw attention to the stock by declaring a 3 per cent dividend but then had decided against listing the shares because of the panic triggered by Jay Cooke's collapse in September.* Nearly a year later Collis proposed that they repeat the strategy on a bigger scale. The others agreed and declared a 5 per cent dividend out of net earnings of $7.5 million— about half a million to each of the associates. The next year they repeated

---

* The 3 per cent was based on the par figure of $100 and applied to 537,750 shares, the bulk of them held by the five associates. Ed Crocker, by this time, was helplessly paralyzed and his estate was being managed by his brother Charles.

the process with semiannual dividends totalling 10 per cent—approximately a million to each man out of an operating net that had dipped to $5.7 million.

The associates deposited much of this annual harvest, at interest, in the Western Development Company, the construction firm which had succeeded their original Contract & Finance Company and which was building the Southern Pacific.[10] The rest the California associates used for rearing ponderous palaces atop San Francisco's Nob Hill, the most sensational residence lots, probably, in the nation. Their wives—even Mark Hopkins' placid Mary Francis—were very happy.

So easy an inpouring of gold after years of waiting gave them second thoughts about selling their stock. Why not meet the floating debt by selling land-grant bonds instead, bonds which would not have to be redeemed until . . . well, sometime later on? Meanwhile, life was beautiful. When a would-be investor offered eighty-eight for five hundred shares of Central Pacific stock none of them except Huntington was willing to part with his proportionate share in order to make up the amount.[11] To have done so would, of course, have established a precedent, and they did not want Huntington selling their stock as *he* saw fit in New York.

Collis was furious. He was still living in relative simplicity in his old house at 65 Park Avenue. Against his better judgment he had consented to an issue of land-grant bonds and was doing his best to market them under adverse conditions created by the nation's continuing economic slump. In his mind the antics of his partners were unjustifiable.

When he went West with Elizabeth in the summer of 1875, he spoke his mind. He promised that he would not reduce the value of the shares by dumping a lot of them onto the market at once, but he did insist that it was time to begin a cautious selling program. The others nodded their heads, or he thought they did. But no stock followed him to New York for sale, even though he was having to borrow heavily in order to meet January interest on the road's first-mortgage bonds.[12]

Poverty in the midst of plenty—it was an exasperating situation to have to explain. Bankers began questioning. Why should a road that was declaring fat dividends and supporting turreted palaces above the Bay need to borrow so much money? Was another Gould-type piece of stockjobbery in the making?[13]

For still other reasons, the ostentation in California hurt. Attacks on the railroad were growing increasingly virulent. John Luttrell, one of the state's newly elected Democratic Congressmen, rose in the House of Representatives on January 12, 1874, dug up a spadeful of figures from a copy of Sam Brannan's old suit against the Central Pacific, and used them to demand still another full-scale investigation of the associates' allegedly unreasonable profits. Huntington retorted with a long, vigorous letter to Philetus Sawyer, Chairman of the House Committee on Pacific Railroads. In it he presented, in a far more masterful style than Luttrell commanded, the railroad's version of income. After balancing this against his own selected figures concerning cost, he declared, with deep hurt, that the Central Pacific had reaped no undue gains at the government's expense.

The letter was intended for more eyes than Sawyer's. Printed copies were distributed throughout the land—with negligible effect.[14] At best, people tend to remember lurid accusations longer than defenses, and when the mansions appeared on Nob Hill, Collis' justifications died under the lofty turrets and the tons of ornately carved granite. Meanwhile, demands in Congress for loan repayment and in the Sacramento legislature for state control of rates continued unabated.

The California agitation reached a climax early in 1876, when Assemblyman Laurence Archer introduced a bill to cut the road's freight rates by almost one half and passenger fares by one third. The springboard for one of Archer's speeches in support of his proposed legislation was, inevitably, a ringing reference to the American Revolution. "The battle we are fighting today . . . is no less important than was the question which the patriots of 1776 were dealing with, when they made their declaration of independence. The wrongs and injuries under which they suffered . . . were not [sic] comparable to the wrongs and injuries which the people of California are suffering now."[15] One wrong adduced during the debates was favoritism to the Huntington & Hopkins Hardware Company. Discriminatory freight rates, opponents charged, placed it in so unassailable a position that it had achieved a near-monopoly in the hardware business from British Columbia to Mexico.

The assembly passed the bill with a roar of outrage, sixty-eight to eight. Stanford at last took alarm. Summoning a corps of experts, he opened a barrage on the state senate's committee on corporations, pelting its bewildered members, one commentator wrote, "with figures, deluging them with statistics, and enveloping them in the mysteries of railroad bookkeeping, until what the gentlemen were pleased to call their minds revolted from the whole subject" and they let the bill die.[16] But before the demise the whole state had read, on the front page of nearly every

301

California newspaper, a series of scathing legislative denunciations of the associates and their creation.

The debates on the Archer bill were accompanied by two sensational lawsuits. The first was an action by the Central Pacific Railroad against Alfred A. Cohen. Once upon a time Cohen had been a friend. He had arranged the sale of the Oakland and Alameda short lines, in which he was a principal shareholder, to the associates, and then had gone to work for them as an attorney. He had tried to put together a syndicate to buy the Central Pacific during the days of Huntington's discouragement. He had then been entrusted with arranging certain contracts and purchasing certain real estate for the railroad. The associates—or, more specifically, Charles Crocker—developed a notion that in performing these duties Cohen had abused their trust and had pocketed for himself many thousands of dollars. The railroad thereupon sued for an accounting.

Immediately, the Big Four (Ed Crocker had died in July 1875) discovered that they had tried to lay hold of a hornet. Cohen dug up their ancient enemy, John Robinson of the erstwhile Sacramento Valley Railroad, learned that he owned ten shares of Central Pacific stock purchased in 1863, and persuaded him to bring suit after the manner of Sam Brannan. Cohen, indeed, used Brannan's very figures, just as Luttrell had in Congress. But Cohen's use was more damaging. He printed the allegations in a complaint that he distributed throughout California, and thousands of people who had missed Brannan's earlier charges could now read them wide-eyed as emanating from John Robinson.[17]

Cohen's own suit was heard without a jury before Judge W. P. Dangerfield in San Francisco. He acted as his own attorney. To the intense delight of the spectators and newspaper reporters, he resorted to such slashing personal attacks that Dangerfield later remarked, "Perhaps never since the organization of Courts in this state has such wholesale abuse and vituperation been indulged in in a Court of Justice. . . . Surely these things must have been done to please the multitude, for they certainly have no place in a Court. . . ."

Cohen mocked Crocker's appearance: "too fat of diaphragm for genteel comedy, and too fat of wit for low comedy," useful only to "light the lamps and sweep the stage." Stanford, the heavy of the play, "sullen, remorseless, grand and peculiar," moved about the stage "with the ambition of an Emperor and the spite of a peanut-vendor." As for Huntington, "if ever a witness left the stand with the brand of perjury indelibly impressed upon his forehead, that man was **C. P. Huntington.**" And on and on, including those Nob Hill houses:

> With absence of shame and decency, they parade the results of their crimes in the face of the world by erecting edifices to crown the heights of our city, which, instead of being, as they assert, monuments of honest enterprise, are to the thoughtful mind glaring and conspicuous . . . emblems of shame and dishonor.

Although Judge Dangerfield publicly rebuked Cohen for such billingsgate, he found in his favor against the railroad.[18] And so the associates had nothing to show for their action other than one more smear of bad publicity where they could afford it least, in the persistently hostile city of San Francisco.

Why did they incur this unabated enmity after all they had done for the state, Huntington kept asking himself. Finally he decided that one paramount reason, aside from the almost universal anti-railroad feeling of the times, was the Californians' flaunting of their wealth. He told them so to their faces, and for the rest of his life, whenever the question of the road's extreme unpopularity was raised, he divided a large share of the blame between San Francisco's sensation-seeking newspapers and those awesome mansions towering like sultans' palaces high above the Bay.[19]

Western Union and the Associated Press, angered still by the Central Pacific's tie-in of its telegraph lines with the rival Atlantic & Pacific Telegraph Company, spread the accumulation of unfavorable reports throughout the nation.[20] From Huntington's standpoint the timing could hardly have been worse. Tom Scott was turning his fight for a southern transcontinental into an intensely emotional issue, based on the resurgent South's demand for justice and equal opportunity. Anything that denigrated the Central Pacific was ammunition for his already powerful arsenal.

Because of the financial panic of September 1873, the battle had gathered momentum slowly. Scott had needed a year to put his own affairs and those of the Pennsylvania Railroad back into order. Fortunately for his long-range plans, his friends in the construction company that hoped to build the Texas & Pacific Railroad had made lavish use of their personal credit to keep that firm alive. Grenville Dodge, battling floods and yellow fever in his construction camps, had laid enough rail in eastern Texas to prevent forfeiture of the state land grants—meanwhile fleeing hither and yon in various disguises to keep from being served with subpoenas that would have compelled him to testify before Congress concerning Crédit Mobilier.[21] Thus by the fall of 1874 Scott was ready to start driving westward again.

The great problem was money. Bonds on unbuilt railroads were unsalable, and he could expect no help from the nervous, depression-haunted directorate of the Pennsylvania Railroad, even though he had just been elevated to its presidency on the death of J. Edgar Thomson. So far as the Texas & Pacific was concerned, they told him, he was on his own.

He turned to Congress, offering through legislative friends a bill that would authorize a government loan of $100 million secured by a first mortgage on the Texas & Pacific's presumptive land grants in Texas, Louisiana, New Mexico, Arizona, and California. In this bill he also asked permission to change his route through Southern California.

The original act chartering the T&P had envisioned a line running due west from Yuma on the Colorado River to San Diego. The mountains in that direction would be expensive to cross, however. Accordingly Scott proposed in his new bill to bend the tracks northwest at Yuma, skirt the deep trough that later became known as Imperial Valley, and thus reach San Gorgonio Pass, an easy gap some hundred miles east of Los Angeles. From San Gorgonio he would dip back south to San Diego.

The flaw in the plan was the Southern Pacific's franchise, which allowed the associates to build a line from San Gorgonio to Yuma.

Blandly Scott called on Huntington, showed him copies of the bill, and remarked that there was no point in both of them building parallel lines out there in the desert. Would it not be better for the Southern Pacific to meet him at San Gorgonio and spare itself the expense of building all the way to the Colorado River?

Huntington shook his head. He had long since determined not to let a rival transcontinental reach San Diego and develop it into a rival port from which commerce could be sent by cheap water freight to San Francisco, Portland, Australia, and all the Orient. With matching blandness he told Scott that he really had no choice but to meet his charter requirements by constructing the line to Yuma. Would it not be better for Scott simply to stop there beside the river?

No, said Scott. He had promised the good people of San Diego that he would build a line to their city (where, as Huntington knew, he owned valuable property) and the route through San Gorgonio Pass was the only feasible way. He must go ahead.

Don't fret, said Huntington. The Southern Pacific would be glad to provide all those good people of San Diego with a branch to San Gorgonio and connections there with either Los Angeles or the East. In short, Scott might just as well get the message: Yuma was the end of his line.

Scott of course had no more desire to be stopped in the middle of the desert than the associates had been when threatened in similar fashion by the Union Pacific ten years before. Crisply he told Huntington that he would pass his bill and use part of the money to parallel the Southern Pacific not just to San Gorgonio Pass but to San Francisco, too, if that was the only way to bring the light of understanding to his Western opponents.[22] And with that the battle was on.

Attack, with Huntington, was always the best defense. He would kill the San Diego and San Francisco threats by killing Scott's bill *in toto,* even though that would involve the death of the entire Texas & Pacific system as well.

It would not be easy. Scott was relying on an appeal of tremendous emotional strength. Since the founding of the nation, his argument ran, the South had been slighted in the matter of government aid for internal improvements. Between 1789 and 1873, the North had drained from the federal treasury for wagon roads, canals, and railroads $100 million, whereas the South had received only $4.5 million. Moreover, the lion's share of that $100 million had gone to the Union Pacific and Central Pacific railroads, on a vote rammed through Congress when Southern representatives were not in Washington to protest the inferior central route. It was time to adjust the balance. The only real opposition to his proposed act of eminent fair play was the Central Pacific, which controlled the Southern Pacific and was using the latter as a tool to defend a monopoly under whose grinding heel the people of California were crying out in despair.[23]

If such arguments were not enough, then Scott had other means. For the sake of his bill, the Pennsylvanian was prepared to use unlimited sums of money currying a Congress that, in Huntington's words, promised to be "composed of the hungriest set of men ever got together."[24]

When necessary, Huntington, too, was willing to spend lavishly, making the payments not directly but through his suave and knowledgeable chief lobbyist in Washington, Gen. Richard Franchot.[25] But he did not trust to money alone, for he could always be outbid. He preferred striking at an opponent's weakness. In this case it was Scott's appeal for subsidies during an era when sentiment against subsidies was growing increasingly strong. He would capitalize on the feeling by declaring to the whole country that the Southern Pacific would build, by itself, without government aid, the transcontinental that the South wanted. Why then should millions be doled out to feather the nest of Thomas Alexander Scott and Grenville M. Dodge?

To be convincing, such talk had to be backed by a show of strength. Construction on the Southern Pacific, which had all but halted in 1873, had to be stepped up. And that meant having Crocker push his construction crews into the formidable mountains that still separated the main line from the spidery rails that William Hyde had been laying beyond the mountain barrier, near Los Angeles, in order to collect the subsidy that the county had voted in 1872.

The only practicable route was serpentine. From Bakersfield in the southern part of the San Joaquin Valley, the tracks would have to thrust southeast to Tehachapi Pass, the lowest gap in the shaggy uplift that enclosed the valley's southern end. Surveys had already indicated that surmounting the Tehachapis, even at that pass, would necessitate a bewildering complex of curves and tunnels. Along one tight stretch Crocker's Chinese—two thousand or more of them—would have to blast out six tunnels and lay seven miles of track in order to achieve a net forward gain of only a single mile. In another spot the rails would have to describe a complete spiral and cross over themselves above another tunnel in order to rise a meager seventy-seven feet in altitude.[26]

On the far side of the mountains, the tracks would drop down to the desert town of Mojave. From there they would have an easy run south to the precipitate drainage system of the Santa Clara River. The rails would follow the stream back westward for a few miles and then strike south again into the San Fernando Mountains. There the associates would have to drill the fourth longest tunnel in the United States, through fault-shattered rock filled with water and oozing gravel—hazards unknown, of course, at the time of planning. The drilling on the San Fernando tunnel was to begin simultaneously with the thrust from Bakersfield toward Tehachapi Pass.[27]

Those were the major jobs, but not the only ones. As part of the subsidy bargain with Los Angeles, track had already been laid between San Fernando and Los Angeles, and from Los Angeles eastward to the now vanished town of Spadra. While the mountain track and the San Fernando tunnel were under construction, still more roustabouts could start grading from Spadra east to San Gorgonio.

It was a massive project. Nothing comparable to it was being undertaken anywhere else in the United States at the time. It certainly should look convincing both to Tom Scott and to Congress. But it was going to burden Huntington with the same sort of financial, purchasing, and

306

lobbying details that had almost overwhelmed him during the rush days of the Central Pacific. On top of that he had still another railroad to worry about, the Chesapeake & Ohio. It had paid no interest on its bonds since the crash of September 1873. Its debt had reached a staggering $31 million. In an effort to stave off receivership, Huntington was engaged in an acrimonious battle with a faction of rebellious shareholders, William Aspinwall and David Stewart of his original syndicate included.

He needed more help than he could count on his associates to provide. Hopkins was ill. Crocker was of no great use apart from construction matters. Stanford was increasingly absorbed in raising race horses on an eight-thousand-acre farm he had bought near Palo Alto and in seeking to answer, through a series of camera studies, the profound riddle of how many of a trotting horse's feet were ever off the ground at a given moment.

As Collis searched the rosters of the company's proliferating organizations for someone he could lift into a position of trust, his eyes fell on the name of David Douty Colton. Colton's background was varied and turbulent. He was red-haired, stocky, and aggressive. During the days of the gold rush he had served as sheriff of Siskiyou County and once had staved off a mob that had tried to storm his jail. A little later, in the 1850s, he had served as part of David Broderick's kitchen cabinet when the latter had been brawling with William Gwin for control of California's Democratic party. When Broderick had fought his fatal duel with David Terry of the state supreme court, Colton had been Broderick's second. Afterwards he had come into possession of some of Broderick's choice real estate, no one ever quite knew how. Appointed a general in the state militia, he had resigned without seeing active service, but he still liked to be called by that title. During the Civil War he had studied law in the East and after his return to California he had prospered as a nimble wheeler-dealer in various trading ventures.

Colton and Jolly Charley Crocker were great friends. At Crocker's suggestion, Colton was allowed to buy an interest in the associates' lucrative Rocky Mountain Coal and Iron Company of Wyoming. Soon he became president of the firm and then built a $250,000 mansion on Nob Hill, a development that drew the others' attention in that direction. He was accustomed to meet with Huntington during Collis' trips to California, and as early as June 1874, while Crocker was still abroad on his traffic-soliciting trip, the general was hinting that he would like to find a place for his talents in the Southern Pacific.[28] Under pressure of heavy work, Huntington agreed.

Even Colton may have been surprised at the contract he was offered. He received twenty thousand shares of Central Pacific stock and twenty thousand of Southern Pacific. In return he gave the associates his promissory note for one million dollars, due in five years, and guaranteed his services to the company without stint throughout that period. Unless the stock reached an average value of fifty dollars a share (at the time he signed the contract, Southern Pacific securities were not salable at any price), he would be in a precarious position. But if the railroad succeeded, he would make a killing.[29] Moreover, he was allowed to buy, later on, a one-ninth interest in the associates' construction firm, the Western Development Company. The other four each held two ninths.

Shortly after Colton became a partner of the associates, Huntington summoned him East. A new strategy of falsification was needed. Scott was flooding Southern newspapers with articles denouncing the Central Pacific as the real force behind the North's opposition to his subsidy bill. In an effort to deny a close connection between the Southern Pacific and the Central Pacific, Huntington resigned as president and director of the SP and spread word that control was now in the hands of David D. Colton and his friends. He equipped Colton with passes and money to use in Washington and sent him to the Capitol as the Southern Pacific's chief representative before the congressional committees that were conducting hearings on the bill. Collis meantime stayed carefully out of sight, going quietly to some obscure hotel room in Washington only when Franchot summoned him to lend a little extra weight.[30]

It is not likely that Colton's lobbying played a significant part in killing Scott's request for aid. The Granger movement was at its height—"Communists" being Huntington's epithet for the radicals, a scare word even then—and a railroad subsidy of $100 million, unsupported by other considerations, had scant hope of even emerging from committee. Scott's bill didn't.

As soon as word reached California that the bill was dead, Stanford decided to use the event to gain friends for the Central Pacific in San Francisco. He summoned a reporter from the *Chronicle* to his office and staged an interview that Huntington read a few days later with shuddering incredulity.

There was, Stanford told the reporter, "mistrust abroad in the community against myself and the management of this great railroad enterprise; but I shall outlive it." Though the people of the Bay City might not appreciate the full significance of the congressional truimph as yet, they owed the Central Pacific undying gratitude, "for had Tom Scott built his road, he would have given San Francisco a blow from which she never would have recovered." But now the future was assured. He pointed upward toward his mansion, still under construction. "I shall hope to live to sit upon yonder balcony and look down upon a city embracing . . . a million of people. I shall see railroads . . . fleets of ocean steamers . . . thronged and busy streets . . . and I shall say to myself, 'I have aided to bring this prosperity and this wealth to the State of my adoption and to the city in which I have chosen my home.' "[31]

Stanford, the strutter, publicly claiming that he and the *Central Pacific* had wrought all this! What in the name of the Eternal—a favorite oath in those days—did the man suppose had been Huntington's motive in trying to keep the Central Pacific hidden throughout the congressional maneuvers?

Nor was that all. The California associates were not yet prepared to swallow Colton as president of the Southern Pacific. Instead, they elected Charles Crocker to the place that Huntington had vacated. That finished washing out Collis' pretense that the railroads were separate. Though he continued saying lamely that Colton really was the key figure in the Southern Pacific, no one took him seriously and he did not even bother to bring Colton to Washington when Scott resumed the battle at the next sitting of Congress.[32]

The skill of the Pennsylvanian's attack shook Huntington's confidence. First, Scott reduced the magnitude of his requests: this time he asked only that the government help make his bonds salable by guaranteeing the interest on forty million dollars' worth, to be issued on a scale of no more than $35,000 to $40,000 a mile, depending on the nature of the terrain. Then, with Grenville Dodge doing most of the organizational work, he sent representatives throughout the South. They visited legislatures, chambers of commerce, boards of trade, even Grange chapters. They urged those bodies to pass resolutions favoring the bill and to bombard individual Congressmen with mail in support of it. Conventions on behalf of the Texas & Pacific were held in both St. Louis and Memphis; at them such magic figures as Jefferson Davis stirred up paroxysms of enthusiasm.[33] Under the impact of the demonstrations, the Texas & Pacific bill became a symbol of "justice to the South," and its effect soared far beyond the confines of mere logic.

Huntington was not without comparable weapons. Opponents of more largesse to railroads were as emotional on the point as Southerners were in their support of the Texas & Pacific. Accordingly Collis intensified his promises that the Southern Pacific would build a transcontinental through the South without government aid.

Mockers asked him how he intended to do it under the terms of his congressional charter. That document allowed the California road to go east only as far as the Colorado River, and Scott's forces in Congress would do all in their power to block an amendment granting him more. Hoping to find an effective counter, Huntington urged his associates in California to obtain franchises for the Southern Pacific from the legislature of Arizona Territory, even if they had to spend $25,000 doing it. He would then use the territorial charters as a lever on Congress for a right-of-way through federal lands.[34] He even began searching for a Texas railroad with which he could reach an understanding, to lend substance to his declaration that the Southern Pacific did not mean to stop until it reached New Orleans.[35]

All of this frightened his associates. They did not mind Collis' talking about building a railroad through the Southwest, but suppose he really got carried away with the idea? To hold him down to earth they dragged their feet about seeking a charter in Arizona. From their viewpoint, halting Scott at Yuma was ample for the protection of their monopoly. Why build a new transcontinental which, in essence, would simply be a competitor of the Central Pacific?

Meanwhile Huntington was fighting Scott in the South with the Pennsylvanian's own weapons. The Central Pacific was corrupt, was it? Then what of this: Tom Scott had offered both the Republican and Democratic national committees $300,000 if they would pass resolutions in favor of his bill.[36] Monopoly? What about this: Scott's real intent was to bend the Texas & Pacific northward from Texarkana, on the boundary between Texas and Arkansas, to a connection with the Pennsylvania Railroad at St. Louis. The fraud! He had no intention whatsoever of helping the South, once he had pocketed the taxpayers' money.

To give the charges wide circulation in strategic spots, Huntington hired secret emissaries who supposedly had no connection with him. He sent them throughout the South from Virginia to Texas. They, too, visited legislatures, boards of trade, and chambers of commerce, and quietly revealed to those hostile bodies the "truth" about the Pennsylvania Napoleon. Huntington thought their work was effective. Whether or not it really was is impossible to determine.[37]

In Washington, Grenville Dodge, a one-time Congressman and a personal friend of President Grant, led Scott's lobby. It was a blow, at that juncture, to have Richard Franchot die. "We have lost a good man," Huntington wrote Colton on November 27. "I do not know his equal." But there was an equal—Huntington himself. Abandoning the tattered pretense that there was no connection between the Central Pacific and

310

the Southern Pacific, he stepped into Franchot's shoes and openly led a successful fight to have his choice, Michael Kerr of Indiana, elected speaker of the House of Representatives over Scott's favorite, Samuel Randall of Pennsylvania. That done, the struggle to control the committees began.*

Somehow or other, Representative Luttrell of California, who only a year before had been demanding a full-scale investigation of the Central Pacific, was won to Huntington's side. Except for William A. Piper of San Francisco ("a damned hog" in Collis' opinion) the California House delegation was now solidly behind him.[38] That gain, however, was offset by more of Stanford's bungling in California.

Out on the Coast, Governor Newton Booth had split the Republican party by a maverick campaign for a seat in the U. S. Senate, a move that ran afoul of Aaron Sargent and the old-line Republican machine that Sargent had taken over on his own election to the Senate in 1871. Fearing Booth's strong anti-railroad prejudices, Stanford and his chief Sacramento strategist, William B. Carr, decided that the surest way to defeat him would be to support the Democrats. All they did was wreck Sargent's machine. Booth emerged triumphant. In a fury Sargent and George C. Gorham, the latter a one-time bondholder in the Southern Pacific and the Republican secretary of the Senate since 1869, swung their support to Scott.[39] It took Huntington months of effort to woo back Sargent's vote—they had been personal friends for more than a decade—and he never did succeed in placating Gorham. Not that it made much difference. The congressional situation was completely fluid, with Scott's forces and Huntington's checkmating each other at every turn. By the fall of 1876 the two titans of American railroading were in a complete deadlock.

An apparent break came with the contested presidential election between Samuel Tilden and Rutherford B. Hayes. Although Tilden, the Democrats' candidate, won the popular vote, charges of massive corruption in Louisiana, Florida, and South Carolina gave Hayes and the Republicans a thin chance of upsetting him in the electoral college. Their strategy was to woo the Southern Democrats to their side with promises that the national government would withdraw troops from the defeated states, would refrain from further interference in racial matters, and would divert federal funds to the South for "internal improvements," words that in many Southern minds meant the Texas & Pacific Railroad.

* Charles H. Sherrill, a very able lobbyist, soon took Franchot's place as, to use the official title, "Adviser and Agent of the Central Pacific Railroad in the City of Washington before Congress and the Departments."

The behind-the-scenes swing of the Republican strategists to Scott's side seemed to bring irresistible strength to the Pennsylvanian. Reluctantly Huntington decided to come to terms with him. This in turn involved reaching an understanding with Jay Gould and the Union Pacific.

Gould had been eying the Southern Pacific askance for some time, for if the line really did go to New Orleans it would of course be a competitor of the Union Pacific, unless the needs of the Central Pacific kept traffic flowing to the UP in Utah. Yet Gould did not want to block Huntington openly, for that would help Scott, potentially an even more formidable competitor.

Searching for a way to show his claws, Gould discovered the little Los Angeles & Independence Railroad. Independence was a hamlet in Owens Valley, at the eastern base of the precipitous Sierra Nevada mountains. On the eastern side of Owens Valley, in the Inyo Mountains, was the prosperous mining camp of Cerro Gordo. Southeast of Cerro Gordo was the newer, richer silver camp of Panamint, on the bleak edges of Death Valley. The principal Panamint mines were controlled by William Stewart of Nevada, long-time friend of the associates who had just lost his Senate seat; by John P. Jones, who at a reputed cost of $500,000 had recently won a Nevada senatorship (not Stewart's); and by Trenor W. Park, a canny speculator who hunted sharklike in Gould's turbulent wake. Park owned stock in the Pacific Mail Steamship Company; in addition, he and Jones both held shares in the Panama Railroad. These things brought them into contact—and sometimes into conflict—with Gould.

Jones thought that he could control the mining camps of Cerro Gordo and Panamint by building a supply railroad from Independence south through Cajon Pass to the vicinity of San Bernardino. From there he would run the rails to a new seaport which he planned to create on ranch lands he owned due west of Los Angeles.

Santa Monica, as he named the would-be terminus of his road, was half a day closer by ship to San Francisco than was the harbor at Wilmington, south of Los Angeles, which was the terminus of the associates' Los Angeles & San Pedro Railroad. Thus Santa Monica was a potential threat to the Southern Pacific's strangle hold on all freight that moved into and out of Los Angeles.

Local traffic was only part of the worry, however. Jones and Trenor Park were appealing to Jay Gould for help in constructing the new Los Angeles & Independence Railroad. Their chief selling point was an argument that the Utah Southern, which Gould controlled, could build west through southern Nevada to a hookup with the Los Angeles & Independence. In that way the Union Pacific would have an outlet to the sea independent of the Central Pacific. Such a connection, as Gould realized at once, would reduce the effectiveness of the Central Pacific and thus provide him with a riposte in case Huntington really was serious about pushing the Southern Pacific all the way to New Orleans.

While waiting for Gould to make up his mind, Senator Jones built, with his own funds, the last section of the line, from Los Angeles to Santa Monica. At Santa Monica he constructed a deep-water pier capable of handling ocean steamers. He advertised this pier as the probable terminus of both the Union Pacific and Texas & Pacific railroads. Using that and cut-rate excursion trains to the beach as real estate bait, he began selling building lots in Santa Monica.

The alarmed associates in San Francisco responded by cutting fares on their Los Angeles & San Pedro Railroad to rock bottom. Huntington meantime called on Gould several times, showed him maps of the arid West, and told him that the Los Angeles & Independence would be a very poor investment. As he had anticipated, Gould backed away. The man was not as interested in building lines as he was in manipulating them. Moreover, his chief concern had been to warn Huntington, not to help Jones, and he had made his point. But more of that in a moment.

About the time that Jones realized he had been left in the lurch, the stock of his Comstock mines crashed. There was a simultaneous break in the shares of the Panama road. Shivering in the sudden chill, Jones sought out Huntington and offered to sell the railroad between Los Angeles and Santa Monica to the Southern Pacific.

The associates in California objected. Jones was broke. Let him shiver. Besides, Crocker argued, the purchase would give the agitators who were crying out about monopoly something more to fume against—and it was monopoly, he said, rather than the size of the houses on Nob Hill that bred enmity. Huntington, however, wanted Jones's vote in the Senate. He insisted on making the purchase, mainly to keep Jones friendly. The associates then tore up the Los Angeles & Independence tracks, dismantled the pier, let infant Santa Monica die, and raised the rate on their Los Angeles & San Pedro line to a higher point than ever before. The citizens of Los Angeles held indignant mass meetings, implored Sacramento to pass a rate-regulation bill, sent representatives to Washington, and implored Tom Scott to save them. Crocker had the sour satisfaction of writing "I told you so!" to Huntington, but Collis paid no attention.[40] By that time the local tempest no longer mattered either to him or to Jay Gould.

313

As indicated earlier, the contested presidential election between Hayes and Tilden had upset old alignments. As the time for counting the electoral votes drew near, a frenzy swept much of the country. Hotheaded Tilden supporters began to arm, vowing to fight a new civil war rather than be robbed of victory. Republican strategists sought feverishly to forestall such violence and at the same time hang onto the presidency by working out, with Southern Democrats, a compromise that involved, as one of its items, a recommendation of subsidies for the Texas & Pacific.

Opponents of federal bounty to railroads dissented sharply, as Huntington of course knew. Hayes had been nominated as a reform candidate by Republicans disgusted with the scandals of the Grant administration. Carl Schurz warned the new candidate, "Remember the Crédit Mobilier. . . . It looks almost as if a railroad could not come within a hundred miles of a legislative body without corrupting it."[41] Thus advised, Hayes remained publicly noncommittal. Not so his energetic promoters. They worked so diligently and so skillfully throughout the border states and among wavering northern Republicans that Huntington, who seldom misjudged the mood of Congress, made a mistake this time. He decided the Scott bandwagon was the one to ride.

The prospect of cash in hard times was one of his motives. Southern Pacific bonds were proving almost unsalable. This meant that the mountain track laying and tunnel digging in California had to be paid for by drawing on the Central Pacific's annual earnings, by selling Central Pacific land-grant bonds and diverting the receipts to unauthorized purposes, and, during times of crisis, by a dangerous juggling of short-term loans.[42] In California his associates were growing increasingly opposed to his unrestrained warfare on Scott and at any moment might rebel. Under the circumstances, a share of the subsidies Scott wanted might prove an escape from a precarious situation.

Scott of course would resist. Needing an ally, Collis called on Jay Gould. After the episode of the Los Angeles & Independence, he did not dare do otherwise.

Gould's price was high—a ten-twenty-seconds share in the construction company that was to build whatever tracks were allotted to the Southern Pacific.[43]

That arrangement secured, Huntington went to Scott and demanded a right to construct part of the southern transcontinental and thus share in whatever benefits Congress assigned to the Texas & Pacific. Scott refused. He thought he had loaded the key congressional committees in his favor and could ram his bill through without knuckling under to these raiders from the West. But then he discovered that between them Gould

314

and Huntington controlled as many committeemen as he did. Neither side could bring a bill onto the floor of Congress without the other's consent. Convinced of that fact, the Pennsylvanian at last consented to talk.

During the bargaining several flare-ups crackled between the two men.[44] That and the confusion in Congress led Huntington to wonder whether he had been correct in estimating the values of an alliance with the Pennsylvanian, whom he did not trust.

In an effort to copper his bets, he ordered ten thousand tons of steel rail, suggested to his partners the advisability of buying or leasing enough shallow-draft river boats to ferry the material from the Gulf of California up the Colorado River to Yuma, and directed Colton to pry a franchise out of the Arizona legislature. He knew the others would not like the implications behind the orders, but never mind. No matter what happened to his fragile truce with Scott, he meant to lay the rail deep into Arizona— with or without his partners' approval.[45]

Conniving did not end there. The turmoil in Congress led him and Gould to consider additional legislation that they might slip past the agitated watchdogs of the Treasury, this time a funding bill that would let the Union Pacific and Central Pacific pay their debts to the government on practically their own terms. The matter was growing acute. During the past summer the Senate Judiciary Committee had reported out a rigorous bill, authored by Allen Thurman of Ohio. If Thurman's measure passed, the Pacific railroads would have to meet their debts to the United States by paying 25 per cent of their net earnings into a government-managed sinking fund.

For some time Collis had been working on gentler substitutes. What he proposed was to return to the government six million acres of the Central Pacific's unsold land in the sagebrush wastes of Nevada and western Utah and receive for them a credit of $2.50 an acre to be applied against the road's debt. The rest of the debt could then be met with relatively little trouble.

To him the matter was one of simple justice. When making the grants to the Pacific railroads in 1862 and 1864, the government had supposed that the companies would sell the land to settlers in order to reimburse themselves for the cost of construction. Settlers, however, had failed to bid as anticipated, and in Huntington's opinion it was up to the government to make amends. Anti-subsidy congressmen rejected the appeals. The government's offer of the land, they said, had been made in good faith. The railroads had accepted it, and now must live with it. Certainly the plaints did not come with good grace from a railroad that was paying high dividends.

315

Although Gould's potent lobby had joined with Huntington's in an effort to change Congress' views, they had made little headway at first. But as the time for canvassing the electoral votes drew near and tension mounted on Capitol Hill, the two men decided to take advantage of the new opportunities for horse trading and try again. Once more their legislative errand boys drew up fresh land-credit funding bills for submission to the distracted lawmakers.[46]

The concerted attacks began in January 1877, when Lucius Quintus Cincinnatus Lamar of Mississippi submitted the Texas & Pacific bill to the Senate. It was an astounding grab bag. The Texas & Pacific, working westward, and the Southern Pacific, working eastward, were to build 1,187 miles of track between Marshall, Texas, near the Louisiana border, and Yuma, Arizona. The road was to be bonded at forty thousand dollars per mile, with the government promoting the sale of the bonds by guaranteeing their interest for fifty years. The railroads' land grants were to serve as security.

Five branches were involved. The Southern Pacific was to build a hundred-mile branch from San Gorgonio Pass to San Diego.* In the East there were to be four branches. One would run from the main trunk line to Vinita, Indian Territory (now Oklahoma), there to meet the remnants of the Atlantic & Pacific. Other branches would lead from Marshall to Memphis, Vicksburg, and New Orleans. Those branches, too, asked for government aid.

The total amount of construction proposed came to 2,307 miles. The cost was estimated at some $85 million. Five per cent interest on this amount for fifty years came to another $220 million.

It was too much. Much of the nation's press reacted in hot indignation to what seemed the cynical advantage that both Thomas Scott and Collis Huntington were trying to take of their county's travail. For months Scott had been crying out that he meant to break the unholy monopoly being exercised by the Central Pacific and Southern Pacific. Now he was in league with the monopoly. During those same months, Huntington had proclaimed far and wide that he would build the southern transcontinental without government aid. Now he was reaching into the Treasury with both hands—and on top of that, trying, with the help of the notorious Jay

---

* By this time, the Tehachapi Mountains had been surmounted and the San Fernando tunnel holed through. In September 1876, Charles Crocker drove a golden spike that symbolized the linking of Los Angeles to San Francisco by way of the San Joaquin Valley and Oakland. SP tracklayers pushed through San Gorgonio Pass and began driving southeast through desolate wastes toward the Colorado River and Yuma.

Gould, to pass a sinking fund bill that would enable him, opponents charged, to sidestep part of the Pacific railroads' just debt to the government.[47]

Anti-subsidy forces shook themselves awake with far more vigor than Huntington had anticipated. Although Hayes was elected (on other grounds than railroad considerations), the subsidy and sinking fund bills were crushed. The defeat automatically ended the truce with Scott, and the old war was on again. But this time ten thousand tons of rail were loaded on shipboard, destined for California. And that, Huntington vowed —he never accepted defeat—was going to make the difference.

24   Connivings and Scandal

Tom Scott was an optimist. He knew that President Hayes was eager to conciliate a South aroused by his election, and a promise of government help for the Texas & Pacific might help him along his thorny path. The Pennsylvanian felt, too, that the alliance with Huntington had been a mistake because of the antagonism stirred up in Congress over the sinking fund bill. He accordingly dropped Collis completely and returned with undiminished zeal to his original attack, trying to line up favorable committees in the new Congress as the first step in bringing a favorable bill to the attention of the nation.

Huntington reacted by also returning to his old strategy, struggling with Scott for control of the committees and sounding anew his promise to build the southern transcontinental without aid. For a time his associates in California complied with his demands almost as if mesmerized. They purchased the Colorado River steamers that he wanted for hauling rail and other material to the Yuma docks from ocean ships anchored far down the Gulf of California. Crocker prevailed on the Arizona legislature to grant the Southern Pacific a franchise across the territory. That done, the territorial governor, vigorous little Anson Peacely-Killen Safford, promised that he would urge Congress to approve the franchise and give the Southern Pacific a right-of-way across Arizona's public lands on the basis that the railroad would bring prosperity to the Southwest.[1]

Another problem involved getting into Arizona. As matters stood, the Southern Pacific's franchise from Congress extended, ambiguously, to the Colorado River in the vicinity of Yuma. At the time the bill passed, bored eastern Congressmen had probably understood this to mean a terminus at the California-Arizona border. The border, however, snaked along the middle of the Colorado River. Arguing that a terminus there was un-

318

reasonable, the associates decided to push on into the town of Yuma, which was clearly past the river and firmly inside Arizona. In pursuit of this goal, which Scott would certainly object to, they obtained a bridge charter from both California and Arizona. Crocker then journeyed to Yuma in the spring of 1877 to select the best site for the structure. Inasmuch as satisfactory sites were scarce in the vicinity, he was able to pick one that amounted almost to a blockade so far as Scott's long-range plans were concerned.

Reaching the bridge site presented difficulties. The west (California) bank of the river was engulfed by the Fort Yuma Military Reservation. Tracks could not reach Crocker's bridge site without crossing a corner of the reservation lands. Permission to build there would have to come from Hayes's new Secretary of War, George McCrary.[2] This would allow Scott to strike counterblows, for McCrary was friendly both to him and to Grenville Dodge.

In spite of this, the associates went ahead with engineering studies for a drawbridge that would allow passage to river boats. They planned to prefabricate parts of the structure and ship them to the site by water. As soon as preliminary drawings had been made, Crocker carried the specifications and the bridge charter to Gen. Irvin McDowell, commander of the Army's Department of the Pacific. Obviously, he said, the bridge would not be very useful unless the Southern Pacific was allowed to lay the necessary tracks across a few miles of the reservation.

After the usual amount of buck-passing, a compromise order arrived from Secretary McCrary. Ultimately, he said, the issue of a right-of-way across government land would have to be settled by Congress. Until Congress could take up the matter, the SP would be allowed to lay "temporary" tracks across the reservation, with the understanding that the company must remove the rails if Congress later denied the right-of-way. The same privilege was extended to the Texas & Pacific—a somewhat meaningless provision since its trackhead was 1,200 miles away. Still, Scott's hand may have been behind the mushy order. It did not amount to a refusal, which would have brought Huntington up fighting, but it left the future so uncertain that perhaps the Southern Pacific would suspend work until it could obtain a more definite pronouncement.

If this was Scott's reasoning, he was partly right. The associates began work on the bridge in July—and that was to be the end of the line, so far as the directors in California were concerned. Yuma, fine. The strategic bridge would preserve their monopoly. But that, they told Huntington, was as far as they would go. Let Scott have the rest if he wanted it.

They were frightened. Times were hard. The winter of 1876–77 had been inordinately dry. Wheat died in the fields; livestock perished; creeks turned to dust and hydraulic mining ceased. Simultaneously, the output of the great Nevada silver mines began to drop. To complete the gloomy picture, the full pinch of the depression that had been crippling the East at last reached California. Credit constricted, unemployment leaped. Receipts on the railroad dwindled. San Francisco filled with men out of work. Their mood was explosive.

Huntington, who reached the city on July 9 for the annual board of directors' meeting, soon received a graphic example of local feelings. On July 23 a huge mass meeting was called in the center of the city. Its purpose was to express sympathy with railroad strikers in the East, and to protest the use of troops in dealing with the unrest.

During the course of the meeting, a rowdy fringe of the gathering began chanting slogans against the Chinese. Because the Orientals would work for low wages, they had replaced whites extensively, first on railroad construction and then in many fields—digging irrigation canals, mining old claims, harvesting crops, making cigars, and so on. Caucasians believed that California's depression was largely attributable to this "coolie competition."

Excited by the emotionalism generated at the mass meeting, a segment of the group broke away and began hunting Asiatics. They burned one laundry and destroyed several others. Liking the sport, the more violent of the rioters ordered all Orientals out of San Francisco under threat of general incineration.

The small police force of 150 men was unable to cope with the situation. Fearing that a widespread assault on wooden Chinatown might result in a city-wide conflagration, agitated property owners gathered in a public meeting of their own and voted to form a Committee of Safety under the presidency of William T. Coleman.

The name awoke memories for Huntington. When Coleman had been head of the famous San Francisco vigilance committee of 1856, Collis, as corresponding secretary of the Sacramento group, had called on him for advice in matters of organization. Later Coleman had leased a building that the associates had erected on the Mission Bay property donated to them by the city in 1868. Though no surviving record says so, it would not be strange if the two men met again during these newest days of public alarm.

Coleman enrolled a citizens' army of about 5,500 men. A finance committee raised a war chest of $7,500; almost surely the railroad contributed. Prodded by Senator Sargent, the Secretary of War ordered

General McDowell by telegraph to turn over to Coleman 1,760 rifles, five hundred carbines, and ammunition for arming them. The Secretary of the Navy ordered five small warships to take up positions at intervals off the city wharves.

The volunteer militia formed companies, elected officers, and began to drill. Coleman distributed a few rifles and then, sobered by the fiery temper of the peacemakers, decided to substitute pick handles instead.

On the night of the twenty-fifth, three hundred cavalrymen patrolled the outskirts of the city. Other volunteers were stationed aboard vessels moored to different piers. About 1,500 men, divided into numerous watches, walked assigned beats throughout the city.

The ill-organized mob met the challenge by swarming down to the foot of Brannan Street—ironic name—to attack the docks owned jointly by the Pacific Mail Steamship Company and the associates' Occidental & Oriental line. The year before, upwards of 22,000 Chinese immigrants had landed on those docks. The O&O line was accustomed to crowding up to a thousand of them per trip, at fifty dollars a head, into the mephitic holds of its three steamers, and the Pacific Mail Company was equally busy in the trade. By destroying the docks the rioters hoped to underscore their demand that "The Chinese Must Go!" The associates, all of them in the city at that time, were naturally upset by the threats.

Shock waves of Coleman's pick-handle brigade met the mob in a fierce melee and drove it back. The frustrated rioters then ignited several nearby lumber yards and attacked the fire engines that arrived to quell the flames. Fresh vigilantes poured into the district. For two hours guerrilla warfare raged through the streets. Four men were killed and many injured. By midnight quiet had been restored. There were no further eruptions, and on July 28 the Committee of Safety disbanded.[8]

Strong-arm tactics had worked again, as they had in 1856, and it is likely that the restorers of law and order did not see any marked distinction between the hoodlums whom the weak city government of '56 had not been able to handle, and the unemployed of '77, who wanted help from their government and were receiving none. But there was a marked difference. No one fled the city in '77. Instead, the bloody encounters of the night of July 25 brought disaffection to a boil and was a powerful stimulus in the secret formation of the California Workingmen's party.

When the party emerged into the open that fall (after Huntington had returned to New York), its favorite rallying point was a vacant lot across from the city hall—hence the name "sand-lotters" for the group. On the lot, hungry men applauded the spellbinding harangues of Denis Kearney. They marched behind Kearney to the top of Nob Hill and shouted imprecations outside the mansions of the California associates. More seriously, so far as the railroad was concerned, their party was a leading force in legislative rebellions that finally resulted in the calling of a convention to rewrite the state's obsolete constitution. A primary goal of the sand-lotters was the imposition of strong curbs on the railroad monopoly and upon land speculators in general.

These things Huntington of course could not foresee in July, any more than he could guess the outcome of the Thurman sinking fund bill that was still under debate in Congress. Quiet restored in the streets, he and his partners resumed their acrimonious debate about the future course of the Southern Pacific.

Apparently no firm decisions were reached. The associates did agree to apply to the legislature of New Mexico for a charter to build in that territory, as well as in Arizona, but the charter would not commit them to actual work. They agreed further—or Huntington thought they did—that they would not declare a fall dividend, a restraint which, he said, would make his borrowing in the East much easier.[4] On August 9, mollified by these sops, he left for New York.

While the associates argued in California, the Nez Percé Indian "uprising" occurred in Idaho and touched their fortunes to this extent: troops from throughout the Department of the Pacific were hurried into the Northwest to join Gen. O. O. Howard's punitive pursuit of Chief Joseph's retreating band. Fort Yuma was stripped of all but four men— Maj. T. S. Dunn, who was in command, one sergeant, and two privates.[5]

Early in August Major Dunn inspected the "temporary" tracks that the Southern Pacific was edging into the reservation. They looked permanent to him, and he so notified the Secretary of War. McCrary responded on September 1 by ordering all work halted, at which time the rails were within a few rods of touching the half-built bridge. Huntington was convinced that Gould as well as Scott had a hand in the harassment.

Crocker was not nonplused for long. He called on General McDowell, pointed out that the bridge over the Colorado River was incomplete, and said that it would be ruined by the treacherous stream if the company was not allowed to carry out certain salvage operations. Would the Army relent that much?

Again telegrams flew, and on September 6 McCrary authorized enough work to prevent waste. The bridge builders sprang to intensive action. Their intent, of course, was to push a permanent structure the rest of the way across the stream. That done, a special crew would lay track over the span before the four-man army could stop them, and would then run a train into Yuma.

It was characteristic Central Pacific-Southern Pacific strategy: seize and then defend—or, as Colton outlined matters to Huntington with underscoring:

I told Arthur Brown when he went down, to get all ready to lay the steel, which he said he could do in two hours after the completion of the bridge. . . . I do not believe they [the government] will interfere with the mails and passengers, after the track is completed, *but at any rate I think it is a good climate on the Arizona side in which to winter an S.P. locomotive*, should they cut us off, & it will be a check to our friend Thos. A. Scott.

As soon as word reached Crocker that the bridge was ready, he ordered a train prepared in San Francisco for hauling mail and passengers to Yuma, knowing well the excitement that its arrival would create in the remote desert town. He scheduled the event for Sunday morning. That meant that the tracks would have to be run across the bridge on Saturday night.

Sensing that something might be afoot, Major Dunn and his garrison stood guard until 11 P.M. Not a human sound met them. Soothing themselves with the thought that the railroaders would not work on Sunday, the sleepy quartet went back to the barracks to bed. About 2 A.M. they were awakened by the clang of a dropped rail. Marching forth, they took up a position athwart the right-of-way and ordered the several score workers to desist—only to have to scramble out of the way when a carload of rails was pushed toward them by a switch engine. Angrily Major Dunn thereupon ordered the man in charge of the work to consider himself under arrest. The fellow replied impolitely, and the outnumbered army, its duty done as it saw it, marched back to the fort.

All told, the workers laid half a mile of track, across the bridge and into Yuma as far as Madison Avenue and First Street. About sunrise a work engine halted at tracks' end, tolled its bell and blew blast after blast from its whistle. Sleepers tumbled from their beds and rushed from their homes, rubbing their eyes. A locomotive in Arizona! A bit later along came a handcar, making sure of the track. Behind it chuffed Crocker's San Francisco Express, the engine bedecked in American flags.

More telegrams flew. General McDowell ordered reinforcements to Yuma—by train—twelve troopers and a laundress, with orders to open the draw and let no more trains across. With a speed that suggests prior preparation, the major and leading merchants of Yuma, and Governor Safford and the chief politicos in the capital of Tucson fired petitions and telegrams to Washington: Don't take away our railroad!

The West was agog. In its leading Sunday (October 7) editorial, entitled "The Iron Horse Has Snorted in the Ear of National Authority," the San Francisco *Alta California* demanded, "Now what are you going to do about it, Uncle Samuel? Will you set Stanford and Company to work pulling up those piles with their teeth? . . . Will you set us back to the days of Forty-Nine, when we crossed the river in a basket covered with the skin of a dead mule? . . . Uncle, what will you do?"

The best answer is provided by Huntington's letter of October 10, 1877, to Colton:[6]

> I went to Washington night before last and returned last night. I think I have the bridge question settled. . . . I found it harder to do than I expected. The Secretary of War told me that they had it up in two Cabinet meetings and had concluded not to do anything, as Congress would come together next week; but I got him out of that idea in about twenty minutes. I then saw three others of the Cabinet; then I went and saw the President. He was a little cross at first; said we had defied the Government, etc., but I soon got him out of that idea. . . . He then said, "What do you propose to do if we let you run over the bridge?" I said, "Push the road right on through Arizona." He said, "Will you do that? If you will that will suit me first rate."

An executive order allowing train service to Yuma followed. There was, however, no building eastward into Arizona. The California associates flatly refused to go ahead, in spite of Huntington's promise to the President of the United States. The matter had become an obsession; they simply would not authorize additional construction until they saw some way of reducing the Central Pacific's huge floating debt. Hopkins, dangerously ill in bed, was particularly obdurate. When Huntington wired a request for his colleagues to endorse jointly a hundred notes with the amounts left blank so he could fill them in as required and then use them one by one for desperately needed collateral, Mark shook his thin head back and forth on the pillow. Their building program in Southern California had been, as Colton reported Hopkins' words, "madness and if we all wanted to go to the D——l much as he liked us he would not [be a party to the folly]." To which the others, in a flood of letters, added fervent approval. They were through.[7]

Huntington had to acquiesce. Finances were as desperate as his associates said, although in his opinion their own ill-considered conduct and not the costs of construction was the cause. In spite of published reports of the Central Pacific's huge floating debt, the Californians had ignored his violent objections and had declared a dividend for the fall of 1877. It looked like stockjobbery, and, as he had predicted, created enormous difficulties in the way of selling Central Pacific securities or borrowing money for current needs[8]—hence his need for the blank notes that Mark would not sign. The bitter quarrel had its effect, however. No more dividends were publicly announced during 1878 or 1879.

Underneath those rifts about policy ran an even more difficult personality problem. Stanford for some time had been declining to let his full share of the dividends remain on deposit with the Western Development Company so that the money could be used for meeting construction bills. The funds he withdrew, Crocker wrote Huntington, were being used to purchase land and to further a company that planned to use a newly invented cable car for climbing San Francisco's steep hills. The governor had made similar withdrawals in 1873, taking the money then from the Contract & Finance Company in order to buy real estate in the Twin Peaks district of San Francisco. It had looked to his associates during those desperate days as if he had feared bankruptcy for the Central Pacific and was building up a private bulwark. Perhaps he was equally afraid, in 1877, of bankruptcy for the Southern Pacific and was sliding off around the corner, even though their unwritten agreement had always been to sink or swim together.

Finally Crocker enticed Stanford over to Hopkins' house, where Mark was still abed. Gathering their nerve, the two bearded the Central Pacific president about his disloyal conduct. He told them bluntly that they could go to hell. He had done nothing illegal. The money was due him, and he would withdraw it whenever he saw fit.[9] It was not the sort of reply to add to Huntington's peace of mind, off on the other side of the continent.

Meanwhile Congress had convened and the Washington visitations began again. Scott had to be forestalled; the bridge affair had to be repeatedly defended; Senator Thurman's sinking fund measure had to be modified, if possible. The constant strain exhausted Huntington. Repeated lamentations run through his letters: "Of all things, I do most dread this Washington business." . . . "I do not feel so much like doing battle with the whole human race as I once did." . . . "I am having a rough fight." . . . "I do not think I have had one hour's sleep in the last four days and am getting very nervous. . . ." To which Colton replied, yes, it was a "terable strain," but things weren't easy in California either. There were runs on Sacramento banks to which the Central Pacific was heavily indebted; the sand-lotters were demonstrating; the Chinese-carrying business of the O&O line was falling off badly. He wasn't sleeping well, either. "All my hair in the front has droped out or turned *gray*."[10]

During these days, ailing Mark Hopkins was being treated by a Chinese herb doctor, Li Po Tai. Feeling better and thinking that warm weather would speed his recovery, he decided to visit Yuma and see the bridge that had caused so much uproar. He went down in a private car with a group of company brass, including Dr. A. B. Nixon, the railroad's official physician and one of the founders of California's Republican party. On the morning of March 29, 1878, while the car was standing on a siding at Yuma, he did not awake. When Nixon was summoned, it was too late.

The loss of his partner of a quarter of a century was a profound shock to Huntington, and yet he made no effort to go to California for the funeral. The Thurman act was scheduled for final debate in the Senate, and he was doing what he could, not to prevent passage, which he considered inevitable, but to have amendments added that would reduce its rigors. Part of his trouble was Jay Gould. The Union Pacific president swept into Washington to put his weight against the measure but was so crass about it that he succeeded only in raising hackles.[11]

The Senate passed the bill on April 9; the House concurred a month later. Henceforth 25 per cent of the net earnings of the Union Pacific and the Central Pacific—even the earnings of the branch lines that had received no government aid—must go, under a complex formula, into a sinking fund for retiring the bonded debt due the government. The railroads' word about profits would not be accepted; all books and records were to be examined by a government auditor.[12]

Huntington, coldly furious, ascribed Thurman's activities to his desire to be President, "He turned demagogue for political purposes" and unearthed unsuspected talents: "lying was his best forte." After making standard remarks to the effect that "it is almost a crime to own any property," Jolly Charley Crocker decided that the company could learn to live with the bill. Colton sputtered with indignation: "Congressional Persecution. . . . ROBBERS. . . ." He then fired off an aphorism that encapsulated the opinions of his class and era: "No government can last long when the rights of the *Individual* are ignored to gratify the many."[13]

Despite the gloom, Huntington's financial antennae were beginning to quiver. Money was growing easier. In California crops promised to be plentiful again. And in Texas, Col. Tom Peirce was eager to thrust a little short line, the Galveston, Harrisburg & San Antonio, westward toward El Paso. (Harrisburg has since been swallowed by Houston.) All Peirce needed was money—and during secret talks in New York, Huntington said that perhaps he could provide funds in return for a share of the Texas road.[14]

He never let go. He had said once that he meant to build a road through the South, and he refused to let his partners' pessimism dissuade him. When he attended the board of directors' meeting in San Francisco in August and September 1878, he heaped them with arguments.

Now that money was growing easier, he said, giant combines were stirring. Someone was going to build that southern transcontinental. Scott might find eastern capitalists who, for the sake of the Texas & Pacific's land grants, might extend the aid that Congress refused. Gould, working through the Missouri Pacific, might strike both south to New Orleans and southwest toward El Paso in order to complete his dominion over the central part of the United States. Why let them? No one else was in as good a strategic position as the associates were. If the Southern Pacific worked east and the Galveston, Harrisburg & San Antonio worked west to a junction near El Paso, they could obtain an opening on Gulf of Mexico waters—perhaps even at New Orleans—and at the same time would completely outflank any other cross-country system. As for money, he would find it somehow. That was his business.

Ambition and the zest of battle were probably his chief motives. But he knew his associates well enough that he played on them with three clear-cut economic arguments as well. First, if the Southern Pacific was completed to the Gulf of Mexico, they could divert Central Pacific traffic over the new line. This would reduce the CP's net earnings and cut down on the payments they would have to make to the government. Secondly, if they planned carefully and got control of the Galveston, Harrisburg & San Antonio, they would not have to share proceeds with anyone, as the Central Pacific had to do with the Union Pacific. And finally, luck was on their side. Recent mineral strikes at Tombstone and Wickenberg, Arizona, were developing into a real stampede. And so, just as the Central Pacific had drawn early sustenance from mining traffic to Virginia City, the SP could count on lucrative local profits in Arizona to help it along its way.

He carried the argument and returned to New York, there to begin searching for money. Stanford and Crocker, mindful of the ten thousand tons of steel rail that he had already provided, issued orders to their engineers to launch construction at Yuma in November, when the desert heat would have abated. They then went off on holiday junkets, Stanford to the East and Crocker to London. Affairs in California were left to David Douty Colton, whose wife and younger daughter were visiting relatives in Iowa, and to two heirs apparent, Charles F. Crocker, Jolly Charley's eldest son, still in his mid-twenties, and Timothy Hopkins, childless Mark's nephew and adopted child.

On the evening of October 8, 1878, Colton was brought unconscious to his home. There he died. Rumor said that he had been stabbed. The physicians who were called to attend him denied this and said that the sudden death had resulted from the aftereffects of his being thrown from a horse a day or two earlier. Still other rumors declared that he had died of a "dreadful tumor." It is not likely that the truth will ever be known.[15] He was forty-seven years old.

Two deaths occurring so close together demanded a major reorganization. Although Huntington remained in New York, Stanford and Charles Crocker returned to California as rapidly as they could. On November 4, 1878, the Pacific Improvement Company replaced the Western Development Company as the associates' construction firm for building the Southern Pacific and, later, for extending the California & Oregon into the north. Offices were redistributed, and a routine check of the books began.

Illness plagued the survivors that winter. Crocker was troubled with rheumatism. Stanford fell into a long decline. His baffled doctors finally decided that his troubles arose from his having breathed, for two years, the air of a privy vault beneath his ranch house at Palo Alto. They said another year might pass before he recovered, but in April 1879 he threw away his medicines and began to improve.[16]

A far more serious ailment was unearthed by the bookkeepers. Colton, whose one-million-dollar note to the associates fell due in October 1879, had sensed that he was not going to be able to meet it from the normal profits of the company. Desperate, he had misappropriated funds and had assigned himself stock certificates to which he had no right.

The ill wind had its uses. The associates wanted to get rid of Mrs. Colton, who was a shrewd and tough-minded woman. During the spring of 1879, Stanford and Crocker presented her with the million-dollar note and offered to cancel it if she would return to them all of Colton's stocks and bonds in the railroad enterprises—the securities he had picked up in the Central Pacific, Southern Pacific, O&O Steamship Company, the Western Development Company, the Rocky Mountain

Coal Company, and so on. They assured her that they were making the offer from the kindness of their hearts. The securities were not worth a million dollars, they said, and the stock in the Western Development Company would soon be heavily assessed in order to meet the costs of the new construction program.

She hesitated longer than they liked. During the summer, when Huntington was in San Francisco for a directors' meeting, they applied force. Pretending that they must have an answer before he left, they sent granite-faced lawyers to her with word of her husband's alleged defalcations. Unless she did as requested, they would drag Colton's name through the mire of all the newspapers in the land. At that she surrendered.* Later, when Hopkins' estate was probated, she decided from accounts in the papers that she had been bilked. According to her calculations the securities she had given up were worth much more than a million dollars. In May 1882 she opened suit. She charged the associates with fraud, denied her husband's wrongdoing, and demanded a return of the securities, after which she would pay the note.

The case was long, complex, and expensive for all concerned. In need of the best legal talent available, the associates made peace with vituperative A. A. Cohen. He and a battery of attorneys fought the case all the way to the state's supreme court.[17] At each trial Mrs. Colton lost.

It was a costly victory for Huntington. During the course of the litigation, Mrs. Colton's attorneys read into the record several hundred of the unguarded letters about hungry Congressmen, legislative manipulation, and financial juggling that Collis had written Colton. The San Francisco *Chronicle* seized on these and syndicated them throughout the country. They were widely printed in December 1883, and immediately supplanted the discredited Brannan charges as a source of ammunition for men attacking the railroad. Throughout the rest of Huntington's life they would be used against him during political campaigns and in repeated congressional investigations. By then, however, he had developed a hide like a rhinoceros toward public defamation. He serenely said that the letters did not bother him and that quotations made from them out of context did not mean a thing. He was not ashamed, he told more than one reporter, of any business transaction he had ever made.

California hostility toward the railroad continued to mount nevertheless. The constitutional convention in Sacramento, held during the winter of 1878–79, rang with charges. The railroad, opponents declared, used

---

* She was not left destitute. Colton had set aside enough property beyond the associates' reach to provide her and her daughters with about $28,000 a year, no small sum in those days.

its monopolistic powers to impose unfair and discriminatory rates. It avoided taxation. Its officials diverted public funds to their own use. Its agents tried to force subsidies from towns along its proposed routes; if the communities refused to open their purses, the company formed rival communities nearby. It refused to show its records to duly appointed commissions. "Its managers," Delegate Volney Howard declaimed, "have controlled the political organization and conventions of both parties. . . . The Central Pacific elects their man and sends him to Washington with a collar around his neck, on which is inscribed in golden letters, 'Central Pacific,' so if he is lost or strayed he may be recaptured and returned to his lawful owners."[18]

Worst of all, to Californians, the railroad imported Chinese labor to the detriment of white American workers.

Defenders insisted that the railroad had not corrupted California. The state had done that to herself during the frenzies of the gold rush, the Nevada silver excitement, and the speculative crazes of the mid-1870s. Legislators expected pay for votes. If it was not forthcoming, they introduced outrageous "cinch bills" so that the railroad could not survive and then demanded that the railroad buy them off. When the state had cried for transportation, the Big Four had provided it under the promise of rates set by the legislature itself as being fair. And now the people who benefited from the railroad cried that the promised rates were too high. Nor were the builders diverting funds to themselves. Rather, they were using income derived from the Central Pacific to build the Southern Pacific. This in turn was creating new jobs and outlets for the produce of hundreds of new farms. Wherever their rails ran, land values had soared. Were they to be punished for all this?

The arguments made little impression. The convention wrote into the new constitution detailed provisions for a railroad commission of three elective members. They gave the commission extensive powers of review and regulation. The first trio, J. S. Cone, C. J. Beerstecher, and George B. Stoneman, went into office in 1880. They accomplished nothing. During his time in office, Cone, a rancher of the Sacramento Valley, made large profits through dealings in railroad grant land. Beerstecher, who was more lacking in subtlety, apparently required that his bribes be made out of hand. George Stoneman, who hoped to become governor, raised some hue and cry about monopolies but in general avoided stumbling over opposition as powerful as the railroad's.[19] A new constitution, the people of California learned, was not necessarily a cure-all for major ills.

Violence meanwhile was building in Mussel Slough, where overflow water from the Kings River drained toward Tulare Lake and was easily diverted by communal irrigation systems.* Hence the land was desirable. But who owned it?

It will be recalled that during the late 1860s, the Southern Pacific had changed its proposed route from the coastal counties to the San Joaquin Valley. Its grant had then been revoked and reinstated by two Secretaries of the Interior. Even after the route and grant had finally been confirmed, a hundred-mile stretch of so-called main-line track between Tres Pinos and Goshen had remained unbuilt, although the railroad, in order to hold onto the grant, had kept promising to fill the gap.

In 1877, when forfeiture loomed, the railroad at last ran a forty-mile piece of track westward along the prescribed route from Goshen through Hanford toward Huron. As soon as the track was approved by government inspectors, title to a checkerboard of mile-square sections in a belt twenty miles wide passed to the Southern Pacific, or so its officials claimed. The only formality remaining was for surveyors of the government's General Land Office to mark the corners of each section.

Rather than wait for this, the railroad sent its own surveyors into the area to make preliminary determinations so that the land could be put onto the market. The surveyors immediately found that many of the sections claimed by the railroad were occupied by belligerent squatter families. Some of them had been living on the land since the confused days when the grant had been twice revoked and twice approved, and no one had been sure what would happen.

Settlers who had followed the firstcomers into the fertile area contested the grant on still other grounds. A partial closing of the gap between Goshen and Tres Pinos, they argued, was not enough. The whole line had to be completed or the entire grant was subject to forfeiture. And the time for building had, by charter, expired on July 18, 1878.

The farmers of the area, most of them truculent southerners, pooled their resources to carry the matter to the courts. They also formed a vigilante committee called the Settlers League. Abetted by the enthusiastic encouragement of Denis Kearney's Workingmen's party, the league announced that it would protect its members from eviction until the courts had rendered a decision. As a side issue the league also warred on farmers who, having purchased land from the railroad, defended its title, and on local cattlemen. They leased grazing rights from the railroad at modest fees and wanted no sodbusters breaking up their range.

League members drilled in secret, wore masks, applauded and perhaps

---

* Mussel Slough, now called Lucerne Valley, is a few miles north of the San Joaquin Valley town of Hanford.

sheltered bandits who preyed on company trains throughout the San Joaquin Valley. Raiders dressed like Indians burned the homes of men who dared speak out against the league and its methods. Land sales dwindled at a time when the railroad needed every source of revenue for the push toward Texas.

On December 15, 1879, Judge Lorenzo Sawyer of the San Jose district court held in favor of the railroad. Their title was sound. Infuriated, the settlers vowed to carry the case to the supreme court and warned the railroad not to try evicting any of the league's members until a final decision had been rendered.

The railroad refused to be coerced.* With Sawyer's decree as their authority, they sold certain pieces of land to a pair of strong-arm boys who probably had been hired for the purpose. After obtaining writs of eviction from the court, local SP agents set about establishing the buyers on the contested property.[20] On May 11, 1880, a gun battle flared. Eight men died, including both "purchasers."

Seven settlers were arrested. They were taken to San Jose and tried before Judge Sawyer. A jury found five of them guilty of resisting a marshal. Sawyer fined them three hundred dollars each and sentenced them to eight months in the San Jose jail. They became pampered martyrs. The wives of three of them lived with their husbands on the top floor of the structure. They all sauntered over to the post office each day to pick up fan mail sent from all parts of the nation. Local merchants delivered choice food to them without charge. A bachelor among them was so little confined that he was able to woo and win the daughter of the jailer. At the end of their terms they were escorted from town by a brass band. Refusing to touch a Central Pacific railroad car, they traveled to Hanford in wagons and were received as conquering heroes by three thousand cheering neighbors. But the railroad won the court cases and kept the land.

Throughout the episode, newspaper cartoons from one end of the state to the other savagely caricatured the associates. The favorite picture was that of a tentacled monster reaching clawlike into every vale and factory. Through the windows of the creature's baleful eyes peered the bloated heads of the partners, Crocker and Stanford in particular. The emotionalism was such that even today it is difficult to find in California histories a dispassionate account of the Battle of Mussel Slough.[21]

And still no controls were placed on the railroad. Stanford, a leader of the state's Republican party, played the most cynical politics. In 1882,

* Stanford made a few conciliatory gestures that at this distance seem to have been designed to woo public opinion rather than placate the settlers.

he secretly backed a Democrat, Railway Commissioner George Stoneman, for the governorship. Stoneman campaigned as a reformer and won. The new railroad commissioners who rode Stoneman's coattails into office were Democrats named Carpenter, Foote, and Humphrey. Carpenter and Foote turned out to be subservient to the railroad and created tremendous antagonism with their decisions. One of Carpenter's pro-railroad rulings at a hearing held in the San Joaquin Valley so infuriated the spectators that one of them threw an egg into the commissioner's face. The crowd of farmers and reporters present applauded enthusiastically. Carpenter's son, who happened to be present, knocked the egg-thrower to the floor. A wild scuffle ensued—but the ruling stood.

Governor Stoneman meantime had called a special session of the legislature to carry out the promises of reform that he had made during the campaign. Not a single effective law against the railroad was passed —"for the usual reason," said one commentator. "The legislators preferred railroad gold to railroad legislation." Since the administration that year was Democratic, much of the largesse was doled out, at no loss to himself, by the Democratic boss of San Francisco, Christopher Augustine Buckley, a rough, genial ex-bartender who was totally blind and recognized men by their voices.[22]

25 The Potentate

The excitement in California touched only the edges of Huntington's attention. He was engrossed in plans of extraordinary boldness and complexity. If they had worked—and they almost did—he would have held in the cup of his hand, insofar as railroads could bring it to him, most of the southern half of the United States. Unfortunately for his purposes, the vision intoxicated him and turned him, at an age when most men are growing conservative, into a plunger.

As he had foreseen, money grew easier. Late in 1878 he sold to Speyer & Company one million dollars' worth of Southern Pacific bonds at eighty-six, plus accrued interest, and also an option under which the firm could purchase several more million. In 1880 the Central Pacific resumed paying dividends, and Huntington was able, after a long drought, to move large blocks of its stock at prices of seventy-five dollars a share or higher.*

The inpouring of funds enabled the Southern Pacific to push at a rapid pace across the gaunt lands of southern Arizona, following survey stakes set out years before by engineers of the hapless Texas & Pacific. Jay Gould watched askance. He did not want the Union Pacific hurt by a diversion of traffic over this new line. Nor did he want the Southern Pacific to enter Texas, a region he meant to have for himself. Accordingly he decided to block the Californians at El Paso on the Rio Grande.

His first step was to form a construction firm, backed by eastern capitalists, for building the Texas & Pacific westward from Fort Worth. Scott was delighted. The fruitless struggle for congressional support and the violent labor strikes against the Pennsylvania Railroad in 1877 had ex-

---

* Southern Pacific stock remained almost unsalable, however, and so the associates clung to it themselves, counting on the future to repay them for their risks as handsomely as their long-held Central Pacific stock was at last doing.

334

hausted him and he had suffered a stroke. Seeing a way to ease his burdens, he let Gould take him to his gnomelike breast, where so many others had been wooed and then crushed.

Had the contest depended on the Southern Pacific alone, the outcome would not have been in doubt. In the early fall of 1880 its tracklayers crossed into New Mexico, and the Rio Grande was only two hundred miles away. The key to victory lay east of El Paso, however, in broken, rugged country that stretched to the hamlet of Sierra Blanca, ninety miles away. There was room in some of those canyons for only a single railroad —and the Southern Pacific had no charter to build in Texas. It would have to halt across the river from El Paso and wait for Peirce's Galveston, Harrisburg & San Antonio to come to it across the dry plains of western Texas. Yet Peirce was showing no disposition to hurry, perhaps because he was seeking better terms than Huntington was inclined to give him. Under those circumstances, Gould might well be able to push the Texas & Pacific into Sierra Blanca from farther north and seize the canyons ahead of his rivals.

To distract Huntington with flank attacks, he announced plans for two Union Pacific extensions to the Coast. One was the Oregon Short Line, designed to follow the old Oregon Trail from Granger, Wyoming, to the Columbia River. The other projected line was to dip through southern Utah and Nevada into California.

Although Huntington had been in touch for some time with B. J. Pengra and other Oregon railroad promoters, including the Portland Board of Trade, he had not been able to work out means for halting the Oregon Short Line.[1] The Union Pacific was going to reach the Coast at last—and so, too, was the recently reinvigorated Northern Pacific. The best the associates could do in that direction was to complete the California & Oregon, acquire its counterpart, the Oregon & California, and thus prevent either the UP or NP from building along the coast to San Francisco. This they managed to do in 1887, after arduous construction around Mt. Shasta, through sixteen tunnels and over a 4,100-foot pass.

In the South their luck was better. Crocker, who was itching for a fight, sent surveyors out east of Ogden. Huntington told Jay Gould where the engineers were working and asked his rival whether he'd like to see a Central Pacific counterpart of the Oregon Short Line reaching into the Missouri Valley. Gould, who was already having troubles enough with the Burlington in the Midwest, decided that he wasn't interested in that line through Nevada to California after all. The fight settled back into a straightaway contest between the Texas & Pacific and the Southern Pacific.

It wasn't quite the gladiatorial contest it had once been; Scott and Gould soon disagreed. Ill and unable to battle longer, the Pennsylvanian in April 1881 sold to Gould every interest he had in the railroad. A few weeks later he was dead. Huntington grieved. Tom Scott had been a mighty adversary, winning affection even in the heat of conflict. Gould's icy veins would never elicit that kind of response.

Meanwhile Collis had resolved his problems with Peirce. In July 1881 the Southern Pacific took over a controlling interest in the Galveston, Harrisburg & San Antonio. That subsidiary road thereupon executed a contract for the Southern Development Company (which was a New Mexico name for the associates' Pacific Improvement Company) to do its construction work in Texas. Thus it was no longer necessary to wait for the Galveston, Harrisburg & San Antonio to come to the canyons from the east. Using the same crews that had built the SP track across the Southwest, the Southern Development Company, under the legal fiction of acting for the Texas-chartered GH&SA, sprang out of El Paso into the strategic canyons. Gould was beaten. The Texas & Pacific, once designed to reach at least as far as San Diego, halted at tiny Sierra Blanca, ninety miles southeast of El Paso.

The SP crews from El Paso met those working from San Antonio on January 12, 1883, just outside a long tunnel near the canyoned junction of the Pecos and Rio Grande. Huntington meantime had been busy absorbing the capital stock of other Texas and Louisiana railroads at a cost of over $7.5 million. By February 1883, San Francisco passengers were able to ride a single line all the way from their bayside city to New Orleans. By 1885 they could do more. The Southern Pacific added a fleet of steamships to its holdings and opened connections with New York City.[2] Shippers could now send goods from coast to coast under a single bill of lading, a decided advantage to accountants wearied of the multiplication of forms and the long delays experienced on combination routes. But this success did not eliminate the threat of still other southern transcontinentals—and that brings us back once more to Jay Gould.

As soon as Gould realized that he could not beat Huntington, he joined him. In November 1881 they agreed to share the track between Sierra Blanca and El Paso and prorate long-haul traffic; some would move through Texas to New Orleans over the Texas & Pacific and some would use the Southern Pacific line through San Antonio as soon as it was completed. In exchange for this share of the Far West's business, Gould assigned the Texas & Pacific land grant in Arizona and New Mexico to the SP—and at that point some of Huntington's earlier bombast came home to roost. He had declared far and wide that he would build the Southern

Pacific without governmental aid, and had done so. It ill behooved him now, congressional opponents said, to ask that the Texas & Pacific grants be transferred to him. In spite of Huntington's urgent lobbying, the entire western part of the grant was declared forfeit.

Peace in Texas achieved, the two titans became allies on a broad front. Huntington took a seat on the boards of the Pacific Mail Steamship line and of Western Union, which had succumbed to Gould's attacks, and thus ended his long troubles with the latter company. Together the pair then cast unfriendly eyes upon the Atchison, Topeka & Santa Fe, latest entry, thanks to a variety of complex happenings, in the cross-country field.

Years earlier, the hard-luck Atlantic & Pacific Railroad had gone bankrupt. The pieces had been picked up, for the sake of its charter and potential land grants, by the owners of a road called the St. Louis & San Francisco, more commonly, the Frisco. Lacking funds to build west along the A&P's chartered route beside the thirty-fifth parallel, the managers of the Frisco entered into a joint construction arrangement with the Santa Fe.

Repercussions reached as far as San Diego, where the frustrated residents jubilated once again. A railroad at last! With the blessings and backing of the Atchison, Topeka & Santa Fe, to whose officers they donated valuable real estate, the San Diegans incorporated a new California Southern. Their plan was to build northeast through San Bernardino and Cajon Pass to a junction with the new transcontinental in the vicinity of present-day Needles. The Santa Fe, the San Diegans hoped, would then use their city as its outlet and develop a major port in competition with San Francisco. Actually, the Santa Fe still meant to reach San Francisco by rail, but did not say so aloud in San Diego.

Neither Gould nor Huntington wanted a new, competitive transcontinental. As a first step in obstructionism, Collis dusted off the Southern Pacific's original charter, which allowed the road to build its main line to Needles (the Yuma line was, legally, a branch) and sent construction crews eastward from the town of Mojave to the Colorado River. Gould meantime sought to buy enough Frisco stock that he would be able to club the new line into talks at a conference table. The men he approached refused to sell. Huntington then took up the search and somehow located in the brokerage house of Seligman & Company a cache of Frisco certificates. Gould and he purchased them jointly. They forced themselves onto the enemy's board of directors and cooled the Santa Fe's aspirations of building toward San Francisco. But they did have to yield the new-

337

comer trackage rights as far as Mojave. It wasn't much, but it did let the newcomer get a foot into the door.

By that time the little California Southern had managed to push defiantly across the Southern Pacific's tracks at the town of Colton and reach San Bernardino. There they ran out of money and had to halt. Although they had achieved roundabout rail connections with the outside world through their junction with the SP at Colton, it benefited them little. The larger road harassed them so with red tape and outrageous freight rates that very little traffic moved down their line into languishing San Diego. Then floods took out large chunks of their track. Appeals to the Santa Fe for help fell on ears all at once strangely deaf, and again it became clear to the dejected people of San Diego that rail commerce still moved in California only as the associates decreed.[3]

Gould perhaps supposed that this achievement was Huntington's main goal in purchasing the Frisco stock. Actually Collis' aims were far broader. He wanted to span the continent.

As noted earlier, the panic of 1873 had thrust the Chesapeake & Ohio into receivership. After involved jockeying, Huntington was able to put together a syndicate that in 1878 purchased the road back at a forced bankruptcy auction on the steps of the Richmond courthouse—price, $2.7 million. He then began a program of headlong expansion. He replaced the worn iron of the C&O tracks with new steel rail. He ran a seventy-five-mile line from Richmond, Virginia, down the peninsula to sleepy Newport News. Under the name of the Old Dominion Land Company, he bought choice acreage in the vicinity, constructed a hotel, stores, and dwellings. He built piers, wharves, a grain elevator, and coal bunkers where steamers could refuel. He leased freighters to run to Liverpool and founded the Old Dominion Steamship Company to link the towns along the navigable rivers of tidewater Virginia. He organized the United States & Brazil Mail Steamship line to run from New York via Newport News and the West Indies to Rio de Janeiro.

Concurrently with those developments, he began thrusting extensions of the Chesapeake & Ohio westward into Kentucky. He bought bankrupt roads and reinvigorated them. He picked up forgotten charters and built new lines. Some bent north to Covington, Kentucky, on the south bank of the Ohio River opposite Cincinnati. Another bent south from Louisville to Memphis, 1,136 miles from Newport News.[4] A key assistant in this western work was his nephew, Henry Edwards Huntington, who had knit the family ties still tighter by marrying Mary Alice Prentice, eldest sister of Clara Prentice, who had been living with Collis and Elizabeth since the death of the girls' father in Sacramento in 1862.*

As the web of steel expanded in Kentucky and Tennessee, Collis planned two mighty extensions. One would cross the Ohio River over a great bridge to be erected between Covington and Cincinnati. From there the rails would drive west and northwest to the Great Lakes, in order to seize midwestern farm produce and manufactured goods and bring them for shipment to the vast ice-free harbor that he envisioned at Newport News.

The other extension would leap the Mississippi at Memphis, drive west across Arkansas, and join the Atlantic & Pacific-Frisco-Santa Fe system in Indian Territory, now Oklahoma.

In 1882 he was not ready to tackle the powerful railroads north of the Ohio River. But he was ready, he thought, for the drive west, where his own growing Southern Pacific system was waiting to receive him at Mojave. That tie-in achieved, the next step, still carefully concealed, would be to elbow Gould out of the way and capture the new Santa Fe system for himself and his associates. He would then dump everything —Santa Fe, Southern Pacific, Central Pacific, Chesapeake & Ohio and related lines—into one great bin, form a giant holding company to lease and operate them all, and so bring into being the only continent-wide rail system in the United States. After that he would turn toward the Great Lakes.

It was a bold plan and nearer attainment, it seemed, than anything that either Tom Scott or Jay Gould had dared contemplate. Yet he had already strained himself to the utmost to build to Newport News and to construct the lines in Kentucky and Tennessee. He could go no farther without help. Early in 1883, therefore, he turned to Crocker. Would the old crew join him, under the banner of the Pacific Improvement Company, in building the first vital link in the cross-country thrust, the road across Arkansas?

On March 2 Crocker replied. The answer was no.

There were several reasons. One was corporate debt. During the period of easy money Huntington had pushed the Texas work so recklessly that the short-term obligations of the Southern Pacific and of the Pacific Improvement Company had reached twenty million dollars.[5] That, on

---

* Henry E. Huntington, it will be recalled, had first gone to West Virginia to operate his uncle's sawmill at St. Albans. Forming a partnership with lobbyist Richard Franchot, he purchased the mill from Huntington, then bought out Franchot. After operating the property on his own for a year, he sold it in 1876 for a good profit and returned to Oneonta to help his ailing father, Solon Huntington. He rejoined his uncle's fold in 1881.

top of the road's long-range commitments, Crocker said, was as much as the companies could stand for a few years. Besides, the old zest was gone. "We are not working together as we used to work." In a later letter he was more explicit.[6] Stanford no longer seemed to care about railroad matters. He had bought a 19,000-acre wheat ranch in Butte County in the Sacramento Valley and, not far away, a tract eighty-five square miles in size. There he was planting 3,500 acres of wine grapes.[7] "He has not," Crocker finished, "put any of his interest received from railroad securities to his credit on the books of the P. I. [Pacific Improvement] Co. for over a year while I have been putting in all of mine as usual, and I believe you have done the same. This weakens us."

Weakness in dealings with William Strong, aggressive head of the Santa Fe, would be fatal. Strong was already complaining (as was Gould) that the Southern Pacific was violating its traffic-sharing agreements and was hogging more than its just portion of freight originating in California. As a counter, the Santa Fe pushed its tracks south to join a railroad that it had acquired in Sonora, Mexico. This let it reach the port of Guaymas on the Gulf of California. From Guaymas it ran steamers to San Francisco —a roundabout challenge, to be sure, but it frightened the California associates. They told Huntington that his hope of overwhelming so energetic a company by coming at it with a railroad through Arkansas was absurd.

As usual, he did not yield at once but offered a substitute idea. He already controlled a few short, run-down lines south of Memphis. Why not repair them, do such new construction as was necessary and so join the Chesapeake & Ohio system to the Southern Pacific at New Orleans? Reluctantly Crocker and Stanford agreed and, in conjunction with other friends they launched what became the Louisville, New Orleans & Texas Railroad.[8]

When the 450-mile project was finished in October 1884, Collis Huntington became the only man in the United States ever to be able to ride in his own railroad car from the Atlantic Ocean to the Pacific over tracks that he either owned completely or in a large measure controlled. It was a satisfaction, surely, but it was not the direct slash through the heart of the country that he had dreamed of.

Well before the Louisville, New Orleans & Texas was completed, disaster threatened again. The country's financial establishment was going through another of its violent readjustments. Credit tightened; stocks plunged.

The railroads controlled by the associates had relatively few resources left with which to weather the blasts. During the years of rising prices the partners had exuberantly sold more than 70 per cent of their Central Pacific stock and now controlled the road largely through proxies. During the same period, Huntington had sold Southern Pacific bonds as fast as brokers would absorb them, and now the railroad had relatively few left as a buttress against the sudden shocks of '84. Inasmuch as Collis had been simultaneously pouring his own fortune into his projects in Virginia and the border states, he faced ruin along with the collapse of the associates' empire.[9]

In desperation the Central Pacific skipped its dividends in 1884, and Huntington undertook, with amazing success considering the circumstances, to placate a representative of the English stockholders who came storming across the ocean to learn what was wrong. Producing ready funds proved more difficult. When the pinch first began to develop in 1883, Collis proposed so shady a bond juggling scheme that even Crocker protested.[10] Left with no other alternatives, Huntington then sold his Frisco stock, ending the dream of a direct transcontinental to the Pacific. That hope gone, he entered into discussions with the Santa Fe about an entry into California. The upshot was an arrangement whereby the associates sold the Needles–Mojave section to the invader for $7.2 million and leased passage rights from Mojave to Oakland for $1,200 per mile per year. The sale enabled the Southern Pacific to keep its head above water, but for the first time a rival had succeeded in opening the California door.[11]

Promptly the Santa Fe made connections through Cajon Pass with the California Southern. San Diego had a railway at last, but it came too late. By that time (1885) Los Angeles was established as the metropolis of Southern California. The Santa Fe paralleled the Southern Pacific tracks into the bustling little city and launched a fierce rate war; at one point it carried excursionists from Kansas City to Los Angeles for a dollar each. Both roads issued floods of alluring publicity about the region. In the end the Southern Pacific benefited far more than did its rival, for it had thousands of acres of grant land to sell and moved them at heady profits. Dozens of towns mushroomed; thousands of citrus ranches were planted.[12] When Collis Huntington declared, as he often did, that he and his associates had done more for California than any other group of men, he was not entirely wrong;[13] he just did not bother to listen when opponents sought to tell him the other side of the story.

A longer-range effort than emergency sales to create stability for the railroads was Huntington's proposal to form a holding company that would embrace all of the lines in which he was interested, so that the stronger could carry the weaker and prevent the latter from setting off a domino-style collapse. The holding company would also produce efficiencies in management and operation. In March 1884, accordingly, he obtained a broad charter from the state of Kentucky for the Southern Pacific Company.* Shortly thereafter the associates began assembling in New York to work out the arduous details of the organization. Charles Crocker represented his own interests and those of his brother's estate. Timothy Hopkins was on hand for his aunt.

The Stanfords were late, not arriving until May 4. They were crushed with grief. During the winter, which they had spent in Europe, their only child, Leland Stanford, Jr., had fallen ill and had died in Florence, Italy, on March 13, 1884, just short of sixteen years of age. Already the distraught parents were contemplating founding a university to bear his name and serve as a lasting memorial.

Huntington was gentler than usual with his partner. He, too, had had a confrontation with death. Early in 1883, Elizabeth had been stricken with cancer.[14] After a long, painful illness, she had died on October 5, 1883.

She had been a gentle, quiet, self-effacing woman, an essential source of strength to Collis during the years when their home had been hot, tight rooms above the hardware store at 54 K Street in Sacramento. But there had been intimacy then, and in New York matters had changed. He was often away, in Washington, Virginia, Kentucky, California, everywhere. When he was home, he spent evening after evening in long meetings, sometimes in hotel lobbies or offices but often in his own house at 65 Park Avenue. The men who assembled there—Gould, Scott, Pullman, Franchot, Senator Conkling, and dozens of others—talked a hard, cryptic commercial language that she did not understand and could not share. As has happened in other situations where business becomes all-absorptive, the links between them had imperceptibly slackened one by one, save for Clara, then growing into her teens. Thus death came to Collis as a blunt ending to what he had been gradually losing for a long time. Nevertheless the emptiness was, for a time, profound. When he wrote a relative that "it is lonesome here" at 65 Park Avenue, he was speaking out of as deep a desolation as he would ever know.

He was soon distracted by the critical state of his business affairs and by the need to plan for the holding company. Then, as winter softened,

* Note that the word "railroad" does not appear in the title. The Southern Pacific Railroad Company would be just one component within the Southern Pacific Company.

he began to seek the company of a young woman and long-time friend, Arabella Duval Yarrington Worsham, or Belle, as Collis called her.

Considerable conjecture has surrounded Arabella Yarrington, to use her maiden name. Efforts to discover information about her background lead to such blank walls as to leave one wondering whether she may have systematically eliminated traces of her youth. Though she became one of the prominent women of America, neither the place nor the date of her birth have been firmly established, apart from her own not wholly convincing statements. She may have been born in Virginia—or Alabama —and the date may have been June 1, 1850—or earlier.

She is said variously to have been a cook, a housekeeper, a governess, and a very effective Washington lobbyist. Sometime late in the 1860s she married a Mr. Worsham. He may have been a river-boat gambler, as is said, but more probably was John A. Worsham, a minor banker in New York City. He either disappeared or died shortly after the wedding. Pregnant, she may have gone to Texas to be near her relatives for the birth of her son, Archer, an event that occurred on March 10, 1870, or she may have stayed in New York.

She was a big, handsome, vivacious woman. Near-sighted, she habitually wore pince-nez glasses. Whatever her origins, she had made herself into a cultured woman, fluent in French, at home in literature, and an avid collector of expensive *objets d'art*. She was also a clever real estate speculator.

The Huntingtons had known her for a long time. In 1871 she was living on Lexington Avenue, New York City, in a house owned by Collis Huntington. By 1877 she was able to start putting together several lots on West Fifty-fourth Street near Fifth Avenue. She built a house on them and soon her investment had reached $330,000, a sizable sum for a young widow with a son to support. In 1883 she sold part of the property to William H. Vanderbilt. The following year she sold the rest, including the house, to John D. Rockefeller. Her net profits on the two transactions came to at least $300,000.[15]

At ten o'clock on Saturday morning, July 12, 1884, at Arabella's home, which had not yet passed into Mr. Rockefeller's possession, she and Collis Huntington were married. The ceremony was performed by Henry Ward Beecher, to whom the bridegroom handed an envelope containing four thousand-dollar bills. Collis was sixty-three; his bride, thirty-four or so.

Only a few relatives were present at the ceremony. Among them were Arabella's mother, sister, and teen-age son Archer, a tall, studious lad whom Collis soon adopted. There is no record that any of his California associates, all of whom were in the city, attended the function. The New York press ignored it, although it was the sort of thing that made good copy. Precautions may have been taken to keep reporters away.[16]

The honeymoon was brief. Business affairs remained critical and the reorganizations had to be hurried through. Huntington wanted the Southern Pacific Company to spread its umbrella over his eastern lines as well as over the western. Crocker and Stanford demurred; the patchwork in the border states looked flimsy to them and they did not want it dragging down their profits. Except for the New Orleans terminus, the Southern Pacific Company accordingly stayed west of the Mississippi, leasing and operating, under complex terms, a system that reached from Portland, Oregon, to New Orleans, including a proliferation of feeders in Texas and western Louisiana, and from San Francisco to Ogden. Stanford was elected president of the new firm.

In order to consolidate his eastern roads, Huntington formed, under charter from the state of Connecticut, another holding organization named the Newport News and Mississippi Valley Company. He was its president. The first vice-president was Isaac Gates, who, trained as a minister, had married Collis' youngest sister, Ellen, and then had left the pulpit to function as Huntington's confidential secretary. The second vice-president was J. D. Yarrington, Arabella's brother. He had gone to work for the Chesapeake & Ohio some twelve years before as a conductor.

While the work of reorganization was going on, Grover Cleveland was nominated for the presidency by the Democrats, and it began to look as though that party might sweep to victory in November. As Huntington weighed these prospects, wondering what would happen to his voice in Congress, he encountered an old Republican friend, Aaron A. Sargent.

After leaving the Senate in 1879, Sargent had been appointed minister to Germany. There he had become *persona non grata* because of his overheated opposition to German quota restrictions on American pork. Now he was looking for another job.

Records do not agree concerning what followed. Sargent many have decided on his own initiative to seek another term in the Senate and have come around to Huntington's new offices at 23 Broad Street to seek help.* Or, as he said, he may have preferred returning to his long-neglected law practice but finally yielded to Huntington's importunities that he run.

---

* This was the Mills Building, one of the first skyscrapers. It had been erected recently by Huntington's old Sacramento and San Francisco friend, Banker Darius Ogden Mills. Huntington's offices, now employing forty clerks, occupied much of the seventh floor.

Huntington was sure that he could guarantee success. Election would be by the California legislature in January 1885. If the Republicans captured the legislature, as reports from the West said that they would, then a nod from Stanford would be enough.

Would Stanford nod? He and Sargent had been at swords' points ever since Stanford's meddling in the election of 1875 had derailed Sargent's political machine.

That was a long time ago, Huntington said. He persuaded the two men to come together at his home and sat over them most of the night, patiently explaining the practicalities of the situation. At last they agreed to forgive and forget.

The Republicans captured the California legislature as predicted and Stanford hurried to Sacramento. He did no nodding on Sargent's behalf, however. Gradually it appeared that a strange draft was being generated for—it was almost beyond Sargent's credence—for Leland Stanford. He notified Huntington, who immediately wired his associate: "IT IS REPORTED THAT YOU ARE IN THE FIELD AGAINST SARGENT. I CANNOT BELIEVE IT. PLEASE TELEGRAPH AT ONCE."

This forced Stanford's hand; until then he had been staying quietly in the background. He said that after a thorough canvass of the situation, his political advisers in Sacramento had decided that an attempt to elect Sargent would only cause a crippling breach in the Republican party. In fact, as the new candidate explained the situation, his advisers had insisted that Leland Stanford was the only man capable of preventing a party rift and checking the well-financed bid of mining magnate George Hearst, the Democrats' candidate.

In due time Stanford was elected. Several prominent California Republicans assured the enraged Huntington that Stanford's version was the unadulterated truth. The tellers were all good friends of Stanford's, however. Huntington and Sargent both remained convinced that they had been double-crossed.[17]

As usual Huntington refused to give up. Six weeks after Stanford had been elected, California's other senator, John F. Miller, died in office. The Democratic governor, George Stoneman, appointed Hearst to serve for a few weeks, when a special session of the legislature would elect a successor to fill out Miller's term, which ended March 4, 1887. Why Stoneman did not simply appoint Hearst to serve until March remains a mystery.

Huntington was determined that Sargent should be elected at the special session. He flooded Stanford and other leading Republicans in California with letters, received heartening replies, and assured Sargent

345

that "I cannot believe but what he [Stanford] is honestly and fairly working for you." Stanford was doing no such thing, however. The interim choice fell on an unknown, Abram P. Williams. In a rage Collis wrote Creed Haymond, a Southern Pacific attorney and a political power, "You and some others in California were trifling with me"—others obviously referring to Stanford.

Stanford would not be derelict again, Collis assured the dejected Sargent on August 30. Huntington meant to go to California himself that fall. There he would set the politicians to rights or "at least have some kind of time that the monkey and parrot had when they were left alone together in one cage." More specifically, he would elect a Republican legislature committed to sending Sargent to Washington for the full term that began March 4, 1887.

He left New York on September 4 and stayed in California until October 17. He returned confident and was dumfounded when the Democrats carried the election. This in turn guaranteed that George Hearst, raining out gold through San Francisco's blind boss, Chris Buckley, would be California's next senator.

It was the only time in Huntington's life that he had been beaten three times in a row and he did not like it. This last defeat, he growled to a friend, was the fault of the Southern Pacific's machine for failing to push as hard as they had promised him that they would. They'd learn. "I don't forget those," he warned, "who have played me false."[18] And he didn't, as shall become evident.

During these uproars the tenor of his life was changing completely. Although he had started burrowing into the classics during the 1870s (he knew many of George Crabbe's poems by heart and occasionally let loose lines from Shakespeare in his letters), although he had bought a few paintings and went to the theater now and then, he and Elizabeth had lived simply and quietly. Arabella was different. Restless, intense, and exacting, she wanted lavish surroundings. Shortly after their marriage, she prevailed on Collis to buy a 113-acre estate at Throg's Neck in Westchester County, where there was a broad, cool view of Long Island Sound. Simultaneously they purchased a town house at 5 West Fifty-first Street, installed an elevator, made other improvements—and then Arabella decided that she did not like it. Early in 1887 Huntington sold the place to Andrew Carnegie for $170,000 plus the cost of the improvements.[19] They moved back to 65 Park Avenue and there Arabella began drawing plans for a home that she fully intended to be the envy of New York.

346

She and her husband were not in agreement about its location. Collis wanted to build on lots he owned at Eightieth Street and Fifth Avenue; Arabella favored the northeast corner of Seventy-second and Fifth—a parcel of property that had cost Huntington $400,000.[20] Eventually they rejected both places in favor of a more central location, and bought the corner at Fifty-seventh and Fifth where Tiffany is now located. There between 1889 and 1893 they erected a heavily ornate pile that cost upwards of $2.5 million—a domed interior court, a sweeping central staircase of marble and onyx, gilt ceilings, and tapestries and paintings that they traveled to Europe to buy. It was far more pretentious than his associates' Nob Hill mansions, of which he had once been so critical.

Clara, who got on famously with her new foster mother, shared the excitement of these expanded horizons of living. As a child she had been docile, as Elizabeth had been. As a young woman she had sometimes tried to find relief from boredom by going on train trips with her foster father and painting genteel watercolors of local scenes while he was engaged in business. Belle's independence changed her. First, she decided to plunge into real estate, as Arabella had. Huntington was opposed. "It is very dangerous," he said, ignoring his own wife's example, "for young ladies to get the idea that money is to be made by speculating in land and stocks." But finally she and Belle prevailed on him, and he grudgingly sent five thousand dollars to the Southern Pacific's land agent in California, with instructions that he buy a little something for her that would be a sound investment and not a high-flying speculation.[21]

The girl's next shocker was a proposal that she travel alone to Europe. After all, she said, she was twenty-eight years old and capable of fending for herself. Again there were domestic thunders. Belle and Clara emerged partially triumphant but yielded to Collis' demand that his foster daughter travel with a chaperone and maid. Thus equipped, and armed with letters of introduction to Huntington's broker friends, mainly in Germany, she sailed on November 17, 1888.[22]

She was no longer docile. The chaperone reported her "capricious and somewhat wilful." At Aix, where they spent part of the winter, she met Prince Francis von Hatzfeldt de Wildenberg, an impoverished but dashing nephew of the German ambassador to England. After contemplating her charms and perhaps reading up on her foster father's accomplishments, the prince forsook his Parisian mistress (or so the scandal sheet *Gil Blas* slyly hinted) and borrowed money to pursue her about Europe. In the early summer of 1889 she wrote home, not to ask permission to marry him, but to say that she was going to.

The rest of the script is predictable. Collis and Arabella departed immediately for Paris, where they met the lovers. Huntington insisted that the foolishness end. Clara defied him. Collis hurried to Germany to investigate the prince's qualifications and returned faintly mollified. Then the prince stated his estimate of a proper dowry. To a one-time Yankee peddler and California gold-rusher the entire concept was monstrous. Never! Scenes, tears, anger. Well, all right, but the wedding would have to be in New York the following year.

It was solemnized in Brompton Oratory, St. Wilfrid's Chapel, London, on October 28. After a wedding breakfast at the German embassy, the couple left for Italy. According to the London *Mail and Express* of October 28, Huntington gave the bride a necklace of eighty diamonds, "the stones being of two and three carats each; also a magnificent brooch. Mrs. Huntington gave her a superb diamond star, with a very large stone in the center." The New York *Morning Journal* proclaimed that the prince did better: "$10,000,000 for a coronet!" But perhaps this was newspaper inflation; the press of two continents had a field day over the affair.[23] As for the young couple, they evidently lived happily, or reasonably so, ever after.

The conspicuousness of Huntington's new way of living brought new problems. Dozens of would-be entrepreneurs importuned him to help them launch new enterprises. He answered an amazing number of these requests personally, using two stock responses for turning them down: either his money was tied up in other enterprises, or he had made it a rule not to invest in companies that he could not control. Meanwhile he continued his habitual position as family patriarch, supervising the business affairs of his brothers and sisters and of many of Elizabeth's relatives as well. Again and again he came to the aid of a multitude of nieces and nephews, even though some of them annoyed him repeatedly by their persistent improvidence. He even responded to the appeal of a certain Agnes Huntington and her mother, distant cousins from Iowa with whom he had never had any communication until they suddenly appeared at his door, as it were. They wished to go to Europe, they told him, so that Agnes could study voice. He spent $7,000 on her, to no avail so far as her career was concerned.[24]

Then there was charity. He soon developed his own stern ideas about it. An incredible number of young men and women wrote out of the blue asking help so that they could finish their education or devote themselves to some exemplary project. Such people invariably received long personal letters of advice about the virtues of self-reliance and hard

348

work, and of saving each week a little more than one spent. No money accompanied the letters.

When friends were in need the reaction was different. On learning that Kate Chase Sprague, daughter of Salmon Chase, former chief justice of the United States, was destitute, he joined J. P. Morgan, Seth Low, president of Columbia University, Senator Price of Ohio, and others in paying the mortgage on her home and canceling her debts.[25] He gave Jessie Benton Frémont tickets and money to take her ailing husband to a warmer climate in California and tactfully soothed the embarrassed general's pride by telling him, "You forget our road goes over your buried campfires and climbs many a grade you jogged over on a mule; I think we rather owe you this." Later he directed John Boyd, his agent in Washington after Sherrill's death, to support a bill in Congress that would give Frémont a pension with the rank of major general.[26]

When Anna Judah, Theodore Judah's widow, appealed to him in 1878 and again in 1886, he persuaded his associates to join him in a gesture of good will that might end the long bitterness. They would "lend" her money, taking mortgages on bits of property she owned so that she would not feel that she was the victim of charity, yet they agreed among themselves not to press her about the notes. The second time she asked for help turned out to be sticky. Crocker still bore grudges against her long-dead husband and against her, too, for joining Brannan and the Lambards in suing them. Once was enough for her. But eventually Collis won him around—and then Anna grew skittish, deeming that the mortgage they proposed would leave her "embarrassed and chained to a rock." Collis tried to jolly her with his favorite meteorological theory, the effects of weather on the mind. "When the wind is in the northeast, for instance, people begin to talk about ebb tides in business, disordered lives, rheumatism, hard luck &c, &c, and when the wind shifts they wonder how they saw all those dismal things." Unfortunately, surviving records do not reveal the conclusion of Anna's second appeal.[27]

He could be impulsive and quixotic. The moment he read of the Chicago fire, he sent $5,000 to be used in relief work, for he knew the meaning of fire after his own experiences in Sacramento. When the police ejected two old ladies, a Margaret O'Brien and a Mrs. Wood, and their fruit stands from Central Park, he invited them onto his $400,000 lots at Seventy-second and Fifth Avenue, then discovered that he had embraced their feud as well and built a fence between them. When that was not enough, he ordered them to make peace or leave. But when the law harassed them again for some minor infraction, he stormed to the rescue, as ruffled, one newspaper account said, "as if he had heard of

349

a side of the continent along which he had forgotten to build a railroad. . . . His language was of that strong kind which sometimes gets mixed with good deeds."[28]

He was an early user of the "matching funds" approach to wealthy men. When Jeanette Thurber was campaigning in support of the American Opera Company, he gave her letters of introduction to George Westinghouse, Jesse Seligman, and others, and promised to match each $5,000-donation that they made—which, of course, led them to respond. He used the same tactic to help the director of the Metropolitan Museum, L. P. di Cesnola, purchase a certain collection he wanted.[29]

He built a small library in Westchester "to draw away from the drinking saloons at least a part of the men who frequent them." He built a granite chapel in Harwinton, Connecticut, in memory of his mother, and occasionally supported other churches and YMCA projects, although at times it seemed to him that every religious group in every town through which his railroads passed felt entitled to call on him for help.

He refused an appeal to help restore Sutter's Fort in Sacramento. What good was there in those old mud walls? But he did say that he would build a park on the site, "to be used by the people of all colors and nationalities," an offer rejected by the restorationists. He refused to give money to colleges. In his opinion a person who got that far should be able to continue on his own.*

His favorite charity was the Hampton Normal and Agricultural Institute near Newport News. It had been founded shortly after the Civil War by the American Missionary Association to help educate some of the children of the ten thousand black refugees who had huddled there close to Fortress Monroe. After 1876 Indians were also admitted. Collis, who had always been distressed by the plight of the Negro, became interested during an inspection trip of the region for the Chesapeake & Ohio. He approved particularly of Hampton's vocational courses, for he believed that the freedman's best hope of self-sufficiency lay in learning a trade. He built a steam sawmill for the school, and he and Arabella together donated ten or more seventy-dollar scholarships each year, seventy dollars being enough to cover annual tuition. They also helped one of Hampton's most illustrious graduates, Booker T. Washington, launch Tuskegee Institute in Alabama, where Huntington Hall was named for them. Collis personally urged railroad superintendents throughout the

* One exception was the Pacific Theological Seminary in Oakland. He gave it ten thousand dollars and helped solicit an additional twenty-five for endowing a professorship. When J. E. Dwinnell, the president of the Seminary, suggested calling the chair the Huntington professorship, Collis declined.[30]

South to employ Negro laborers wherever possible. He was, Booker T. Washington later wrote Arabella, "one of the best friends my race ever had."[31]

He could be distressing in his manner of going about it. He asked that Hampton's financial reports be sent to him regularly, and in acknowledging one of them he remarked that he was thinking about donating a new building. Then he let loose this thunderbolt:[32]

> As I write these last words my eye falls upon the enclosed sheet of account paper, which came with your letter, which is blank and has been carelessly thrown away in this correspondence. I return it herewith, simply remarking that . . . 'Straws show the way the wind blows.'

His censure about a half-cent sheet of paper was not intended to make his correspondent squirm, though no doubt the recipient did. It was not an example of either attempted humor or of stinginess. It was Huntington's way of underlining a creed about which he was growing increasingly vocal: waste could not be tolerated in business. It was very well to spend, outside of business, ten thousand dollars on a painting, if you had ten thousand, but the work of the world demanded precision and attention. It was not a lesson that persons outside of his orbit absorbed readily. Why should a man who could afford a house that cost $2.5 million worry about a sheet of paper? Yet Huntington always insisted that the point was fundamental. You made $2.5 million by not tossing away paper or anything else.

So far as records show, no one ever quite dared suggest to him that although he had perhaps saved his pennies, preciseness of that sort was not really the method by which he had made his millions. As for waste, few construction jobs in history have exceeded the inevitable prodigality that accompanied the Central Pacific's headlong effort to outrace the Union Pacific. But, then, Collis Huntington was not the first self-generated millionaire to develop, as age crept up, a chasm-sized dichotomy between what he thought had happened and what actually had occurred. As to the reason for the self-deception, the point is perhaps best left to the psychologists.

26 Slings and Arrows

During the murk of the depression of 1893, Huntington wrote to young Fred Crocker (Charles F. Crocker), who had become president of the Southern Pacific Railroad, urging him not to grow downhearted. "I am," he said, "decidedly against yielding to anything except the inevitable."[1]

He considered very few things to be immediately inevitable, death included. Cheerily he predicted that he would live to be a hundred, and as his seventieth birthday drew near (it fell on October 22, 1891), he looked as if he might. Although he had put on weight after his second marriage, until he tipped the scales at more than two hundred pounds, his massive frame kept him from looking gross, as stubby Charles Crocker had looked. Grizzled hair added to the impressiveness of his big, rocklike head. He trimmed his beard close (one newspaper reporter said that the cropping made him look like Stanford, which undoubtedly displeased him[2]), and in his office he habitually covered his bald pate with a rabbinical-style skullcap of black silk, an affectation popular among some financiers. As befitted his looks, he was given on occasion to oracular utterances concerning the state of the nation.

For years he believed that the payment of the principal and interest arising from the second-mortgage bonds which represented the Central Pacific's debt to the government, could be, like death, postponed indefinitely. To anyone else the sums involved might well have seemed terrifying. Including the bonds that had been issued to the Western Pacific, the principal amounted to $27,855,680. The annual simple interest on this, paid by the government, came to $1,671,340. Thus by the time the bonds began maturing in 1895, the government would have paid out on behalf of the Central Pacific nearly $76 million.[3] At the most, credits available to be applied against this sum—transportation of troops and mail, deposits in the meager sinking fund, and so on—would be about sixteen million.*

As chief Washington representative of the heavily indebted railroad, Huntington the moneyman bore scant resemblance to Huntington the moralist who read periodic sermons to young people concerning the virtues of solvency. Realizing at once that the government had made inadequate provisions for debt retirement and being recurrently faced with more pressing crises, he had, as we have seen, resorted to every loophole to hold down the amounts he turned over to the Treasury.

The government's response had been the Thurman Act, designed to bring about increased contributions to the sinking funds, but because the bill's teeth could bite only into net profits, it failed to hurt very much. The Central Pacific's profits were in decline. Part of the shrinkage reflected a drying up of traffic to and from the Nevada mines and part from losses to competitive transcontinentals—the Oregon Short Line, the Northern Pacific, the Atchison, Topeka & Santa Fe, and even the Canadian Pacific. But an even greater shrinkage had come about through the associates' deliberate diversion of traffic to the Southern Pacific.

Stanford believed that the railroad would be fully justified in asking that the Central Pacific's debt to the government be canceled entirely. Huntington did not go to this extreme. Instead, he sought ways of making repayment painless. First he concocted plans which, if accepted, would allow the railroad to receive credit for turning back the less valuable portions of its land grant. After continued rebuffs had at last convinced him that Congress would not agree to accepting the land on his terms, he turned to plans for refunding. He proposed that the bonds be replaced as they fell due with new issues bearing interest of 2 per cent or so and redeemable over long periods of time—a hundred years or more.

The proposal was poor psychology on Huntington's part. Meager interest and an extension of a hundred years looked to people who were worried about the government's mounting expenditures like some sort of scheme leading toward eventual repudiation of the debt. Moreover, his suggestion came at a time when laissez-faire capitalism was under strenuous attack; any plan whatsoever that he offered was certain to be whipped about through the halls of Congress, no matter what its merits might be. He fought back, of course. As a consequence he found himself plunged headlong, during the closing years of his life, into a battle whose emotional pitch reached levels he never comprehended.

* First-mortgage bonds held by private investors amounted to another $28.8 million. Every semiannual interest payment on these had been met on time, often by dint of considerable ingenuity and effort on Huntington's part.

The beginning of the struggle was a congressional bill which, if passed, would establish a three-man commission with broad powers to investigate every phase of the Central Pacific and Union Pacific—their origins, financing, organization, operating characteristics, political manipulations, and so on. Piquancy was lent to the debates by a series of what the New York *World* called "exposures." These pryings into the iniquities of the railroads had been prepared by one Theophilus French, a former government auditor of railroads. First he had tried to blackmail Huntington with them, and when Collis refused to pay him off, French sold the stories to the *World*. Foolishly he had made his approach to Huntington by mail, and so Collis was able to reveal the man's motives by publishing the correspondence in a paper called *The Financier*.[4] This of course did not answer the charges that French was making, and, anyway, defamations are more widely read and remembered than are retorts. The agitation over the *World* stories reached a considerable pitch and probably had some effect on Congress. On March 3, 1887, the lawmakers established the United States Pacific Railway Commission, granting it extraordinary powers to hire expert help, summon witnesses and documents, and require compliance.

Huntington, after growling that "we shall have to suffer, as the weaker party always does in dealing with unscrupulous strength," was the first man grilled, on April 27.[5] The commissioners then traveled slowly across the country to San Francisco, listening along the way to every witness they could unearth who had had any sort of connection with either the Union Pacific or the Central Pacific since the days of their inception. Some of those who were called on to testify in San Francisco were voluble and unfriendly; others were afflicted with failing memories. A. A. Cohen, for example, pled that an attack of paralysis "has somewhat impaired . . . my recollection as to details." Crocker, ill at the time of his interrogation, was nevertheless defiant and cantankerous, but equally unable to remember anything significant.

After careful coaching by the company's lawyers, Stanford presented, in a session at the Palace Hotel in San Francisco, a vigorous and able defense of policies in general. He startled the commission by insisting that the government owed the company $62 million, rather than the other way around. The Central Pacific, he declared, had lost money by having to sell the aid bonds at heavy discount; it had saved the Post Office and the War Department at least $21 million by completing the job seven years ahead of time in spite of almost unbelievable difficulties in the Sierra; it had lost another million in revenues because the government had subsidized other railroads in competition to it, and so on.

354

It was, so long as he had his notes with him, a masterful counterattack. But when he was unexpectedly confronted with about four million dollars' worth of vouchers listed vaguely on the company books as being for "expenses" and was asked to account for them—influencing legislation, perhaps?—he grew abruptly silent. Exasperated, the commission haled him into the California circuit court, hoping to have him declared in contempt unless he answered. The inquisitors served themselves poorly, for the court was presided over by Stanford's long-time crony, Justice Stephen Field. Field ruled in the defendant's favor, declaring that the commission was not a judicial body and could not encroach, as it was endeavoring to do, on personal security and liberty.[6] From today's viewpoint concerning individual rights, the doctrine was sound, but one still wonders a little about the justice's motives.

During its western travels the commission laid hold of copies of Huntington's correspondence with David Colton, which had been published a few years earlier in the San Francisco *Chronicle*. On returning to New York in September, the inquisitors used the letters as the basis for another merciless examination. A. A. Cohen, acting as Huntington's lawyer, advised him that he need not reply. He scorned silence, however, and resorted to his own stratagems, rambling on and on, sarcastic sometimes, evasive often, forgetful when that was convenient, and on occasion treading close to perjury in circuitous, almost-denials that he was the author of certain damaging lines that were thrown at him again and again. It was not one of his better performances.[7]

The commissioners roundly condemned the associates' first construction firm, the Contract & Finance Company. They offered their opinion that "large sums of money were expended by Mr. Huntington in his efforts to defeat the passage of various bills pending in Congress." They charged the railroad with an apparently willful attempt to avoid repayment of its debt to the government, and concluded ruefully that there was scant chance of the Central Pacific's being able to meet its obligations when the second-mortgage bonds fell due.*

What next?

The minority report, offered by the commission's chairman, Robert Pattison of Pennsylvania, suggested that the government foreclose and take over the operation of the road. Obviously this would involve prodigious problems relative to the unsubsidized portions of the line and the equities of its stock and bondholders, by then widely distributed.

The majority recommended a funding of the debt as it stood on July

---

* The Union Pacific was also tried and found wanting, but its affairs lie apart from our considerations.

1, 1888, by means of fifty-year, 3 per cent bonds. Security would be a lien on the entire Central Pacific system and not just those portions that had received government aid.

President Cleveland sent the majority report to Congress for consideration. In due time the matter reached a select committee of the Senate for hearings.

Alignments quickly took shape. Sentiment in California, examples of which were sent by the barrelful to the Senate committee, leaned toward foreclosure. The railroad took the other extreme: the government should recognize the Central Pacific's great services to the country by canceling the debt outright. If that proved impossible, then refunding should be on liberal terms—century-long payments at minimum interest. In between stood a large body of Congressmen who wanted to obtain maximum return for the government without injuring investors in the railroad or imposing burdens beyond the Central Pacific's ability to meet. Since neither the railroad nor the advocates of foreclosure were willing to yield, the long string of bills proposed by the moderate middle made no progress.[8]

During this period of ill will, Huntington created more turbulence by deciding to oust Stanford from the presidency of the Southern Pacific Company. His reasons were complex. One had to do with the disintegration of his Newport News and Mississippi Valley system.

The key part of the organization, the Chesapeake & Ohio, did not command enough local traffic to sustain the ambitions that Huntington had for it and for its terminus at Newport News. In an effort to develop more freight, he began adding, as previously noted, feeder lines in Kentucky and Tennessee, intending to use them eventually as springboards for reaching the Pacific Coast and the Great Lakes. Although the junction that he achieved with the Southern Pacific at New Orleans was not the through route to the Coast that he really wanted, he accepted it and turned next toward the Great Lakes.

His first step followed a well-tested pattern. He formed a construction firm, the Contracting and Building Company, and awarded it a contract to build a subsidiary line for the Chesapeake & Ohio. This was called the Maysville and Big Sandy and was to run from the Big Sandy River near Huntington, West Virginia, along the south bank of the Ohio River to Covington, Kentucky. The Contracting & Building Company was also employed by the C&O to supervise the construction of a bridge over the Ohio River from Covington to Cincinnati. The structure would measure, if its approach viaducts were included, nearly a mile and a half in length. Its central span of 550 feet would be the longest of its type in the

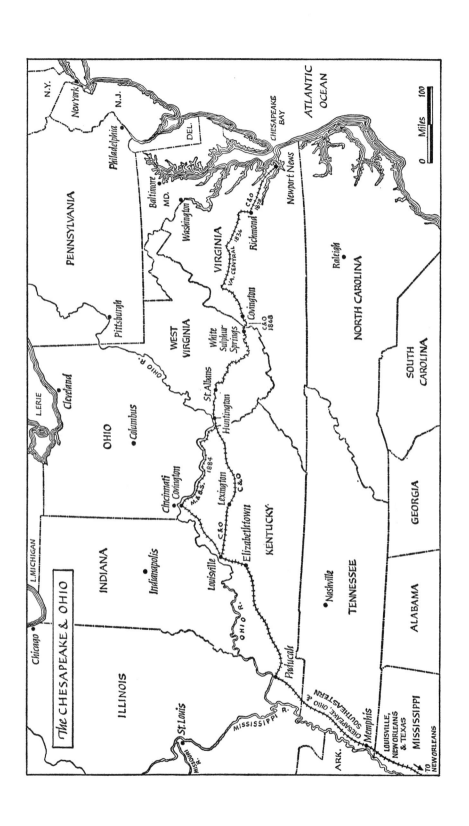

The CHESAPEAKE & OHIO

world.[9] It would carry two tracks, two wagon ways, and a walk for pedestrians, would cost about $8.8 million, and would give employment to two thousand men.

While work was going on between 1886 and 1888, Huntington quietly bought up two million dollars' worth of bonds in the Scioto Valley Railroad of Ohio. This was to be the wedge that he would use for breaking into the Lakes area. His rationale was double-pronged: first, Chicago and St. Paul were somewhat closer to salt water at Newport News than at any other major port, and, second, the C&O had easier grades across the Allegheny Mountains than did its rivals.

Marvelous though the plan looked on paper, he could not complete it. As his California associates had realized when refusing to put the Southern Pacific under the same umbrella as the eastern lines, the patchwork that he had thrown together in Kentucky and Tennessee was flimsy. In his driving ambition to conquer the continent, he had overextended. The Chesapeake & Ohio, key road of the system, had been neglected. Tracks and equipment were wearing out, traffic had not reached the levels he had anticipated, and competition was forcing down rates.

As conditions worsened, rebellious security holders forced the road into receivership again, hoping to free it from its loose-jointed connections. Drexel, Morgan & Company were hired to effect a reorganization. The personal advances that Collis had made to the C&O, the Maysville & Big Sandy, and to the "great Huntington bridge," as it was called, were paid off and he was deprived of control.* The lease of the C&O to the Newport News and Mississippi Valley Company was canceled. With only detached short-line feeder roads left to supervise, the holding company no longer had a sound reason for existence.

Here was an inevitability that even Huntington could recognize. Gone were the plans of straddling the continent, and he had always said that what he could not control he did not want. Early in 1889 he announced that he was selling his interests east of the Mississippi.[10]

He moved slowly, not letting any of the lines go until he could command a profit.[11] There was one thing he would not yield—the Chesapeake Dry Dock & Construction Company, for which he had broken ground in February 1887 on a site owned by his Old Dominion Land Company.

From repairing ships in a dry dock to building them was a logical next step, provided that one could find clients—and that brings us back,

* He owned a large enough block of stock that he stayed on the C&O's board of directors, but no longer in a commanding position.

358

through the amazing convolutions in the thinking of this restless, insatiable old man, to the Southern Pacific.

It followed as the night the day that if Collis Huntington disposed of his interests east of the Mississippi, the only focus left for his still undimmed energies would be the lines west of the river, all of them under control of a holding company presided over by Leland Stanford. There was no possibility that the two of them could get along, and no peacemakers capable of standing between them remained alive. Crocker, fat Jolly Charley Crocker, had died in August 1888 at the opulent Del Monte resort hotel that he had recently erected at Monterey, California. His eldest son, Col. Charles Frederick Crocker, who liked to be addressed by his state militia title but who was generally called Fred by the older generation, had stepped into his father's shoes in the organization. Huntington, however, disdained the young man as "weak."[12] With no fear of any effective brakes being applied to him, Huntington prepared to remove Stanford from any position of responsibility in the company.

Meantime Stanford went his way lulled by habit. For decades his election first as president of the Central Pacific and then of the Southern Pacific Company had been a stately routine at each annual meeting. Why should it be different in 1890? Besides, he was absorbed in schemes to guarantee the election of a Republican legislature that would be committed to returning him to the United States Senate during its balloting in the fall.

Huntington all this while was sharpening his bayonets. He assiduously cultivated Edward T. Searles, a young interior decorator who had married his elderly client, the widow of Mark Hopkins. As soon as Collis was sure that the Hopkins-Searles holdings in the Southern Pacific Company would be voted as he asked, he felt safe to exert a bit of blackmail of his own—he who so often had railed against blackmailers. He had in his possession papers which, presumably, would show Stanford's breach of faith in the Sargent affair.* Publication of them would be damaging to Stanford's political hopes, and when he realized that Huntington was serious about revealing them, he caved in. What did Collis want?

At a meeting in New York on February 28, 1890, attended by Huntington, Stanford, and representatives of the Crocker and Hopkins estates, Collis explained what he wanted—to be elected president of the Southern Pacific at the next annual meeting in San Francisco on April 9. Fred Crocker stirred a little, but when the attorneys representing Mr. and Mrs. Searles sat as still as stone, he subsided.

* These papers have since disappeared.

Being deprived of the leadership of one of the country's great corporations was a blow to Stanford's vanity, but loss of his Senate seat amidst an odorous scandal would have been a greater one. He began to dicker. What would Huntington yield in return?

Collis agreed to surrender the papers concerning the Sargent affair. He and the others at the meeting also promised to "refrain from hostile or injurious expressions concerning each other and shall in good faith co-operate for the election of Leland Stanford as senator to the next term of the United States Senate."[13]

The agreement was reduced to writing and signed by all those present. Then, after the others had departed, Huntington sat down at his desk and prepared, out of years of resentment, a document dripping with vitriol—a document that cast strange light on his written promise to "refrain from hostile or injurious expressions."[14] It went as follows*:

STANFORD MATTERS—SUGGESTED INTERVIEW

Q: I see it stated in the papers that Governor Stanford is to resign the presidency of the Southern Pacific.

A: Mr. Stanford is very clever in some things, but his strong point is his vanity. We have thought for some years of electing someone else to the Presidency, but he wanted the place so much that some of the directors did not wish to wound his feelings and so let him hold on.

Q: Do you think it would be safe for the Company to lose his services before a settlement is effected between the Central Pacific and the government?

A: Mr. Stanford has about as much to do with this settlement as he has with the revolving of the earth.

Q: He had much to do with the building of the road, did he not?

A: Not that I know of.

Q: I have been told that you were very much displeased with the way Mr. Stanford treated A. A. Sargent when the latter ran for Senator.

A: That is a page so dark that it should not be recorded. I would rather the act should die with the actor, the treason with the traitor.

This fantasy interview was mere malice. Realizing in time how petty it would look in print, Huntington set it aside and prepared an attack that would really damage. The opening was a short speech that he delivered on the occasion of his formal election to the company presidency on

* This reproduction is slightly condensed.

360

April 9 in San Francisco. He was honored and so on. And then came the thrust that he knew would be picked up by every newspaper in the state: "In no case will I use this great corporation to advance my personal ambition at the expense of its owners [the stockholders], or put my hands in its treasury to defeat the people's choice, and thereby put myself in positions that should be filled by others."

The instant the release was handed out, reporters came swarming. He meant Stanford, didn't he? He certainly did. And he added, during a talk with a reporter from William Randolph Hearst's San Francisco *Examiner,* "Politics have worked enough demoralization in our company already, and they have gone out the door never to return." Henceforth the Southern Pacific would confine itself to business.

After two days of shaken silence Stanford wrote an open letter to the board of directors, demanding an investigation of the charges so that he could be vindicated. Simultaneously Creed Haymond told the *Examiner* that Mr. Huntington had let personal dislikes sway his judgment. He did not understand the California situation and had not attempted to inform himself. If he had, he would know that Stanford had neither double-crossed Sargent, who could not have been elected under any circumstances, nor had the Senator used either his money or the railroad's to secure his seat. To which Huntington replied, through a reporter from the New York *Morning Journal,* "Stanford has a lot of little satellites flickering around him who, I suppose, will set up a howl because their pap is taken away."

Wringing their hands over the notoriety the company was receiving, Fred Crocker and other members of the board called on Huntington in his suite at the Palace Hotel, showed him the agreement he had signed in New York, and prevailed on him to write Stanford a letter of apology. In return, Stanford would drop his demands for an investigation, a threat which, if carried out, could only result in embarrassment for everyone.

Huntington gagged, but he could not get around his own signature. On April 15, he composed a letter of tortured sententiousness. Near its end he finally got around to saying that he had not intended to make a personal attack "or to charge that you had used the Company's money to advance your own personal interest."[15]

The retraction, of course, received less attention than the charge. Reporters continued to surround Huntington wherever he went, and he continued to let slip barbs which showed how little his heart had been in the apology. Tensions were so little resolved, indeed, that when Huntington returned east and paid one of his regular visits to Washington, he was summoned to meet with Secretary of State James G. Blaine, several leading Republican senators, and, according to some reports, with President Harrison himself. They advised him to speak more softly. It would not do to have a Democrat elected in California. Besides, there was the matter of a favorable funding bill then pending before Congress.[16]

His rancor, finally out and rioting, could not heed even those admonitions. When the editor of the Kern County *Californian* wrote him about the affair, Collis replied on August 8, 1890, knowing that the letter would be printed, "I can endorse all you say about the rottenness of the politics of the state as conducted by Leland Stanford, through which he used the Southern Pacific, very much to its own disadvantage, in order to accomplish his own selfish purpose." Political corruption, he continued, resulted from the habit of voting for party rather than for men, because "bad men have been put forward to represent the party preferred," and when that happened all considerations of public welfare disappeared.[17]

Papers throughout the land picked up and published the outburst. Hoping to capitalize on the feud, Stephen Mallory White, a Democratic aspirant for Stanford's Senate seat, sought Huntington's support in the forthcoming campaign. At that point Collis belatedly remembered his promises and turned White away with the remark that he was not going to work against Stanford in the election—although it is difficult to see what else his public utterances amounted to. In October, Stanford, who fled from the scene to Europe on the plea of poor health, returned to California, stumped the state and was rewarded by a Republican legislature. This, supporters said, was the result of his energy and popularity. More cynical observers charged him with dealing with George Hearst: if Democrat George Hearst would support him in 1890, Stanford would return the favor in 1893. Hearst agreed, Stanford opened wide his purse to the bosses of both parties, Bill Higgins of the Republicans and blind Chris Buckley of the Democrats, and soared to triumph.[18]

Back East in Virginia, Huntington on July 30, 1890, executed between himself as representative of the Pacific Improvement Company and himself as head of the Newport News Shipbuilding and Dry Dock Company a contract for building a tug and two freighters to be used on the Southern Pacific's ocean run between New Orleans and New York. Contracts for two more Southern Pacific freighters soon followed. Having proved the yard's capabilities with those pilot operations, Huntington began to bid for government jobs and in 1895 undertook the first of several mammoth battleships. When he visited the humming scene, of which he was very proud, he was wont to stump around the scaffolding, exclaiming every now and then, "I have always been in the habit of looking as carefully after small expenses as large ones," and pointing with his cane to some bolt or rivet that had been dropped, until finally he had halfway convinced himself that frugality and not the fortunate circumstance of his being able to assign himself million-dollar contracts was the true secret of the huge plant's successful beginnings.[19]

His moral opinions were as adaptable as his economic views. Having publicly justified his ousting of Stanford for political malfeasance—"If you or I," he wrote W. H. Mills of the San Francisco office, "had done what he has done we should have been put behind bars"—he then set about removing the railroad from political entanglements. He cut off a ten-thousand-dollar annual payment to the newspaper *Argonaut.* By letter he officially ordered Mills "to do all you can to get the Southern Pacific out of politics," and added that as soon as he had disposed of his eastern railroads, he intended to spend most of his time in California, supervising matters. His goal, he said, was to serve the state, the nation, and all people.[20]

In an extraordinary adaptation of the policy of using a thief to catch a thief, he made overtures to W. W. Stow, Stanford's chief fixer, who had helped implement the senator's re-election and then had resigned from the company. Huntington wanted Stow back, this time for higher purposes.

Let's work in the interest of the shareholders and not in devious ways and by crooked lines. . . . I want the railroads conducted in such a manner as to be of the greatest service to the people who use them, being willing to have the rates of fares and freights so that they will only pay the fixed and current charges, waiting for the state to increase in population and business for any dividends. . . . I am devising all the ways and means that I can to develope (sic) the resources of California.[21]

The approach, novel to Stow, bemused him to such an extent that he returned to the company, charged this time not with manipulating its political reins but with discarding them!

One stumbling block in the way of reform, or so Huntington thought, was Fred Crocker, who also had political ambitions. At first, Collis considered ejecting him from his inherited position as president of the Southern Pacific Railroad (as distinct from the Southern Pacific Company) but was dissuaded.[22] One upheaval of that sort had been enough.

363

Instead, he neutralized Crocker by bringing in Henry Edwards Huntington and naming him, in April 1892, first assistant to the president of the Southern Pacific Company and his alter ego whenever the president was away. The appointment stirred considerable jealousy and apprehension in the entrenched bureaucracy at Fourth and Townsend streets, San Francisco, the railroad headquarters.

Simultaneously Collis made gestures toward fulfilling his promise of spending more time in the West. Searching for a house that might please Arabella, he chose, of all places, the old Colton mansion atop Nob Hill; either he was careless about or indifferent to the connotations about honesty in politics that the place might suggest to San Franciscans. He and his wife remodeled it extensively—"Belle, as you know, is exceedingly particular."[23] One addition was an imposing gallery to hold some of the art work that they were collecting. Restless Arabella, however, did not really like the new plaything and they seldom spent more than two or three months each year, in installments, in San Francisco.

In spite of his exhortations, the political laundering made slow progress. When he complained, General Superintendent A. N. Towne, assisted by a B. Worthington, prepared for his edification a long report, dated September 3, 1892, about the California situation.[24] Matters, they insisted, really were improving. They submitted figures in proof. In 1887, "legal expenses," which the writers admitted were a euphemism for political expenditures, had totaled $722,683. In 1891, the first full year of the purification program, the cash outlay had dropped to $538,000. Expenditures made during the first seven months of 1892 suggested a further reduction for the year to the neighborhood of $350,000.

Under the circumstances, the writers said, it was an admirable showing. After all, they had to be practical. The railroad could be hurt by municipalities and legislatures from Oregon to Louisiana. Many councils and assemblies cynically debated "cinch bills" whose sole purpose was to frighten the Southern Pacific into buying them off. In creating armor for defending itself, the company had become involved in so complex a system of alliances with local bosses, ward heelers, and even organized crime syndicates, and in regular payoffs to petty fixers and influence peddlers that instantaneous disengagement could not be expected—and would not be advisable.

Keep trying, Huntington ordered, and would continue ordering it in California for the rest of his life.[25]

Elsewhere matters were different. At the very time that he was writing of his high-minded intentions to W. W. Stow, he was ordering a lobbyist in Virginia to kill a bill that he felt would be harmful to Newport News.

He turned from writing W. H. Mills of his abhorrence of Stanford's activities to instructing John Boyd in Washington about his wishes concerning appointments to the Interstate Commerce Commission and to the Senate's judicial and railway committees. He told Boyd whom to work for when the House of Representatives met to choose its speaker.[26]

He did not always get his way, of course, and letters which survive from the period of the early 1890s do not reveal anything about the means which Boyd was supposed to use. A few letters written during the month of December 1886 to Boyd's predecessor, Charles H. Sherrill, may be indicative, however.

In 1886 a Mr. Guthrie, a clerk in the Treasury Department, was, in Huntington's words, "in our employ" and probably not just for mere innocent moonlighting. On December 7, Collis asked Sherrill how Senator Cockrell of Missouri "stands with us?" A certain man thinks that, with adequate support, he can defeat Cockrell, but do we want the Missourian defeated? On December 15, he told Sherrill to decide whether or not to spend three thousand dollars to bring about victory in a Democratic-Republican struggle for control of the Indiana legislature. The next day, December 16, Sherrill, who must have been a busy man, was directed to kill the proposed Interstate Commerce bill, to arrange for the passage of a certain desirable lighthouse measure, and to obtain less rigorous specifications for the great Huntington bridge that Collis wanted to build across the Ohio River between Covington and Cincinnati.[27]

And then there was the time when it was necessary to hurry a thousand dollars to needy Congressman H. Libbey of Newport News. Huntington wrote detailed instructions to Gen. Williams C. Wickham, vice-president of the Chesapeake & Ohio, who seems to have been naïve about such matters. The money was to be placed in an envelope and sent by messenger to the lobby of a pre-selected hotel in a town where neither Libbey, Wickham, nor the messenger resided. "Of course," finished Collis, "you understand you want to send him this in currency and let no one know it but yourself, not even the man who takes the money down. Merely give him the envelope to hand it [sic] to Mr. Libbey."[28]

And yet he wanted to clean up the Southern Pacific in California. By what rationalization, half-instinctive probably, did he reconcile the two stands?

As noted earlier, his ferocious attacks on Stanford's corruption required him to adopt, for the benefit of Westerners, what he sometimes called "the high road." He did it without strain. Stanford had politicked not for the railroad's advantage but for Stanford's—and that, in Huntington's mind, was true venality. Huntington looked on the railroad with a profound pride of creation that Stanford never felt; when Collis indulged in questionable manipulations, it was to achieve what was for him the ultimate good, the well-being of his company. This company was just as much private property to him as was the Huntington-Hopkins hardware store, which also served the public. He had, he felt, an inalienable right to further its prosperity and to defend it against attack by whatever means were necessary.

To that end he employed expert representatives in Washington and in several state capitals. Their duty was to "explain" to legislators what was "right," and he did not inquire closely into the methods of the explanation. Like any American he insisted on his privilege to support the election of officials whose theories coincided with his own. He preferred not to use crude means to obtain what the railroad needed, but if he must, he would. Payments in the form of free passes on his multitudinous lines, of contributions to campaign expenses, or even the passing of cash under the table were not, under those circumstances, bribery. This was especially true when the payments were defensive. A bribe, by contrast, was a voluntary buying for personal gratification, like meeting a prostitute in an alleyway. That was the nature of Stanford's corruption, as Huntington saw it, and he would have none of it.

These distinctions, so clear to Huntington, eluded most Californians. The clamor against the Southern Pacific increased as the depression of the 1890s began to cripple the nation. He was bewildered. Had not the railroad, he asked again and again, contributed more to California than any other agency? The state's two major cities answered with a resounding "No!" They considered the Southern Pacific—and now Collis P. Huntington *was* the Southern Pacific—a mortal enemy. He never really comprehended why.

The Southern Pacific's trouble with Los Angeles had begun in 1877 when the road had absorbed Senator John P. Jones's little Los Angeles & Independence and then had boosted rates on its own branch to the harbor at San Pedro. That twenty-mile branch, Los Angeles' only rail link with the ocean, was a key line in the SP monopoly. By controlling it, the railroad was able to negate what otherwise would have been the ameliorating effects of water transport. It was able to maintain higher rates between San Pedro and Los Angeles than existed between Hong Kong and San Pedro, and the gouging did not stop there. Los Angeles was the distribution center for southern California, and since water rates exerted no effect in the city, land rates stayed high in the rest of the area as well—

so long as the Santa Fe Railroad co-operated, a matter arranged through the formation of transportation pools.

The control was soon threatened. Los Angeles, fed mightily by the population boom of the late 1880s, outgrew the primitive facilities of the rickety piers at San Pedro and Wilmington. Civic boosters, fearful of San Diego's competition, began to talk of creating a huge artificial port by deep dredging and extensive breakwaters. Financing the project exceeded the young city's abilities, however, and so in 1888 a vigorous new chamber of commerce began agitating for federal help. Its members assiduously cultivated Senator Stanford, and he told them that he saw much merit in the proposal. Why not? Would not the Southern Pacific benefit, too?

To Huntington this was one more example of Stanford's folly. Couldn't he hear the reformers, who were already declaring that if the government financed the harbor, then it should be open to all railroads? In addition, geography was such that the Southern Pacific could not cover every approach. One determined rival was already in the making—the so-called Terminal Line, which was surveying a right-of-way from Glendale through Los Angeles to Terminal Island on the outer side of the harbor. If it succeeded, rates were bound to slip drastically.

Huntington, his confidence in no wise sapped by age, decided that the best counter was to find a harbor whose approaches he could control absolutely. He would then induce the federal government to forget San Pedro and spend its money developing *his* choice.

Senator Jones of Nevada may have helped germinate the plan. He still owned the old Santa Monica ranch bordering the northern part of Santa Monica Bay, and had built a sprawling redwood home atop one of its bluffs; he lived in Nevada only long enough to qualify as a senator. At some point or another he told Huntington of the virtues of the place: a narrow beach backed by cliffs that could be approached only through one tight little canyon. No other railroad could interfere with a harbor there. That was the main reason, he said, that he had chosen it as the terminus of his short-lived Los Angeles & Independence.

Whatever the beginnings of the scheme, no steps were taken until after Huntington had ousted Stanford. Then, during the course of a regal inspection trip of the Southern Pacific's western system, Collis visited Los Angeles. He called on Jones. Despite Fred Crocker's opposition, he bought for $125,000 a quarter interest in Jones's Santa Monica ranch, the money to be paid later from the sale of building lots. He also employed an old friend, Abbott Robinson, and a new agent, Fred Davis, to buy up more land in the vicinity. The only other landholders of consequence in the area, Col. Robert Baker and his wife Arcadia, owners of Southern California's most luxurious resort hotel, the Arcadia, joined the syndicate, and now Santa Monica harbor was fenced-off, in the words of a later commentator, as tightly as if by the Great Wall of China.[29]

All of this was kept very secret, of course. Huntington, however, did give the thoughtful something to chew on by remarking casually that the Southern Pacific was considering building a "commercial wharf" at Santa Monica—this at the very time that a board of army engineers, sent out by the government to examine potential harbor sites throughout the Los Angeles area, was announcing in favor of San Pedro.[30] No, age had not softened him one bit.

A year passed. Abruptly, in 1891, the Southern Pacific stopped work on a new pier at San Pedro. Its engineer, William Hood, announced that satisfactory footing for piles could not be found in the vicinity; therefore the railroad was transferring operations to Santa Monica, which he expected to become the port of the future.

San Pedro was too well established to be so summarily dismissed, especially since the Terminal Railroad (which hoped for connections with Salt Lake City) had just arrived on Terminal Island. Their port was the gateway of the future, they retorted, and a bitter tug of war over federal appropriations began. For years the struggle was deadlocked. Boards of investigating engineers regularly reported in favor of San Pedro. Just as regularly, the Rivers and Harbors Committee of the United States Senate, which was manned with Huntington friends, William M. Stewart of Nevada among them, reported out bills which, if they had passed, would have awarded the money for development to Santa Monica.

While this inconclusive struggle was raging, an even more vitriolic one gathered force in San Francisco. Ever since the inception of the railroad, the city's jobbers, who controlled the merchandising of most of the Far West, had looked on the associates as avowed enemies. When it had seemed that the terminus of the first transcontinental would be Sacramento rather than San Francisco, they had joined stage lines and steamboat companies in a fruitless effort to keep their city from donating money to the venture. Next, the railroad's effort to obtain Goat Island had been taken as the first step in a plan to build a rival metropolis in the Bay. That threat ended, the railroad had established at Port Costa, not at San Francisco, the greatest wheat shipping facilities of the Pacific Coast. What, asked many a businessman, did these things add up to other than deliberate malice on the part of the Southern Pacific?

Quarrels over rate structures increased the animosity. San Francisco wholesalers wanted to pay water-scale freight on goods shipped from the East. In the palmy days before the railroad, they had imported supplies in shipload lots and had distributed them throughout the hinterland by means of their own intricate and profitable system. After the rails had been finished, they had demanded that they receive trainload lots in a similar way, so that the gains of distribution to the interior would still be theirs. They threatened that unless this was done, they would return to steamships, which could transship goods via the Panama Railroad more cheaply than locomotives could cross the Sierra.

The Central and Union Pacific roads retorted by subsidizing the Pacific Mail Steamship Company so that it would keep its rates as high as the trains'. For a while that had worked. Eventually, however, the Central Pacific, now a part of the Southern Pacific Company, had been forced to grant special terminal rates to cities that could be reached by water—San Francisco first and then Sacramento, Oakland, Stockton, Monterey, and similar spots. Before long, this arrangement, too, proved inadequate. As the cities of the interior grew, their wholesalers, hoping to eliminate San Francisco's profit taking, began to demand carload rates on material shipped directly to their doors. Instead of setting a firm policy, the Southern Pacific's traffic department drifted along from case to case, negotiating each contract as the conditions of the moment suggested. Gradually, and probably with no premeditated intent to harm the San Francisco jobbers, the Southern Pacific began sending more and more merchandise directly into areas that once had been wholly dominated by the Bay City.

Just as this development flowered, the depression of the 1890s further restricted the flow of commerce. The railroad's rate structure, which indeed was arbitrary and discriminatory, received the full blame. The Southern Pacific, hotheads charged, was deliberately trying to reduce the importance of San Francisco, just as it had once tried to set up a rival metropolis right in the Bay itself.

Extraordinary emotionalism accompanied these economic pangs. Public mass meetings were called and citizens' committees were appointed to study ways of combatting the Octopus, a name that by then was guaranteed to generate howls of execration just by being mentioned.

The upshot was the formation of the Traffic Association of California, a sort of wholesale union designed to bargain collectively with the Southern Pacific.[31] When the railroad proved obdurate, the Traffic Association launched campaigns to raise funds for supporting competitive ventures. One scheme involved financing a line of clipper ships sailing around the Horn, as in the days of yore. Under another plan, a group of merchants sponsored by the Traffic Association leased steamships and entered into carrying contracts with the Panama Railroad, which had fallen into one of its periodic squabbles with the Pacific Mail Steamship Company. Both efforts probably cost their backers far more money than was returned to them through the savings they realized from rate reductions gained from the Southern Pacific.

The principal hope, long discussed but not launched until 1895, was the building of another railroad southward through the San Joaquin Valley. It was designed to serve as a distributive line for San Francisco and in time might hook up with the Sante Fe. In order to gain popular backing for it, its promoters solicited stock subscriptions at huge public rallies where orators belabored the wicked Southern Pacific much more eloquently than they praised their own line. But they did give the new project an apt name. It was, they declared with ringing fervor, the People's Road—the movement came during the height of the Populist agitations—and skimmed over the fact that the real power behind it was not the people but Claus Spreckels, a millionaire sugar refiner, and two of his sons.*

Inevitably the furor over rates soon became entangled with opposition to the railroad's plan of extending its payment of the debt to the government. Orators in California cried out that the railroad proposal would increase rates still more: the Central Pacific had been paying no interest on its bonds for thirty years; if the company were now to begin paying 2 per cent over a hundred years or so, it would simply raise the price of tickets and freight high enough to meet the increase. Would it not be better for the government to foreclose on both the Union Pacific and Central Pacific and operate them for the benefit of the nation? In that way California would at last receive fair rates and regulations beyond control of the venal state legislature.

This argument of course overlooked the fact that the government's lien covered only the original Central Pacific-Western Pacific track. Foreclosure would leave the bulk of the lines operated throughout the state by the Southern Pacific Company untouched. Many people, however, did not grasp the point and went home from the rallies with the belief that the whole system would be nationalized if only the funding bill were defeated and the government were left with no recourse but foreclosure.

The Populist party of California was particularly energetic in its opposition to refunding. To lead them in the fray they selected as eccentric an opponent as Huntington ever faced, German-born Adolph Sutro, his round face graced with puffy mutton-chop whiskers and a fine Prussian

---

* As formally incorporated, the road was named the San Francisco and San Joaquin Valley Railroad.

mustache. He owned more property in San Francisco than any other man —as much as one twelfth of the city's area, it was said.[32]

Sutro had made his money by drilling a long tunnel under the mines of the Comstock Lode in Nevada, providing them with ventilation, drainage, and improved ore-hauling facilities. He used part of the fortune to buy a magnificent view site at the tip of the continent, overlooking both the Pacific and the entrance to the Golden Gate. There he lived in a small house amidst spacious gardens decorated by statues scattered about the sward and even tucked into niches in the cliffs above the crashing surf. Nearby he built a big salt-water aquarium that was filled at high tide by ocean water pouring through a 150-foot tunnel. Next to the aquarium he erected a gargantuan bathhouse where ten thousand swimmers a day could dip themselves into warmed sea water.

The gardens, bath, Cliff House restaurant, and adjoining entertainment pavilions were served by the Park & Ocean Railway Company, which charged twenty cents for a round-trip fare—too much, Sutro felt, for a clerk making twelve dollars a week. Because he really was a philanthropist at heart, even though he had spies watch his workmen lest they loaf on the job, he countered by helping finance the Powell Street Railroad Company. As his price he made the railroad agree to serve Sutro Gardens for a five-cent fare. In 1893, the company, which was losing money, sold out to the Market Street Railroad, a subsidiary of the Southern Pacific. Fares immediately rose.

At a luncheon meeting with Huntington, Sutro tried to have the five-cent fare reinstated. Collis refused. It was a losing rate, and besides, he suspected Sutro of wanting to use the low fare as bait to lure customers to, as Collis deemed them, his unsavory establishments.

Thoroughly enraged, Sutro retaliated by charging anyone who rode to the gardens on a Market Street car an admission fee of twenty-five cents. All others entered free. He also began building a rival line out from the city.[33] Most damaging of all, he plunged into the fight against the refunding bill, sending telegrams to President Cleveland—"History will record you as the greatest benefactor of the American people if you will recommend, by special message to Congress, the foreclosure of the mortgages on the Pacific Railroads"—and actively collected signatures to add to a mammoth petition against refunding which was being promoted by Hearst's San Francisco *Examiner*.

These interests, the Populists decided, made the millionaire real estate baron just the man to run for mayor of San Francisco. In July 1894 Sutro agreed and campaigned almost entirely on an anti-Southern Pacific platform.

It was a time of wretched suffering and deep bitterness. The depression continued unabated. A strike against the Pullman Company spread to California, where the Southern Pacific insisted on its right to move trains with sleeping cars attached. The strikers seized engines, burned bridges, dynamited property. In a confrontation between militia and strikers in Sacramento, two civilians were killed and one wounded.

Polemics against the railroad appeared on every hand. John P. Robinson, Huntington's old enemy from the Sacramento Valley Railroad, cleared the way for Frank Norris' later novel of the same name by going to press with a book called *The Octopus: A History of the Construction, Conspiracies, Extortions, Robberies and Villainous Acts of the Central Pacific, Southern Pacific . . . and Other Subsidized Railroads.* Hearst's reporters and cartoonists poured out acid.[84] Mass meetings listened to unbridled denunciations. Although the Pullman strike failed, largely in the East, it and an accompanying statewide emotional binge against the railroad swept Sutro into office with a whooping majority.

Committee hearings on the funding bill were conducted during the winter of 1895–96. Huntington's grilling came during February and March. Hearst sent Ambrose Bierce and cartoonists James Swinnerton and Homer Davenport to Washington to cover Huntington's appearances. From their joint efforts a picture emerged that was repeated over and over in caricature and words: "The dromedary head of Mr. Huntington, with its tandem bumps of cupidity and self-esteem . . . bulbous bulk . . . one leg in the grave, one arm in the Treasury, and one eye on the police. . . ." It was a thorough hatchet job of the sort that Hearst knew so well how to engineer.

Mayor Sutro contributed his bit, summoning a mass meeting in San Francisco that named him head of a Committee of Fifty to keep the opposition alive. He obliged, using his own money to mail each day to Congressmen (until the Post Office checked him) big envelopes on whose faces different slogans were printed in screaming red: "HOW CONGRESSMEN ARE BRIBED!" "HUNTINGTON THINKS CONGESSMEN ARE HUNGRY!" "HUNTINGTON WOULD NOT STEAL A RED-HOT STOVE!" "OH! WHAT A HOG!" Inside the envelopes were choice quotations lifted from the old Colton letters. Sutro even wrote the legislature of Kentucky, appealing that it cancel the Southern Pacific's charter: "Rid us of the horrible monster which is devouring our substance, and which is debauching our people, and by its devilish instincts is every day more firmly grasping us in its tentacles."[35]

At the hearings Huntington was questioned, as he had been by the

Pacific Railway Commission in 1887, on every phase of the railroad's career. Again he resorted to evasion, forgetfulness, and occasional sharp exchanges of sarcasm with his chief inquisitor, Senator John Morgan.[36] Bierce mocked the performance cruelly, but some of the press came to Collis' defense. On March 2, the New York *Daily Financial News* editorialized, "Mr. Huntington has remained unpretending in his greatness. . . . He has been content to abide by the results of his labors, and to leave his case, if need be, to the verdict of posterity. . . . In the light of [his] achievements, it is pitiable to hear men who have never been anything better than political parasites talk of the selfishness of Mr. Huntington."

Though Collis himself generally maintained silence outside of the committee room, exasperation did provoke him to one verbal slash at Hearst and Sutro. "These people who are fighting me in California," he told a reporter from the *Daily Financial News,* "are about as uncanny a set of vagabonds as was ever found sneaking around a farmer's hen roost in the short hours of the night." The riposte and the *News*'s editorials were wasted breath. Hearst's papers had far greater circulation, and Bierce's continuing vituperation was the voice the nation heard.

Midway through the Senate hearings Huntington sent a message to the committee, asking for a postponement on the grounds of illness. When he returned, his speech was blurred and hesitant. Ever alert, Bierce abruptly changed his theme from Huntington, the malevolent bandit ("Of the modern Forty Thieves, Mr. Huntington is the surviving thirty-six") to Huntington the senile buffoon, "shuffling, falsifying, cowering. . . . Perhaps the impediment in his speech, like the erratic and purposeless lies that were its immediate occasion, may be the mark of a failing mind." A more probable explanation is that Collis Huntington had suffered a slight stroke. He was then seventy-four years old.

Because 1896 was an election year, the refunding measure that Huntington wanted was put over until January 1897. When at last it was brought to a vote, it was roundly defeated. In San Francisco, Mayor James Phelan, who had succeeded the ailing Sutro, declared a city-wide holiday of rejoicing and fireworks.

At Santa Monica, too, things were going badly. In 1896, just after the close of the hearings on the funding bill, Congress had agreed to accept and follow through with whatever harbor recommendations were made to it by yet another board of blue-ribbon army engineers. Their choice went to San Pedro. Secretary of War Russell A. Alger, who was said to have had business relations with Huntington, thereupon reacted by bottling the report in his office, refusing under one pretext or another to turn it over to Congress, until finally California's Democratic Senator, Stephen M. White, and General Rosecrans went to President McKinley and forced its release. And still Huntington struggled against the new bill that was based on the report, until Senator James H. Berry of Arkansas rose from his seat in exasperation to say that there was no man in the United States "save and except Mr. Huntington, who would have the assurance, in the face of reports of these army officers, to have come to the United States, and asked them to give him $3,000,000 in money to build a breakwater to serve his private interests." When the vote came, San Pedro won, and this time Southern California rejoiced.[87]

Meanwhile the debt to the government had matured. Something had to be done, either refunding or foreclosure—and it would not be the latter. Huntington could conceivably form a syndicate and at a forced sale buy back his own line free of encumbrances. Nor was government operation likely. William Jennings Bryan's challenge to the vested interests of American capitalism had been defeated. McKinley's gold-standard Republicans were in control, the depression was ending, and a new climate bathed Capitol Hill. On July 7, 1898, Congress appointed three Cabinet members, the Secretary of the Treasury, the Secretary of the Interior, and the Attorney General, as a commission to arrange a settlement, subject to the President's approval. McKinley himself followed all stages of the negotiations with close attention.

In the midst of the deliberations, James Speyer offered himself as mediator. His firm, Speyer & Company, had marketed scores of millions of dollars' worth of railroad bonds for Huntington, and Speyer had full confidence in and admiration for Collis' integrity and ability in transactions connected with the handling of securities. He was able to smooth the old man's hackles and quell suspicions born of years of buffeting at the hands of the lawmakers.

In 1899 the Central Pacific's debt, after application of credits in the sinking fund, amounted to nearly $59 million. It was agreed that the railroad should liquidate this sum in twenty installments spread over a ten-year period, issuing 3 per cent notes against the unpaid balance. Stockholders and bondholders were quieted by a complex reorganization formula, and both Speyer and the Southern Pacific undertook to guarantee the notes. The latter point was crucial. When payment had rested on the earning abilities of the main line of the Central Pacific alone, Huntington had declared that settlement would be impossible unless spread across several decades. But when he was faced at last with the inevitable, he consented to put the entire Southern Pacific system behind the plan.

374

Under those circumstances a single decade proved adequate, and in 1909 the settlement with the government was completed.[88]

During these involved and troubled times, Huntington continued serenely with his duties as head of one of America's largest corporations, the Southern Pacific Company. Although his step had slowed and the shaggy hair around his bald pate had long since turned completely white, he had lost none of his zest for work, perhaps because little else was truly meaningful to him. Thoughts of retirement seem never to have crossed his mind. He declined to sell the Central Pacific to E. H. Harriman, who had recently gained control of the Union Pacific, and he kept pouring money and energy into the shipyards at Newport News—on March 24, 1898, two huge battleships, the *Kentucky* and the *Kearsarge* were launched simultaneously and contracts for others quickly followed —just as if he fully intended to be around for years to come. "When life is no longer a struggle," he told one of his officials in San Francisco, "it is no longer worth living."

And yet the final inevitability was approaching more swiftly than he knew. Foreseeing it, Arabella had spent five years and a quarter of a million dollars erecting at Woodland Cemetery, near Throg's Neck, a mausoleum patterned after a Roman temple. It was 42 feet long, 28 feet wide, and 24 feet high. Collis refused to look at it.

The sudden end came at Pine Knot Lodge beside Raquette Lake in the Adirondack Mountains of New York. Another of the strange interlockings of Huntington's life was at work there. The land around Raquette Lake was owned by William West Durant, son of Thomas C. Durant, Huntington's arch enemy during the building of the Pacific railroad. Young Durant developed the area around the lake as a super-resort for the very rich—J. Pierpont Morgan, Alfred Gwynne Vanderbilt, and Collis P. Huntington among others. In order to facilitate access to the place, Huntington and young Durant collaborated in building—shades of Thomas C.!—a nineteen-mile railroad to connect with the Delaware & Hudson.

At Raquette Lake the Huntingtons had a rustic camp—they called it a camp—purchased for $100,000 and improved for another $150,000. There, during a vacation in August, 1900, Huntington spent several days taking short walks in the emerald woods. On the warm evening of the 13th, he sat out on the lawn talking to friends until eleven o'clock. Shortly after retiring, he groaned with pain and lapsed into a coma. He died at five minutes before midnight from a heart attack.[89]

Only a few close friends and relatives attended the funeral services, which were held at his own home at eleven o'clock in the morning on August 17. At that moment and for seven minutes thereafter, "5000 men [his employees] became idle, engines paused upon the rails, ships floated motionless upon the water, telegraph instruments ceased to click, and busy offices became silent."

One third of his estate went to Arabella's son, Archer Huntington, one third to Arabella, and one third to Henry E. Huntington. The last two thirds, considerably augmented, were eventually reunited. Finding San Francisco uncongenial, Henry E. Huntington yielded, as did Arabella, to the importunities of E. H. Harriman of the Union Pacific. They sold control of the Southern Pacific to him, and Henry Huntington moved to Southern California, where he became engrossed in electric interurban lines and in real estate development. He and his wife, Mary Prentice Huntington, were divorced, and in 1913 Henry married his uncle's widow, Arabella.

From the union of their fortunes flowed hospitals and the world-famed Henry E. Huntington Library and Art Gallery, surrounded by majestic gardens. Archer, renowned as a scholar of Spanish civilization, founded the Hispanic Society Museum of New York City, the beautiful Mariner's Museum at Newport News, and Brookgreen Gardens near Myrtle Beach, South Carolina. Partly because of these benefactions, the odium that once attached to the name has evaporated. And yet, nearly three quarters of a century after Collis Huntington's death, an appraisal of his career remains difficult. As Professor Grodinsky has remarked, the repeated attacks made on him in Congress and in the newspapers during the last part of his life still prevent adequate recognition of his creative work "as the leading railroad builder of the United States."[40]

The long-continued din, especially in California, about destructiveness, treasury-raiding, selfishness, and the corrupting of public officials have beclouded the less sensational truth of his achievements. For he did have vision—a vision that first straddled the Sierra when few believed the feat possible and then spanned the continent. Others, too, saw that much. But Huntington saw *how* to do it.

Other railroads faltered. His western lines never did. Of the nation's major transcontinental systems, only the Central and Southern Pacific avoided bankruptcy and foreclosure. By keeping the network expanding throughout the nation's recurrent cycles of economic distress, he performed a major service to the phenomenal growth not only of California but of the entire Southwest.

He benefited personally from the doing—he made very sure of that— and his procedures were often questionable even by the lax standards of his times. His scruples were highly adaptable. Hard-tempered first by the poverty of his youth and then by the gold-rush crucible of California, he returned roughshod to the East, took the burgeoning *laissez faire* spirit of industrial America as he found it, and bent it to his purposes. In a milieu of cutthroat competition, he was unyielding, tireless, ruthless, and fertile of stratagems. But unlike Jay Gould and other manipulators of transportation finance, he never sold out on his railroads. They and the great shipyards at Newport News were his life. Inevitably, too, they were an influential factor as well in the life of his nation.

Notes

The principal manuscript sources for the first four chapters are letters which Collis Huntington (and a few others) wrote to Solon Huntington. They are now in the possession of Mr. Collis Holladay of San Marino, California, and are used with his permission. References to these letters are so frequent that it would be unwieldy to repeat the location each time: the Holladay Collection. In the absence of other citation, this location of all letters and documents involving Solon Huntington is to be understood.

1 THE START

1. School material from an article by schoolmate T. E. Nunan in the San Francisco *Call*, February 2, 1896, and Huntington's answer in the Sacramento *Record-Union*, March 3, 1896, both reproduced in Cerinda W. Evans, *Collis Potter Huntington* (Newport News, Va., 1954). For his life in Poverty Hollow, see Lewis S. Mills, "Collis Potter Huntington," *The Lure of the Litchfield Hills*, Vol. XIII, No. 1, December 1954, and Joseph F. Doherty, "Smooth is the Road," *Tracks* (house organ of the Chesapeake and Ohio Railway), February 1951.

2. There are two dictations, Bancroft's "Huntington Manuscript" and the "Huntington Typescript," with notes by David Sessions, both in the Bancroft Library, University of California, Berkeley. The fulsome sketch based on them, "Life of Collis P. Huntington," is Chapter II, Vol. V of Bancroft's *Chronicles of the Builders* (San Francisco, 1891).

3. Mahlon D. Fairchild, "Reminiscences of a Forty-Niner," *California Historical Society Quarterly*, March 1934.

4. The contract for erecting the building, executed with Elihu Brown on March 25, 1841, is in the Holladay Collection.

5. The contract between the brothers is in ibid.

6. Willard V. Huntington, *Oneonta Memories* (San Francisco, 1891).

7. Egbert Sabin, who went to California with Huntington in 1849, regularly referred to him as "The Old Man"—Collis to Solon Huntington, July 12, 1851.

8. Collis to Solon, March 25, 1850.
9. The California contract is in the Holladay Collection. Data concerned with preparations for the trip are drawn from several letters to Solon. George Murray discusses his debt to Solon and Dr. Case in letters of May 18, 1850, and September 22, 1850. Collis refers to the Ford mortgage in letters of February 14, 1853, July 30, 1854, etc.
10. The route is indicated by Collis' record of Egbert's expenses, to Solon, July 12, 1851.
11. Collis to Solon, March 14, 1849.
12. Jessie Benton Frémont, *A Year of American Travel* (New York, 1878), pp. 22 ff.

2 ALMOST THE FINISH

1. Murray's account unfortunately ends with the arrival of the *Crescent City* at Chagres.
2. In his reminiscences Huntington coalesced the committees into one— "Huntington Manuscript" and "Huntington Typescript." Murray's letter-journal to Solon and Dr. Case shows that there were two and locates Huntington and Parbert on different ones.
3. For contemporary accounts of Panama, see the early pages of Bayard Taylor, *Eldorado* (New York, 1850); Frank Marryat, *Mountains and Molehills* (Lippincott paperback ed.: Philadelphia and New York, 1962); the journal of Stephen Chapin Davis, published as *California Gold Rush Merchant*, edited by Benjamin B. Richards (San Marino, Calif., 1956); Joseph W. Gregory, *Guide for California Travelers via the Isthmus of Panama* (New York, 1850). The definitive modern study is John H. Kemble, *The Panama Route, 1848–1869* (Berkeley, Calif., 1943).
4. From Collis' letter to Solon of July 12, 1851. This letter, occasioned by Egbert Sabin's suit against the brothers for mistreatment, is the principal source of information concerning Huntington's whereabouts during the early months of the California adventure.
5. For the *Humboldt:* Theodore H. Hittell, *History of California*, Vol. III (San Francisco, 1898), pp. 248–49. Hittell's statement that the forcible provisioning of the ship took place before the departure from Panama is apparently in error. See "The Humboldt Association," 30th Anniversary Pamphlet (a copy is in the Henry E. Huntington Library, San Marino, Calif.), and James E. Gordon, secretary of the Humboldt Association, "Voyage of the Old Ship *Humboldt*" in *The Traveler*, August 1893. One other small discrepancy: Hittell gives the cost of a steerage ticket as $100; Collis to Solon Huntington, July 12, 1851, says it cost $175.

3 THE NIGHTMARE CITIES

1. *Digging for Gold—Without a Shovel: The Letters of Daniel Wadsworth Coit*, edited by George P. Hammond (Denver, 1967), p. 81.
2. John N. Stone, "Brief Notes . . ." in *California Gold Rush Voyages*, edited by John E. Pomfret (San Marino, Calif., 1954), p. 167.

3. Huntington's dictation to Bancroft's scribe, David Sessions, the so-called "Huntington Typescript."
4. Ibid. In recounting the incident of the schooner to Sessions, Huntington does not mention Egbert. I deduce the boy's presence from the record Huntington kept of his expenses. There are entries for the stops in Panama and Acapulco, but none for San Francisco. Presumably Egbert earned his own way there, probably by carrying boxes with Collis— Collis to Solon, July 12, 1851.
5. The date has not been established. Rodman Paul, *The California Gold Discovery: Sources, Documents, Accounts and Memoirs* . . . (Georgetown, Calif., 1966).
6. See Paul Bailey, *Sam Brannan and the California Mormons* (rev. ed., Los Angeles, 1953), and Reva Scott, *Sam Brannan and the Golden Fleece* (New York, 1944). For Sutter: James P. Zollinger, *Sutter, the Man and His Empire* (New York, 1939), and Richard Dillon, *Fool's Gold* (New York, 1967). For early Sacramento: John Frederick Morse (who had been on the *Humboldt* with Huntington), *The First History of Sacramento City* (reprint ed., Sacramento, 1945).
7. Collis to Solon, July 12, 1851.
8. Quoted in J. S. Holliday, "The California Gold Rush Reconsidered," *Probing The American West* (Santa Fe, N.M., 1963), p. 41.
9. George R. Stewart, *The California Trail* (New York, 1962), p. 292. Stewart's 21,000 is a modest estimate. Dale Morgan suggests 30,000, *The Overland Diary of James A. Pritchard* (Denver, 1959), p. 17. Holliday, op. cit., p. 36, would put the figure even higher.
10. Collis to Solon, July 12, 1851.
11. "Huntington Typescript."
12. For the flood: Morse, op. cit., pp. 58–62; Morgan, op. cit., pp. 141, 172; Coit, *Digging for Gold*, p. 101; Dillon, op. cit., pp. 323–24.
13. Collis to Solon, March 25, 1850. George Murray to Solon, May 18, 1850.
14. Collis to Solon, March 25, 1850.
15. Collis to Solon, July 12, 1851.
16. Ibid.
17. Collis to Solon, March 25 and June 17, 1850.

4 THE EDUCATION OF A GOLD-RUSH MERCHANT

1. Collis to Solon, June 17, 1850. Solon did not make the trip. Perhaps he should have. The unsupervised shovels did not reach San Francisco until a year after they had been ordered and were too rusted to be salable.

   The shovels raise another question about the accuracy of Huntington's image-making reminiscences of 1888 or 1889. During their compilation he bragged to Bancroft's interviewers that in 1850, when shovels were overabundant and prices low, he bought all that were available, 1,200 dozen according to the "Huntington Manuscript." He then ran up prices by spreading rumors of shortages and sold out at from $120 to $240 a dozen, a potential profit of over $100,000. He made a similar killing, he said, by cornering the market in potatoes.

The stories seem doubtful. There are no echoes in letters to Solon, who was waiting impatiently for money due him, or in the reminiscences of other California merchants. Moreover, the timing of Huntington's reminiscences is again suggestive. In the spring of 1888, Creed Haymond, attorney for the Central Pacific Railroad, had delivered a vigorous defense of his clients to the investigators of the U. S. Pacific Railway Commission. Among other things Haymond insisted that they had been wealthy men at the time of the building of the railroad and that the government's loans, far from being a help, had been a hindrance because of the strings attached. Creed Haymond, *The Central Pacific Railroad Company: Its Relations to the Government* (San Francisco, 1888), pp. 29, 47–56, 222–23.

As will appear further on, tax rolls, though not conclusive, suggest that when the Big Four undertook the railroad, they were not wealthy in any sweeping sense of the word. But in 1888 they needed to seem so, for the sake of Haymond's arguments. Hence the shovels, the potatoes, and so on.

2. Collis to Solon, November 10, 1851, and March 28, 1852.
3. "Huntington Manuscript." How often Huntington made these aquatic dashes and how many other merchants bestirred themselves to similar activity cannot be said. Huntington's 1888 telling suggests that he alone thought up and pursued the stratagem, but this probably was more gilding.
4. July 17, 1850. Later estimates of damage were $3,000,000. H. H. Bancroft, *History of California* (San Francisco, 1888), Vol. VI, pp. 202–03.
5. Hittell, *History of California*, Vol. III, pp. 669 ff.
6. Bancroft, op. cit., Vol. VII, pp. 130–35. Coit, op. cit., pp. 96–97.
7. Morse, *History of Sacramento*, pp. 90–94; Thompson and West, *History of Sacramento County* (Oakland, 1880), p. 56. Among those who died was Mayor Biglow of Sacramento, weakened by the amputation of his arm. Hittell, op. cit., Vol. III, pp. 176–77.
8. Elizabeth to Collis' mother and sister in Oneonta, June 24, 1851. All details of the journey are from this letter.
9. Frank Marryat, *Mountains and Molehills* (Lippincott paperback ed.: Philadelphia and New York, 1962), p. 93.
10. Elizabeth gives some of the rumors in the letter cited in note 8 above.
11. Elizabeth's sister Mary to Collis' sister Phoebe, July 9, 1851, copying from a letter received the week before from Elizabeth.
12. Collis to Solon, June 28 and December 13, 1851.
13. Collis to Solon, June 28, 1851.
14. As in 8 above.
15. Collis to Solon, November 10, 1851. Most Sacramentans shared Huntington's opinion. After the executions the citizens assembled in a mass meeting in front of the Orleans Hotel (there is no way of knowing whether Collis was with them), passed resolutions calling on the governor to resign, and then burned him in effigy for having pardoned one of the convicted men. See H. H. Bancroft, *Popular Tribunals* (San Francisco, 1887), Vol. I, pp. 441–48, and Thompson and West's *History of Sacramento County*, pp. 125–26.

16. Collis to Solon, August 14, September 11, December 13, 1851; March 28, 1852.
17. Stewart, *The California Trail*, pp. 301–02. Several factors caused the drop. The primary ones were pessimistic reports by stampeders who had returned stone broke from the goldfields and the counter-attraction of newly liberalized laws for the acquisition of land in Oregon.
18. Collis to Solon, September 11 and October 11, 1851.
19. Collis to Solon, September 11, October 11, November 10, December 13, 1851.
20. Collis to Solon, May 30, 1852.
21. Ibid.
22. For the fire, see Collis to Solon, November 14, 1852; Elizabeth to Phoebe Pardee, January 1, 1853. Also, the Sacramento *Daily Bee*, November 3, 1862, reprinting the same paper's story of November 3, 1852.
    The Stanfords' Sacramento store was run by Josiah and Philip Stanford. Their brother Leland had only recently arrived from the East and was managing a branch store at Cold Springs, a mining camp midway between Coloma and Placerville.
23. Colville's *Sacramento Directory*, 1854.
24. Collis to Solon, February 14, 1853.
25. Elizabeth to Phoebe Pardee, January 1, 1853. The context suggests that the letter was misdated. She may have meant January 10 or 11.
26. Israel Minor & Co. to Solon, December 15, 1852; November 19, 1853.
27. A Henry Merwin was also involved, I do not know exactly how.
28. References to money sent for Ellen's education run through several letters to Solon, beginning May 31, 1853. In time Collis had the satisfaction of seeing his sister established as a minor religious poet with published volumes of inspirational verse and hymns to her credit. *The Huntington Family in America* (Hartford, Conn., 1915), p. 844.
29. Collis to Solon, September 14, 1853.
30. Oscar Lewis, *The Big Four* (New York, 1938), p. 213; Bancroft, *Chronicles of the Builders*, Vol. V, p. 37.
31. Collis to Solon, October 15, 1854, outlining his financial standing at that point. This contemporary statement is far more relevant, obviously, than the statements about his wealth that he made years later to Bancroft's researchers.
32. On this point see Earl Pomeroy, *The Pacific Slope* (New York, 1965), pp. 67–69.
33. This according to Charles Crocker: "Crocker Manuscript," Bancroft Library.

5 CALIFORNIA FERMENT

1. The description is based on a photograph reproduced in Ralph Cioffi, "Mark Hopkins, Inside Man of the Big Four" (unpublished M.A. thesis, University of California, Berkeley, 1950). I am indebted to Mr. Cioffi for permission to obtain microfilm of this work.

2. E. H. Miller, Jr., dictation concerning Mark Hopkins, Bancroft Library, p. 5.

3. There may have been two men named Mark Hopkins keeping store in Sacramento during the 1850s, one from North Carolina and one from New York. At least such is the contention of Estelle Latta in *Controversial Mark Hopkins* (New York, 1952). She makes a good case for the point, then uses it to buttress a less tenable theory that the North Carolina Hopkins was the true member of the Big Four and that after his death his associates rang in the other Hopkins in an involved plot to keep control of his estate. Variant tellings of this deep-dyed villainy have stirred the blood pressures of scandal-hunting Californians for decades. No court has been convinced by the available evidence, however, and I have followed their decisions in confining this account to a single Hopkins from New York.

4. Latta, op. cit., interleaf pp. 86–87, presents a photostat of the marriage certificate. Mark Hopkins was not, as is sometimes said, nearly twice the age of his bride.

5. Robert O. Briggs, "The Sacramento Valley Railroad" (unpublished M.A. thesis, Sacramento State College, 1954), p. 14, quoting official papers of the Sacramento Valley Railroad Co. Most of my data on the early days of the railroad is drawn from this thesis and from Gilbert H. Kneiss, *Bonanza Railroads* (Stanford University Press, 1941), pp. 3–29.

6. The beginning point of any study of Judah is Carl Wheat, "A Sketch of the Life of Theodore D. Judah," *California Historical Society Quarterly*, September 1928, based on Judah's own engineering reports and on the reminiscences of his wife, Anna.

7. For the long Broderick-Gwin feud, which continued until Broderick was mortally wounded in 1859 in a duel with a Gwin supporter, Judge David S. Terry of the state supreme court, see Hittell, *History of California*, Vol. IV, passim. Also Donald Hargis, "The Issues in the Broderick-Gwin Debates of 1859," *California Historical Society Quarterly*, December 1953.

8. Cornelius Cole, *Memoirs* (New York, 1908), pp. 92–96.

9. For Crocker's early career: his dictation to Bancroft, the "Crocker Manuscript," Bancroft Library; Bancroft's *Chronicles of the Builders*, Vol. VI. pp. 33–47; Bunyan Hadley Andrew, "Charles Crocker" (unpublished M.A. thesis, University of California, Berkeley, 1931), pp. 1–32.

10. Hittell, op. cit., Vol. IV, p. 173.

11. An assumption. However, William Stoddard is listed in Sacramento directories for 1856–58, and since he must have needed a few months to establish his business, a guess that he came West with Elizabeth in September 1855 is not unwarranted.

12. Collis to Solon, September 19, 1855. Collis added cynically that the agents of the line reported only one hundred deaths lest the truth turn travel back to the rival Panama route. The official account, probably not as falsified as Collis believed (but the point is that he and others *did* believe it) was set at 104 dead on shipboard, nine after docking. Oscar Lewis, *Sea Routes to the Goldfields* (New York, 1949), pp.

243–44. Lewis, pp. 244–54, summarizes other marine disasters of the early 1850s with which the Hungtingtons must have been familiar.

13. Overland figures estimated by Stewart, *The California Trail*, pp. 312–13. Weller's speech is in the *Congressional Globe*, Vol. XXV (1855–56), p. 1252.

14. For the wagon roads: Chester White, "Surmounting the Sierras: The Campaign for a Wagon Road," *California Historical Society Quarterly*, March 1928; W. Turrentine Jackson, *Wagon Roads West* (Berkeley and Los Angeles, 1952), pp. 161–67; Francis P. Farquhar, *History of the Sierra Nevada* (Berkeley and Los Angeles, 1965), Chapter XI.

6 UPSTAIRS AT 54 K

1. Collis to Solon January 3 and April 19, 1856. The relatives with whom they boarded were Elizabeth's sister Clarissa and Clarissa's husband, E. D. Prentice. Prentice had come to California in 1849, had run a store built of tule reeds in Stockton, and then had gone home to marry Clarissa Stoddard. In the summer of 1853 he returned to California with his wife and a baby daughter, who soon died. By 1856 he had entered the mercantile business with William Stoddard, one of Elizabeth's many brothers. Several of these brothers and half brothers (Elizabeth's father had children by three wives) followed her to California at different intervals. For Prentice, see *Letters of Edwin Dwight Prentice to his Mother, Sister and Friends, 1850–1856* (San Francisco, 1916).

2. The tale of the clerks is in the "Huntington Manuscript" and, suitably revised, in Bancroft's *Chronicles of the Builders*, Vol. V, pp. 38–39. The paternalism was not as unique as Huntington remembered; Crocker's clerks also boarded at the Crocker store. And, wrote Mary Crocker's brother John to a friend inquiring about employment, "I might mention that Charles Crocker has no desire to employ any more clerks that smoke cigars." John G. Deming to John T. Griffitts, January 5, 1856, in the transportation section of the California State Library, Sacramento.

3. Cole, *Memoirs*, pp. 112–13.

4. Sacramento *Union*, March 9, 1856.

5. The original signed document is in the Estelle Doheny Collection, St. John's Seminary, Camarillo, California.

6. Sacramento *Union*, May 12, 1856. Cole, *Memoirs*, pp. 113–14, quotes the handbill in full.

7. Bancroft, *Popular Tribunals*, Vol. II, p. 203. There is a plethora of material on the San Francisco committee, little on the Sacramento group. For a starting point, see Bancroft, op. cit., and Hittell's *History of California*, Vol. III, pp. 460–649.

8. "Huntington Manuscript." Huntington's words: ". . . circumstances arise sometimes when power gets into the hands of corrupt men, who withhold justice and are perfectly willing to ruin others to sustain themselves . . . and when the only possible way of obtaining justice is by the use of influence in whatever form is essential and inevitable; in such cases bribery may be the last and only means left to honest men. . . . All

theory is opposed to this, I know, but there is a knowledge [illegible] to all philosophizing, that comes from the depths of human experience."

9. Quoted in Catherine Coffin Phillips, *Cornelius Cole* (San Francisco, 1929), p. 89.
10. George T. Clark, *Leland Stanford* (Stanford University Press, 1931), pp. 76–79.
11. Bancroft, *Chronicles of the Builders*, Vol. V, p. 42.
12. Clark, op. cit., pp. 26, 31. My summary of Stanford's early career is based largely on the first three chapters of Clark's biography.
13. Sacramento *Union*, February 23, 1856; Kneiss, *Bonanza Railroads*, pp. 14–18.
14. Phillips, op. cit., p. 95.
15. Jackson, *Wagon Roads West*, pp. 175–76.
16. Wheat, "Judah," pp. 225–26.
17. Sacramento *Union*, April 19, June 30, July 18, 1856.
18. Wheat, op. cit., pp. 229–32.
19. Jackson, op. cit., note 50, p. 355. For the maneuvering in general, ibid, pp. 174–75, 201.
20. Chester L. White, "Surmounting the Sierras," pp. 17–18.
21. Jackson, op. cit., pp. 201–05, 216–17.
22. Clark, *Leland Stanford*, pp. 68–69; Collis to Solon Huntington, February 11, 1858; Sacramento *Union*, January 19, 1861.
23. Hittell, *History of California*, Vol. IV, pp. 218–20, 257. Clark, op. cit., pp. 82–91.
24. Hittell, op. cit., pp. 223–29.

7 THE CATALYST

1. Bancroft, *Chronicles of the Builders*, Vol. VI, p. 118.
2. Ibid., pp. 131–34.
3. *The Sacramento Valley Railroad, Report of the President, Trustee and Superintendent. . . . December 31, 1860* (San Francisco, 1861). See also James John Campilio, "A History of the Sacramento Valley Railroad up to 1865" (unpublished M.A. thesis, University of Southern California, 1934).
4. See Judah's letter to the Sacramento *Union*, September 26, 1860; also, the convention's own official "The Address to the People," printed in the *Union*, November 8, 1859. For summaries of the convention's work: Bancroft, *Chronicles of the Builders*, Vol. VI, pp. 206 ff.; Robert A. Russel, *Improvements of Communication with the Pacific Coast as an Issue in American Politics, 1783–1864* (Cedar Rapids, Iowa, 1948), pp. 174–76.
5. For the shifting national and congressional attitudes toward the Pacific railroad: Russel, op. cit.; Robert W. Fogel, *The Union Pacific Railroad, A Case Study in Premature Enterprise* (Baltimore, 1960), pp. 1–50; Allen Kline, "The Attitude of Congress Toward the Pacific Railway, 1856–1862," *Annual Report of the American Historical Association . . . 1910* (Washington, 1912), pp. 191–98.

6. For an introduction to the complex and still largely hidden story of the influence exerted on national railway legislation by local entrepreneurs, see Wallace D. Farnham, "The Pacific Railroad Act of 1862," *Nebraska History*, XLIII, September 1962, pp. 141 ff.; Charles N. Glaab, *Kansas City and the Railroads* (Madison, Wisconsin, 1962); William R. Petrowski, "The Kansas Pacific Railroad in the Southwest," *Arizona and the West*, Summer 1969, pp. 129 ff., and the early chapters of Stanley W. Hirschon's biography, *Grenville Dodge* (Bloomington, Indiana, 1967). On reaching Washington, Judah trimmed his sails to the winds he found blowing there, a matter that California historians, who like to mount Judah on a white charger, tend to overlook. They dwell, for instance, on a bill which Judah prepared while traveling East with Congressman John C. Burch in the fall of 1859. Actually the bill was without effect. It was not until Judah had aligned himself with the midwestern promoters that his knowledge of the situation in California finally began to receive a hearing.

7. Judah described the method of selecting the recipients of government aid in his first sales appeal to California investors. The favored company, he said, could be designated "by inserting the name of this company directly in the bill, as the company to whom these appropriations should come, or by an arrangement with the incorporators or trustees named in the bill." Theodore Judah, "The Central Pacific Railroad of California" (San Francisco, November 1, 1860).

8. The Anna Judah manuscript, Judah papers, Bancroft Library. This is a long letter about her husband, written in 1890 or so to an old friend, Amos P. Catlin, once of Mormon Island, later a member of Bancroft's staff. Anna's reminiscence needs to be used with caution. She had no more comprehension of the involved nature of her husband's activities than most wives have. Moreover, she wrote her letter out of an abiding bitterness over what she considered to be the shabby treatment accorded her husband by Collis Huntington and his associates.

9. Sacramento *Union*, July 25, 1860.

10. This surmise is based on the fact that the Robinsons a little later did build a road from Dutch Flat to the Henness Pass wagon road. From a speech by N. W. Winton, "The Pacific Railroad," to the Nevada Senate, February 27, 1865. In Vol. V of the Central Pacific Railroad Pamphlets, Huntington Library, San Marino, California.

11. Judah's report of 1862 to the stockholders of the Central Pacific Railroad discusses the engineering problems in detail (Sacramento, 1862). For a modern-day civil engineer's appraisal of the route: John Debo Galloway, *The First Transcontinental Railroad* (New York, 1950), pp. 120–32.

12. Testimony of D. W. Strong in the report of the investigations of the United States Pacific Railway Commission, 50th Cong., 1st Sess., Sen. Exec. Doc. 51 (8 vols., Serials 2505–09), p. 2959. Hereafter cited as Pac. Ry. Commission.

13. Ibid., pp. 2838–39.

14. Anna Judah manuscript. For Marsh: a clipping from the *Journal of* Nevada City, California, November 9, 1860, Judah papers, Bancroft

Library. For the Johnson Pass country: Judah's report of October 1, 1861, to the Central Pacific Railroad (Sacramento, 1861).
15. So Judah stated in his first pamphlet, November 1, 1860, loc. cit. When the company's articles of incorporation were filed with the state eight months later, however (June 28, 1862), only fourteen mountain subscribers were named, including Strong and Marsh. They were listed as signing for 265 shares, a face value of $26,500, exactly $20,000 short of what Judah had reported in November. Either some of the original subscribers had got cold feet and backed out or Judah, a practised engineer, had made a slip in his addition.
16. The pamphlet of November 1. On November 10 Judah condensed its eighteen pages into a circular which, presumably, he distributed more widely.
17. Pac. Ry. Commission, p. 2961.
18. Anna Judah manuscript.

8   THE INCREDIBLE LEAP

1. Elijah R. Kennedy, *The Contest for California in 1861* (Boston, 1912). See also Winfield J. Davis, *History of Political Conventions in California, 1849–92* (Sacramento, 1893). The vote figures: Lincoln, 38,-699; Douglas, 37,957; Breckinridge, 33,969.
2. Clark, *Leland Stanford*, pp. 95–97.
3. Strong's testimony, Pac. Ry. Commission, p. 2838. My account of the formation of the Central Pacific Railroad Company is patched together out of Strong's account, Judah's known theories, and the reminiscences which Huntington, Charles Crocker, Stanford, and Anna Judah passed on years after the event to Hubert Howe Bancroft's researchers. Additional odds and ends came from Cole's *Memoirs* and tales given to author Robert Fulton, *Epic of the Overland* (San Francisco, 1924), by B. F. Leete, a surveyor who worked for Judah. In 1899 Huntington repeated a garbled version of his Bancroft reminiscences to banker James Speyer of New York City (letter, Holladay Collection). William L. Willis, *History of Sacramento County* (Los Angeles, 1913), p. 193, adds other small details supposedly emanating from primary sources.
    None of these accounts, written a quarter of a century or more after the event, is satisfactory as an historical document. For one thing, they scarcely allude to politics, although politics must have been a primary consideration. Anna Judah did not understand the convolutions involved; and Huntington, Crocker, and Stanford, who at the time of the reminiscing were under scrutiny by Congress for alleged political malfeasance, naturally gave the topic of politics wide berth.
4. "Huntington Manuscript."
5. Some accounts say the wagon road was a major cause of the later breach between Judah and the Big Four. Yet Anna Judah's manuscript letter is definite about the road's being part of her husband's bait to draw the financiers on.
6. In both the "Huntington Manuscript" and the "Huntington Typescript"

and in his 1899 letter to James Speyer, loc. cit., Huntington says that he raised $35,000 for the surveys. The figure simply is not so and was part of Collis' latter-day pretense of having been affluent at the time of launching the company. Better evidence comes from Judah, who recorded the survey's actual cost in the back of a stock journal of the California Granite Company, which shipped thousands of tons of building stone over the Sacramento Valley Railroad. This record, now among the Judah papers at the Bancroft Library, shows that the company expended on the survey $5,563.14, plus Judah's salary of $100 a month from March 1 through September 30, 1861. The total cost of the survey was thus $6,263.14.

I reach the figure of $1,500 for each contributor, rather than Huntington's $5,000, on the ground that five of those who backed the survey (Huntington, Hopkins, Crocker, Stanford, James Bailey) are shown in the original list of stockholders as having subscribed to 150 shares of stock each—i.e., a down payment of $1,500 apiece. Judah states in his account book that his preliminary work in organizing the company was recognized with a bookkeeping deposit of $1,500, applicable to 150 shares of stock. So far, so good. But then came two minor stockholders whom Huntington also names among the backers of the survey (after a mysterious James Peel had dropped out): Charles Marsh, who held fifty shares, and Lucius Booth, who pledged himself for only ten. I am inclined to think the inclusion of this pair represents another slip of memory. They were on the company's first board of directors and Huntington may therefore have supposed, years after the event, that he had lined them up as backers along with the others.

7. When Sam Brannan sued the railroad for an accounting in 1870 (in the District Court of the Fifteenth Judicial District of the State of California . . . a copy of the complaint is among the railroad pamphlets in the Bancroft Library), he estimated the resources of the founders at the time of incorporation as follows: Leland Stanford (whose grubstake share in the Lincoln Mine on Sutter Creek was just beginning to pay) and Collis Huntington, $50,000 each; Mark Hopkins and Charles Crocker, $30,000 each. In view of the assessed valuations noted in the text, Sam's evaluations were probably fair, except perhaps in Stanford's case—see note 8 below. James Bailey, it might be added, was generally considered to be the wealthiest of the original promoters, Fulton, *Epic of the Overland*, p. 14.

8. "Crocker Manuscript." For Mills: Huntington's letter to Speyer. The Speyer letter also states that Stanford delayed coming in because his older brother Charles controlled the purse strings and would not release the money. This soft slur, it is worth noting, came after Huntington and Stanford had broken completely. Sacramento tax rolls assessed Stanford's real and personal property in 1861 at $43,600, five times Huntington's. Stanford's biographer, George Clark, op. cit., p. 97, sets his fortune in 1861 at $250,000. Leland hardly needed to go begging to Charles for $1,500.

9. Cole, *Memoirs*.

10. Russel, *Improvements of Communication*, p. 285–95.
11. Clark, *Leland Stanford*, pp. 98–99. The letters were prompted by more considerations, of course, than just the railroad.
12. See note 15, Chapter 7.
13. In this account of the choice of directors I follow Strong, Pac. Ry. Commission, pp. 2838 ff., even though Strong obviously errs in saying that Stanford, who was in the East, attended the meeting.
14. Strong, as above, note 13.
15. Sacramento *Union*, July 8, 1860.
16. Pac. Ry. Commission, p. 2469. There is a slightly different version in Clark, op. cit., p. 173.
17. Pac. Ry. Commission, p. 2964.
18. Stuart Daggett, *Chapters on the History of the Southern Pacific* (New York, 1922), p. 48. Judah's account book, loc. cit., note 6 above.
19. E. B. Crocker to Cornelius Cole, April 9, 1864, Cole papers, University of California at Los Angeles.
20. This is assumption, based on the otherwise inexplicable fact that the first version of the bill reported to the House by the Select Committee on Pacific Railroads did include the California Central, the California Northern, and other dinky north-bound roads as recipients for generous federal grants. *Congressional Globe*, 37th Cong., 2d Sess. Also the Sacramento *Union*, February 25, 1862.
21. I reconstruct the trip from Strong's account in Pac. Ry. Commission, p. 2845, which is not entirely clear. There is a possibility, too, that this trip and the one described by Stanford (see note 16 above) are the same and that Huntington threaded Donner Pass only once that year, and not twice, as I have assumed.
22. A Sam Silliman, presumably a Nevada figurehead for the Californians, was also involved in the franchise manipulations. Though Todman won a franchise for his "Virginia, Carson & Truckee Railroad," he was never able to raise enough money to build it. Kneiss, *Bonanza Railroads*, p. 52; Thompson and West, *History of the State of Nevada* (facsimile edition, Berkeley, 1958), p. 274.
23. Bancroft, *Chronicles of the Builders*, Vol. VI, p. 217. Timothy Hopkins, *Hopkins Documents*, Vol. I, p. 8, Manuscript Collections, Stanford University Libraries, hereafter cited as Stanford University Manuscripts, sets the capitalization at $400,000. This seems high. For one thing, the incorporators—Huntington, Mark Hopkins, Charles Crocker, Strong, and E. L. Bradley of Dutch Flat, who together controlled three quarters of the stock—might have had trouble, at that particular juncture, in raising the 10 per cent down payment of $40,000 required by law.
24. Collis to Solon Huntington, December 26, 1861.
25. On August 11, 1862, the Sacramento *Union* carried a feature story, "The Railroad Bill—How It Passed Congress," by "Our Special Correspondent." The correspondent's style, his obvious intimacy with Sargent, and the close relationship between Judah and the *Union*, have led me to identify Judah as the author and to put into his mouth phrases from the article.

26. Glaab, *Kansas City and the Railroads*, pp. 104 ff.; Farnham, "The Pacific Railroad Act of 1862"; and the testimony which some of the Kansans who were engaged in the lobbying gave to the United States Pacific Railway Commission—pp. 1595 ff., 1672 ff., 3849 ff.

27. Huntington admired Stevens. "If anyone should crack the Pennsylvanian's skull it would let out the brains of the Republican party." Stevens was "a man who dared stand up for the right, as he understood it, regardless of clamor, prejudice, or any other influence which sways a mere politician." Bancroft, *Chronicles of the Builders*, Vol. V, p. 68.

28. Testimony of James C. Stone, one of the Kansas promoters, in Pac. Ry. Commission, p. 1609.

29. Pac. Ry. Commission, p. 4783. In addition to his salary of $150 a month and his expenses (he hit Huntington for another $200 in Washington—Judah account book), Judah received $25,000 in CP stock (face value) for his work in Washington—ibid.

30. It is fair to Judah to add that at the close of the session he was presented with a testimonial praising "his indefatigable exertions and intelligent explanations of the practical features of the enterprise." This unusual document was signed by forty-four representatives and seventeen senators. Judah, understandably pleased, reprinted it in his "Report of Chief Engineer of the Central Pacific Railroad Company on His Operations in the Atlantic States" (Sacramento, October 22, 1862).

31. *Congressional Globe*, 37th Cong., 2d Sess., p. 1708.

32. Bancroft and others have stated that Judah had reached an understanding on this point with Dame et. al. before leaving San Francisco for Washington on October 11, 1861. The contention overlooks the fact that the San Francisco & San José was named in the first version of the act but not in the second. Judah himself says ("Report . . ." cited in note 30 above) that he made the agreement in Washington with Senator McDougall and Representative Phelps in order, presumably, to gain their support for the revised bill. On three separate occasions, however, Huntington declared that he participated in the deal and that it was made in Washington directly with the San Franciscans concerned— Pac. Ry. Commission, p. 15; "Arguments Before the Committee on Military Affairs in the Senate" concerning Goat Island, in Vol. VI of the Central Pacific Railroad Pamphlets; and again during the 1896 congressional hearings concerning the railroad refunding bills. No doubt Phelps and McDougall were also involved.

33. Daggett, *Southern Pacific*, p. 47. Other commentators assign the credit to Senator James Harlan of Iowa—James McCague, *Moguls and Iron Men* (New York, 1964), pp. 29–30.

34. Sacramento *Union*, April 10, 1862.

35. In later years Huntington liked to brag that he personally collected the necessary arguments (they were worn threadbare by his time) and single-handedly pushed through the Pacific Railroad Act of 1862. California historians like to give the kudos for its passage to Judah—Oscar Lewis, *The Big Four*, for one example. Judah gives the major credit to Sargent —Sacramento *Union*, August 11, 1862. Wallace Farnham, close student

of the Union Pacific, ascribes success to the Kansas promoters, op. cit., p. 151. Stanley Hirschon, biographer of Grenville Dodge, nods toward the railroad boomers of Iowa and Chicago, p. 60. The bill itself was named for Congressman Rollins of Missouri. All had a part, but basically the bill passed because the popular mind was at last ready for it. The different special interests involved, Huntington included, simply maneuvered among themselves in an effort to catch a ride on the coattails.

9 PREPARATIONS

1. Sacramento *Daily Union* (hereafter cited as *Union*), "Record of Events," January 1, 1863. Clark, *Leland Stanford*, pp. 114–15. Phillips, *Cornelius Cole*, pp. 112–13. For Prentice: *Union*, March 22, 1862, and family notes from David Huntington.
2. Morrill: *Congressional Globe*, 37th Cong., 2d Sess., p. 1947. For the maneuvering that accompanied the act: Farnham, op. cit., and the same author's "The Weakened Spring of Government," *American Historical Review*, LXVIII (April 1963).
3. For the wagon road: Pac. Ry. Commission, pp. 2962–63. *Union*, June 5, 1862.
4. *Union*, July 4, 1862.
5. *Union*, July 12, August 6, 1862. Unauthenticated legend attributes to Judah a victory telegram reading, "We have drawn the elephant. Now let us see if we can harness him up." Huntington, who knew a good line when he saw one, told Bancroft that he was the author of that message, a manifest impossibility since Collis was not in Washington at the time of the alleged dispatch.
6. Of these 163 incorporating commissioners, 158 were named by Congress from twenty-five northern states; five were named by the Secretary of the Interior. California was represented by fifteen congressional and one secretarial appointees. Half of these sixteen were allied with the Central Pacific—Huntington, Judah, Bailey, and Marsh of the CP board; Donahue, Dame, and McLaughlin, who hoped to build the Sacramento–San Francisco link; and banker Darius O. Mills of Sacramento.

   The other eight appointees were bitter enemies of the first eight. One was John P. Robinson of the Sacramento Valley Railroad, which would be destroyed if the Central Pacific supplanted it in the foothills. Another was S. J. Hensley, head of the California Steam Navigation Company. That firm held a monopoly on water traffic between San Francisco and Sacramento and wanted no competition from a railroad. There was Louis McLane. He was involved in stagecoach lines that held lucrative contracts with the Wells Fargo Express Company. (Louis' brother Charles was president of Wells Fargo Express Company; their brother Allan McLane was an official of the Pacific Mail Steamship Company, which monopolized traffic across Panama; the steamship line and the stagecoaches would lose their shirts to a continental railroad.) There was George Mowe, a director of the Pioneer Stage Lines that ran over Johnson Pass to Nevada. Why would he want a railroad? Why would C. R. Hosmer, president of the Pacific Postal Telegraph Company, which would be injured by the railroad's telegraphic facilities? O. M. Wozencraft, nominee of the Secretary of the Interior, had once tried to promote a northern wagon road to Honey Lake; he was still opposed to a rail crossing of the Sierra as far south as Donner Summit.

It was a real bagful of fighting tomcats. And yet Congress, in its obscure wisdom, put them all onto the same gigantic board responsible for forming the Union Pacific.

7. *Union*, August 17, 1862. Bailey returned on August 31.
8. *Union*, November 11, 1862; January 1, 1863.
9. The company's full answer to routes proposed as substitutes for Donner Pass is in Judah's report of October 22, 1862.
10. Judah "Report of the Chief Engineer to the Board of Directors and President of the Central Pacific Railroad" (Sacramento, July 1, 1863). See also Winton, Speech to the Nevada Senate.
11. The Sacramento Valley Railroad's line of attack is revealed in letters written by Lester L. Robinson, February 3 and 23, 1865, to the Joint Committee on Railroads of the Nevada legislature and in Stanford's and Crocker's replies, written to the same body on February 14, 1865— Vol. V, CPRR Pamphlets.
12. Judah's report of October 22, 1862.
13. So Huntington said when reminiscing to Bancroft's researcher twenty-six years or so after the event, "Huntington Manuscript."
14. Data on the company's early bond issues can be found in the circulars of Fisk and Hatch (Vol. I, CPRR Pamphlets), a New York bond house which began handling the securities "when," one prospectus read, "the road was but a strip of rails over which a man could walk in a day."
15. *Union*, November 12 and 22, 1862. Hittell, *History of California*, Vol. IV, pp. 348–49.
16. "Huntington Manuscript."
17. Boruck's testimony, Pac. Ry. Commission, p. 3421.
18. "Crocker Manuscript," p. 14. See also Crocker's testimony to Pac. Ry. Commission, p. 3651.
19. *Union*, February 6, 1863.
20. Bancroft, *Chronicles of the Builders*, Vol. VI, p. 119.
21. *Union*, December 10, 1862.
22. Ernest Wiltsee, *Gold Rush Steamers* (San Francisco, 1938).

10 THE QUAGMIRE

1. *Union*, February 17, March 5 and 9, 1863. Wesley S. Griswold, *A Work of Giants* (New York, 1962), pp. 42–47. Glaab, *Kansas City and the Railroads*, pp. 111–14.
2. *Union*, January 24, February 17 and 19, 1863. The "Huntington Manuscript" gives an involved and in places almost incoherent account of Collis' activities on behalf of the five-foot standard.

3. Charles E. Russell, "The Great Millionaire Mill," *Hampton's Magazine,* April 1910.

4. Huntington's account of the rupture with Flint, Peabody & Company is in Bancroft, *Chronicles of the Builders,* Vol. V, pp. 56–58. Unmentioned in that summary is the fact that on August 1, 1863, James P. Flint received thirty $1,000 Central Pacific Railroad bonds "for services as per arrangement"—Pac. Ry. Commission, p. 4783. In view of the failure of Flint, Peabody & Company to sell CPRR securities, the payment could hardly have been a commission. It may represent a penalty for the breaking of the sales contract. It is my guess (but only a guess), however, that it may have been a good will offering to counter the blandishments of John P. and Lester L. Robinson, who were desperately trying to put together a California railroad network in opposition to the Central Pacific. According to the Sacramento *Union* of February 17, 1863, John Robinson was in the East doing all he could to harm the CP. Whether or not he made contact with Flint, Peabody & Company in furtherance of these designs is impossible to say. Anyway, James Flint received $30,000 in Central Pacific bonds for some unspecified reason.

5. Henry Thomas Holmes, a Sacramento friend of Huntington's, claimed to have had these details directly from Collis—Holmes interview, Bancroft Library. See also Bancroft, *Chronicles of the Builders,* Vol. V, p. 58.

6. Stanford's first report to the company, July 14, 1863, as printed in the *Union,* July 15. In addition to listing the equipment purchased, the report adds that Huntington successfully disposed of 900 bonds in the East. One of the many tables in the U. S. Pacific Railway Commission report says that 783 bonds were marketed during 1863. The difference may be the bonds held by Oliver Ames as security for his loan. For costs, see E. H. Miller, Jr., in *Letter to Montanya et al.,* Vol. V, CPRR Pamphlets.

7. The amounts of county bond issues to be used for purchasing Central Pacific stock were as follows: Placer County, $250,000 in 8 per cent twenty-year bonds; Sacramento County, $300,000; San Francisco County, $600,000. For purchasing Western Pacific stock: Santa Clara County, $150,000; San Joaquin County, $250,000; San Francisco County, $400,000. The San Francisco & San José Railroad, which was controlled by the people who hoped to build the Western Pacific, had already received from the city and county of San Francisco bond aid of $300,000; from Santa Clara County, $200,000; from San Mateo County, $100,000. (Hittell, *History of California,* Vol. IV, pp. 467–71).

8. This fantasy was aired on the floor of the Nevada senate on February 27, 1865, by N. W. Winton. McDougall of California also warned the U. S. Senate about French-Mexican designs on the Coast states, but did not involve Pioche and Bayerque by name—*Union,* February 4, 1863.

9. *Union,* May 21, 1863.

10. Daggett, *Southern Pacific,* pp. 32–33.

11. "The Pacific Railroad, A Defense against Its Enemies," n.p., December 1864, Vol. V, CPRR Pamphlets.

12. Huntington's opinion of Phil Stanford was voiced in a letter to Mark Hopkins, April 11, 1867—Stanford University Manuscripts.
13. For the injunctions: *Union*, May 19, 20, 21, 1863.
14. W. W. Robinson, *Lawyers of Los Angeles* (Los Angeles, 1955), p. 337.
15. *Union*, March 5, 1863. "Crocker Manuscript," p. 29.
16. *Union*, July 15, 1863. The rate of shrinkage is indicated by Stanford's letter to the San Francisco *Alta California*, May 15, wherein he declared that subscriptions at that time amounted to $800,000.
17. Bancroft, *History of California*, Vol. VII, p. 352; Clark, *Leland Stanford*, pp. 149–60.
18. In his report to the company of July 1, 1863, Judah, though not mentioning the wagon road specifically, dwelt on the need of care in meeting congressional requirements. For his resentment of the highway, see Anna Judah manuscript.
19. Pac. Ry. Commission, pp. 3568–70, 3643, 3680. The U.S. surveyor-general for California, Edward Fitzgerald Beale, favored an equally flat point nine miles from Sacramento.
20. Lewis, *The Big Four*, p. 45. Pac. Ry. Commission, p. 2861.
21. Ibid., pp. 2965–66.
22. Judah's report of July 1, 1863. *Union*, July 2 and 16, 1863. For costs: Miller, *Letter to Montanya et al.*
23. Wheat, "Judah," p. 262. Earle Heath, "From Trail to Rail," *Southern Pacific Bulletin*, May 1927.
24. Judah's account book. By the summer of 1863 he had been able to pay in $10,403.33 of the $25,000 due on the stock.
25. Collis to E. B. Crocker, Jr., May 1868: "If you should see [Grenville] Dodge you would swear that it was Judah . . . the same low cunning . . . a large amount of that kind of cheap dignity that Judah had." *Letters from Collis P. Huntington to Mark Hopkins, Leland Stanford, Charles Crocker, E. B. Crocker, and D. D. Cotton [sic] Aug. 20, 1867—Aug. 5, 1869* (privately printed, New York, 1892). Hereafter cited as *Collected Letters*. For additional data see bibliographic note.
26. Strong in Pac. Ry. Commission, pp. 2965–66.
27. This summary for the battle for control is pieced together from both the "Huntington Manuscript" and "Huntington Typescript," Huntington's 1899 letter to James Speyer, and Bancroft, *Chronicles of the Builders*, Vol. V, pp. 62–64. The *Union*, July 16, 1863, dates the decision to shift the tracks to I Street as having been made the day before, which indicates that the Big Four made their position on the board secure before opening the battle, a strategic necessity unmentioned in Huntington's various reminiscences.
28. "Huntington Manuscript."
29. Wheat, op. cit., p. 262. Evans, *Collis Potter Huntington*, pp. 74, 98. Lester L. Robinson, "Letter to the Joint Committee on Railroads of the Nevada Legislature," February 3, 1865, Vol. V, CPRR Pamphlets, says that the $100,000 in bonds were given Judah to keep him silent about the impossibility of building a railroad over Donner Pass.
30. Stanford to the Senate Committee of the Nevada Legislature, February

14, 1865, Vol. V, CPRR Pamphlets; Clark, *Leland Stanford*, p. 191; Strong in Pac. Ry. Commission, p. 2967; Anna Judah manuscript.
31. *Union*, November 10 and 11, 1863.
32. Pac. Ry. Commission, P. 3113.

11 ANTICLIMAX

1. Figures from a letter of E. B. Crocker to Cornelius Cole, March 2, 1864, Cole Papers, University of California, Los Angeles.
2. McCague, *Moguls and Iron Men*, p. 99.
3. Farnham, "The Weakened Spring of Government," p. 662–80.
4. Evans, *Collis Potter Huntington*, pp. 213–14.
5. Glaab, *Kansas City and the Railroads*, pp. 112–229.
6. Pac. Ry. Commission, p. 3037.
7. "Crocker Manuscript."
8. Sargent to Cole, May 11, 1864, Cole Papers, indicates the feelings of the Republicans toward the Union Democrats who had outwitted them: "The Conness horde is the mean, dirty fringe of the Democratic party . . . contemptible in purpose . . . but firmly settled upon the abdicated throne of Republicanism." Huntington's problem appears in a letter of his to Hopkins, December 22, 1865, Stanford University Manuscripts: "[Cole] likes you or for that matter all my associates better than he dus me . . . for the Reason that when I went to Washington I counted on him as oure friend . . . and as we did not expect so much good feeling from Conness I of course went with him (Conness) but all the time being friendly with Cole and doing all that I could to bring about a good and friendly feeling between him and Conness."
9. David L. Joslyn, "The Romance of the Railroads Entering Sacramento," *Bulletin 48* of the Railway and Locomotive Society, March 1939.
10. Thomas G. and Maria Robins Belden, *So Fell the Angels* (Boston, 1956), p. 80–127, passim.
11. House Report 78 [of the so-called Wilson Committee], 43d Cong., 3rd Sess. Cf. the Poland Committee on Crédit Mobilier, House Report 77, ibid.
12. Phillips, *Cornelius Cole*, p. 255.
13. Belden, op. cit., p. 56
14. David Sessions, handwritten note appended to the typescript of his interview with Huntington.
15. Another indication that Huntington did not keep close tabs on the Senate version of the bill lies in provisions that would have granted aid to two California short lines. One was the San Francisco & Sacramento. As early as 1857 Judah had predicted that the line, projected to run from the west side of the Sacramento River opposite Sacramento City in a straight line to the port of Benicia (from whence it would jump to San Francisco by ferryboat), was certain to become the western end of the transcontinental, for it was the shortest possible route. The other line the Senate proposed to aid was the Sacramento, Stockton & San Francisco. This company hoped to drive due west from Stockton to Oakland,

run trestles from there over shoal water to Yerba Buena Island (currently an anchor of the Bay Bridge) and build ferry facilities for connecting Yerba Buena with San Francisco.

Both roads would offer quicker service to San Francisco than the Western Pacific's long line around the Bay's south shore, and hence were threats to it. Huntington, however, was committed to helping the Western Pacific. When he belatedly learned, from the debates on the floor of the Senate, of the presumptions of the rival roads, he went to work on Conness and Cole, and the clauses favoring them were stricken from the final version of the bill.

Another clause that would have confirmed the CP's assignment of its Sacramento–San Francisco rights to McLaughlin, Houston, and associates was also deleted from the Senate bill, in spite of Huntington's protests. The lawmakers were reluctant to award franchises to individuals and would not approve the transfer until it was applied for in the name of the Western Pacific. This was finally accomplished in October 1864.

A summary of all these maneuvers is in Russel, *Improvements of Communication*, pp. 319–20.

16. House Report 77, 42d Cong., 3d Sess., p. xviii.
17. *Union*, March 21, 1864.
18. In his *Memoirs*, pp. 179–81, Cole declared that he was the only man on the House Select Committee who had crossed the continent by stagecoach and as a result commanded the full confidence of committee chairman Thaddeus Stevens. "It is not too much to say that I had my own way on the committee." And he added, with no apparent notion that the remark might raise eyebrows, that he was able to promote Huntington's wishes "in almost every particular." Time, obviously, was softening some of the harsher realities, since Huntington's wishes were not observed in almost every particular. For a more dispassionate view, see Russel, op. cit.; Lewis B. Haney, *Congressional History of Railroads* (Madison, Wis., 1910); Griswold, *A Work of Giants*, pp. 62–75.
19. *Congressional Globe*, 38th Cong., June 21, 1864.
20. Washburne in the *Congressional Globe*, 40th Cong., 2d Sess., p. 2135.
21. In 1866 both Conness and Representative Thaddeus Stevens declared, in brazen contradiction of what is printed in the *Congressional Globe*, 38th Cong., May 23, 1864, that the 150-mile limit was never contained in the bill passed by Congress, but was "smuggled" in later, during the printing of the act—Conness, *Congressional Globe*, 39th Cong., 1st Sess., p. 3261. Stevens, ibid., p. 3422. Huntington carried on the same pretense when interviewed by Bancroft's scribes, adding that he had not worried. "I said to Mr. Union Pacific I would take it [the limitation] out when I wanted." "Huntington Manuscript." Actually, it is very unlikely that in 1864 he would have risked saying any such thing to Thomas C. Durant.
22. Certain iron manufacturers did accept his Sacramento and Placer county bonds, and also a few company bonds, in payment for about 5,500 tons of rail—Central Pacific, Annual Report, September 1864, summarized in Bancroft, *Chronicles of the Builders*, Vol. VI.

1. The road cost $195,000. Huntington to the Senate's Committee on Military Affairs re the Goat Island lease, Vol. VI, CPRR Pamphlets.
2. A series of stories that appeared in the Sacramento *Union* during the last weeks of August 1864, reflects the city's pain over the new road.
3. For years afterward, Bishop's figures, which were never put to test, were quoted by Nevadans to "prove" that the Central Pacific's construction costs in the Sierra were outrageously padded. For instance, see Thompson and West's *History of the State of Nevada,* pp. 272–75.
4. Stanford's speech was successful enough that the Central Pacific printed it in pamphlet form in 1865—Vol. V, CPRR Pamphlets.
5. Bancroft, *Chronicles of the Builders,* Vol. VI, pp. 135–36. A possible sidelight: in August 1864, Sheriff McClatchy received ten shares of Central Pacific stock in return for unspecified services—Pac. Ry. Commission, p. 4784.
6. Kneiss, *Bonanza Railroads,* pp. 27–28. E. B. Crocker to C. Cole, December, n.d., 1864, Cole Papers.
7. Pac. Ry. Commission, pp. 2779, 4531. Brannan, it should be noted, never finished the last seven miles of the Yuba Railroad to Marysville.
8. Daggett, *Southern Pacific,* p. 21.
9. Griswold, *A Work of Giants,* pp. 108–12.
10. "Huntington Manuscript."
11. Daggett, op. cit., p. 21.
12. Presumably these figures included the cost of rails, timber, work trains, sidings, depots in the little mountain towns, etc. Most fabricated material could be purchased in the East in greenbacks and the freight around the Horn paid the same way. Thus the company's insistence that it had to convert *all* its paper into gold was not fully accurate. Even so the depreciation was onerous—more onerous than later critics of the company were inclined to admit when making charges about excessive profits.
13. Winton, speech to the Nevada Senate.
14. Company report of September 1864, summarized in Bancroft, *Chronicles of the Builders,* Vol. VI, p. 226. There seems no way to determine how much stock (in addition to the 5,500 shares held by Sacramento and Placer counties) was ever in the hands of private investors. Almost certainly it was less than ten thousand shares.
15. E. B. Crocker gave Cole credit for passage of the bill. Letter to Cole of April 12, 1865, Cole Papers.
16. Brannan's suit against the Central Pacific et al., in the District Court of the Fifteenth Judicial District of the State of California, in and for the City and County of San Francisco. Hereafter cited as Brannan Suit.
17. Winton, op. cit.
18. That Phil Stanford was one of the original six (not four as is generally stated) participants in Charles Crocker & Company and that Huntington did not trust him is made clear by Huntington's letter to Hopkins of

May 11, 1864, Stanford University Manuscripts. Soon thereafter Phil Stanford was eliminated from the construction company.

19. Wearisome speculations have been substituted for the unrecoverable facts about Charles Crocker & Company and its successor, the Contract & Finance Company. The nearest thing to evidence is the testimony scattered throughout the reports of the Pacific Railway Commission of 1887 —pp. 2630 ff., 3045 ff., 3207, 3436 ff., 3608, 3640–66, passim—and the transcripts of congressional hearings held in connection with the refunding bills of 1896—House Report 1497 and Senate Report 778, 54th Cong., 1st Sess., 1896–97, serials 3462 and 3365. For summaries: Daggett, op. cit., pp. 71 ff.; Henry T. Carmen and Charles H. Mueller, "The Contract and Finance Company of the Central Pacific Railroad," *Mississippi Valley Historical Review*, December 1927.

20. Cole Papers.

21. *Union*, January 8, 1866.

22. The letter is in the Holladay Collection.

23. Conness, a Democrat, was still trying to control California politics through the Union party that he and Stanford had patched together in 1862. In 1865, the glue did not hold, mainly because Conness tried to gerrymander the state in such wise that the new legislature of 1865 would be composed of men committed to electing his protégé Governor Frederick Low to the U. S. Senate in place of James McDougall, whose term was due to expire on March 4, 1867. The Sacramento County nominating caucus rebelled. "Hickory canes were first plied; and then resort was had to spittoons, which flew from side to side like bombs on a battle field. . . . finally chairs were broken up to supply clubs." Hittell, *History of California*, Vol. IV, p. 394. Eventually the legislature elected Cole instead of Low to the Senate. Thereafter, California's two Senators, Conness and Cole, scarcely nodded to each other in passing, a hostility that eventually would roughen the way for some of Huntington's own machinations.

24. Collis to Hopkins, April 4, 1866: "We have used of railroad money sinse I came here [in the fall of 1863 presumably] $50,201.91." On May 11, 1866: "I used $15,000 of the railroad Co. money for H & H." On August 3, 1866: "I took today $10,000 of railroad money for H & H." Huntington to Hopkins Correspondence, Stanford University Manuscripts.

25. Ibid., January 3, 1866; August 8, 1866.

26. Ibid., December 22, 1865; April 20, 1866.

27. For Charles Stanford: Huntington to Hopkins, ibid., April 4, 1866. The next year Charles tried again to buy an interest and was again turned down—ibid., August 29, 1867. For Emmons: ibid., April 16, May 17, 1866. For Phil Stanford: ibid., May 11, 1866.

28. The expensive stimulus to the Union Pacific of the race with the Eastern Division is not always recognized by historians, although Oakes Ames was vocal on the point—Bancroft, *Chronicles of the Builders*, Vol. V, 586–87. Ames also recognized Durant's mistake in yielding 150 miles to Huntington in 1864. That much conceded, Collis inevitably was going to ask for more.

29. For the debates: *Congressional Globe,* 39th Cong., 1st Sess., pp. 3224, 3256–57, 3261–66.
30. So Huntington ("Manuscript") told the story to Bancroft twenty years later. Bancroft, alert to libel laws, omitted Alley's name in repeating the yarn in *Chronicles of the Builders,* Vol. V, p. 68–69. Huntington, incidentally, recalled that the bill passed the Senate by a vote of 34–8. Actually, it was closer: 20–12, with seventeen members, including McDougall of California, absent.
31. Cole to E. Burke, December 12, 1866, Cole Papers. "I hereby . . . empower you to . . . manage my interest in the California and Oregon Railroad Company . . ."
32. In telling the tale years later Huntington gave the number of tons purchased as sixty thousand—Bancroft, op. cit., pp. 60–62. As usual he was exaggerating, or else Bancroft doctored the figures to make them more impressive. In round figures, a hundred tons of the light rail used in those days would make one mile of track. ("This 33,000 tons of rails will lay 350 miles of road." Huntington to E. B. Crocker, December 7, 1867, *Collected Letters,* Vol. I.) Since the distance from Sacramento to Promontory Point, Utah, is less than seven hundred miles, the Central Pacific obviously did not need sixty thousand tons in 1866; and did not have it, either, for Huntington went on buying rail in ten-thousand-ton lots during 1867 and 1868. Moreover, twenty-three ships would not carry sixty thousand tons. Rails went in sailing vessels carrying two to three hundred tons each—Huntington to Hopkins, March 7, 1868, ibid. Thus twenty-three vessels would carry about six thousand tons. But what's an extra zero in the spinning of a good yarn?

13 THE TENTACLES BEGIN TO GROW

1. Griswold, *A Work of Giants,* p. 200.
2. Theodore Pease, "Browning," *Dictionary of American Biography.*
3. Lengthy excerpts from the speech are in Clark, *Leland Stanford,* pp. 228–30.
4. Hittell, *History of California,* Vol. IV, p. 487.
5. Stanford University Manuscripts.
6. The growth of Huntington's concept can be followed in part in the bond prospectuses issued for the Central Pacific by the brokerage firm of Fisk and Hatch, Vol. I, CPRR Pamphlets. The map in the first broadside, dated March 1867 but prepared some weeks earlier, shows the CP's projected rail line running south of Great Salt Lake and ending at Salt Lake City. By May 1867, the line had shifted north of the lake and was thrusting up Weber Canyon through "The Great Coal Basin" to Ft. Bridger, Wyoming, on one of the tributaries of the Green River.

   In testifying before the Pacific Railroad Commission of 1887, Huntington frankly declared (p. 2469) that he wanted to reach Green River in order to shut the Union Pacific out of Portland. He discusses the other rewards of reaching Green River in letters to Stanford on November 22, 1867, and to E. B. Crocker, December 7, 27, 1867—*Collected Letters,* Vol. I.

7. Griswold, *A Work of Giants,* p. 233. Since construction costs in general were padded, these figures may have been, too.

8. Huntington to E. B. Crocker, October 3, 1867, *Collected Letters,* Vol. I.

9. Clark, *Leland Stanford,* p. 224.

10. Huntington to Stanford, September 28, 1867, *Collected Letters,* Vol. I: "I have got Fisk & Hatch to sell our bonds on the road east of the Cala. State line. They would not do it for some time. . . ."

11. Franchot was selling CP bonds as early as April 1866—Huntington to Hopkins, April 4, 1866, Stanford University Manuscripts. For his effectiveness in the Schenectady area: Huntington to E. B. Crocker, October 9, 1867, *Collected Letters,* Vol. I. For placing bonds "in small lots amongst the people": Huntington to Stanford, September 28, 1867, ibid.; to E. B. Crocker, September 30, 1867, ibid.

12. Clark, *Leland Stanford,* pp. 224–25, quotes some of Stanford's letters on the subject of securing recommendations.

13. Ibid., pp. 225–27. In his reminiscences Huntington told David Sessions ("Huntington Typescript") that he personally borrowed *all* the money needed for crossing the Sierra (as usual, he exaggerated) and set the figure at seven million dollars. Stanford in Pac. Ry. Commission, pp. 2758–60, says that by the time the railroad had crossed the mountains, the floating debt stood between six and seven million. The figures probably are inflated. They are related to the company's justification of the Contract & Finance Company on the grounds of financial desperation, a questionable assertion that will be considered later in this chapter. There was a heavy debt, however, even if the exact amount is unascertainable.

14. Huntington to E. B. Crocker, September 27, 1867, *Collected Letters,* Vol. I: "The money market is rather tight now, but I borrowed $450,000 when money was easy." See also ibid., October 26 to Stanford.

15. Pac. Ry. Commission, p. 2759.

16. Letters concerning the sale are in the Stanford University Manuscripts, Huntington to Hopkins: January 3, June 7, 1866; March 29, May 24, November 13, 15, 16, 19, 20, December 8, 1867. See also Evans, *Collis Potter Huntington,* pp. 42–45, and Cioffi, "Mark Hopkins," pp. 100 ff.

A tenth interest in Huntington, Hopkins & Company was not as paltry as it may sound. It became one of the largest hardware companies in North America. By 1890 the firm had a five-story granite and iron headquarters building in San Francisco, an enlarged three-story building in Sacramento, branches in several other California cities, in Hawaii, British Columbia, and Mexico. The partners, in addition to Huntington and Hopkins, were Albert Gallatin, William Foye, Charles Miller (a relative of E. H. Miller, Jr. of the Central Pacific), and Horace Seaton (a nephew of Elizabeth Huntington).

17. Huntington to Hopkins, March 15 and December 8, 1867, Stanford University Manuscripts.

18. Huntington to E. B. Crocker, September 18, 1867; to Hopkins, November 17, 1867—*Collected Letters,* Vol. I.

19. A highly colored account of Elliott's Oregon activities may be found in Henry Villard's posthumous *The Early History of Transportation in Oregon,* edited by Oswald Villard (Eugene, Ore., 1944). Several other accounts of the Oregon railway shenanigans are available in early (1902–06, 1924) issues of the *Oregon Historical Quarterly.* Unfortunately, the antics of Elliott and his heirs in California have not received equal attention.

20. Huntington to E. B. Crocker, September 23, 1867, *Collected Letters,* Vol. I: "The owners of the Cala. and Oregon Rail Road say that they are going to Congress next winter and get that land grant away from us. . . . I would like to see them do it."

21. Huntington to E. B. Crocker, August 24, 1867, *Collected Letters,* Vol. I. To Hopkins, August 29, 1867, Stanford University Manuscripts. One reason prompting Wilson to suppose that he could gain the ear of the Union Pacific was the Lambard brothers, one of whom lived in Sacramento. Stockholders in Crédit Mobilier, the Lambards also owned bonds of the California Central and Yuba roads—Huntington to E. B. Crocker August 23, 1867, *Collected Letters,* Vol. I.

22. E. B. Crocker to Hopkins, quoted in Clark, *Leland Stanford,* p. 235. Several other letters concerning the clash are in ibid., pp. 233–42.

23. Daggett, *Southern Pacific,* pp. 86–87.

24. Bancroft, *Chronicles of the Builders,* Vol. VI, pp. 154–56.

25. Clark, op. cit., p. 235.

26. Stanford to Hopkins, April 19, 1867: "We are waiting for answer from Huntington with such patience as we can command." More of the same, E. B. Crocker to Hopkins, April 29, Clark, op. cit., p. 242.

27. Ibid., pp. 238, 241.

28. Ibid., p. 243.

14 OVERCONFIDENCE

1. Evans, *Collis Potter Huntington,* pp. 167–69.

2. Huntington to E. B. Crocker, September 9, 18, 23, 1867, *Collected Letters,* Vol. I.

3. Huntington to E. B. Crocker, August 30, September 7, ibid. To Hopkins, October 2, 1867, ibid.

4. Huntington to E. B. Crocker, September 11, 1867, ibid. See also the photograph in Evans, op. cit., p. 254.

5. For Fisk and Hatch: Huntington to Stanford, September 28, 1867, *Collected Letters,* Vol. I. For grapes: Huntington to Hopkins, October 17, ibid. References in *Collected Letters,* Vol. I, to improved bond sales after the holing through of the tunnel are so numerous that it is impractical to cite them individually.

6. Huntington to Hopkins, August 29, 1867, Stanford University Manuscripts.

7. He spent part of Christmas Day, 1867, writing a long letter to E. B. Crocker (*Collected Letters,* Vol. I) in which he said, concerning the Articles of Association of Contract & Finance Company, "If you are all

pleased with it I have nothing to say, but if we could work on as we have been doing it would have been as well in my opinion."

8. Huntington to Hopkins, March 31, 1876, *Collected Letters,* Vol. III, p. 481: "We used up something over $64,000 in bonds per mile in building the road in Nevada and Utah. The bonds we sold at about par in currency. . . . If I remember correctly, Crocker says the road lost about $17,000 per mile. You can burn this." In the endless speculation concerning the profits of the Contract & Finance Company, these figures seem never to have been noticed before. For the figures that the associates paraded in public, see Pac. Ry. Commission, p. 2979.

9. See citations in Note 19, Chapter 12.

10. Huntington to C. Crocker, December 27, September 9, 1867, *Collected Letters,* Vol. I.

11. Stanford University Manuscripts. On May 30, 1868, Stanford gave his wife nine thousand shares of C&F stock and wrote her (ibid.) that the stock was "worth in all probability much more than par. . . . They [the certificates] are for you and will secure you a competence in case of accident to your devoted husband." Nine million dollars, especially in those days, was indeed a competence. So much for the poor state of C&F stock.

12. Huntington to E. B. Crocker, August 24, September 27, November 1, 1867, *Collected Letters,* Vol. I.

13. Huntington to E. B. Crocker, December 29, 1867; February 25, 1868, ibid. Control of the California Central's extension, the Yuba Railroad, eluded them for another year, however.

14. Huntington to Hopkins, December 29, 1867, ibid.

15. Huntington to E. B. Crocker, October 29, 1867, ibid.

16. Huntington to Hopkins, November 17, December 21, 1867; to E. B. Crocker, October 29, 1867, all ibid.

17. Huntington to E. B. Crocker, October 29, 1867; February 21, March 13, 1868; to Hopkins, November 19, 29, December 16, 1867, all ibid.

18. Huntington to Hopkins, November 19, 1867, ibid.

19. There are cryptic allusions to this waterfront property in Huntington to Crocker, November 26, 1867, and to Hopkins, November 27, 1867, January 27, 1868, *Collected Letters,* Vol. I. The details of the scheme as it existed at that time are obscure.

20. Huntington to Stanford, November 20, 1867, ibid.

15 THE RACE HEATS UP

NB: Unless otherwise noted, all citations in this chapter and the next are to letters written by Huntington and reproduced in *Collected Letters,* Vol. I.

1. To C. Crocker, October 9, December 7, 1867; April 21, 1868.
2. To C. Crocker, December 27, 1867.
3. To C. Crocker, December 7, 1867.
4. To Hopkins, February 5, 1868.
5. To C. Crocker, January 1, 3, 26, 1868. To Hopkins, February 24, 1868. To E. B. Crocker, January 1, February 21, 1868.
6. To C. Crocker, January 21, February 3, 1868.

7. To C. Crocker, January 1, February 22, 1868.
8. To C. Crocker, February 22, 1868.
9. To Hopkins, February 5, 1868.
10. Huntington's letter to Browning apparently has not survived. I deduce its contents from Collis' own summary to Crocker, April 21, 1868.
11. To Hopkins, November 14, 1867.
12. To C. Crocker, April 21, 1868.
13. To Hopkins, April 13, 1868. To C. Crocker, June 8, 13, 23, 1868.
14. Stanford to Huntington, May 20, 1868. CP telegram book, Stanford University Manuscripts.
15. To Hopkins, May 16, 1868. To Stanford, May 22, 1868.
16. To Hopkins, May 23, 30, 1868.
17. To Stanford, May 29, 1868.
18. Leland Stanford to Jane Stanford, May 30, 1868, Stanford University Manuscripts.
19. Stanford to Hopkins, June 9, 1868, quoted in Clark, *Leland Stanford*, p. 245.
20. To Hopkins January 27, June 6, 1868; to E. B. Crocker, April 6, 24, June 9, 1868.
21. To Stanford, June 8, 1868.
22. Ibid.; to E. B. Crocker, June 13, 1868. During this period one of the government's directors on the UP board was also complaining to Browning about the UP's shoddy work—Griswold, *A Work of Giants*, p. 268.
23. To C. Crocker, June 23, 1868.
24. To C. Crocker, June 9, 1868; to Hopkins, June 10, 1868.
25. To C. Crocker, June 9, 1868. The strictures on Stanford's work habits were not wholly justified. He was up at five on at least one morning to look over Weber Canyon with Engineer George Gray—Clark, *Leland Stanford*, p. 245.
26. To Charles Crocker, July 1, 1868.
27. Montague to Huntington, June 30, 1868, CP telegram book.
28. To Charles Crocker, July 20, 1868. Allusions to the scheme are frequent in the letters Huntington wrote during this period. For example: to [E.B.?] Crocker, June 12, 13, and to all the associates throughout October and November.

In connection with amoral standards, consider the following extract from a letter Huntington wrote Ed Crocker on March 28, 1868: "As the Union Company are so very corrupt that it has to a considerable extent demoralized all the roads being built under the Pacific Railroad Act, I should not be surprised if Congress should order a committee to overhaul all the companies, and while I know everything is all right with the Central Pacific, I would be very careful that the company's books should make it so plain that anyone could so see it." In other words, *rig the record*.

To censure on this point, Collis would no doubt have replied that he was forced to act as he did. Congress, too, was corrupt. In May, President Andrew Johnson would come within one vote of being impeached. The administration was discredited, confused, adrift. "Bidding" for favor was often the only way anything could be accomplished in

Washington. Collis felt quite sincerely that in order to save himself and the Central Pacific he had to fight fire with fire. His letters are studded with references not to Congressmen he seduced, but to Congressmen and administrative officials demanding pay for their favors. In the case of adultery, *who* is guilty?

29. To Stanford, July 17, 1868.
30. To Crocker, July 1, 1868.

16 GUARDING THE FLANKS

1. E. H. Miller, Jr., to the Wilson Committee of Congress in 1873, as quoted in Galloway, *The First Transcontinental Railroad*, p. 113. The figures proclaimed by Fisk and Hatch were approximately the same: $664,206 in 1866 and $1,139,740 in 1867—Pamphlet 20, Vol. I, CPRR Pamphlets.
2. Daggett, *Southern Pacific*, pp. 41–42; Hittell, *History of California*, Vol. IV, pp. 482–83.
3. Huntington to Hopkins, April 11, 1867, Stanford University Manuscripts.
4. Huntington to [E.B.?] Crocker, February 25, 1868.
5. "Crocker Manuscript," p. 35. Huntington to James Speyer, undated, 1899, Holladay Collection; Hopkins to Huntington, February 15, 1873, *Collected Letters*, Vol. IV.
6. Daggett, op. cit., p. 122.
7. Huntington to E. B. Crocker, May 4, 1868.
8. Ibid. and February 21, 1868.
9. Huntington to Hopkins, January 27, 1868; to E. B. Crocker, January 29. Under Tevis' leadership, the Southern Pacific finished acquiring control of the San Francisco & San José on February 4, 1868—Clark, *Leland Stanford*, p. 261. Although the same men now dominated both lines, the companies were maintained as separate entities and, so far as the law was concerned, would have to be dealt with separately.
10. William A. Bell, a young Englishman who accompanied the surveyors, left a lively account of the West as he saw it in Palmer's company, *New Tracks in North America* (London, 1869).
11. For the acquisition of the SP: Huntington to E. B. Crocker, March 13 (a postscript), March 18, April 28, May 4, July 2, 1868; to Hopkins, March 31, April 17, May 26, June 6, 1868, all *Collected Letters*, Vol. I; also January 26, 1870, *Collected Letters*, Vol. II; to Stanford, May 29, July 17, 20, 1868, *Collected Letters*, Vol. I. The associates paid for their five-eighths interest about $360,000. Part was paid in the form of Central Pacific bonds and part as Central Pacific stock. The associates also took an option on the San Francisco & San José. Since this was an operating railroad, the cost was far higher—$3.25 million in gold. The associates did not succeed in raising that much hard cash until well into the 1870s—an interesting sidelight concerning the millions they were reputed already to have at their fingertips.
12. Daggett, op. cit., p. 98.
13. Ibid., pp. 85–91. Stanford conducted the Oakland negotiations, which

involved his pet road, the Western Pacific, without keeping Huntington abreast of developments. On April 24, 1868, Collis wrote querulously to E. B. Crocker, "I notice a kind of water property at Oakland, Tevis, Stanford, and other trustees. What of it, and who owns it?"

14. For the Perry-Scott-Huntington negotiations: Huntington's letters to E. B. Crocker, March 21, April 21, 25, May 4, 1868. To Hopkins, March 31, April 13, 17, 1868.

15. Huntington to Hopkins, April 14, 1868.

16. Huntington to Charles Crocker, May 9, 1868.

17. Haney, *Congressional History of Railways,* p. 81. Also Huntington to E. B. Crocker, May 5, 1868: "The [New York] *Tribune* has been very strongly opposed to aiding any railroads . . . but I have had several talks with them lately and I think they are going to be pleasant." Diffidence about his ability to handle people was not one of Huntington's more notable characteristics.

18. Huntington to Hopkins, June 6, 1868.

19. For Donnelly, Ames, and Goat Island: Huntington to E. B. Crocker, December 7, 1867; July 2, and 28, 1868. To Stanford, July 30, 1868.

17 SCHEMING FOR VICTORY

Once again all citations, unless otherwise specified, are to Huntington's letters in *Collected Letters,* Vol. I.

1. To Charles Crocker, October 22, 1868.

2. To Hopkins, September 14, 1868.

3. Even today, reading several letters on the subject side by side, it is difficult to unravel the details of the scheme. Huntington was improvising and not always consistent. Moreover, his writing was not always lucid. He outlines the plan as succinctly as anywhere in a letter to Crocker of October 22, 1868—but October 22 was late for him to start clarifying himself. The whole affair is a classic example of a communications gap between business associates who supposedly understood each other well.

4. To Stanford, November 2, 1868: "I have written you occasionally for the last six months . . . but up to this time if there has been anything done, I can only say that I have not heard of it, and it is just possible that you think it is not important."

5. To Stanford, September 29, 1868.

6. The letter to Browning is in *Papers Submitted to the House Committee on the Pacific Railroad . . . Relative to the Issue of Bonds to the Central Pacific Railroad Company,* Washington, 1869, Vol. VIII, CPRR Pamphlets.

7. My reconstruction of events is synthesized from Huntington's letters to Crocker, October 14, 17, 21, 1868, plus *The Diary of Orville Hickman Browning,* Vol. II (Springfield, Illinois, 1933), pp. 221–22. The only open mention of undue influence at this point occurs in a letter, Huntington to Hopkins, October 23, 1868: "Mr. John Bloss is chief clerk in the Interior Department and has helped me much in my matters, and I told him I would give him an interest in some of our new towns."

8. Telegram, E. B. Crocker to Huntington, October 19, 1868, CP telegram book.
9. To Hopkins, October 23, 1868.
10. To Crocker, October 22, 1868.
11. To Crocker, October 29, 1868. "You will take possission of this whole line to Echo, but we must be within 300 miles before the Union Company has laid rails to Echo."
12. Stanford to Hopkins, November 9, 1868, quoted in Clark, *Leland Stanford*, p. 247.
13. Stanford to Hopkins, November 9, 1868, in ibid., pp. 248–50.
14. Huntington to Crocker, November 7, 1868.
15. To Hopkins, November 9, 1868.
16. To Stanford, November 13, 1868.
17. Clark, op. cit., pp. 251–58.
18. To Hopkins, November 18, 1868.

18 BY THE SKIN OF THEIR TEETH

Unless otherwise specified, all citations are to Huntington's letters in *Collected Letters*, Vol. I.

1. To Hopkins, December 2, 1868.
2. Browning, *Diary*, Vol. II, p. 229.
3. Quoted by Fisk and Hatch in their brochures, as Huntington naturally made sure it would be. The full report is in *Papers Submitted to the House Committee on the Pacific Railroad . . . Relative to the Issue of Bonds to the Central Pacific Railroad Company.*
4. To Crocker, December 16, 1868. It was in connection with this special commission that Crocker told his oft quoted (and unlikely) story about filling a glass of water to the brim, setting it on the floor, and ordering the engineer to drive fifty miles per hour over a new stretch of track. Not a drop spilled. Obviously the roadbed was in better shape than the unfriendly editors of the Sacramento *Union* were charging—"Crocker Manuscript."
5. No record of the actual conversations has survived. I am deducing Huntington's reactions from a plethora of uncomplimentary remarks he fired off in letters after his return to New York. For instance: to Stanford, January 25, 30, 1869 ("I want the responsibility to rest where it belongs —on the party having the construction in charge"); to Hopkins, January 26, 27, 1869 ("our *miserable failure*").
6. To Hopkins, January 20, 1869.
7. Elizabeth apparently did not return with him. At least the several telegrams announcing Huntington's westward progress all mention her, but those concerning his return trip do not—CP telegram book. She may have wanted to visit friends and relatives in Sacramento a little longer, or she may have found her bruising adventure with Collis in a stagecoach less pleasant than anticipated and have decided to return by train after the transcontinental was in operation.

8. See documents in *Papers* . . . , note 3 above. Browning's new commission consisted of Lt. Col. R. S. Williamson, a friend of the CP's; Gen. Gouverneur Warren, an army engineer who Collis feared might lean toward the UP; and Jacob Blickensderfer, Jr., a civil engineer employed by the Union Pacific. In order to neutralize Blickensderfer, Collis marched California's entire congressional delegation to Browning's office and demanded that he add Lewis Clement, an engineer employed by the Central Pacific, to the examining body. Browning complied. Browning, *Diary*, Vol. II, February 12, 1869, p. 239.

9. To Stanford, January 25, 1869. To Hopkins, January 26, 1869.

10. To Hopkins, January 20, 26, 1869. To Crocker, February 11, 1869.

11. To Stanford, January 30, 1869.

12. To [E.B.?] Crocker, February 5, 1869. To Hopkins, February 20, 1869.

13. To E. B. Crocker, February 22, 1869. To Hopkins, March 5, 1869. Browning, *Diary*, Vol. II, entries for February 26, March 1, 1869. *Congressional Globe*, House of Representatives, March 29, 1869. For the exact amount that Collis collected (a figure often inaccurately given), see *Papers* . . . , note 3 above.

14. To Hopkins, March 5, 1869. In reminiscing to Bancroft's scribes ("Huntington Manuscript"), Collis told an involved tale about Secretary McCulloch's reluctance to part with the bonds. He finally got them, he said, by parking himself in the Secretary's office and refusing to budge until the securities were delivered. In view of Browning's diary entry of February 26, 1869—"Mr. McCulloch and I were in favor of giving them"—the story seems questionable. But it was prettier than the truer tale of wholesale bribery would have been and of course protected McCulloch as well as Huntington.

15. To Hopkins, March 5, 1869. To C. Crocker, March 6, 1869.

16. To Stanford, still in Salt Lake City, March 8, 1869.

17. See document in *Papers*, note 3 above.

18. To Stanford, March 30, April 3, 1869. To Hopkins, April, undated.

19. The litigants were Col. Henry McComb, Duff Green, Ed Learned—Huntington to Stanford, March 22, 1869. The 1869 suits were quieted. Later, in 1872, McComb launched another court action that blew the Crédit Mobilier scandal wide open.

20. Huntington to [E.B.?] Crocker, April 13, May 17, 1869.

21. To Stanford, April 12, 1869.

22. To E. B. Crocker, May 17, 1869. To Stanford, August 2, 1870, *Collected Letters*, Vol. II.

23. To Stanford, May 26, 1869. The reports themselves are in *Papers* . . . , note 3 above.

24. To C. Crocker, May 10, 1869.

19 NEW VISTAS IN VIRGINIA

1. To Hopkins, August 6, 1869, *Collected Letters*, Vol. II.

2. For the early days of the Chesapeake and Ohio: Doherty, "Smooth is

the Road," *Tracks* (house organ of the Chesapeake and Ohio Railway), March 1951 through August 1951.
3. Ibid., September 1951.
4. According to figures submitted to the Wilson Committee of Congress by E. H. Miller, Jr. (summarized in Galloway, *The First Transcontinental Railroad*, pp. 106–17), the Central Pacific owed its construction firm, the Contract & Finance Company, $12.5 million. As the next chapter will indicate, the figure was a smoke screen designed to hide a far more serious state of affairs.

Huntington's own statements concerning the cost of the Central Pacific are in a public letter of May 1874 (later printed) to Philetus Sawyer, chairman of the House Select Committee on the Pacific Railroad (San Francisco, 1874). In that letter, Collis convincingly refutes some of the charges of excessive profits leveled at the company; however, he has picked his figures with care and offers no bookkeeping records in substantiation of his remarks. For these reasons, and because of decades of animus toward the man, historians incline to overlook Huntington's own testimony, though some of it could be used to advantage.

Testimony given the U. S. Pacific Railway Commission in 1887 by Lloyd Tevis and Alfred A. Cohen corroborates the associates' own statements about the unhappy state of their finances. "When this road was finished," Cohen said (p. 2399), "every one of the directors was mortgaged up to all that his credit would carry. Their notes were out everywhere . . . many of them bearing from 12 to 15% interest." Tevis added (p. 3134) that he had refused to have any financial dealings with the Central Pacific because of "the great indebtedness of the road." In evaluating these statements it should be remembered that both Tevis and Cohen were friendly witnesses—but not necessarily to the point of perjury.

5. To Stanford, August 21, 1869, *Collected Letters*, Vol. II.
6. To Hopkins, March 5, July 17, 1869; to E. B. Crocker, March 17, May 8, 1869, *Collected Letters*, Vol. II.
7. To C. Crocker, May 8, 12, 17, 1869; to Stanford, June 21, 1869, *Collected Letters*, Vol. I. Huntington every now and then suggested lowering rates to points below those considered feasible by his associates.
8. Doherty, op. cit., September 1951.
9. Catherine C. Phillips, *Jessie Benton Frémont* (San Francisco, 1935).
10. Doherty, op. cit., September 1951. Evans, *Collis Potter Huntington*, pp. 510 ff. Huntington to Hopkins, January 14, 1870, *Collected Letters*, Vol. II.
11. Doherty, op. cit., September 1951.

20 CONSOLIDATION IN CALIFORNIA

1. Huntington to Towne, August 23, 1869; to Charles Crocker, August 14, 25, 1869, *Collected Letters*, Vol. II. *Union*, September 17 and 18, 1869, lists the names of some of the travelers.
2. Huntington's hopes for the city emerge in intermittent correspondence

with Crocker, Hopkins, and Stanford from November 19, 1869, through July 7, 1870, *Collected Letters,* Vol. II.
3. *Union,* September 17.
4. Ibid.
5. See note 8, Chapter 14.
6. Senate Report 778, 54th Cong., 1st Sess., p. 38.
7. The Alameda road cost $337,718—Huntington to Hopkins, December 16, 1869, *Collected Letters,* Vol. II. And the Oakland road $487,218— *Hopkins Documents,* Vol. II, Stanford University Manuscripts.
8. Festivities were scheduled for the opening of that branch on November 8, 1869. Unhappily the first train, loaded with dignitaries, ran through a switch and was wrecked. Fourteen persons, some of them very prominent, were killed. The show went on, nevertheless. A substitute train was hurried into Oakland just after dark. Spectators warming themselves by bonfires beside the track raised a cheer, speakers orated by candle-light, and a burst of skyrockets was fired to let San Francisco know that triumphant Oakland was now the terminus of the great Pacific railroad. (Myron Wood, *History of Alameda County;* Earle Heath, "From Trail to Rail," *Southern Pacific Bulletin,* April 1928.)

    The big wreck and a series of smaller accidents led Huntington to heavy sarcasm: "I would suggest that you buy some mustangs and hire some boys to always ride just ahead of the machines, so as to give notice when the engines are coming together; and have them furnished with bells so that when they run in a fog they can ring, and in that way all will know when a collision is taking place."—to Hopkins, November 30, 1869, *Collected Letters,* Vol. II.
9. Deduced from an angry letter to Hopkins, January 10, 1870—*Collected Letters,* Vol. II—in which Huntington refers to the California agreement and objects to the way in which it is being broken.

    The California associates seemed to think they could raise some of the money they needed by an appeal to the public. They asked the city of Stockton to aid the San Joaquin with grants of land for marshaling yards and with rights-of-way along the streets. The municipal officers, who previously had carried on a vendetta with the Western Pacific, re-fused. To punish the citizens, the railroad moved a few miles away, formed the town of Lathrop (named for home-loving Jane Lathrop Stanford), and built south from there. Construction began December 31, 1869.

    Bills were also introduced into the legislature that would have au-thorized five San Joaquin Valley counties—Stanislaus, Merced, Fresno, Tulare, and Kern—to hold bond elections to approve a donation, in county bonds, of six thousand dollars a mile to the new road. The bills passed, but were vetoed by Governor Henry Haight in March 1870. The San Joaquin Railroad, which by then had built eleven miles from Lathrop, thereupon came to a sulking halt and did not resume con-struction until September.
10. Figures from Stanford's testimony to the U. S. Pacific Railway Com-

mission. Huntington's figures, as nearly as they can be resurrected, are slightly different (537,774 shares), and also show an additional, unexplained 53,330 shares "held in trust"—for whom or what, I have no idea. To Hopkins, February 3, 1871; March 22, 1872, *Collected Letters,* Vol. II.

11. In their accounting to the government early in 1873, the associates pretended that the Central Pacific still owed the Contract & Finance Company $12.5 million for work done—House Report 77, 42d Cong. 3d Sess. *A series of coded letters written at about the same time shows that this statement to the government was completely false. Instead, the Contract & Finance Company owed the railroad $5.7 million.* Some of this debt was incurred after the period under discussion in this chapter, but enough was owed in 1869 to make matters potentially very touchy indeed. After the Crédit Mobilier scandal had broken, the associates resorted to hurried bookkeeping manipulation "so that," in Hopkins' words, "the Notes shall be owned and held by *us* instead of continuing so large a C&F . . . debt owing to the Badger Co." [code word for Central Pacific]—Hopkins to Huntington, September 27, 1873, *Collected Letters,* Vol. IV. For other indications of the alarm of the associates when things threatened to come to a head, see the same volume, Hopkins to Huntington, February 21, November 15, 1873; Stanford to Huntington, February 23, 1873. When the laundered accounting was presented to the Pac. Ry. Commission, sure enough the C&F owed the associates $5.7 million, quite legally.

12. Echoes of the controversy are in Huntington to Stanford, March 3, 1870; to Hopkins, June 24, 1870, *Collected Letters,* Vol. II.

13. Echoes of the land grant and Rosecrans matters are in Huntington to Hopkins February 4, 14, March 29, December 23, 1870, *Collected Letters,* Vol. II. Cf. Robert M. Fogelson, *The Fragmented Metropolis, Los Angeles, 1850–1930* (Cambridge, Mass., 1967), pp. 44–45. The California Southern was not actually incorporated until January 1870, but Rosecrans' intent had become clear some months earlier.

14. There were many peripheral matters to be attended to. Both the Union Pacific and the Central Pacific had built telegraph lines in connection with their railroads. Rival telegraph companies, the Western Union and the Atlantic and Pacific (no connection with the railroad of the same name) wanted to use the railroad wires in forming coastal hookups. By choosing the Atlantic & Pacific, the associates incurred the bitter enmity of Western Union, which thereafter spread stories unfavorable to the CP and refused to carry laudatory dispatches. Huntington believed that the Western Union even invented unfavorable stories to spread— Huntington to Stanford, January 11, 23, 1870, *Collected Letters,* Vol. II. Since James W. Simonton, head of the Associated Press and part owner of the San Francisco *Bulletin,* was also involved in the Western Union, there were ample opportunities for low blows, and Simonton seems to have taken full advantage of them.

Other problems concerned sleeping cars; the associates decided to reject George Pullman's overtures and use ornate Silver Palace cars of their own manufacture. Another highly intricate matter involved traffic-sharing agreements whereby the Union Pacific and Central Pacific divided freight and freight revenues with the Pacific Mail Steamship Company and the related Panama Railroad.

15. It was often charged that the associates did not even pay full price for the 150 shares of stock to which they subscribed at the time the Central Pacific was organized—Brannan Suit. A. A. Cohen was slightly more generous and said that Mark Hopkins may have paid the full $15,000 but that the others never went past the initial 10 per cent down payment—A. A. Cohen, *An Address on the Railroad Evil and Its Remedy* (San Francisco, 1879). The charges are probably true, but somewhat irrelevant. Before state and federal aid became available, the associates dug into their own pockets for as much as they had, and if the advances were not applied against the original 150 shares of stock, it was partly a matter of bookkeeping.

16. In this connection it is worth recalling that under California law stock-holders were personally liable, in proportion to their holdings, for *all* of the debts incurred by any California corporation in which they had invested.

17. Fogel, *The Union Pacific Railroad, A Case Study in Premature Enter-prise,* has worked out an elaborate formula for determining what "fair" profits in the construction of the Union Pacific might have been. He points out, first, that the profits figured by the government were ex-panded by a heated combination of politics and outrage engendered by the Crédit Mobilier scandal. After unraveling the Crédit Mobilier's ob-scure bookkeeping as best he could, Professor Fogel has decided that Crédit Mobilier profits amounted not to the $44 million charged by the government, but, at the most, to $16.5 million. By weighing the enormous risks involved, Fogel then decides, by means of his complicated formula, that the UP promoters were entitled to a profit of $11.1 million. Thus their gains were unreasonable but not outrageous. Al-though he condemns the promoters for the political corruption they employed in reducing their risks, he also blames the permissiveness and greed of Congress for much of what developed.

What Fogel says of Crédit Mobilier probably applies to the Central Pacific and the Contract & Finance Company as well. There is no way of applying his formula, however, since the Contract & Finance Company books were deliberately destroyed. Because of that hasty act of destruc-tion, the Big Four condemned themselves to being forever judged by unfriendly figures only.

18. This was the period when an ill-digested extension of Darwin's theories were being eagerly applied to social as well as to natural organisms. For one summary of the phenomenon, see Richard Hofstadter, William Miller, Daniel Aaron, *The United States, The History of a Republic* (New York, 1957), pp. 529–38.

19. The philosophy is implicit in Huntington's remarks about using bribery to achieve what is "right." See note 8, Chapter 6.

21. BLACKMAIL AND OTHER AILMENTS

1. For the launching and building of the Chesapeake & Ohio: Doherty, "Smooth is the Road," October 1951, February–March 1952. Because the state of Virginia held stock in the Chesapeake & Ohio, Huntington's syndicate did not risk setting up its own construction company but let the work on bids.

2. Doherty, op. cit., February 1952. Evans, *Collis Potter Huntington,* pp. 524–26.

3. Doherty, op. cit.; *The Huntington Family in America,* p. 838. Another nephew, Scott Hammond, fared less well. Scott's father, Daniel Hammond, had gone to California with Huntington in 1849, and in Sacramento had married Elizabeth's sister Hannah. Through his uncle Collis, Scott, who was not yet out of his teens, obtained a summer job with a Chesapeake & Ohio construction gang. On July 20, 1870, in the course of his work, he drowned in the New River. Collis and Elizabeth, very upset, had the body brought to New York; funeral services were held in their home at 65 Park Avenue—Oneonta *Herald,* August 17, 1870, Holladay Collection.

4. Quoted in Julius Grodinsky, *Transcontinental Railway Strategy, 1869–1893* (Philadelphia, 1962), p. 28.

5. Oneonta *Herald,* June 1, 1871, Holladay Collection.

6. Huntington to E. B. Crocker, December 13, 1869, *Collected Letters,* Vol. II.

7. To Hopkins, November 29, 1869; to Stanford, November 19, 29, December 4, 6, 13, 24, 1869; to C. Crocker, December 21, 28, 1869, ibid.

8. To Hopkins, February 5, 25, March 1, 1870; to C. Crocker, July 7, 1870, ibid. From such evidence as survives, it would seem that Stanford's position on the matter was sounder than Huntington's.

9. To Stanford, December 7, 1869; January 19, 1870; to Hopkins, December 24, 28, 1869; January 25, 26, 1870, ibid.

10. To Hopkins, December 16, 1869, ibid.

11. To Hopkins, December 10, 1869; March 4, April 13, 1870, ibid.

12. To Hopkins, March 7, April 21, 1870; to Crocker, June 9, 1870, ibid.

13. To Hopkins, January 20, 25, February 9, 1870; to Tevis, January 26, 1870, ibid. Later, when the Southern Pacific undertook to raise money by bonding its holdings, Tevis' undivided interest created knotty legal problems that this account has no space to deal with.

14. For a start on available literature concerning the sinking fund, Haney, *Congressional History of Railways in the United States,* pp. 85 ff.; Daggett, *Southern Pacific,* pp. 370 ff. For citations to documents poured out by the railroads in defense of their position, Evans, *Collis Potter Huntington,* pp. 412 ff.

15. To Stanford, December 16, 1869; to Hopkins, December 17, 1869, *Collected Letters,* Vol. II.

16. The figures are from Brannan's complaint, *Brannan Suit,* as later filed in the district court in San Francisco.

17. For Tevis: Cobb's testimony to the U. S. Pacific Railway Commission, p. 3246. *Union,* July 4, 1870. Huntington's views on motives are in letters to Hopkins, May 8, 1870, and Stanford, May 10, 1870, *Collected Letters,* Vol. II.

18. Brannan's suit charges Mills with engineering the purchases from both counties. Huntington (to Hopkins, April 14, 1870, *Collected Letters,* Vol. II) seems, somewhat inconclusively, to say that Hopkins obtained the Sacramento County stock for 70 per cent of face value in gold, or close to par in currency. When the officials of Placer County learned that other stockholders had received more than par for their holdings, they sued not for an accounting but, foolishly, for as much as the other fellows got. They lost.

19. To Hopkins, April 9, May 16, 1870, *Collected Letters,* Vol. II.

20. Huntington's correspondence concerning the suits is in *Collected Letters,* Vol. II. It begins April 9, 1870, and runs throughout the rest of the year, with the biggest concentration coming in the spring. It is too numerous for individual citation. There is additional data in Vol. I of the *Hopkins Documents,* Stanford University Manuscripts.

21. To Crocker, June 14, 1870; to Stanford, June 30, 1870, *Collected Letters,* Vol. II. Testimony in Pac. Ry. Commission, p. 3655, suggests that the associates paid from $250 to $1,700 a share in their hurry. The New York *Sun,* July 19, 1873, suggested prices up to $1,187 a share. A. A. Cohen, in his furious controversy with the associates, gives a top of $550—*CPRR* v. *Alfred A. Cohen,* 1876, District Court, Twelfth Judicial District, State of California. Huntington's own purchases seem to have been made at considerably less than that amount. Since the correspondence is not complete, particularly in respect to the California purchases, there is no way of reaching firm conclusions.

22. Moses Cobb, in Pac. Ry. Commission, p. 3246. Cf. Doherty, "Smooth is the Road," January 1952. For Aspinwall and Stewart (who in 1875 fell out bitterly with Collis over a receivership for the Chesapeake & Ohio): Huntington to Hopkins, March 30, 1876, *Collected Letters,* Vol. III.

22   THE DESPERATE YEARS

1. Pamphlet 20, Vol. I, CPRR Pamphlets, indicates the sweeping promotional uses made of the consolidation.

2. Rosecrans later regretted his decision and tried to edge back into the company. Huntington advised Stanford—December 23, 1870, *Collected Letters,* Vol. II—to tell the general that they would consider a cash offer—a demand which, Collis hoped, would quiet the general without offending him. Rosecrans, however, was offended and with singular lack of imagination organized the California Southern Coast Railroad. This repeat run of the California Southern did not interest Scott or anyone else and Rosecrans slowly faded from the railroad scene.

3. Hopkins to Huntington, October 16, 1870, *Collected Letters,* Vol. IV. Also Huntington to Hopkins, October 26, 1870; March 17, 27, May 2, 19, June 6, 1871; to Stanford, April 10, 20, 1871; to Crocker, May 17, 1871, *Collected Letters,* Vol. II.

4. New York *Sun,* February 13, 1875.

5. *Collected Letters,* Vol. II, January 1871 through August 1871, contains several of Huntington's letters on the subject, mostly to Stanford. The letters, however, do not reveal who devised the counterattack that was finally used. See also the San Francisco *Alta California,* May 24, 1871; Bancroft, *Chronicles of the Builders,* Vol. VI, p. 151.

6. The quotation is from a letter to Crocker, August 21, 1874, *Collected Letters,* Vol. III. For a typical stockholder suit: *Complaint of Charles Main et al.,* filed in the District Court in San Francisco in 1880. There is a copy in the Cohen Papers, Huntington Library. Cohen was attorney for the complainants. See also the summary of the California Pacific takeover in Daggett, op. cit., pp. 108–18.

7. For Goat Island: *Collected Letters,* Vol. II, March 16–May 11, 1872, passim.

8. Clark, *Leland Stanford,* pp. 315–26. Bancroft, *Chronicles of the Builders,* Vol. VI, pp. 301–02. The Committee of One Hundred also tried to dredge up other plans for breaking the associates' monopoly. The quarrelsome members could not agree on any one line of attack, however. After listening to the blandishments of the Atlantic & Pacific, some of the committee suggested that the city buy stock in the A&P and and finance an independent road that would build east to connect with that organization. Others wanted the independent road to hook up with the Texas & Pacific. Still others thought that the city should buy the Southern Pacific. Bills embodying the proposals got onto the November ballots and hurt the Central Pacific briefly. None of the measures passed.

9. Clark, op. cit., pp. 334–36. Even Huntington gave Stanford credit for the plan—to Stanford, November 25, 1871, *Collected Letters,* Vol. II—but worried over its legality: "the devil only knows what the Interior Department will do" if controversies developed as a result of the long skip—to Hopkins, November 13, 1871, ibid.

10. To Hopkins, December 26, 1872, ibid.

11. Fogelson, *The Fragmented Metropolis,* pp. 52–56. Remi A. Nadeau, *City-Makers* (New York, 1948), pp. 71–87.

12. To Hopkins, February 20, 27, March 3, 1873, *Collected Letters,* Vol. II.

13. To Hopkins, December 2, 19, 1872. The letters leave scant doubt that the figures were doctored according to need. Later on, the associates grew more cautious and reduced the sums they displayed in public. See the reports of the Pac. Ry. Commission, and Galloway, *The First Transcontinental Railroad,* pp. 106–17.

14. To Hopkins, March 14, 1873, *Collected Letters,* Vol. II. Hopkins to Huntington, February 21, September 27, November 6, 15, 1873, *Collected Letters,* Vol. IV.

15. To Hopkins, April 16, 1873, *Collected Letters,* Vol. II. The doleful

tale of the fruitless efforts to place the stock on the market runs through several letters from the fall of 1872 to early 1874, *Collected Letters*, Vols. II and III. No effort is made here to cite them individually.

16. Reports on the efforts to sell, chiefly to Scott or to a San Francisco syndicate put together by A. A. Cohen, also fill a bulky place in the volume cited above. Huntington suspected that Stanford, who liked being a railroad president and who wanted to leave a little something for his frail son, dragged his feet during some of the negotiations with deliberate intent to kill them—to Hopkins, January 23, March 7, 1873, *Collected Letters*, Vol. II.

17. Once again it would be impractical to make individual citations from the great number of references in the last part of *Collected Letters*, Vol. II, and the first part of Vol. III. For a summary, see Grodinsky, *Transcontinental Railway Strategy*, pp. 15–54, passim.

18. To Hopkins, September 26, 1873, *Collected Letters*, Vol. III.

19. Crocker to Huntington, November 5, 1873, et seq., *Collected Letters*, Vol. IV.

23 NEW BATTLEFIELDS

1. For Gould, the Pacific Mail, and the railroads, see Bancroft, *Chronicles of the Builders*, Vol. V, pp. 418–46, passim; Julius Grodinsky, *Jay Gould: His Business Career, 1867–1892* (Philadelphia, 1957), pp. 112–29 passim.

2. Huntington to Stanford, June 29, 1874, *Collected Letters*, Vol. III. Though no evidence survives on the point, Crocker may have been hurried to the Orient to expound on the virtues of the railroad not only over Suez but over Panama as well.

3. Huntington was very worried about Hopkins' health. "You are worn down with work and now need a change of climate and rest." To Hopkins, June 24, 1874, ibid.

4. To Crocker, September 14, November 6, 14, 18, 1874; to Stanford, September 17, November 10, 1874; to David D. Colton, November 9, 1874, ibid.

5. To Stanford, November 28, 1874, ibid.

6. To the associates' surprise, the O&O proved very profitable. In time, too, Huntington became first a director of the Pacific Mail Steamship Company and eventually the firm's president.

7. To Stanford, December 18, 1874, March 16, 1875; to Colton, November 13, 1874, April 3, 1875, ibid.

8. Doherty, "Smooth is the Road," December 1952.

9. To Hopkins, January 12, 14, 16, February 19, March 28, 1874; to Stanford, January 8, April 14, 18, 1874; to C. Crocker, January 17, 1874, *Collected Letters*, Vol. III.

10. Figures from Daggett, *Southern Pacific*, pp. 169, 365. There is no way to determine what proportion of each dividend was left with the Western Development Company; the amount increased when the race with Scott heated up. Meantime other investments were paying handsomely, notably

Wells Fargo and the Rocky Mountain Coal and Iron Company in Wyoming, the latter of which sold coal to the railroad and to many San Francisco manufacturing establishments and paid each owner eight thousand dollars a month.

11. To Hopkins, May 7, 1875, *Collected Letters,* Vol. III.

12. To Hopkins, September 13, 1875; to Crocker, December 18, 31, 1875, ibid.

13. To Hopkins, September 25, 1875, *Collected Letters,* Vol. III. To Colton, May 9, 1877, as published in San Francisco *Chronicle,* December 23, 1883.

14. *Letter to the Hon. Philetus Sawyer* . . . (Published by the Central Pacific in San Francisco, 1874).

15. *Union,* February 26, 1876.

16. Cohen, *An Address on the Railroad Evil and Its Remedy.* See also the second paragraph of note 25 below.

17. *John R. [sic] Robinson* vs. *The Central Pacific Et Als.,* in the District Court of the Fourth Judicial District of the State of California, in and for the City and County of San Francisco. A bit later Cohen prevailed on San Joaquin County, as a sometime holder of Western Pacific stock, to enter a similar complaint. Again the old Brannan material formed the substance of the allegations. Neither Robinson nor the county collected. As a further devilment Cohen made several speeches on behalf of the Archer rate-regulation bill.

18. There is a copy of Dangerfield's opinion and a transcript of the case in Pardee Scrapbook No. 2, Henry E. Huntington Library, San Marino, Calif.

19. To Crocker, March 14, 1876, *Collected Letters,* Vol. III; to James Speyer, n.d., 1899, Holladay Collection.

20. Colton to Huntington, May 22, 1876, Cohen Papers, Huntington Library.

21. Hirschon, *Grenville Dodge,* pp. 191–93.

22. Some of the Scott-Huntington correspondence is in *Collected Letters,* Vol. III. Huntington to Stanford, September 18, 1874, ibid., describes earlier meetings during which Scott "showed a good deal of feeling about his San Diego hopes." See also Huntington's letters to Crocker during November 1874, ibid., and Lewis Lesley, "A Southern Transcontinental Railroad into California: Texas and Pacific vs. Southern Pacific, 1865–1885," *Pacific Historical Review,* Vol. V, 1936.

23. C. Van Woodward, *Reunion and Reaction* (Boston, 1951), pp. 58–60.

24. Huntington to Colton, November 20, 1874, *Collected Letters,* Vol. III.

25. Overt bribery was never proved against Huntington. The Pacific Railway Commission of 1887 dug up vouchers issued during the years of the Scott fight (1873–79) totaling $4.8 million and charged simply to "legal expenses." Many were drawn in favor of Richard Franchot, who was not a practising lawyer. Collis parried the questions that resulted by saying that he did not recall the incidents in detail but was sure all was proper. Franchot was a man of integrity; "when he said to me, 'I want $10,000,' I knew it was proper to let him have it." Besides, "I have

given instructions to my people never to use any money in any immoral or illegal sense, but to bring proper influences to bear to get votes"— these proper influences being objective explanations about what was "right" and in the public interest. Pac. Ry. Commission, pp. 3697, 3700–01, 3706, 3715.

The commission also unearthed other heavy payments made by Stanford and charged to "expenses" during the time the Archer rate-regulation bill was under discussion in Sacramento—expenses whose exact nature slipped Stanford's mind on the witness stand, even though one item cost $111,431. Ibid., p. 2999. In view of everyone's lack of candor, the majority report of the commission assumed that the object of the $4.8 million expenditures was "illegitimate." Ibid., pp. 84–87.

26. Nadeau, *City-Makers*, pp. 202–10.
27. A summary of the work authorized by the directors that fall is in Huntington to Colton, November 7, 1874, *Collected Letters*, Vol. III.
28. William B. Hyde to Henry Bacon, August 22, 1873, Huntington Library. Huntington to Stanford, May 5, June 27, September 24, 1874, *Collected Letters*, Vol. III. It is not fully accurate to say, as is sometimes done, that Crocker alone fobbed Colton off onto the company.
29. Daggett, *Southern Pacific*, pp. 154–57.
30. Huntington resigned as president on December 21, 1874. Colton arrived in New York on December 28. For the situation in general: Huntington to Colton, December 8, 1874; March 3, 1875; to Crocker, December 21, 29, 1874; to Stanford, January 1, 6, 1875, *Collected Letters*, Vol. III. Mentions of Huntington's own trips to Washington are to Hopkins, January 11, February 25, 1875, ibid.
31. Quoted in Clark, *Leland Stanford*, pp. 309–11, 337.
32. To Colton, September 18, October 6, December 22, 1875; and, angrily, to Hopkins, February 12, 1876, *Collected Letters*, Vol. III.
33. Woodward, *Reunion and Reaction*, pp. 76–98 passim.
34. To Colton, September 27, October 4, 29, November 10, 1875. The letter of September 27 suggests the figure of $25,000 for the franchise. That of October 29 raises the proposed ante to $50,000, as printed in *Collected Letters*, Vol. III. As printed in the San Francisco *Chronicle*'s airing of the notorious Colton Letters, December 23, 1883, the figure is $5,000. Evidently one of the publications contains a typographical error; since the original letter has vanished, no firm resolution is possible.
35. To Colton, October 18, November 3, 1875; to Hopkins, February 19, 1876, *Collected Letters*, Vol. III.
36. To Hopkins, February 19, 1876, ibid.
37. To Colton, October 26, November 30, 1875; February 26, 1876; to Hopkins, October 8, November 19, December 2, 1875; to Stanford, December 1, 1875, ibid. The emissaries whom Huntington employed included a still mysterious Mr. Budd, a Harvey Brown, a Judge Evans, and, not least, William Gwin, one-time senator from California and a fire-breathing Confederate who still had wide connections below the

Mason-Dixon line. Gwin was ordered never to communicate directly with Huntington, but to report to Huntington's chief writer of publicity and advertising, Richard Colburn of New Jersey.

38. To Colton, January 29, 1876, ibid.

39. To Colton, December 13, 1875; January 29, March 6, 1876, ibid. See also the introductory notes to the Colton Letters as published in the San Francisco *Chronicle,* December 23, 1883. In his anger, Sargent even introduced a bill into the Senate asking for still another investigation of the Central Pacific and the Contract & Finance Company—to Colton, May 12, 1876, ibid. For Sargent's resolution: *Congressional Record,* January 7, 1876.

40. This account of the Los Angeles & Independence is pieced together from more correspondence in *Collected Letters,* Vol. III, April 1875 intermittently through March 1876, and *Collected Letters,* Vol. IV, May 1877 through September 1877, than can be cited in detail. See also, Franklin Hoyt, "The Los Angeles and Independence Railroad," The Historical Society of Southern California *Quarterly,* December 1950.

41. Quoted in Woodward, op. cit., p. 167.

42. In California the associates did sell some Southern Pacific bonds at sixty (par was 100). This raised interest to prohibitive rates, and so Collis repudiated the sale. A few years later, when Southern Pacific bonds reached par, he had the satisfaction of unloading a safeful of them and netting some fourteen million dollars more than his associates would have made through their premature sales, "Huntington Manuscript." A summary of his financial nimbleness during the construction of the Southern Pacific is in Grodinsky, *Transcontinental Railway Strategy,* pp. 60–63. Impressed by the skill with which Huntington kept the SP moving ahead and opening uninhabited areas to settlement during depression years, Professor Grodinsky declares, p. 63, "He was in this sense a public servant and performed a notable public service."

43. Huntington to Colton, December 25, 1876, *Chronicle* reprints, December 23, 1883. Gould was primarily interested in the railroad's stock, but Huntington insisted on doling it out to him through the construction company, then the Western Development Company, which had first absorbed the shares as part of its price for building the track. This device, if the subsidy bill passed, would keep Gould interested in furthering the progress of the road.

44. To Colton, November 15, December 4, December 20, 1876; January 22, 1877, ibid.

45. To Colton, December 4, 1876; January 22, 1877, ibid.

46. To Colton, February 14, June 24, 1876; January 22, 1877, ibid. It seems likely that William B. Carr was used to "influence" at least part of the California delegation to support the sinking fund bill. See cryptic letters to Colton, December 23, 1875, January 14, 1876, ibid., and Huntington to Hopkins, January 7, 1876, Cohen Papers, Huntington Library.

47. Woodward, op. cit., pp. 127–42.

1. Huntington to Colton, March 8, 1877, *Chronicle* reprints. Crocker to Huntington, April 20, May 15, 1877; Gov. Safford to Crocker and Crocker to Safford, April 11 and 25, 1877, *Collected Letters,* Vol. IV. Colton to Huntington, May, n.d., 1877, Cohen Papers.

   Safford was an old friend of the associates. A gold-rusher, he had left California for the Nevada silver fields and there had entered politics. He attended the golden spike ceremony at Promontory in 1869. Shortly thereafter he had been appointed governor of Arizona.

   When Crocker journeyed back and forth to Arizona, he occasionally took visiting VIPs with him. He was supposed to impress them and all others with the resources of the land, so that the resultant publicity would make Huntington's bond selling easier. It was difficult to wax eloquent about the blistered sands of the Colorado Desert, however. Snapping back at Huntington's requests for material, Crocker growled, on June 5, 1877, *Collected Letters,* Vol. IV, that he would like to take Collis over the line and "hear you expatiate on the loveliness of that charming country. . . . I shall enjoy it better than I would reading the latest novel."

2. Citations as above, note 1. It seems that during the summer of 1876, Grant's Secretary of War, James Cameron, visited California and in the hearing of Gen. W. T. Sherman assured the associates of permission to cross the reservation when the time came. At least the associates later made a great point of this unwritten and somewhat nebulous authorization—Colton to Huntington, October 7, 1877, *Collected Letters,* Vol. IV.

3. For the riots and the Workingmen's party; Hittell, *History of California,* Vol. IV, pp. 594–614.

4. Deduced from Huntington's later letters to Colton, *Chronicle* reprints, and from Colton to Huntington during the same period, Cohen Papers and *Collected Letters,* Vol. IV.

5. For the bridge: San Francisco *Chronicle,* October 4, 5, 9, 10, 1877; *Alta California,* October 7, 1877; Crocker's letters to Huntington, September 5 through October 9, 1877, *Collected Letters,* Vol. IV; Colton to Huntington, September 24, 25, October 5, 1877, Cohen Papers.

6. *Chronicle* reprints.

7. Colton to Huntington, January 31, 1878, Cohen Papers. Colton finally persuaded Hopkins to endorse twenty of the notes; later in March, Mark signed the remaining eighty, March 9, 1878, ibid. At this period, all of the associates were vociferously opposed to Huntington's desire to extend the Southern Pacific. Colton to Huntington, February 14, March 28, 1878; Crocker to Huntington, February 12, March 4, 10, 18, 19, 28, 1878, *Collected Letters,* Vol. IV.

8. Huntington to Colton, October 29, November 16, 23, 1877, *Chronicle* reprints.

9. Stanford withdrew from the Western Development Company in the

course of two or three years $816,000 *more* than Huntington did, $1 million more than Crocker, and $1.5 more than Hopkins. During the last five months of 1877, withdrawals went as follows: Hopkins, $800; Colton, $9000; Crocker, $32,000; Huntington, $57,600—and Stanford, $276,000. (Crocker to Huntington, October 29, November 22, 1877; July 25, 1878 (*Collected Letters*, Vol. IV.) Colton to Huntington, January 4, 1877 (Cohen Papers, loc. cit.). Huntington to James Speyer, n.d., 1899 (Holladay Collection).

10. Huntington to Colton, October 31, November 9, 30, 1877; February 25, 1878, *Chronicle* reprints. Colton to Huntingon, November 30, 1877; January 5, 14, 22, February 7, 1878, Cohen Papers.

11. Huntington to Colton, April 19, 1878, *Chronicle* reprints.

12. For a discussion of the bill: Daggett, *Southern Pacific*, pp. 370–94; Haney, *Congressional History of Railroads*, pp. 94 ff.

    Through Albert Gallatin, a partner in the Huntington-Hopkins hardware store and owner of five shares of CP stock, the railroad sued the government, contending that the Thurman Act, which arbitrarily amended the government's 1862 and 1864 contracts with the railroads, amounted to confiscation of property, inasmuch as the government had no right to anticipate a default in payment of the bonded debt before the default actually occurred. The nation's Supreme Court upheld the government in a split decision. Arguing vigorously on behalf of the railroad was Justice Stephen Field, a close friend of Stanford's. Carl B. Swisher, *Stephen J. Field* (Washington, 1930), pp. 246–49.

13. "Huntington Manuscript," pp. 76–77. Crocker to Huntington, April 27, 1878, *Collected Letters*, Vol. IV; Colton to Huntington, May 8, 1878, Cohen Papers.

14. The date of the Southern Pacific's acquisition of the Galveston, Harrisburg & San Antonio is uncertain. Evans, *Collis Potter Huntington*, p. 252, gives 1877. S. G. Reed, *A History of the Texas Railroads* (Houston, 1941), pp. 544–51 says that the purchase occurred "about" 1880. Grodinsky, *Jay Gould*, p. 347, favors 1881. On purely inferential grounds, I am inclined to think that Huntington's initial interest, perhaps a small one, was acquired in 1878.

15. Lewis, *The Big Four*, pp. 301–02. Evans, op. cit., p. 345. Charles F. Crocker wrote Huntington on October 11, 1878, *Collected Letters*, Vol. IV, that Mrs. Colton was rushing back from Iowa aboard special trains provided by the Burlington and Union Pacific railroads as fast as possible. There was need for haste: "The embalming process has not been entirely successful, and the remains cannot be kept many days."

16. Crocker to Huntington, February 25, March 10, April 3, 1879, *Collected Letters*, Vol. IV.

17. The lengthy decision of Judge Jackson Temple of the superior court at Sonoma, California, was printed in full in the San Francisco *Evening Post*, October 8, 1885. The case itself—*Ellen M. Colton* v. *Leland Stanford et al.*, in the Superior Court of the State of California in and for the County of Sonoma—runs to thousands of pages of testimony, documents, and depositions.

18. Volney Howard, "Regulating Railroad Corporations," a speech delivered to the convention on November 23, 1878. See also Carl B. Swisher, *Motivations and Political Techniques in the California Constitutional Convention, 1878–79* (Claremont, Calif., 1930).

19. See the "Report of the Committee on Corporations," *Appendix to the Journals of the Senate and Assembly of the Legislature of the State of California.* Daggett, op. cit., pp. 181–98. A. N. Towne and B. Worthington of the railroad, reviewing the California political scene for Huntington on September 3, 1892, H. E. Huntington Biographical File, Box P-1, Huntington Library, saw matters differently. Cone and Beerstecher were good men, they said; lazy George Stoneman, by contrast, loafed into just enough of the meetings to be able to draw his pay.

20. In this account I avoid the controversial matter of the circulars issued by the railroad inviting settlers onto its land and promising, somewhat ambiguously, that when patents were issued by the General Land Office and sales could be formally consummated, the company would not charge purchasers for the improvements they had made on the farms in the interim. When the time for collecting came, however, the local land agents of the railroad did ask some squatters for more than the circulars had seemed to promise. There is evidence that the railroad did not consider the extra charge as being for improvements, but as back rent for lands that had been occupied for many years free of charge. On the other hand, there is also evidence that Crocker and Huntington may have concocted the circular as a means of bringing the dispute with the settlers to a head—pay now or get out. Crocker to Huntington, November 30, 1878, May 7, 31, 1879, *Collected Letters*, Vol. IV.

21. Frank Norris' novel *The Octopus* is, of course, the average reader's main contact with the affray. Although effective as protest literature, *The Octopus* is a poor historical document. Norris never saw the Hanford area but described the countryside around Hollister, more than a hundred miles away. He locates a Spanish mission where none ever existed. More seriously, his ranchers are bonanza wheat farmers, not modest homesteaders. He makes little mention of the vigilante activities of the Settlers League, and skims over Sawyer's court decision, a significant omission since the decree was sound from a legal point of view and furnished the railroad with ample justification for going ahead with the evictions.

     For more objective accounts, see James L. Brown, *The Mussel Slough Tragedy* (Fresno, Calif., 1958); Wallace Smith, *Garden of the Sun* (Los Angeles, 1939), pp. 259–87; Irving McKee, "Notable Memorials to Mussel Slough," *Pacific Historical Review*, Vol. XVII, 1948, pp. 19–27.

22. These strictures of Stoneman and his railroad commissioners are based on Towne and Worthington (see note 19 above). A different contemporary opinion is in Hittell, *History of California*, Vol. IV, pp. 667 ff. See also Alexander Callow, Jr., "San Francisco's Blind Boss," *Pacific Historical Review*, August 1956.

     Huntington viewed Stoneman's election with frank distaste. On February 6, 1883, he told a reporter from the New York *Journal*, "Out in California the hoodlums have elected a lot of representatives who are without brains or money, and these men are just now trying to pass laws giving the railroad corporations no right to exist. . . . They forget that without the aid of money to build their railroads or work their mines they would yet be living in a wilderness; that California and the entire West and the Southwest owe what they are to the energy and enterprise of the men who have risked their money to build them up."

25 THE POTENTATE

1. James B. Hedges, *Henry Villard and the Railways of the Northwest* (New Haven, 1930), pp. 36–59.
2. Reed, *A History of the Texas Railroads,* pp. 195–96, 242–80, passim; Grodinsky, *Jay Gould,* pp. 345–50; and the same author's *Transcontinental Railway Strategy,* pp. 170–73.
3. Grodinsky, *Jay Gould,* pp. 378–80, and *Transcontinental Railway Strategy,* pp. 216–18; Fogelson, *The Fragmented Metropolis,* pp. 58–60; Franklin Hoyt, "San Diego's First Railroad, the California Southern," *Pacific Historical Review,* May 1854.
4. The Newport News and Chesapeake & Ohio affairs are summarized from Evans, *Collis Potter Huntington,* pp. 530–68, and Doherty, "Smooth Is the Road," March and April 1953.
5. Grodinsky, *Transcontinental Railway Strategy,* p. 211.
6. Crocker to Huntington, March 2, 7, 1883, *Collected Letters,* Vol. IV.
7. Biographers say that Stanford meant to produce fine wine—Clark, op. cit., p. 393. By contrast, geographers David Lantis, Rodney Steiner, and Arthur Karinen, *California, Land of Contrast* (Belmont, Calif., 1963) state, p. 365, that he intended a volume output of a cheap product. Stanford also planned to distill brandy, a project that drew scorn from the abstemious Huntington.
8. Grodinsky, *Transcontinental Railway Strategy,* p. 164; Doherty, op. cit., March 1953, pp. 44–45. Stanford was rewarded for his participation by having Leland, Mississippi (near Greenville) named for him.
9. Grodinsky, op. cit., pp. 212–13. Daggett, *Southern Pacific,* pp. 146–48.
10. Crocker to Huntington, several letters, July and August 1883, *Collected Letters,* Vol. IV.
11. Grodinsky, op. cit., pp. 217–18; Hoyt, op. cit.
12. The standard account is Glen Dumke, *The Boom of the Eighties in Southern California* (San Marino, 1944).
13. "If there is anybody who has done more for this country than my associates and myself I would like a chromo of them, I would." Huntington in an interview, New York *Daily Tribune,* September 23, 1887.
14. The death certificate from the New York City Board of Health records gives the cause of death as "epithelioma of the vulva and pudendum," with "asthenia" as a contributing cause.

15. Robert Wark, director of the Huntington Art Galleries, "Arabella Huntington and the Beginnings of the Huntington Art Collection" (San Marino, California, 1969).

16. The Sacramento *Record-Union*, which the associates then controlled, announced the nuptials on July 15, 1884, and gave this biography of the bride: "Mrs. Huntington's early home was in the South. . . . Her family and that of Mr. Huntington have been on terms of the closest intimacy. She is wealthy in her own right. Her first husband died several years ago."

 According to Arthur McEwen, writing in the Los Angeles *Express*, April 19, 1890, the Stanfords, Crockers, and all of their connections refused to recognize Arabella; they may have stayed away from the wedding by choice. McEwen attributes Huntington's deepening hatred of Stanford to these slights. The theory probably has about as much to recommend it as most newspaper tittle-tattle.

17. The standard Sargent-eye view of the affair is in Lewis, *The Big Four*, pp. 242–47. Clark, *Leland Stanford*, pp. 428–36, defends Stanford. Mr. Lewis would increase the odium of the double cross, if there really was one, by having Sargent and Stanford close personal friends. Remarks scattered through the Huntington correspondence lead me to a different conclusion about the intimacy.

18. Huntington to George Whitney, December 9, 1886, C. P. Huntington, Personal Letterbook, 1881–89, Huntington Library, San Marino. These follow-up efforts on Sargent's behalf have generally been overlooked. This account is pieced together from a run of letters to Sargent, Charles F. Crocker, Creed Haymond, and others, June 14, 1886 to December 29, 1886 ibid., and Letterbook, 1885–87. This correspondence of course reveals Huntington's estimate of the situation. Several correspondents tried to assure him that he was wrong, that his employees had worked hard, but that the efforts were hopeless. Sargent, they said, was a complete has-been so far as California politics was concerned. Huntington refused to believe that he had made such a mistake and blamed Stanford for the rest of his days.

19. Letters to the Otis Elevator Company, Andrew Carnegie, and others, Letterbook, 1881–89.

20. To E. H. Ludlow and Company, September 23, 1887, ibid.

21. To Joseph D. Redding, February 6, 1888; to W. H. Mills, February 21, 1888, Letterbook, 1888–89.

22. Ibid., letters on pp. 383 ff.

23. This account is based on contemporary newspaper clippings and is not necessarily authentic in every detail.

24. To R. M. Huntington, Boone, Iowa, August 7, 1888, Letterbook, 1888–89. The personal letterbooks of 1881–89 and 1888–89 contain a plethora of such incidents, and they are only two of three surviving letterbooks of the 1880s; several others have vanished. The standard aspersion that Huntington was a tightwad does not hold up under investigation. He just wasn't lavish; also, he made so many public ut-

terances about saving pennies that people concluded he did not spend any, either.

25. Belden, *So Fell the Angels,* p. 347.
26. Phillips, *Jessie Benton Frémont,* pp. 310–11. Also Huntington's letters to Mrs. Frémont, April 14, 1888, and John Boyd, April 23, 1888, Letterbook, 1888–89.
27. Stanford to Huntington, March 6, 1878; Charles F. Crocker to Huntington, November 18, 1878, *Collected Letters,* Vol. IV. Huntington to Anna Judah, January 5, 20, March 5, June 3, 11, 1886; to Stanford, March 27, 1886, Letterbook, 1881–89.

    Concerning meteorology: Huntington used to say that the northeast wind also affected the stock market: "There is always a point's difference between the northeast and the northwest." Doherty, "Smooth Is the Road," May 1953.
28. *Alta California,* August 2, 1886. Huntington to Margaret O'Brien, March 24, 1887; to James Waddell, April 29, 1887, Letterbook, 1881–89.
29. To Jeanette Thurber, November 20, 1888; to Luigi P. di Cesnola, June 18, 1888, ibid. Presumably these cultural interests were a result of Arabella's influence.
30. To Dwinnell, November 30, 1888, ibid.
31. To Mrs. M. J. Sherman, May 31, 1888; to F. N. Gilman, May 31, July 5, 1888, ibid. Evans, *Collis Potter Huntington,* p. 691.
32. To Gilman, August 7, 1888, ibid.

    This may be as good a place as any to repeat the story about *The Man with the Hoe,* a poem written by Edwin Markham, an Oakland schoolteacher, purchased by Hearst's San Francisco *Examiner* for forty dollars and printed on January 15, 1899. It swept the country, a symbol, said William Jennings Bryan, of "humanity's protest against human greed." Huntington, who for a quarter of a century had been helping Hampton Institute's hard struggle to put tools into the hands of the wretched, did not see it that way. The man to pity, he retorted, was the man who had no hoe—in other words, let there be more Hamptons— and he offered a prize of $750 for a poem in rebuttal. The nation jeered his unfortunately worded statement: he was as insensitive as the man with the hoe and had missed Markham's point. He may indeed have done so—he never really indicated—but the nation had missed his point, too. Literary mythology is not likely to readjust the account, however. The yarn is too good the way it stands. For one of many versions of the hoe story, see Lewis, *The Big Four,* pp. 240–41.

26 SLINGS AND ARROWS

1. To C. F. Crocker, July 18, 1893, Holladay Collection.
2. San Francisco *Call,* March 29, 1888.
3. The most lucid account of the involved problems attending the railroads' debts to the government is in Daggett, *Southern Pacific,* pp. 370–424.
4. Theophilus French to I. E. Gates (Huntington's chief expediter), December 3 and 30, 1886; Huntington to French, January 6, 1887, as printed

in an undated clipping from *The Financier,* Pardee Scrapbook No. 1, Huntington Library. Also Huntington to Sargent, January 21, 1887, and to lobbyist John Boyd, January 18, 1887, Letterbook, 1881–89. In the letter to Boyd, Huntington suggested putting a detective on French's trail to learn whether the man was vulnerable to retaliation. Results do not appear.

5. Quotation from a letter to George B. Williams, January 28, 1887, ibid.
6. Swisher, *Stephen J. Field,* pp. 264–65.
7. The commission's 5,560-page report was printed as Senate Executive Document No. 51, 50th Cong., 1st Sess. Stanford's testimony is on pp. 2452–95, 2620–48, 2758–60, 2829, etc. Huntington's: pp. 8–43, 3696 ff.
8. Daggett, op. cit., pp. 395–401. The most dazzling performance on behalf of the Central Pacific was by Creed Haymond, attorney for the Southern Pacific system. Haymond spoke extemporaneously before the select committee on three different days in March and April 1888. The associates, he declaimed, were paragons of virtue and patriotism, responsible for "the greatest achievement of the human race on earth." Far from enriching themselves at the expense of the government, they had lost their fortunes in racing the Union Pacific—a race made inevitable by the iniquitous acts of the government. He whirled figures like Indian clubs, censured Congress for the Thurman bill, challenged the world to prove a single instance of either bribery, tampering with legislative processes, or illegal diversion of funds. It was a particularly remarkable achievement in view of the fact that ten years before, when campaigning for office in California, Haymond had stumped the state "in violent opposition to the corporation, even advising his hearers to tear up its tracks"—Graves, *California Memories.* The raiload thought well enough of his newer opinions that they rushed his marathon speeches, which had been transcribed stenographically, to press in California and distributed them widely. The effect was negligible. Haymond, *The Central Pacific Railroad Company.*
9. Figures from Doherty, "Smooth Is the Road," December 1953. They differ from those in Evans, *Collis Potter Huntington,* p. 543.
10. Evans, op. cit., p. 582.
11. The H. E. Huntington Biographical File, Folders 3, 4, and 5, Huntington Library, contain considerable correspondence between Collis and his nephew Henry Edwards Huntington, then general manager of the Kentucky Central, concerning the sales of the various properties.
12. To W. H. Mills, November 28, 1891; to A. N. Towne, December 21, 1891, Letterbook, November 1891–January 1892, Huntington Library.
13. Clark, *Leland Stanford,* p. 436–38.
14. Holladay Collection.
15. San Francisco *Examiner,* April 10, 13, 1890; New York *Morning Journal,* April 14; Los Angeles *Express,* April 19; Los Angeles *Times,* April 24, and on and on. Cf. Clark, op. cit., pp. 438–41.
16. The Washington pressure is reported by the Oakland *Times,* July 13, 1890, and the San Francisco *Argonaut,* August 18, 1890.

17. Printed in the Kern County *Californian,* August 23, 1890, and widely copied throughout the nation.

18. Clark, op. cit., p. 443–48, presents the favorable side. Callow, "San Francisco's Blind Boss," and Edith Dobie, *The Political Career of Stephen Mallory White* (Stanford, Calif., 1927), pp. 118–19, present rather more convincing accounts of a totally corrupt use of money and bargain making.

19. Evans, op. cit., pp. 601–41 passim.

20. To W. H. Mills, August 27, 1890, Letterbook, June 1890–June 1891. The ending of the *Argonaut* payments is recorded on the back of the draft of "Stanford Matters—Suggested Interview," Holladay Collection.

21. The quotation is compounded from two letters to Stow, December 3 and 24, 1891, Letterbooks.
    Although it was not a field wherein his talents lay, Huntington frequently pondered increasing traffic by developing new agricultural resources. One example: on October 29, 1894, he wrote a long letter to W. H. Mills (Holladay Collection) concerning foreign crops that might be adaptable to California—licorice from Asia Minor, filberts from Spain, wild thyme from Palestine for honey. He also suggested experiments to spread the growing range of date palms.

22. To Mills, December 22, 1891; to Towne, December 21, 1891, Letterbooks.

23. C. P. Huntington to H. E. Huntington, June 1, 1896, H. E. Huntington Biographical File, Box H-1-1. Arabella seems not to have liked letter writing. At least Collis was the one who dispatched directive after directive concerning the house, even down to detailed instructions concerning the tiles in Arabella's bathroom.

24. Towne and Worthington to Huntington, September 3, 1892, H. E. Huntington Biographical File, Box P-1, which was the company's designation for letters dealing with political subjects. This P-1 file is occasionally suggestive. For example, a letter from Isaac Gates to H. E. Huntington, January 14, 1893, announced that a certain amount of currency had been sent from New York. That's all that is said. But the filing is under "Politics." Was currency perhaps sent from New York so that there would be no damaging record of withdrawals from the banks in San Francisco?

25. For example, C. P. Huntington to J. O'H. Cosgrave, June 5, 1900, two months before Collis' death.

26. To Henry Wickham, December 4, 1891; to John Boyd, December 4, 8, 18, 1891, Letterbooks.

27. Letterbooks, 1881–89 and 1885–87. See index under Sherrill.

28. To W. C. Wickham, August 13, 1886, Letterbook, 1885–87.

29. Huntington to Abbott Robinson, December 7, 1891, Letterbook, November 1891–January 1892. New York *World,* June 26, 1894.

30. For the San Pedro-Santa Monica rivalry: Charles Dwight Willard's participant's account, *The Free Harbor Contest at Los Angeles* (Los Angeles, 1899); Boyle Workman, *The City That Grew* (Los Angeles, 1936); Fogelson, *The Fragmented Metropolis,* pp. 108 ff.; Marshall

Stimson, "A Short History of Los Angeles Harbor," The Historical Society of Southern California *Quarterly,* March 1945; and the opening
sections of Albert Clodius, *The Quest for Good Government in Los
Angeles, 1890–1910* (unpublished Ph.D. dissertation, Claremont [Calif.]
Graduate School, 1953).

31. For the antecedents and outgrowths of the Traffic Association: Daggett,
Southern Pacific, pp. 293–346.

32. Robert E. Stewart, Jr., and Mary Frances Stewart, *Adolph Sutro, A
Biography* (Berkeley, 1962).

33. Ibid., pp. 181–200 passim. San Francisco *Chronicle,* February 1, 1896.
San Francisco *Examiner,* January 28 and 29, 1896. Sutro reported to
Huntington's charges by saying that the Southern Pacific wanted to keep
people away from his establishments so that he would fail; the railroad
would then buy his land and erect an aristocratic resort hotel where
once the common people had been wont to frolic.

34. This was the period of the railroad's disputed payoff to Hearst. On
June 29, 1892, Southern Pacific officials in San Francisco bought $30,000
worth of advertising in the *Examiner* and appended a secret agreement to
the effect that although the company would not be immune to criticism,
the tone of it would henceforth be gentler. In the spring of 1894, enraged by attacks that could by no means be called gentle, Huntington
canceled the contract, with eight thousand dollars still unpaid. The *Examiner* did not sue, as it was entitled to do on a straight advertising
contract, but neither did anyone on the Southern Pacific staff swear under
oath, as they were often requested to do, that the contract was primarily
a payoff and not a straightforward advertising transaction. Huntington
certainly believed that his subordinates had signed a subsidizing agreement and that its cancellation explained Hearst's fierce enmity—Huntington, marked "Private," to F. H. Gassaway of the *Examiner,* October
22, 1894, Holladay Collection. Hearst just as sincerely believed that his
staff had not been guilty of accepting a payoff—W. A. Swanberg,
Citizen Hearst (soft-cover edition, New York, 1963), pp. 107–18.

35. A copy of Sutro's Kentucky letter, which was printed for distribution
in California, is in the Huntington Library. The same library has several examples of Sutro's broadsides to Congressmen. For models of scur-
rility, see Ambrose Bierce's Washington dispatches, beginning in the San
Francisco *Examiner* on February 1, 1896. Huntington's only revenge was
a remark to a reporter from the San Francisco *Call,* a competitor of
the *Examiner*'s, that, "Willie Hearst is a dirty boy, too nasty to touch
with a pair of tongs," a bon mot that the *Call* joyfully headlined on
May 1, 1898.

36. The hearings were published as Senate Document 314, 54th Cong., 1st
Sess.

37. Dobie, op. cit., p. 184; Stimson, op. cit.

38. For the settlement: Daggett, op. cit., pp. 412–24.

39. Doherty, "Smooth Is the Road," October 1953.

40. Grodinsky, *Jay Gould,* p. 346.

Sources and Acknowledgments

This book was suggested to me by David Huntington, who turned over to me the voluminous notes that he had been collecting on Collis P. Huntington. Without this generosity, the writing would have been, for me, next to impossible.

Collis Huntington Holladay of San Marino, California, made available many documents and letters written by his great-uncle. They are cited in the Notes as "Holladay Collection." The letters sent by Collis Huntington to his brother Solon during the gold-rush period and the subsequent years in Sacramento, form a significant part of the Holladay Collection and were particularly valuable in allowing a reconstruction of a hitherto little-known period of Collis' life.

The trustees of the Henry E. Huntington Library, San Marino, California, and the director, Dr. James Thorpe, graciously allowed me to go through its extensive and hitherto restricted collection of material known as the Henry E. Huntington Biographical File. This collection insofar as it relates to Collis Huntington, can be divided roughly into two parts:

1. Letterpress copies of correspondence mailed by Collis P. Huntington. Each letterbook contains five hundred or more pages. There are three books extant covering the period of the 1880s: one, 1881–89, marked "Private"; one, 1885–87; and one, June 12, 1888 to January 21, 1889. Several other letterbooks cover the early 1890s. Most of these letterbooks are concerned with matters apart from Huntington's railroads and shipyards. Occasionally, however, as the text indicates, a revealing letter pops up in the midst of a long run of routine correspondence.

2. A great mass of loose originals, carbons, documents, and so on dealing with the period from Henry E. Huntington's arrival in San Francisco in 1892 to the close of the century. Many of the telegrams and some of the letters are in cipher. The Huntington Library possesses two of the company's cipher books, but these do not cover all of the coded documents. A long struggle with this coded material led to a conclusion that it was mostly for word saving and privacy in the telegraph office, that the gist could be gathered from follow-up letters, and that inability to "break" all of the codes has not

resulted in an overlooking of significant data. Some future sleuth may wish to pursue the matter further.

The letters and telegrams in this collection had been filed originally by the company according to a cataloguing key recorded in blue pencil in the upper right-hand corner of the front page. Tony Bliss of the Huntington Library staff solved the key and recatalogued much of the material. The convenience of this to research is self-evident.

Another Huntington Library collection of usefulness to this study were the A. A. Cohen Papers.

The other great collection of original manuscript material—letters, contracts, and whatnot—concerning the railroad builders is at Stanford University. Once known variously as the George Clark collection and as the Hopkins Transportation Library, this material is now classified broadly as part of the Manuscript Collections, Stanford University Libraries. The Wyles Collection of the University of California at Santa Barbara has microfilm of the Stanford material.

The Bancroft Library of the University of California at Berkeley has manuscript dictations of autobiographical accounts by Charles Crocker, Leland Stanford, Collis Huntington, and a few others connected with them. These dictations should be used with more caution than they generally receive. Though by no means valueless, still they were composed at a time when the associates were under searching examination by congressional investigating committees, and the dictators spoke to Bancroft's scribes with full awareness that they should not contradict testimony given to the government inquisitors. The Bancroft Library also holds a file of Theodore Judah material, including the reminiscences of his widow, Anna.

Certain printed materials qualify as primary documents. These include the four following volumes of letters, cited in the Notes as *Collected Letters*, Vol. I, II, III, and IV.

I. Letters from Collis P. Huntington to Mark Hopkins, Leland Stanford, Charles Crocker, E. B. Crocker, Charles F. Crocker, and D. D. Cotton (sic) from August 20, 1867, to August 5, 1869. New York, 1892.

II. Letters from Collis P. Huntington to Mark Hopkins, Leland Stanford, Charles Crocker, and E. B. Crocker from August 5, 1869, to March 26, 1873. New York, 1892.

III. Letters from Collis P. Huntington to Mark Hopkins, Leland Stanford, Charles Crocker, and D. D. Colton from April 2, 1873, to March 31, 1876. New York, 1894.

IV. Letters from Mark Hopkins, Leland Stanford, Charles Crocker, Charles F. Crocker, and David D. Colton to Collis P. Huntington from August 27, 1869 to December 30, 1879. New York: John C. Rankin Co., 1891.

I know of only two sets of these books. One is at the Mariners' Museum, Newport News, Virginia. The other is at the Huntington Library. Their provenance baffles me. They are said to have been compiled by Archer Huntington for the use of his stepfather. Apparently Archer used letterpress copies in Collis' possession as his source. The letterpress books have since disappeared.

At the time of doing this work Archer was in his early twenties and must have been somewhat startled at what the documents revealed (if, indeed, he was the editor). In the hands of a government board of inquiry, the volumes could have been highly embarrassing. Why Collis Huntington had these four volumes printed I cannot imagine.

How extensively were they edited? A comparison with some of the originals in the Stanford collection suggests that changes were limited to rectifying Collis' free-wheeling spelling, grammar, and punctuation. A few words illegible in the originals have been left blank. Now and then a name emerges incorrectly because of difficulties with penmanship; Casserly, for example, will be rendered Connely. Otherwise there seems to have been no altering of the originals, a reassuring conclusion, since these four volumes are the single most important source for the present study.

Another printed source is the so-called Colton Letters. These were originally part of the testimony in Mrs. David Colton's lawsuit against the associates, and were reprinted extensively (but not wholly) by the San Francisco *Chronicle,* the Chicago *Tribune,* and the New York *World.* I used the *Chronicle* reprints, December 23, 1883. A spot comparison of several of these letters with those printed in the *Collected Letters* cited above and with a handful of original letters from Huntington to Colton, in the Huntington Library, again suggests that no significant omissions or changes in the text have occurred during the process of transcription.

Another primary source relied on heavily in this work is a series of congressional documents issued by various investigation committees. The most useful by far was the 5,560-page report of the United States Pacific Railway Commission of 1887; full citation is in the Notes.

Copies of legal complaints issued by those who sued the associates for various reasons have been useful, but of course had to be handled with care since the complainants were naturally charging the defendants with all the wrongdoings that they could think of. Again the Notes will indicate the suits that were most frequently consulted. Newspapers, especially the Sacramento *Union* during the days when the Central Pacific was under construction, and the San Francisco *Examiner* during Hearst's campaign against the Southern Pacific, were regularly consulted. See the Notes for specific citations. Finally, the Huntington Library contains several bulky volumes of pamphlet material relating to the Central Pacific, its aquisitions, and its enemies. These pamphlets consist of engineering reports, financial statements, bond sales prospectuses, transcriptions of congressional hearings, and whatnot—a treasuretrove not to be overlooked by any student of the associates' work.

The Notes will serve as a bibliography of the books and articles used during the preparation of this work.

I should like to express my appreciation for help rendered, to David Huntington, Collis Huntington Holladay, the trustees of the Huntington Library and its staff: Mary Isabel Fry of the reference department; Cary Bliss, the curator of the Rare Book Room—and also to Robert Wark, director of the Henry E. Huntington Art Galleries. Helpful, too, were Ralph Hansen, archivist, Stanford University, Robert Becker of the Bancroft Library, University of California at Berkeley, and Richard Dillon of the Sutro Library, San Francisco.

Since the name Huntington appears so often in these acknowledgments, perhaps I should say that this is in no sense an "official" biography and that, as a reading of the text will substantiate, questions of censorship were not raised, a liberality of action not always extended by the holders of family papers.

As usual, the unabated zeal and nimble typing of my wife Mildred were the chief sustaining factors throughout.

Index

Alameda, Cal., 186–87, 221, 246, 258
Alger, Russell A., as Secretary of War, 373
Alley, Sen. John B., of Mass., 174, 196
Ames, Oakes, 129, 144, 145, 165, 171, 174, 196, 198, 206, 211n., 221, 223, 237, 238, 239, 240, 292
Ames, Oliver, 129, 144, 165, 174, 196, 221, 237, 240, 254, 255
Anderson, Joseph R., 253
Archer, Laurence, as California assemblyman, 301
Aspinwall, William, 253, 279, 280, 307
Associated Press, 286, 303
Associates of Central Pacific R.R.: and stock arrangement with Charles Crocker & Co., 167, 193; dissension among, over take-over of Western Pacific, 183–89; and Contract & Finance Co., 194–95, 246, 261; moves of, to gain control of northern railroads and of Goat Island, 196; strategy of, to control rail traffic to deep water around San Francisco, 197; and intensification of construction race with Union Pacific, 198–209; take-over of Southern Pacific by, 214–15, 222, 223; and exclusive rights to Wells Fargo for carrying express on Central Pacific, 217; and Oakland waterfront, 217, 221; quarrel between Huntington and Stanford over CP policy on location line in Utah, 228, 232–33; Huntington's driving of, for more speed in construction, 236–37, 239; standard California denigration of, 248n.; failure of Huntington to inform of his C & O plans, 252–53, 271; criticism of UP roadbed and tracks by, 255; month-long meeting of, in fall of 1869, on company financing and policies, 255–63, 267; and eliminating possible competitors, 257–59; and consolidation of all of its roads (except Southern Pacific) under a single management, 260, 263, 264, 277, 282; and scheme for watering CP stock under consolidation, 260; and manner of obtaining the many short-line acquisitions, 261; and inquiries in California Legislature about source of money being used by CP in acquiring so many California short lines, 261, 263; carelessness of, about their minority stockholders, 263; need and greed appear to have blinded them in their stock manipulations, 263; polarization of opinions about, 267, 281; attitude of, toward profits made, 268; appraisal of themselves as public benefactors, 268, 269; replies of, to their critics and detractors, 268–69; philosophy of, 269; increasing friction between Huntington and Stanford, 273–74, 275; financial problems because of extravagances in construction, 274; Huntington's criticism of activities of other associates, 277; panic of, at threatened suit by minority stockholders, 278; scramble of, to buy up all CP stock in hands of minority shareholders, 278–80; suits against CP for stock accounting, 280–81; and "evidence" about CP stock as shown in their books, 281; and incorporation of Southern Pacific Railroad Company, 283; buy holdings of Charles and E. B. Crocker in CP, 284; and plans to sell one of their systems, CP or SP, 285, 293; and gaining of control of California Pacific R.R. by questionable means, 286; and the 1872 bill for control of Goat Island, 287–88; and junction of CP and SP at Goshen, Cal., 289; books of Contract & Finance Co. burned by, 292, 293; and saving of CP and SP in 1873 financial panic, 293–95; and Huntington's plans for their full measure of profit, 295; and dividends declared on CP earnings, 299–30; mansions of, atop San Francisco's Nob Hill, 300, 301, 303, 307, 321–22, 364; and hard times of winter of 1876–77, 320; refusal of the California associates to authorize SP construction eastward beyond Yuma, 324; rifts about policy, and difficult personality problem, 325; and Huntington's determination to build Southern transcontinental, 327; major reorganization of, 328; and financial difficulties, in 1884, of railroads controlled by 340–41
Atchison, Topeka & Santa Fe R.R., 337, 353
Atlantic & Pacific R.R., 170, 174, 191, 192, 213, 214, 218, 223–24, 250, 257, 265, 266, 283, 337
Atlantic & Pacific Telegraph Co., 303

Bailey, James: as investor in planned Central Pacific R.R., 95, 97; as secretary of Central Pacific R.R., 98, 100; and factional split in management of Central Pacific R.R., 136, 138, 139, 140; forced out of Central Pacific management by Huntington, 140

Baker, Col. Robert, and his wife Arcadia, 368

Bancroft, Hubert Howe, and biography of Collis Huntington, 3, 15, 19, 66, 67

Barber, Orson, Collis Huntington as apprenticed farm-hand to, 3

Beckworth Pass threat to Central Pacific, 171

Beecher, Henry Ward, 343

Beerstecher, C. J., 330

Bennett, Henry, 107, 108

Benson, Farr & West, 226

Benton, Sen. Thomas Hart, of Missouri, 9, 10, 59

Berry, Sen. James H., of Arkansas, 374

Bierce, Ambrose, 372; cruel reporting by, of Huntington at Senate committee hearings, 373

Big Four of Central Pacific R.R., *See* Crocker, Charles; Hopkins, Mark; Huntington, Collis; Stanford, Leland

Bingham, Rep. John, of Ohio, 239

Bishop, F. A., 159, 163

Black Friday in California (February 23, 1855), 56

Blaine, James G., 291; as Secretary of State, 361–62

Blue Ridge R.R., 245, 252

Booth, Lucius A.: as member of board of directors of Central Pacific R.R., 98, 136, 138, 139; forced out of Central Pacific management by Huntington, 140

Booth, Gov. Newton, of California, 296, 311

Boruck, Marcus D., 121

Bowles, Samuel, 168

Boyd, John, 198, 349

Bradbury, George, 297

Bragg, George, 162–63

Brannan, Sam: as wharf operator in San Francisco, 22, 23; activities of, in early California, 24–25, 26, 35; and discovery of gold near Sacramento, 26; and growth of Sacramento, 27; as promoter without equal, 27; and squatters in Sacramento, 36; and vigilante committee in San Francisco (1951), 41; and California Central R.R., 102, 105, 108, 124–26, 247; and Yuba R.R., 125, 160, 247; and Northern Pacific R.R., 154; and Central Pacific R.R., 160–61; crumbling of his California-wide empire, 184; as holder of CP stock, 260, 277; suit of, for stock accounting, against Central Pacific, 280, 301

Bribery of Congressmen, Collis Huntington on, 66

Broderick, David C.: and California politics in the 1850s, 52–53, 74–75, 307; death of, in politically instigated duel, 75–76

Brookgreen Gardens near Myrtle Beach, S.C., 376

Brooks, Rep. James, of N.Y., 292

Brown, Arthur, 180, 225

Brown, John, and Collis Huntington, 4, 53

Browning, Orville, as Secretary of Interior, 176, 179, 191, 202, 204, 206, 207, 208, 222, 226, 229–30, 231, 233, 234, 237–38, 265

Bryan, William Jennings, 374

Buckley, Christopher Augustine, 333, 346, 362

Burlington R.R., 335

Bushnell, Cornelius S., 147, 164, 198

California: hazards of conducting business in early 1850s, 34; and proposals that government help finance railway across continent, 34; admission of, to the Union (1850), 37–38; cholera epidemic in (1850), 38; and vigilantism in the 1850s, 41, 65–66; and politics in the 1850s, 52–53, 54, 56, 62–64, 66–67, 70, 74–76; gubernatorial 1859 campaign, 74–75; secessionist sentiment and prowar demonstrations of Union clubs in, 98; and polarized opinions about Central Pacific as state benefactor, 267, 281; dominant group in post-Civil War economy of, 269; unfavorable publicity triggered in, by Congressional railroad investigations, 291; and legislative bills to curb the railroads, 296; unabated hostility in, toward Central Pacific, 303, 329; charges against CP made at constitutional convention, winter of 1878–79, 329–30; defenders' replies to charges against CP, 330; and railroad commission with extensive powers of review and regulation, 330, 333; boast of Huntington about what he and his associates had done for, 341, 366; clamor against Southern Pacific in, 366

California Central R.R., 77, 90, 102, 105, 108, 124–26, 128, 140, 160, 171, 184, 185, 186, 196, 247, 258; control of, gained by Central Pacific R.R., 196, 247, 258

California Daily Times, and 1856 presidential campaign, 67, 69

California feeder to Pacific R.R.: rivalries and scramble over, 84–91; organizing and promotion of Central Pacific R.R. by Judah, 89–91

California Northern R.R., 102, 108, 125, 160, 161, 171, 184, 185, 186

California & Oregon R.R., 170, 171, 174, 184, 185, 190, 247, 258, 259, 264, 274, 275, 284, 286, 293, 328, 335; control of, gained by Central Pacific, 247, 258

California Pacific Eastern Extension, 285

California Pacific R.R., 171, 178, 186, 190–91, 221, 264, 285–86, 294; Central Pacific gains control of, by involved and illegal means, 286

California Southern R.R., 266, 283; Central Pacific gains control of, 283

California Southern R.R. (new), incorporated by San Diegans, 337, 338, 341

California Stage Co., 160

California State Board of Agriculture, Collis Huntington as member of, 109

California Steam Navigation Co., 264

California Workingmen's party (sand-lotters), 321–22, 331

Campbell, James A., 105

Canadian Pacific R.R., 353

Capitalization: of Central Pacific R.R., 256, 261; of Southern Pacific R.R. Company, 283

Carnegie, Andrew, 215, 346

Carpentier, Horace W., 186, 187, 192, 216

Carr, William B., 188, 192, 215, 260n., 283, 311

Casement, Dan, 173

Casement, John, 173, 198, 233

Mrs. Colton of his stocks and bonds in their railroad enterprises, 328–29
Colton, Mrs. David D., suit of, against CP associates, 329; letters damaging to Huntington read into the record and widely circulated by hostile press, 329
Comstock Lode, in Nevada Territory, 85, 91, 122, 134, 153, 313, 371; determining of wagon road to, 85–89, 90
Cone, J. S., 330
Congressional investigation of railroad financing, 291–92; Huntington as witness at, 291–92, 293; demand for investigation of CP associates' allegedly unreasonable profits, 301. See also United States Pacific Railway Commission
Conkling, Roscoe, as Central Pacific's legal counsel in the East, 234, 280, 288
Conness, John, 134, 135; as senator from California, 150, 151, 153, 156, 164, 171, 173–74, 191, 213, 220
Construction contracts: profit possibilities in, 146, 166, 168, 256; Huntington quoted on crimes committed under cover of, 286–87
Continent-wide rail system, Huntington's 1882 plan for, 339; and his CP associates, 339–40; completion of modified form of, in October 1884, 340
Contract & Finance Co.: as construction firm of Central Pacific R.R., 194–95, 200, 246, 247, 255, 259, 261, 277, 278, 284, 325, 355; Central Pacific stock held by, 256, 260, 263; as rebuilders of California Pacific's substandard lines, 286; fear of CP associates of public display of books of, 292; books of, burned by CP associates, 292, 293
Contracting and Building Co., as construction firm for subsidiary line for C & O, 356
Cooke, Jay, 150, 181, 255, 258, 294, 299
Corning, Rep. Erastus, of New York, 128
County taxpayers in California, and dissatisfaction over bonds voted for stock in Central Pacific, 210–12
Covington and Ohio R.R., 245
Cox, Jacob, as Secretary of Interior, 265, 266, 267, 283
CP. See Central Pacific R.R.
Crandall, Jared B., of Pioneer Stage Lines, 73
Crédit Mobilier, 147, 152, 154, 164–65, 171, 174, 240, 280, 304, 314; and the scandal about, 195, 196, 211n., 280, 288, 289, 291; and factional disputes, 196; presidential 1872 election, and Crédit Mobilier scandal, 291; irregularities inside Congress revealed by Congressional hearings, 292
Credit structure of Central Pacific, Huntington's work to improve (1874), 299
Crocker, Charles, 102, 103, 118, 136, 152, 161, 180, 185, 187, 188, 204, 214, 220, 225, 229, 231, 234, 236, 242, 243, 252, 254, 273, 302, 306, 307, 318, 319, 322, 323, 325, 326, 327–28, 339–40, 342; and Know-Nothing politics in California in the 1850s, 54, 64; background and early history of, 54–56; and Republican activities in late 1850s, 64, 67, 70, 75, 92; as state legislator, 92; as investor in planned Central Pacific R.R., 95, 99, 100; as president of Contract & Finance Co., 194, 200; upon completion of Pacific railroad, 249–50; associates of CP buy his interest in

Central Pacific, 284; rejoins Central Pacific as second vice-president, 294–95; death of (1888), 359. See also Associates of Central Pacific Railroad
Crocker, Charles & Co.: as construction company for Central Pacific R.R., 123, 134, 137, 142, 148, 167, 168, 171, 180; and Central Pacific stock, 166–68, 172, 193, 195
Crocker, Edwin Bryant, 54, 55, 188, 189, 192, 193, 214, 252, 302; and launching of Republican party in California, 63; activities of, in 1856 presidential campaign, 67; appointment of, by Governor Stanford, as chief justice of California Supreme Court, 134; as Central Pacific's attorney, 143–44, 148, 149, 183, 185, 186; and Charles Crocker-Central Pacific stock deal, 167; and Contract & Finance Co., 194; CP associates buy his holdings in the railroad, 284. See also Associates of Central Pacific R.R.
Crocker, Fred (Charles F.), 328, 361, 363, 367; as president of Southern Pacific R.R., 352, 363; as successor to his father in CP organization, 359
Crocker, H. S., 212
Crocker, Mary Deming (Mrs. Charles), 55–56, 254
Cross-country highway. See Wagon road, cross-country
Curtis, Rep. Samuel R., of Iowa, 81–84, 100n.

Dame, Judge Timothy, 100, 108, 122
Dangerfield, Judge W. P., 302, 303
Davenport, Homer, 372
Davis, Fred, 367
Davis, Jefferson, 251, 309
Day, Sherman, California state senator, 60, 70, 77, 234
Debts of UP and CP to government. See Government loans for railroad construction
Democratic party in California, feuding factions in, 52–53, 74–76; Broderick-Terry duel, 75–76
Denver, Rep. James, of California, 71
Depression of the 1890s, 352, 366, 369, 372, 374
Dey, Peter, 145, 164
Di Cesnola, L. P., 350
Dividend payments on Central Pacific's earnings, 299–300, 325, 334, 341
Dix, John Adams, 174
Dodge, Grenville, 173, 198, 220, 237, 285, 303, 306, 309, 310, 319
Donahue, Peter, 100, 108, 122
Donner Summit, Central Pacific construction drive over, 172
Drew, Daniel, 240
Drexel, Morgan & Co., 357
Dry Diggings, Cal., and the gold-rush, 28–30, 49
Dunn, Major T. S., 322, 323
Durant, Thomas C.: and Union Pacific R.R., 127, 142, 145–47, 152–56, 164–65, 174, 176, 196, 198, 199, 220, 231, 235, 240; and Crédit Mobilier, 147, 152, 154, 164–65, 196
Durant, William West, 375
Dutch Flat and Donner Lake Wagon Road Company, 104–5, 112, 118, 133, 136, 148,

158, 168; "Dutch Flat swindle pamphlet" issued by enemies in San Francisco, 158, 163
Dwinnel, J. E., 350n.

Economic slump in fall of 1951, 42
Elliott, Simon G., 170, 184
Emmet, C. Temple, 184
Emmons, Delos, 172n., 272
Erie R.R., stock raid on, 240
Estate of Collis Huntington, division of, at his death, 376
Europe, marketing of Central Pacific securities in, 181–82, 193–94, 259
Ewing, Thomas, Jr., 106, 108, 127, 147, 176, 202, 206, 208, 222, 230

Farnsworth, Rep. John, of Illinois, 254
Felton, John B., 277
Field, Justice Stephen, 355
Field, Stephen J., 134
54 K Street, Sacramento, Collis Huntington's building at, 42, 43–44, 62; housekeeping of Collis and Elizabeth Huntington upstairs at, 45–46, 62; as center of political activities in organizing of Republican party in California, 62–63; as upstairs rendezvous of Republicans, 67, 70, 75, 92
Financial panic of September 1873, 294, 303, 338
Fisk, Harvey, 244, 246, 247, 248, 249, 251, 253
Fisk, Jim, 240
Fisk and Hatch, of N.Y.C.: marketing of Central Pacific securities by, 169, 181, 182, 193, 210, 220, 229, 244, 246; debts of Huntington's railroads to (1873), 294; insolvency of, 294
Five Eminent Citizens committee appointed by Grant to investigate the Transcontinental, 242, 247; report of, 273, 276
Flint, James P., and Yuba R.R., 125
Flint, Peabody & Co. of Boston, 125; marketing of Central Pacific bonds through, 128, 129
Fort Yuma Military Reservation, 319, 322
Franchot, Richard, 105–6, 143, 172, 181, 240, 305, 308, 310, 339n.; as lobbyist of Central Pacific R.R., 106, 197, 254
Frémont, Jessie Benton (Mrs. John Charles), 9, 13–14, 17, 250, 349
Frémont, John C.: and Collis Huntington, 9, 250, 349; and exploratory trip for route of transcontinental railroad, 59; as Republican presidential nominee in 1856 campaign, 67; and Leavenworth, Pawnee & Western R.R., 127, 142, 147; and Union Pacific, Eastern Division, 147, 166; and Atlantic & Pacific R.R., 170, 250; and Kansas Pacific R.R., 250; and Memphis, El Paso and Pacific R.R., 250–51, 266, 282; and proposed transcontinental from Norfolk to San Diego, 251, 266
French, Theophilus, and attempt to bribe Huntington over pryings into iniquities of railroads, 354
Funding bill, Senate committee hearings on, 356, 372–73; questioning of Huntington, 372–73; illness of Huntington during hearings, 373

Galveston, Harrisburg & San Antonio R.R., 327, 335; controlling interest in, taken over by Southern Pacific, 336
Garfield, James, 291

Garrison, C. K., as president of Sacramento Valley R.R., 57
Gates, Isaac, 344
Gauge of railroads, and problem of, for transcontinental and feeder lines, 125–26, 128
George, Henry, 36
Germany, marketing of Central Pacific securities in, 182, 193, 259, 275, 280
Glidden brothers, as CP stockholders, 279
Goat Island, in San Francisco Bay, 178, 186, 187, 188, 190, 192, 196, 214, 216, 220, 221, 223, 246, 259, 368; Huntington's lobbying in Washington about control of, 196–97, 222, 223, 287; and the 1872 bill on control of, 287–88
Goddard, George, 60, 70
Gold, discovery of, in California, 1, 25–26
Gold market, Jay Gould's assault on (1869), 271
Gold mine of Leland Stanford, 182, 297n.
Gold-rush party from Oneonta, N.Y., to California, 1–2, 6–10; journey of, from New York across Panama to California, 11–20; reactions of, on arrival in San Francisco, 22–23; activities of, around Dry Diggings, 28–30
Gorham, George C., 213, 215, 260n., 283, 311
Gould, Jay, 271, 312, 315–16, 322, 326, 327, 334–36, 339, 377; and control of UP and of Pacific Mail Co., 297; and battle of Huntington and his associates with, over oriental commerce, 297–98; and the Los Angeles & Independence R.R., 312–13; and compromise agreement reached between Texas & Pacific R.R. and Southern Pacific R.R., 314; and land-grant funding bill, 315–16, 317; beaten by Huntington in eastern advance of SP, 336; and Huntington as allies, 336–37
Government bonds for railroad construction, 82, 83, 163, 238–39, 241, 273; arrears of UP and CP in interest payments on, 276; sinking fund for repayment of principal and interest, 276; and amount of CP's debt to government, 352
Government loans for railroad construction, 113–14, 163; demands by Congress for repayment of, 296, 301, 315; and land-grant funding bill of Jay Gould and Huntington, 315–16, 317; sinking fund act for repayment by UP and CP, 315, 326, 353; Huntington's attitude toward delaying payment of, 352–53; Stanford's attitude toward repayment of, 353; refunding measure that Huntington wanted defeated, 373; negotiated settlement of CP's debt agreed upon, 374; settlement of CP's indebtedness completed in 1909, 375
Grant, President Ulysses S., 242, 247, 265, 266, 288, 291; scandals in administration of, 314
Gray, George M., 168, 169, 231, 232
Greeley, Horace, 36, 75, 168, 287
Green River, Utah, Huntington's drive for meeting with Union Pacific at, 176, 179, 182, 185, 193, 196, 197, 199, 242, 257
Grodinsky, Professor, quoted on Huntington "as the leading railroad builder of the U.S.," 376
Gwin, Sen. William M., and California politics in the 1950s and '60s, 52–53, 63, 72, 74–75, 96, 101, 307

Huntington Hall at Tuskegee Institute, 350
Huntington, Hammond & Schultz: trading firm of, organized by Collis Huntington in Sacramento (1850), 32; building erected by, on K Street, 32; Huntington as buyer for, 35; selling activities of Huntington in San Francisco (1851), 40 41; and salvage of goods from wreck of ship *Tagus*, 41; dissolution of (1852), 42
Huntington, Henry E., 38, 143, 272, 338, 339n.; as first assistant to president of Southern Pacific Co., 364; as heir of one-third of estate of Collis Huntington, 376; and sale of Southern Pacific to E. H. Harriman, 376; divorce of, from Mary Prentice Huntington, and marriage to uncle's widow, Arabella, 376; and development of electric interurban lines and real estate in Southern California, 376
Huntington, Mary Alice Prentice (Mrs. Henry E.), 338; divorce of, 376
Huntington, Massol & Co., trading firm in Sacramento, 45–46, 47, 49
Huntington, S. & C. P., general store in Oneonta, N.Y.: partnership of Solon and Collis in, 5, 8; Collis' role in developing and expanding business of, 6; plans for branch store in goldfields of West, 7–8; Egbert Sabin's suit against, 39
Huntington, Solon: as owner, with brother, of general store in Oneonta, N.Y., 1, 5, 8; and promotion of Oneontans' gold-rush to California, 1–2; equity of, in profits earned by Collis in California, 32; and Collis Huntington, ending of half interests in each other's concerns, 45
Huntington, W. Va., 272
Huntington, William (father), 2, 38
Huntington-Hopkins Hardware Co. in Sacramento, 49–50, 56, 57, 62, 129, 171, 301; store as center of Republican party organizing activity, 62, 63; and deals involving Central Pacific money, 171–72; sold to their clerks, and becomes Huntington-Hopkins & Company, 182–83
Hyde, William B., 221–22, 223, 287, 290, 306

Income bonds issued by railroads against anticipated earnings, 256
Industrial capitalism, and Collis Huntington's entrepreneurship, 248n.
Irish labor in railroad construction in West, 168, 173
Isaacs, A. J., 106
Israel Minor & Co., as N.Y. suppliers of Collis Huntington in California, 43, 45

Johnson, President Andrew, 174, 230
Johnson, Gov. John Neely of California, and the 1856 vigilantism, 66
Jones, Sen. John P., 312, 313, 366, 367
Judah, Anna (Mrs. Theodore), 50, 51, 71, 84, 89, 90, 140, 277, 349
Judah, Theodore, 91, 95, 96, 115, 122, 141; as surveying engineer for Sacramento Valley R.R., 50–51, 57, 69; evaluation by, of types of exploratory trips being made for possible route of transcontinental railroad, 59; and jealousies and self-defeating legislative maneuvers for construction of transcontinental road, 61; advocacy of, for federal expenditure for railroad building within California, 71; and debates in Congress over wagon road bills, 71; survey

by, for paper San Francisco & Sacramento R.R., 71; pamphlet of, on practical plan for building Pacific R.R., 71–72, 79; and 1859 convention for promoting Pacific R.R., 79–80; as lobbyist in Congress for Pacific R.R., 80, 82, 83, 100, 105, 107–8; activities of, on potential feeder line to Pacific R.R., 84–85; surveys by, for proposed wagon road to Comstock Lode area, 86–89, 90; and organizing of Central Pacific as feeder line to Pacific R.R., 89–91; survey for Central Pacific R.R. by, 96, 97, 98–99; as chief engineer of Central Pacific R.R., 98; as clerk of House subcommittee for drafting new Pacific R.R. bill, 106, 107; as secretary of Senate Committee on Pacific Railroads, 106; and factional split in board of directors of Central Pacific R.R., 136, 137–39; forced out of Central Pacific management by Huntington, 139–40; death of, 140, 141

Kansas Pacific R.R., 223, 250, 282
Kearney, Denis, 321, 331
Kern County *Californian*, Huntington's continuation of feud with Stanford, in published remarks in, 362
Kerr, Rep. Michael, of Indiana, 311
King, James, 65
Kirk, John, 70–71, 72, 73
Know-Nothings (American party): and California politics in the 1850s, 53–54, 56, 62; Mark Hopkins, as member of, 54, 56, 64

Labor shortages in Central Pacific construction forces because of new silver strikes in Nevada, 148, 225
Lamar, Sen. L. Q. C., of Mississippi, 316
Lambard, Charles A., 129, 165, 247, 248, 277, 278, 279, 280
Lambard, Orville, 129, 165, 247, 248, 277, 280
Land grants for railroad construction, 82, 83, 108, 113, 154, 174, 184, 213, 214, 220, 247, 250, 265, 267, 275, 282, 283, 285, 289, 295, 303, 304, 315, 316, 327, 336–37; land-grant bonds, 256, 300, 314; land-grant funding bill of Jay Gould and Huntington, 315–16, 317
Land speculators, imposition of curbs on, as goal of California Workingmen's party, 322
Latham, Milton, 101, 181–82, 286
Law-and-Order Party in California in the 1850s, 65, 66
Leavenworth, Pawnee & Western R.R., 106–8, 113, 114, 127, 142; renamed Union Pacific Railway, Eastern Division, 142
Lee, Robert E., 246
Libbey, Rep. Harry, of Newport News, 365
Library in Westchester built by Huntington, 350
Lincoln, President Abraham, 92, 96, 113, 126, 128, 136, 144n., 145, 147, 156, 162, 164
Li Po Tai, Chinese herb doctor, 326
Lobbying in Washington: for railroad legislation, 150–54, 176, 284, 305, 310, 311n.; by Huntington and his lobbyists, 142, 150–57, 163–64, 171, 173–74, 196–97, 220, 222, 223, 229–30, 238–39, 247, 265, 283, 287–88, 311, 324, 325, 365, 366

Presidential 1876 election, and contest between Tilden and Hayes, 311, 314

Press in California, and hostility toward Central Pacific, 211–12, 216, 301–2, 303; during the Mussel Slough episode, 332

Progress and Poverty (George), 36

Promontory, Utah: union of CP and UP at, with driving of golden spike into place, 242; absence of Huntington at celebrations marking completion of Pacific railroad, 242, 249; discordant meeting of officials of CP and UP at, 255

Public benefactions: of Collis Huntington, 350–51; of heirs of Huntington, 376

Pullman Company, strike against, and Southern Pacific, 372

Race in construction progress between Central Pacific and Union Pacific, 172, 175, 179, 194, 198–209, 220, 225–33, 351; and map scheme of Huntington, 202–3, 204, 206; and questionable manipulations, illegalities, and recklessness of Huntington, 203, 204–5, 206; Huntington's procuring and shipping of materials, 203–4; Huntington's about-face and decision "to play virtuous," 206; and legal location line in Utah, 226–33, 235–36, 237–38; compromise on meeting place of two roads, and end of long battle between, 241; Central Pacific, and meeting exorbitant cost of, 255, 261

Railroad acts: act of 1862, 113–15, 121, 127, 261; act of 1864, 150–57, 261; amendment of 1865, 164, 173–74; Huntington's interpretation of, with reference to work beyond the three-hundred-mile limit, 227, 228

Railroad-created towns, Huntington's interest in speculative opportunities in, 250

Railroad king, Richmond *Dispatch* on Huntington as, 272

Railroads: California ferment over, in the 1850s, 51; and prices for equipment and materials during Civil War, 129–30; milking of, during process of construction, 146, 166, 168, 194; *See also* Transcontinental railroad; specific names of railroads

Ralston, W. C., 181

Randall, Alexander, 230

Randall, Rep. Samuel, of Pennsylvania, 311

Raquette Lake in Adirondacks, the Huntingtons' rustic camp at, 375

Rates and fares: of Central Pacific, 210–11; on Pacific railroads, 1867 congressional bill on, 211*n;* Archer bill in California legislature to regulate CP's (1876), 301–2

Reed, Samuel, 207

Reno, Nev., new town of, 194, 196

Republican party in California: launching of (1856), 62–64; and 1856 presidential campaign, 66, 67, 70; and 1859 state elections, 74–75; in early 1860s, 92

Richardson, Albert, 168

Rivers and Harbors Committee of U. S. Senate, 368

Robinson, Abbott, 367

Robinson, John P. and Lester L.: and Sacramento Valley R.R., 51, 57, 69, 117–18, 123, 124, 131; and Sacramento, Placer & Nevada R.R., 78–79, 87, 96–97, 117, 132, 148, 158; and wagon road to Comstock Lode area, 85–87; strategy of, against Central Pacific R.R., 131–32, 134; setback for, in Nevada, 159; and obstruc-

tionist moves by directors of Central Pacific, 160; and loss of race between their line and Central Pacific, together with stagecoach lines, 160; sale of their controlling stock interests in California railroad lines to Central Pacific, 162–63, 257; stock manipulations of, in railroad construction, 166

Robinson, John: suit of, against Central Pacific, 302; polemics of, against Southern Pacific, 372

Rocky Mountain Coal and Iron Company, of CP associates, 307

Rosecrans, Gen. William S., 266, 275, 283, 374

Roughing It (Mark Twain), 103–4

Sabin, Egbert, of Oneonta's gold-rush party, 7, 9, 13, 16, 23, 29–30, 31–32, 33, 39

Sacramento: Huntington and other Oneontans leave San Francisco for, 23–24, 26, 27; early history of, 24, 26–27; and long series of floods (1850), 30–31; Huntington, Hammond & Schultz trading firm in, 32; titles to real estate in, and squatter movement and riots, 36–37; Law-and-Order Party in, 37; home of Collis and Elizabeth Huntington, on Second Street, 40; vigilante committee in (1851), 41; building erected by Huntington at 54 K Street, 42, 43–44; city-wide fire in (Nov. 1852), 43–44; rebuilding of, after fire, 44; Huntington, Massol & Co. trading firm in, 45; housekeeping of the Huntingtons over store at 54 K Street, 45–46, 62; Huntington-Hopkins hardware company in, 49–50, 56, 57, 62; named state capital, 52; and vigilantism in the 1850s, 65–66; and 1862 floods, 111

Sacramento, Placer & Nevada R.R., 77–79, 84, 85, 86, 87, 90, 96–97, 100, 117, 132, 148, 158

Sacramento Public Library, founding of (1857), 74

Sacramento Valley R.R., 50–51, 53, 57, 69–70, 78–79, 84, 86, 87, 90, 117–18, 121, 123, 124, 131, 257, 302

Stafford, Anson Peacely-Killen, 318, 324

St. Louis & San Francisco R.R. (the Frisco), 337

Salt Lake City, by-passing of, by northern route for meeting of CP and UP, 202, 204, 205, 206

San Diego: and the Texas & Pacific R.R., 290–91, 304, 336; and the Santa Fe Railroad system, 337, 338, 341

San Diego & Gila Railroad, 250, 266, 282, 283

San Francisco: in 1849, 21–22, 23; series of major fires (in the 1850s), 36, 37–38, 40; tensions in (1851), and vigilante committee, 41; vigilantism in (1856), 65–66; failure of Central Pacific R.R. bonds to sell in, 121; and the 1872 Goat Island bill, 287–88; and Committee of One Hundred, 288; and the Southern Pacific, 368–72, 373

San Francisco, China, and Japan Mail Steamship Line, 177

San Francisco Bay, and Central Pacific's would-be wall around, 221, 258, 264, 288

San Francisco *Chronicle*, and publication of damaging letters written by Huntington to Colton, 329, 355

San Francisco & Sacramento R.R., 71, 170

441

San Francisco & San Joaquin Valley R.R., 370n.
San Francisco and San José R.R., 84, 97, 100, 101, 102, 108, 109, 122, 186, 188, 192, 212, 213, 214, 216, 246, 257, 260, 275, 278n., 283
San Francisco & Washoe R.R., 159, 163n.
San Joaquin R.R., 213, 214, 215, 218, 222, 224, 247, 259, 289, 293; as subsidiary of Central Pacific, 257–58, 289
San Pedro, and plans for developing harbor at, 367, 368, 373–74
Sand-lotters. See California Workingmen's party
Santa Clara and Pajaro Valley R.R., 223n., 283
Santa Fe R.R. system, 337, 339, 340, 367; entry of, into California, 341
Santa Monica, Cal., 312, 313; Huntington's plans for developing harbor at, 367–68, 373–74
Sargent, Aaron A.: as representative from California, 100, 102, 113, 135, 287n., 288; as member of House Select Committee on Pacific Railroad, 105, 125; as senator from California, 287n., 311, 320; as minister to Germany, 344; defeat of, for Senate, and Stanford's role in, 344–45; second defeat of, for Senate, and Huntington's anger over, 346
Sawyer, Judge Lorenzo, 332
Sawyer, Philetus, 301
Schultz, Edward, of Huntington, Hammond & Schultz, 32, 34
Schurz, Carl, 314
Scioto Valley R.R. of Ohio, 358
Scott, Thomas A., 214, 215, 217–20, 229, 282, 283, 285, 286, 290, 291, 293, 295, 296, 299, 303–6, 309, 313, 314–15, 317, 318, 319, 323, 327, 334–35, 336, 339
Searles, Edward T., 359
Seligman, Jesse, 350
Seward, William Henry, 63, 67, 75, 92, 95, 96
Sherman, William Tecumseh: as vice-president of Sacramento Valley R.R., 57; supporter of building of federal wagon roads, 59–60; and vigilantism in California in the 1850s, 66
Sherrill, Charles H., 311n., 365
Sierra construction push of Central Pacific, meeting money demands of, 182
Silver strikes: in Nevada, 148, 153, 155; in Arizona, 327
Simonton, James W., 286, 287
Slavery: opposition of Mark Hopkins and Collis Huntington to, 53; and the Andy case, 53–54
Snow as hazard in Central Pacific's construction progress, 180, 200
Southern Development Co., as construction firm for SP in New Mexico and Texas, 336
Southern Pacific Co.: as holding company for CP associates' railroads, 342, 344; Leland Stanford, as president of, 344; Huntington forces Stanford out as president, and has himself elected instead (1890), 356, 359; Huntington's speech at his election to the presidency and its derogatory references to Stanford, 360–61; Stanford's open letter to board of directors on Huntington's charges, 361; unsavory newspaper publicity over the Stanford-Huntington conflict, 361; Huntington's de-

clared noble purpose of taking it out of politics, 363, 364, 365; Henry E. Huntington named as first assistant to president, by his uncle, 364; and Populist Party, 370, 371; and Adolph Sutro's battle with, 370–71, 372; Huntington agrees to put entire system of, behind plan for settlement of CP's indebtedness to government, 374; control of, sold to E. H. Harriman by heirs of Collis Huntington, 376
Southern Pacific R.R., 170, 174, 191, 192, 212, 213, 214, 216, 218, 220, 221, 223n., 224, 247, 258, 260n., 265–67, 275, 283, 284–85, 289, 293, 300, 304, 305, 307, 309, 312, 313, 314, 322, 327, 330, 340, 341, 352; Central Pacific gains control of, 215, 222, 223, 257, 265, 282; and difficulties over land titles at Mussel Slough, 264, 267, 330; gains possession of San Francisco & San José R.R., 275, 278n.; consolidation of other southern railroads of CP with, to form Southern Pacific R.R. Company, 283; junction with CP at Goshen, Cal., 289; and routing of, through Los Angeles, 289–91; stepped up construction on, in Huntington-Scott battle over southern transcontinental railroad, 306; Huntington's strategy about, in battle with Scott, 308; Charles Crocker as president of, 309; franchise for, across Arizona Territory, 318; and access into Arizona, 318–19, 322; reaches Yuma, 322–23; construction eastward stopped at Yuma by California CP associates, 324; construction push of, across southern Arizona, 334; stock of, and CP associates, 334n.; Jay Gould's maneuvers to keep it out of Texas, 334–35; construction of, into New Mexico, 335; construction work of, in Texas, 336; continuous route of, to New Orleans by 1885, 336; fleet of steamships added to holdings, 336; diversion of traffic, by the associates, from CP to, 353
Southern transcontinental railroad: planned by Pennsylvania R.R. and Union Pacific, Eastern Division, 217–18; bargaining by Scott and Perry with Huntington over, 217–20; lobbying in Washington by Huntington for, 220, 222; failure of plan for, 223; Scott's ambitions for, and renewed fight for, 282–83, 299, 303–6, 308; Huntington's fight against Scott on, 304–6, 308; failure of Scott's bill for government subsidy for, 308; Scott's resumption of battle for bill in next session of Congress, 309; Huntington's continued battle against Scott, 309–11; promise of Huntington to build without government aid, 309–10, 318, 336–37; compromise agreement reached between Huntington and Scott on, 312, 314–15, 316; Texas & Pacific compromise bill of Huntington and Scott on, 316; defeat of Texas & Pacific bill, 317; return of Scott to his original battle for, 318; return of Huntington to his original battle with Scott over, 318; Huntington's determination to build, 327
SP. See Southern Pacific Co.; Southern Pacific R.R.
Speyer & Co., 182, 246, 299, 334, 374
Speyer, James, 374
Sprague, Kate Chase (Mrs. William), 150, 349
Sprague, Sen. William, of Rhode Island, 150

Spreckles, Claus, 370
Stanford, Charles, 172, 260
Stanford, Jane Lathrop (Mrs. Leland), 68, 69, 204
Stanford, Leland, 64, 67, 70, 73, 74, 75, 92, 97, 102, 103, 141, 143, 152, 159, 168, 172, 177, 180, 181, 182, 183, 185, 186, 187, 188, 189, 192, 194, 204, 205, 206, 214, 226, 247, 249, 252, 254, 268, 287n., 288, 289, 297, 307, 311, 327-28, 367; background and early history of, 68-69; as investor in and promoter of planned Central Pacific R.R., 95, 96, 99; as president of Central Pacific R.R., 98, 134; as Republican governor of California, 100, 111, 130, 133, 135; and factional alignment in board of directors of Central Pacific R.R., 136, 139; and Crocker-Central Pacific stock deal, 167; and Contract & Finance Co., 194; Huntington's appraisal of, 194, 206-7, 225, 252, 273-74; and accusation of monopoly brought against Central Pacific, 212-13, 216; and San Joaquin R.R., 213, 215; and Oakland Water Front Co., 217; dislike of, for Huntington, 228; and bill in California legislature to regulate rates and fares of CP, 301; interview of, in *Chronicle*, about failure of Scott's bill for southern transcontinental railroad, 308-9; real estate investments of, 325; cynical politics played by (1882), 332-33; and loss of interest in railroad matters, 340; as president of Southern Pacific Co., 344; election of, as senator, 345, 362; forced out, as president of Southern Pacific, by Huntington, 356, 359. *See also* Associates of Central Pacific R.R.
Stanford, Leland, Jr.: birth of, 195, 204; death of, at sixteen, 342; plan of parents for university as memorial to, 342
"Stanford Matters—Suggested Interview," vitriolic fantasy interview written by Huntington, 360
Stanford, Philip, 133, 158, 172, 260; as member of board of Central Pacific R.R., 139, 167
Stanton, Edwin M., 161
Starr, A. D., 18, 178
State Agricultural Society, Huntington's association with, in the 1850s, 74
Steele, Rep. John B., of New York, 143, 144-45
Stevens, Thaddeus, 107, 144
Stewart, David O., 253, 279, 280, 307
Stewart, James, 150
Stewart, William Morris, 103, 159, 174, 220, 240, 241-42, 312, 368
Stillman, Dr. James, 30, 48, 49
Stock of Central Pacific R.R.: Huntington's determination to protect against effects of excessive bonding, 256, 260; amount held by Contract & Finance Co., 256, 260, 263; maintaining value of, by eliminating possible competitors, 257-59; par and market value of, 257; possibilities of stock manipulation in consolidation of all of CP roads under a single management, 260, 264; minority stockholders, 260-61; to Congressmen as expression of gratitude for votes, 260; listing of, of New York exchange, 263, 292, 293, 299; new issue under consolidation of roads under single management, 263, 277; stock bonus to minority shareholders at time of floating new issue, 263, 277; pressure from Congressmen and minority stockholders for accounting on, 276-77; discrepancy between sales propaganda evaluation of, and real value of, 276-77; Huntington's sworn testimony at Congressional hearings about ownership of, 292; Huntington's plan for marketing (1874), 295; in 1878, 334
Stock manipulations during railroad construction, 146, 166. *See also* Contract & Finance Co.; Crédit Mobilier; Crocker, Charles & Co.
Stockton & Copperopolis short line railroad, 286
Stoddard, Elizabeth. *See* Huntington, Elizabeth (Mrs. Collis)
Stoddard, Hannah, 38, 39, 41
Stoddard, William, 57
Stone, James C., 106
Stoneman, George B.: as railway commissioner, 330; as governor of California, 333, 345
Stow, W. W., 363, 364
Strong, Daniel W., 87-89, 92; as member of board of directors of Central Pacific R.R., 98, 102, 103, 136, 137, 138, 139; forced out of Central Pacific management by Huntington, 140
Strong, William, 340
Suez Canal, 192n., 296
Suit against Central Pacific by group of minority stockholders, 277-81; extraordinary document drawn up by lawyers, 277-78, 292; accusations of blackmail made by Huntington against plaintiffs, 278; scramble of associates to buy up all CP stock, 279-80; damage done to CP by, 280-81
Suit of Central Pacific against Alfred A. Cohen, 302-3
Sutro, Adolph, 370-71; as mayor of San Francisco, 372; Huntington's verbal slash at, 373
Sutter, John: trading post of, near primitive Sacramento, 24, 25; and discovery of gold in California, 25; and titles to Sacramento real estate, 27, 36

Talcott, O. A., 147, 166
Terminal Central Pacific R.R., 190, 191, 192, 196, 213, 217, 221, 223; sale of, to Central Pacific R.R., 287
Terminal R.R., 367, 368
Terry, David S., and duel with David Broderick, 75-76, 307
Tevis, Lloyd, 191, 192, 195, 212, 213, 214, 215, 216, 217, 222, 223, 234, 275, 278; as one of the great landholders of California, 275-76
Texas, railroad peace achieved in, between Jay Gould and Huntington, 336-37
Texas & Pacific R.R., 282, 283, 284, 285, 290, 293, 295, 299, 303, 304, 305, 309, 311, 314, 319, 327, 334, 336, 337
Thompson, J. Edgar, 215, 220, 304
Throgs Neck in Westchester County, Huntington's purchase of estate at, 346
Thurber, Jeanette, and campaign for American Opera Co., 350
Thurman Act on sinking fund for repayment by UP and CP of government loans, 315, 326, 353
Thurman, Sen. Allen, of Ohio, 315, 326
Tilden, Samuel, 311, 314
Todman, J. H., 104
Towne, Alban N., 254, 364

443

444